THE STATE OF PUBLIC ADMINISTRATION

THE STATE OF PUBLIC ADMINISTRATION

ISSUES, CHALLENGES, AND OPPORTUNITIES

DONALD C. MENZEL AND
HARVEY L. WHITE, EDITORS

M.E.Sharpe
Armonk, New York
London, England

Library of Congress Cataloging-in-Publication Data

The state of public administration : issues, challenges, and opportunities / edited by Donald C. Menzel and
Harvey L. White.
    p. cm.
Includes bibliographical references and index.
ISBN 978-0-7656-2504-5 (hardcover : alk. paper)
    1. Public administration—United States. 2. Administrative agencies—United States—Management.
3. Executive departments—United States—Management. I. Menzel, Donald C. II. White, Harvey L.

JK421.S718 2011
351.73—dc22   2010022573

Printed in the United States of America

The paper used in this publication meets the minimum requirements of
American National Standard for Information Sciences
Permanence of Paper for Printed Library Materials,
ANSI Z 39.48-1984.

EB (c)   10   9   8   7   6   5   4   3   2   1

CONTENTS

FOREWORD

RICHARD STILLMAN

Editor-in-Chief
Public Administration Review
University of Colorado

The past decade witnessed one of the most turbulent eras in American history. Indeed, it ranks among the top ten cataclysmic epochs—the Revolutionary War in the 1770s, the ratification of the U.S. Constitution in the 1780s, the Jacksonian populist movement of the 1820s, the American Civil War in the 1860s, the Progressive reforms and World War I in the 1910s, the Great Depression of the 1930s, World War II and the start of the Cold War in the 1940s, and civil rights, feminist rights, and gay liberation movements of the 1960s. The decade of 2000–2010 rightly belongs in the record books as another rare period reflecting enormous historic transformations. The decade opened with the controversial, razor-close 2000 presidential election, which spawned a national crisis involving the nation's very constitutional legitimacy; the 9/11 terrorist attacks, which sparked a global war on terrorism; the double whammy of the dot-com meltdown and the housing-bubble bust, which ushered in the worst economic crisis since the Great Depression; and, of course, the unforgettable Katrina tragedy.

At the heart of all these socioeconomic-political-military shocks stood public administration for good or ill, or for good AND ill. Yes, "ill" because the 2000 Florida election hung in perilous balance precisely due to inconsistencies in how county elections designed ballots and how they counted votes. In the case of 9/11, the hijackers slipped under the FBI radar screen because bureau field agents in Minnesota and Arizona could not convince their superiors at Washington headquarters that the threats they reported were real and imminent. Regulatory management at every governmental level was lax and negligent, thus precipitating market excesses that brought both the domestic and global economies to their knees. Unquestionably, the lengthy chain of federal-state-local misman-agement and faulty planning contributed directly to the deaths of more than a thousand people and the destruction of a trillion dollars-plus worth of property in the wake of Katrina.

Still, abundant good resulted from public administration actions throughout the decade. Votes were counted (for the most part) correctly in 2008, resulting in the election of America's first African-American president. Two far-flung wars were fought in Iraq and Afghanistan thanks to the courage and professionalism of many brave men and women in the U.S. Armed Forces. A rapid response by the Federal Reserve and Treasury dramatically blunted the free fall of the U.S. and world economies. Universal health care was for the first time successfully debated, enacted, and its implementation began.

At the core of all these momentous crises stood public administration, intricately and intimately. Making government work—or fail—is the essence of public administration. Whether we are consciously aware of it or not, public administration decisively shapes and reshapes modern life and contemporary events, with innumerable apparent and not-so-apparent consequences.

Yet, what is public administration today, given that it is everywhere and influences everything in modern society? How can we comprehend its key trends as well as unforeseen consequences? How do we ensure that it serves the public? After all, is not *public* the first word in *public administration*?

Professors Donald C. Menzel and Harvey L. White, both former presidents of the American Society for Public Administration (America's premier professional association of administrative academics and practitioners), edited this remarkable book, which examines the state of the field; a field at the heart of myriad, complicated, even life-and-death domestic and worldwide challenges at the dawn of the twenty-first century. Wisely, the editors recruited more than thirty of the best and brightest administrative scholars to think deeply and broadly about critical public administration issues: What are the new challenges as well as opportunities facing public administration? What are the underlying factors influencing new or emerging trends? What priority issues remain unsolved and why? What do we know and not know about this seminal subject?

Certainly no hard-and-fast answers are found in these pages. Complex conundrums do not—cannot—yield easy solutions. Rather, these essays are probative and exploratory. Individually and collectively they compose a snapshot of today's leading-edge issues, and propose vital, even provocative, suggestions about where we should head tomorrow in order to advance the public interest as well avoid the glaring mistakes of yesterday. Complexity, uncertainty, and tentativeness pervade these penetrating analyses. This book is a timely, necessary first step toward charting potential alternative routes and possibilities to move forward in the decade ahead.

PREFACE

Dateline: Beijing, People's Republic of China, October 2007. This volume was conceived in China while the editors were conferencing with colleagues in Chengdu and Beijing. Why China? The answer is disarmingly simple—China's rise as a world power turns in no small part on the ability of its leaders to govern with efficiency, effectiveness, fairness, and the creative application of public administration concepts and practices. The contrast in the value placed on public administration as a field of study and practice in China and in the United States is striking and worrisome. Public administration in the United States has been pillaged and demeaned throughout government and academia in recent decades. The time is at hand to recognize, respect, and value the profession and practice of public administration. Thus, one key objective of this volume is to draw together the very best contemporary, cutting-edge scholarship in the field.

The chapters in this volume have been prepared by known scholars and aspiring scholars who value public administration and appreciate the difference that theory and practice can make in good governance. This volume is not a handbook, however. Rather, it is a compendium of essays that address leading-edge issues, challenges, and opportunities that confront public administration as a professional field of study and practice in the twenty-first century. The trends and practices that mark the field are ever changing and essential to administrators and policy makers worldwide. It is therefore imperative that the field be surveyed from time to time. The calamities of recent years—9/11, Katrina, war profiteering, privatization miscues, the hollowing out of government, the dismantling of civil service, and more recently, the collapse of the financial industry as well as international calamities such as the SARS crisis in China, the Asian tsunami, Ebola, famine and genocide in Africa, and the Haitian earthquake disaster—have turned on its head Ronald Reagan's famous line that "government is the problem, not the solution." Thus, the need for a state-of-the-art book is ever more pressing.

We approached contributors who possessed expertise and knowledge of the subject matter and could bring broad coverage of relevant topics. From a content perspective, authors were advised to not dwell on "old" public administration issues, even though they may be relevant to the subject matter (e.g., politics-administration dichotomy, science of administration, the identity crisis). Rather, authors were asked to emphasize contemporary problems, issues, and challenges, taking note of recent trends and future developments. Each author was invited to approach topics in a manner that was both comfortable to him or her and sensible given what is known and important in stimulating the reader. Innovation, creativity, and invention were welcomed.

The following questions served as guideposts, although authors were not required to address each one:

1. What are the new issues, challenges, and opportunities? Are there trends?
2. What are the underlying factors influencing new or emerging trends, for example, socioeconomic, environment, technology, and so forth?
3. What issues are unresolved? Why?
4. What do we know or not know about the subject?
5. How can we find out more? What research is needed?

Our vision is a book that will find professional and classroom use and will be on every professor's and practitioner's must-have list. The collection should serve serious-minded students, thoughtful practitioners, and motivated faculty. It was conceived and created in the spirit of an intellectual tradition that asserts a compelling need to update the field. The last effort along these lines, *Public Administration: The State of the Discipline* (Chatham House, 1990), was coedited by Naomi B. Lynn and Aaron Wildavsky. This volume thus seeks to bridge a twenty-year gap.

While the treatment of public administration in the chapters that follow often takes place in the context of the American experience and no claim is made that the volume is the definitive examination of the field worldwide, we believe the analyses offer much to those who labor across the globe to advance the field as a profession and instrument of good governance.

ACKNOWLEDGMENTS

The quality of the chapters in this volume is the product of many hands, certainly but not exclusively those of the authors themselves. The editors turned to many scholars worldwide to serve as external reviewers in a double-blind review process. We acknowledge their excellent reviews and contributions and offer many thanks for the time and energy that went into the assessments. In alphabetical order, they are: Robert Agranoff, Indiana University; Jennifer Alexander, Cleveland State University; Howard Balanoff, Texas State University; Enid Beaumont, George Mason University; J. Edwin Benton, University of South Florida; Geert Bouckaert, Catholic University of Leuven, Belgium; Gerald Caiden, University of Southern California; Naomi Caiden, California State University–Los Angeles; Crystal Carlucci, National Association of Schools of Public Affairs and Administration; Dale Krane, University of Nebraska–Omaha; Dennis Daley, North Carolina State University; John Daly, University of South Forida; Ruth deHoog, University of North Carolina–Greensboro; Janet Denhardt, Arizona State University; Kathy Denhardt, University of Delaware; Pat Dobel, University of Washington; Melvin Dubnick, University of New Hampshire; Frances Edwards, San Jose State University; Andrew Ewoh, Kennesaw State University; Catherine Horiuchi, University of San Francisco; Edward Jennings, University of Kentucky; Patricia Julnes, University of Baltimore; Carole L. Jurkiewicz, Louisiana State University; Naim Kapucu, University of Central Florida; Anne M. Khademian, Virginia Tech; Judith Kirchoff, Rutgers University–Newark; Heidi Koenig, Northern Illinois University; Myrna Mandell, California State University–Northridge; Michael McGuire, Indiana University; Fred Meine, Troy University; Berhanu Mengistu, Old Dominion University; Katherine Naff, San Francisco State University; John Nalbandian, University of Kansas; Kathryn Newcomer, George Washington University; Larry O'Toole, University of Georgia; Jerry Pops, West Virginia University; Joan Pynes, University of South Florida; Jo Raadschelders, University of Oklahoma; Beryl Radin, American University; Dianne Rahm, Texas State University; David Schultz, Hamline University; Kevin B. Smith, University of Nebraska–Lincoln; Rodney Smith, University of Sydney, Australia; Camilla Stivers, Cleveland State University; James Thompson, University of Illinois–Chicago; Mary Timney, Pace University; Carol Weissert, Florida State University; Jonathan West, University of Miami; Howard Whitton, Ethicos Group; Ethel Williams, University of Nebraska–Omaha; Gary Zajac, Pennsylvania Department of Corrections.

Finally, a note of enduring thanks and appreciation to our families, who came to know more about the study of public administration than they may have wished as the months passed while we labored to put this volume together. Don would especially like to acknowledge his partner, Kay, for the fifty years of marriage that came to pass on August 22, 2009, in Carmel, California, where he and she uttered those famous last words, *I do*. Harvey would like to recognize his wife, Velma, who became the "wind beneath his wings" on November 4, 1989, in Pittsburgh, Pennsylvania.

INTRODUCTION

DONALD C. MENZEL AND HARVEY L. WHITE

The study and practice of public administration are robust, healthy, and moving forward in America and abroad as the second decade of the twenty-first century gets under way. The challenges of the past, both theoretical and practical, have somewhat though not entirely moved to the sidelines. The debate over practice-driven theory versus theory-driven practice, while important, no longer has the cachet it once had. Nor, for that matter, does the exchange over the administration-policy nexus confound and confuse as it once did. Indeed, in this volume Robert F. Durant and John Marvel (chapter 20) take this often controversial topic to a new, more sophisticated level by examining the implications that several theoretical developments drawn from "new institutionalism" have for future research on the dynamic relationship between policy and administration in the study of American bureaucracy.

Another issue—methodological pluralism—has receded in attention as well over the past decade or two. In addition, downsized to a large extent is the identity crisis, at least as characterized in years past. Public administration no longer suffers from the "Who am I?" syndrome, although one author, David Schultz (chapter 27), reframes the question as a postglobal issue. Public administration has become an acknowledged, legitimate enterprise in the academy and the real world of governance; it is knowable and, in the judgment of many, essential to good governance. Finally, it might be said with confidence that the grand quest for a science of administration has run its course.

While the past is just that, it is no less important to bring into focus the issues, challenges, and opportunities that define the state of public administration in the new millennium. The twenty-seven chapters in this volume, each in its own way, are directed toward this end. As noted in the preface, contributors were invited to address a set of questions.

While it would be tedious and redundant to search through each chapter for answers to all the questions, it is appropriate in this introductory section to provide the reader with a glimpse of the contributors' answers to some. At the same time, the topic-chapter matrix (Figure I.1) enables the reader to connect issues, challenges, and opportunities across selected topics and chapters.

WHAT ARE THE NEW ISSUES, CHALLENGES, AND OPPORTUNITIES FACING PUBLIC ADMINISTRATION?

This is a significant question that generates a wide spectrum of responses by topical area. They range from the need "to emphasize the processual nature of theory creation"—theorizing according to Laurence E. Lynn Jr. (chapter 1)—to the role of public administration in a postglobal world, that is, how does the new global economic order challenge public administration theory as it is now formulated (David Schultz, chapter 27)? Along the way, the challenge of understanding "why

Figure 1.1 **Topic-Chapter Matrix**

		Topics					
		Theory	Profession	Compe-tencies	History	Leadership	Ethics
1	Public Administration Theory	X	X				
Part I	THE PROFESSION						
2	Public Administration as a Profession		X	X	X		X
3	Public Service Professionals	X	X	X		X	X
4	Professional Associations and Public Administration	X	X	X		X	X
5	Accreditation and Competencies in Education for Leadership in Public Service		X	X	X	X	
6	Changing Dynamics of Administrative Leadership			X		X	X
7	Ethics and Integrity in Public Service	X	X	X		X	X
Part II	PUBLIC MANAGEMENT ISSUES						
8	Human Resources Management	X		X	X		
9	New Directions in Public Budgeting		X				
10	The Proxy-Partnership Governance Continuum	X		X		X	
11	The Pursuit of Accountability	X			X	X	X
12	Technology and Public Management Information Systems				X		
13	Emergency and Crisis Management		X	X	X		
Part III	NETWORKING AND PARTNERSHIPS						
14	Federal Contracting				X		X
15	Citizen-Driven Administration and Civic Engagement		X	X	X	X	
16	Network Theory and Practice in Public Administration	X	X	X			
17	Collaborating Public Organizations	X		X		X	
Part IV	GOVERNANCE AND REFORM						
18	Historic Relevance Confronting Contemporary Obsolescence?	X	X		X		
19	Neglected Aspects of Intergovernmental Relations and Federalism	X					
20	Politics, Bureaucratic Dynamics, and Public Policy	X			X		
21	Civil Service Reform		X		X		
22	Pubic Administration's Legal Dimensions	X	X	X	X		
23	Governance in the Midst of Diversity		X			X	X
Part V	INTERNATIONAL AND GLOBAL CHALLENGES						
24	New Public Management	X	X	X	X	X	
25	Governance					X	X
26	Development Management		X		X		
27	The Crisis of Public Administration in a Postglobal World	X	X		X		
	Number of chapters	13	17	14	15	12	9

Topics										
Human Resources	Fiscal	Nonprofits	Account-ability	Technology	Information Systems	Crisis Manage-ment	Contracting	Federalism	Intergov-ernmental	Civil Service
			X							
			X							X
		X				X				
X		X								X
X										
X										
										X
X										X
	X						X	X		
		X	X				X			
			X				X			
			X	X	X		X			
					X	X		X	X	
	X		X				X			
			X							
				X	X	X			X	
		X					X	X	X	
	X						X	X	X	X
								X	X	
			X						X	
X			X				X	X	X	X
			X					X		X
X										
			X							
					X					
	X									
			X							
6	4	5	12	2	4	3	8	7	7	7

(continued)

Figure 1.1 *(continued)*

		Topics						
		Legal	Diversity	Collab- oration	Net- working	New Public Manage- ment	Global- ization	Citizen Engage- ment
1	Public Administration Theory							
Part I	THE PROFESSION							
2	Public Administration as a Profession					X		
3	Public Service Professionals		X	X				
4	Professional Associations and Public Administration		X	X	X	X		
5	Accreditation and Competencies in Education for Leadership in Public Service							
6	Changing Dynamics of Administrative Leadership			X	X	X		
7	Ethics and Integrity in Public Service							
Part II	PUBLIC MANAGEMENT ISSUES							
8	Human Resources Management	X	X					
9	New Directions in Public Budgeting							X
10	The Proxy-Partnership Governance Continuum			X	X			
11	The Pursuit of Accountability							
12	Technology and Public Management Information Systems			X	X			
13	Emergency and Crisis Management	X		X	X		X	
Part III	NETWORKING AND PARTNERSHIPS							
14	Federal Contracting	X						
15	Citizen-Driven Administration and Civic Engagement			X	X			X
16	Network Theory and Practice in Public Administration			X	X			
17	Collaborating Public Organizations			X	X			X
Part IV	GOVERNANCE AND REFORM							
18	Historic Relevance Confronting Contemporary Obsolescence?	X		X	X			
19	Neglected Aspects of Intergovernmental Relations and Federalism	X		X	X		X	
20	Politics, Bureaucratic Dynamics, and Public Policy				X	X		X
21	Civil Service Reform	X				X		
22	Pubic Administration's Legal Dimensions	X						
23	Governance in the Midst of Diversity	X	X	X	X	X	X	
Part V	INTERNATIONAL AND GLOBAL CHALLENGES							
24	New Public Management			X	X	X	X	
25	Governance	X		X	X	X	X	
26	Development Management						X	
27	The Crisis of Public Administration in a Postglobal World					X	X	
	Number of chapters	9	5	14	14	8	7	4

good governance is vital for the overall development of a society" is addressed head on by Jamil Jreisat (chapter 25) and Louis A. Picard (chapter 26).

Different challenges and opportunities are examined by others. Patricia M. Shields and Nandhini Rangarajan (chapter 3) focus on the challenges that faced three pioneering women who, "individually and collectively, laid the historic foundation for a new kind of approach to administration where scientific rigor and sensitivity go hand in hand." Norma M. Riccucci (chapter 8) lays out a number of challenges in human resources management, noting that four in particular are the most enduring: affirmative action, labor-management relations, performance management, and succession planning. Human resources issues and challenges, while centermost in contemporary organizations, occur alongside huge changes in information and telecommunication technology, which Stuart I. Bretschneider and Ines Mergel explore in chapter 12. Among other things, they provide an historical review of changing technology over the past fifty years and present forward thinking about the potential impact that information technology may have on both the structure of government organizations and management in the years ahead.

New issues and opportunities abound for practitioners and scholars interested in the emerging profession of emergency and crisis management. Although the public administration community has been slow to pick up the challenge, William L. Waugh Jr. asserts in chapter 13 that this is changing rapidly both domestically and internationally. As he puts it, "The professional emergency management community is increasingly international and collaborative. The same is true of the disaster research community." It is also becoming much more multidisciplinary, which equally characterizes the field of public administration.

WHAT ARE THE UNDERLYING FACTORS INFLUENCING NEW OR EMERGING TRENDS?

There is little question that key influencing factors in the study and practice of public administration include (1) globalization, which has brought forth a degree of economic interdependency never experienced before, (2) breathtaking new communication technologies and information systems, (3) cultural assimilation and resistance, and (4) political change, with the explosive growth of aspiring democracies and supranational organizations such as the European Union, the World Trade Organization, and others.

The era of diversity is here as well and is having a significant influence on public administration worldwide. Harvey L. White (chapter 23) tracks the mosaic of language, racial, cultural, ethnic, age, economic, gender, and sexual influences as well as the diversity of services and technologies that enmesh contemporary administrators in their workplace. Governance in the midst of diversity, he contends, is both a challenge and an opportunity that together make public administration a fascinating profession.

Yet another influence on contemporary public management is the rapidly growing interdependencies among governmental entities, nonprofit organizations, and private businesses. Public management in this environment is changing dramatically. Networking and collaborative management are the new waves sweeping across the continent and across the globe and are likely to shape the future for years to come. As Louise K. Comfort, Clayton Wukich, Steve Scheinert, and Leonard Huggins note in chapter 16, "ineffective hierarchical structures are giving way to informal methods of addressing shared problems among multiple entities in metropolitan regions . . . [which in turn] are leading to significant change in the administrative framework of urban regions." Robert Agranoff notes in chapter 17: "the work of government is changing by rapid externalization . . . changes [that] predominantly involve linkage, partnering and networking activities with NGOs, and emergent forms of collaborative leadership." This exciting new world of government and governance is described by other authors (see Deil S. Wright, Carl W. Stenberg, and Chung-Lae Cho, chapter 18) as a near-tsunami force that is quickly enveloping public administration practice and scholarship.

Irene S. Rubin (chapter 9) points out that there is a powerful trend toward greater politicization of budgeting, which is a direct result of the increased scope of government and the different tools and program designs that are now in frequent use. The time has arrived, she claims, for significant reform in budgeting practices at all levels of government that enables budgetary actors and processes to be able to deal with increased scope, increased politicization, and increased conflict.

Efforts to reform the civil service in the United States continue unabated. "The tension between neutral competence and political responsiveness," assert Stephen E. Condrey and Jonathan P. West (chapter 21), "will continue to influence how civil service systems are managed, reformed, modernized and modified." Reformers who lose sight of the need to balance managerial flexibility and employee rights may well be responsible for a return to a past where cronyism and spoils prevailed.

WHAT ISSUES ARE UNRESOLVED? WHY?

There are many. Among them are leadership, accountability, and intergovernmental relations and federalism (in the American context). Administrative leadership has a long history of benign neglect, theoretical confusion, and subjugation as a distinct field of study. What are the boundaries and context of public leadership? How does it resemble or differ from corporate leadership and nonprofit organizational leadership? What might be a postmodern paradigm wherein public leadership can evolve? These difficult and unresolved issues and questions are addressed by Montgomery Van Wart (chapter 6), who contends that the field of administrative (public) leadership has achieved a critical mass to be considered a recognizable and maturing field of interest. His claim is bolstered by the growing interest in educating men and women for leadership in public service. Jeffrey A. Raffel, Steven M. Maser, and Crystal Calarusse (chapter 5) outline new directions in accreditation standards recently promulgated by the National Association of Schools of Public Affairs and Administration to advance competencies deemed essential for effective leadership.

Accountability issues remain perplexing and difficult to resolve. As Melvin J. Dubnick and Kaifeng Yang (chapter 11) note, "all major schools of thought in American public administration are arguably about accountability." This ubiquity is not necessarily a virtue, however, as it confounds the best efforts to facilitate and foster responsible, trustworthy behavior. Dubnick and Yang challenge the reader to not abandon efforts to understand the concept and its use.

WHAT DO WE KNOW OR NOT KNOW ABOUT THE SUBJECT?

This is a double-barreled question. While there is much that is known about all of the subjects in this volume, there is a great deal yet to learn. Consider the following (certainly not a comprehensive list):

Federal Contracting

How can the notion of "inherently governmental function" be made more clear and operational? What more needs to be done to slow the revolving door? In administering the occluded world of federal outsourcing, how can public administrators increase transparency, enforcement, and accountability? (See Nicholas Henry, chapter 14.)

Citizen-Centered Civic Engagement

What are the new institutional forms that need to be designed to connect local engagement institutions with federal policy initiatives? What do elected officials need to learn in order to work with citizens beyond election campaigns? (See Terry L. Cooper, chapter 15.)

The Profession

James S. Bowman and Jonathan P. West in chapter 2 and Donald C. Menzel in chapter 7 highlight several important unknowns. They include questions regarding: What can be done to ensure that a public service ethos animates the work of governing and government? What can be done to eliminate the "trust deficit" that has arisen between citizen and state? What constitutes ethical competency, and how is it achieved among those who administer the state?

Intergovernmental Relations and Federalism

The study of intergovernmental relations and federalism, asserts Beverly A. Cigler (chapter 19), is long on "vertical federalism" but quite lacking in other dimensions. Neglected issues that so little is known about include multistate legal action, coordinated initiatives, cooperative horizontal federalism, state-local relations, intermunicipal relations including city-county consolidation and shared services, regional economic collaboration, and internationalizing federalism. She contends that these neglected dimensions must be explored by scholars and is confident that the "state of the practice" can help shape future academic research in federalism and intergovernmental relations.

Legal Dimensions

David H. Rosenbloom (chapter 22) asks, "Why is not law more central to U.S. public administration?" He offers several explanations including the view that "public administration and law incorporate different mind-sets that act to frustrate their integration. U.S. constitutional law tends to be contractarian in outlook, whereas public administration is utilitarian (benefit-cost) and instrumental (cost-effectiveness)." Perhaps by turning more attention to how public administrators actually do their jobs, he concludes, can the field gain a better understanding and appreciation of its legal dimensions.

HOW CAN WE FIND OUT MORE? WHAT RESEARCH IS NEEDED?

Theory

Laurence E. Lynn Jr. (chapter 1) contends that the blend of intellectual curiosity and passion for effective democratic governance is a hallmark of public administration as a profession, with important implications for theorizing. Heterodoxy rather than orthodoxy is the norm for public administration research, which if carefully conceived and theoretically framed and executed with skill, can produce contingent findings that are sufficiently robust to provide useful contributions to conceptual and practical understanding.

The Profession

Public administration as a lifelong career has many ups and downs. Working in the public sector under the glare of public scrutiny and transparency can produce much stress among even the most well-balanced professionals. Research is needed that informs managers and workers how to cope with work-induced stress and build resilient cultures. Wendy Haynes and Beth Gazley (chapter 4) suggest that studies are needed as well that explore the activities of professionals and professional associations—why they join, stay, or exit, and how professional associations make a difference in the quality of public service. They correctly observe that little empirical research has addressed professional associations and even less has examined their activities in the public sector.

Public Management

The research needed in public management covers a broad spectrum of issues. Consider the relationship between job satisfaction and job training. As Riccucci points out (chapter 8), "a number of studies examine the relationship between job satisfaction and job training, but research needs to examine the potential linkage between job training and enhanced employee performance." Moreover, in the area of succession planning, she asserts that very little research has been conducted. A survey of state and local governments as well as federal agencies to discover the extent to which it is actually being relied upon would be a significant first step. Other needed research could focus on the efficacy of diversity as well as the link between public service motivation and performance. On the subject of diversity, White (chapter 23) adds, "theoretical and empirical research is sorely needed on questions concerning the limits of differences or bounded diversity and who has the rights to set these limits."

Networking and Partnerships

Judith R. Saidel (chapter 10) calls for future research to build on the solid base of empirical research literature in the area of bilateral and network contracting relationships. "Researchers could examine consequences such as information availability, authority sharing, discretion permitted, frequency and intensity of monitoring, and extent of access to bureaucratic policy making." Comfort and colleagues (chapter 16) add that "current technologies for information exchange . . . speed the flow of information rapidly across large numbers of people in spontaneous and undirected ways. Understanding these dynamic information processes and how they influence civic engagement in, or resistance to, governmental action is critical to maintaining an open, responsible, democratic society."

Governance and Reform

Among the major reform initiatives advanced over the past decade or two is new public management (NPM), which has been described by some scholars as a global revolution. Alan Lawton and Frédérique Six (chapter 24) are not so certain. They explore this initiative in considerable depth and advise that "the first lesson for scholars researching NPM is to be clear about what exactly is being researched. If the concern is with values, then politics cannot be ignored. If the focus is on management, then design and implementation issues need to be addressed." Much more research is needed on NPM's adoption and implementation outside the Anglo-American-European cultures.

International and Global Challenges

Like other areas previously discussed, the research needs in the international and global domain are wide-ranging. To offer but one example, consider development management. Picard (chapter 26) notes that globalism has brought about an increasing role for international organizations, including the United Nations, the world and regional financial institutions, and security organizations, which has expanded the role for development management in terms of both theories and operational practices. Yet, there is a research gap in the conceptual needs for and practical applications of development management.

While this brief introduction is a starting point for this volume, it barely scratches the surface of the many exciting and important issues, challenges, and opportunities that await the reader.

THE STATE OF
PUBLIC
ADMINISTRATION

CHAPTER 1

PUBLIC ADMINISTRATION THEORY

Which Side Are You On?

LAURENCE E. LYNN JR.

Sometimes characterized as an occupation, an area of interest, or an academic discipline, public administration as a field of scholarship, teaching, and practice is most widely understood as a profession (Denhardt 1990, 63). As with professions such as business administration, social work, and education, public administration scholarship necessarily draws on the theoretical resources of many disciplines, fields, and intellectual traditions in order to address problems and issues that reside in no single domain of inquiry (Frederickson and Smith 2003).

A recognizable theoretical bent was evident in the earliest days of public administration. How and why does our system of government work? What do the answers imply for the policies and practices of public administration? As Lynn (2008) has noted, that curiosity was seldom dispassionate or narrowly "academic." It reflected awareness that the rapid transformation of American life made research to support the creation of competent governments a matter of urgency. That blend of intellectual curiosity and passion for effective democratic governance remains the hallmark of public administration as a profession, with important implications for theorizing.

The profession's theoretical resourcefulness is regarded by many as healthy (Evans and Lowery 2008; Frederickson and Smith 2003; O'Toole 1995; Waldo 1955). Yet critics view public administration theory as incoherent and inadequate. Rosenbloom (1983, 219) complains that "the discipline of public administration is plagued by a weak or absent theoretical core." Hummel (2007, 292) notes the profession's "present state of theoretical anarchy." Savoie argues that public administration has a chronic identity crisis because it "has no integrative theory and borrows from a variety of disciplines" (Savoie 2008, 187). Of such divergent views, Denhardt (1990, 43) observes that "public administration theory draws its greatest strength and its most serious limitation from [its] diversity."

A sense of inadequacy is symptomatic of another characteristic of theorizing in public administration: the philosophical partisanship among many of its theorists. The often sardonic tone of symposia in *Administrative Theory and Praxis* and the "Disputatio Sine Fine" feature of *Administration and Society* reveals a real animosity between adherents of different "ways of knowing" that aspire to inform practice that is both humane and efficient. Such tensions are inimical to creating an integrated account of how and why public administration contributes to democratic governance. Theorizing is an arena where diverse, passionately held values compete for the soul of the profession.

This chapter provides a broad overview of public administration *theorizing*—this word is chosen to emphasize the processual nature of theory creation—in the context of the tensions that pervade it. The next section discusses the special challenges of theorizing for professional practice, discussing the meaning of both *profession* and *theory*. Next come three sections on public administration theorizing itself. The first sketches three metaperspectives that reflect the major epistemologies that constitute the foundations for theorizing in public administration. The second presents examples of the kind of theorizing that is associated with the dominant mode of research in public administration: theory-based empirical investigation reflecting a positivist epistemology. The third provides examples of theorizing associated with other foundational epistemologies. The concluding section argues that, because the diversity of theory and tensions among theorists reflects the existential reality of administrative practice, heterodoxy is the profession's identity, not a threat to that identity.

THEORIZING IN AND FOR A PROFESSION

Theorizing is essential in a professional field as diverse as public administration, say Frederickson and Smith (2003). This assertion is not self-evident, however. Many if not most practitioners in humanistic professions believe that the competence and expertise required of them is largely experiential and tacit, comprising lessons, principles, best practices, and wisdom acquired by doing, not by abstract reasoning. To such practitioners, theory tends to be viewed in an Aristotelian sense, as the pursuit of truth for its own sake and, as such, of only occasional relevance to practice. It is revealing that the national selection committee for the Ford Foundation-Kennedy School of Government annual innovation in government awards "has not been favorably disposed to programs that attempt to communicate a theoretical construct as the basis of their innovation" (Christopher 2003, 685).

While most public administration scholars and many administrators reject a dismissive view of theory, the inherent tension between theory and practice is a major reason for the diversity, and divergence, of the profession's theorizing and for the passion infusing the arguments over epistemology put forward in professional forums. Theoretical passion reflects the passions of the public sphere.

The Meaning of Profession

The concept of *profession* implies *practice* (or praxis), that is, the purposeful application of specialized knowledge and skills by those who have been attracted to an occupation requiring them. To define public administration as a profession is not only to associate it with practice but also to assert a jurisdictional claim: the authority to control its knowledge base and its membership, which implies in turn authority over the field's boundaries. In Eliot Friedson's view, "'Profession' is synonymous with 'occupation': it refers to specialized work by which one gains a living in an exchange economy. But it is not just *any* kind of work that professionals do. The kind of work they do is esoteric, complex, and discretionary in character: it requires theoretical knowledge, skill, and judgment that ordinary people do not possess, may not wholly comprehend, and cannot readily evaluate" (Friedson 1974, 200). Thus a profession is founded on theory-based knowledge and specific opportunities to use it, offering the possibility of ascending to higher levels of responsibility and reward.

Early in the history of public administration, academics such as Woodrow Wilson, Frank Goodnow, and Leonard White drew on European antecedents to initiate a literature of ideas concerning the practice of public administration. Formulating a "science of administration" became an early goal of scholars and reformers alike. However, theorizing as it is now understood in the social sciences—conditional causal reasoning leading to explanation, prediction, or prescription—was difficult to distinguish from political philosophy, or normative reasoning (Lynn 2008). For early theorists, creating competent administrative institutions at municipal, state, and federal levels was a compelling goal. Many drawn to the profession were, and still are, concerned as much with promoting effective democracy as with narrowly academic concerns.

It was fateful, therefore, when, in response to the Depression-era expansion of the public sector, universities began to assume a dominant role in training public administrators, usurping the role then performed by private institutions and municipal research bureaus. From then on, theory and theorizing increasingly reflected the university's role in defining the field's boundaries, content, and membership. University programs in public administration and affairs now claim, implicitly if not explicitly, to possess both uniquely valuable knowledge on which to ground training for practice and legitimate authority to graduate, certify, and honor practitioners. This means, however, that content and boundary defining are affected not only by the needs of practice but also by the economic, political, and sociological pressures that confront members of academic communities.

Just as there can be no separation of politics and administration, then, there can be no separation of the relatively insular world of the academy and the engaged world of praxis. This truth has important implications for theorizing.

The Meaning of Theory

Creating an authoritative knowledge base for professional practice conceived in politics (in the Aristotelian sense of collective action by a polity or community) raises philosophical, ontological, epistemological, and methodological questions: What should a public administration professional know? What are the sources of such knowledge? How can "theorizing" and theory-based scholarship contribute to creating an appropriate knowledge base for practice?

Choices among epistemologies might be assumed to reflect scientific considerations. Such an assumption is only partly true in public administration. Theorizing may reflect policy and political ideologies, with differences reflecting, for example, the relative priority placed on equity, participation, and social justice or on property rights and personal freedom. Theorists may have a priori philosophical commitments, for example, to realism or to postpositivism, with their associated epistemologies and methodologies. Choices may reflect the kinds of questions scholars find most interesting: Why does the administrative system work as it does? How can the administrative state be made to work better? How and by whom should the administrative state be organized?

An enduring view is that theory *follows* practice. As sociologist Robert Park put it long ago, "As a matter of fact and natural history, the problems which attract public attention are usually problems of administration. When emergencies arise, we meet them with some novel administrative measures. But later on we formulate a policy to justify the innovation; we do this by interpreting our legislative and administrative experiments. . . . On the whole, theory follows practice and serves to generalize, justify, and rationalize it" (Park 1917, 64–65, quoted by Rein and Peattie 1981, 527).

This view characterizes much but not all theorizing within public administration. Stillman has argued that "a succession of American theorists have attempted to impose the 'correct' or 'efficient' administrative models on the American state . . . with little or partial success—not to mention considerable frustration" (Stillman 1991, 71). In recent decades, normative theorists have aspired to transform the values underlying practice, sometimes creating tensions with practitioners (Mostel 2009).

Theorizing itself can take many forms, which have been categorized in various ways. Rosenbloom (1983) identifies three "theoretical approaches" corresponding to the three branches of government: political, managerial, and legal. Denhardt's (1990) classification has two dimensions: the objectivity ↔ subjectivity of epistemologies and the political ↔ organizational focus of the objects of theorizing. To Frederickson and Smith (2003), *theory* takes three forms: deductive, causal explanations; the ordering and classification of information; and normative arguments. O'Toole (1995) distinguishes what he calls explanatory, interpretive, and critical approaches to theorizing; with similar meaning, Denhardt (1990, 64) acknowledges "contending epistemological positions, with positivism, phenomenology, and critical theory being most prominent." This latter scheme will frame the subsequent discussion of theorizing.

The Purposes of Theorizing

In America, the basic frame for mainstream theorizing is, explicitly or implicitly, our constitutional scheme of governance and the administrative institutions created within and legitimated by it. The purpose of theorizing is to explain the workings of this scheme toward the goals of explaining, predicting, and improving its performance.

As just suggested, however, theorists have different purposes, and some adopt frames of reference that that lie outside the prevailing scheme—in other words, outside the status quo—and that would premise the legitimacy of public administration on other than existing systems of power and influence. Their purposes may be to interpret administrative systems from perspectives that reveal their ethical or moral defects, to criticize existing administrative systems from explicitly political perspectives, or both. Their goal is to reconceptualize, reformulate, and reconstruct the status quo based on different ethical, moral, and political precepts, with radical implications for governance and for Madisonian politics.

To illustrate the varieties of approaches that constitute public administration's theoretical enterprise, it is useful to sketch the general assumptions associated with the three dominant purposes of theorizing in public administration depicted by O'Toole and Denhardt: positive/explanatory, interpretive/phenomenological, and critical. The first perspective is generally realist in its philosophical orientation, whereas the latter two are regarded as "postmodern" or "postpositive," that is, reactive to and critical of realist philosophy.

Explaining

Theorists of a "positive" or "positivist" orientation are generally interested in devising explanations for how and why individuals, groups, institutions, and other social entities work as they do. Their question is, Why does governance take the form that it does in any given constitutional system and with what kinds of consequences? Drawing on such explanations, positivist scholars may formulate prescriptions for "interventions," such as public policies, managerial strategies, and organizational reforms, intended to improve the efficiency, effectiveness, and availability of services. In that respect, positivist scholars can be said to have an "instrumental," means-ends orientation to public administration.

Positivism is the philosophical foundation of what are generally termed "the scientific method" and "normal science" (Cruise 1997; Doubuzinskis 2003; Meier 2005). Positivism assumes the existence of a "reality," that is, a factual world, or a world of broad intersubjective agreement as to what "exists," that can be observed, categorized, measured, and analyzed so as to reveal correlations and causal relationships that explain the observed "real world." Thus explanations are not to be deduced from metaphysical systems of thought. Valid, that is, well-founded, explanations are those that can be shown to explain the facts of the observed world through appropriate applications of the scientific method. Positivists tend to assume, often without an inculcated self-awareness of the implications of doing so, that the processes that create and sustain political and administrative institutions are legitimate, and, therefore, so are the institutions themselves and the outcomes that are their consequences.

A scrupulous adherence to scientific method, in particular the methodologies that have been adapted to questions that arise in the social and behavioral sciences and in humanist professions, is believed to guarantee the objectivity, that is, the absence of intentional and corrupting bias, of theory-based research. Such objectivity is a consequence of the transparency and self-correcting nature of the scientific approach, whereby all aspects of an investigation are available for critical scrutiny. Commitment to confirmation or disconfirmation of findings through independent replication is sine qua non to professional judgments concerning what can be held to be "true" and actionable by policy makers and administrators. In public administration education, the approach is taken for granted to such an extent that students may not become aware that there are alternative philosophies for theorizing and research.

Positivist theorizing in public administration reflects the influence of many disciplines and scholarly traditions. The scope of theory-based explanation can be as broad as the administrative state and the constitutional order that underlies it or as narrow as organizing the delivery of one type of service in a given jurisdiction. Potential explanations can be a product of deductive or inductive reasoning. Theorizing and model development can be highly reductive and parsimonious so as to isolate specific causal mechanisms or more expansive or broadly cognizant of potentially influential factors so as to produce insights of greater verisimilitude. Though positivists tend toward methodological individualism and the assumption that choice is rational (or boundedly rational), units of analysis and associated behavioral assumptions can also be organizations, social units, or polities that are said to act on the basis of incentives, norms, rules, shared purposes, or canons of appropriateness. Methods and data employed in the testing of potential explanations can be quantitative, qualitative, or, many would say preferably, both.

Interpreting

An alternative to positivism is phenomenology, a philosophy that holds that "reality" consists of the lived experiences of individuals, of the meanings individuals attribute to specific objects—a Social Security check received, an application to be filled out—within their consciousness, and of how individuals make sense of their environments. Phenomenological assumptions lead, according to Kahn, "to a particular type of methodological pursuit, namely, describing people's conscious experiences as nakedly as possible" (Kahn 2003). As he sees it, phenomenologists tend to prefer qualitative methods, the results of which become the basis "for interpretations that allow for more abstract concepts and theories" (330).

Phenomenological theorizing thus is regarded as "interpretive" rather than "explanatory." In this respect, phenomenology is related to a class of approaches that hold that

> the chief purpose of social theory and research is to interpret the lived experience of intentional agents. . . . Its members include hermeneutics [the process of reflecting on the assumptions behind interpretations, especially in light of their political ramifications], ethnomethodology [describing how people make sense of things], symbolic interactionism [individuals act toward objects based on the meanings of those objects established through social interaction], various "standpoint epistemologies" (feminist theory being the most prominent of these), depth psychology (mainly Freudian and Jungian), the structuralism of Levi-Strauss [identifying the mental structures underlying human behavior], and, finally, the

post-structuralist approaches [emphasizing the plurality or instability of mental structures or meanings] of Foucault, Derrida, and Baudrillard. (Harmon 1995, 297)

From a phenomenological perspective, all "truth statements," such as those about political behavior, have moral implications, that is, conform to a greater or lesser extent to standards of right or just conduct. It follows that all instrumental decisions that have implications for individuals' lived experiences are moral decisions and must be evaluated on their intrinsic morality, not on their "results." Indeed, "without privileging the moral, a person is not a complete human being" (Farmer 2005, 583).

It follows that theories and theory-based research employing phenomenological assumptions are normative in that they depend on value judgments concerning the nature of right or just conduct. That this is true raises difficult issues. As Spicer notes (2008, 57), "The questions of normative theory in politics and administration such as 'Who should govern?' 'What should government do?' 'What should be the role of administrators in a democracy?' or 'What role should citizens play in governance?' do not admit to an answer using some clear-cut sort of methodology. . . . There is no generally accepted way of either answering or, for that matter, even to begin thinking about how one might answer these questions given the availability of sufficient data or time to think."

Phenomenologists are sharply critical of positivism. The study of human experience is regarded as "tainted to the extent that [it is] clothed in the researcher's own biases, presuppositions, or interpretations" (Kahn 2003, 330). Argues Spicer (2008, 57–58), "The meanings of words like public administration, government, constitution, law, democracy, citizen, and legislature are inherently ambiguous and are never precise or neutral in any scientific sense. They are inevitably tied, in the final analysis, to what sort of institution we think government is, can be, or, for that matter, ought to be. They are inextricably linked through our mental frameworks to what it is that we think government does, can do, or ought to do."

Thus, he says, "in our desire either to be more practical or to meet the canons of a more precise and value-free social science, we often express [philosophical] ideas unconsciously or without thinking. As a result, we may be led to embrace political values that are incoherent with, or that even contradict those which we ourselves hold to be dear and true" (Spicer 2008, 59–60).

The difficulties of doing so notwithstanding, scholars within this philosophical realm advocate a movement from the "is" to the "ought" in public administration: from putatively neutral or instrumental positivist formulations to self-aware normative statements. Denhardt assigns a reconstitutive role to theorists, favoring theorizing that is concerned with "the quality of the public service and the responsiveness of the public bureaucracy in a democratic society" (1990, 65). At the very least, phenomenologists would urge all public administration scholars to bring a philosophical self-awareness to bear on their use of abstractions, categories, terms of art, and analytical constructs such as causality and correlation, recognize the moral implications of their interventions, and include such implications in their instrumental prescriptions. Denhardt believes that "the vocation and obligation of the theorist" is to understand the moral obligations of his or her work, an obligation theorists share with practitioners (66).

Criticizing

The point of departure for critical theorists is a critique of the social, economic, and political order. Their presumption (Boyd and Kyle 2004, 255) is that "humans are enmeshed in relations that facilitate the domination of some by others which limits our freedom. These relations are not maintained solely by overt force (i.e., state power) and economic forces (e.g., capitalist economic arrangements), but they are also legitimated by approaches to governance and administration (e.g., new public management) and by ideological beliefs in things like the possibility and desirability of objectivity, professionalism, and expert knowledge."

The extent and persistence of oppression, discrimination, and hegemony are themes of critical theory. The individual's essential humanity is assumed to be diminished as power accumulates in the large, formal organizations of the public and private sectors and is wielded by Weberian bureaucracies through "scientifically justified" uses of various instruments of control and regulation, that is, technical, means-ends definitions of rationality.

Critical theory is the most overtly and programmatically political of the three theoretical perspectives under discussion. Using critical theory as a strategy for promoting democratic redistributions of power and reconceptualizations of reason, "critical theorists hope to engender crises of confidence in a society's ideological and institutional framework" (Sementelli and Abel 2000, 459). "Ideally," says Box, "critical theory aims to create conditions in which a fully conscious public enacts change" (Box 1995, 5). "The space of the economy and of formal organizations," say Salm, Candler, and Ventriss (2006, 527), "needs to be delimited, in a democratic manner, so that the phenonomic and isonomic spaces necessary to a full human existence can be preserved." Clearly, then, critical theorizing is also normative.

The critical theorists' political argument is succinctly summarized by Box: "The freedom of the individual has been twisted into freedom of private corporations to dictate the conditions of life and the physical environment of the world's population" (2004, 590). This development produces a conundrum. People come to realize that "government could be their only protection from the powerful, but government may be the 'property' of the people from whom they seek protection," or, as phenomenologists argue, government itself may, perhaps unconsciously, become an agent of oppression. "In contemporary societies based on liberalism, public institutions are used, in the words of Bowles and Gintis (1986, 17), to 'render democracy safe for elites—democracy is confined to a realm (the state) relatively unlikely to interfere with the wielding of economic power. . . . ' In this situation, democratic practice is 'limited to forms (representative government) insufficient for the consolidation of popular power'" (Box 2004, 590).

Such a corruption of governance is, however, not inevitable, Box insists. "Centralization can result in greater democracy in the long term, even when it appears coercive at the moment" (2004, 590), although a clever politics is essential to a good result. "Advances in democracy may be possible without causing such consternation amongst the powerful that they intervene to curtail them" (592). Continues Box, "discourse theory . . . is an important approach to involving the public in . . . deciding what to do" (598). This will be true, however, only if issues such as access to information, the quality of deliberation, the role of professionals in administration, and the functioning of representative institutions are properly addressed. Doing so may be as much a matter as changing perceptions of the purpose of government and the appropriate locus of decision making as of changing formal legal structures and, on the part of professional public administration, a commitment to social relevance rather than scientific legitimacy.

This pragmatic perspective is controversial, however. Fox argues, for example, that "ultimately constitutionalism fails us because it is simply too conservative; it is reactionary in the noble but still fettering Burkean sense. To defend the administrative state by constitutional inquiry looks back instead of forward" (Fox 1993, 56).

Axes of Reconciliation and Conflict

It should be apparent that phenomenological and critical perspectives are complementary rather than antagonistic. They share a commitment to symbolic and communicative interaction, to the objective of unifying theory and praxis, and to creating widely shared interpretations of objects and circumstances. This synthesis may, however, require phenomenologists to pay greater attention to the material conditions affecting interpretation that are central to critical theory, but there would appear to be no principled objection to doing so. The goal is that "the field of symbolic or communicative interaction will eventually become embedded in the emergent field of purposive/ rational action, now the basis for the new legitimation of the structure of social power" (Denhardt 1981, 630).

Thus, mutually reinforcing normative theorizing might have as its purpose that which Denhardt has claimed for critical theory: "It is the role of theory to reveal . . . contradictions [between human strivings and the limitations imposed on them by social conditions] and, thus, permit us to pursue our own freedom." The objective is "to transcend the tension and to abolish the opposition between the individual's purposefulness, spontaneity, and rationality, and those work-process relationships on which society is built" (Denhardt 1981, 629).

Some positivists acknowledge the influence on their thinking of various normative perspectives and are sympathetic to their broad purpose of critique that facilitates greater personal freedom and dignity. In the course of their work, positivists may employ phenomenological ideas. For example, in their empirical analysis of public organizational performance, Brewer and Selden acknowledge that "organizational performance is a socially constructed phenomenon that is subjective, complex, and particularly hard to measure in the public sector" (Brewer and Selden 2000, 688).

Indeed, positivists have asserted that propositions derived within normative perspectives might be subject to confirmation or disconfirmation through application of their methods. Most, however, are likely to agree with Sementelli and Abel that "there seems to be no evidence that any immanent critique currently propels or guides the action of any movement, party, interest group or regime. Moreover, forms of life that are distinctly non-emancipatory thrive in many places, even within societies dedicated to an ongoing self-criticism of its institutions and regimes" (Sementelli and Abel 2000, 464–465). "In brief," they continue, "non-emancipatory discourses, institutions and process that do not respect the integrity of the individual (in the sense of self-rule) seem to be working, and nowhere do we find a working model of critical theory as delineated by modern critical theorists" (465).

The possibilities of reconciliation among these three orientations on behalf of a comprehensive and coherent "theory of public administration" must confront the implications of their own premises. Positivists are inherently distrustful of theorizing they regard as tainted by unexamined biases, subjectivity, and self-affirming reasoning. For their part, normative theorists are inherently distrustful of the technical rationality that, by providing apparent scientific legitimacy for agents of hierarchical control of human behavior and experience, are profoundly antidemocratic and inimical to unfettered discourse among equal citizens. Because of these axes of tension, theorizing in public administration is an arena for contentious debate over the profession's values and epistemologies.

VARIETIES OF EXPLANATION

As noted earlier, most theorizing in public administration involves explaining administrative activity or performance through empirical investigation: testing or identifying theoretical propositions in the light of "facts," that is, actual (recorded, measured, observed, and described) events or phenomena: behavior, administrative acts, decisions, legal and organizational structures and processes, service utilization, and the like. The intended uses of such explanations include, in addition to further theory building, contingent predictions—if-then statements—held with sufficient confidence to support arguments on behalf of specific policies, management strategies, and service-delivery practices.

While the tradition of theory-based empirical explanation has its historical roots in the Progressive Era's scientific management movement, empiricism began to assume its present form in the 1930s in investigations by Ridley and Simon (1938; Simon et al. [1941]), Stone, Price, and Stone (1940), and Lipson ([1939] 1968) (for further discussion, see Bertelli and Lynn 2006). Additional momentum was provided by the emergence of the policy sciences, operations research, and systems/policy analysis movements and of Herbert Simon's Carnegie School of behavioral research following World War II, which increased the emphasis on research-based decision making in public administration. The policy sciences, as developed by H.D. Lasswell (1971) and his colleagues, "proposed intellectual tools to aid practitioners in the identification and specification of policy problems and the development of sensible, useful, and politically viable solutions to them" (deLeon and Steelman 2001, 164). Training for understanding and engaging in such research gradually became a staple of professional education in public administration.

Aaron Wildavsky, a seminal figure in the public policy movement, described "the art of policy analysis" as follows (1979, 16): "Policy analysis must create problems that decision-makers are able to handle with the variables under their control and in the time available . . . by specifying a desired relationship between manipulable means and obtainable objectives. . . . Unlike social science, policy analysis must be prescriptive; arguments about correct policy, which deal with the future, cannot help but be willful and therefore political." Policy analysis became firmly institutionalized in public deliberation and decision making in the executive and legislative branches and in legal deliberations at all levels of government.

Further impetus for theory-based empirical research in public administration has come from the recent emphasis on performance: of agencies and organizations, policies, programs, and public officials, specifically on performance measurement and management and on evidence-based policy making and practice. Nonprofit and for-profit research institutes and think tanks have joined universities in meeting steadily growing demands for research and analysis and for theories that explain important facts and predict consequences of policy, regulatory, and service interventions.

A useful characterization of theory that explains administrative phenomena has been formulated by Rockman (2000, 6). "Theory," he says, "constitutes a logical concatenation of ideas that may be formally derived and axiomatic or merely verbal formulations that represent a logical set of hunches about how things work." He elaborates: "An important theory provides us with the power to draw inferences that would not be self-evident but for the organizing principle the theory provides. A powerful theory also helps us understand the mundane by pulling together in a conceptually coherent way a set of behaviors or phenomena we would otherwise see only in isolated terms." Theorizing of this kind seeks to provide logical, empirically verifiable explanations of what Rockman calls the peculiarities of political institutions, and it is enjoying growing global prominence within public administration and management.

The Scope of Explanation

Empirically oriented theorizing varies widely in scope and purpose. A growing body of research is concerned with the determinants of "government performance" (Boyne et al. 2006; Forbes, Hill, and Lynn 2006; Robichau and Lynn 2009). But investigators' more focused concerns, together with limitations of data and analytical methods, mean that much theorizing occurs in the middle range of practical concerns about particular propositions within broader conceptual frameworks, such as the efficacy of particular kinds of incentives, for example, pay for performance, within a given organizational or institutional context, such as a tenured civil service.

To illustrate the character of this type of theorizing, several examples have been chosen for their quality and representation of the contemporary empirical research agenda. Their scope ranges from explanations of particular propositions to explanations intended to provide more general, or generalizable, insights into organizational and administrative system operation and performance.

Explanations: Partial Theories

Rockman's "logical concatenation of ideas," both verbal formulations and more formally derived hypotheses, provide the basis for deriving administrative propositions intended to have implications for practice.

Are Public Sector–Private Sector Differences Significant? How, why, and with what implications does administration in the public sector differ from that in the private sector? The characteristics that differentiate public from private organizations, the consequences of those differences for performance, and the relationships between characteristics and consequences offer countless possibilities for theory-based empirical research on public-private differences (Rainey and Chun 2005).

An example is Nutt's investigation of differences in the decision-making practices of public and private sector organizations. His theoretical proposition is that these practices differ because "organizations with public features are seen as being constrained in ways that limit what they can do when making strategic choices" (2006, 290). By comparing decision making in a tax-supported public agency with that in a private firm that sells to a market, he seeks to assess "problems and prospects in the oft-repeated call for public sector organizations to adopt private sector practices" (290).

Employing a complex research design involving a simulation, Nutt tests five specific hypotheses concerning "how mid-level managers in [a state department of natural resources and an automotive company] view the prospects of approval and the risk" in budget decisions. His explanatory variables include "sector, budgeting practices, the cognitive makeup of the participant, and level of controversy. The budgeting practices draw on the modes of understanding found in four kinds of decision-making cultures and are applied to controversial and noncontroversial budget requests" (290).

Nutt's broad conclusion is that "managers in the private sector seem to place too much reliance on analytics and too little on bargaining. Those in the public sector may place too great an emphasis on [internal] bargaining and too little on networking [with external actors], but they do seem to understand the limits of analysis" (311). His policy implication is that those who "seek to reform government by calling for the use of private sector business practices . . . should pay more attention to the barriers to using analysis, real and imagined, if they hope to see their recommendations followed. The recommended practices invariably call for analytic procedures and practices [that are] difficult to carry out" in a political setting (312).

How Can Better Client Outcomes Be Achieved? How do program structures, management strategies, operating practices, and client characteristics interact to determine program outputs and outcomes? Theorizing concerning this question varies widely in scope. The object to be explained is usually the outputs or outcomes of a particular type of agency, a specific agency, or a specific program (Heinrich 2003).

Bloom, Hill, and Riccio (2003) conducted a multilevel study of measured impacts on clients of welfare-to-work programs. They were able to pool data "from a series of large-sample, multi-site experiments of mandatory welfare-to-work programs conducted by MDRC during the past 15 years." The authors' theorizing assimilates the conjectures and propositions of other investigators of the determinants of a program's impact on client outcomes. It focuses on the influence of four sets of implementation-related factors on the effectiveness of welfare-to-work programs: program management and treatment practices, client activities, the economic environment in which programs operate, and client characteristics. Their dependent variable is an outcome measure: "the estimated impact on sample members' mean total earnings (measured in constant 1996 dollars) for the first 2 years after random assignment" to a control or treatment group (557).

The authors found that "the emphasis placed by programs on quick client employment has by far the largest, most statistically significant, and most robust effect on program impacts of all that we observed" (565). In addition, "findings for personalized client attention are also striking, statistically significant, and robust" (565). Their policy implication is that "management choices for how welfare-to-work programs are implemented matter a great deal to their success. In particular: a strong employment message is a powerful medium for stimulating clients to find jobs, a clear staff focus on personal client attention can markedly increase their success, [but] large client caseloads can undercut program effectiveness" (571).

How Can Bureaucratic Accountability Be Assured? The importance of bureaucratic responsiveness and accountability to political control has greatly increased as political emphasis on performance and transparency has grown. Questions that arise include those concerning both bureaucratic responsiveness to political authority and worker responsiveness to clients affected by their work.

Based on the literature, Potoski (1999) argues both that bureaucracies can be responsive and that bureaucracies can be independent and even influential in their own right. He chooses to address a question concerning the conditions under which bureaucracies are either more politically responsive or more autonomous. The problem, as he sees it, is that "theories offer widely different and sometimes conflicting predictions about how politicians use administrative procedures to control agencies" (624).

Potoski proposes "a positive (transaction costs) theory of how politicians use administrative procedures to reduce uncertainty about agency behavior." He differentiates between ex ante procedures that "stack the deck" "so that agencies' policy decisions favor the political interests that the legislators target" (625) and ex post "fire alarms," such as transparency requirements, that "reduce the various forms of politicians' uncertainty surrounding bureaucratic performance" (625). Three types of procedures were chosen for study based on discussions with state clean air officials: policy analysis procedures, political consultation procedures, and group consultation procedures" (630). Data for the study were from a survey of administrative procedures used by state air pollution control agencies. Explanatory variables that affect political transaction costs—strength of interest groups, complexity, strength of legislative staff and committees, and political turnover—were included in a multivariate regression model.

His contingent results, Potoski claims, confirm his expectations. "When they face the uncertainty of a turbulent political environment, politicians hardwire agencies by establishing policy analysis procedures. In response to the uncertainty of complex policy problems, politicians expand agency autonomy, reducing oversight procedures in order to capitalize on the technical expertise of unfettered clean air bureaucrats. Finally, politicians with stronger legislative committee and staff resources can use fire alarm procedures to combat the principal-agent problem of overseeing clean air agencies" (637).

Explanations: Organizational Performance

Organizational theory adapted from sociology, economics, social psychology, and other fields has long been featured in public administration theorizing because of the profession's focus on public agencies. In empirical research, such theorizing has focused on the determinants of the performance both of specific agencies or types of agencies and of the public sector, that is, tax-supported organizations more generally.

Why Are Some Organizations More Effective Than Others? How can the fact that some public organizations are more effective than others be explained? Theorizing must contend with the undoubted but difficult-to-assess influence of, among other things, political context, policy design, management, organizational cultures, street-level worker values, skills and practices, and characteristics and behaviors of beneficiaries themselves.

In a well-known article, Rainey and Steinbauer (1999) draw on the literature and research on effective government organizations to select and develop conceptual elements of a theory that would explain their effectiveness. Rather than deductive theorizing based on concepts from public choice theory or the economics of organization, their approach "draws . . . on case studies and empirical research in public administration and public bureaucracy as well as concepts from organization and management theory[,] . . . conclusions from many of the authors on successful leadership and management . . . [and] efforts to characterize government agencies that perform efficiently" (8).

The authors' concept of effectiveness, that is, their generalized dependent variable, "refers to whether the agency does well that which it is supposed to do, whether people in the agency work hard and well, whether the actions and procedures of the agency and its members are well suited to achieving its mission, and whether the agency actually achieves its mission" (13). Their theory is meant to suggest the kinds of complex causal relationships that must be considered in thinking about the determination of organizational performance and in designing empirical research.

What Specific Factors Affect Organizational Performance? An analytic framework such as that of Rainey and Steinbauer is bound to become a point of departure for more focused investigations. For example, Brewer and Selden (2000) contend that both agency-level and individual factors affect organizational performance. They identify five agency-level factors: organizational culture, human capital and capacity, agency support for the National Performance Review (the Clinton administration's public management reform), leadership and supervision, and red tape. Their four individual-level factors are structure of task or work, task motivation, public service motivation, and individual performance.

The authors test their theory using data from the 1996 Merit Systems Protection Board's Merit Principles Survey, which questioned a random sample of 18,163 permanent, full-time employees in the twenty-three largest federal government agencies, and ordinary least squares regression methods. The dependent variable was a measure of organizational performance based on responses to six survey questions. The authors found that agency-level factors most affect organizational performance; organizational culture in particular, which comprises efficacy, teamwork, protection of employees, and concern for the public interest, is "a powerful predictor of organizational performance in federal agencies" (703). Individual-level variables were "modestly important predictors of organizational performance." They claim that their findings have clear implications for the teaching and practice of administration and management.

Does Management Affect Results? Though theory-based empirical research has established that "management matters" to organization results, questions still remain concerning how management matters to government performance.

"Although theoretical ideas about public management and how it shapes governance action proliferate like populations without predators," say Meier and O'Toole (2007), "much of that work is ambiguous in character and unsystematic in sketching causal links between public management and public program performance" (505). Based on theoretical and empirical (mostly case-study) literature in both hierarchical and networked environments, the authors constructed a formal model of the management-performance relationship. According to the authors, in the model governing the relationship between public management and program performance: current outputs reflect prior outputs; fundamental causal relationships are nonlinear; and performance is properly conceptualized in terms of outputs and outcomes.

The Meier and O'Toole model has spawned a large empirical literature by the authors themselves and by colleagues testing the model's logic. The results tend to confirm the authors' reductive theory. That this is so is in contrast to models like that of Rainey and Steinbauer, which, because they are constrained by little or no formal logic, tend to spawn research of considerable theoretical variability. This advantage of the Meier-O'Toole model is offset in part by the ambiguity of the model's variable constructs: "a measure of stability"; "management," which comprises "management's contribution to organizational stability through additions to hierarchy/structure as well as regular operations," management's efforts to exploit the environment of the organization, and management's effort to buffer the unit from the environmental shocks"; and "a vector of environmental forces" (505). With such formulations, construct comparability across studies becomes an important issue.

Explanations: Government Performance

If organizational cultures matter most, according to one study, political support according to another, might their relative influence be assessed? Some of the most ambitious theorizing for empirical research seeks to explain "government performance" within a broad framework that explains the outputs or outcomes (or both) of policies, programs, organizations, or complex administrative systems operating in multilevel political contexts (Boyne 2003; Lynn, Heinrich, and Hill 2001). Such theorizing may encompass both hierarchical and networked or consociation arrangements, multiple levels of hierarchical interaction, and complex dimensions of management and service delivery.

How Can We Understand the Performance of Multilevel Governance? Findings from individual studies suggest that the relationship between public policies and their outcomes is mediated by factors at multiple levels of governance. Lynn, Heinrich, and Hill (2001) have constructed an analytic framework they term a "logic of governance," which identifies these levels of interaction, thus establishing a nexus among policy makers, public managers, service providers, service recipients, and the public. They propose that this framework be used not only to inform theorizing concerning how political-administrative systems are implicated in the shaping and implementation of public policies but also as a framework for synthesizing findings across studies, leading to insights that might otherwise be opaque.

Hill and Lynn (2005), for example, used the logic of governance to synthesize findings from more than eight hundred published studies that investigated interrelationships between two or more levels of governance. A striking finding of their analysis was that, in the vast majority of studies, "influence is modeled as flowing downward from legislation and management toward treatments [service delivery] and consequences, and this general pattern is evident for virtually every level of governance being modeled" (179). Moreover, "variables at virtually every level of the governance hierarchy both influence and are influenced by variables at other levels, and these relationships can be (but are not always) statistically and substantively significant" (181). Of particular interest, they say, "are constructs . . . over which public managers and their agents have influence: formal organizational structure, public management [strategies], and [service delivery]" (181).

How Do Politics and Management Interact? As managerialism—letting, or making, managers manage—in various guises became a fashionable theme of public administrative reform, theorizing turned to the question of how and why management matters in politically designed, complex government organizations (Hill and Lynn 2005; Meier and O'Toole 2007). Though much empirical research focuses on identifying best practices, effort devoted to theory-based investigations of political influences on management and performance has increased.

For example, Moynihan and Pandey (2005) focus on "key environmental and organizational predictors of performance" (424). They test a number of specific hypotheses concerning "the impact [on organizational effectiveness] of a number of environmental factors (the support of elected officials, the influence of clients, the influence of the public) and organizational factors (culture, centralization of decision authority, goal clarity, barriers to reorganization)" (424). Variables in their study were based on responses from a survey of 274 managers from eighty-three organizations across the fifty states who were engaged in information-management activities in state-level primary health and human services agencies. Based on ordinary least squares regression analysis, the authors conclude that "results . . . support the proposition that organizational performance is shaped both by external environmental factors and internal management factors" (430). Evidence concerning the importance of political support is particularly strong. Further, they note, "the positive impact of public/media influence on performance supports this claim, suggesting that bureaucrats understand performance in terms of responsiveness to the broader public" (432).

How Does Policy Affect Service Delivery? Management matters, but what about the policy designs that those managers are directed to implement? A growing body of theory-based empirical research embeds management in a matrix of interdependent relationships with policy makers and service workers: Management, in other words, is both dependent and independent variable (Hill and Lynn 2005; Forbes, Hill, and Lynn 2006).

Based on their survey of empirical literature, May and Winter (2009) argue that previous research "provides little understanding of the importance of political and managerial influences in the implementation equation" (2). The authors seek to explain the extent to which the actions of street-level bureaucrats reflect higher-level policy goals in reformed Danish employment programs. Their model includes municipal-level considerations such as "municipal policy goals, political attention, and managerial actions, along with . . . attitudinal and contextual variables that relate to individual caseworkers" (12).

With data drawn mainly from a nationwide survey of a sample of municipal caseworkers who are responsible for implementing the laws and intentions of the reform as well as from surveys of employment functions of chief executive officers and municipal middle managers in all Danish municipalities, the authors use hierarchical linear modeling (HLM) estimation methods to investigate "the extent to which caseworkers take actions that are consistent with the national goal of getting people into work" (12). They found that "on the one hand, higher level political [attention of relevant municipal politicians to employment issues] and managerial [supervision, communicating specific goals] factors influence the policy emphases of frontline workers. On the other hand, the strength of the effects is relatively limited" (16).

VARIETIES OF CRITICAL INTERPRETATION

In contrast to positivist theorizing, what can theorizing within interpretive and critical traditions contribute to the practice of public administration and management? Several classic papers suggest some possibilities.

The Social Construction of Reality

Among the most well-known ideas emerging from nonpositivist theorizing is that the reality that motivates political and administrative behavior is "socially constructed." A social construction is a phenomenon that is held to be real by those who constitute a culture or subculture. Social constructions are "normative and evaluative," not "objective"; homelessness and the homeless, poverty and poor people, veterans, and gender and gender roles are examples of socially embedded constructions implying certain perceived (as well as measured) characteristics and cultural (as well as expert) judgments.

Schneider and Ingram (1993), for example, put forward a theory of the social construction of "target populations"—populations that are the objects of public policy—contending that social constructions become embedded in public policies, "send[ing] messages about what government is supposed to do, which citizens are deserving (and which not), and what kinds of attitudes and participatory patterns are appropriate in a democratic society" (334).

The authors' theory offers not only an interpretation of the behavior of societal actors but also an explanation of political outcomes: who gets what, when, and how. It bridges the divide between phenomenology and positivism in that, as they put it, "target populations are assumed to have boundaries that are empirically verifiable (indeed, policies create these empirical boundaries) and to exist within objective conditions even though those conditions are subject to multiple evaluations" (335). In other words, phenomena that are regarded by positivists as facts are better understood as the resultants of a process of social construction that selects a particular evaluative interpretation of perceived phenomena.

What Is a "Problem" Requiring a Policy Response?

From the wide variety of social constructions that might motivate a political response, only some reach the agenda for political action at national, state, and local levels of policy making. The question is, which culturally identified situations, difficulties, and problems reach that agenda?

This question is addressed by Stone (1989). "Problem definition," she argues, "is a process of image making, where the images have to do fundamentally with attributing cause, blame, and responsibility" (282). That is, political actors must be able to conceive of difficulties as having a cause, and a locus of responsibility, that they can ameliorate by use of the legislative and regulatory tools at their disposal. The causal arguments embraced by political actors may or may not be valid in a scientific sense; policy makers persist in their faith in performance-based pay for civil servants despite the absence of evidence of their efficacy (Perry, Engbers, and Jun 2009). Causal arguments that do have a degree of validity that is convincing to scholars may fail to move policy makers because such arguments do not readily translate into a convincing policy argument. Government performance may have multiple, complex determinants, but rewarding measured performance is an easily grasped idea with popular appeal.

Can Policy Making Be More Democratic?

The relationship between research and practice with respect to public policy and administration has often been characterized as a relationship between specialist professionals and their practitioner "clients." Critical theorists see this relationship differently, as representing "the capitulation of social science to the instrumental and rationalizing processes of the modern techno-industrial system and its state apparatus" (Fischer 1993, 165).

To remedy the technocratic bias inherent in policy making based on positivist policy research, Fischer (1993) puts forward a postpositivist conception of "practical reason," which is a product of "deliberation" and "giving good reasons" and, therefore, of a non-Madisonian politics in which citizens participate directly and equally in the policy-making process (167). The role of experts is transformed from proffering their best technical judgments on problems they themselves define to facilitating citizen efforts to learn and choose for themselves the problems that concern them and reasonable approaches to them. "It involves the creation of institutional and intellectual contexts that help people pose questions and examine technical analyses in their own ordinary (or everyday) languages and decide which issues are important to them" (171). Thus, experts immerse themselves in the very cultural processes described by Schneider and Ingram and by Stone and facilitate social constructions that are democratic. Such "collaborative research" is perhaps best suited to those difficulties or problems that are especially complex, both intellectually and institutionally.

To the objection that widespread participation is difficult to achieve in a mass society subject to competing demands on collective attention, Dryzek (2001) responds by defining the legitimacy of deliberative democracy in terms not of head counts but of "the resonance of collective decisions with public opinion, defined in terms of the provisional outcome of the contestation of discourses in the public sphere as transmitted to the state" (666). The difference between this formulation and contemporary arrangements is subtle: the extent to which discourses are undistorted by elite interests and constructions.

PUBLIC ADMINISTRATION THEORY: A HETERODOXY

Taken together, the preceding three sections have an important implication. The achievement of an integrated, more coherent understanding of public administration that resolves the identity crisis long perceived by many within the profession is not only a vain hope; it is a misguided one. The controversies that infuse theorizing in public administration reflect the existential reality of public administration's moral, humanistic, democratic, and pragmatic professional concerns. Indeed, because philosophical differences among theorists turn on moral questions, because the suppression of such differences would be greeted with opprobrium by all concerned, and, finally, because advocates of the dominant philosophy, positivism, are hardly unified themselves, public administration theory is fated to remain a heterodoxy of dissenters from orthodoxies favored by one or another philosophical protagonist.

The positivist orthodoxy appears to be, on the whole, more self-critical than the normative orthodoxies. The oft-acknowledged difficulties of conducting research on political and organizational phenomena notwithstanding (Bradley and Schaefer 1998), Lynn, Heinrich, and Hill have argued that "research—carefully conceived and theoretically framed, executed with skill, and appropriately qualified—can produce contingent findings that are sufficiently robust to provide useful contributions to conceptual and practical understanding, contributions that, on the whole, are at least as useful as those provided by any other high-quality research approach" (Lynn, Heinrich, and Hill 2008, 105; cf. Cruise 1997).

As a practical matter—as a matter of professional ethos—theory-based empirical research in public administration is most usefully regarded as a potentially credible source of heuristics for practice, that is, as a source of stimulants to constructive, creative, or critical thought about administrative phenomena and of ideas for deliberation and, if suitably vetted, for action. Well-executed, theory-based empirical research can be insightful about practical matters, cutting through what might otherwise appear to be incoherent complexity. Normative critics must be able to show that they can do better than positivists when confronting administrative problems as they present themselves in practice.

What constitutes "doing better" is a judgment call, however, arguably no more free of ideological bias than normative assertions. Confirmed antipositivists will be disinclined to accept the "highest-quality" positivist research as a legitimate basis for action because positivism tends to ignore the lived experiences of those affected by such action, the cultural bases of social constructions, and the moral implications of acting.

In the light of these difficulties, what the profession might aspire to has been articulated by Evans and Lowery (2006, 2008). They note that "scholars in the field of public administration . . . are generally less free to advance normative claims in so uncritical a fashion than are practitioners, political actors, the general public and even writers of popular fiction. . . . We know, however, that normative claims that set out to answer [important] questions are often advanced with something less than a full articulation of the various philosophical, social, and political beliefs and commitments on which they are grounded. More is needed if a normative claim is to be considered scholarly" (Evans and Lowery 2006, 158). In their view (2008, 21–22):

> Should we choose to see ourselves as a multidisciplinary field of study in support of a broad array of professional practices, our eyes (and hearts) can bask in the beauty shared in a wide range of scholarly arguments, some of them innovative and surprising. The insights embodied in these arguments may have the capacity to open doors to both past experiences and new opportunities. They could evoke the significance inherent in the mundane, practical, and daily experienced truths of those whose explorations into the realm of meaningful practice we profess to guide, even if these truths fly in the face of conventional wisdom.

If that range of scholarly arguments—for example, over reconciling moral imperatives such as the universality of access to health care, educational opportunity, and income security with resource scarcity and individual liberty—includes those put forward undogmatically by individuals who would explain, or interpret, or criticize, then both the symbiosis and the serendipity among theorists and between theorizing and practice on which a healthy sense of professional identity depends may be within reach.

REFERENCES

Bertelli, Anthony M., and Laurence E. Lynn Jr. 2006. *Madison's Managers: Public Administration and the Constitution.* Baltimore, MD: Johns Hopkins University Press.

Bloom, Howard S., Carolyn J. Hill, and James A. Riccio. 2003. Linking program implementation and effectiveness: Lessons from a pooled sample of welfare-to-work experiments. *Journal of Policy Analysis and Management* 22 (4): 551–575.

Bowles, S., and H. Gintis. 1986. *Democracy and Capitalism: Property, Community and the Contradictions of Modern Social Thought.* New York: Basic Books.

Box, Richard C. 1995. Critical theory and the paradox of discourse. *The American Review of Public Administration* 25 (1): 1–19.

———. 2004. Alternatives to representative primacy and administrative efficiency. *Administrative Theory and Praxis* 26 (4): 588–608.

Boyd, Neil M., and Ken Kyle. 2004. Expanding the view of performance appraisal by introducing justice concerns. *Administrative Theory and Praxis* 26 (3): 249–277.

Boyne, George A. 2003. Sources of public service improvement: A critical review and research agenda. *Journal of Public Administration Research and Theory* 13 (3): 367–394.

Boyne, George, Kenneth Meier, Laurence O'Toole Jr., and Richard Walker, eds. 2006. *Public Services Performance: Perspectives on Measurement and Management.* Cambridge: Cambridge University Press.

Bradley,W.J., and K.C. Schaefer. 1998. *The Uses and Misuses of Data and Models: The Mathematization of the Human Sciences.* Thousand Oaks, CA: Sage.

Brewer, Gene A., and Sally Coleman Selden. 2000. Why elephants gallop: Assessing and predicting organizational performance in federal agencies. *Journal of Public Administration Research and Theory* 10 (4): 685–711.

Christopher, Gail C. 2003. Innovative government practice: Considerations for policy analysts and practitioners. *Journal of Policy Analysis and Management* 22 (4): 683–688.

Cruise, Peter L. 1997. Are proverbs really so bad? Herbert Simon and the logical positivist perspective in American public administration. *Journal of Management History* 3 (4): 342–359.

deLeon, Peter D., and Toddi A. Steelman. 2001. Making public policy programs effective and relevant: the role of the policy sciences. *Journal of Policy Analysis and Management* 20 (1): 163–171.

Denhardt, Robert B. 1981. Toward a critical theory of public organization. *Public Administration Review* 41 (6): 628–635.

———. 1990. Public administration theory: The state of the discipline. In *Public Administration: The State of the Discipline,* ed. Naomi Lynn and Aaron Wildavsky, 43–72. Chatham, NJ: Chatham House.

Doubuzinskis, Laurent. 2003. Logical positivism and public administration. In *Encyclopedia of Public Administration and Public Policy,* ed. Jack Rabin and T. Aaron Wachhaus, 739–43. New York: Marcel Dekker.

Dryzek, John S. 2001. Legitimacy and economy in deliberative democracy. *Political Theory* 29 (5): 651–669.

Evans, Karen G., and Daniel Lowery. 2006. Prescriptive thinking: Normative claims as scholarship. *Administration and Society* 38:147–165.

———. 2008. The scholarship of elegance and significance: Expressive and aesthetic truth claims. *Administration and Society* 40:3–24.

Farmer, David John. 2005. The moral first, the technical second! *Administrative Theory and Praxis* 27:581–594.

Fischer, Frank. 1993. Citizen participation and the democratization of policy expertise: From theoretical inquiry to practical source. *Policy Sciences* 26 (3): 165–187.

Forbes, Melissa K., Carolyn J. Hill, and Laurence E. Lynn Jr. 2006. Public management and government performance: An international review. In *Public Services Performance: Perspectives on Measurement and Management,* ed. George Boyne, Kenneth Meier, Laurence O'Toole Jr., and Richard Walker, 254–274. Cambridge: Cambridge University Press.

Fox, Charles J. 1993. Alternatives to orthodoxy: Constitutionalism, communitarianism, and discourse. *Administrative Theory and Praxis* 15 (2): 52–70.

Frederickson, H. George, and Kevin B. Smith. 2003. *The Public Administration Theory Primer.* Boulder, CO: Westview Press.

Friedson, Eliot. 1974. Dominant professions, bureaucracy, and client services. In *Human Service Organizations: A Book of Readings,* ed. Yeheskel Hasenfeld and Richard A. English, 428–448. Ann Arbor: University of Michigan Press.

Harmon, Michael. 1995. Diversity of social science theories. *Public Administration Review* 55 (3): 296–297.

Heinrich, Carolyn J. 2003. Measuring public sector performance effectiveness. In *Handbook of Public Administration,* ed. Guy Peters and Jon Pierre, 25–37. London: Sage Publications.

Hill, Carolyn J., and Laurence E. Lynn Jr. 2005. Is hierarchical governance in decline? Evidence from empirical research. *Journal of Public Administration Research and Theory* 15 (2): 173–195.

Hummel, Ralph P. 2007. What do theorists do? *Administrative Theory and Praxis* 29 (2): 292–296.

Kahn, William A. 2003. Review of *Toward Phenomenology of Groups and Group Membership.* In *Administrative Science Quarterly,* ed. H, Sondak, M, Neale, and E, Mannix, 330–332. Oxford: Elsevier Science.

Lasswell, H.D. 1971. *A Preview of Policy Sciences.* New York: American Elsevier.

Lipson, Leslie. [1939] 1968. *The American Governor, from Figurehead to Leader.* New York: Greenwood.

Lynn, Laurence E., Jr. 2008. The 2007 John Gaus Lecture: New frontiers of public administration: The practice of theory and the theory of practice. *PS: Political Science and Politics* 41:3–9.

Lynn, Laurence E., Jr., Carolyn J. Heinrich, and Carolyn J. Hill. 2001. *Improving Governance: A New Logic for Empirical Research.* Washington, DC: Georgetown University Press.

———. 2008. The empiricist goose has not been cooked. *Administration and Society* 40:104–109.

May, Peter J., and Søren C. Winter. 2009. Politicians, managers, and street-level bureaucrats: Influences on policy implementation. *Journal of Public Administration Research and Theory* 19 (3): 453–476.

Meier, Kenneth J. 2005. Public administration and the myth of positivism: The Antichrist's view. *Administrative Theory and Praxis* 27 (4): 650–668.

Meier, Kenneth J., and Laurence J. O'Toole Jr. 2007. Modeling public management: Empirical analysis of the management-performance nexus. *Public Management Review* 9 (4): 503–527.

Mostel, Claire. 2009. Finding the heart and soul of bureaucrats: A practitioner talks back. *Public Administration Review* 69 (3): 544–547.

Moynihan, Donald P., and Sanjay K. Pandey. 2005. Testing how management matters in an era of government by performance management. *Journal of Public Administration Research and Theory* 15 (3): 421–439.

Nutt, Paul C. 2006. Comparing public and private sector decision-making practices. *Journal of Public Administration Research and Theory* 16 (2): 289–318.

O'Toole, Laurence J., Jr. 1995. Diversity or cacophony? The research enterprise in public administration. Review of *Research in Public Administration: Reflections on Theory and Practice,* by Jay D. White and Guy B. Adams. *Public Administration Review* 55 (3): 293–297.

Park, Robert E. 1917. The social sciences and the war. *American Journal of Sociology* 23:64–66.

Perry, James L., Trent Engbers, and So Yun Jun. 2009. Back to the future? Performance-related pay, empirical research, and the perils of persistence. *Public Administration Review* 69 (1): 1–31.

Potoski, Matthew. 1999. Managing uncertainty through bureaucratic design: Administrative procedures and state air pollution control agencies. *Journal of Public Administration Research and Theory* 9 (4): 623–639.

Rainey, Hal G., and Young Han Chun. 2005. Public and private management compared. In *The Oxford Handbook of Public Management,* ed. Ewan Ferlie, Laurence E. Lynn Jr., and Christopher Pollitt, 72–102. Oxford: Oxford University Press.

Rainey, Hal G., and Paula Steinbauer. 1999. Galloping elephants: Developing a theory of effective government organizations. *Journal of Public Administration Research and Theory* 9 (1): 1–32.

Rein, Martin, and Lisa Peattie. 1981. Knowledge for policy. *Social Service Review* 55 (4): 525–543.

Ridley, Clarence E., and Herbert A. Simon. 1938. *Measuring Municipal Activities: A Survey of Suggested Criteria and Reporting Forms for Appraising Administration.* Chicago, IL: International City Managers Association.

Robichau, Robbie Waters, and Laurence E. Lynn Jr. 2009. Public policy implementation: Still the missing link. *Policy Studies Journal* 37 (1): 21–36.

Rockman, Bert A. 2000. Theory and inference in the study of bureaucracy: Micro- and neoinstitutionalist foundations of choice. *Journal of Public Administration Research and Theory* 11 (1): 3–27.

Rosenbloom, David H. 1983. Public administration theory and separation of powers. *Public Administration Review* 43 (3): 219–227.

Salm, José Francisco, Gaylord George Candler, and Curtis Ventriss. 2006. The theory of social systems delimitation and the reconceptualization of public administration. *Administrative Theory and Praxis* 28 (4): 522–539.

Savoie, Donald J. 2008. Searching for answers by retracing the roots of public administration and looking to economics. *Public Administration Review* 68 (1): 187–490.

Schneider, Anne, and Helen Ingram. 1993. Social construction of target populations: Implications for politics and policy. *American Political Science Review* 87 (2): 334–347.

Sementelli, Arthur, and Charles F. Abel. 2000. Recasting critical theory: Veblen, deconstruction, and the theory-praxis gap. *Administrative Theory and Praxis* 22 (3): 458–478.

Simon, Herbert A., William R. Divine, E. Myles Cooper, and Milton Chemnitz. 1941. *Determining Work Loads for Professional Staff in a Public Welfare Agency.* Berkeley, CA: Bureau of Public Administration, University of California.

Spicer, Michael W. 2008. The history of ideas and normative research in public administration: Some personal reflections. *Administrative Theory and Praxis* 30 (1): 50–70.

Stillman, Richard J., II. 1991. *Preface to Public Administration: A Search for Themes and Direction.* New York: St. Martin's Press.

Stone, Deborah A. 1989. Causal stories and the formation of policy agendas. *Political Science Quarterly* 104 (2): 281–300.

Stone, Harold, Don K. Price, and Kathryn H. Stone. 1940. *City Manager Government in the United States: A Review after Twenty-Five Years.* Chicago: Public Administration Service.

Waldo, Dwight. 1955. *The Study of Public Administration.* New York: Random House.

Wildavsky, Aaron. 1979. *Speaking Truth to Power: The Art and Craft of Policy Analysis.* Boston: Little, Brown.

PART I

THE PROFESSION

The long-standing consideration of public administration as a profession has engendered a stimulating discourse. The chapters in this section are an expansion of this discourse. They add to the insightful work in Richard L. Schott's 1976 *Public Administration Review* article, "Public Administration as a Profession: Problems and Prospects," and the exchanges around it.

Foresight in the dialogue fostered by Schott is intriguing. Writing nearly thirty-five years ago, authors involved in the exchange seem to foretell many of the challenges facing public administration that are considered in this section. The emergence of public policy as a field of study and the National Association of Schools of Public Affairs and Administration (NASPAA) as a mechanism for accreditation were a part of this discourse. The effects of technology, albeit a different set of technologies, the development of sectionalism (health, budgeting, human resources, and so on) within the profession, and the increasingly interdisciplinary nature of public administration were also discussed. How could they know these issues would be so salient in public administration today? Or did they know? Fortuitously, they provide an answer, including those in *Public Administration: The State of the Discipline,* edited by Naomi B. Lynn and Aaron Wildavsky (1990).

A careful reading of the dialogue reveals that these scholars were not merely attempting to foretell the future of public administration but rather were prescribing what it should become as a profession. Their quest was for "a revitalization of public administration" and, as leaders in the profession, they accepted the challenge of prescribing how this could be achieved. As David Fauri (1976, 722) notes in this commentary on Schott's article: "Public administration educators [and scholars] will eventually lead the way in professionalization, and while this may involve some frustration, the long-range prospect is for better educated graduates, stronger educational programs, and improved government administration." The contributors to this section are equally committed to the revitalization of public administration, and their prescriptions for achieving it are also very insightful.

Fortuitously and appropriately, this section starts with Bowman and West's chapter, "The Profession of Public Administration: Promise, Problems, and Prospects." Similar to Schott's work, Bowman and West's essay does not shy away from controversy. They highlight the impact of misguided reforms that "'placed their faith in oversimplified and discredited management nostrums.'" This includes reforms that provide a form of private sector business management, "'whilst hollowing-out the substance of the public sector ethos and ethics.'" Bowman and West also discuss a restoration of public administration as a profession that could be taking place. As they note, "signs exist that public employment will, once again, be seen as an employer of choice." Other contributors to this section also address the restoration of public administration as a profession.

Patricia Shields and Nandhini Rangarajan expand the discussion of professionalism by analyzing several pioneering women's contributions to the development of public administration. A major point in their work is that "these early women and their organizations . . . uncovered ideas and practices [that] are an integral but neglected influence on . . . public administration as a field of practice and study." Moreover, they insist that women have demonstrated their talents in many public service endeavors and current challenges demand that we bring our full capacity—which includes the talents of women—to the task.

Wendy Haynes and Beth Gazley's work considers the impact of professional associations on public administration, and their potential for fostering public service excellence. Of importance is the special capacity of these associations to educate, train, and credential people in many occupations and provide commercial services to professionals. As they surmise, "It is quite possible that every career public official belongs to one or more professional associations."

Jeffrey A. Raffel, Steven M. Maser, and Crystal Calarusse chronicle the accreditation process and standards promulgated by the NASPAA over the past twenty-five years. Through this chronology, they highlight NASPAA's role in promoting accountability, transparency, professionalism, equity, trust, and responsiveness as the values that define the field. They also give thought to the future of public service education and NASPAA's role in shaping it.

Montgomery Van Wart focuses on the increasing importance of administrative leadership in public administration. This is crucial because leaders of "public organizations can bring in resources, set a positive tone, encourage a can-do attitude, or, alternatively, run the organization like a fiefdom, stamp out creativity, make poor judgment calls, or be slow to react to external events." For Van Wart, the biographies of outstanding leaders are encouraging because they "not only commemorate the qualities of professionalism and perseverance, but serve as valuable teaching tools as well."

Although ethics and integrity in public service are the focus of Donald C. Menzel's work, it traverses all of the topics discussed in this section. The professions, gender, associations, standards, and leadership are given varying degrees of attention in his probe of the relationship between ethics and individual and organizational performance. As such, Menzel's chapter is a fitting conclusion to this section on the profession of public administration.

REFERENCES

Fauri, D.P. 1976. Thoughts on public administration as a profession. *Public Administration Review* 36 (6): 722–723.

Lynn, N.B. and A. Wildavsky (eds). 1990. *The State of Public Administration.* Chatham, NJ: Chatham House.

Schott, R.L. Public administration as a profession: Problems and prospects. *Public Administration Review* 36 (3): 253–259.

CHAPTER 2

THE PROFESSION OF PUBLIC ADMINISTRATION

Promise, Problems, and Prospects

JAMES S. BOWMAN AND JONATHAN P. WEST

George Washington envisioned the ideal that people of character and competence—the hallmarks of professionalism—would fill the ranks of his administration. Rather than mere employees, the Constitution (article 2, section 2) refers to officers of government. Imbued with an obligation of civic duty, the job of serving the nation's citizens was understood to be more than simply the application of business economics. The federal service would be what Ben Franklin called "posts of honor," the foundation of democracy.

As might be expected, the nature of public service would undergo considerable change over the years. Indeed U.S. history is one of competing administrative doctrines: the guardian model (a politically neutral, merit-based, career bureaucracy) versus the politico model (a politically sensitive, patronage-based, noncareer bureaucracy). Since the management of human capital reflects societal norms and clashing values, the result has been shifting preferences for professional expertise and political appointment over time (Dionne 1998).

This chapter examines these changes with a focus on the last generation. The promise of the profession is traced from the 1883 Pendleton Act through the middle of the past century. Its problems are then discussed, with particular attention to the last several decades. Finally, prospects are outlined in the context of the Obama administration.

PROMISE

With the emergence of political parties, Washington's ideal would come under pressure as partisans sought to repay their supporters with the rewards of victory. The plundering and pillaging of office—favoritism, cronyism, intimidation, corruption—during the ensuing spoils system prevailed for much of the nineteenth century. Set in motion during Andrew Jackson's presidency, this pattern of arrogance, greed, and opportunism engulfed integrity, competence, and prudence. Degradation of public service, rather than the celebration of good government and politics, was characteristic of the era as the carnival-like system encouraged mediocre governance and damaged democratic institutions. It became increasingly evident, however, that a large, growing, industrializing nation could not be effectively managed in such a predatory, scandal-ridden manner (Van Riper 1958).

To protect the legitimacy of the state from private interests, and to cleanse the public service from partisan interference, English merit principles (entrance examinations, career tenure, political neutrality) were adopted in the Pendleton Act. Reformers believed that the moral and economic virtue of responsible and efficient government meant that it should be shielded from unscrupulous politicians and operated in a professional, disinterested, businesslike fashion. Most states and many localities, placing policy above party, eventually established their own centralized merit systems to reduce corruption and enhance productivity. Such developments were a reaffirmation of Alexander Hamilton's belief that government should be judged by the quality of its administration. Public office could, once again, be a public trust; the civil service would belong to the people it served, not to the administration temporarily in power. It was seldom necessary to explain, much less defend, doing the public's business on the basis of merit.

With the demise of the spoils system, administrators began to see themselves as depending upon no party or personage and serving without fear or favor. They did not see every business that they came in contact with as a potential employer and did not feel that job security relied on currying favor with their superiors. Indeed, before midcentury, the public service would be staffed by its share of the most able members of society. "Government work," wrote Patricia Ingraham (2007, 71), "was as much about defining government as in carrying out its tasks." Cloaked in the mantle of stewardship and instilled with a sense of duty, it was a noble calling, as illustrated by the "greatest generation" of World War II.

Echoing Plato and Weber, a professional ethos—a principled framework for action—developed that privileged the public good over private interest. Although it is difficult to prescribe in detail what flows from such an ethic, it does include "the sum of ideals which define . . . the public service"—integrity, political independence, anonymity, and impartiality—at its core (Organization for Economic Cooperation and Development 1996, 14). Through the presence of exemplary public servants, merit-system legislation, professional associations and publications, and widely understood administrative norms, the distinctive character of the civil service was genuine. Like the public interest, "its genius lies not in its clarity, but in its . . . moral intrusion upon the internal and external discourse of ruler and ruled alike" (Bailey 1965, 106).

The professional, politically neutral civil service, one permanently staffed on the basis of competence and devoted to the public interest, became the central organizing principle in government. As a formative principle, a premise that cannot be derived from something else, it summarized the essential nature of political and administrative life. While it would be imprudent to romanticize the ethos, there was a profession of public administration, a spirit of stewardship, and an esprit de corps; an ethic of public service was seen "as a necessary condition of good government" (Crewson 1995, ii).

This legitimating myth, a unifying belief system, empowered the nation to modernize, win world wars, deal with the Great Depression, and amass an extraordinary record of policy achievement (see, especially, Light 2002; Rouban 2003; McDonough 2006). Professional qualifications secured delivery of services and checked political influence. Public service was a sentinel to which its members could point with pride, was regarded by citizens with respect, and was viewed by other nations as worthy of emulation. The quality of life in contemporary history was substantially improved due in large part to professionalism, which ensured "higher standards of competence, expanding research frontiers, [and] quicker application of new knowledge" (Caiden 2008, 11).

Through understanding the inevitable strains between bureaucracy and democracy, leaders such as Frederick Mosher (1968), John Macy (1971), and Hugh Heclo (2002) saw the tension between the administrative need for continuity and the political demand for change as cooperative and creative because both bureaucrats and politicians shared the responsibilities of office and a sense of public service. As Heclo put it, "The spirit [public administration] does not split the difference between idealism and realism, but unites them into one realm" (691).

While not unproblematic, as an "ideal type" this public service ethos was animated by loyalty, integrity, respect for bureaucratic expertise and democratic processes, and the pursuit of the common good (Dillman 1998). There may never have been a golden age of public administration in the form of a pure concern for civic duty, but as with all ideal types, there was an essential truth: a norm of a unified career service that functioned as an inspirational guide for official behavior. Public employees in these institutions may not have been saints, but neither were they sheer opportunists. What gives institutions "direction and worth," wrote Mark Blitz, "is always something of an aspiration," and what defines administrative practice "is not automatic or self-perpetuating but requires effort and risk" (2005, 4). Indeed, the civil service could be understood only by appreciating the profound sense of responsibility that became associated with it—a critical factor that many of its leaders did so much to honor (see, e.g., Cooper and Wright 1992).

However fundamental—and fragile—a professional ethos in government may be, the public service nonetheless has been historically an undervalued and much-maligned idea. In fact, Gerald Caiden (2008, 5) argued that "public administration has had to struggle for recognition, never quite succeeding to claim its rightful place in the sun. . . . No matter how essential its role in contemporary society, its enemies have never been . . . relaxed in their attacks and criticisms. . . . Indeed, the more successful public administration becomes, the more resentful and uncompromising its critics become."[1] During the past one hundred years, for example, there have been no less than twelve major reform efforts (Kellough and Selden 2003), averaging one about every eight years.

Most reforms prior to the contemporary civil service reform movement occurred in the context of legislative and executive conflicts over controlling bureaucracy, spoils and merit, and budgets and employees (Lee, Cayer, and Lan 2006, 38). However, few questioned the need for the merit system or argued for a different type of workforce. To do so without careful consideration of evidence and consequences would be foolhardy and counterproductive. Yet reform in government, driven by cyclic, shifting values—neutral competence, representativeness, executive leadership (Kaufman 1956, 2008)—had been under way for some time during the latter part of the last millennium.

PROBLEMS

New public management (NPM) and reinvented entrepreneurial government came into full flower in the 1990s (Lane 2000). Challenging the traditional ethics, it boldly asserted that twenty-first-century issues could not be met with twentieth-century administration. McDonough held that in the orthodox approach, "the public good is about . . . implementing the democratic principles that protect the interests of every citizen. Charged with realizing this ideal . . . public servants are expected to be accountable, demonstrate bureaucratic behavior [honesty, integrity, impartiality, and objectivity], believe in the public interest, be motivated by the intrinsic rewards of their work rather than profit, and be loyal to their departments, professions, and communities" (2006, 631).

The new strategy, in contrast, defined the public good as receipt of services provided with maximum efficiency, claimed that performance can be achieved only by relying on the private sector and its management techniques, most notably competition and customer service (Pollitt 1993).

Having run against "Washington," presidents after Lyndon Johnson sought to shrink, decentralize, and privatize government, eroding the idea that public servants provide value to citizens. Instead of seeing the state as a benefit to society, they saw it as an impediment; rather than viewing the civil service system as serving the people, they viewed it as serving itself (see, e.g., Howard 1994).

Given its size and cost, it was an easy target, a convenient scapegoat for political failures. "By vilifying the administrative state in general and public servants in particular," according to

Lawrence Terry, reformers sought "to create a sense of crisis to achieve wide ranging restructuring of the public sector" (2005, 429). Government agencies were expected to emulate commercial styles of management, leading to deinstitutionalization and marketization of public organizations, privatization of large portions of civil service, and the commodification of its services. This would transform much of the structure, culture, and personnel of the central bureaucracy, potentially producing a more politically compliant workforce. Merit-system procedures for recruiting, rewarding, and disciplining employees were altered. Performance was defined as being responsive to political goals rather than responsible to the common good, thereby undermining the capacity for effective governance.

Based on public choice and market theories, NPM assumed as self-evidently true that the private and public sectors are essentially alike in purpose, people, and process; thus, the public service should be subject to the same set of economic incentives and disincentives as business (Dillman 1998). Officials were seen as utility maximizers, and therefore their actions were governed by self-interest, not a generalized concern for the commonweal. Public duty was no longer seen as necessarily the most important reason for being a civil servant. Rather than serving the nation, working for the country was just a job.

Devoid of larger public purpose, the approach accorded no special role for either the civil service or the national interest. As Robert Durant (2007, 183) pointed out, "unlike Progressives and New Dealers who saw government as the solution to market failures, [NPM] reformers see markets as the solution to government failures" (a view that would be overtaken by the events of the Great American Bailout of 2009). Institutions of government should be shaped in ways that maximize performance and hence serve as solely instrumental; diminished was its fundamental constitutive role, as part of the organic law of the land, to help clarify duties of government and preserve the rights of the people. Instead, the public service ethos was taken for granted, ignored, or treated with disdain, as rules and restraints were removed with little concern for consequence. Lip service was paid to the common good and public duty while reforms that undermined their basis were promoted. Values of impartiality, integrity, objective merit, and accountability may be important in civil service, but NPM did little to protect them; doing the public's business was frequently based on glib aphorisms, symbolic actions, and political expediency.

Many interests would benefit from this transformation, but there were also losers. Among them was the public interest, as standards of probity in politics and administration no longer enjoyed the protection of administrative tradition. One British critic argued, for instance, that reforms provide "the form of private sector business management, whilst hollowing-out the substance of the public sector ethos and ethics" (Massey 1995, 30). With the loss of the ability to see management as a single, comprehensive function came the disaggregation of government, which meant that agencies sought to establish their own missions, select their favorite citizens ("customers"), follow their own rules, and define their own standards of success (Moe and Gilmour 1995). As concepts of the civil service ethos and public duty were jeopardized, radical change accelerated and illegal and unethical behavior increased (see, e.g., Buzenberg and Kaplan 2008). The capacity to achieve traditionally accepted values such as improved living standards, social equity, and public goods (e.g., environmental quality and health care) was eroded.

Reforms—devoted to a different way of conducting the business of government—taken to their logical conclusion, alter government in largely predictable ways that the Pendleton Act sought to prevent. Notably, rules for hiring, managing, and terminating personnel were changed, with departments authorized to create less formalized, uniform management methods. Civil service professionals went from being vital to protecting the citizenry from graft to having virtually no role in shielding the public from political abuse; changes had little to do with improving the effectiveness of government and everything to do with the ability of political leadership to implement ideological agendas (Anonymous 2007, 5).

The September 11, 2001, disaster, for example, transformed civil service reform issues from a micropolitical to a macropolitical environment, where rhetoric can be particularly influential (Brook and King 2007; the next several paragraphs are adapted from Bowman 2009). Like the assassination of a president that led to civil service change in 1883, the tragedy emboldened reformists. The terrorist attacks offered an opportunity to use national security as a justification to achieve political aims in reforming the public service. The emphasis was placed on agency mission, not management of the bureaucracy. Thus, the departments of Homeland Security and Defense, as well as the Transportation Security Agency, were authorized to create new human resource management systems, which were seen as blueprints for dismantling the government-wide merit system. Unlike the reforms of yesteryear, the programs were enacted in a response to national security arguments, not because of the need to improve personnel administration by rooting out corruption.

Although a comprehensive assessment of contemporary reform does not exist, two former senior government executives (Underhill and Oman 2007) find that there is little relationship between the difficulties that the civil service faces and the goals of change. Either most of the common criticisms of the bureaucracy were not addressed, or the changes have, at best, marginal significance. For instance, the growing number of political appointees, as well as the impending wave of retirements, are largely overlooked, and new classification, pay, and disciplinary policies, if even well executed, are unlikely to effect genuine change.

Political movements in general, and NPM in particular, tend to exaggerate the evils they seek to conquer, with the result that change often makes things worse. This may not be surprising, because the underlying purpose of new policies was not better management (Moffit 2001; Perry 2008), but rather the perceived need for personnel flexibility in the war on terror. In light of the counterproductive consequences of reform (Bowman and West 2007), the challenge today is to eschew reckless change by revitalizing the public service ethos, the ideal of stewardship, and the fiduciary responsibility in the spirit of public administration.

PROSPECTS

The public service, in short, has been the object of one of the most determined and sustained efforts to reform government in many years. The concept of a public servant has been consistently debased, and "the changes have undermined the public service and ideal of public service which inspired that ethos" (O'Toole 2006b, 203). "Reforms such as reinventing government and new public management," Patricia Ingraham pointed out, "placed their faith in oversimplified and discredited management nostrums" (2007, 82). By grounding efforts in economics, the value base of change was one-dimensional, with the outcome that the ability of officials to shape government was limited, except to emphasize efficiency.

Much has been lost in recent years in terms of values and ethics in public service. Although it may not "simply be too late to maintain that the civil service . . . exists for public purposes" (O'Toole 2006a, 45), NPM has shifted governmental administration toward managerialism, entrepreneurism, and efficiency and away from promotion of the "general welfare" (as stated in the preamble to the U.S. Constitution). If the traditional notion of public service still enjoys any currency, it is attributable to the cultural lag between changing circumstances and their impact on civil service and its members. Yet "it is by believing in the public service ethos," wrote Barry O'Toole, "that it will be saved" (1998, 99).

Such a revitalization may occur in the wake of the 2008–2009 financial crisis which has shaken the nation into rethinking "the magic of the market," the idea that "business is good and government is bad," and the efficacy and benevolence of the once-vaunted, now disgraced, private sector (Martinez 2009). As Sylvia Horton argued, the displacement of the old public service ethos with "accountability to the market is not a substitute for political accountability and a strong administrative system that can act as the guardian of the constitution" (2008, 29). If the NPM-contrived management crisis provoked change, then the very real current economic calamity produces the urgency and opportunity to provide resources and act responsibly. There may be a growing recognition of the value of a professional career corps as the keystone of the state in service to the public interest.

If so, then the time is propitious to rebuild the public service. More than any other presidential candidates since John F. Kennedy, Barack Obama and John McCain put a focus on service to the country and sacrifice for the common good, an appeal like Kennedy's that could become a self-fulfilling prophecy. Rather than scoring political points by running against Washington and federal bureaucrats, Obama in particular sought to rebrand government, to "make it cool again." He saw this as critically important not only to the American people, but also to the well-being of free markets (Newell 2008).

The country's problems today are so daunting that pretense and pride must give way to recognition that government will be central to their solution. The bipartisan hostility to the very idea of using the state to serve the greater good (Reagan's "government is the problem"; Clinton's "the era of big government is over") has run amok. As Melvin Dubnick observed, "Such a commitment to an unframed and untested set of beliefs is unwise at best, for these promises have proven dangerously powerful when put in action and can generate costly consequences, not merely in terms of time and other wasted resources, but in the distortions and perverse behavior they produce" (2007, 3).

Contempt for government, especially evident during the George W. Bush administration, deeply corrupted the discipline of self-government and the notion of public service. It appeared that the Bush administration saw little point in governing well because of their belief that the public sector contributed little to society. Ruled by instinct and ideology, the administration treated citizens as consumers, seeded the bureaucracy with political ideologues, hived off public services to contractors, thinned the ranks of contract monitors, and emasculated regulatory agencies.

Rather than, in the words of the Constitution, taking "care that the laws be faithfully executed" (article 1, section 3), the consequence has been "one of the most destructive in our public life," according to political scientist Thomas Mann (Buzenberg and Kaplan 2008). As systematically chronicled by a nonpartisan good-government organization (the Center for Public Integrity), it is an extraordinary, self-defeating record of underfunded programs co-opted by political appointees, with lax oversight, limited accountability, and leadership based on ideology, not competence. To take one example among many, government auditors report that the Department of the Interior has been so enfeebled that it is unable to perform many of its core missions, with the result that its personnel and the public are at risk (Carlstrom 2009)—as the 2010 Gulf oil spill amply demonstrated. "We are constantly bombarded with stories of government breakdowns, from the failure to keep contaminated peanuts off the market to the Securities and Exchange Commission's bungling of the Bernie Madoff case to Hurricane Katrina," opined Max Stier (2009a) of the Partnership for Public Service.

With Republican and Democratic administrations approving massive subsidies to the private sector, the era of demonizing government and glorifying the market may have ended. "The axis of the field of public administration," wrote James D. Carroll, "should shift from a preoccupation with service delivery, 'customer satisfaction' and immediate gratification, to reinvestment to meet evolving needs in public action for which public administrators are responsible" (2009, 21).

The 2008 election was a repudiation of the shortsighted, antigovernment philosophy that celebrated self-interest, denigrated the public interest, and claimed that it was possible to govern successfully while relentlessly disparaging government. Gone was the "you're on your own" ethos that had come to define the relationship between government and citizens. Instead, the election can be plausibly interpreted as a rediscovery of the belief that the greater good should come first, that the economy should serve society and not the other way around. It revealed the socially constructed nature of the status quo, showed that the old social constructs passing as reality were not immutable, and promised emancipatory change.

After years of being defiled and defunded, an emasculated government has been presented with an historic opportunity full of peril and possibility to prove itself—ironically by rescuing the business sector. The key is to enhance governmental capacity and honor its constitutional role in democracy, something not easily achieved. In so doing, the profession is responsible for focusing on process and structure to fulfill the constitutional obligations of public administration. This will involve strengthening the organizational, analytical, and managerial capacities of the organs of government and encouraging investment-oriented initiatives (e.g., infrastructure, research, children's health) relative to consumption-oriented entitlement and transfer-payment programs (e.g., farm subsidies).

Smart policies and more funding may be necessary, but success depends upon the president's ability to lead government. The president has an opportunity to reverse the long-standing erosion of federal service by reenergizing government (Light 2008). Donald Klingner cautioned, "The current U.S. economic crisis is not like the Great Depression in at least one crucial respect. Seventy-five years ago, the experts who led us out of the dark were public servants like Harold Ickes, David Lilienthal, Frances Perkins, Luther Gulick, and Louis Brownlow. Today, the players occupying center stage are the Wall Street financiers and bankers whose corporate lobbyists pushed federal policy-makers to approve, in the name of free markets, the deregulation that caused this problem to begin with" (2009, 16). The fact remains that the Obama administration has an opportunity to reverse the long decline of federal service by reenergizing government.

Having an engaged workforce will not ensure success, but not having one will produce failure; personnel *is* policy, as ultimate success depends on the ability to act effectively. Indeed, the drive is not merely to improve government operations, but to devote as much energy to policy execution as to policy development, as evidenced by the following:

- the proactive 2008 presidential transition process,
- appointments made at twice the rate of those in earlier administrations,
- establishment of a chief performance officer position,
- giving the director of the Office of Personnel Management a seat at Cabinet meetings,
- early executive orders on governmental transparency and professional standards,
- in-sourcing of previously contracted-out jobs,
- commitments to hire six hundred thousand new public servants in the next four years, and
- presidential visits to agencies (Stier 2009b; 2008).

To foster more competent, professional government involves reducing the number of political appointees, flattening the federal hierarchy, restaffing hollowed-out agencies, emphasizing to top agency leadership that a quality workforce is a priority, reforming the lengthy hiring process, seeking pay comparability with the private sector, supporting enactment of a ROTC-like program for civil service or the proposed National Service Academy, or both, and investing in workforce training and development (Light 2008).

In other words, recruitment and retention initiatives like these will increase the number of those doing government work who, unlike contractors, will have absorbed the culture of public service and taken the oath to uphold the constitution. Bilmes and Gould (2009) have offered a detailed outline of what this new civil service would look like and how to pay for it. Federal chief human capital officers and the Government Performance Coalition also have provided "roadmaps to reform" that identify ways to elevate the federal workforce and strengthen organizational capacity (Kamensky 2008). Such initiatives may help shape the administration's plans to overhaul the civil service. One conceptual framework within which such initiatives might reside is supplied by Denhardt and Denhardt's (2007) "new" public service, which describes "the role of government as brokering interests among citizens and other groups so as to create shared values."

Encouraging signs exist that public employment will, once again, be seen as an employer of choice. Widespread unemployment, baby boomer retirements, presidential appreciation of public service, the economic stimulus package, in-sourcing of programs, and disillusionment with business all combine to furnish an opportunity to bolster the civil service. Whereas graduates and would-be graduates in medicine, engineering, and law once sought fortunes in banking and finance, government and public service occupations were the most popular of forty-six career fields among college students in early 2008. A year later, career counselors at two hundred colleges and universities found that 90 percent of students were interested in federal jobs or internships (Davidson 2009; also see Light 2003; Rosenberg 2009; Goldin and Katz 2008). Indeed, a position in today's cerebral White House would become the ultimate status symbol among job seekers.

A leading nonprofit group sees such indicators as a reflection of "a new generation . . . choosing to use their tech savvy and advanced degrees to bring about change" (Partnership for Public Service 2009). Another survey found that among newly hired public employees, nearly half of those under thirty years of age and four-fifths of those over thirty expect to make government their career (Yoder 2008). Moreover, according to the Federal Human Capital Survey, more than 90 percent of personnel report that they believe that their work is important (U.S. Office of Personnel Management 2008).

Buttressed by far more job applications than received by previous administrations (Woodrow Wilson School Task Force 2009), as well as a substantial increase in applicants to the Presidential Management Fellows program (Vogel 2009), public service may once again become less of a contractual relationship focused on personal gain and more of a covenantal commitment to country. This suggests a change in the claim that neither the politico nor the guardian administrative doctrine holds public favor (Dionne 1998). With the governing assumptions of the last three decades largely discredited,[2] a restoration of the idea that the function of government is to maintain the conditions in society so that morality is possible could be taking place.

An appreciation that public administrators are "the *only* officials that pay attention to governmental activities all the time" and as such hold a special duty to protect and serve the public interest (Goodsell 2006, 63; emphasis in original) may be growing. As E.J. Dionne suggested, extreme individualism is an infantile approach to governance, "one that must be supplanted by a more adult sense of personal and collective responsibility" (2009, A17). Perhaps it is *not* surprising, then, that eight of ten Americans say they would encourage a young person to work for the federal government (Adams and Infeld 2009).

There are, in summary, many reasons to suspect that the state of public administration in the future may be quite different from that in the initial decade of the new century. It is important to note, however, that facts and documentation can be remarkably insignificant when assessing trends in government and confronting national identity, narratives, and myths. Politics often only requires beliefs, not evidence. As the 2009–10 health-care debates demonstrated, unless deeply ingrained distrust of government can be overcome—if change does not supersede national myth—reform may be stymied. (Malloy 2009). In the end, public administration is an ethical activity because public office is a public trust and because of the nature of the civil servant who "must be prepared to apply a moral measure in the public interest to every act or decision" (Macy 1971, 249). The Founders understood the need not only for an educated citizenry, but also for public-spirited officials. The challenge of 1789 remains today: to produce the conditions for responsible government by effectively managing the professional civil service.

NOTES

1. Nobel Prize winner and *New York Times* columnist Paul Krugman argued that a "good-as-bad" political philosophy mandates that government must be prevented from solving problems even if it can because "the more good a proposed government program would do, the more fiercely it must be opposed" (2007). "Even when they (these ideologues) failed on the job . . . , they could claim that very failure as vindication of their anti-government ideology, a demonstration that the public sector can't do anything right" (Krugman 2008).

2. As Krugman (2007) pointed out, however, it would be a mistake to overemphasize this development. For instance, despite the near collapse of the nation's financial system, reflexive antigovernment forces are so powerful that efforts to regulate the banking industry.are generally limited to revising existing institutions responsible for the crisis. Narrowly avoiding a depression, paradoxically, reduced the political pressure for a fundamental restructuring of the economy.

REFERENCES

Adams, W., and L. Infeld. 2009. Surprising majority of Americans endorse careers in government. *PA Times* 32 (7): 1–2.

Anonymous. 2007. Merit, morality, and administration: The forgotten legacy of civil service reform. Unpublished manuscript submitted to *Administration and Society.*

Bailey, S. 1965. The public interest: Some operational definitions. In *Nomos V: The Public Interest,* ed. C. Friedrich, 96–106. New York: Atherton.

Bilmes, L., and W. Gould. 2009. *The People Factor: Strengthening America By Investing in Public Service.* Washington, DC: Brookings Institution.

Blitz, M. 2005. *Duty Bound: Responsibility and American Public Life.* London: Rowman and Littlefield.

Bowman, J. 2009. Turbulence in civil service: Whither the public service ethos? In *Public Human Resource Management: Problems and Prospects.* 5th ed., ed. S. Hays, R. Kearney, and J. Coggburn, 327–338. Englewood Cliffs, NJ: Longman.

Bowman, J., and J. West, eds. 2007. *American Public Service: Radical Reform and the Merit System.* New York: Taylor and Francis.

Brook, D., and C. King. 2007. Civil service reform as national security: The Homeland Security Act of 2002. *Public Administration Review* 67:399–407.

Buzenberg, B., and D. Kaplan. 2008. Broken government: By the numbers. Paper Trail: The Center Blog. Center for Public Integrity, December 9. www.publicintegrity.org/blog/entry/1076 (accessed December 9, 2008).

Caiden, G. 2008. The hollowing out of public administration. Unpublished manuscript. University of Southern California.

Carlstrom, G. 2009. Interior unable to perform many core missions, auditors say. *Federal Times,* March 9, 5.

Carroll, J. 2009. The public administration of reinvestment. *PA Times* (March): 21–22.

Cooper, T., and N. Wright, eds. 1992. *Exemplary Public Administrators.* San Francisco: Jossey-Bass.

Crewson, P. 1995. The public service ethic. Ph.D.diss., American University.

Davidson, J. 2009. Government gets high marks from student job seekers. *Washington Post,* January 15, D04.

Denhardt, J., and R. Denhardt. 2007. *The New Public Service: Serving, not Steering.* Armonk, NY: M.E. Sharpe.

Dillman, D. 1998. Leadership in the American public service. In *Reform, Ethics, and Leadership in Public Service: A Festschrift in Honour of Richard A. Chapman*, ed. M. Hunt and B. O'Toole, 142–158. Brookfield, VT: Ashgate.

Dionne, E.J., Jr. 1998. "Bureaucrats": Can't public service get some respect? *Brookings Review* 19 (2): 8–11.

———. 2009. Old, true, and radical. *Washington Post*, January 22, A17.

Dubnick, M. 2007. Pathologies of governance reform: Promises, pervasions, and perversions in the age of accountability. *PA Times* (October): 3.

Durant, R. 2007. Institutional values and the future of the administrative state. In *Revisiting Waldo's Administrative State: Constancy and Change in Public Administration*, ed. D. Rosenbloom and H. McCurdy, 179–202. Washington, DC: Georgetown University Press.

Goldin, C., and L. Katz. 2008. Transitions: Career and family life cycles of the educational elite. *American Economic Review: Papers and Proceedings* 98 (2): 363–369.

Goodsell, C. 2006. A new vision for public administration. *Public Administration Review* 66 (4): 623–635.

Heclo, H. 2002. The state of public administration. *PS: Political Science and Politics* 35 (4): 689–694.

Horton, S. 2008. History and persistence of an idea and an ideal. In *Motivation in Public Service*, ed. J. Perry and A. Hondeghem, 17–32. Oxford: Oxford University Press.

Howard, P. 1994. *The Death of Common Sense*. New York: Random House.

Ingraham, P. 2007. Who should rule? In *Revisiting Waldo's Administrative State: Constancy and Change in Public Administration*, ed. D. Rosenbloom and H. McCurdy, 71–84. Washington, DC: Georgetown University Press.

Kamensky, J. 2008. Performance advice for Obama administration. The Presidential Transition: A Weblog by the IBM Center for the Business of Government, December 5. http://transition2008.wordpress.com/2008/12/05/ (accessed January 15, 2009).

Kaufman, H. 1956. Emerging conflicts in the doctrines of public administration. *American Political Science Review* 50 (4): 1057–1073.

———. 2008. Ruminations on the study of American public bureaucracy. *American Review of Public Administration* 38 (3): 256–263.

Kellough, J., and S. Selden. 2003. The reinvention of public personnel administration. *Public Administration Review* 63 (2): 165–176.

Klingner, D. 2009. Beyond the bailout: Facing the big issues. *PA Times* (January): 16.

Krugman, P. 2007. Don't cry for Reagan. *New York Times*, March 19. http://select.nytimes.com/2007/03/19/opinion/19krugman.html?_r=1 (accessed March 19, 2007).

———. 2008. Barack be good. *New York Times*, December 26. www.nytimes.com/2008/12/26/opinion/26krugman.html (accessed December 26, 2008).

Lane, J. 2000. *New Public Management*. London: Routledge.

Lee, H., N. Cayer, and G. Lan. 2006. Changing federal government employee attitudes since the Civil Service Reform Act of 1978. *Review of Public Personnel Administration* 26: 21–50.

Light, P. 2002. *Government's Greatest Achievements*. Washington, DC: Brookings Institution.

———. 2003. *In Search of Public Service*. Washington, DC, and New York: Center for Public Service, Brookings Institution, and Wagner School of Public Service.

———. 2008. A government ill executed: The depletion of the federal service. *Public Administration Review* 67 (3): 413–419.

Macy, J. 1971. *Public Service: The Human Side of Government*. New York: Harper and Row.

Madrick, J. 2009. *The Case for Big Government*. Princeton, NJ: Princeton University Press.

Malloy, J. 2009. The health-care debate, from up north. *Washington Post*, September 15. www.washingtonpost.com/wp-dyn/content/article/2009/09/14/AR2009091402707.html (accessed September 15, 2009).

Martinez, M. 2009. *The Myth of the Free Market: The Role of the State in a Capitalist Economy*. Sterling, VA: Kumarian Press.

Massey, A. 1995. Civil service reform and accountability. *Public Policy and Administration* 10:16–33.

McDonough, P. 2006. Habitus and the practice of public service. *Work, Employment, and Society* 20 (4): 629–647.

Moe, R., and R. Gilmour. 1995. Rediscovering principles of public administration: The neglected foundation of public law. *Public Administration Review* 55 (2): 135–146.

Moffit, R. 2001. Taking charge of federal personnel. Background Paper no. 1404, Heritage Foundation, Washington, DC.

Mosher, F. 1968. *Democracy and the Public Service.* New York: Oxford University Press.

Newell, E. 2008. Candidates stress need to restore faith in government. GovernmentExecutive.com, September 12. www.govexec.com/dailyfed/0908/091208e1.htm (accessed September 12, 2008).

Organization for Economic Cooperation and Development. 1996. Ethics in public service: Current issues and practice. PUMA Occasional Papers 14, Organization for Economic Cooperation and Development, Paris.

O'Toole, B. 1998. "We work by faith, not by sight": The ethos of public service. In *Reform, Ethics and Leadership in Public Service: A Festschrift in Honour of Richard A. Chapman,* ed. M. Hunt and B. O'Toole, 84–106. Aldershot, England: Ashgate.

———. 2006a. The emergence of a "new" ethical framework for civil servants. *Public Money and Management* 26 (1): 39–45.

———. 2006b. *The Ideal of Public Service: Reflections on Higher Civil Service in Britain.* London: Routledge.

Partnership for Public Service. 2009. EPA's Taddonio illustrates a new generation of thinking. *Washington Post,* February 23. www.washingtonpost.com/wp-dyn/content/article/2009/02/20/AR2009022002491. html (accessed February 23, 2009).

Perry, J. 2008. The Civil Service Reform Act of 1978: Symposium introduction. *Review of Public Personnel Administration* 28 (June): 200–204.

Pollitt, C. 1993. *Managerialism and the Public Services.* Oxford: Oxford University Press.

Rosenberg, A. 2009. Polls find Uncle Sam's popularity up among job seekers. GovernmentExecutive.com, May 7. www.govexec.com/dailyfed/0509/050709ar1.htm (accessed May 7, 2009).

Rouban, L. 2003. Politicization of the civil service. In *Politicization of the Civil Service in Comparative Perspective: The Quest for Control,* ed. B. Peters and J. Pierre, 310–320. London: Routledge.

Schlesinger, A. 1986. *The Cycles of American History.* Boston: Houghton Mifflin.

Stier, M. 2008. A lesson for Obama on reaching out to the federal workforce. *Washington Post,* December 26. www.washingtonpost.com/wp-dyn/content/article/2008/12/25/AR2008122500832.html (accessed January 21, 2009).

———. 2009a. Managers: Ignore Washington at your peril. BusinessWeek.com, March 23. www.businessweek.com/managing/content/mar2009/ca20090323_058018.htm (accessed March 27, 2009).

———. 2009b. Obama signals shift in governing philosophy. *Washington Post,* January 26. www. washingtonpost.com/wp-dyn/content/article/2009/01/26/AR2009012600742.html (accessed January 26, 2009).Terry, L. 2005. The thinning of administrative institution in the hollow state. *Administration & Society* 37 (4): 426–444.

Underhill, J., and R. Oman. 2007. A critical review of the sweeping federal civil service changes. *Review of Public Personnel Administration* 27 (4): 401–420.

U.S. Office of Personnel Management. 2008. *Federal Human Capital Survey.* Washington, DC: Office of Personnel Management.

Van Riper, P. 1958. *History of the United States Civil Service.* Westport, CT: Greenwood Press.

Vogel, S. 2009. More young people lining up for government jobs. *Washington Post,* March 26, A19.

Woodrow Wilson School Task Force. 2009. *The Changing Nature of Government Service: Final Report.* Princeton, NJ: Woodrow Wilson School.

Yoder, E. 2008. The newcomer's guide to the federal government. *Washington Post,* November 14. www. washingtonpost.com/wp-dyn/content/article/2008/11/13/AR2008111303296.html (accessed November 14, 2008).

CHAPTER 3

PUBLIC SERVICE PROFESSIONALS

The Legacy of Florence Nightingale,
Mary Livermore, and Jane Addams

PATRICIA M. SHIELDS AND NANDHINI RANGARAJAN

Florence Nightingale, Mary Livermore, and Jane Addams, individually and collectively, laid the historic foundation for a new kind of approach to administration where scientific rigor and sensitivity go hand in hand; where evidence-based administration is infused with emotional intelligence; where professionalism coexists with consideration. They sowed the seeds for what would blossom into customer-oriented public service delivery. The ideas of these women have been buried, distorted, or hidden in plain sight—waiting to be discovered.[1] This chapter focuses on the contributions of these women and their organizations because their uncovered ideas and practices are an integral but neglected influence on the evolution of public administration as a field of practice and study. The chapter concludes with a discussion of how the work of these women has contemporary relevance, and how their insights may shape the future of public administration.

REINTERPRETING THE PAST

Perhaps it is not surprising that this story of women in public administration begins during the Victorian Era (1837–1901), the apex of the British Empire. There, in plain sight, we see a great leader in Queen Victoria, who was also a devoted wife and mother. By happenstance of birth she was placed at the helm of the British Empire. Yet in Queen Victoria's time most women lived and worked at home, well outside the wider public sphere of men. This chapter focuses on three women who came into their own as influential public administrators during the Victorian Era. Their route to influence and public responsibility was blocked by cultural norms that kept them out of the public sphere.

For a millennium the human race has raised armies to fight wars. Like it or not, military leaders and their subordinate officers were and are among the first public administrators working to advance the goals of their governments. It is perhaps not surprising that two wars (the Crimean War and the U.S. Civil War) offered women early opportunities to develop and use administrative skills. During the Crimean War (1853–56), Great Britain and France fought the Russians in Turkey. British troops suffered severe losses. The sick and wounded were treated through a poorly supplied, unsanitary, and disorganized system (Woodham-Smith 1951, 99). News of the heavy losses and suffering troops traveled quickly via new technology—the telegraph. The British Sanitary Commission was an official response to the disaster.

Florence Nightingale was an architect of the British Sanitary Commission. Her analysis revealed that the neglect of soldier needs was based on "total oblivion" among the powerful that "the soldier is a mortal man subject to ills" such as wet, cold, bad food, fatigue, and so on (Nightingale 1862, 3). She used scientific and statistical methods to show that the high initial death-by-disease rate among wounded British troops could be reduced with simple hygienic changes, more supplies, and good food (Woodham-Smith 1951, 204–206). British Sanitary Commission Reports (authored by Nightingale) showed that army barracks in Great Britain were also unhealthy. The mortality rate among soldiers was markedly higher than among similar civilian men (Nightingale 1862). In fact, the British army, presumably one of the world's best and most well organized, had barracks that threatened the lives of their soldiers.

In the early days of the American Civil War, two conditions collided to create the U.S. Sanitary Commission. The first was the recognition of a groundswell of energy in the populace to provide soldiers' desperately needed supplemental supplies. This relief effort needed to be organized if it was to make a difference. Second, the unsanitary conditions in camps and hospitals threatened the health and safety of Union soldiers. Well-publicized British Sanitary Commission reports revealed the roles of overcrowding, cleanliness, drainage, ventilation, and hospital comforts in the health and recovery of soldiers (Nightingale 1858, 23). Using these findings, leaders in the U.S. medical community argued that the science of sanitation should be applied to the Army Medical Bureau and to general camp organization. The United States did not have a systemwide capacity to meet the everyday needs of the massive numbers of new troops (sick or healthy), and clearly, if science had uncovered that service in the British army held health risks, so much more so for hastily gathered regiments organized at the local level with leaders untrained in military discipline.

Upper-class medical doctors, led by a minister, traveled to Washington during the early days of the war. They called for the creation of an agency of inquiry that could investigate the sanitary needs of the Union army and organize the chaotic, often counterproductive system of civilian relief. On June 6, 1861, Abraham Lincoln authorized the U.S. Sanitary Commission. The two missions were intertwined. Nevertheless, men organized a system of camp and hospital inspections, and women managed the relief efforts and were often called to nurse the sick.

In the official histories of the U.S. Sanitary Commission, the authors often cited the British disaster in the Crimea and credited Florence Nightingale with stimulating the reform that saved thousands of British soldiers (Sanitary Commission of the United States Army [1864] 1972; Stillé 1866). The British Sanitary Commission looked backward and investigated the causes of the crisis and the consequences of an intervention. The U.S. Sanitary Commission learned from the British experience and created the largest and most complex civilian organization the U.S. government had ever authorized. Women administrators were critical to its success.

NIGHTINGALE: CARING, EVIDENCE-BASED HOSPITAL REFORM

> *It may seem a strange principle to enunciate as the very first requirement in a Hospital that it should do the sick no harm.*
> (Nightingale 1863, iii)

How did an elite, pampered young woman born in 1820 become a noted statistician, a leading expert on hospital administration, a pioneer in hospital architecture, and the crusader who virtually created the nursing profession? When she was a child, her father recognized her intellect and indulged her boundless curiosity and love of mathematics. At seventeen she experienced a profound, life-altering call to serve the Lord. By her mid-twenties this call had crystallized into a focus on serving the sick and the poor in hospitals. Her parents placed almost insurmountable barriers before her because the foul, vermin-infested hospitals were no place for a lady. Further, the few women employed at public hospitals had reputations as alcoholic prostitutes (Woodham-Smith 1951). To overcome these roadblocks, Nightingale traveled widely, observing and training in hospitals in continental Europe. She also carefully studied the scientific ideas of John Pringle, physician and father of military medicine, and applied them as she pored through records from English hospitals. Her mission was to use science to reduce suffering and save lives by understanding what did and did not work.

She socialized widely in elite circles and shared her knowledge and passion for hospital reform with like-minded elites. She developed theories about how to improve hospitals. By the mid-1850s she was recognized as an expert on hospital reform and administration. Eventually she was given an opportunity and successfully applied her ideas in a small, failing hospital designed to serve gentlewomen in distressed circumstances (Woodham-Smith 1951).

When the Crimean War broke out, reports of disorganized, rat-infested, poorly supplied, moldy hospitals and extraordinary soldier death-by-disease rates reached an outraged public. Nightingale's close friend Lord Herbert, the secretary of war, approached her, asked her to investigate, and empowered her to take action. She organized a group of thirty-eight upstanding women nurses (twenty-four of whom were members of religious orders), collected supplies, and traveled to a hospital in Scutari, Turkey (Woodham-Smith 1951).

In a letter to Florence Nightingale, Herbert indicates, "There is but one person who would be capable of organizing and supervising such a scheme." He credits her knowledge and "*power of administration*" (emphasis added; as cited in Woodham-Smith 1951, 88). Thus, from the inception Nightingale was charged with saving lives by fixing a broken administrative system—a system frozen in "bureaucratic ineptitude" (Hobbs 1997, 1). A "byzantine system of transport and supply had been designed to prevent fraud, and basic provisions were delayed by complicated rules for requisition" (Hobbs 1997, 53).

Nightingale's mission trampled cultural norms. Upstanding women were authorized to enter and change military practices—in the army, the heart of the male sphere. Further, the nurses' mission represented a type of radical reform. The introduction of women as nurses is particularly relevant here. Nightingale understood that hospitals needed caring nurses who were willing to incorporate the basic hygiene needed for healing. Hence, she argued that respectable women caregivers belonged in hospitals and should receive training. If the nursing role had dignity, patients would be more likely to heal. She connected nursing to the dignity and moral authority of the "caring mother" who operated within the family sphere. These skills were needed to save sick soldiers and finally for nations to win wars. Armies that fell to disease were of no use to the empire. She adopted the "mother of the troops" passion for suffering soldiers. She advocated capturing the caring and emotional connection of the women's traditional sphere to make hospitals places of healing. This would require a normative sea change from the armed forces and society (Reverby 1987).

She and her group of nurses applied her ideas to a horrifying situation. Not surprising to twenty-first-century sensibilities, they showed that making sure wounded soldiers did not lie in the soiled sheets of the recently deceased, scrubbing and painting moldy walls, clearing and cleansing backed-up sewers, and providing good food led to a remarkable turnaround in death-by-disease rates. The hospital mortality rate plummeted. Still, skeptical and defensive hospital doctors often thwarted her work. Luckily, when her political battles seemed hopeless, Queen Victoria stepped in and supported her. Queen Victoria's powerful women's sphere extended to her country's sons fighting in the Crimea. Nightingale is remembered as the selfless "Lady with the Lamp" because returning, recovered soldiers told their friends and families of her after-dark bedside visits and life-saving changes in the hospital (Woodham-Smith 1851). Perhaps she needed the daylight to ensure that reforms were implemented and had time to visit only after the sun had fallen.

The medical and nursing profession has rediscovered Nightingale the statistician and her focus on evidence-based decision making. She is applauded for measuring outcomes well before her time (McDonald 2001, 1). What the medical profession does not emphasize is another aspect of Nightingale's work—analysis of ineffective administrative processes. So, aside from summary tables and charts, she used persuasive narrative to show why, for example, wounded soldiers lacked adequate supplies such as shirts, towels, socks, undergarments, spoons, and forks. The problem stemmed from a regulation that mandated that these supplies come from the soldiers' packs. Unfortunately, wounded soldiers usually got separated from their kits. Further, regulations mandated that "the contents of the kits could not be replaced" (Nightingale 1858, 73). Thus, the seemingly mundane everyday problem of a wounded soldier being separated from his pack coupled with a thoughtless regulation led to a breakdown of the supply system. Obviously, the supply of undergarments and towels would have traditionally been within the women's sphere. Inattention to these details could have disastrous consequences.

Putting It in Perspective

> *A slop pail should never be brought into a sick room.*
> (Nightingale [1860] 1922, 23)

Nightingale was driven by the passion to serve and change the lives of ordinary persons through administrative reforms. Her innovations changed the policies, practices, and images of hospitals and hospital administration. She tirelessly argued that reforms were needed. One key reform involved the nature of nursing. Ongoing patient care should be a noble profession performed by respected, knowledgeable women. The hospital would never "work" if nursing continued to be a disorganized occupation filled by men and women a step above criminals. For this to happen, nurses needed a sterling reputation and training. The nursing schools she subsequently established represent some of the earliest formal training directed at women working outside the home. Nursing reform was but one pillar in a larger strategy to bring evidence-based decision making to hospitals. Nightingale saw that suffering and needless death could be prevented by simple changes in the way hospitals were run. She articulated the causal links between seemingly minor rules and dying men. The young men who served Her Majesty became her surrogate children.

Nightingale's work contains themes that were carried forward across the Atlantic and to subsequent generations. Of course, she brought the benefits of sanitary science, experimental design, and data analysis to the art of running a military hospital. She showed how regulations that ignored commonplace experience (soldiers separated from packs) could lead to misery and inefficiencies. Nightingale also brought a sympathetic understanding to human suffering. She and others like her laid the foundation for what is termed "emotional labor" in the contemporary world. She sought to bring a new dignity to the soldier and to the caregivers that attended to their everyday needs and by implication showed that failure to incorporate women's-sphere activities to army administration had disastrous consequences. Nightingale's approach, which illustrates a bottom-up view of administration, broadens the women's sphere by connecting it to the army hospital. She showed that the complex army hospital is more effective if it cares for its soldiers. Care is consistent with evidence-based reform, an emphasis on human dignity (soldier and nurse), and attention to the commonplace (food, sewers). This conception of care linked to administration is a contribution hidden in plain sight. Nightingale's work and the British experience became the clarion call for another sanitary commission—this one run by Yankee men and women as they supplied the Union.

THE U.S. SANITARY COMMISSION

Chapin Hall was filled with ladies who came together to inquire how the charity of women could best serve her country in its impending peril.
(Mary Brayton and Ellen Terry, Official Historians,
Cleveland Branch, USSC [Brayton and Terry 1869, 17])

During the American Civil War, the U.S. Sanitary Commission (USSC), a short-lived civilian organization, inspected army facilities and provided relief supplies and a variety of services to Union troops and their families. The inspection arm took its direction from Nightingale's reports and applied "sanitary science" to camps, hospitals, and transportation systems for the wounded. Spurred on by the national mission and deep sympathy for the troops, the women of the North transformed seven thousand ladies aid societies into local relief agencies that funneled supplies to the troops through regional hubs led by women.

President Lincoln authorized this "gigantic national agency" (Hoge 1867, 21), which raised and spent $25 million. The Sanitary Commission was financed through voluntary contributions because the founders wanted official U.S. agency status but did not want to rely on tax dollars and be accused of profiting from the war (or be touched by contractor scandal) (Stillé 1866).

The women involved in this story included Miss Libby McGrath, the secretary of the Frogsville, Ohio, branch, and the more worldly Louisa Schuyler, the manager of the New York City branch (aka the Women's Central Association of Relief) (Brayton and Terry 1869, 477). Most of these women had their lives turned upside down when a beloved male family member left home to serve the Union. Though they were overwhelmingly in the minority, some women coupled their desire to serve with an existing reform agenda. For them, the USSC was a vehicle to prove women's ability and further women's rights. Louisa Schuyler and Elizabeth Blackwell are important examples.

Whatever the motivation, the administrative experience gained through successfully organizing the ladies aid societies and delivering tons of needed supplies changed the way women were perceived and how they perceived themselves. Given their success, by war's end the country was more ready to grant women additional rights and opportunities (education, employment, legal and political rights). Moreover, women had a new vision of their place and the skills to make it happen. Knowingly and unknowingly, the women of this bottom-up organization pushed the boundaries of the women's sphere as they invented new ways to serve the troops, created administrative structures, mastered the challenges of transcontinental collaboration, and reconceptualized the role of government.

Inexperience Breeds Peril

Most of them had no experience whatever of campaigning and their knowledge of a soldier's duty was confined to the requirements of a holiday parade.
(Charles Stillé, Official Historian, USSC [Stillé 1866, 21])

Over the course of the war, more than 2 million men served in the Union Army. At the start of the war, the regular army had fewer than twenty thousand soldiers. The additional 1.98 million troops were drawn from local volunteers. Initially these green recruits were organized into volunteer regiments and led by local men untrained and usually unfamiliar with military ways. Tragically, many of the early volunteer regiments were led by men who, oblivious to the women's sphere, neglected to plan for food, bedding, clothes, and cleanliness—all things their wives or mothers attended to (Maxwell 1956, 34). Further, the army's medical bureau was overextended and often neglected these basic necessities. The health and efficiency of the army was jeopardized by this neglect (Stillé 1866).

Furthermore, the supplies generated through the haphazard relief efforts that sprang up spontaneously across Northern villages and towns seldom met military needs. The leaders of the USSC recognized that chaotic, inefficient volunteer actions needed to "harmonize with that of the regular authorities" (Stillé 1866, 168). In addition, local relief efforts undermined the war effort by splintering support for the troops geographically. Hence, the Sanitary Commission's local offices were told to shed their commitment to community regiments in favor of a national mission. "The task of aiding the government in this matter, seemed to devolve peculiarly on the women of the country" (Stillé 1866, 169).

Cooperative Women Serving the State

This is the first example of cooperative womanhood serving the state the world had ever witnessed.
(Mary Livermore, Northwestern Branch Manager [Livermore 1891, 285])

Women's influence in this initiative is clearly pervasive. Nightingale provided the stimulus and conceptual foundation for the camp and hospital inspections. Women provided key midlevel leadership and administrative skills for the massive relief enterprise. For four long years, tens of thousands of wives, mothers, and sisters worked tirelessly behind the scenes running local relief societies, coordinating a regional supply network, participating in the commission decision making, raising funds, publishing bulletins, providing sick and wounded lists from the front, and volunteering to nurse and carry relief work to the field (Giesberg 2000, xi). In so doing, they built collaborative networks and developed insights into public administration that have been hidden in plain sight.

Most United States women of the early nineteenth century focused on the care of their families and devoted themselves to upholding Christian morality. The ideal mother provided good food, clean clothing, and tender care to her family. She met her family's emotional needs, particularly when her husband and children faced sickness. She remained ignorant of the marketplace and party politics. In contrast, her husband resided in the public sphere and looked outward. Mary Livermore (1891), former manager of the USSC Chicago Branch, explained that this inward focus resulted in a near consensus among women and men that women's limited perspective and tendency toward petty gossip made women ill suited for executive tasks.

During crises, the nineteenth-century women's sphere widened a bit to serve the local community. Ladies aid societies, for example, were designed to render aid when fire or flood devastated local families. The seven thousand soldiers aid societies of the USSC were a natural extension of this system and were patched together from home mission societies, church organizations, sewing circles, and other benevolence organizations (Brayton and Terry 1869, 27). They became an effective bottom-up supply network that provided critical sustained support to the U.S. Army.

The leadership and networks did not occur spontaneously. During the 1820s and 1830s some women were active in moral reform societies and local benevolent organizations. Drawn together by a common purpose (usually abolition), these local reform societies worked for political change.

This network of female institutions articulated an "original political language that allowed them to expand women's sphere into the public world while not directly challenging the separation of spheres. When the war came, women extended the focus of their local reform efforts even further," often taking leadership positions in the USSC (Giesberg 2000, 24).

Over time, the mission of the supply arm of the Sanitary Commission expanded to include an incredible variety of services. It partnered with and supplemented army organizations that focused on the health and welfare of the troops. It filled gaps in the medical and nonweapon-related supply chain. For example, when scurvy began interfering with soldier recovery, large gardens sprang up on hospital grounds, thanks to the commission. The Union medical system focused on acute care; the USSC opened convalescent homes to serve disabled troops. Drawing on the women's tradition of fund-raising by church bazaars, women organized huge sanitary fairs that added millions to commission coffers (Livermore [1887] 1995, 412). They saw needs and experimented.

Like Nightingale, they used a "'scientific approach' to reform, one that emphasized organization, efficiency and professionalism" (Venet 2005, 73). Branch leaders, for example, were known for conducting surveys to find new ways to serve and to gather insights from those who labored in the local societies. With the exception of the U.S. Postal Service, the Sanitary Commission was the first organization to penetrate the federal system and knit together the United States as a continental power.

Twenty-six years after the USSC closed its doors, Mary Livermore (1891, 286) reflected on how women absorbed the big picture while responding to day-to-day administrative challenges.

> While they were working for the relief of the army, women studied the policy of government, and learned what tremendous issues were at stake. . . . Not only did these women broaden in their views; they grew in practical and executive work. They learned how to cooperate intelligently with men; became an expert in conducting public business, in calling and presiding over public meetings, even when men made a large part of the audience; learned how to draft constitutions and bylaws, to act as secretaries and committees; how to keep accounts with precision and system; how to answer, indorse, and file letters; how to sort their stores and keep accurate account of stock; they attended meetings with regularity and promptness, and became punctilious in observance of official etiquette; in short, they developed rapidly a remarkable aptitude for business, on which men looked and wondered. "Where were these superior women before the war?"

As women took up these new administrative functions, they created a transcontinental cooperative network of supplies and services unlike any the world had ever seen. Surely, there are lessons for public administration.

Women's Role as Nurses

> *In every ward the men greeted me gladly. They stretched out their hands to take mine; they talked freely of their home. . . . I was told by the poor fellows; "I've got a good mother at home, one of the best."*
> (Mary Livermore, USSC Nurse [Livermore (1887) 1995, 205])

Thus far only the role of women as administrators has been stressed in this chapter. Many women affiliated with the USSC also went to the field and served as nurses. In June 1861, Dorothea Dix was appointed superintendent of nursing (Giesberg 2000, 43). Perhaps to ensure their reputations, Dix required that nurses "be over thirty years of age, plain almost to repulsion in dress, and devoid of personal attractions" (Livermore [1887] 1995, 246). The nurses that eventually served did not all meet Dix's unusual specifications. Nevertheless, by insisting that nurses be older, Dix unwittingly filled their ranks with mature women who viewed the wounded and sick soldiers as their surrogate sons. A strong, caring, mother-son bond grew between the nurses and their young patients. The sick and dying men missed the embrace, sound, and scent of their mothers. They welcomed the maternal presence (Wood 1972; Shields, 2004).

Often working fourteen-hour days for weeks on end, the women nurses of the Civil War proved in yet another way that women's capabilities far outstripped those assigned them by society and often by themselves (Schultz 2004). The nurses used the mother-son bond as a moral wedge to protect their "boys" by advocating for change in senseless military regulations and sidestepping drunk or corrupt surgeons (Wood 1972). Although most would not have been familiar with Nightingale's science, the Union nurses stressed the "motherly" virtues of cleanliness and good nutrition and in so doing saved countless lives (Silber 1995, xi). These experiences brought the dignity of the mother-son relationship into army hospitals. They also reinforced and expanded women's sphere into often hostile male bastions.

Livermore ([1887] 1995, 206) describes the experiences of nurse Mary Safford. When first she entered the hospital, "there was no system, no organization, no knowledge what to do, and no means with which to work. As far as possible she brought order out of chaos, systematized the first rude hospitals. . . . Surgeons and officers everywhere opposed her, but she disarmed by the sweetness of her manner." There she was in the deplorable hospital, bringing "order out of chaos" and at the same time maintaining her sweetness of manner. Livermore points to this as one of many instances where the moral authority of the caring mother combined with other womanly traits (a sweet manner) to save lives.

A New Reform Agenda

I registered a vow that when the war was over I would take up a new work—the work of making law and justice synonymous for women. I have kept my vow religiously.
(Livermore [1887] 1995, 437)

The USSC experience left a lasting imprint on women's political agenda. The extended sense of sisterhood combined with a new awareness of women's unequal place in society ignited a women's reform movement. Why had women worked so hard for a nation that refused them the right to vote, acquire higher education, hold property, or keep their wages? These questions spurred new organizations, and the USSC experience gave them the confidence and skills to effect change.

In Great Britain, class lines marked political cleavages. In the United States, where all white men had the right to vote, political cleavages occurred across gender lines and were reinforced by the way men and women organized their lives (Skocpol 1992). Domesticity, however, "did not merely act to exclude women from the public sphere." It also created an opportunity "to begin to develop collective consciousness and the sense of sisterhood" (Giesberg 2000, 24). Throughout the war, these women "*created a model organizational structure* for women's organization in the post war era" (Giesberg 2000, 7). Prior to the Civil War there were a few women and organizations dedicated to promoting women's rights. These organizations were thwarted by a culture that placed women in a narrow sphere. The success of the Sanitary Commission relief efforts dispelled ingrained myths about women's abilities.

In the decades after the Civil War, women's political activism became both visible and successful. For example, the doors of higher education were constructed and opened, the suffrage movement gained momentum, policies to help women and children were proposed, and a temperance coalition was formed. In *Civil War Sisterhood,* Judith Giesberg (2000, 11) rediscovers the USSC and shows how women's participation was the missing link between "female activism of the first half of the century and the mass women's movements of the late nineteenth and early twentieth century." The USSC experience activated women such as Mary Livermore, who used her pen and voice to tell women it "was their destiny to play a greater role in public life" (Venet 2005, 7).

As the war neared its end, the women of the USSC were increasingly involved with providing assistance to the returning soldier and his family (including burial of children, heating, rent, and medical care). They were committed to taking work beyond mobilization. "As part of a new political culture, women saw beyond the demands of a single campaign and embraced the need for continued collaborative efforts on behalf of their communities" (Giesberg 2000, 135).

Putting It in Perspective

> *Until our civil war, it was considered inevitable that for every soldier killed in battle four must die of disease. . . . In the Crimean War seven-eighths of the mortality of British troops was due to disease. . . . But during our national struggle, for every soldier who fell in battle only two died of disease,—the splendid result of the beneficent work of the commission.*
> (Livermore 1895, 587)

Livermore (1891), Giesberg (2000), and Venet (2005) have made a compelling case for the USSC as a vehicle that helped transform women's role in politics and society. Its implications for public administration are of course outside their interest or frame of reference. If the USSC was a missing link that propelled women's political reform, it was also a key organization for providing women with the sustained administrative experience needed for them to contribute to public administration theory and practice.

Clearly the insights to public administration are found in the ways the women's sphere expanded. The mother-son bond reveals the importance of sympathetic understanding and the dignity of the everyday. The supplies reached their surrogate sons through a collaborative effort. Women increased their willingness to push the boundaries of the men's vision for the USSC, which surely did not include convalescent homes, sanitary fairs, bulletins, aid to soldiers' families, or help with pension-request forms. These women showed a willingness to experiment and reimagine how government could serve citizens.

The following vignette relayed by Mrs. Hoge (1867, 99) in the *The Boys in Blue* captures the compassion and efficiency that women brought to their work. Although the woman does not have a name, as the president of the Dixon Indiana Aid Society she is clearly a local leader who is part of a complicated supply network. "Her son has returned home on sick furlough, and said to his mother, 'I never received any sanitary stores when I was in the hospital.' 'Did you receive not green tea, and white sugar or codfish or eggs or farina?' 'Yes, I did. . . . ' 'All that you have enumerated are doubtless furnished by the Commission.'"

The mother knows that these everyday items (green tea, white sugar, codfish) were not army issue but supplied through the USSC network. The women's efforts were invisible to her son yet there in plain sight. "At night, when he had taken his bath, and thrown aside his soiled undergarments, she gathered them up and found them all marked 'North Western Sanitary Commission.' Yet so silently and unobtrusively had the work been done, that he knew not."

What could be more part of the women's sphere than a son's underwear and food? Yet these were found in an army hospital thousands of miles from home. There, hidden in plain sight, stamped in his undergarments, was the sign of the USSC. While new undergarments may not have made the difference between life and death, they were a signal of a viable supply chain that included basic necessities—necessities that were usually missing at the beginning of the war and were missing in Nightingale's Crimea. The sign of the USSC was invisible to her son; for his mother it was "proof sufficient of the blessed effects of the commission"—and motivated her and countless others to "work till the war should close."

Incidents like this show how the relief efforts had expanded the women's sphere and how the everyday occurrence of a mother picking up a son's soiled garments could be infused with meaning and inspire a woman to serve the commission and the Union in a sustained way.

URBANIZATION AND INDUSTRIALIZATION

> *Country doctors testify as to the outbreak of scarlet fever . . . each autumn after the children begin to wear infected coats sent from city sweatshops . . . when the tailoring of the family is done in the distant city under conditions which the mother cannot possibly control. The sanitary regulations of the sweatshops by city officials is all that can be depended upon to prevent such needless destruction.*
> (Addams 1910, 174–175)

The story of women in public administration now shifts to the well-educated daughters of the Civil War sisterhood as they address the problems of urbanization and industrialization. Jane Addams and the Settlement Movement are spotlighted. Addams is emphasized because she was one of the leading founders of the twentieth-century American administrative state (Stillman 1998). More important, she skillfully and coherently applied and refined key themes developed earlier, such as the women's sphere, scientific attitude, collaboration, sympathetic understanding, and the dignity of the everyday. These themes became the basis for her social ethics and democracy—a theory with widespread implications for public administration practice and theory (Addams 1902), a theory that should help public administration meet present-day challenges.

American women's exclusion from suffrage stimulated collective consciousness and counterorganization outside of the parties and regular electoral politics. Compared to their European counterparts, American women reacted more intensely, both ideologically and organizationally, against their exclusion from a fully democratized male polity. Theda Skocpol (1992, 52) argues that during the "nineteenth century, no major industrializing country differentiated worlds of politic—understood in the broadest sense as patterns of participation in public affairs—so *sharply on strictly gender* lines as did the United States." [Skocpol's emphasis]

As an alternative to formal electoral politics, many middle-class American women established local voluntary associations for charitable, religious, and welfare purposes. By the end of the century, these associations were "knit together into huge nation-spanning federations, networks that paralleled the local-state-nation structure. . . . And as this knitting together occurred, American women increasingly thought of themselves as uniquely moral political actors who had the duty to 'mother the nation.' Achieving a remarkable kind of maternalist political consciousness . . . American women used their clubs and federations to engage in municipal housekeeping" and to successfully propose new social programs (child labor laws, juvenile courts, laws that restricted hours worked, factory inspections for health) to help mothers and families around the nation (Skocpol 1992, 529). Building on existing networks of women's clubs, American women organized to influence social policy in the years between the Civil War and suffrage.

Moreover, American women were ready to take on this task. Increased opportunities for higher education resulted in a highly educated generation of women capable of taking over the reins of reform in the newly urbanized and industrialized nation. Education also "fostered an unusual sense of independence and determination in an elite minority of women." Unlike their mothers, however, they formed separatist organizations and created "single-sex institutions where they lived permanently outside the home" (Skocpol 1992, 343). Jane Addams's Hull House was one of these institutions.

JANE ADDAMS

Jane Addams is best known for her more than forty years of work with low-income immigrants at Hull House, her settlement house in the industrial Nineteenth Ward of Chicago. In addition, Addams was a public administrator, social worker, peace activist, philosopher, and gifted writer. She was a tireless advocate for those who had the least, pushing for social reform on countless issues. Her work (and that of the women and men of Hull House) provided the framework for social policy change, particularly during the institution of the New Deal policies (Lundblad 1995). Like Florence Nightingale, she came from an upper-class background and at a young age felt the call to serve. Addams's work was also a forerunner to several New Deal and Great Society programs that expand our understanding of public administration.

Addams approached her work and life with a sense of critical optimism, the sense that one has "the potential to make a difference and connect to the common good" (Shields 2003, 533). Her life and work were built upon a foundation of values and ethics and a steadfast commitment to the principles of democracy. Throughout her lifetime, as demonstrated through her work at Hull House, Addams sought practical ways to seek social change through democracy, for "as democracy modifies our conception of life, it constantly raises the value and function of each member of the community" (Addams 1902, 80). Addams felt that it was due to a lack of democracy that the needs of the poor and the working men and women went unanswered by society (Addams 1902, 96–97). Therefore, she advocated for democracy through the "mutual interpretation of the social classes to one another" (Elshtain 2001, 88).

A common, understandable misconception is that Hull House was an 1890s version of a contemporary soup kitchen or homeless shelter. Hull House had a broader objective. The residents of Hull House were creating community and citizens (Elshtain 2002, 152–153). The large Hull House complex became part of the community as it addressed the needs of the nearby impoverished, diverse, immigrant community. Labor and art museums, a day nursery, college extension courses (which emphasized art, literature, language, mathematics, history, music, and drawing), a coffeehouse, Sunday concerts, a summer school, a choir, at least twenty-five clubs, cooking classes, free kindergarten, facilities for organized labor to meet, speaker series, dances, a gymnasium, and a public dispensary (drugstore) were all found within its walls. John Dewey, George Herbert Mead, W.E.B. DuBois, Susan B. Anthony, and Theodore Roosevelt lectured at Hull House. Hull House was also a source of neighborhood activism, often going head-to-head with Chicago's corrupt political machine.

Expanding Women's Sphere: Social Claim

> *In short, if woman would keep on with her old business of caring for her house and rearing her children she will have to have some conscience in regard to public affairs lying quite outside of her immediate household. The individual conscience and devotion are no longer effective.*
> (Addams 1910, 174)

Obviously, the woman's sphere came with many claims on time and talent. Traditionally, women met their duty or claim by caring for their families. In an agrarian society, where families were separated from one another by great distances, women had control over their households. Their duty was narrowly circumscribed. In the urbanized and industrialized world of late-nineteenth- and early-twentieth-century America, assumptions about a woman's control over her family's welfare broke down. Addams argued that a singular focus on care within the home could be counterproductive and even harmful. "In a crowded city quarter, if the street is not cleared by the city authorities no amount of private sweeping will keep the tenement free from grime; if the garbage is not properly collected and destroyed a tenement-house mother may see her children sicken and die of diseases from which she alone is powerless to shield" (Addams 1910, 174).

To truly serve their families, women must widen their sphere to incorporate larger social issues. The claim or corresponding duty was now social, for unless a woman paid attention to the larger public, no amount of care inside the home would guarantee the health and safety of her family (her foremost duty).

Jane Addams and other well-educated women of that period were drawn to the social claim. Their desire to move outside the traditional sphere challenged long-standing belief systems about the roles of men and women in society. In *Democracy and Social Ethics* (1902), Addams examines the conflict many young women faced as they were pulled to social activism (social claim) and challenged by their families for neglecting their family duties (in favor of moving into the male, or public, sphere).

Drawing on themes already well developed in the women's reform movement, Addams makes a strong case for reconceptualizing the role of the city in citizens' lives so that the concerns of the family can be met more fully. For example, men conceptualize the city as a citadel or as a mighty economic engine. Using the expanded women's sphere and the social claim, Addams argues that the city should be reconceptualized as a civic household. As a civic household, the city would ensure the health and safety of its citizens through safe sewers, clean water, and clean streets. If city leaders and administration are oblivious to the social claim, babies die unnecessarily. "The family claim is no private matter; it is a social claim of the most basic kind. Addams's challenge was to see the family as a part of a web of social imperatives and forces without ever losing sight of that one little hand" (Elshtain 2002, 97).

Scientific Attitude

> *A Special Investigation of the "Slums of Great City's" was undertaken,*
> *the spring of 1893, by the United States Department of Labor, by order of*
> *Congress; and as Mrs. Florence Kelly, the Special Agent Expert in charge in*
> *Chicago, resided at Hull House while conducting the investigation, the information*
> *collected by the government officials was brought within the very doors.*
> (Holbrook [1895] 1970, 6–7)

Clearly, Hull House was a homelike environment where women could practice the art of civic housekeeping, in other words, seek solutions to social problems. Early on, Addams realized that she did not want to impose solutions on the neighborhood. She developed an approach that focused on inquiry. So, as the Sanitary Commission was an agency "organized for the purpose of inquiry" (Sanitary Commission of the United States Army [1864] 1972, 5), so too was Hull House. If the residents were to learn the connection between industrial practices and disease, or filthy streets and infant mortality, they would need to experiment and collect data.

"The Settlement, then, is an experimental effort to aid in the solution of the social and industrial problems which are engendered by the modern conditions of life in a great city. . . . It must be hospitable and *ready for experiment.* It should demand from its residents a *scientific patience in the accumulation of facts*" (Addams [1910] 1930, 126–127; emphasis added).

Like Nightingale, Addams combined an "experimental" approach to problem solving with "scientific patience in the accumulation of facts." This belief in the necessity of depending upon valid and reliable data for scientific inquiry led the residents of Hull House to develop innovative research design and cartographic techniques to explore the ethnic geography of Chicago neighborhoods (Deegan 1990).

DIGNITY OF THE EVERYDAY

> *The children of our neighborhood twenty years ago played their games in and around huge garbage boxes. They were the first objects a toddling child learned to climb.*
> (Addams [1910] 1930, 164)

Because she was close to the people, Addams's experiential social ethics led her to recognize and celebrate the dignity of people's daily lives. Her democracy is a type of lived experience that takes into account the small things in order to see the whole (Elshtain 2002, 172). Addams found dignity in the everyday tasks of tending to the well-being of the old and young—sewing and sowing, planting and harvesting. She celebrated the everyday with its undramatic practices and values (Elshtain 2002, 64).

The everyday problem of grossly inadequate garbage collection illustrates the importance of humble activities and propelled Addams into the sphere of public administration. The sights, smells, health hazards, and Chicago's obvious corruption stimulated Addams and the women's clubs of Hull House to action. During a hot summer, Addams organized neighborhood women to "carefully [investigate] the conditions of the alleys." After two months, they reported 1,037 violations to the health department (Addams [1910] 1930, 284–285). In spite of their efforts, violations persisted and the infant mortality rate remained high. Corrupt contractors continued to win bids. Eventually, Chicago City Hall recognized the community's concern and appointed Jane Addams the first female garbage inspector. She used her office to force contractors to clean the streets. Her efforts dramatically reduced the infant mortality rate in the Nineteenth Ward. Society may take women's work for granted, yet if it is left undone, society's survival is threatened (Addams [1910] 1930, 284–285).

Addams celebrated the dignity of the everyday and made the connection between democracy and the humble, yet important, nature of human experience. Since public administration is a field of study and a field of practice, it incorporates the lived experiences of practicing street-level administrators. Just as Nightingale knew that hospitals needed a way to give dignity to patient and caregiver, so, too, Addams's insight gives meaning and dignity to the everyday interactions of public servant and citizen. In addition to administrators the status of expert, she showed how the work itself has inherent dignity. Addams infused even the most humble task with dignity and meaning and connected them to her vision of an ethical, social democracy.

Sympathetic Understanding

> *We are learning that a standard of social ethics is not attained by traveling a sequestered byway, but by mixing on the thronged and common road where all must turn out for one another, and at least see the size of one another's burdens.*
> (Addams 1902, 6)

Nightingale demonstrated the importance of sympathetic understanding to patient, hospital administration, and the nursing profession. Addams showed its importance to a newly urbanized America. Addams's faith in a social democracy where human beings in concrete situations could work out social claims depended upon the ability of each to sympathetically understand the other or "at least see the size of one another's burdens." The concept of sympathetic understanding is the cornerstone of her larger social ethics. An ethical social democracy works when this component is practiced and understood. Sympathetic understanding and the resultant fellowship were her alternative to dogmatism, rigid moralism, and self-centered righteousness. "To perform too many good deeds may be to lose the power of recognizing good in others" (Addams 1902, 146).

Sympathetic understanding is facilitated when the everyday is given dignity. Connections between people are deepened. Democracy is about connections between people.

Collaboration—Participatory Democracy

> *It is most difficult to hold to our political democracy and to make it in any*
> *sense a social expression and not a mere governmental contrivance,*
> *unless we take pains to keep common ground in our human experience.*
> (Addams 1902, 221)

Addams's democracy is a way to examine relationships in the new expanded sphere, where people understand and feel the social claim. This is clearly a bottom-up vision of democracy—one consistent with a public service ethic. The active women's networks that formed outside politics were an obvious way to think about the nature of these relationships. The power of collaboration and networks gave Addams insight into a participatory democracy that complemented political democracy. Addams drew on these experiences as she incorporated an expanded notion of participation into her theory of democracy.

Addams's democracy is a kind of cooperative experiment (Seigfried 1996, 92). The values of democratic community (mutual respect, mutual toleration, give-and-take, the pooling of experience) are connected by sympathetic understanding. The success of the community depends upon cooperative efforts to seek the common good in a democratic way. We may be drawn together to solve our problems, but it is the togetherness, not the solution, that is the primary result (Campbell 1998, 40). Public administration and the public its professionals serve are united in a new way through Addams's vision of democracy.

Embodiments of Emotional Labor

The women highlighted in this chapter are synonymous with evidence-based, rigorous, scientific work that is infused with care, compassion, kindness, empathy, understanding, and nurturance, and their work is highly evocative of emotional labor. As Hsieh and Guy (2009) observe, emotional labor is a concept introduced to public administration by Mary Ellen Guy and Meredith Newman (2004) and refers to the expression of appropriate emotions during service transactions by both men and women (Ashworth and Humphrey 1993).

The main arguments presented in the literature on emotional labor in public administration could serve as an explanation for why the work of exemplary women such as Nightingale, Addams, and others has not received due recognition. Mastracci, Guy, and Newman (2006, 126–127) observe that more than one-half of all working women have jobs that require emotional labor and that women are expected to perform "more emotional labor than men in the same occupation" and even within predominantly female occupations. Guy and Newman (2004, 289) note that although men and women perform emotional labor, "it is the softer emotions, those required in relational tasks such as caring and nurturing, that disappear most often from job descriptions, performance evaluations and salary calculations. These are the emotions that are a mainstay of health and human service professions, public education, paraprofessional jobs and most support positions, such as administrative assistants, receptionists, clerical staff and secretaries. Simply stated, acts that grease the wheels so that people cooperate, stay on task and work well together are essential for job completion but they are rewarded more with a pat on the back than with money."

They also observe (292) that emotional labor by women is worth less than emotional labor by men. Guy and Newman illustrate that even in female-dominated occupations, emotional labor is compensated less when performed by a woman than by a man (292). Furthermore, in the context of emotional labor in academia, they note that work that involves extensive amounts of emotional labor is seen as work that does not require special training and is therefore rewarded less than administration and research. However, Meier, Mastracci, and Wilson (2006, 899) have shown in the context of education that "organizations with more women at the street level have higher overall organizational performance" and that, therefore, emotional labor has the potential to reduce teacher turnover and increase student attendance and productivity. Interestingly, a United Nations Economic and Social Commission report shows that if women were paid at the same rate that men were, the GDP of the United States would go up by 9 percent, that of the European nations would go up by 10 percent, and that of Japan would go up by 16 percent. According to a UNICEF report, women perform 66 percent of the world's work, produce 50 percent of the food, but earn 10 percent of the income and own 1 percent of the property (United Nations Development Fund for Women 2010).

The discrepancy in recognition and compensation of women's labor and in particular women's and men's emotional labor is a significant issue that has historical roots. If in today's world, when laws and other mechanisms are in place to ensure that women enjoy the same rights as men, the work of women could be eclipsed in the aforementioned ways, it is no surprise that the work of Nightingale and Addams has simply not received the acknowledgment that it deserves. Highlighting the contributions of Nightingale and Addams is one way to make "emotional labor visible" (Guy and Newman 2004, 296).

Contemporary Relevance

The historical cases highlighted in this chapter have irrefutable insights for present-day public administration. First, women such as Nightingale, Livermore, and Addams serve as exemplars for women in addressing present-day issues associated with obesity, teen pregnancy, general education, domestic violence, and microeconomics, to name just a few. Nightingale, Livermore, and Addams were able to foresee the immense opportunity that their situations presented and were able to leave an indelible impression on administrative history by being optimistic in deplorable situations. They had access to information and, most important, the ability to process that information in a useful way. Women of today face no less an opportunity. As repositories of information as a result of their everyday interactions with the sick, the elderly, young children, and students and as a result of their roles as daughters, mothers, wives, coworkers, and caregivers, their everyday experiences can strengthen the foundation of public administration reform. Second, current realities, including war-torn nations such as Iraq and Afghanistan, and nations in humanitarian crises such as Sudan and Sri Lanka, mirror the realities faced by Nightingale and Addams. A staggering statistic in this regard is that 72 percent of the world's refugees are women and children and close to 50 percent of women experience partner violence in their lives (USAID 2009). The fact that they were able, through their work, to instill a sense of hope and dignity in those in their care should serve as inspiration. Third, the work of these women has major implications for public personnel management. Their work is the perfect blend of hard-core management skills, emotional intelligence, and emotional labor. If such work has the potential to go unrecognized in today's world, it can have serious implications for workplace motivation and morale. It is essential to consider institutional and organizational changes that would put emotional labor on par with knowledge work. Newman, Guy, and Mastracci (2009, 6) emphasize the centrality of emotional labor in a multitude of work contexts. They conclude that the most compelling challenge for public managers is to infuse a sense of caring and humanity (embodied by the likes of Nightingale and Addams) in the workplace as opposed to just efficiency (18).

CONCLUSION

The three historical cases presented here show how women developed a new conceptualization of administration. Inattention to the traditional women's sphere led to much suffering. In each case, this reconceptualization was lost from the historical legacy. Nightingale is the "Lady with the Lamp," the USSC itself has been lost from our historical memory, and Jane Addams's administrative and philosophic contributions were buried (Seigfried 1996; Deegan 1990). Social work, a field that often claims Addams as a founder, adopted the case method of Sigmund Freud as a way to gain professional legitimacy and in doing this de-emphasized its Settlement tradition (Shields 1989).

This chapter shows us a way to reconnect to a fuller and more complete historical legacy. It is a legacy that provides a bottom-up perspective and shows how a broader definition of the women's sphere served society well. Perhaps more important, connections across the three cases show how Addams's social ethic and democracy are a logical extension of early women's contributions. Addams provides us with an organic vision of democracy that can connect us to the people we serve in helpful ways.

Addams's ideas have the potential to inspire practicing public administrators. If they incorporate her vision of democracy, practitioners will see their actions and experiences as creating democracy. This is not the political or legal democratic framework; rather, democracy is experienced in their conversations with citizens, clients, coworkers, and so on. Addams imagined a kind of democracy that can be actively practiced in public administrators' day-to-day life. The humble activities of public administration have the potential to be part of ongoing democratic processes—processes that involve people every day—not just on Election Day or through the activities in a distant state capitol building. This kind of democracy has the potential to energize the field.

Further, it shows the importance of incorporating a diversity of views as we confront contemporary public problems. These challenges demand that we bring our full capacity to the task. Seemingly insurmountable problems—global warming, pandemics, financial crises, war, poverty, an inadequate health-care system—all are best resolved if multiple perspectives are incorporated into discourse, decision making, and implementation.

NOTE

1. Camilla Stivers (1993, 2000, 2002) has done much to integrate women's history and feminist ideas into public administration. Her study of the late-nineteenth- and early-twentieth-century Settlement women articulated their alternative model of public administration, one that differed markedly from the reform-minded men of the New York Municipal Research Bureau (Stivers 2000). She argues for a reformulation of public administration's past that takes into account both perspectives. Stivers's quest for a usable past helps

us make better sense of our present, which in turn could fuel our efforts in the future. We draw on Stivers's insights and highlight the achievements of an even earlier generation of women, who, like their Settlement daughters, engaged in and were transformed by their public administration experience. Jane Addams and Florence Nightingale emerge as key figures. They are linked through their shared desire to expand the narrow domestic sphere as a way to deal with larger societal problems (child labor, filthy streets, deadly water and sewer systems, dangerous hospitals). In addition, these women were careful to advance their ideas using evidence-based research techniques. Both women wrote extensively and literally got their hands dirty as they gathered the evidence needed for serious reform. Their volumes of written work reveal a public service philosophy that incorporated an expanded women's sphere, the dignity of the everyday, caring, practice, sympathy, and a willingness to experiment. It is this sense of women's contribution to public administration that is missing.

REFERENCES

Addams, Jane. 1902. *Democracy and Social Ethics.* New York: Macmillan.

———. 1910. Why women should vote. *Ladies Home Journal* 27:21–22. In *Selected Articles on Woman Suffrage,* comp. Edith Phelps, 173–183. Minneapolis, MN: H.W. Wilson.

———. [1910] 1930. *Twenty Years at Hull-House.* New York. Macmillan.

Ashworth, Blake E., and Ronald H. Humphrey. 1993. Emotional labor in service roles: The influence of identity. *Academy of Management Review* 18 (1): 88–115.

Brayton, Mary, and Ellen Terry. 1869. *Our Acre and Its Harvest: Historical Sketch of the Soldiers' Aid Society of Northern Ohio, Cleveland Branch of the United States Sanitary Commission.* Cleveland: Fairbanks, Benedict.

Campbell, James. 1998. Dewey's conception of community. In *Reading Dewey: Interpretations for a Postmodern Generation,* ed. Larry Hickman, 23–42. Bloomington: Indiana University Press.

Deegan, M. 1990. *Jane Addams, and the Men of the Chicago School.* New Brunswick, NJ: Transaction Books.

Elshtain, Jean Bethke. 2001. Jane Addams and the social claim. *Public Interest* 145 (Fall): 82–92.

———. 2002. *Jane Addams and the Dream of American Democracy.* New York: Basic Books.

Giesberg, Judith. 2000. *Civil War Sisterhood: The U.S. Sanitary Commission and Women's Politics in Transition.* Boston: Northeastern University Press.

Guy, Mary Ellen, and Meredith Newman. 2004. Women's jobs, men's jobs: Sex segregation and emotional labor. *Public Administration Review* 64 (3): 289–298.

Hobbs, Colleen. 1997. *Florence Nightingale.* New York. Twayne Publishers.

Holbrook, Agnes. [1895] 1970. Map notes and comments. In *Hull-House Maps and Papers,* by Residents of Hull House, 3–26. New York: Arno Press.

Hoge, A.H. 1867. *The Boys in Blue; or Heroes of the "Rank and File."* New York: E.B. Treat.

Hsieh, Chih-Wei, and Mary Ellen Guy. 2009. Performance outcomes: The relationship between managing the "heart" and managing client satisfaction. *Review of Public Personnel Administration* 29 (1): 41–57.

Linn, James. 1968. *Jane Addams: A Biography.* New York: Greenwood Press.

Livermore, Mary. [1887] 1995. *My Story of the War: The Civil War Memories of the Famous Nurse, Relief Organizer and Suffragette.* New York: Da Capo Press.

———. 1891. Cooperative womanhood in the state. *North American Review* 153 (September): 283–295.

———. 1895. Massachusetts women in the Civil War. In *Massachusetts in the Army and Navy During the War of 1816–65,* ed. T. Higginson, 586–602. Boston: Wright and Potter.

Lundblad, Karen Shafer. 1995. Jane Addams and social reform: A role model for the 1990s. *Social Work* 40: 661–669.

Mastracci, Sharon, Mary Ellen Guy, and Meredith Newman. 2006. Appraising emotion work: Determining whether emotional labor is valued in government jobs. *American Review of Public Administration* 36 (2): 123–138.

Maxwell, William Q. 1956. *Lincoln's Fifth Wheel: The Political History of the United States Sanitary Commission.* New York: Longmans, Green.

McDonald. Lynn. 2001. Florence Nightingale and the early origins of evidence-based nursing. *Evidence-Based Nursing* 4 (3): 68–71.

Meier, Kenneth, Sharon Mastracci, and Kristin Wilson. 2006. Gender and emotional labor in public organizations: An empirical examination of the link to performance. *Public Administration Review* 66 (6): 899–909.

Newman, Meredith, Mary Ellen Guy, and Sharon Mastracci. 2009. Beyond cognition: Affective leadership and emotional labor. *Public Administration Review* 69 (1): 6–20.

Nightingale, Florence. 1858. *Notes on Matters Affecting the Health, Efficiency and Hospital Administration of the British Army, Founded Chiefly on the Experience of the Late War.* London: Harrison and Sons. Reprinted in Neuhauser, Duncan. 1999. *Florence Nightingale: Measuring Hospital Care Outcomes.* Oakbrook Terrace, IL: Joint Commission on Accreditation of Healthcare Organizations.

———. [1860] 1922. *Notes on Nursing: What It Is, and What It Is Not.* New York: D. Appleton.

———. 1862. *Army Sanitary Administration and Its Reform Under the Late Lord Herbert.* London: Mc-Corquodale.

———. 1863. *Notes on Hospitals.* 3d ed., enlarged and for the most part rewritten. London: Longman, Green, Longman, Roberts, and Green.

Reverby, Susan. 1987. A caring dilemma: Womanhood and nursing in historical perspective. *Nursing Research* 36 (1): 5–11.

Sanitary Commission of the United States Army. [1864] 1972. *A Succinct Narrative of Its Works and Purposes.* New York: Arno Press and the *New York Times.*

Schultz, Jane. 2004. *Women at the Front: Hospital Workers in Civil War America.* Chapel Hill: University of North Carolina Press.

Seigfried, Charlene 1996. *Pragmatism and Feminism: Reweaving the Social Fabric.* Chicago: University of Chicago Press.

Shields, Patricia. 1989. Freud, efficiency and pragmatism. *Transaction/Society* 26 (2): 67–72.

———. 2003. "The Community of Inquiry: Classical Pragmatism and Public Administration." *Administration & Society* 35, (5): 510–538.

———. 2004. Mary Livermore: A legacy of caring and cooperative womanhood in service to the state. In *Outstanding Women in Pubic Administration: Leaders, Mentors, and Pioneers,* ed. Claire Felbinger and Wendy Hanes. New York: M.E. Sharpe.

Silber, N. 1995. Introduction. In *My Story of the War: The Civil War Memories of the Famous Nurse, Relief Organizer and Suffragette,* ed. M. Livermore, i–xxi. New York: Da Capo Press.

Skocpol, Theda. 1992. *Protecting Soldiers and Mothers: The Political Origins of Social Policy in the United States.* Cambridge, MA: Belknap Press of Harvard University Press.

Stillé, Charles J. 1866. *History of the United States Sanitary Commission: Being the General Report of Its Work During the War of the Rebellion.* Philadelphia: J.B. Lippincott.

Stillman II, Richard. 1998. *Creating the American State: The Moral Reformers and the Modern Administrative World They Made.* Tuscaloosa, AL: University of Alabama Press.

Stivers, Camilla. 2000. *Bureau Men, Settlement Women: Constructing Public Administration in the Progressive Era.* Lawrence: University Press of Kansas.

———. 1993. *Gender Issues in Public Administration: Legitimacy and the Administrative State.* Thousand Oaks, CA: Sage.

———. 2002. *Gender Issues in Public Administration: Legitimacy and the Administrative State.* 2d ed. Thousand Oaks, CA: Sage.

Ulrich, Beth. 1997. *Management and Leadership According to Florence Nightingale.* Upper Saddle River, NJ: Prentice-Hall.

United Nations Development Fund for Women (UNIFEM). 2010. Facts & figures on women, poverty & economics. www.unifem.org/gender_issues/women_poverty_economics/facts_figures.php#1, accessed September 10, 2010.

USAID. 2009. Women in development: Gender statistics. www.usaid.gov/our_work/cross-cutting_programs/wid/wid_stats.html, accessed September 10, 2010.

Venet, Wendy H. 2005. *A Strong Minded Woman: The Life of Mary Livermore.* Amherst: University of Massachusetts Press.

Woodham-Smith, C. 1959. *Lonely Crusader: The Life of Florence Nightingale 1820–1910.* New York: Whittlesey House.

Wood, A. 1972. The war within a war: Women nurses in the Union army. *Civil War History* 18 (3): 197–212.

CHAPTER 4

PROFESSIONAL ASSOCIATIONS AND PUBLIC ADMINISTRATION

Making a Difference?

WENDY HAYNES AND BETH GAZLEY

This chapter examines the literature on professional associations in the public management arena and identifies future lines of inquiry for empirical research and theoretical development. Little empirical research has addressed professional associations, and even less has examined their activities in the public sector. However, there is considerable conceptual literature that lends itself to an improved understanding of the range of associations available to public professionals, their impact on public administration, and their potential for fostering public service excellence. This disparate and sometimes entirely conceptual literature is connected, in this chapter, to the very practical question of how professional associations support public sector management.

THE ASSOCIATION ARENA IN THE UNITED STATES

Associations are the common name for numerous not-for-profit, mutual benefit organizations that serve the interests of social, political, cultural, religious, and professional groups. They include communes, homeowners associations, producer cooperatives, trade and occupational associations, religious congregations, recreational clubs, fraternities and sororities, and political organizations. Their names are familiar—the Rotary Club, the American Heart Association, and the American Bar Association—and not so familiar—the National Association of Professional Pet Sitters, the National Association of Female Executives, and the United Daughters of the Confederacy.

Quantifying the number of member-serving organizations depends on how inclusively the terms *association* and *membership* are applied. From a broad perspective, associations can be organized under several classes of the federal tax code governing nonprofits. The family of organizations incorporated under the 501(c)(5), (c)(6), (c)(7), and other sections of the tax code include chambers of commerce, social clubs, labor unions, and fraternal societies. One-quarter of all nonprofit organizations (about 336,000 entities in 2008) are organized legally as these mutual benefit organizations, created by individuals who join together to promote and protect collective interests (National Center for Charitable Statistics [NCCS] 2009).

Trade and professional associations represent a subfield of these organizations, numbering about seventy-two thousand in 2008 (NCCS 2009). Since some charities and other public benefit organizations also operate under a membership structure and provide educational services to warrant a charitable status, the actual number of associations may be considerably larger. It is worth noting that a few associations have found that a for-profit status better serves their interests. For

Table 4.1

A Selective List of Associations Organized by Representational Level

Jurisdictions and Authorities	Professions	Functions
National Association of Counties	Government Finance Officers Association	National Association of State Charity Officials
Florida League of Cities	California State Firefighters Association	Association of Public Health Laboratories
Pennsylvania State Association of Township Supervisors	National Forum for Black Public Administrators	American Public Works Association
Public Library Association	Federal Managers Association	American Public Transportation Association
Metropolitan Washington Council of Governments	Council for Excellence in Government	Public Risk Management Association
Regional Council of Rural Counties	Association of Government Accountants	National Emergency Management Association
Public Housing Authorities Directors Association		

example, the New York Stock Exchange converted from a not-for-profit business league to a publicly traded corporation in 2006.

Collectively, professional associations educate, train, and credential people in many occupations (e.g., engineering, medicine, education), provide commercial services to professionals, and advocate for member interests in the public policy arena. In the public sector, hundreds of professional associations represent the interests of governmental *jurisdictions* and *authorities* (e.g., the National Association of Counties), *professions* (e.g., the Government Finance Officers Association), and *functions* (e.g., the National Association of State Charity Officials). Association membership can be open to individuals, institutions, businesses, or governments. It is quite possible that every career public official belongs to one or more professional associations (see Table 4.1).

THE PUBLIC VALUE OF PROFESSIONAL ASSOCIATIONS

The authors conducted a review of thirty textbooks commonly used in introductory public administration courses and advanced courses in leadership and ethics and found only sixteen books that address the benefits and values that professional associations contribute to public management. Thirteen books provide a paragraph or so, while only three describe the value of associations in acculturating graduate students to the core values of public administration.[1] In fact, one text—Starling's *Managing the Public Sector*—describes the professional codes issued by professional associations as of "limited usefulness" (2008, 181).

Rather than accept this casual dismissal of the importance of professional associations, we suggest the need for a broader appreciation of their value in public administration. Haynes and Samuel (2006) contend that associations serve multiple purposes, including enabling members to participate in wider communities beyond those experienced in the workplace (e.g., global connections) and contributing to policy development and implementation, especially at the national level. Associations also provide leadership training and experience through participation in the governance of membership organizations.

No research has yet asked public managers to identify systematically the professional associations they consider most useful in their work, nor the benefits they value the most. A content analysis of organizational Web sites mentioned by leaders of the American Society for Public Administration (ASPA) suggests a typology of organizational benefits for public managers.[2]

These benefits include training and development, awards and recognition, research and knowledge creation, certification and standard setting, ethical guidance and codes of conduct, professional networking and career development, leadership opportunities, and public service value advocacy. The following sections describe ways in which associations provide these benefits.

Training and Development

Most associations offer training and professional development opportunities. Public administrators can acquire new skills and hone those acquired earlier in their careers. A study of seventeen thousand association members conducted by the American Society of Association Executives in 2006 found training and development to be the most important function that associations provide (Dalton and Dignam 2007). Training opportunities vary widely, from webinar offerings by the Association of Government Accountants and ASPA to extensive professional development by the Association of Inspectors General and the International City/County Management Association (ICMA).

Awards and Recognition

Associations also recognize practitioner and scholarly achievements. For example, ASPA and the National Academy of Public Administration cosponsor the National Public Service Awards and collaborate with the National Association of Schools of Public Affairs and Administration to recognize outstanding contributions in faculty research, service, and teaching. Indeed, ASPA's award listing continues for many pages and covers the field from chapter newsletters to lifetime achievement awards (www.aspanet.org/scriptcontent/index_awards_about.cfm). The ICMA offers an extensive awards program that recognizes extraordinary accomplishments as well as dedicated service to the profession of city and county management.

Research and Knowledge Creation

Associations offer a wealth of publications, including glossy magazines, learned books, newsletters, scholarly journals, white papers, and other commentary. Associations also provide a venue for those who wish to have their own research published and shared with peers. Often, associations serve as the principal means by which professionals obtain timely information about scientific and technical developments in their field (Dalton and Dignam 2007).

Certification and Standard Setting

Many associations have programs that certify expertise and accredit academic programs that meet published standards. For example, a section of ASPA advocates for the Certified Public Manager designation, which indicates completion of training accredited by the Certified Public Manager Consortium and is offered through authorized stated-based entities. Similarly, the Association of Government Accountants has developed the Certified Government Financial Manager program. To achieve and maintain the designation, members undergo extensive testing, complete continuing professional education hours, and must adhere to the Association of Government Accountants' code of ethics. The ICMA has a voluntary credentialing program that allows public managers to earn the designation of ICMA-CM (for "credentialed manager"). The certified public manager program includes an Applied Knowledge Assessment (AKA) tool that is based on ICMA's

Practices for Effective Local Government (Streib and Rivera 2010). As discussed in this volume, the National Association of Schools of Public Affairs and Administration establishes rigorous standards for accrediting master's programs in public policy, affairs, and administration (see chapter 5, "Accreditation and Competencies in Education for Leadership in Public Service").

Ethical Guidance and Codes of Conduct

Most, if not all, associations that serve public administrators promulgate ethical standards and issue codes of conduct. Indeed, it is only in this area that introductory public administration textbooks make more than a passing mention of professional associations. Most often noted are the codes of conduct for members of the ASPA and the ICMA.

Jeremy Plant (2000, 317–318) explores the history of ethical standards and codes of conduct, noting that a "fruitful source of insights is provided by the literature on public professional associations, many of which have a long and rich involvement in ethical issues, as well as a strong historical connection to the field and practice of public administration." In the case of the ICMA, Plant observes that no other association has the wealth of experience or duration of interest in promoting ethical practices and behavior. Plant asserts that the lasting significance of codes of ethics is that "they can lift individual public servants above the 'do's and don't's' of ordinary organizational life to give meaning and reality to the highest values of a democratic society" (328).

According to Plant (325), four types of associations are most likely to have a formal code of conduct:

1. Engineering associations, including such public sector associations as the American Association of State Highway and Transportation Officials (AASHTO) and the American Public Works Association;
2. Associations representing professionals in administration of justice or regulatory activities using the law as an enforcement approach [including the many well-known state trooper associations, the Professional Law Enforcement Association, and more esoteric organizations, such as the American Working Dog Council, which sets standards for police dog training];
3. Associations with a clearly public sort of professionalism, including ICMA, American Planning Association/American Institute of Certified Planners, GFOA [Government Finance Officers Association], and ASPA; and
4. Associations representing professionals in education [such as the National Association of Elementary School Principals and the National Council of Teachers of Mathematics, which has developed a professional oath].

Professional Networking and Career Development

Associations enable professionals to interact with and observe colleagues across generations, sectors, and levels of experience. Many associations, including ASPA, the Partnership for Public Service, ICMA, the National Association of Redevelopment Officers, the Association of Government Accountants, the Association of Inspectors General, the Government Financial Officers Association, and others, offer recruitment and job placement opportunities. Conferences, local chapter meetings, and workshops provide a venue for meeting people in the field one might ordinarily not encounter. Online resources provide electronic networking opportunities through blogs, Listservs, and social networking sites. Some associations become important recruitment mechanisms for the functional areas they represent (such as civil engineers, government accountants, or foreign service officers), with programs that encourage young professionals to enter their fields.

Leadership Opportunities

In addition to professional paid staff, associations have a member-led governance structure (non-profit organizations are legally required to have an operating board). Beyond the formal governance structure, numerous committees of lay members help achieve associations' operational objectives, including conference programming, review of professional standards, and the creation of training curricula. Association governance and committee activities can and do provide members with valuable leadership experiences. These leadership opportunities provide a means for honing interpersonal skills and developing better citizens for the association and the community at large.

Public Service Value Advocacy

Associations offer a venue for connecting members with others who hold similar values and advocate for public policy initiatives that promote those values, such as fairness, social equity, and transparency. Association representatives from both the private and public sectors regularly participate in local, state, and national legislative hearings as expert witnesses, advocates, or lobbyists.

RESEARCH ON PROFESSIONAL ASSOCIATIONS

Scholars from many disciplines—sociology, social psychology, political science, economics—have been interested in why and how individuals with common interests organize themselves in groups. In the beginning of his famous work on collective action, Mancur Olson (1965, 17) cites Aristotle's argument that humans have a predisposition for group formation. The remarks of Alexis de Tocqueville, the renowned French observer of 1830s America, are also used today to suggest that Americans have a strong disposition to solve problems through volunteer associations (Dalton 2008, 138–160).

Along this historical path, the reasons behind association formation have been widely debated. The lack of agreement stems, no doubt, from the tremendous diversity of the field, the variety of intellectual frameworks that can be brought to bear on associational activity, and the difficulty in categorizing associations into defined groups according to purpose, legal form, or representation. Abbott (1988), Knoke (1986), and Tschirhart (2006) have produced the most comprehensive work on associations, although none of them has addressed associational activity in a public service context. Their perspectives, however, not only help build an understanding of associations but also help to identify the association field's lack of a core theory or conceptual framework. Multiple perspectives are offered as explanations for the formation of associations.

WHY WE JOIN

An economic perspective relies on exchange theories to suggest that individuals join associations when they derive sufficient benefits beyond the cost of their dues and time. Political scientists emphasize the representative nature of associations and their ability to serve a pluralist function and to organize group interests. Sociologists and human ecologists view associations as social units that organize collective life, build social capital, and contribute to collective (though not necessarily majority) interests (Hawley 1950; Putnam 2000). Rational actor and institutional theories, widely applied in public management, describe the ability of associations to set standards of conduct and legitimize their actions by imposing behavioral expectations on other institutional actors (Brignall and Modell 2000; DiMaggio and Powell 1983).

Many scholars have observed that underlying the challenge in understanding public sector association activity, a substantial empirical and theoretical gap exists in the general research on mutual benefit associations (Hudson and Hudson 2002). As Knoke (1986, 2) writes, "Put bluntly, association research remains a largely unintegrated set of disparate findings, in dire need of a compelling theory. . . . [Without it], students of associations and interest groups seem destined to leave their subject in scientific immaturity." Two decades later, Tschirhart (2006, 535–536) suggests that "these earlier assessments still hold today. . . . We need more theories and empirical work" about the role of associations in American civic life. Tschirhart notes in particular the dearth of high-quality, cross-sector research that can produce generalizable models of association effectiveness.

As noted, observers also suggest that associations do not necessarily offer societal benefits. Although voluntary associations can support democratic processes and diffuse knowledge, they can also suppress minority voices and promote inequities (Tschirhart 2006, 526). Many associations represent powerful special interests. The typology of nonprofit organizational forms makes a crucial legal distinction between those organized for public or general societal benefit and those organized for collective or mutual benefit. Associations as mutual benefit organizations are under no particular obligation to benefit the public. They can exclude individuals from receiving benefits by imposing membership criteria or high entry fees and can advocate for public policies that do not serve the public interest as a whole.

To reiterate, very little research addresses the particular context of the public sector associations with their distinct accountability expectations. (See chapter 11, "The Pursuit of Accountability: Promise, Problems, and Prospects.") Many theoretical perspectives described previously have not been verified either in the particular context of association activity or, more specifically, in public sector contexts. However, it is important to do so given the unique political and legal obligations under which public sector professionals operate, the greater public scrutiny of their actions, and the value in bringing the best training and education to bear on solving public problems. Indeed, Guy B. Adams joins Terry L. Cooper and others in concern over the "tension between a meaningful democratic politics on the one hand, and a professionalized, scientized, expert administration on the other" (Adams 2000, 300). Beverly Cigler expresses the problem as a "paradox of professionalization." She observes that "as the professionalization of permanent career bureaucrats at all levels increased significantly, bureaucracy's acceptance by its clients—citizens and political elites alike—decreased" (1990, 638). This phenomenon suggests a risk in public sector associational activity if the greater expertise within government creates a disconnect between the work of professionals and the citizenry, and leads these professionals to discount public views.

Theories of the Underlying Function of Professional Associations in a Public Sector Context

Complicating the landscape on professional association research are the multiple functions these associations provide and their status as instruments of collective action. As Cigler and Adams observe, the multiple roles of public associations as representatives of jurisdictional, institutional, or individual interests means that broad assumptions should be avoided with respect to the potential benefits, limitations, or influences on effective public management, public policy, and public regulatory systems. However, some conceptual frameworks are helpful in both capturing the differences and describing the common ground.

Recent research on the challenges public administrators face as they engage with nongovernmental organizations in networked activities yields fertile ground for examining nonprofit association activities. Agranoff (chapter 17, "Collaborative Public Agencies in the Network Era," in this volume) opens the door to further exploration when he notes that "the literature on networking points to the importance of expanding information and access to expertise of other organizations." Political and collective-action perspectives also are essential in understanding that managers can find from time to time that their professional and institutional affiliations clash with one another. The following five perspectives are not intended to be inclusive but are presented to illustrate that associations introduce both benefits and challenges to public professional life.

Public Professional Associations as Regulatory Agents and Promulgators of Institutional Rules

One widely cited argument about organizational behavior has particular relevance to association activity. DiMaggio and Powell (1983, 147) describe professions as some of the "great rationalizers" of the latter twentieth century in terms of their ability to impose standard operating procedures and other "rituals of conformity" (150) on their members. Brignall and Modell (2000), and Greenwood, Suddaby, and Hinings (2002) lump professional associations together with public regulatory agencies in their common ability to define institutional norms and regulate behavior. Associations allow professional communities to represent themselves to others both within and outside their field, and they develop, monitor, and enforce norms of behavior for their fields. Their influence is reflected in their ability to enforce standards of conduct even to the point where association membership is required for advancement.

Haynes and Samuel's (2006) work, titled *Value of Membership in Professional Associations,* discusses the potential for associations to influence public professionals positively. This view, however, requires empirical confirmation since the phenomenon they describe may also suggest that association participation might have unintended consequences. While association participation can expose professionals to radically different perspectives and encourage tolerance for diversity, alternatively, long-term affiliation with a professional association could homogenize perspectives and dilute rather than promote tolerance for differences. Haynes and Samuel note the importance of shifting from "assimilating" members of different cultural backgrounds and viewpoints to "raising awareness of differences, valuing them, and making use of them" (5).

With respect to the influence that association activity has on organizational behavior, DiMaggio and Powell (1983) suggest that there is a relationship between managerial participation in trade and professional associations and the level of institutional isomorphism that occurs. This isomorphism is a form of organizational conformity driven by various external pressures. It manifests itself through behaviors surrounding professional activity: *Coercive* isomorphism occurs as a response to regulations, licensing, and accreditation expectations; *normative* isomorphism may result from the imposition of societal or professional standards on an industry's members; and *mimetic* isomorphism can happen as organizations adopt performance standards and benchmarks from peer institutions (DiMaggio and Powell 1983; Frumkin and Galaskiewicz 2004). These *behaviors* can be found in all three sectors of economic activity—nonprofit, commercial, and governmental. Frumkin and Galaskiewicz (2004) have compared these three sectors to understand the relative influence of associational activity on isomorphic behavior. They find that a public manager's membership in professional associations can be a powerful external influence on a public agency's behavior and structure, possibly rivaling internal forces (such as a bureaucracy's tendency to mimic other bureaucracies). For example, they find that government agencies with stronger associational tendencies are less centralized and formal in their operations. Their findings suggest the potential for an influential role for professional associations in shaping the organizational culture, strategic direction, and performance of public agencies. Further, with respect to the influence of associations on organizational performance, Heugens and Lander (2009) performed a meta-analysis of DiMaggio and Powell's arguments and validated the role that associations have in improving organizational performance. Although sometimes limited in their claims, these studies reveal potentially important differences between the sectors in terms of how associational activity influences the behavior of public managers or agencies.

Public Professional Associations as Sources of Ethical Standards

Whether or not associations can impose codes of conduct, they often offer standards of behavior that managers can follow voluntarily. In the wake of controversial policies and governmental scandals during the 1970s and 1980s—the Vietnam War, Watergate, and Irangate, among others—a survey of ASPA members found that "promoting ethics is perceived to be the single most important activity that ASPA performs" (Bowman 1990, 352). A "skills triangle" developed by Bowman, West, and Beck (2009) emphasizes technical, ethical, and leadership competencies and argues that their mastery is essential for the consummate professional. Referencing Menzel (2009), Bowman notes that each public servant "should strive to become ethically competent. This means being committed to high standards, possessing knowledge of relevant ethical codes and laws, engaging in ethical reasoning, acting upon public service ethics and values, and promoting ethical behavior in organizations" (Bowman, West, and Beck 2009, 92).

Public Professional Associations as Sources of Role Conflict or Culture Clash

Another perspective suggests that public managers with strong professional affiliations can find their functional and professional roles in conflict with one another. From a public administration perspective, Starling (2008, 448) suggests that increased professionalization has revived the politics/administration debate. He quotes Dennis L. Dresang, who argues, "A professional, almost by definition, typically seeks autonomy and a status that commands deference. The mixing in a common arena of a political official pursuing the mandates of the ballot box and a professional expecting to dominate in the policymaking process is bound to generate conflict and distrust. There are likely to be frustrations, too, because a politician and the professional need each other."

From a policy-making perspective, conflicts are caused when competing goals are introduced. For example, Susskind (2003, 273–274) observes that many public managers responsible for community mediation have a planning or public administration background. They may identify themselves as mediators and belong to umbrella organizations such as the Association of Conflict Resolution, but they also "continue to maintain their affiliation with professional planning and public management associations. This means that the interveners who seek to mediate public policy disputes are sometimes part of the city's planning staff. From the standpoint of a neighborhood upset with what the government has proposed to do in its area, the idea that someone in city hall, regardless of the skills he or she might have, could be neutral is almost impossible to accept." Susskind concludes that public managers who attempt to mediate public policy disputes must be able to separate their professional and governmental identities.

Public Professional Associations as Sources of Hierarchical Conflict

Yeatman (1987, 346) observes the potential for conflicting ideologies or values—not in Susskind's context of a public manager with a dual identity, but in the sense that managers at different supervisory or functional levels view their objectives differently:

> Professionalization of the upper and middle ranks of public servants is confined within the model of professional management. This is a technical or methodological professionalism. It vies with and even overrides the professionalism of substantive expertise. Thus professional engineers, doctors, social workers, lawyers and so on in the public sector may find that the discretionary authority they require to interpret their task and to respond to needs has been seriously circumscribed by the requirements placed on them by professional managers. The rise to power of professional managers in the public service is not only at the expense of the erstwhile authority of substantive professional positions in the public service. It leads also to a deskilling of the latter by reducing, as far as possible, the type of work involved to technical input and output measures.

One persuasive argument in support of this perspective is offered by Romzek and Dubnick (1987, 235) who attribute the 1986 explosion of the *Challenger* space shuttle to a clash between political responsiveness and professionalism. In the *Challenger* tragedy, engineers who held essential information about shuttle safety by virtue of their professional training were relegated to a subordinate role in the managerial decision-making process, which favored other, competing forms of accountability (political, hierarchical): "Had NASA relied exclusively on a professional system of accountability in making the decision to launch the *Challenger* space shuttle, perhaps deference would have been given to the technical expertise of the engineers. Their recommendation against launch might never have been challenged."

Public Professional Associations as Institutions That Build Social Capital and Support Civic Connectedness

In *Bowling Alone* (2000), Robert Putnam addresses the relationship between associations and civic participation. With respect to work-based organizations, Putnam argues that these organizations represent an "important locus of social solidarity, a mechanism for mutual assistance and shared expertise" (80). Indeed, he asserts that work-related organizations have been among the most common forms of civic connectedness in America. However, like community and church-based organizations, Putnam has observed a decline in membership among professional organizations during the latter part of the twentieth century.

Putnam does not distinguish associations by economic sector. The professional organizations he addresses (e.g., the American Bar Association, American Medical Association, American Institute of Architects) rely on broad memberships that transcend public and private sector distinctions. Nonetheless, Putnam develops the notion of "social capital"—that is, "social networks and the norms of reciprocity and trustworthiness that arise from them"—in ways that prove useful to observing the role of professional associations in public administration, as well as in the actual practice of public administration (2000, 19). Recent research on networks and collaborative management underscores the importance of social capital—of trust and reciprocity—to public management across sectors in the twenty-first century. (See chapter 17, "Collaborative Public Agencies in the Network Era," in this volume.)

Not all commentators have agreed with Putnam's bleak portrayal of a decline in civic engagement. In *The Good Citizen* (2008), Russell Dalton argues that "the good news is . . . the bad news is wrong" (161). Rather than attribute the decline in social capital to the "slow, steady, and ineluctable replacement of older, civic-minded generations by the disaffected Generation X" (3), Dalton challenges the "norms of citizenship" and the definition of what it means to be a good citizen. According to Dalton, a host of social changes have affected how the American public acts and thinks about politics. At an earlier time, traditional norms of American citizenship—voting, paying taxes, belonging to a political party—have evolved into what he calls "engaged citizenship." Dalton asserts that "engaged citizenship emphasizes a more assertive role for the citizen and a broader definition of the elements of citizenship to include social concerns and the welfare of others."[3]

There are several significant connections among Dalton's description of active citizenship, the role of public administrators, and professional associations. The public administration professionals of today and tomorrow rise from the very citizens Dalton describes. Schools of public affairs and administration can find much to ponder in the literature on the "knowledge workers" and the "creative class" that Dalton and others explore (see, for example, Florida 2002). Moreover, public administrators of today and tomorrow serve the citizenry Dalton describes. Their concerns, inclination toward engagement, and perspective on government affect how public administrators engage their publics and respond to an ever-changing policy landscape. Broad-based professional associations may offer a venue in which public administrators explore the implications of these societal changes and seek ways to respond to emerging needs of the "new" citizenship. (See chapter 15, "Citizen-Driven Administration: Civic Engagement in the United States," in this volume.)

Strengthening Research on Associations

A further limit on understanding association activity in the public sector is the fact that no comprehensive empirical effort has been made to document association activity. The lack of even basic descriptive statistics on the extent of association activity has limited hypothesis testing and sophisticated theoretical development. In some instances, promising theoretical groundwork has been produced in related fields but lacks testing in the context of association activity.

The principal limit to generalizable research is that most associations collect data only about their own members' characteristics and preferences. Although many peer-reviewed studies have made use of such data, especially in management journals, this effort has little value in understanding sector-wide patterns of behavior. We challenge the assumption that associations have no incentive to collect data about nonmembers. It is very likely that they would find cross-organizational comparisons useful. However, it is clear that the incentives to do so are limited. The most significant effort to collect generalizable data has come from the American Society of Association Executives. This organization represents the interests of the association sector generally, and trains and credentials professionals who manage associations. Recent surveys involving a half dozen to nearly one hundred separate associations have investigated membership satisfaction, member philanthropic activity (volunteerism, giving), and the impact of the 2009 economic recession on associational activity (Dalton and Dignam 2007; Dignam 2009; Gazley and Dignam 2008).

The American Society of Association Executives data shed limited light on public sector participation in professional association activity. These data are useful for studying the considerable variation in association participation by public managers: In one recent study involving twenty-one associations (including a variety of professional groups such as nursing, education, and engineering) the percentage of respondents who work in the public sector varied from 1 percent to 19 percent depending on the organization (see Table 4.2).

Table 4.2

Sectoral Representation of Selected Association Members (in percent)

	Government sector	Nonprofit sector	Academia	Business sector	Self-employed
American Nurses Association	13	32	29	21	5
American Society of Civil Engineers	16	1	4	75	4
American College of Healthcare Executives	16	55	6	20	3
American Industrial Hygiene Association	17	3	8	62	10
Institute of Electrical and Electronic Engineers	7	3	19	61	10
American Institute of Certified Public Accountants	5	5	4	59	27

Source: Gazley and Dignam 2008.

The data also reveal that members who work in the public sector are more likely to indicate that there are too many associations in their field, but they are similar to the private sector members on many other measures of membership satisfaction, especially on the benefits of joining an association. Public employees agreed with private sector members about the value of associations in providing members with technical information, training and professional development, networking opportunities, standards of practice, timely information about their field, and advocacy for the field when dealing with government agencies and the public (Dalton and Dignam 2007). No data were collected in this particular study about where government employees worked. Thus, while additional attention to the American Society of Association Executives data might shed light on how attitudes about the value of association participation vary across the public and private sectors, they do not provide sufficient detail about the market penetration of professional associations into governmental agencies or occupations.

Further Directions for Research

The state of theoretical and empirical knowledge about public administrators' participation in professional associations points to many opportunities for scholarly inquiry. The following lines of research might be pursued to develop more inclusive knowledge and information about association activity in the public sector.

First, to understand the influence of associations on public managerial behavior, it would be useful to organize them according to several possible dimensions. The typology shown in Figure 4.1 is offered as a starting point.

Associations can be organized and compared in the following ways:

- According to the jurisdictional interests they represent within the public sector (such as ICMA for cities, National Association of Counties for counties)
- By the nature of their representation (jurisdictions/communities, institutions/agencies, individual managers, citizens/consumers of public services, or perhaps all of these)
- By their emphasis on professions across (or regardless of) the entire employment sector (such as nursing, teaching, engineering)
- By industries or functions (such as emergency management)
- By mission and purpose (labor representation, regulatory change, and so on)

Figure 4.1 **Typology of Association Characteristics**

- By their membership requirements: Some associations are open to any dues-paying individual interested in their mission, while others impose strict educational, experiential, or behavioral criteria
- By the services they provide to members (education, advocacy, research, credentialing) and members' perceived benefit of those services
- By level of coercion or influence on members or nonmembers; Tschirhart (2006) observes that some ideas about association activity apply only to the majority of associations where membership is voluntary, while others have relevance for the more coercive, guild-like organizations where membership becomes almost compulsory for managerial performance or professional success[4]
- By market conditions such as the number of associations representing any particular occupation or field and the subsequent level of competition for members
- By the level of professionalization to which an association or an occupational field aspires. Professionalization can be measured according to "the universality of credential requirements, the robustness of . . . training programs," the proportion of managers in an occupational field who belong to a professional association, the size of those associations, and other variables that signify the vitality of a professional or trade association (DiMaggio and Powell 1983, 156). (Given that defining "professionalism" can be a moving target, we suggest the strongest reliance on measures of professional activity that have good qualitative value and broad agreement about their worth to a field.)

The value in this research effort is to understand at a much more comprehensive level the influence that associations have on managerial outlooks or performance. For example, one might apply such a professional association framework to studies that seek to understand effective public leadership, to managers' perspectives on public sector accountability, and to the growing body of work on public service motivation. The research on public service motivation is actively interested in why employees enter the public workforce, how they professionalize themselves as public managers, and how these factors influence their performance (see also Perry, Hondeghem, and Wise 2009). Scholars in this field of research could make a much stronger and deliberate connection between a manager's professional association activity and his or her public service outlook.

We note that the role that these professional associations play in supporting performance at managerial or organizational levels is contextual, and causal connections are difficult to make. However, the contextual nature of their influence is as much of an argument to consider their role as it is to discard their influence. In certain instances, for example, association membership plays such a central role in a public manager's ethical perspective, values, or daily work that aspects of that association experience must be included in a research model for the model to be adequately specified. In the public service motivation research and elsewhere, scholars can increase their understanding of the impact of professional training on managerial behavior by treating associational activity as a multidimensional construct with distinct qualitative variations.

The Impact of Professional Training and Education on Managerial Performance

This dimension of association activity can be examined from several perspectives. First, what contributions do professional associations make to educating public managers? Can these contributions be connected to organizational or managerial performance? Romzek and Dubnick (1987) argue, at least indirectly, in favor of this perspective. More recently, in the context of emergency management services, McGuire and Silvia (2010) and Brudney and Gazley (2009) find that professional training in emergency management (such as the training provided by the International Association of Emergency Managers) is related to a county emergency manager's perception that his or her jurisdiction is adequately prepared for disasters, and to the amount of intergovernmental collaboration and networking in which the manager participates. The study on which these authors relied is notable in gathering specific data about emergency management certification trends and the educational level of the respondents.

In addition, one might ask whether public affairs graduate degree programs are missing opportunities to teach students important lessons about the value (or limits) of associational activity in the public sector. Courses in human resources management, emergency management, planning, performance management, network management, leadership, and ethics would all be appropriate places to discuss the role of professional associations and societies in training public managers. Yet professional associations receive little attention in commonly used textbooks, and there is little evidence to indicate that faculty members in master of public administration programs strongly or consistently encourage graduate students to participate in professional associations.

Membership Behavior and Associational Activity in a Public Sector Context

Why do public managers join or not join associations? Tschirhart (2006) observes three research approaches in the general scholarship on joining behavior: research that examines how members calculate the cost-benefits of joining an association, research on the demographic predictors of membership, and research on external environmental factors that encourage or discourage joining behavior (such as economic or immigration trends). None of these frameworks has been applied yet to public management, but they could certainly be used to strengthen an understanding of where and how public managers decide to obtain their training. There is value in closer collaborative activity between public administration scholars and the associations that serve the public sector, such as ASPA and ICMA. Joint data collection and analysis might help to identify information with both practical and scholarly value, such as trends in public sector professional association activity, how member preferences have changed over time, and what programs and services could meet public managers' future needs.

CONCLUSION

This chapter describes a broad field of professional activity: the associations and societies that train, support, and advocate for hundreds of managerial functions, public service sectors, and jurisdictional interests. This diffuse field of study has weak theoretical and empirical foundations. Nonetheless, conceptual literature lends itself to understanding the role and behavior of professional associations in supporting public management. Studying public sector associational activity is worthwhile because professional associations can, through training, advocacy, and other mission-related endeavors, play a role in addressing much larger public administration issues. Associational activity and training can support effective performance management, help public managers learn to operate within complex service networks and informal management systems, and possibly stem the brain drain in the public sector workforce. Are professional associations making a difference? The answer is an unequivocal *yes!*

Data collection may not be the main challenge to these research efforts. Rather, the barriers may be perceptual. Greenwood, Suddaby, and Hinings (2002, 65) observe that "professional associations are notable for their attention to documentation." As noted earlier, some associations are increasingly interested in collecting data on member activities and preferences and in engaging both academics and practitioners in that effort. However, most membership data are still carefully guarded based on their commercial value. A greater acknowledgment in academia of the value of association research may also help reinvigorate public administration scholarship in this neglected but important field.

NOTES

1. The authors thank Amanda Donovan and Stella Ngugi for assistance in reviewing the texts; the list of texts with citations is available upon request (whaynes@bridgew.edu). The three texts that accorded fuller coverage of the topic were written by T.L. Cooper (*The Responsible Administrator*), H.G. Frederickson and K.B. Smith (*The Public Administration Theory Primer*), and W. Bruce (*Classics of Administrative Ethics*).

2. For purposes of this chapter, we focus on associations with missions oriented toward practitioner professionals, including public administrators. Academic associations such as the Association of Public Policy and Management, the American Political Science Association, and the Policy Studies Organization merit separate treatment but are not addressed in this chapter. The American Society for Public Administration provides a forum for both practitioners and scholars, so it is included in our discussion.

3. For a fine exploration of civic engagement and citizenship, see Terry L. Cooper's chapter in this volume: chapter 15, "Citizen-Driven Administration: Civic Engagement in the United States."

4. Associations range from those whose membership is entirely voluntary to guild-like organizations that can restrict some professional activity by nonmembers. The ability in the United States of occupational associations to require membership as a condition of employment in a field was abolished by the U.S. Supreme Court in 1978 (Tschirhart 2006).

REFERENCES

Abbott, Andrew D. 1988. *The System of Professions: An Essay on the Division of Expert Labor.* Chicago: University of Chicago Press.

Adams, Guy B. 2000. Administrative ethics and the chimera of professionalism: The historical context of public service ethics. In *Handbook of Administrative Ethics.* 2d ed., ed. Terry L. Cooper. New York: Marcel Dekker.

Bowman, James S. 1990. Ethics in government: A national survey of public administrators. *Public Administration Review* 50 (3): 345–353.

Bowman, James S., Jonathan P. West, and Marcia A. Beck. 2009. *Achieving Competencies in Public Service: The Professional Edge.* 2d ed. Armonk, NY: M.E. Sharpe.

Brignall, Stan, and Sven Modell. 2000. An institutional perspective on performance measurement and management in the "new public sector." *Management Accounting Research* 11:281–306.

Brudney, Jeffrey L. and Beth Gazley. 2009. Planning to be prepared: An empirical examination of the role of voluntary organizations in county government emergency planning. *Public Performance and Management Review* 32 (3): 372–398.

Cigler, Beverly A. 1990. Public administration and the paradox of professionalization. *Public Administration Review* 50 (6): 637–653.

Dalton, James, and Monica Dignam. 2007. *The Decision to Join.* Washington, DC: American Society of Association Executives and the Center for Association Leadership.

Dalton, Russell J. 2008. *The Good Citizen: How a Younger Generation Is Reshaping American Politics.* Washington, DC: CQ Press.

Dignam, Monica. 2009. *Beliefs, Behaviors, and Attitudes in Response to the Economy.* Washington, DC: American Society of Association Executives and the Center for Association Leadership.

DiMaggio, Paul J., and Walter W. Powell. 1983. The iron cage revisited: Institutional isomorphism in organizational fields. *American Sociological Review* 48:147–160.

Florida, Richard. 2002. *The Rise of the Creative Class: And How It's Transforming Work, Leisure, Community and Everyday Life.* New York: Perseus Books.

Frumkin, Peter, and Joseph Galaskiewicz. 2004. Institutional isomorphism and public sector organizations. *Journal of Public Administration Research and Theory* 14 (3): 283–307.

Gazley, Beth, and Monica Dignam. 2008. *The Decision to Volunteer.* Washington, DC: American Society of Association Executives and the Center for Association Leadership.

Greenwood, Royston, Roy Suddaby, and C.R. Hinings. 2002. Theorizing change: The role of professional associations in the transformation of institutionalized fields. *Academy of Management Journal* 45 (1): 58–80.

Hawley, Amos H. 1950. *Human Ecology: A Theory of Community Structure.* New York: Ronald Press.

Haynes, Wendy, and Antoinette A. Samuel. 2006. *Value of Membership in Professional Associations— American Society for Public Administration: A Stellar Case in Point.* Parkville, MO: Park University International Center for Civic Engagement.

Heugens, Pursey P.M.A.R., and Michael W. Lander. 2009. Structure! Agency! (And other quarrels): A meta-analysis of institutional theories of organization. *Academy of Management Journal* 52 (1): 61–85.

Hudson, James R., and Patricia A. Hudson. 2002. Getting started: The founding of membership-based organizations. Paper presented at the annual meeting of the Association for Research on Nonprofit Organizations and Voluntary Action, Montreal, Quebec, Canada, November 14–16.

Knoke, David. 1986. Associations and interest groups. *Annual Review of Sociology* 12:1–21.

McGuire, Michael, and Chris Silvia. 2010. The effect of problem severity, managerial and organizational capacity, and agency structure on intergovernmental collaboration: Evidence from local emergency management. *Public Administration Review* 70 (2): 279–288.

Menzel, Donald. 2009. *Ethics Moments in Local Government: Cases and Controversies.* New York: Taylor and Francis.

National Center for Charitable Statistics (NCCS). 2009. Number of nonprofit organizations in the United States, 1998–2008. Washington, DC: Urban Institute. Accessed at http://nccsdataweb.urban.org/PubApps/profile1.php?state=US.

Olson, Mancur. 1965. *The Logic of Collective Action.* Cambridge, MA: Harvard University Press.

Perry, James L., Annie Hondeghem, and Lois R. Wise. 2009. Revisiting the motivational bases of public service: Twenty years of research and an agenda for the future. Paper presented at the International Public Service Motivation Research Conference, cosponsored by the School of Public and Environmental Affairs, Indiana University, Bloomington and the Public Management Institute, Katholieke Universiteit Leuven, Bloomington, Indiana, June 7–9.

Plant, Jeremy F. 2000. Codes of ethics. In *Handbook of Administrative Ethics.* 2d ed., ed. Terry L. Cooper. New York: Taylor and Francis.

Putnam, Robert D. 2000. *Bowling Alone.* New York: Simon and Schuster.

Romzek, Barbara S., and Melvin J. Dubnick. 1987. Accountability in the public sector: Lessons from the *Challenger* tragedy. *Public Administration Review* 47 (3): 227–238.

Starling, Grover. 2008. *Managing the Public Sector.* 8th ed. Boston: Thomson Wadsworth.

Streib, Greg, and Mark Rivera. 2010. Assessing the ethical knowledge of city managers. *Public Integrity* 12 (1): 9–23.

Susskind, Lawrence. 2003. Collective bargaining and public policy dispute resolution. In *Negotiations and Change: From the Workplace to Society,* ed. Thomas A. Kochan and David B. Lipsky, 269–278. Ithaca, NY: Cornell University Press.

Tschirhart, Mary. 2006. Nonprofit membership associations. In *The Nonprofit Sector: A Research Handbook,* ed. Walter W. Powell and Richard Steinberg. New Haven, CT: Yale University Press.

Yeatman, Anna. 1987. The concept of public management and the Australian state in the 1980s. *Australian Journal of Public Administration* 46 (4): 339–356.

CHAPTER 5

ACCREDITATION AND COMPETENCIES IN EDUCATION FOR LEADERSHIP IN PUBLIC SERVICE

JEFFREY A. RAFFEL, STEVEN M. MASER, AND CRYSTAL CALARUSSE

What competencies do professionals in public administration need? That is, what knowledge, skills, and aptitudes does a public administration professional need to have in order to produce results that serve the public? What does the profession consider to be the characteristics of exemplary educational programs that educate professionals in the field?

The answers matter because they inform decision makers: program directors and faculty working to improve their programs, attract students, and serve their communities with their graduates; prospective students choosing among alternative programs and careers; employers who want validation that the employees they hire have the competencies they value; and university administrators and policy makers who want independent affirmation that the resources they invest in their programs are paying off.

The answers can be found in the accreditation process and standards promulgated by the National Association of Schools of Public Affairs and Administration (NASPAA). For more than twenty-five years, NASPAA has been accrediting programs in the United States at the master's level to "prepare students . . . for leadership positions in public affairs, policy, and administration" (NASPAA 2008, 6).[1] Accreditation involves a process of peer review meant to ensure and improve the quality of educational programs. By establishing a set of standards, accreditation agencies define the content of a professional or academic field. The standards establish the competencies to be required of professionals in the field and set thresholds of acceptability and quality for programs whose missions include helping students master them.

NASPAA's accreditation process embodies the values that define the field: accountability, transparency, professionalism, equity, trust, and responsiveness—all in the public interest. It involves a rigorous peer review. Defining the standards employed by the reviewers is the critically important precursor to accreditation. The evolution of NASPAA's accreditation standards reflects the history of the profession since 1970, as well as its direction.

Amid a changing environment for accreditation, public administration, and public policy, in 2006 NASPAA launched a review of its standards and accreditation process, ten years after it adopted its existing standards. The effort sought input from a variety of constituencies, including faculty members and employers, about the competencies every graduate of a program accredited by NASPAA should acquire to be a successful public servant. This chapter outlines the history that informed the recent review, the reasons and the process for the review, the competencies that have been defined in the standards adopted in 2009, and the challenges of assessing student learning.

THE EMERGENCE OF ACCREDITATION FOR U.S. PUBLIC AFFAIRS, ADMINISTRATION, AND POLICY PROGRAMS

NASPAA is an institutional membership organization with a twofold mission: to ensure excellence in education and training for public service and to promote the ideals of public service. NASPAA was founded in 1970 as a satellite of the American Society for Public Administration, a professional society for public service (Henry 1995). NASPAA's institutional membership grew along with the expanding numbers of public administration programs in the United States. In 1977 member institutions of NASPAA voted to adopt a program of voluntary peer review evaluation of master's degree programs in public affairs and administration and adopted *Standards for Professional Masters Degree Programs in Public Affairs, Policy and Administration.*

NASPAA-accredited programs demonstrate compliance with the NASPAA standards during a rigorous process of self-study and peer review.[2] Many nonaccredited programs in the United States and abroad shadow the standards.[3] Prior to 1992, NASPAA's standards were relatively input oriented, requiring, for example, curriculum coverage of specific topics such as human resources, budgeting, and financial management. In 1992, NASPAA added a mission-based layer to the standards, making them more output oriented. Mission-based accreditation allows each program to articulate its mission and the process by which it develops and implements it. The program must assess the extent to which it meets its mission and describe changes the program adopted in light of the assessment. Mission-based accreditation was designed in part to allow a broader array of programs, including public policy, into the fold of accreditation (Ellwood 2006).

In 2004, the Commission on Peer Review and Accreditation (COPRA), NASPAA's accrediting arm, altered slightly its self-study instructions—the guidance it gives to programs preparing their reports—introducing a larger philosophical change. It anticipated the third generation of NASPAA's accreditation standards, giving greater prominence to the requirement that programs articulate the extent to which their students learn a set of competencies. Programs had to "identify the general competencies that are consistent with the program mission" (NASPAA 2006a, 8), encouraging them to be more outcome oriented. However, this change did not have a major impact on programs seeking accreditation, in part because programs promulgated and COPRA accepted broad, almost generic missions that by inference allowed broad, generic competencies, and in part because defining and measuring competencies proved to be difficult.

ACCREDITATION, PROGRAM DIVERSITY, AND THE CORE CURRICULUM OF THE TWENTIETH CENTURY

Several histories of NASPAA and education for the public service strike consistent themes: the diversity of programs in the field, the continued responsiveness of NASPAA and accreditation to the public service environment, a lack of a uniform approach to the field, and a foundation built on POSDCORB. In 1937 Gulick and Urwick created the POSDCORB acronym to define the competencies required of public administrators: planning, organizing, staffing, directing, coordinating, reporting, and budgeting. In 1985, Elwood's *A Morphology of Graduate Education for Public Service in the United States* began with the statement "Graduate education for public service in the United States is characterized by its diversity—a diversity to meet the differing needs of the various levels of American government and the variety of professions which dominate employment in the public sector" (1). Almost a quarter of a century later, Riccucci (2007) echoed Ellwood's themes, recognizing the interdisciplinary roots of the field and the variety of organizational forms, and concluding that no "one best approach to public administration" exists (762).

Laurin Henry's opus (1995) on NASPAA's history highlights similar themes of balancing program diversity with other goals, the responsiveness of NASPAA to its environment, and the difficulties in finding a common core. Henry refers to NASPAA as a "dependent variable" (2), responding to the challenges faced by deans and directors from the "unstable seas of national politics" (3). Describing the roots of the accreditation process, initially a peer review exercise, Henry highlighted the development of a "matrix of competencies" in 1973–74 by a NASPAA Standards Committee. The matrix "was summarized on a spreadsheet that began with several subject-matter areas listed down the left side: Political, Social, and Economic Context; Analytical Tools; Individual, Group, and Organizational Behavior; Policy Analysis; and Administrative/Management Processes. For each subject-matter area, appropriate knowledge, skills, and behavior were elaborated in successive columns to the right" (14). This approach helped to diffuse a conflict over accreditation standards between elite programs, which wanted to focus on institutional characteristics such as the number of faculty as indicators of quality, and smaller programs, which lacked resources and size.

Eleanor Laudicina (2007) described a layered approach to curriculum and standards rather than an integrated and coherent approach. For example, describing trends in the 1950s, she indicated, "In general courses and curricula continued to reflect the traditional emphasis on organization and management, administrative technique, public personnel, budgeting, and finance" (732). During the 1980s, the challenges to NASPAA and public service education included the emergence of public policy programs, the burgeoning use of microcomputers, and privatization, associated with distrust in and the downsizing of government—just as "some consensus on curriculum finally emerged" (743). Observing NASPAA's response, she concluded, "Those who seek a real synthesis or a universal paradigm probably are doomed to disappointment" (750). According to Laudicina, NASPAA had yet to respond to the necessity for "new competencies in team building, communication, employee involvement, cultural awareness and labor relations" (749) likely to be needed by public managers.

At the turn of the century, NASPAA's curricular requirements in the accreditation standards were defined as follows (2007):

> 4.21 *Common Curriculum Components.* The common curriculum components shall enhance the student's values, knowledge, and skills to act ethically and effectively

In the Management of Public Service Organizations, the components of which include:

- Human resources
- Budgeting and financial processes
- Information management, technology applications, and policy.

In the Application of Quantitative and Qualitative Techniques of Analysis, the components of which include:

- Policy and program formulation, implementation and evaluation
- Decision-making and problem-solving.

With an Understanding of the Public Policy and Organizational Environment, the components of which include:

- Political and legal institutions and processes
- Economic and social institutions and processes
- Organization and management concepts and behavior.

The standards also called for programs to "prepare students to work in and contribute to diverse workplaces and communities."

ACCREDITATION AND THE CORE CURRICULUM IN THE TWENTY-FIRST CENTURY

In spring 2006, NASPAA president Daniel Mazmanian, with the support of NASPAA's Executive Council as per an October 2005 vote, appointed the NASPAA Standards 2009 Steering Committee. The committee included representatives from the profession and academic programs. The executive council, supplemented by representatives from the committee, held a March 2006 retreat in Tucson, Arizona, led by strategic planning expert, John Bryson, to consider the future of public service education (NASPAA 2006e). The outcome was a process for drafting a set of new standards, ultimately voted upon and approved by accredited members at NASPAA's 2009 fall conference.

NASPAA committed to thoroughly evaluating and revising the public service degree curriculum and the NASPAA Accreditation Standards to ensure that accredited degree programs serve the profession and give graduates the competitive skills they need to lead the public sector.

During the years following the retreat, NASPAA's annual conference titles included "The Future of the Public Sector" (2006), "Embracing the Certainty of Uncertainty: Creating the Future of Public Affairs Education" (2007), and "NASPAA Meets the Future" (2008). At about the same time, other national associations in the fields of public administration, affairs, and policy built their conferences around the topic. The Association for Public Policy and Management, for example, held a conference titled "Charting the Next Twenty Years of Public Policy and Management Education," generating more than a dozen papers (APPAM 2006). In sum, the profession focused on updating the collected wisdom its degree programs conveyed.

Forces in the environment of public service education set the stage for reexamining NASPAA's standards, including projections of the future state of the world of public affairs, administration and policy, national accreditation issues, and trends in quality review and assessment (see, in general, the chapters in Liou 2001, especially Durant's [2001], and, of course, all of the chapters in this volume). Other forces originated with the degree programs themselves, as they attempted to address the increasing demand for innovative offerings. These included executive programs attending to midcareer and senior learners with leadership offerings and flexible course scheduling (NASPAA 2006c); new program delivery mechanisms, such as online courses or satellite campuses facilitated by improved technologies and electronic information sharing; contracting to educate entire cohorts of international public servants and opening campuses overseas, requiring an understanding of the international context of public service in curriculum and in program design; and cooperation with academic programs outside of the traditional public service fields to develop curricula and offerings that prepare graduates for the multisectoral workforce (NAPA 2005).

Given these forces, what, then, makes a program accreditable in terms of its core curriculum? Specifically, what are the competencies that future public servants are expected to master as a result of experiencing the curricula offered by accredited programs as the twenty-first century progresses? The answers provided in this chapter derive from four sources: statements by academic leaders in the profession, advice from practitioners, the literature on public service education, and comments solicited during the accreditation review process.

Visions of Academic Leaders

During the first decade of the twenty-first century, several visionaries challenged the field of public service education to address change. Barbara Nelson, in her NASPAA Conference Plenary address in October 2002, "Education for the Public Interest," suggested that curricula should encompass problem solving across boundaries, educating students for shared power and shifting alliances, citizen engagement and diversity, and the realities of public opinion, including declining support for the public sector. Focusing on the federal government, Abramson, Breul, and Kamensky (2003)—practitioners who were elected to the National Academy of Public Administration—believed that "the next decade will best be categorized by a topsy-turvy ride for government leaders" as government learned to respond to four trends: (1) changing rules, (2) emphasizing performance, (3) improving service delivery, and (4) increasing collaboration.

Similarly, Astrid Merget, in her 2003 Donald Stone Lecture to the meeting of the American Society for Public Administration, challenged the profession to confront a "sampler of changes," including (1) the globalization of the political economy, (2) technology, (3) the imperative for public, private, and nonprofit partnerships, (4) a renewed and amplified view of institution building, (5) complexity, and (6) the importance of research while asserting a healthy respect for the political milieu. Jeffrey Straussman, in a discussion paper for the Association for Public Policy Analysis and Management spring 2006 conference (2008), cited several of the same trends but brought an empirical analysis of management and policy process course syllabi to his analysis. Among the topics he found to be necessary in today's world: (1) globalization, (2) managing across sectors, (3) collaborative management, and (4) being reflective yet evidence based. Lester Salamon's address to NASPAA in 2005 called for preparing "professional citizens": people educated for jobs that involve solving public problems, again, across sectors.

In 2007, American Society for Public Administration president Harvey White appointed a five-person committee to address "several disturbing developments pushing public administration towards academic obfuscation" and "an increasing propensity to prepare students for almost everything except careers in public administration" (quoted in Henry et al. 2009, 118). The committee called for the master of public administration (MPA) degree to be distinctive from degrees in public policy and public affairs, emphasizing public administration values—albeit U.S.-centric (Raffel 2009)—such as a focus on the U.S. Constitution and principles of "individual rights, due process of law, equal protection, and the separation of powers" (123).

Employer Expectations

In 2006, more than four hundred city managers responded to an online survey conducted by NASPAA and the International City/County Management Association. The city managers were given fifteen types of management knowledge and skills and asked to consider how important each was for their organization's management needs. Decision making and problem solving were rated as "extremely important" by 82 percent of the respondents. The other items receiving over 70 percent in the highest category were communications skills (77 percent), leadership (72 percent), and teamwork (71 percent). Items receiving few ratings of extreme or high importance included statistical analysis and marketing. When asked to check the three most important skills in their organizations, respondents added budgeting and financial management to this list, but e-governance, information technology, policy analysis, and statistical analysis never made it above ground level. A list of public service knowledge and skills indicated that ethics and integrity topped the city managers' list, although many other topics were also considered important, such as openness to citizen participation and involvement, organization and group behavior, and political and legal institutions.

A 2007 federal survey (NASPAA 2007) mirrored the city manager survey in the skills most frequently identified, with the addition of program evaluation and accountability to the list of important topics. In a 2007 survey of students, which included many practitioners seeking their MPA degrees, respondents perceived the most important skills desired by potential employers to be written and oral communication, decision making, leadership, and teamwork, quite similar to the skills selected by the local and federal practitioner surveys (NASPAA 2007).

Individual employers are not shy about expressing their needs. Angela Evans, deputy director of the Congressional Research Service (CRS), identified the core competencies required by that organization (2006). These included knowledge, skills, and abilities (KSAs) to perform analysis and to operate in a public policy community, as well as a good work ethic and a commitment to public service. Among these KSAs were old academic standbys such as "establishes conceptual frameworks," "speaks and communicates effectively," and "conducts public policy analysis." She also included more organizational abilities such as "leads and tasks effectively," "negotiates and resolves disputes," and "innovates and creates." Value considerations also played a strong role; KSAs included "desires to serve the public," "behaves with honestly and integrity," and "behaves professionally" (Evans 2006).

Sallyanne Harper, chief financial and administrative officer of the Government Accountability Office (GAO), summarized a study of factors associated with the success of entry-level hires in the GAO (2006). The GAO's study used the ratings of 534 analysts hired in fiscal years 2002–4 supplemented by discussions with managing directors. The factors identified as differentiating the highest-rated performers from others included critical thinking, written and oral communication, and collaborating with others. Other significant factors included showing initiative, demonstrating flexibility, detail orientation, adapting quickly to the GAO, and seeing the big picture.

Thus, a gap appeared between the needs of employers and NASPAA's accreditation standards for curricula in place at the time: people and leadership skills. Although the standards begin with the statement that accredited programs prepare leaders for public service, the core curriculum as defined in the standards remained focused on POSDCORB. The standards did not address leadership competencies. Practitioners began asking whether the MPA curriculum, for example, was strictly a management curriculum. Was there a place, indeed, a need for, explicit leadership content and skill development (Fairholm 2006; NASPAA 2005)? Even some policy analysts, whose programs had been focused on methods, not process, recognized the need for "people skills" in their curriculum (Mintrom 2003) because designing and implementing a policy successfully is a social and political as well as a technical matter.

The Literature on Public Service Education

The academic literature on the KSAs expected of public servants during the twenty-first century repackages existing competencies and identifies new ones. For example, research on networks of both people and organizations that are dealing with complex public problems, as opposed to unitary, purposeful, and hierarchical organizations dealing with similar problems, reinforces the importance of leadership (Milward and Provan 2006). Public service degree holders need to understand not just *government* but also *governance* that moves across boundaries (Berry and Brower 2005; Goldsmith and Eggers 2004; NAPA 2005; Salamon 2005). Defining the competencies of leadership in these environments will provoke healthy debate and inspired pedagogy (Crosby and Bryson 2005).

Changes in technology, like changes in governing structures, have led to a new set of needed competencies. Competency using e-government refers to using the Internet and the World Wide Web as tools not only to reduce the cost of transacting business with government but also to transform the relationship between the government and the governed. Student competencies with word processing, spreadsheets, and even databases and global information systems no longer prepare them adequately for e-government. Technology today makes possible the reengineering of administrative processes and services, assuming practitioners are competent to manage privacy, security, and Americans with Disability Act concerns (Kim and Layne 2001), as well as to plan and execute the organizational changes associated with process reengineering.

Risk management revisits the elements of POSDCORB with an eye on the exposure of agencies and their clients to liability by virtue of administrative actions. This broader view encompasses legal, financial, occupational safety, employment, contract performance, and reputational risks. It entails broadening the traditional way of teaching administrative law in MPA programs to include, for example, contract law and public employment law (Roberts 2008).

A case exists for de-emphasizing traditional statistical tools drawn from the social science roots of public service education in favor of statistical tools drawn from management science. As technology trickles down, public servants are moving from consuming statistical reports delivered by others to producing models, forecasts, projects, and decisions. This involves tools beyond testing hypotheses and regression analyses to include decision and value trees, linear programming, Program Evaluation and Review Technique/critical path analysis, and payoff matrices (Aristigueta and Raffel 2001; Caulkins 1999; Horne 2008).

The literature also reveals a debate about whether public administration students should learn policy analysis and whether policy analysts should learn management. Piskulich and Mandell (2007) prepared a white paper on curricular competencies for the standards review process, addressing the "balance between maintaining a common identity without limiting the ability of programs to experiment and to respond to perceived changes in the public sector environment" (4). They advocated specifying a minimal number of competencies consistent with the changed world of public service. Because the changing world needs policy analysts, for example, they should understand how public administrators manage projects in an organizational context so the policies that analysts propose can be implemented feasibly; moreover, public administrators should understand, if not conduct, policy research so their implementation achieves the objectives of the analysts. A quarter century after Behn called for the same thing (1980), Ellwood (2006) concluded that public administration and public policy programs were converging in just this way.

New competencies might come from new paradigms of management. One is "design science" (Dunne and Martin 2006; Barzelay and Thompson 2007). This is less a concept of managerial decision making than one of managerial problem solving. It encourages students to think broadly, to integrate, and to consider sustainability; to focus on the needs of those who will be served by the solution to the problem; and to welcome constraints, as opposed to limiting them, on the grounds that the more complex the problem, the more inspired and satisfying the solution.

New competencies might emerge from new technologies, as well. Will new competencies be required to manage a virtual workplace built around telecommunication (Cascio 2000)? What will the impact on government workplaces be from information technologies that allow collaborative work to be done away from central office buildings or even in virtual worlds such as Second Life (www.secondlife.com)? To the extent that government is not immune to these technical changes, managers will have to focus even less on time at work and more on results.

Feedback from the Standards Review Process

In April 2008, after distributing a draft of the proposed standards, NASPAA sponsored fourteen focus groups around the nation. Participants—approximately 160 in all—reacted with constructive criticism to a draft of the new standards. When it came to curriculum content, the theme that emerged from reviewing notes of the group meetings was the importance of branding—distinguishing degrees in the field from others chosen by students as pathways to enter and advance in the public sector. This concern has a history. In 1971 Frank Marini, writing about the first Minnowbrook conference on public administration, predicted optimistically, "Public administration will deal with its relationships to its old foes—law and business administration—more intelligently while it is dealing with its old disciplinary base—political science—more intelligently" (357).

Dealing with these relationships continues to be problematic. Federal employees with an MBA degree have salaries, grades, and supervisory authority comparable to those who earned an MPA; those holding law degrees command higher salaries (Lewis and Oh 2008; see also Yeager et al. 2007). The 2006 Association for Public Policy Analysis and Management conference revisited master of public policy curricula in light of competing degree programs (Radin 2008, 636). Branding can be an intelligent way for public administration to deal with its old foes, but only if the brand associated with the public administration degree signals substance: a promise and an experience that are distinctive and valuable.

What competencies in public administration make its degree distinctive and valuable?

First, consider competencies of concern to NASPAA's focus group participants that should be part of the public service curriculum but are not necessarily distinctive: to manage complex organizations, to manage change, to manage high-performing organizations, to conduct economic as well as political analyses, and to manage in cross-cultural and international contexts. To be culturally competent, for example, requires a manager not only to acknowledge different pathways to leadership among people with whom he or she is working, different concepts of career success, and different demands for and responses to authority and services (Boxall and Gilbert 2007), but also to respect and honor these differences, as well as to have the capacity for cultural self-assessment (Rice 2007, 2008). These are competencies expected of managers in business, government, and nonprofit organizations, so educational programs in business include them, too. (See also Friedman 2005; NASPAA 2004.)

Second, consider competencies of concern to NASPAA's focus group participants that appear to be cross-sectoral but that, as applied in the public sector, are distinctive: to manage the policy process, to measure and manage performance, to manage relationships and communication. Managers—at least enlightened ones—in business recognize the interdependence of business and government. This requires them to understand and participate in the public policy process because its outcomes impact their activities. Managers in the public sector, however, not only have to work within that process; they participate in creating and making the process work with citizen engagement (Morse et al. 2005). At least in modern democracies, where efficiency can take second place to due process and equity, the process is not businesslike, which is one reason why managers with only business experience who move into government roles absent prior public service experience can have a rocky start.

The third set of competencies of concern to NASPAA's focus group participants speaks to competencies they saw as distinctive to public service: managing diversity, adhering to public values, and leading. The government of any jurisdiction is by definition inclusive. It discriminates at its peril. Businesses succeed by discriminating, matching their products and services to segments of the market. They create inclusive workplaces when advantage can be gained in creativity and productivity. For public servants, inclusiveness is a raison d'être. A community chooses the government it wants to be served by; a business chooses the community it wants to serve. Community and government are synonymous in a way that business and community are not. In that sense, diversity is a core public service value, and managing it is a core competency in public service degree programs. Other public values, such as due process, equity (see also Svara and Brunet 2005), and ethics are as important and distinctive to public service as diversity is.

The final category of competencies that participants in NAPSAA's focus groups perceived to be distinctive is leadership. Yet public, private, and nonprofit organizations all have leaders. Indeed, the new accreditation standards embrace an expansive definition of leadership, one likely to be interpreted by the accrediting body to include generic competencies, such as creativity and innovation, conflict management, vision, and building coalitions, that complement, if not exceed, management skills. The career paths of students, wherever they work, will move them from less authority to more, from more supervision to less, and from well-defined tasks requiring technical skills to ill-defined tasks requiring adaptive capacities: different leadership competencies at different times and places (Bartlett and Ghoshal 1997; Charan, Drotter, and Noel 2001). Regardless, one can lead throughout one's career, even without having achieved nominal authority, high position, and significant discretion. Leadership in pursuit of public service values and leadership within a group in similar pursuit involve distinctive competencies.

Limits on Predicting the Future

While defining the world of public service has been the subject of thoughtful academic and professional leaders, defining the future of public service education is problematic. Are the generals in the field fighting the last war; that is, are these the changes of the last decade? What changes will the next decade bring? Are these changes overstated; that is, will *all* graduates really confront a globalized, IT-dominated, multisector world, or are these trends at the edge of the field? Will a counterforce, as there often is in history and politics, swing the pendulum back to more traditional forms of government?

During the 2006 NASPAA Executive Council retreat on the future of public service education, one speaker noted that ten years earlier few, if any, would have predicted the issues that vex us today (NASPAA 2006e). Another way to view this reflection is that the challenges confronting our graduates in ten years may be quite different from those they confront today, so what educational program can prepare them for a world that cannot be imagined? Of course, the financial meltdown of 2008 and the Democratic victory and election of America's first African American president highlight the difficulty of predicting changes even two years out. In a fast-paced world, the relevance of public administration programs depends on their ability to respond quickly to changes in the environment of public administrators.

Predicting the future will be much easier than determining what NASPAA should do about it. The consensus on the future, and our ability to add one more prediction on top of many others, makes this exercise relatively noncontroversial. Translating these predictions into policies and standards, the difficulties become apparent. Major questions include the following:

- Will the consensus on what to add to the core curriculum be stronger than the consensus on what to reduce or eliminate? For example, practitioners and others have made a good argument for adding leadership competencies to the list of requirements, but how many would support removing competencies in human resources management? Adding is easier than subtracting.

- How can programs maintain a set of standards in a fast-paced world where the context changes so rapidly? Will NASPAA's mission-based approach be sufficient?
- Where will programs obtain the resources to move from traditional public administration to programs incorporating topics such as managing information technology, security, and contracts? For example, many NASPAA programs have struggled to meet the five-faculty minimum and to find faculty to teach basic information technology.

ASSESSING STUDENT COMPETENCY

The best practices in accreditation now include the evaluation of student learning outcomes, and the Council for Higher Education Accreditation (2003) and U.S. regional accreditors require it.[4] What is a "student learning outcome"? According to CHEA (2006a), an "outcome is something that happens to an individual student as a result of his or her attendance at a higher education institution or participation in a particular course of study. . . . A 'student learning outcome,' in contrast, is properly defined in terms of the particular levels of knowledge, skills and abilities that a student has attained at the end (or as a result) of his or her engagement in a particular set of collegiate experiences."

Huba and Freed (2000) provided a brief political and pedagogical explanation for the movement from a teacher-centered paradigm, focused on curriculum, to a learner-centered paradigm, emphasizing learning outcomes. The latter requires direct measures of not only what students know and understand but also what they can do, for example, on projects, performances, portfolios. "As the goal of a college education for all became more widespread . . . concerns that college graduates did not have the skills and abilities needed in the workplace surfaced" (16). This led to calls for reform and accountability. "In part to curtail the direct involvement of state legislatures in higher education, regional accrediting institutions . . . became involved and began requiring member colleges and universities to perform outcomes assessments" (17).

Huba and Freed also credited the continuous improvement movement with pushing higher education institutions to conduct outcomes measurement. Ewell (2001) recognized the role that distance learning has played because these programs try to show their impacts on student learning compared to traditional classroom methods. Outcomes assessment is viewed as one means to address issues such as grade inflation, employers' concerns about the relevance of program content to their needs, programmatic versus individual course learning, and comparability across institutions.

Requiring student learning assessments is still new to many accrediting bodies that may have been encouraging it. Comprehensive surveys of current practices in accreditation are lacking, so most data are anecdotal from conversations with other accreditors and Web site surveys. NASPAA held an informal accreditation summit in the summer of 2007 with representatives of three accreditation assessment leaders: the Accreditation Board of Engineering Technologies, the Association to Advance Collegiate Schools of Business, and the Council on Accreditation of Healthcare Management Education. The most common path for specialized accreditors appears to be to either establish, or to have the program establish, a set of competencies for student achievement based on the needs of the profession. The programs are then expected to demonstrate that students achieve those competencies to be accredited. Typically, it is up to the program to determine the method of student assessment, usually within some parameters (Kershenstein 2002).

CHEA (2002, 2) specified a typology of outcomes assessment measures: direct (sources of evidence: capstone performance, professional/clinical performances, third-party testing, such as licensure, and faculty-designed examinations) and indirect (portfolios and work samples, follow-up of graduates, employee ratings of performance, self-reported growth by graduates). While assessment may be widespread and includes measures from job placement through student satisfaction, few assessment measures are "*direct* evidence of student learning outcomes of the kind currently being asked for by external stakeholders" (Ewell 2001, 1). Whatever measures are used, the recognition standards for CHEA stated that "to be recognized, the accrediting organization provides evidence that it has implemented: . . . accreditation standards or policies that require institutions or programs routinely to provide reliable information to the public on their performance, including student achievement as determined by the institution or program" (CHEA 2006b).

NASPAA has not been at the forefront of the outcome assessment movement, although it has periodically mobilized to address outcomes issues. NASPAA program surveys have found a reliance on indirect outcomes measures, with some programs using capstone evaluations. Measures used in other fields are not necessarily appropriate for public service education. MPA programs have no analog to the passage rate in bar exams used by law schools. Nor is salary necessarily an indicator of the market's assessment of student learning, as it might be for graduates from business schools.

In late 1991 NASPAA's Outcomes Assessment Committee published its report and a symposium in the *American Review of Public Administration* (Poister and Ingraham 1991). At the time fewer than half of the 216 schools and programs in their survey were assessing outcomes, and the most prevalent techniques were alumni and student surveys. Few were using employer surveys, focus groups, or assessment centers. The committee concluded, "NASPAA should implement a decentralized model of outcomes assessment, requiring programs to engage in some form of assessment but allowing wide flexibility in how it is implemented and utilized" (180). This would allow schools and programs to continue to develop appropriate approaches for their situations, but "as schools experiment further in refining assessment methods, more systematic research into the strengths and weaknesses of various approaches and their applicability in different program settings will be necessary."

To update information on the use of outcomes measurement, NASPAA staff conducted a Web survey of NASPAA programs during the summer of 2006. Seventy-six programs responded to the survey. Not surprisingly, a majority (58.1 percent) reported relying heavily on the traditional methods of course and assignment grades. Slightly less than a majority relied heavily on a semester-long capstone course and a capstone project. Student surveys were the next most popular means. Few programs extensively used theses, portfolios, or one-day capstone exercises to measure student learning. About one-quarter of the programs relied heavily on a comprehensive exam (29.6 percent) or an employer survey (26 percent).

Newcomer and Allen (2008) recently analyzed the state of outcomes measurement in the field of public service education. They concluded that, consistent with the previous NASPAA surveys, "the measurement of these student learning outcomes rarely goes past the surveying of students, alumni, and occasionally employers about the change in student knowledge, skills, and abilities from classroom and field learning experiences" (5). They cite Donald Kirkpatrick's typology, which proposed four possible outcomes of training programs (Newcomer and Allen 2008, 6–7): "first, the student' perception of the quality/value/worth of the program at the conclusion of the program typically captured in end-of-course or program feedback forms; second, actual use of the knowledge and skills in the workplace some months after the completion of the program; third, some positive changes in the work processes that resulted from the students' employment of the skills and knowledge they learned; and fourth, increases in the productivity of the organizations where the program alumni worked."

They conclude, however, "Due to the resources and time required to follow-up program alumni, as well as the analytical challenges to attributing organizational changes to specific student/alumni contributions, evaluation of educational programs rarely goes further than Kirkpatrick's second level." Indeed, the extensive use of surveys "rarely reach[es] beyond Kirkpatrick's first level" (12). The new standards require all programs to assess student learning outcomes but leave the means of assessment to individual programs, thus begging the question of how high programs will venture on Kirkpatrick's scale.

RESULTS AND IMPLICATIONS OF CHANGING THE ACCREDITATION CURRICULUM STANDARDS

Building on the foundations outlined above, the new standard on curriculum content requires the following:

> 5.1 Universal Required Competencies: As the basis for its curriculum, the program will adopt a set of required competencies related to its mission and public service values. The required competencies will include five domains: the ability
>
> - to lead and manage in public governance;
> - to participate in and contribute to the policy process;
> - to analyze, synthesize, think critically, solve problems and make decisions;
> - to articulate and apply a public service perspective;
> - to communicate and interact productively with diverse and changing workforce and citizenry.

The new standard differs from the old in several ways. First, reflecting the verities at the core of public service education, the proposed NASPAA standard expects all accredited programs to demonstrate that their graduates are competent in five general domains rather than three. Remaining, although in a different form, are decision making and understanding and participating in the policy process. Leadership has been added to management. The target of these domains is no longer just public sector organizations but governance more generally. Governance is what a government does, exercising management power and policy.

Second, the new standard requires demonstrable functional competencies rather than coverage of curriculum topics. For example, the new standard lists competencies such as to "lead and manage in public governance" rather than traditional courses such as human resources management. Third, the new standard clarifies what it means to act effectively and ethically. Fourth, and most important, the new standard expects programs to distinguish themselves as public service education by embedding public service values in every competency (Raffel 2007; Raffel, Maser, and McFarland 2007). This revitalizes the profession's commitment to a public service ethos (see chapter 7, "Ethics and Integrity in Public Service," and chapter 2, "The Profession of Public Administration," in this volume).

Reflecting the inevitability of change in their environments and the need to be responsive, the new standard moves the most specific curriculum coverage requirements, such as "human resources," "budgeting and financial processes," and "political and economic institutions and processes," into the self-study instructions. The self-study instructions, prepared by COPRA, allow NASPAA to update its expectations through the guidance it provides without submitting changes to a majority vote of its accredited members. At the same, by specifying the standard on curriculum in terms of competencies—outcomes—rather than subjects, individual programs have

Figure 5.1   **NASPAA Standards, 2009**

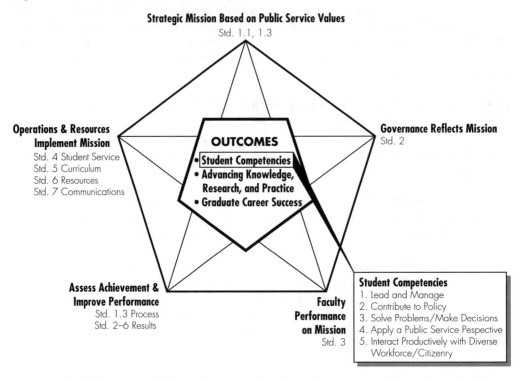

more freedom to design their curricula around competencies dictated by their missions. Figure 5.1 depicts the foci of accreditation, linking the standards with each of five interrelated components of a management system designed to ensure that graduates learn competencies consistent with a program's mission.

The passage of the new standards will require programs to make a series of decisions about the competencies they are fostering in students and how to measure students' achievement. Discussions with public administration program directors and others indicate that all programs will need to address the following:

- Defining competencies for each of the five areas defined in the new standards for required curricula: What process is appropriate; for example, should it involve stakeholders such as professionals, employers, and students?
- Adding program-specific competencies: What makes this program unique, and how does this relate to competencies?
- Measuring the achievement of competencies: What measures will be inside versus outside of courses? Will competencies and students be sampled? What should be the level of attainment, for example, all students or some percentage? What should be the criteria for selecting measures, for example, reliability? Are absolute or value-added measures, or both, for example, pre- and post-tests, more appropriate?
- Validating the measurement of competencies: Should professionals, employers, academics, or some combination of the three from outside the program become involved in the assessment?

- How can benchmarks be identified or established, for example, through NASPAA? (See Jennings 1989.)
- What resources will this require, and where will they come from?
- How transparent will the results be? Which stakeholders will be able to see which results?

Given that programs have been required to measure student mastery of competencies for well over a decade but remain at a low level of sophistication in doing so, will the revised standards lead to increased sophistication? There are several reasons for a positive answer. First, regional and other professional accrediting agencies are requiring competency-based standards and measurement. This has changed the environment on campuses, raising the expectations for programs setting learning objectives and measuring student learning. Professional accreditors also are offering help to programs. For example, the business accrediting agency the Association to Advance Collegiate Schools of Business specified a phased transition process for meeting their new outcomes-based standards and maintained a complete question-and-answer section on its Assessment Resource Center Web site to address many of the most difficult issues. The Accreditation Board of Engineering Technologies, the accreditor for college and university programs in applied science, computing, engineering, and technology, sponsors assessment seminars, and the Council on Accreditation of Healthcare Management Education, the health policy and management accreditor, collects information on assessment from its members.

Second, practitioners in both the private and public sectors have been adopting competency models, using them for decades as tools in recruiting, developing, and promoting employees. This provides a base of knowledge from which public administration and policy degree programs can build. Tim Mau (2009) has catalogued leadership competencies for the public sector employed in the United States, Canada, and around the world.

Third, requiring competency-based education is at the heart of the new standards, not an add-on requirement. For example, the self-study report instructions drafted by a NASPAA task force provide detailed guidance on what is expected of programs. Finally, NASPAA has linked the revision of accreditation standards and the new self-study instructions to a data warehouse and a renewed commitment to transparency. This will make it easier to study public affairs education and, thereby, to improve it. That stated, NASPAA and COPRA still must take a leadership role for full implementation of competency-based accreditation.

With the adoption of its new standards, NASPAA accreditation has moved from focusing on inputs to focusing on outputs, and then to outcomes, and finally to performance. In each case, NASPAA's accreditation has sought to be state-of-the-art, guiding programs in generating more value for their stakeholders and the public. NASPAA's emerging role as an information clearinghouse for the profession, supported by new information technology infrastructure, will facilitate COPRA's holding programs accountable throughout successive accreditation cycles. This increases the validity and promise of accreditation as a vehicle for helping programs improve and for serving the public.

CHALLENGES AND CONCLUSIONS

The list of competencies for those in public service early in the twenty-first century, as incorporated into the new accreditation standards that include leadership and management, decision making, and communications, is not conclusive. Given recent history, is presuming prescience folly? Questions remain, but the processes for answering them are in place.

What will students need to know in ten years? What profound changes will surface in the decade ahead that redefine the knowledge, skills, and abilities required of students working in public service? Shifting details from standards to the documentation requirements outlined in the self-study instructions should allow the field to respond appropriately and quickly to the challenges ahead.

Will the field continue to move toward the big-tent approach or will it divide more, for example, with a profusion of degrees in areas such as nonprofit management and health policy and management? Will separate degrees proliferate? Will public administration and public policy degrees stay together under the NASPAA banner? Will these degrees be distinguishable from other degrees as sector lines blur? Specialization is a trend long in the making and likely to continue, but the new standards will allow NASPAA to advance the field by providing guidance to educational programs, whatever their specialization, that are committed to public service values.

Can accreditation and the field keep up with the demands of technology? Will new instructional delivery mechanisms make it increasing difficult to set standards? In every endeavor, people learn from the advance of technology, finding ways to assess quality and improve performance. The academy, which is at its core about learning but is one of the last social institutions to undergo renovation under the onslaught of information technology, will be no different. Accreditation is not likely to become an anachronism. It could become more decentralized and democratic in the sense of increased input from more stakeholders.

Will NASPAA have the capacity and model to allow programs outside the United States to seek and gain accreditation? Is the tent big enough to include a broad range of programs beyond the nation's borders? Will the entrance of non-U.S. programs lead to changes in expectations for performance of U.S. programs? Globalization appears to be inevitable and with it the globalization of accreditation. Changing expectations likely will follow, inducing U.S. programs to become more globalized and cognizant of alternative models of governance and service delivery.

Given the proliferation of competencies required for success in public service, will programs be able to identify curricula and competencies not required of all students? What current competencies will programs drop without harming the competitive position of their graduates? Forces such as specialization, technological change, and globalization likely will induce programs to experiment. NASPAA, which has always encouraged accreditation standards that allow for program innovation, may play an increasingly important role as a clearinghouse for best practices and as an accreditor of quality.

What research is needed to improve the definition, measurement, and use of student learning outcomes? What competencies are needed for various types of positions and careers, for instance, city management or nonprofit leaders? What are efficient and valid measures of the levels of competency acquired by students as a result of their formal education when they bring different backgrounds into programs, especially given the growth of executive education? Institutions of higher education and their accrediting bodies increasingly have accepted contributions to the scholarship of learning as a part of faculty performance portfolios. Faculty members, along with practitioners using competency models in their human resource management practices, will provide the answers to these questions, especially if they wish to continue serving the public interest and attract highly motivated students into the profession.

Whatever competencies will be required of master of public administration and master of public policy graduates during the twenty-first century, the curricula of 2025 and 2050 will have elements that look like the curricula of 2010. Some elements must be different. Upgrading master of public administration and master of public policy curricula to reflect current realities has not made sufficient progress; the necessity for change is increasingly clear (Forrer, Kee, and Gabriel 2007). If MPA programs are to remain relevant, foreseeable changes in communication, information technology, partnering and contracting, and global forces make curricular changes inevitable

(Holzer and Lin 2007). Accreditation plays a role in this, not only by establishing expectations for curricular content, but also by encouraging programs to adapt, to serve their communities, and to pursue their missions by attending to those who employ their graduates (Bremer and El Baradei 2008). In sum, accreditation of programs in public service education is a work in progress with many substantive challenges and opportunities to invigorate the profession.

NOTES

1. NASPAA is an association of programs of "public affairs and administration"; the current standards refer to preparing students for leadership positions in "public affairs, policy, and administration," and as noted in the text, the accreditation process increasingly involves "public policy" programs and preparing students for leadership in the nonprofit sector (see NASPAA 2006b and Nonprofit Academic Centers Council 2003). NASPAA's journal is the *Journal of Public Affairs Education.* This chapter refers to education for the "public service" and standards to be inclusive of the fields of public affairs, public administration, and public policy.

2. In part because public service is not a licensed profession in the United States, the NASPAA accreditation process is voluntary. (See the NASPAA accreditation Web page for details on the process and the standards: http://naspaa.org/accreditation/seeking/reference/reference.asp.) Not all NASPAA institutional members have sought accreditation from the Commission on Peer Review and Accreditation. Its membership includes 271 university programs in public affairs, public policy, and public administration. Of the total number of programs eligible to participate in peer review in 2009, 169 programs at 160 schools (59 percent of member institutions) have been accredited by the commission.

3. NASPAA does not review undergraduate or PhD programs or programs outside of the United States. However, NASPAA standards have become a benchmark for the burgeoning number of public service degree programs internationally, and NASPAA is expanding the jurisdiction of its accreditation. Changes to curriculum expectations or to the assessment of student learning thus have a wide impact on public affairs education globally.

4. In 1983, the members of the association voted to apply to the Council on Postsecondary Accreditation (COPA) to become recognized as a specialized agency to accredit master's degrees in public affairs and administration. COPA granted recognition in October 1986. In 2003, the Council for Higher Education Accreditation (CHEA), COPA's successor association of three thousand colleges and universities recognizing institutional and programmatic accrediting organizations, granted recognition for ten years to NASPAA's Commission on Peer Review and Accreditation (COPRA) to accredit master's degrees in public administration, public affairs, and public policy in the United States. NASPAA and sixty other agencies share CHEA recognition, which results from a process of evaluation and self-scrutiny similar to accreditation. To continue to be recognized as an accrediting body, NASPAA's standard-setting process must meet CHEA's expectations.

REFERENCES

Abramson, Mark A., Jonathan D. Breul, and John M. Kamensky. 2003. *Four Trends Transforming Government.* Washington, DC: IBM Center for the Business of Government.

Aristigueta, Maria P., and Jeffrey A. Raffel. 2001. Teaching techniques of analysis in the MPA curriculum: Research methods, management science, and "the third path." *Journal of Public Affairs Education* 7 (3): 161–169.

Association for Public Policy Analysis and Management (APPAM). 2006. Charting the next twenty years of public policy and management education. Paper presented at the Association for Public Policy Analysis and Management Spring Conference, Park City, UT, June 15–17 (accessed July 21, 2010 from www.appam.org/conferences/spring/parkcity2006/index.asp).

Bartlett, Christopher A., and Sumantral Ghoshal. 1997. The myth of the generic manager. *California Management Review* 40 (1): 92–116.

Barzelay, Michael, and Fred Thompson. 2007. Making public management a design-oriented science. Paper presented at the Eleventh International Research Society for Public Management Symposium, Potsdam, Germany, April 3.

Behn, Robert D. 1980. Policy analysis and public management: What should Jones do? In *Education for the Public Service,* ed. G.S. Birkhead and J.D. Carroll, 17–25. Syracuse, NY: Maxwell School.

Berry, Frances S., and Ralph S. Brower. 2005. Intergovernmental and intersectoral management: Weaving networking, contracting out, and management roles into third party government. *Public Performance and Management Review* 29 (1): 7–17.

Boxall, Peter, and John Gilbert. 2007. The management of managers: A review and conceptual framework. *International Journal of Management Reviews* 9 (2): 95–115.

Bremer, Jennifer, and Laila El Baradei. 2008. Developing public administration and public policy master's programs in Egypt. *Journal of Public Affairs Education* 14 (3): 439–462.

Cascio, Wayne. 2000. Managing a virtual workplace. *Academy of Management Executive* 14 (3): 81–90.

Caulkins, Jonathan. 1999. The revolution in management science instruction. *Journal of Public Affairs Education* 5 (2): 107–117.

Charan, Ram, Stephen Drotter, and James Noel. 2001. *The Leadership Pipeline.* San Francisco: Jossey-Bass.

Council for Higher Education Accreditation. 2002. Student learning outcomes workshop. *CHEA Chronicle* 5 (2): 1–2.

———. 2003. Statement of mutual responsibilities for student learning outcomes: accreditation, institutions, and programs. September. www.chea.org/pdf/StmntStudentLearningOutcomes9–03.pdf.

———. 2006a. Accreditation and accountability: A CHEA special report. CHEA Occasional Paper, December. www.chea.org/pdf/accreditation_and_accountability.pdf.

———. 2006b. Recognition standards. In *Recognition of Accrediting Organizations: Policies and Procedures,* ed. CHEA, 5–8. Washington, DC: Council for Higher Education Accreditation, January 23. www.chea.org/recognition/CHEA_Recognition_Policy_and_Procedures.pdf.

Crosby, Barbara, and John Bryson. 2005. Challenges of introducing leadership into the public affairs curriculum. *Journal of Public Affairs Education* 11 (3): 193–205.

Dunne, David, and Roger Martin. 2006. Design thinking and how it will change management education. *Academy of Management Learning and Education* 5 (4): 512–523.

Durant, Robert F. 2001. Politics, paradox, and the "ecology" of public administration: Challenges, choices, and opportunities for a new century. In *Handbook of Public Management Practice and Reform,* ed. Kuotsai Tom Liou, 1–34. New York: Marcel Dekker.

Ellwood, John W. 1985. *A Morphology of Graduate Education for Public Service in the United States.* Washington, DC: National Association of Schools of Public Affairs and Administration.

———. 2006. Challenges to public policy and management education. Paper presented at the Association for Public Policy Analysis and Management Spring Conference, Park City, UT, June 15–17.

Evans, Angela. 2006. Demand for masters of public policy in public service. Paper presented at the Association for Public Policy Analysis and Management Spring Conference, Park City, UT, June 15–17.

Ewell, Peter T. 2001. *Accreditation and Student Learning Outcomes: A Proposed Point of Departure.* Washington, DC: Council for Higher Education Accreditation.

Fairholm, Matthew R. 2006. Leadership theory and practice in the MPA curriculum: Reason and methods. *Journal of Public Affairs Education* 12 (3): 335–346.

Forrer, John, James Edwin Kee, and Seth Gabriel. 2007. Not your father's public administration. *Journal of Public Affairs Education* 13 (2): 265–280.

Friedman, Thomas. 2005. *The World Is Flat.* New York: Farrar, Straus and Giroux.

Goldsmith, Stephen, and William D. Eggers. 2004. *Governing by Network: The New Shape of the Public Sector.* Washington, DC: Brookings Institution Press.

Gulick, Luther, and Lindal Urwick. 1937. *Papers on the Science of Administration.* New York: Institute for Public Administration.

Henry, Laurin. 1995. History. National Association of Schools of Public Affairs and Administration (NASPAA) (accessed July 21, 2010 from http://www.naspaa.org/about_naspaa/about/history.asp).

Henry, N., C.T. Goodsell, L.E. Lynn Jr., C. Stivers, and G.L. Wamsley. 2009. Understanding excellence in public administration: The report of the task force on educating for excellence in the master of public administration degree of the American Society for Public Administration. *Journal of Public Affairs Education* 15 (2): 117–133.

Holzer, Marc, and Weiwei Lin. 2007. A longitudinal perspective on MPA education in the United States. *Journal of Public Affairs Education* 13 (2): 345–364.

Horne, Christopher. 2008. Teaching what we know: Describing and challenging the neglect of management science methods in MPA programs. *Journal of Public Affairs Education* 14 (3): 427–438.

Huba, Mary E., and Jann E. Freed. 2000. *Learner-Centered Assessment on College Campuses: Shifting the Focus from Teaching to Learning.* Boston: Allyn and Bacon.

Jennings, Edward T. 1989 Accountability, program quality, outcome assessment, and graduate education for public affairs and administration. *Public Administration Review* 49 (5): 438–446.

Kershenstein, Karen. 2002. Some reflections on accreditors' practices in assessing success with respect to student achievement. June. www.aspa-usa.org/documents/Kershenstein.pdf.

Kim, Soonhee, and Karen Layne. 2001. Making the connection: E-government and public administration education. *Journal of Public Affairs Education* 7 (4): 229–240.

Laudicina, Eleanor V. 2007. A history of pedagogy in public administration. In *Handbook of Public Administration.* 3d ed., ed. Jack Rabin, W. Bartley Hildreth, and Gerald J. Miller, 723–755. Boca Raton: Taylor and Francis.

Lewis, Gregory, and Seong Soo Oh. 2008. Graduate education and federal career success: How well does the MPA stack up? *Journal of Public Affairs Education* 14 (3): 463–474.

Liou, Kuotsai Tom. 2001. *Handbook of Public Management Practice and Reform.* New York: Marcel Dekker.

Marini, Frank. 1971. The Minnowbrook perspective and the future of public administration education. In *Toward a New Public Administration,* ed. Frank Marini, 346–367. Scranton, PA: Chandler Publishing.

Mau, Tim. 2009. Is public sector leadership distinct? A comparative analysis of core competencies in the senior executive service. In *Public Sector Leadership: International Challenges and Perspectives,* ed. Jeffrey A. Raffel, Peter Leisink, and Anthony E. Middlebrooks, 313–339. Cheltenham, UK: Edward Elgar.

Merget, Astrid. 2003. Times of turbulence. *Public Administration Review* 63 (4): 390–395.

Milward, H. Brinton, and Keith Provan. 2006. *A Manager's Guide to Choosing and Using Collaborative Networks.* Washington, DC: IBM Center for the Business of Government.

Mintrom, Michael. 2003. *People Skills for Policy Analysts.* Washington, DC: Georgetown University Press.

Morse, Ricardo S., Larkin S. Dudley, James P. Armstrong, and Dong Won-Kim. 2005. Learning and teaching about deliberative democracy on campus and in the field. *Journal of Public Affairs Education* 11 (4): 325–336.

National Academy of Public Administration (NAPA). 2005. *Managing Federal Missions with a Multisectoral Workforce: Leadership of the 21st Century.* Washington, DC: National Academy of Public Administration.

National Association of Schools of Public Affairs and Administration (NASPAA). 2004. Internationalizing the public affairs core curriculum. *Journal of Public Affairs Education* 10 (3): 259–262.

———. 2005. Should leadership be in the core curriculum? *Journal of Public Affairs Education* 11 (3): 207–210.

———. 2006a. General information and standards for professional masters degree programs. January (accessed July 21, 2010 from www.naspaa.org/accreditation/document/OFFICIAL_DOCUMENTS_2008_standards_only.pdf).

———. 2006b. Guidelines for graduate professional education in nonprofit organizations, management and leadership. October (accessed July 21, 2010 from www.naspaa.org/accreditation/document/NASPAA GuidelinesforNP%20Fina12006.doc).

———. 2006c. Sector survey of executive education programs for public service professionals. October (accessed July 21, 2010 from www.naspaa.org/execMPA/doc/2006ExecEduSurveyReport.pdf).

———. 2006d. The future of the public sector. NASPAA Annual Conference, Minneapolis, MN, October 19–21.

———. 2006e. The future of the public sector. NASPAA Executive Council Retreat, Tucson, AZ, March 30–31.

———. 2007. Surveys (accessed July 21, 2010 from www.naspaa.org/naspaa_surveys/main.asp).

———. 2008. Standards: 2008 (accessed July 21, 2010 from www.naspaa.org/accreditation/seeking/reference/standards.asp).

Nelson, Barbara. 2002. Education for the public interest. Plenary address at NASPAA Annual Conference, Los Angeles, CA, October 17 (accessed July 21, 2010 from unpan1.un.org/intradoc/groups/public/documents/ASPA/UNPAN006959.pdf).

Newcomer, Kathryn E., and Heather Allen. 2008. Adding value in the public interest. White paper (accessed July 21, 2010 from naspaa.org/accreditation/standard2009/docs/AddingValueinthePublicInterest.pdf).

Nonprofit Academic Centers Council. 2003. *Curricular Guidelines for Graduate Study in Philanthropy, the Nonprofit Sector, and Nonprofit Leadership.* 2d ed. Cleveland, OH: Nonprofit Academic Centers Council (accessed July 21, 2010 from www.naccouncil.org/pdf/NACC_Guidelines.pdf).

Piskulich, Michelle, and Marvin Mandell. 2007. Curricular competencies. NASPAA White paper. October (accessed July 21, 2010 from www.naspaa.org/accreditation/document/WhitePaperCompetencies.pdf).

Poister, Theodore H., and Patricia Ingraham. 1991. Assessing MPA program outcomes: Current practice and policy alternatives. *American Review of Public Administration* 21 (3): 169–181.

Radin, Beryl. 2008. Discussion report: Process, politics, and management in the curriculum. *Journal of Policy Analysis and Management* 27 (3): 635–640.

Raffel, Jeffrey A. 2007. The uniqueness of NASPAA-accredited programs: The role of public service in accreditation. White paper. September 26. www.naspaa.org/accreditation/document/WhitePaperPublic-ServiceRequirementRaffe110.2007.pdf.

———. 2009. Looking forward: A response to the ASPA task force report on educating for excellence in the MPA. *Journal of Public Affairs Education* 15 (2): 135–144.

Raffel, Jeffrey A., Steven Maser, and Laurel McFarland. 2007. NASPAA standards 2009: Public service values, mission-based accreditation. White paper. Washington, DC: NASPAA (accessed July 21, 2010 from www.naspaa.org/accreditation/document/NASPAAStandardsPhilosophy09.12.2007.pdf).

Riccucci, Norma M. 2007. Public administration pedagogy: What is it? In *Handbook of Public Administration.* 3d ed., ed. Jack Rabin, W. Bartley Hildreth, and Gerald J. Miller, 757–765. Boca Raton, FL: Taylor and Francis.

Rice, Mitchell F. 2007. Promoting cultural competency in public administration delivery: Utilizing self-assessment tools and performance measures. *Journal of Public Affairs Education* 13 (1): 41–57.

———. 2008. A primer for developing a public service agency ethos of cultural competency in public services programming and public services delivery. *Journal of Public Affairs Education* 14 (1): 21–38.

Roberts, Robert. 2008. Teaching law in public administration programs. *Journal of Public Affairs Education* 14 (3): 361–381.

Salamon, Lester M. 2005. Training professional citizens: Getting beyond the right answer to the wrong question in public affairs education. *Journal of Public Affairs Education* 11 (1): 7–19.

Straussman, Jeffrey D. 2008. Public management, politics, and the policy process in the public affairs curriculum. *Journal of Policy Analysis and Management* 27 (3): 624–635.

Svara, James, and James Brunet. 2005. Social equity is a pillar of public administration. *Journal of Public Affairs Education* 11 (3): 253–258.

Yeager, Samuel, W. Bartley Hildreth, Gerald Miller, and Jack Rabin. 2007. What difference does having an MPA make? *Journal of Public Affairs Education* 13 (2): 147–167.

CHAPTER 6

CHANGING DYNAMICS OF ADMINISTRATIVE LEADERSHIP

MONTGOMERY VAN WART

This chapter examines the status of public leadership as a field of scholarship, with a focus on its context in the mainstream literature. In particular, this chapter seeks both to provide an overview of recent trends in leadership research and to provide a sense of where public sector leadership theory has been of late.[1] The chapter first defines the boundaries and context of public leadership. It then presents the "postmodern" paradigm that is likely to supplement rather than supplant the "modern" paradigm in the field of organizational leadership. Coverage is then given to eight specific areas in which either the mainstream or public leadership fields have made advances. The chapter concludes with a review of the opportunities and challenges for a public leadership research agenda.

HISTORICAL BACKGROUND OF ADMINISTRATIVE
LEADERSHIP STUDIES

Although the modern study of leadership is about a hundred years old, interest in leaders and leadership dates back to the beginning of history. There are at least three major reasons that have stimulated enormous interest in the topic. First, leaders have a critical effect on us in the present and future. They can determine on a grand scale the success or failure of a society, country, and community. Leaders of public organizations, especially governments, can bring in resources, set a positive tone, encourage a can-do attitude, or, alternatively, run the organization like a fiefdom, stamp out creativity, make poor judgment calls, or be slow to react to external events (Kaiser, Hogan, and Craig 2008; Trottier, Van Wart, and Wang 2008). At a more tangible level for those not in the senior positions, a bad supervisor can send workers scurrying for new jobs while a good team leader makes a difficult assignment seem easy because of good organization and encouragement. Second, nearly everyone has a leadership role in which he or she wants to do well, no matter whether it is the chief operating officer of a major institution or the lead person in a cross-functional team. Third, there is an intense fascination surrounding those in leadership positions. Human nature is such that there is equal interest in the leader who is a consistent success and the one who is flawed or even a failure. Yet even with what we know about its ancient roots, its effect on citizens and employees, an individual's personal stake in doing it well, and the compulsive fascination it holds, the study of leadership is challenging.

One great guru of organizational leadership, Warren Bennis, noted that "the subject is vast, amorphous, slippery, and, above all, desperately important" (Bennis 2007). It might seem that a special focus on one major context, public administration, would make the task of providing an assessment of the field easier since less scholarship could make it more manageable. However, the challenges in the field of public administration quickly come to the fore. As Chet Newland stated years ago, public administration tends to be a field of strangers in search of a discipline. "American public administration is awesomely multidisciplinary and more—complicatedly multicultural— drawing on the expertise and insights, even the hopes and imaginations, of all sorts of people. But public administration's more than multidisciplinary character is often frenzied, lacking a fair modicum of shared culture and enterprise" (Newland 1994). When discussions of leadership with a public sector thrust occur, it is often as if mainstream topics hit a multifaceted prism and are refracted in distinctly different, and not uniform, directions.

In the first major assessment of administrative leadership research in the last twenty years,[2] Larry Terry noted that in "all this talk about more effective leadership, the topic of *bureaucratic leadership* is conspicuously absent" (Terry 1995, 2; emphasis in original). He noted numerous reasons for this lacuna, elaborated a "conservator" model advocating a balance of stewardship and deliberative action, and urged far greater attention to this important topic. Eight years later, Van Wart's assessment was that the field of administrative leadership was beginning to evolve, albeit slowly and with as many gaps as there were strengths. After an extensive review of the literature, he noted three trends. First, he found that the normative foundations of administrative leadership were being thoroughly discussed because of the debates surrounding reinvention, the new public management, and various public sector reforms such as contracting out that have been slowly but surely changing the face of public administration in the United States and around the world. Second, the importance of administrative leadership, as opposed to management practice, still seemed either to be largely lacking from a research perspective, or supplied with a nonempirical set of assertions—often atheoretical. Finally, the amount and quality of "normal science" research in administrative leadership was scant and weak. In addition, he pointed to two gaps. The need for work in integrated models or frameworks of leadership that can be used to organize the disparate field as well as for teaching purposes was highlighted. Also noted was a need for more consistent clarity in identifying the leadership population vis-à-vis its position in the political-administrative system. Overall, he felt that the "weaknesses were more pronounced than the strengths" (Van Wart 2003, 224).

A third perspective is reflected in a symposium in which Van Slyke and Alexander reviewed the literature on public service leadership. Their assessment includes all types of leadership. One important conclusion that they reach is that "public sector leadership research parallels developments on the private sector side but lags temporally in empirical tests, application, and modifications of leadership concepts and frameworks as they relate to public organizations. Understanding the interactions between the microlevel attributes of the individual leader (traits, characteristics, and competencies) and the macrolevel attributes of the organization (structure, culture, environment, products, people, and partnerships) is critical for discovering and developing appropriate models of public sector leadership" (Van Slyke and Alexander 2006, 366).

Thus, their major focus is to refine the mainstream literature in the public sector context— identifying where it is the same or nearly so, but clarifying where and why it is different. They identify large-scale projects as being particularly useful because of the scope of the leadership environment and the substantial variations across the public sector universe. Although they identify this as a major gap, they present it as an excellent opportunity as well.

A final assessment by Morse, Buss, and Kinghorn echoes Terry's call for more emphasis on administrative leadership in a rapidly evolving world in which the increasing challenges for leaders make it "not a friendly one" (2007, 10). Their emphasis, as shaped by the edited volume, is to better articulate the normative debate on the best style of administrative leadership (strongly entrepreneurial and market driven on one extreme and more restrained and civic guided on the other), to better understand how to achieve successful change in public sector settings, to provide useful models of collaboration, and to investigate theories in relation to specific administrative contexts.

DEFINING THE BOUNDARIES AND THE EVOLVING CONTEXT OF PUBLIC LEADERSHIP

In defining the broad boundaries of public leadership, Morse, Buss, and Kinghorn (2007) note that there are at least three types of public sectors. There is political leadership, which involves legislators, elected executives in the policy process such as presidents, governors, and mayors, and the various stakeholders in the political process. There is organizational leadership, also known as bureaucratic or administrative leadership, primarily aimed at those leading and managing employees, programs, and organizations for the public good. Third, there is collaborative leadership, which focuses on leading in a shared-power world where citizens must have broad access and engagement, where more organizations must be included in policies and solutions, and where accountability is more broadly distributed (see chapter 17, "Collaborative Public Agencies in the Network Era," in this volume). Each of these types is important, and each will be referenced. The primary focus of this chapter, however, is about administrative leadership affecting more than 23 million employees in the United States alone.[3] As Morse, Buss, and Kinghorn (2007) note, it is difficult to disentangle the types because of the enormous overlap; at the same time, it is important to provide a narrower focus of this sweeping topic for heuristic purposes.

While there are many fundamental "eternal verities" related to leadership that seem to defy culture, time, and even biology (Arvey et al. 2007), much of what is interesting about leadership is affected by context. Therefore, when environmental shifts occur, social values evolve, organizational structures adjust, preferred leader styles alter, and competency needs are affected (Bass 2008). Research needs to identify, to the degree possible, the more long-term stable elements of leadership and those that are more topically affected. What are the recent shifts in the organizational environment? Focusing on the American context, the demographics have shifted to a more multicultural and educated society. Communication is much more computer and technology mediated. Organizations are more team based, networked, globally connected, and flatter, and purport to be more empowered and participative. The public at-large as citizens, consumers, and organizational members is much more cynical and distrusting. Global and national wealth distribution trends have been more unequal for thirty years so that the average CEO now gets 262 times what the average worker gets (Mishel, Bernstein, and Sheirholz 2009). Global competition has increased enormously over the last half century.

Abramson, Breul, and Kamensky (2006) point out that in a world in which public sector expectations and mandates, technology, structures, resources, workforce demographics, and norms are evolving, the challenges of management must also evolve. They identify six major trends that have direct or indirect effects on management: (1) changing the formal rules of government in order to allow more flexibility and customization of services, (2) the expanded use of performance measurement, (3) the increased emphasis on competition, choice, and incentives, (4) the expectation of performance on demand, (5) the requirement for greater citizen engagement, and (6) the greater use of networks and partnerships. Ultimately, all these trends make leadership challenging (Van Wart and Berman 1999) and make the business of providing scholarly and applied materials that much more critical (see Cortada et al. 2008 for a list of worldwide drivers affecting government).

These trends and others have had a real impact on leadership. For example, the massive reductions in middle management in the 1980s in the private sector and in the 1990s in the public sector may have been instigated by economic pressures but were made possible by improvements in communication and data processing. This encouraged more use of teams, networks, and the concomitant empowerment strategies, all of which had an enormous effect on the necessity of leaders at all levels to broaden the range of their styles and to shift their emphasis from directive styles toward more participatory and delegated modes. Because these latter styles are no less difficult to implement successfully, it might be argued that they are more difficult to implement; managers-as-leaders have had their work cut out for them in trying to make this transition.

The recent leadership literature adds to or changes ongoing approaches developed over the last century or more. The literature started with a "great-man" approach in the nineteenth century. A "traits" approach dominated the first half of the twentieth century but was very one-dimensional and failed to adequately address the various contexts of leadership. Useful, if simplistic, situational and contingency models, such as the managerial grid (Blake and Mouton 1964) and situational leadership (Hersey and Blanchard 1969), were put forward in the 1960s. In the 1970s somewhat more sophisticated models such as path goal theory (House and Mitchell 1974) and normative decision theory (Vroom and Yetton 1973) were advanced. The field expanded greatly in the 1980s and 1990s with the surge in interest in transformational and charismatic leadership. Executive and external perspectives became foci of the literature. Normative discussions about the personal morality of leaders and the appropriate role of public leaders of various types have been ongoing in the academic literature since the 1940s. No brief synopsis can do justice to a vast and complex field. (See Bass 2008 for a more inclusive review of mainstream literature and Van Wart 2008 for public sector leadership literature.)

THE RISE OF THE POSTMODERN PERSPECTIVE IN LEADERSHIP STUDIES

Several characteristics have dominated the overall approach to leadership studies. First, until recently, leadership research followed "modern" trends, with an emphasis on empiricism, rationalism, positivism, and reductionism. Empiricism holds that all knowledge comes from the senses and that the metaphysical is not an interest of science. Rationalism asserts that the mind organizes knowledge of the external world by observation and contemplation. Positivism (built on empiricism and rationalism) supports an approach that holds that science is testable, cumulative, and neutral and that things are ultimately measurable. Reductionism is an approach that attempts to reduce complexity to the fewest elements or variables and to explain science at the most fundamental level (e.g., reducing classical genetics to molecular biology).

Second, and flowing from the first, the study of leadership (overall) has tended to be objectivist, leader-centric, and status quo oriented. The objectivist trend was manifested by the effort to break leadership down into its constituent parts (traits, skills, behaviors, attitudes, etc.) and analyze the empirical relationship among them, with the hope that increasingly abstract general rules could be interpolated from microlevel studies. Research tended to be leader-centric because the leader in the leadership process has tended to be the major object of study. How does the leader relate to the followers? How does the leader maintain order and productivity? How does the leader use her or his values or change the organization's values? Finally, leadership studies have tended to assume that leadership forms are inherent and that individuals and organizations need to discover and master those forms (sometimes called realism).

Incipient challenges to some of the tenets of modernist research began as early as the late

1970s in the work of people such as Burns (1978), with the introduction of social values, and Greenleaf (1977), with the introduction of individual values and a denial of instrumentalism. Since 2000, leadership studies have been increasingly affected by calls for and approaches reflecting postmodern research trends. The newer journals *Integral Leadership* (2000) and *Leadership* (2005) reverse the modernist emphasis by calling for more eclectic, relational, and holistic approaches. While the tenets underlying modern research are not abandoned, they are likely to be overtaken by a radically different perspective by many leading researchers in the longer term.

Postmodern thought asserts that science is not neutral, science is not necessarily cumulative, sensory knowledge is only one form of knowledge, and nonsensory knowledge can be studied. It also asserts that the structure of knowledge is a form of power and thus accepting that structure is to reify the status quo. An alternative way of knowing and perceiving is constructionism (aka constructivism), which challenges the supremacy of empiricism, rationalism, positivism, and reductionism. It holds that all knowledge is constructed, truth is relative to our purposes (i.e., based on intersubjectivity), the notion of "progress" is largely a myth, and far from being neutral observers of "facts," scientists are active participants in creating reality or distorting it for their own (generally unintentional) ends.

Postmodernism also points out that differences are often as important as or more important than similarities. Postmodernists assert that the myth of neutrality allows personal assumptions to go unchallenged; it is better to state one's values and incorporate them in the research endeavor explicitly than purport to be unbiased. The scientific theory underlying postmodernism is general systems theory to the degree that it emphasizes the importance of the whole as much as or more than the parts, the prospect for external perturbations, and the unexpected effects of seemingly tiny incidents (e.g., tipping points and butterfly effects). Examples of research reflecting strong elements of postmodernism in leadership are identified in the following sections. They relate to such topics as discourse (aka discursive) theory, complexity and relational theory, integral leadership studies, and network and collaboration theory. Public sector examples are integrated in the discussion that follows.

Discourse Theory

Discourse theory has its roots in Foucault (1970, 1972), who examined the reification of social structures through language and customary usage. For example, calling guerrilla military activists in another country either "freedom fighters" or "terrorists" entirely changes the terms of debate. In leadership studies in particular, an interest in discourse theory "began with a more general dissatisfaction with the results and lack of coherence in trait and style based psychological research" (Kelly 2008, 764). Those with a discourse-theory perspective tend to question traditional definitions of leadership (Barker 2001), question and challenge traditional leadership studies as excessively involved in the psychology of leaders (Fairhurst 2007), emphasize the importance of studying followers in context (Alvesson and Sveningsson 2003; Collinson 2006; Gronn 2002), and ask for longer ethnographic studies (Kelly 2008). Chen (2008, 547) notes that the more traditional positivist research tradition of leadership psychology and more constructionist discursive leadership "appear to have little in common." Nonetheless, she "finds ample room for coexistence . . . when one takes into consideration the enormous complexity of the subject matter, coupled with the multiplicity of perspectives for study" (Chen 2008, 549).

Gender theory in leadership is loosely aligned with discourse theory. Gender theory has used a variety of critiques to understand the glass ceiling, but discourse theory is particularly powerful at describing and studying the subtle structures of power that do not necessarily block women from power in the contemporary world, but tend to create amorphous cultural challenges for women to reach the highest levels (e.g., Eagly and Carli 2007 use the labyrinth metaphor).

Complexity Theory

Complexity science suggests a different paradigm for leadership—one that frames leadership as a complex interactive dynamic from which adaptive outcomes emerge (e.g., learning, innovation, and adaptability). Complexity theory is a type of general systems theory that appreciates the massive complexity and interconnectedness of all phenomena, and particularly human social processes such as leadership. Because of this complexity, it points out that the most successful organizations are often ones that have evolving structures that bubble up from below and percolate in from the environment—often called complex adaptive systems (Osborn and Hunt 2007). Complexity theory is very good for studying the multidirectional relational nature of leadership (Uhl-Bien 2006), and the emergence of new organizational and leadership forms (Lichtenstein and Plowman 2009). This approach has reached the popular literature in many subtle and not so subtle ways. For example, in defining leadership, Goffee and Jones (2009) say—to lay audiences—that it is relational, nonhierarchical, and contextual, a far cry from many earlier definitions focusing on leaders' influence, power to change for better or worse, leader traits, and so on.

Integral Leadership

Integral leadership tends to focus on leadership as a community process, democratizing and decentralizing leadership as much as possible. This is the focus of the *Integral Leadership Review*. One example is McCrimmon (2007, 1), who asserts that "leadership needs to be reframed for a digital, postmodern age. The world is losing its stable and hierarchical character. Life is now more dynamic, chaotic; final authorities have vanished." Edwards (2009) is another example of this emphasis, as demonstrated in the title of his essay "Seeing Integral Leadership Through Three Important Lenses: Developmental, Ecological, and Governance," which incorporates the focus on followers, the environment, and community. Integral leadership themes are common in the popular literature because of the concern for corporate social responsibility among leaders and private organizations, as well as the public administration literature because of its focus on serving the community and doing good.

These themes have been expressed in the literature regarding public sector organizations, but in many cases the theoretical or ideological specification has been substantially more muted and related trends are intermingled more freely. An excellent example of discourse (and gender bias) theory is by Ford (2006, 77) who "examines contemporary discourses of leadership and their complex interrelations with gender and identity in the UK public sector. . . . [and] questions dominant hegemonic and stereotypical notions of subjectivity that assume a simple, unitary identity and perpetuate andocentric depictions of organizational life." Crosby and Kiedrowski (2008) provide four levels of integral leadership spanning the individual, group, organization, and society. Schweigert (2007, 325) provides a concrete example in a community setting in which "leadership is rooted in the authority of the followers" and further asserts that "leadership development must focus less on the qualities of individual leaders and more on the social settings, processes, and needs that require and facilitate authoritative action." Critique of the limits of hierarchy and measurement has suggested more integrated and values-oriented public sector leadership models (Loveday 2008).

Network Theory and Collaborative Leadership

The interconnectedness of problems, the regionalization and globalization of solutions, and the decrease in government resources have emphasized the need to move increasingly from government to governance and from hierarchy to networks (Maak and Pless 2006). This requires that leaders have a new worldview, different competencies, and additional tools. Several sets of literature have evolved that overlap with organizational leadership, which is a primary focus of this chapter. One important example relates to a special issue on collaborative management in *Public Administration Review* in 2006. The symposium editors provide two helpful definitions: "Collaborative public management is a concept that describes the process of facilitating and operating in multi-organizational arrangements to solve problems that cannot be solved or easily solved by single organizations. Collaborative means to co-labor, to cooperate to achieve common goals, working across boundaries in multisector relationships. Cooperation is based on the value of reciprocity" (O'Leary, Gerard, and Bingham 2006, 7).

They further note that "participatory governance is the active involvement of citizens in government decision making. Governance means to steer the process that influences decisions and actions within the private, public, and civic sectors." Don Kettl (2006, 10) explains why the contemporary imperative to collaborate is more important than historic boundaries. He notes, "Working effectively at these boundaries requires new strategies of collaboration and new skills for public managers. Failure to develop these strategies—or an instinct to approach boundaries primarily as political symbolism—worsens the performance of the administrative system." Thompson and Perry (2006) dissect collaboration into five variable dimensions that leaders have to understand and master for maximum effectiveness: governance, administration, organizational autonomy, mutuality, and norms of trust and reciprocity. Researchers also point out when collaboration is less than ideal (McGuire 2006) and discuss the limits of collaboration (Bevir 2006).

MAJOR ACTIVITY IN LEADERSHIP STUDIES

Leadership studies have progressed not only because of the additional postmodern perspective, but also because of a maturation of some to the traditional foci. Attention is now given to specific areas in more detail in which there has been significant activity: distributed leadership, transformational leadership, ethics, methods, crisis management, case studies, trait and competency models, and integrated theories.

Distributed Leadership

The attention to followers has not been a major theme in the study of the leadership process in the past. A number of important exceptions existed. For example, Hollander's idiosyncratic credit theory (1958) noted that leaders build up and lose psychological support that they use in their initiatives. However, the traits of leaders, their daily practices (transactions), and the ability to inspire change have tended to be center stage. Contemporary trends have increasingly placed followers in their various guises in an equal light, and have given them far more research attention. Pearce and Conger's (2003) important work, *Shared Leadership: Reframing the Hows and Whys of Leadership,* crystallized the new rethinking about nonleader-centric forms of leadership by incorporating elements of vertical leadership with horizontal leadership (i.e., self-managed teams, leadership of self, and various types of empowering leadership). Horizontal leadership is often called distributed leadership; *Leadership Quarterly* devoted a special issue to it in 2006, as well as one that included followers in 2001. Examples in the follower-distributed vein are numerous; a few noteworthy ones are Kellerman's book on followership (2008), Drath et al.'s call for an "increasingly peer-like and collaborative" framework (2008), and Van Vugt, Hogan, and Kaiser's (2008, 182) historical-evolutionary analysis for why leadership research "tends to ignore the central role of followers." Calls for more emphasis on followers and collective action in public sector settings have become more common around the globe (Dunoon 2002; Alimo-Metcalfe and Alban-Metcalfe 2005; Lawler 2008; Lemay 2009).

Teams started to become important in the 1980s, but research lagged until the 1990s, as did team leadership functions in particular (Burke et al. 2006). The different types of teams (senior management, functional, cross-functional, self-managed, etc.) with their different emphases on regular production, communication, and innovation, as well as vertical versus horizontal (distributed) modalities, have made research in this area complex. Today, with the increased importance of distributed leadership, leadership in teams has become an important topic (Day, Gronn, and Salas 2006). Transformational leadership effects have been formally studied for face-to-face and virtual teams (Purvanova and Bono 2009; Schaubroeck, Lam, and Cha 2007). Significant work has been done on different types of teams such as senior management teams (Wageman et al. 2008), comparing the importance of vertical and shared leadership elements (Pearce, Conger, and Locke 2008), representative teams and organizational democracy (Clarke 2006), and the effects of formal leadership roles on individual performance (Day, Sin, and Chen 2004), among other topics.

Transformational Leadership

Although some studies still usefully point out the utility of transactional approaches (e.g., Vecchio, Justin, and Pearce 2008), the debate over the effectiveness of transformational leadership over transactional leadership (e.g., Schriesheim et al. 2006) has subsided with a more reasonable acknowledgment that both styles are needed in different situations to different degrees (O'Shea et al. 2009). One of the key elements, change, has received a significant amount of research on the public sector side. For example, Fernandez and Pitts (2007) investigated the array of factors enhancing or diminishing change in an educational setting, Wright and Pandey (2009) found more transformational leadership at the municipal level than has been assumed by scholars, Dull (2008) examined the prime importance of credibility for public leaders, and Washington and Hacker (2005) studied the critical need for public managers to fully understand policy changes for better implementation.

Although charismatic leadership is typically considered a subtype of transformational leadership, it continues to receive a great deal of interest. Sosik (2005) found that approximately 11 percent of the positive performance variance was due to the presence of charisma in the case of five organizations, while Rowold and Heinitz in their study (2007) found that charismatic leadership had a significant impact only on subjective perceptions of performance, not on profit. Work by de Hoogh et al. (2005) discriminated the subtle but significant differences in the operation of charisma in the private versus public sectors, finding that leader responsibility makes a difference in charismatic appeal. Javidian and Waldman (2003) also found that charismatic leadership was a potent force in the public sector. Innumerable studies and books have examined negative charisma, among them Cha and Edmondson (2006), which looked at the long-term disenchantment effect, and Tourish and Vatcha (2005), which looked at charisma leading to corruption at Enron. Related to negative charisma is an increase in research on the nature of other types of negative leadership by various names (Rosenthal and Pittinsky 2006; Schilling (2009).

Among the other aspects of transformational leadership that have received considerable attention include the effects of vision (e.g., Strange and Mumford 2005), the role of positive emotions and mood contagion (e.g., Bono and Ilies 2006), and the effect of those positive emotions on service relationships (Liao and Chuang 2007). Strategic leadership is closely aligned with transformational leadership, but it focuses more on how ideas are selected, how decisions are made, and the subsequent implementation (e.g., Boal and Hooijberg 2001; Pajunen 2006). Discussions of strategic leadership at the administrative level have been more muted in the public sector because of issues related to democratic accountability, but it has not been entirely overlooked (Fairholm 2009).

Ethics and Leadership

The mainstream leadership literature has finally started to come of age in looking at ethics in more than an ad hoc framework. Three different perspectives have emerged (Trevino, Weaver, and Reynolds 2006) that are distinctive enough to describe, but the ideal-type models sketched here inevitably have a good deal of overlap as articulated by various theorists. The ethical leadership model (e.g., Brown and Trevino 2006) focuses on moral management at a more transactional level and ethical standards at the organizational level (Waldman and Siegel 2008). What do leaders do to support ethical and moral behavior, and what do they need to do in order to make sure that organizations themselves are ethical?

A second model is the servant leadership model (e.g., Greenleaf 1977; Liden et al. 2008), which focuses more on supporting followers via participation, empowerment, and development. How can leaders make sure that the organization is about the employees and end users? A more recent version of servant leadership is spiritual leadership, which emphasizes membership and calling (Fry, Vitucci, and Cedillo 2005) to balance transformational needs that focus primarily on the organization (Parolini, Patterson and Winston 2009).

A third model is authentic leadership, which tends to focus on self-awareness, honesty, and transparency (Avolio and Gardner 2005; Yammarino et al. 2008). How can leaders have integrity in a multifaceted world? All these themes have been extensively discussed in the public sector literature for some time in journals such as *Public Integrity* and indirectly in both the ethics and management literatures (Menzel 2007). A current example of a relatively new theme in the public sector is "affective" leadership, which stresses the need to take into consideration the emotional labor so common in the public sector (Newman, Guy, and Mastracci 2009).

Trust has continued to be an important topic in the mainstream (no matter the research paradigm) and in the public sector. Trust is invariably highlighted by popular writers such as Covey (2009), and the mainstream literature has shown the power of positive organizational behaviors as emerging from select traits such as hope, optimism, resiliency, and other variables (Luthans 2007), and has provided careful analyses of the subelements of trust (Burke et al. 2007). Extensive research has been done about trust in government. This includes Newell, Reeher, and Ronayne's edited volume (2008) on building trust through values-based leadership, self-awareness, coaching, using teams effectively, providing high performance (good value), collaborating, and using good networking skills. Empirical research has shown that although citizen participation and involvement can positively affect trust, agency or government performance is the stronger factor ultimately (Vigoda-Gadot and Mizrahi 2008; Wang and Van Wart 2007).

Methods

Because of the complexity of approaches, factors, and interactions, the strength of research methods is a major concern relative to the perceived credibility of the field from a scholarly perspective.

Although popular and quasi-academic products are not expected to provide the same level of rigor, the scholarly literature should provide clearly enunciated constructs, carefully conceived hypotheses, and well-crafted empirical arguments (Yammarino and Dansereau 2008). In a 2005 meta-analysis, Yammarino et al. explored the conceptual accuracy of seventeen different approaches to leadership: Ohio State, contingency, participative, charismatic, transformational, leader-member exchange, information processing/implicit, substitutes, romance, self-leadership, multiple linkage, multilevel/leaderplex, individualized, path goal, vertical dyad linkage, situational, and influence tactics. Their concern was that the four major levels of analysis, "individuals or persons (independent human beings), dyads (two person groups and interpersonal relationships), groups (work groups and teams), and organizations (collectives larger than groups and groups of groups)," are commonly but inappropriately blended or conflated, thereby confounding good theoretical modeling practices (Yammarino et al. 2005, 880). They found that "while the literature is vast and growing, relatively few studies in any of the areas of leadership research have addressed levels-of-analysis, and inference drawing. Nevertheless, the findings reported are encouraging, as levels issues are still relatively new to the leadership field and some progress has clearly been made in the last decade" (879). Simultaneously, the postmodern approaches have emphasized qualitative techniques such as biography (Shamir, Dayan-Horesh, and Adler 2005) and narrative inquiry (O'Spina and Dodge 2005).

Leadership in Crisis Management

All organizations can and do have crises from time to time, but their frequency and severity are much affected by the quality of leadership (Tichy and Bennis 2007; Boin and 't Hart 2003). Good leaders have contingency plans (mitigation) to prevent many crises altogether, prepare for a variety of plausible events, respond quickly and effectively when crises occur, and are able to move the affected community and responding organizations back to normalcy after the event in a reasonable timeframe.

Emergency response agencies have a special challenge in dealing with catastrophic events that are very large or unusual, or simply catch agencies off guard (Farazmand 2001). The Katrina/Rita crisis has both entered the national psyche and received tremendous scholarly attention. An entire special issue of *Public Administration Review* in 2007 looked at the roots of administrative failure in the wake of Katrina. The failures of leadership in this event got wide coverage in all the major public administration journals. For example, Kapucu and Van Wart (2006, 2008) compared the administrative successes of the "horde of hurricanes" that inundated Florida in 2004 to the leadership failures experienced in New Orleans with Katrina.

Biographical Case Studies

It was not many years ago that case studies of administrators were scarce and nearly always atheoretical. The biographies of outstanding leaders not only commemorate the qualities of professionalism and perseverance, but serve as valuable teaching tools as well. This deficit has been remedied by numerous biographical case studies, as well as books devoted to significant administrative leaders. In the journal *Public Integrity,* cases include those of George C. Marshall, known for the Marshall Plan (Pops 2006), Dag Hammarskjold, the strong-willed leader of the United Nations from 1953 to 1961 (Lyon 2006–7), and Sam Medina, an everyday moral exemplar (Rugeley and Van Wart 2006). "Administrative profiles" have also been highlighted in *Public Administration Review.* They include the case of Charles Rossotti of the Internal

Revenue Service (Rainey and Thompson 2006), Elmer Staats, who headed the Government Accountability Office (Callahan 2006), and Sean O'Keefe at NASA (Lambright 2008). The IBM Center for the Business of Government provided a volume including short profiles in leadership, specifically seeking out administrative leaders who were not cabinet secretaries (Morales 2007). Of course, many biographies about political and business leaders are published in the popular press, but one that stands out as focusing on an administrative leader is that of Colin Powell (Harari 2002).

Trait and Competency Models

Trait and competency research is alive and well in the organizational world, despite ongoing debates (Hollenbeck, McCall, and Silzer 2006). These debates pit applied and pure researchers against each other. Critics argue that competency models are based on unrealistic assumptions: a single set of characteristics that adequately describes effective leaders, independence of context and trait interaction, and senior management bias for simplistic presentations. Essentially, they argue, competency models are a "descendant of the long-discredited 'great man' theory." Zaccaro (2007), while acknowledging the potential of a trait-competency approach, notes that the value will also be limited unless researchers combine traits and attributes in conceptually meaningful ways that predict leadership. Contemporary critics argue that competency models are excessively individually oriented and leader-centric from discursive and constructionist perspectives (Bolden and Gosling 2006; Carroll, Levy, and Richmond 2008). Proponents argue that competency models have utility because they summarize the experience and insight of seasoned leaders, specify a range of useful behavior, provide a powerful tool for self-development, and outline a framework useful for leadership effectiveness. Yukl, Gordon, and Tabor (2002) use a hierarchical taxonomy with task, relations, and change behavior metacategories that utilizes confirmatory factor analysis to provide empirical support to competency approaches.

Although there are more than eighty-eight thousand units of government in the United States when states, counties, municipalities of various types, school districts, and special districts are counted, the civilian federal government is in a class of its own because of its size, constituting about 11 percent of the employees in American government (U.S. OMB 2009). Because of its resources and prestige, it has unique opportunities to lead when it chooses to do so. One area where it has been generally strong is in leadership research.

One reason for the quality of federal data is because it has been very strong at setting up the systems to critique itself through the Government Accountability Office, Merit Systems Protection Board (MSPB), and inspectors general of the various agencies. The reports of these agencies and offices are, in general, exceptionally well researched and cogently written (see, for example, U.S. Government Accountability Office 2006; Merit System Protection Board 2007). The quality of data provided means that academic research has much to work with, and not only are analyses of the degree of success forthcoming, but so, too, is the analysis of its leadership (e.g., Menzel 2006; Light 2008). The Office of Personnel Management has long tried to provide leadership in applied leadership models (U.S. OPM 1999, 2006), which has encouraged the use of rigorous competency models by academics as well (Van Wart 2003, 2005). Using their own data set, Thach and Thompson (2007) provided a detailed competency comparison of private and public (and nonprofit) organizations. While there was a great deal of similarity, significant differences emerged where business emphasized time management, self-knowledge, and marketing in contrast to the public and nonprofit sectors, which emphasized conflict management and being inspirational.[4]

Integrated Models and Approaches to Leadership

The urge for integrative theories in the popular literature is relatively constant and has led to prescriptive, normative, universalistic, and relatively simplistic models. Though they may be inspiring and provide numerous useful tips, they are not in general rigorous, especially from a contextual perspective.

The most rigorous and elegant integrative model from the scientific community is generally considered to be Bass's "full range" leadership model (1985, 1996), which merges both transactional and transformational approaches. It has found wide support and has been reported to include up to 70 percent of the variance of leadership factors in some studies. As powerful as this may be at a macrolevel, it is still highly universalistic (noncontextual) and simplistic (it accounts for only the broadest behaviors). Thus, there has been a call by the more traditional empiricists for more descriptively precise theories, as well as a call by the newer postmodern theorists for more complex and relational theories.

Avolio (2007) suggests that integrative theories must contain five elements: cognitive elements of leaders and followers, individual and group behaviors, the historical context, the proximal or internal context, and the distal or environmental context. This is a tall order because so many simultaneous spheres are involved, each with numerous factors that make it nearly impossible to represent in more than a descriptive framework. Some examples of such models from the mainstream are Yukl's flexible leadership theory model (2008), Hunt's extended multiple organizational level model (1996), Boal and Hoojiberg's integrated strategic leadership model (2001), Pearce and Conger's shared leadership model (2003, 2008), and Uhl-Bien, Marion, and McKelvey's complexity adaptive systems theory (2007).

One of the significant challenges in organizing leadership research as well as teaching it to practitioners is the enormous situational variety related to different sectors, organizing structures, levels of analysis, and focus of analysis. Even if one narrows the focus to organizational leadership, is one addressing the private or public sector, with their different emphases on profit maximization and competition versus the public good and governance; examining a hierarchical or a team-based organization; distinguishing among the competencies for a frontline supervisor or an agency head; or focusing on managing for results versus the effects of gender, power, or ethics on leadership? While normal science and deep understanding are built upon individual cases, ultimately classes of cases are aligned into categories and types and midlevel theories, which are further aggregated into macrolevel theories. Although mainstream leadership research has been strong at the empirical and middle levels, leadership research has had difficulty agreeing to frameworks to incorporate the disparate theories referenced earlier (i.e., transactional, transformational, distributed, servant).

Integral leadership (aka integrative leadership) focuses on cross-boundary problem solving that elevates the community (Crosby and Bryson 2005; Crosby and Kiedrowski 2008) in the tradition established by Burns (1978). In line with Burns's distinction, it emphasizes "transforming" leadership (raising the consciousness of followers to solve problems through enlightenment as much as self-interest) rather than merely transformational (i.e., change-oriented) leadership, which tends to be more executive and top-down oriented.

Van Wart (2004) frames leadership from an individual and organizational perspective, using a "leadership action cycle" to integrate transactional, transformational, and distributed approaches with particular reference to public sector settings. His model includes five major leader domains—assessments, characteristics, styles, behaviors, and evaluation/development—ultimately incorporating seventy factors. Van Wart's framework is designed to be a useful tool for relating research studies to an overarching context and as a teaching matrix of concrete leadership and management mechanics.

Matthew Fairholm (2004) frames leadership more broadly from a public values perspective. He emphasizes "five leadership perspectives (ranging from leadership as equivalent to scientific management, to leadership being a whole-soul or spiritual endeavor) held by public managers and discusses their implications for public administration." In doing so, he provides a classical apology for administrative leadership. Fernandez (2005) looks at the critical factors leading to superintendent success (educational performance) using an integrative framework and a large data set of Texas school districts. He found that more than half of the variance in organizational performance could be explained by six variables: community support, task difficulty, experience, promotion of change, choice of style, and internal management. While community support had a direct, positive relationship with performance, in other cases variables had nonlinear effects, such as task difficulty, which moderated the choice of style and internal management emphasis, and promotion of change, which had a short-term negative effect because of disruption. Fernandez and Pitts (2007) followed up with a study of leadership change.

RESEARCH GAPS, WEAKNESSES, AND CONCERNS

A number of the major gaps identified by recent reviews have been at least partially addressed. In terms of importance, leadership studies in the public sector have blossomed from being marginalized, when Terry (1995) did his review, to being a recognized area of research interest. In addition to public leadership scholarship, enough materials have been generated with a public sector focus that classes in the area are no longer entirely derivative of materials from business, psychology, and education scholars (Denhardt and Denhardt 2006; Van Wart 2008; Fairholm and Fairholm 2009).

Public leadership theory has followed into more formal aspects of postmodern theory (e.g., complexity and chaos theory) but has integrated collaborative, collective, and network issues with gusto. For example, the affective leadership research of Newman, Guy, and Mastracci (2009) is clearly postmodern in approach. As organizations have flattened in the corporate and agency worlds, distributed theories looking at self-leadership, team leadership, and shared leadership have matured, but more can be done in the administrative leadership arena. Transformational leadership studies have become more careful in their use of constructs and have narrowed their specifications to be more useful and to help build nonuniversalistic theory. Much work needs to be done in this regard. The mainstream has finally caught up with the public sector ethics literature in terms of articulation of conceptual framework. Traditional positivist methods have improved in the field as a whole in terms of levels of analysis and careful model building, but both the mainstream and administrative leadership fields are still rife with impressionistic models utilizing convenience data sets. Some areas in which there has been special interest and need have developed more robustly. Crisis management in the aftermath of 9/11 is one case. The development of teaching materials, case studies, and more sophisticated trait and competency models is another example where materials have blossomed that were formerly scant or out of date with current leadership emphases. Finally, the field as a whole has settled into a better understanding of integrated theory building, from the simplistic trait models of the first half of the twentieth century, the simplistic two-factor matrices of the 1960s through the 1980s, and the interesting but exaggerated debates about leadership versus management and transactional methods versus transformational methods from the late 1970s through the 1990s. Today, with the addition of more theoretically grounded distributed leadership literature, and the enriching nature of postmodern approaches warning us of the excesses of positivism (and its attendant methodologies) and the reification of power, there are finally a variety of comprehensive approaches with a better appreciation of the virtues (and limits) of those approaches.

Nonetheless, there are still a few concerns that are apparent from reviewing the field as well as reviewing manuscripts for publication. One concern is that the strong convictions of many scholars interested in the field tend to lead to implicit if not explicit statements of certitude that they have "the answer" to the leadership question. Such assertions are useful for popular books sold in airports, with their breezy lists of favorite tips and personalized models. This leads to an unhelpful assertion or inference that one type of leadership study is more important than another. An example of this occurred in the mainstream during the 1980s when transformational leadership roared onto the scene and there was a dismissal of management as routine and plentiful, if not downright trivial and potentially insidious. Second, there is still a substantial problem with studies being able to site the context of their "problem" in the bigger picture, which consequently reduces their generalizability and usefulness as normal science. Nevertheless, the recent advances in both the mainstream, in terms of better balance, and the public leadership literature, in terms of self-consciousness and depth, have been impressive.

SUMMARY AND CONCLUSION

The importance of public sector leadership is profound but, historically, has lagged behind the mainstream. However, public sector leadership is slowly becoming its own specialized area of study. Political, organization, and collaborative leadership are distinctive subareas within public sector leadership. An important development in all fields of leadership study is postmodernism. In leadership studies, postmodernism is a broad critique of the literature as being too status quo oriented with an emphasis on leadership from the top down, positivism, empiricism, and static power structures. This perspective aligns with studies emphasizing gender issues, contextual and ethnographic research strategies, complexity and chaos theories, and integral or community approaches, among others. Focusing on organizational leadership, the aspects that have developed most in recent years include distributed or horizontal leadership, biographical case studies, crisis management leadership, analysis of federal leadership and applied competency models useful for government, network and collaborative leadership, and integrated frameworks or holistic perspectives of leadership. The field of public sector leadership is generally more nuanced in terms of specifying types of leadership, the factors involved, and the use of different perspectives. As important, it has achieved a critical mass and can be considered a recognizable and maturing field of interest.

NOTES

1. The review focuses on the last ten years of research but emphasizes the last five years when possible.
2. See Van Wart (2005) for a review of prior literature.
3. OMB historical tables, 2009, reflecting the data from 2007 (U.S. OMB 2009).
4. It should be noted that the first item is similar to other competency priority listings: honesty and integrity. The other matched top competencies are somewhat more highly ranked than on similar lists in the past, but these data reflect holistic assessments discussed above: collaboration (team player) and developing others. Adaptability was fourth for the private sector and fifth for the public and nonprofit sector.

REFERENCES

Abramson, M.A., J.D. Breul, and J.M. Kamensky. 2006. *Six Trends Transforming Government.* Washington, DC: IBM Center for Business of Government.
Alimo-Metcalfe, B., and J. Alban-Metcalfe. 2005. Leadership: Time for a new direction? *Leadership* 1 (1): 51–71.

Alvesson, M., and S. Sveningsson. 2003. Managers doing leadership: The extra ordinarization of the mundane. *Human Relations* 56 (12): 1435–1459.

Arvey, R.D., Z. Zhang, B.J. Avolio, and R.F. Krueger. 2007. Developmental and genetic determinants of leadership role occupancy among women. *Journal of Applied Psychology* 92 (3): 693–706.

Avolio, B.J. 2007. Promoting more integrative strategies for leadership theory-building. *American Psychologist* 62 (1) 25–33.

Avolio, B.J., and W.L. Gardner. 2005. Authentic leadership development: Getting to the root of positive forms of leadership. *Leadership Quarterly* 16:315–338.

Barker, R.A. 2001. The nature of leadership. *Human Relations* 54 (4): 469–494.

Bass, B.M. 1985. *Leadership and Performance Beyond Expectations.* New York: Free Press.

———. 1996. *A New Paradigm of Leadership: An Inquiry into Transformational Leadership.* Alexandria, VA: U.S. Army Research Institute for the Behavioral and Social Sciences.

———. 2008. *The Bass Handbook of Leadership: Theory, Research, and Managerial Applications.* New York: Free Press.

Bennis, W. 2007. The challenges of leadership in the modern world. *American Psychologist* 62 (1): 2–5.

Bevir, M. 2006. Democratic governance: Systems and radical perspective. *Public Administration Review* 66 (3): 426–436.

Blake, R.R., and Mouton, J.S. 1964. *The Managerial Grid.* Houston, TX: Gulf.

Boal, K.B., and R. Hooijberg. 2001. Strategic leadership research: Moving on. *Leadership Quarterly* 11:515–549.

Bolden, R., and J. Gosling. 2006. Leadership competencies: Time to change the tune? *Leadership* 2 (2): 147–163.

Boin, A., and P. 't Hart. 2003. Public leadership in times of crisis: Mission impossible? *Public Administration Review* 63 (5): 544–553.

Bono, J.E., and R. Ilies. 2006. Charisma, positive emotions and mood contagion. *Leadership Quarterly* 17:317–334.

Brown, M.E., and L.K. Trevino. 2006. Ethical leadership: A review and future directions. *Leadership Quarterly* 17:595–616.

Burke, C.S., D.E. Sims, E.H. Lazzara, and E. Salas. 2007. Trust in leadership: A multi-level review and integration. *Leadership Quarterly* 18:606–632.

Burke, C.S., K.C. Stagel, C. Klein, G.F. Goodwin, E. Salas, and S.M. Halpin. 2006. What type of leadership behaviors are functional in teams? A meta-analysis. *Leadership Quarterly* 17:288–307.

Burns, J.M. 1978. *Leadership.* New York: HarperCollins.

Callahan, K. 2006. Elmer Boyd Staats and the pursuit of good government. *Public Administration Review* 66 (2): 159–167.

Carroll, B., L. Levy, and D. Richmond. 2008. Leadership as practice: Challenging the competency paradigm. *Leadership* 4 (4): 363–379.

Cha, S.E., and A.C. Edmondson. 2006. When values backfire: Leadership, attribution, and disenchantment in a values-driven organization. *Leadership Quarterly* 17:57–78.

Chen, L. 2008. Leaders or leadership: Alternative approaches to leadership studies. *Management Communication Quarterly* 21 (4): 547–555.

Clarke, M. 2006. A study of the role of "representative" leadership in stimulating organization democracy. *Leadership* 2 (4): 427–450.

Collinson, D. 2006. Rethinking followership: A poststructuralist analysis of follower identities. *Leadership Quarterly* 17:179–89.

Cortada, J.W., S. Dijkstra, G.M. Mooney, and T. Ramsey. 2008. *Government and the Perpetual Collaboration Mandate: Six Worldwide Drivers Demand Customized Strategies.* Somers, NY: IBM Institute for Business Value.

Covey, S.M.R. 2009. Building trust: How the best leaders do it. *Leadership Excellence* 21 (1): 15.

Crosby, B.C., and J.M. Bryson. 2005. *Leadership for the Common Good: Tackling Public Problems in a Shared-Power World.* San Francisco: Jossey-Bass.

Crosby, B.C., and J. Kiedrowski. 2008. Integrative leadership: Observations from a University of Minnesota seminar series. *Integral Leadership Review* 8 (3): 1–14. www.integralleadershipreview.com/archives/2008–06/2008–06-article-crosby.html (accessed July 2010).

Day, D.V., P. Gronn, and E. Salas. 2006. Leadership in team-based organizations: On the threshold of a new era. *Leadership Quarterly* 17:211–216.

Day, D.V., H. Sin, and T.T. Chen. 2004. Assessing the burdens of leadership: Effects of formal leadership roles on individual performance over time. *Personnel Psychology* 57 (3): 573–605.

De Hoogh, A.H.B., D.N. Den Hartog, P.L. Koopman, H. Thierry, P.T. Van den Berg, J.G. Van der Weide, and C.P.M. Wilderom. 2005. Leader motives, charismatic leadership, and subordinate's work attitude in the profit and voluntary sector. *Leadership Quarterly* 16:17–38.

Denhardt, R.B., and J.V. Denhardt. 2006. *The Dance of Leadership: The Art of Leading Business, Government, and Society.* Armonk, NY: M.E. Sharpe.

Drath, W.H., C.D. McCauley, C.J. Palus, W. Van Velsor, P.M.G. O'Connor, and J.B. McGuire. 2008. Direction, alignment, commitment: Toward a more integrative ontology of leadership. *Leadership Quarterly* 19: 635–653.

Dull, M. 2008. Results-model reform leadership: Questions of credible commitment. *Journal of Public Administration Research and Theory* 19 (2): 255–284.

Dunoon, D. 2002. Rethinking leadership for the public sector. *Australian Journal of Public Administration* 61 (3): 3–18.

Edwards, M. 2009. Seeing integral leadership through three important lenses: Developmental, ecological and governance. *Integral Leadership Review* 9 (1): 1–13.

Eagly, H., and L.L. Carli. 2007. *Through the Labyrinth: The Truth about How Women Become Leaders.* Boston: Harvard Business School Press.

Fairholm, M.R. 2004. Perspectives on the practice of leadership. *Public Administration Review* 64 (5): 577–590.

———. 2009. Leadership and organizational strategy. *Innovation Journal* 14 (1): article 3 (online). http://www.innovation.cc/scholarly-style/fairholm3.pdf (accessed July 2010).

Fairholm, M.R., and G.W. Fairholm. 2009. *Understanding Leadership Perspectives.* New York: Springer.

Fairhurst, G.T. 2007. *Discursive Leadership: In Conversation with Leadership Psychology.* Thousand Oaks, CA: Sage.

Farazmand, A. 2001. Crisis and emergency management. In *Handbook of Crisis and Emergency Management,* ed. A. Farazmand, pp. 1–10. New York: Marcel Dekker.

Fernandez. S. 2005. Developing and testing an integrative framework of public sector leadership: Evidence from the public education arena. *Journal of Public Administration Research and Theory* 15 (2): 197–217.

Fernandez, S., and D.W. Pitts. 2007. Under what conditions do public managers favor and pursue organizational change? *American Review of Public Administration* 37 (3): 324–341.

Foucault, M. 1970. *The Order of Things.* New York: Pantheon.

———. 1972. *Archaeology of Knowledge.* New York: Pantheon.

Ford, J. 2006. Discourses of leadership: Gender, identity and contradiction in a UK public sector organization. *Leadership* 2 (1): 77–99.

Fry, L.W., S. Vitucci, and M. Cedillo. 2005. Spiritual leadership and army transformation: Theory, measurement, and establishing a baseline. *Leadership Quarterly* 16:835–862.

Goffee, R., and G. Jones. 2009. Authentic leadership. *Leadership Excellence* 26 (7): 17.

Greenleaf, R.K. 1977. *Servant Leadership: A Journey into the Nature of Legitimate Power and Greatness.* New York: Paulist Press.

Gronn, P. 2002. Distributed leadership as a unit of analysis. *Leadership Quarterly* 13:481–490.

Hersey, P., and K.H. Blanchard. 1969. Life cycle theory of leadership. *Training and Development Journal* 23 (1): 26–34.

Harari, O. 2002. *The Leadership Secrets of Colin Powell.* New York: McGraw-Hill.

Hollander, E.P. 1958. Conformity, status, and idiosyncrasy credit. *Psychological Review* 65:117–127.

Hollenbeck, G.P., M.W. McCall, and R.F. Silzer. 2006. Leadership competency models. *Leadership Quarterly* 17 (4): 398–413.

House, R.J., and T.R. Mitchell. 1974. Path-goal theory of leadership. *Contemporary Business* 3 (Fall): 81–98.

Hunt, J.G. 1996. *Leadership: A New Synthesis.* Newbury Park, CA: Sage.

Javidian, M., and D.A. Waldman. 2003. Exploring charismatic leadership in the public sector: Measurement and consequences. *Public Administration Review* 63 (2): 229–242.

Kaiser, R.B., R. Hogan, and S.B. Craig. 2008. Leadership and the fate of organizations. *American Psychologist* 63 (2): 96–110.

Kapucu, N., and M. Van Wart. 2006. The evolving role of the public sector in managing catastrophic disasters: Lessons learned. *Administration and Society* 38 (3): 1–30.

————. 2008. Making matters worse: Anatomy of leadership failures in catastrophic events. *Administration and Society* 40 (7): 711–740.

Kellerman, B. 2008. *Followership: How Followers Are Creating Change and Changing Leaders.* Boston: Harvard Business School Press.

Kelly, S. 2008. Leadership: A categorical mistake? *Human Relations* 61 (6): 763–782.

Kettl, D. 2006. Managing boundaries in American administration: The collaboration imperative. *Public Administration Review* 66 (supplement): 10–19.

Lambright, W.H. 2008. Leadership and change at NASA: Sean O'Keefe as administrator. *Public Administration Review* 68 (2): 230–240.

Lawler, J. 2008. Individualization and public sector leadership. *Public Administration* 86 (1): 21–34.

Lemay, L. 2009. The practice of collective and strategic leadership in the public sector. *Innovation Journal: The Public Sector Innovation Journal* 14 (1): 1–19.

Liao, H., and A. Chuang. 2007. Transforming service employees and climate: A multilevel, multisource examination of transformational leadership in building long-term service relationships. *Journal of Applied Psychology* 92 (4): 1006–1019.

Lichtenstein, B.B., and D.A. Plowman. 2009. The leadership of emergence: A complex systems leadership theory of emergence at successive organizational levels. *Leadership Quarterly* 20:617–630.

Liden, R.C., S.J. Wayne, H. Zhao, and D. Henderson. 2008. Servant leadership: Development of a multidimensional measure and multi-level assessment. *Leadership Quarterly* 19:161–177.

Light, P.C. 2008. A government ill executed: The depletion of the federal service. *Public Administration Review* 68 (3): 413–419.

Loveday, B. 2008. Performance management and the decline of leadership within public services in the United Kingdom. *Policing* 2 (1): 120–130.

Luthans, F. 2007. Emerging positive organizational behavior. *Journal of Management* 33 (3): 321–349.

Lyon, A.J. 2006–7. Moral motives and policy actions: The case of Dag Hammarskjold at the United Nations. *Public Integrity* 9 (1): 70–95.

Maak, T., and N.M. Pless, eds. 2006. *Responsible Leadership: A Relational Approach.* London: Routledge.

McCrimmon, M. 2007. Reframing leadership for a modern age. *Integral Leadership Review* 7 (2): 1–6.

McGuirc, M. 2006. Collaborative public management: Assessing what we know and how we know it. *Public Administration Review* 66 (supplement): 33–43.

Menzel, D.C. 2006. The Katrina aftermath: A failure of federalism or leadership? *Public Administration Review* 66 (6): 808–812.

————. 2007. *Ethics Management for Public Administrators: Building Organizations of Integrity.* Armonk, NY: M.E. Sharpe.

Merit System Protection Board. 2007. *Merit Principles Survey: 2007.* www.mspb.gov/netsearch/viewdocs.aspx?docnumber=288965&version=289309&application=ACROBAT (see parts B–D in particular) (accessed July 2010).

Mishel, L., J. Bernstein, and H. Sheirholz. 2009. *The State of Working America: 2008–2009.* Washington, DC: Economic Policy Institute.

Morales, A. 2007. *Management Matters: The Business of Government.* Washington, DC: IBM Global Business Services.

Morse, R.S., T.F. Buss, and C.M. Kinghorn, eds. 2007. *Transforming Public Leadership for the 21st Century.* Armonk, NY: M.E. Sharpe.

Newell, T., G. Reeher, and P. Ronayne, eds. 2008. *The Trusted Leader: Building the Relationships That Make Government Work.* Washington, DC: CQ Press.

Newland, C.A. 1994. A field of strangers in search of a discipline: Separatism of public management research from public administration. *Public Administration Review* 54 (5): 486–495.

Newman, M.A., M.E. Guy, and S.H. Mastracci. 2009. Affective leadership and emotional labor. *Public Administration Review* 69 (1): 6–20.

O'Leary, R., C. Gerard, and L.B. Bingham. 2006. Introduction to the symposium on collaborative public management. *Public Administration Review* 66 (supplement): 6–9.

O'Shea, P.G., R.J. Foti, N.M.A. Hauenstein, and P. Bycio. 2009. Are the best leaders both transformational and transactional? A pattern analysis. *Leadership* 5 (2): 237–259.

O'Spina, S., and J. Dodge. 2005. It's about time: Catching method up to meaning—The usefulness of narrative inquiry in public administration research. *Public Administration Review* 65 (2): 143–157.

Osborn, R.N., and J.G. Hunt. 2007. Leadership and the choice of order: Complexity and hierarchical perspectives near the edge of chaos. *Leadership Quarterly* 18:319–340.

Pajunen, K. 2006. The more things change, the more they remain the same? Evaluating strategic leadership in organizational transformations. *Leadership* 2 (3): 341–366.

Parolini, J., K. Patterson, and B. Winston. 2009. Distinguishing between transformational and servant leadership. *Leadership and Organizational Development Journal* 30 (3): 274–291.

Pearce, C.L., and J.A. Conger. 2003. *Shared Leadership: Reframing the Hows and Whys of Leadership.* Thousand Oaks, CA: Sage.

Pearce, C.L., J.A. Conger, and E. Locke. 2008. Shared leadership theory. *Leadership Quarterly* 19: 622–628.

Pops, G. 2006. The ethical leadership of George C. Marshall. *Public Integrity* 8 (2): 165–185.

Purvanova, R.K., and J.E. Bono. 2009. Transformational leadership in context: Face-to-face and virtual teams. *Leadership Quarterly* 20:343–357.

Rainey, H.G., and J. Thompson. 2006. Leadership and the transformation of a major institution: Charles Rossotti and the Internal Revenue Service. *Public Administration Review* 66 (4): 596–604.

Rosenthal, S.A., and T.L. Pittinsky. 2006. Narcissistic leadership. *Leadership Quarterly* 17:617–633.

Rowold, J., and K. Heinitz. 2007. Transformational and charismatic leadership: Assessing the convergent, divergent and criterion validity of the MLK and the CKS. *Leadership Quarterly* 18:121–133.

Rugeley, C., and M. Van Wart. 2006. Everyday moral exemplars. *Public Integrity* 8 (4): 381–394.

Schaubroeck, J., S.S.K. Lam, and S.E. Cha. 2007. Embracing transformational leadership: Team values and the impact of leader behavior on team performance. *Journal of Applied Psychology* 92 (4): 1020–1030.

Schilling. J. 2009. From ineffectiveness to destruction: A qualitative study on the meaning of negative leadership. *Leadership* 5 (1): 102–128.

Schriesheim, C.A., S.L. Castro, X. Zhou, and L.A. DeChurch. 2006. An investigation of path-goal and transformational leadership theory predictions at the individual level of analysis. *Leadership Quarterly* 17:21–38.

Schweigert, F.J. 2007. Learning to lead: Strengthening the practice of community leadership. *Leadership* 3 (3): 325–342.

Shamir, B., H. Dayan-Horesh, and D. Adler. 2005. Leading by biography: Towards a life-story approach to the study of leadership. *Leadership* 1 (1): 13–29.

Sosik, J.J. 2005. The role of personal values in the charismatic leadership of corporate managers: A model and preliminary field study. *Leadership Quarterly* 16:221–244.

Strange, J.M., and M.D. Mumford. 2005. The origins of vision: Effects of reflection, models, and analysis. *Leadership Quarterly* 16:121–148.

Terry, L. 1995. *Leadership of Public Bureaucracies: The Administrator as Conservator.* Thousand Oaks, CA: Sage.

Thach, E., and K.J. Thompson. 2007. Trading places: Examining leadership competencies between for-profit vs. public and non-profit leaders. *Leadership and Organization Development Journal* 28 (4): 356–375.

Thompson, A.M., and J.L. Perry. 2006. Collaboration processes: Inside the black box. *Public Administration Review* 66 (supplement): 20–32.

Tourish, D., and N. Vatcha. 2005. Charismatic leadership and corporate cultism at Enron: The elimination of dissent, the promotion of conformity and organizational collapse. *Leadership* 1 (4): 455–480.

Tichy, N.M., and W.G. Bennis. 2007. *Judgment: How Winning Leaders Make Great Calls.* New York: Penguin.

Trevino, L.K., G.R. Weaver, and S.J. Reynolds. 2006. Behavioral ethics in organizations: A review. *Journal of Management* 32:951–990.

Trottier, T., M. Van Wart, and X. Wang. 2008. Examining the nature and significance of leadership in government organizations. *Public Administration Review* 68 (2): 319–333.

Uhl-Bien, M. 2006. Relational leadership theory: Exploring the social processes of leadership and organizing. *Leadership Quarterly* 17:654–676.

Uhl-Bien, M., R. Marion, and B. McKelvey. 2007. Complexity leadership theory: Shifting leadership from the industrial age to the knowledge era. *Leadership Quarterly* 18:298–318.

U.S. Government Accountability Office. 2006. *Catastrophic Disasters: Enhanced Leadership, Capabilities, and Accountability Controls Will Improve the Effectiveness of the Nation's Preparedness, Response, and Recovery System.* GAO-06-618. Washington, DC: USGAO.

U.S. Office of Management and Budget (U.S. OMB). 2009. Historical tables (17.5). www.whitehouse.gov/omb/budget/fy2009/pdf/hist.pdf (accessed July 2010).

U.S. Office of Personnel Management (U.S. OPM). 1999. *High Performance Leaders—A Competency Model.* Drafted by L.D. Eyde. D.J. Gregory, T.W. Muldrow, and P.K. Mergen. Report PRDC-99–02. Washington, DC: Employment Service—Personnel and Development Center.

———. 2006. Executive core qualifications. Washington, DC: U.S. OPM. www.chcoc.gov/Transmittals/Attachments/trans751.pdf.

Van Slyke, D.M., and R.W. Alexander. 2006. Public service leadership: Opportunities for clarity and coherence. *American Review of Public Administration* 36 (4): 362–374.

Van Vugt, M., R. Hogan, and R.B. Kaiser. 2008. Leadership, followership, and evolution. *American Psychologist* 63 (3): 182–196.

Van Wart, M. 2003. Public sector leadership theory: An assessment. *Public Administration Review* 6 (2): 214–228.

———. 2004. A comprehensive model of organizational leadership: The leadership action cycle. *International Journal of Organization Theory and Behavior* 7 (2): 173–208.

———. 2005. *Dynamics of Leadership in Public Service: Theory and Practice.* Armonk, NY: M.E. Sharpe.

———. 2008. *Leadership in Public Organizations: An Introduction.* Armonk, NY: M.E. Sharpe.

Van Wart, M., and E. Berman. 1999. Contemporary public sector productivity values: Narrower scope, tougher standards, and new rules of the game. *Public Productivity and Management Review* 22 (3): 326–347.

Vecchio, R.P., J.E. Justin, and C.L. Pearce. 2008. The utility of transactional and transformational leadership for predicting performance and satisfaction with a path-goal theory framework. *Journal of Occupational and Organizational Psychology* 81 (1): 71–82.

Vigoda-Gadot, E., and S. Mizrahi. 2008. Public sector management and the democratic ethos: A 5-year study of key relationships in Israel. *Journal of Public Administration Research and Theory* 18 (1): 79–108.

Vroom, V.H., and P.W. Yetton. 1973. *Leadership and Decision-making.* Pittsburgh: University of Pittsburgh Press.

Wageman, R., D.N. Nunes, J.A. Burruss, and J.R. Hackman. 2008. *Senior Leadership Teams: What It Takes to Make Them Great.* Boston: Harvard Business School Press.

Waldman, D.A., and D. Siegel. 2008. Defining social responsibility. *Leadership Quarterly* 19:117–131.

Wang, X., and M. Van Wart. 2007. When public participation in administration leads to trust: An empirical assessment of managers' perceptions. *Public Administration Review* 67 (2): 265–278.

Washington, M., and M. Hacker. 2005. Why change fails: Knowledge counts. *Leadership and Organizational Development Journal* 26 (5): 400–411.

Wright, B.E., and S.K. Pandey. 2009. Transformational leadership in the public sector: Does structure matter? *Journal of Public Administration Research and Theory:* 20 (1): 75–89.

Yammarino, F.J., and F. Dansereau. 2008. Multi-level nature of and multi-level approaches to leadership. *Leadership Quarterly* 19:135–141.

Yammarino, F.J., S.D. Dionne, J.U. Chun, and F. Dansereau. 2005. Leadership and levels of analysis: A state-of-the-science review. *Leadership Quarterly* 16:879–919.

Yammarino, F.J., S.D. Dionne, C.A. Schriesheim, and F. Dansereau. 2008. Authentic leadership and positive organizational behavior: a meso, multi-level perspective. *Leadership Quarterly* 19:693–707.

Yukl, G. 2008. How leaders influence organizational effectiveness. *Leadership Quarterly* 19:708–722.

Yukl, G., A. Gordon, and T. Taber. 2002. A hierarchical taxonomy of leadership behavior: Integrating a half century of behavior research. *Journal of Leadership and Organizational Studies* 9 (1): 15–32.

Zaccaro, S.J. 2007. Trait-based perspectives of leadership. *American Psychologist* 62 (1): 6–16.

CHAPTER 7

ETHICS AND INTEGRITY IN PUBLIC SERVICE

Issues and Challenges

DONALD C. MENZEL

Public administration as a professional field of study and practice is firmly grounded on understanding and applying ethical behavior and practices in public service. This chapter explores the core values that define ethics and integrity in public service, inventories the research literature regarding ethical issues in public administration, identifies obstacles and challenges that confront public administrators who want to lead with integrity, and offers recommendations for becoming ethically competent.

ETHICS AND INTEGRITY DEFINED

There are endless ethics moments throughout life, those occasions when one just does not know what to do in a "right" and "wrong" situation and sometimes in a "right" and "right" situation. They occur in private life and the workplace. And it is much easier to stumble into an ethics quandary than it is to find a way out. Humans err—sometimes with maliciousness in mind, but most of the time bad judgment and misjudgments are made out of ignorance, intolerance, plain stupidity, or the inability to reason through a complicated ethical situation. While the vast majority of government employees try to do the right thing most of the time, even a handful of employees can cause much devastation in the work of government.

If most public employees are ethically motivated, what is the problem? The answer: It is not always easy to figure out what the right thing to do is, especially in complex organizations that have come to dominate modern governance. Rules and regulations, even laws, are helpful, but doing the right thing often means doing more than just following the rules.

Ethics is a term invoked with considerable frequency in the professions, government, and the corporate world. But how might it be defined? Some define ethics as "morality in action"; others assert that ethics involves "a consensus of moral principles." James Norden (2009) offers this definition: "Ethics are the internal rules that drive one to follow or not to follow external rules. Of course, this definition works best when morals are the external rules. Simply being law-abiding begs the ethical question." The definition used in this chapter is as follows: "Ethics are values and principles that guide right and wrong behavior." The key elements of this definition are (1) values and principles, (2) behavior, and (3) right and wrong.

Values and Principles

A value can be an idea, object, practice, or most anything else to which worth is attached. Of course, ethics does not encompass all values. Consider money or status as a value. Most people attach worth to money and status, but we do not call them values that are essential to a definition of ethics. A value that is translated into an ethic can be thrift (remember Benjamin Franklin), cleanliness (remember the startup of McDonald's), piety (remember the Puritan ethic), work (the Protestant ethic), justice, prudence, compassion, charity, courage, benevolence, and so on.

Principles can be considered values in action. That is, a principle is a prescription for determining how to act in a given situation. Consider the Golden Rule, or treating people with dignity, or telling the truth, or treating others with fairness. These principles prescribe appropriate behavior defined in terms of right and wrong. Violating the principle becomes unethical behavior.

Values and principles are also defined by the professions—medicine, law, clergy, accounting, engineering, and others. Professional associations such as the International City/County Management Association (ICMA), the American Planning Association, and the American Society for Public Administration set forth many values and principles that their members are expected to embrace. These values and principles can be classified broadly as public service values and principles. All call for their members to respect the law, promote the public interest, and serve with integrity. At the same time, more specific behaviors can be proscribed. The ICMA, for example, requires its city managers to serve a community for a minimum of two years unless there are mitigating circumstances (e.g., unexpected illness, family crisis, and so forth). Service of shorter tenure is viewed as harmful to the community. Nor can city managers endorse products that might be used in their city government. Endorsements can lead to both the reality and the appearance of a conflict of interest, which would erode public trust and confidence in the governing body as well as the manager.

Behavior

Ethics is not a spectator sport; it is a contact sport as Carol Lewis (1991) so astutely notes. Ethics is about behavior and consequences. Thinking unethical thoughts is possible, but until those thoughts are translated into behavior, there are no consequences to define "right" or "wrong." Ethics shares with law the notion that it is behavior that matters foremost. Ethics is sometimes equated with morality, as the above definitions suggest. However, the act of thinking immoral thoughts can be defined as immoral itself. Consider the case of former president Jimmy Carter. As a presidential candidate in 1976, he was interviewed by *Playboy* magazine. "The reporter asked me if I had ever been guilty of adultery, and his next question was predictable. I replied truthfully. I've looked on a lot of women with lust. I've committed adultery in my heart many times" (Scheer 1976). To Jimmy Carter, lusting was an immoral act though it was not a behavioral act.

Right and Wrong

The final perhaps most important component in defining ethics is "right and wrong" behavior. In years past right and wrong was typically the province of custom, tradition, and religion. Indeed, one essential reason why ethics has become increasingly important in the modern age is the waning influence of custom, tradition, and religion. Right and wrong are now firmly woven into the fabric of professional occupations and individual choice. Thus right and wrong can be viewed as residing within the individual (some would even contend it is innate) or outside his or her being such as prescribed by codes of ethics or law. Indeed, insanity is commonly defined as the inability to differentiate between right and wrong behavior. Ethical values and principles such as the Golden Rule or the admonishment to treat others with respect share with law and morality a common denominator—prescriptions and proscriptions for right and wrong.

Integrity

Integrity goes hand in hand with ethics but yet has some qualities that differentiate it from ethics. Consider how the ICMA approaches it. The ICMA (2008) identifies three dimensions of integrity: personal, professional, and organizational.

> Integrity: Demonstrating fairness, honesty, and ethical and legal awareness in personal and professional relationships and activities (requires knowledge of business and personal ethics; ability to understand issues of ethics and integrity in specific situations). Practices that contribute to this core content area are:

- *Personal Integrity*   Demonstrating accountability for personal actions; conducting personal relationships and activities fairly and honestly
- *Professional Integrity*   Conducting professional relationships and activities fairly, honestly, legally, and in conformance with the ICMA Code of Ethics—requires knowledge of administrative ethics and specifically the ICMA Code of Ethics
- *Organizational Integrity*   Fostering ethical behavior throughout the organization through personal example, management practices, and training (requires knowledge of administrative ethics; ability to instill accountability into operations; and ability to communicate ethical standards and guidelines to others)

Professor J. Patrick Dobel (1999) has written extensively about public integrity. At the personal level, he asserts "integrity covers the wholeness of our life . . . integrity flows from the process through which individuals balance beliefs, decide on the right action, and then summon the courage and self-control to act upon those decisions" (2009, 10). Administrators, of course, are individuals who hold appointed offices in public, including government and nonprofit, organizations. Consequently, one is not simply a "free agent." Rather, personal integrity must be coupled with the obligations of office. Dobel (1999, 21–22) regards public integrity as a set of commitments. He identifies seven:

1. Be truthfully accountable to relevant authorities and publics.
2. Address the public values of the political regime.
3. Build institutions and procedures to achieve goals.
4. Ensure fair and adequate participation of the relevant stakeholders.
5. Demand competent performance effectiveness in the execution of policy.
6. Work for efficiency in the operation of government.
7. Connect policy and program with the self-interest of the pubic and stakeholders in such a way that the purposes are not subverted.

These seven commitments are substantial and demanding for even the most well-intentioned public administrator.

In the next section, the ethics literature is inventoried, with a focus on five issue areas that have attracted scholarly inquiry and often bedevil public administrators: (1) ethical decision making and moral development, (2) ethics laws and regulatory agencies, (3) ethics and organizational performance, (4) ethics management, and (5) the ethical environment.

THE ETHICS LITERATURE

Ethics as a subject has been the topic of study and prescription by philosophers for many centuries, with Western roots dating to the age of antiquity and the pronouncements of Socrates, Plato, and, most notably, Aristotle. Indeed, ethics is often identified as the fount from which knowledge first flowed, as humankind's search for knowing the difference between right and wrong was a fundamental tenet of civilization. These important and enduring philosophies are not the primary focus of the literature reviewed here. Rather, attention is directed at contemporary empirical theory and research published over the past several decades.

Ethical Decision Making and Moral Development

Central to deontological (principle-based reasoning) and teleological (consequences-based reasoning) approaches to ethics, regardless of whether one is examining Kantian ethics or utilitarianism (as espoused by Jeremy Bentham or John Stuart Mill) or Aristotle's treatises on virtue ethics, are ethical decision making and moral development.

These issues are also central to Lawrence Kohlberg's (1980) six stages of moral development that he contends describe an individual's moral reasoning for better or worse. At what he calls the preconventional stage, one responds to obedience and punishment much as a child responds. At the most developed stage, stage 6, one is acting according to universal principles such as justice and fairness. Gandhi and Martin Luther King Jr. are often held out as examples of stage 6 moral development. Of course different values and behaviors are anticipated for the in-between stages. Kohlberg's theory does not presume that there is a natural evolution; in other words, one's moral development does not always advance. Rather, it presumes that one's moral development can reach one stage (2, 3, 4, 5) and never move beyond it.

A growing number of investigators have been drawn to Kohlberg's theory to test relevant hypotheses. Pamela A. Gibson (2009) launched an investigation of the moral reasoning employed by designated ethics officers in federal agencies. After all, would not one expect those who advise others to "practice what they preach"? Her study involved a questionnaire mailed to 231 ethics officials (100 responded). She found that federal ethics officials operate at the "law and order" reasoning stage as defined by the Kohlbergian model. Principled reasoning is a close second. The dominant reasoning of law and order, she speculates, is likely to be the result of the organizational culture.

Another study based on Kohlberg's theory was conducted by Jurkiewicz and Brown (2000). They examined the link between leadership defined as the effective exercise of power in an organization and ethics. They hypothesized that a positive relationship exists between one's level of ethical reasoning and effective leadership. Forty-two chief executive officers of nonprofit organizations in a large metropolitan community formed their database. Using a sophisticated screening process involving academic and practitioner judges who identified a sample of executives as highly effective, they surveyed two equal-size samples of those judged highly effective and those judged noneffective. Rest's Defining Issues Test was the measurement instrument. Their findings support the primary hypothesis that effective executives are more likely than noneffective executives to evaluate moral decisions on the basis of calculated rights, values, or principles (2000, 205).

The reader may be inclined to think that research on ethical decision making and moral development is driven by Kohlbergian theory and Rest's Defining Issues Test (Rest 1986). This is not so. Other investigators have employed case studies to gain insight into the ethical reasoning and moral development of officeholders. For example, Frederickson and Newman (2001) explored the decision by a high-ranking manager in the U.S. Forest Service to resign her position. She "exited with voice" and, according to the investigators, is a moral exemplar. Their theoretical framework was based on Hart's (1992) notion of a moral episode. The episode had to do with Gloria Flora's judgment that, as the supervisor of a national forest in Nevada, she could no longer carry out her stewardship duties in the face of powerful economic and political pressures to exploit protected federal lands from mining, timber production, and livestock grazing. Gloria Flora's more than twenty years of service with the U.S. Forest Service was terminated with less than three years left before vestment in the civil service retirement system. She paid a high price, emotionally and financially, for her moral courage. Frederickson and Newman then ask, Why would she do this? The answer—because she could not compromise her strong belief to do the "right" thing. "She was motivated to act as she did out of a sense of responsibility" (Newman 2001, 360).

Studies of whistle-blowing also typically focus on ethical decision making. Alan Lovell (2003) investigated the behavior of what might be called "near whistle-blowers" among certified accountants and human resources professionals in seven accounting firms in the United Kingdom. Using an interview methodology, he sought answers to three questions: What types of issues produce "ethical twinges" (i.e., some level of ethical discomfort)? Why were these issues ethically problematic? How were they handled or coped with? Nine case examples of suppressed whistle-blowing were reported. The cases paint a picture of organizational life in which "the fear of impairing one's future career prospects was a significant factor shaping the muteness of many of the managers about their respective ethical dilemmas" (201). Lovell's research points to the often compelling and suppressing influence that organizational imperatives can have on an employee's moral agency. Suppressed whistle-blowing (moral muteness), Lovell contends, is an enduring and troubling phenomenon in modern organizations. What to do about it remains a perplexing problem and a challenge to future researchers.

Rosemary O'Leary, in *The Ethics of Dissent* (2006), presents insightful and compelling accounts of public administrators in federal, state, and county governments who often found themselves caught between the proverbial "rock and a hard place." Should they go along to get along? Or should they resist? If so, what form of resistance should they assume? Blow the whistle, leak information to the media, engage in principled dissent, file a lawsuit, or hunker down in guerrilla warfare? O'Leary's foray into the ethics of dissent led her to conclude that what she describes as "guerrilla government" is here to stay and must be recognized and managed. Left unmanaged, she suggests, it can be devastating to both guerrillas and government.

Ethics Laws and Regulatory Agencies

Ethics statutes and laws are commonplace in governments of all descriptions. American states, for example, have ethics offices, boards, or commissions that are authorized to investigate alleged cases of unethical behavior. Many cities and counties (e.g., Chicago, Los Angeles, Miami–Dade County) have ethics commissions to investigate real and alleged wrongdoing. The U.S. government acted following the Watergate scandal and resignation of President Nixon in 1975. In 1978, Congress passed the Ethics in Government Act, establishing the U.S. Office of Government Ethics.

A number of studies describe and assess ethics regulatory bodies. Smith (2003b) has studied the practices of the Florida Ethics Commission along with those of Connecticut and New York. His comparative case study was based on anonymous interviews with sixty ethics officials and an examination of laws, rules, and regulations employed in these states. The central paradigm that emerged from his study was enforcement (286). By this he means that "complaint making, investigations, and adjudicative proceedings all were geared toward, and products of, this enforcement function" (287). His study primarily compares and contrasts the practices of the state agencies; it does not allow the reader to reach conclusions regarding "best practices" or which state ethics commission is more or less effective than another, nor why this might be the case.

Ethics agencies and practices at the local level of government have also been scrutinized. The city of Houston's zero-gift policy has been assessed by Herbert Fain (2002). He contends that it has deterred unethical behavior by city employees. This policy has also improved the effectiveness of two investigation and enforcement agencies—the Houston Office of Inspector General and the Harris County district attorney. Fain notes that Houston has suffered no further embarrassment due to questionable acceptance of gifts since this policy was put into effect (67).

A contrarian perspective on the zero-gift policy is offered by Denhardt and Gilman (2002, 75). They suggest that while "such a policy leaves no room for doubt abut expectations, it also leaves no room for participating in basic social graces." Public employees sometimes receive unsolicited flowers, cakes, even a basket of apples from aggrieved citizens in appreciation for a deed well done by a competent, caring worker. A zero-gift policy, with its absolutist approach, Denhardt and Gilman contend, can create unnecessarily awkward situations that "defy commonsense standards of reasonableness and propriety" (77). A better solution, in their judgment, is simply to require disclosure of all gifts.

The legal and constitutional aspects of ethics issues have also received considerable attention. John Rohr (2002) offers a constitutional analysis of the ethical aftermath of privatization and contracting out. He explores the arguments developed by the justices of the U.S. Supreme Court and concludes that the "link between ethics and constitutional law is forged by the oath many public servants take to uphold the Constitution of the United States" (1). Robert Gray (2002) reviewed the legal history and justifications for affirmative action with attention to state and federal judiciary decision making.

Comparative international studies have also been launched. Robert Schwartz (2007–8) investigated ethical regulatory failures in Canada and Israel. The Canadian case focused on the drinking-water tragedy in Walkerton, Ontario, in May 2000 when water became infected with E. coli that was discharged from farmers' fields into the town's water supply after a heavy rainstorm. More than twenty-three hundred people among the forty-eight hundred in the town fell ill, some with many long-lasting effects. The Israeli case dealt with building safety: In June 2001 the dance floor in the Versailles Banquet Hall in Jerusalem collapsed, killing twenty-three people and injuring more than four hundred. Both cases involved, in Schwartz's view, breaches in oversight ethics. While the Canadian case resulted in policy changes to strengthen regulatory vigilance, the Israeli case did not. Schwartz puzzled over these contrasting outcomes and concluded that the difference was not due to regulatory capture by industry but was more likely the result of different political circumstances.

These studies add significant insight into ethics laws and the practices of regulatory agencies and, when taken into consideration by reflective public administrators, offer practical guidance in managing the work of their organizations.

Ethics and Organizational Performance

Efficiency, economy, and effectiveness have been the hallmark values of modern public administration ever since Woodrow Wilson declared that "the field of administration is a field of business" (1887, 20). Public officeholders, so presumed Wilson and his intellectual successors, were expected to be men and women of high moral character. Thus there was little reason to be concerned about the need to add a fourth *e*—ethics—to this holy trilogy. Times change, though, and ethics has become academic talk and shop talk.

One might well think that this trend is a result of increasing incidents of wrongdoing. Upon closer examination, however, a more compelling explanation is plausible—the growing recognition that productive, high-performing units can add value to their organization by adhering to practices and behaviors that promote ethics and integrity. Both practicing public managers and public affairs scholars are devoting greater energy to understanding and building ethical workplaces. They are also gaining greater appreciation of the role that professional associations and ethics codes play in fostering organizational integrity.

Still, scandal and well-publicized ethical failings in public agencies are newsworthy and can bring about organizational change. Sadly, there is evidence that even what might be regarded as minor incidents of wrongdoing can breed an organizational climate of deceit, incompetence, and corruption. Taking a case study approach based on fifteen years of experience in federal and state agencies, David W. Haines (2003–4) describes how deceit, incompetence, and corruption became so routinized through minor human failings that the organizations he worked for became the antithesis of the rational, productive, efficient agencies they were designed to be.

In summary, there is a substantial and growing interest in probing the relationship between ethics and organizational performance. On the one hand, the literature suggests that this subject has been thoroughly examined. On the other hand, this is not so evident, because many studies rely on perceptions and attitudes and therefore take only a partial step toward closing the gap in explicating the relationship between ethical behavior and organizational performance.

Ethics Management

Can agency leaders and public officials manage ethics in the workplace in a manner similar to managing budgets, policies, or people? Does ethics management imply controlling the hearts and minds of employees? Perhaps. Yet even simply developing and adopting a code of ethics or a statement of principles is "managing ethics in the workplace." Ethics management is not a new enterprise. What is new is how it is thought about. If it is viewed as the systematic and conscious effort to foster organizational integrity, as article 4 of the American Society for Public Administration's code of ethics declares, then there is such a thing as ethics management. If it is viewed only as control, then it may be disingenuous to contend that there can be effective ethics management.

A number of inquiries have focused on this subject. Among the more resourceful are several conducted by West and Berman. Their research, published in 2003, reports the results of survey of city managers in all 338 U.S. cities with populations over sixty-five thousand. This study focused on the use and effectiveness of municipal audit committees, including an analysis of how audit committees promote accountability and help resolve ethical issues related to financial manage-ment. They report that there is a positive relationship between audit committee activities and the presence of ethics training in a municipality and that audit committees actively seek to detect ethical wrongdoing (2003, 356).

Their study was followed by another (West and Berman 2004) that describes and assesses the state of ethics training in U.S. cities. Three questions were investigated: (1) What are the stated purposes of ethics training? (2) What topics are covered and what are the pedagogical and delivery approaches? (3) What are the correlates of ethics training? A related questions asks, Why do some jurisdictions engage in more—or less—training than other jurisdictions? Also, are those cities that invest more heavily in ethics training more likely to enjoy higher levels of organizational productivity? The first question probes the fit between ethics training and important organizational practices such as hiring and promotion. The second question deals directly with the how-to of training employees. The third explores the factors associated with the use and impact of training such as the ethical leadership of top management, municipal resources and capabilities, and how ethics training influences productivity and the culture of the workplace.

Another investigator who has examined ethics management approaches and strategies is Robert Smith (2003a). His study focused on ethics administrators in government agencies and corporate ethics officers in the private sector. Who and what are ethics administrators and officers? Why are they needed? Are they effective? What difference do they make? His research answers the who, what, and why questions but, as he acknowledges, does not answer the effectiveness questions. He asserts that his inquiry raises more questions than answers. Still, Smith's study offers helpful insight into initiatives that contribute to organizational integrity.

These studies take important steps toward improving our understanding and knowledge of what it means to manage ethics, how it can be done, and what outcomes agency managers can expect. Nonetheless, there remains a need for systematic information about the variation in ethics management strategies and their consequences. While much has been learned about these matters in U.S. local, state, and federal agencies and nonprofit organizations, there is much more to learn about similar practices in countries worldwide.

The Ethical Environment

Studies of the ethical environment are wide-ranging in theory, methodology, and geography. Some question how the ethical environment of one city or community is interwoven with the ethical conduct of public officials (Eimicke, Cohen, and Salazar 2000; Ghere 1996, 1999). Others examine the relationship between ethics and building trust in one's agency and community (De Vries 2002). Still others explore how public managers, elected officials, and citizens view one another ethically and do or do not hold common outlooks that may influence private-public partnerships in their communities.

Privatization, contracting out, and commitment to competition are viewed by some scholars as the tools of entrepreneurial behavior and decision making in the public sector. But are there significant ethical risks associated with employing these tools? Eimicke, Cohen, and Salazar (2000) investigated this question through case studies of Orange County, California; Indianapolis, Indiana; San Diego, California; and Bogota, Columbia. These cases, they contend, are typical of privatization and contracting out in cities and, "although many decisions are carried out without controversy and with beneficial results, ethical questions abound" (240). In other words, public sector entrepreneurialism involves high-level ethical risk taking.

Studies of ethics, leadership, and public trust can also be found in the literature. Justin Marlowe (2004) draws on data from the 1996 General Social Survey to explore public perceptions of the trust placed in public administrators. He observes that it is very difficult to determine whether or not public administrators are part of the problem (declining trust in government) or part of the solution. Indeed, he concludes that they could be both and calls for future investigators to "explore whether citizens are in fact aware of the constraints that shape public administrators' work environments, and whether knowledge of the constraints affects public trust in the same administrators" (108–109). Similar research by Feldheim and Wang (2003–4), who employed survey data of U.S. city officials, examined the relationship between the ethical behavior of public employees and public trust. A key research question was, Does ethical behavior by civil servants influence public trust? They concluded that it does, as they found a positive relationship between the chief administrators' views of the trust placed by the citizens in their city governments and the ethical behaviors of employees. That is, managers who viewed their citizens as placing high levels of trust in city government also viewed their employees as having high levels of ethical behavior. Feldheim and Wang believe that their research findings provide evidence that public trust is increased through the demonstration of "integrity, openness, loyalty, ethical competency," among public employees (73).

It is widely presumed that politicians and administrators find it challenging to act with integrity in carrying out their duties. Systematic research documenting this presumption is, however, uncommon. One rare study is Michiel S. De Vries's (2002) investigation of the honesty of local government politicians and administrators in seventeen countries. His study is also an example of the effort to link traditional ethics theory with empirical research. Four philosophical views—teleological and deontological ethics theories, virtue ethics, and dialogic ethics—are used to frame the work. Nearly ten thousand respondents were asked "questions about their valuation of honesty in general and more specific questions about their opinions on the disclosure of facts and the presentation of one-sided facts" (313). Subsets of fifteen politicians and administrators in each of 408 communities in thirteen countries enabled DeVries and his colleagues to analyze community as well as individual proclivities toward being honest. At the individual level, his statistical model could explain only 5 percent of the variance. However, at the community level, his statistical model performed much better, explaining 26 percent of the variance in the politicians' responses and 13 percent among administrators. These findings, he concludes, suggest that "opinions on ethical behavior are foremost socially-culturally determined" (330). Furthermore, "public officials will tell the truth when they can afford it, and when they are dishonest, this can be explained by the circumstances that do not allow them to tell the truth" (332). How well does ethical theory explain these outcomes? Not very well at all, concludes DeVries. Rather, as suggested above, social-cultural influences appear to make the more significant difference in actual behaviors. Perplexing? So it would seem.

Do ethical communities and cultures beget ethical governments and governance? Or is it the converse? It is, of course, rather difficult to develop a meaningful measure of either an ethical community or an ethical government. Still, the argument is persuasive that one is not likely to find ethical governance in a community rife with an unethical culture. It also seems persuasive to assert that no matter how difficult the challenge might be, managers and public officials that promote and embrace strong ethical values and practices can raise the ethical consciousness of their communities.

Studies of community, ethics, and trust building provide a foundation for further inquiry. There can be little disagreement, however, about the need to more fully understand what community leaders can and should do to foster ethical and trustworthy government, and, by the same measure, what government leaders need to do to build trustworthy relationships with members of their communities.

ETHICS AND INTEGRITY IN ACTION

There are many pitfalls that can ensnare even the most ethically well-intentioned person. A kaleidoscope of rules, regulations, and laws certainly help individuals stay on an ethical path, but no matter how complex an organizational situation might be, it is up to the individual to exercise moral agency. That is why ethical reasoning is so important. For without the ability to reason through a situation, one is largely left to the moral agency of the organization to determine right from wrong. When taken to the dark side of organizational life, the individual's moral agency might be stripped away entirely. "What's good for the organization is good for me" might be the lament—a dangerous supposition, for sure.

Progressive leaders and managers understand the dangers that lurk in the "shadow of organization" and have instituted practices that ensure that an individual's moral agency is not sacrificed on the altar of organizational self-interest. What are those practices? First and foremost is exemplary leadership. Those who pronounce that their supervisors and street-level workers must adhere to the highest ethical standards in the conduct of their work must themselves adhere to those same standards. Leaders must be exemplars in their personal and professional lives. Is this more easily said than done? Certainly, but it is essential. Much the same can be said about peer leadership. Middle managers and even cops on the beat must demonstrate day in and day out their commitment to ethical behavior. Failure to do so can result only in organizations without integrity.

Second, ethics training in cities and counties across America and internationally is becoming more common than uncommon. A study (Berman 1996) of all 554 U.S. cities with populations over fifty thousand reported that there is a great deal of ethics training under way. Two of every three cities reported that they do training. New employees are the target of most training in six of ten cities, while four of ten cities reported that managers are also trained. A smaller number of cities said that ethics training is mandatory.

Third, while government employees are usually subject to state ethics laws, many governments have chosen to adopt a higher standard that is expressed in their own code of ethics. Elected and appointed public managers hold very positive attitudes toward codes of ethics. The conventional wisdom is that codes have a positive influence in governance, especially in deterring unethical acts by ethically motivated public servants. That is, unethical officials are likely to be unethical regardless of whether a code exists or not, but those who want to be ethical find a code helpful in guiding their behavior. Of course, the motivation for adopting a code is often a series of unethical behaviors or a scandal.

Fourth, recruiting and promoting employees based in part on their adherence to ethical standards is growing. Personnel decisions—hiring, evaluating, promoting, firing—are essential features of all organizations. Designing evaluation processes that incorporate an ethical element can be a challenging and complicated task.

Taken together, these practices—exemplary leadership, ethics training, codes, and personnel selection processes that incorporate a standard of conduct—represent a comprehensive approach toward strengthening the ethics culture in public organizations. This is not wishful thinking, as it is happening across America today. Ethics is in action, although the enterprise remains a work in progress. Consider the high-profile story of the impeached and ousted Illinois governor Rod Blagojevich, who is alleged to have offered to sell the Senate seat held by former senator and now President Obama in return for political contributions. At the local level there is yet much work to be done. Consider the recent sordid history of nearly 150 New Jersey state senators, mayors, county executives, and council members who have been arrested and charged with corruption over the past decade (Barbaro 2009).

Obstacles and Challenges

The obstacles and challenges facing those who preside over and administer government organizations are increasingly complex. Among other things, the boundary between those things public and those things private has largely disappeared, leaving in its wake much uncertainty about how to do the right thing. The age of networking and privatization is here and, with it, a vast blur in the ability of citizens, elected officials, and organizational managers to distinguish between public and private organizations, public and private managers, and public and private ethics.

The ethical challenges ushered in by the fast-forward buttons of the Internet, the World Wide Web, electronic mail, direct TV beamed from orbiting satellites, and other breathtaking and powerful communication technologies of the information age are no less daunting. The future is here; it is now. It is both a virtual "now" and a very real "now." Elected officials and public managers, like their private sector counterparts, must not only understand how to harness information technology within their organizations; they must be able to understand and manage the human-technical-organizational dynamics that information technology brings to the workplace.

The knowledge explosion wrought by the electronic age of computers and high-speed, space-age communication has truly transformed the world, giving meaning to the global village and citizen in ways unimaginable a mere decade ago. The globalization of economies, communication, education, commerce, and even warfare and peace is redefining the nation-state and presenting innumerable challenges to public officials in the United States and abroad. Public organizations must add value to their products and services in order to withstand the ever-increasing pressures of worldwide competition. Responsive, high-performing organizations are a necessity, not a luxury. Government agencies are not immune to these pressures, and political executives and career public managers know this. They also know that the forces of globalization can tempt governments to devalue the ethical overhead that is part and parcel of getting things done. Getting things done and staying competitive can be—but are not necessarily—compatible with high ethical standards.

Ethics are involved in all manner of public activities, such as protecting the community from criminals, ensuring that confidential information does not get in the wrong hands, keeping people safe from human-created and environmental hazards, and much more. Ethical behavior, which includes respect for citizens, the promotion of democratic values such as citizen participation in governance, and commitment to the rule of law, is of paramount importance. The citizenry expects those who occupy elected and appointed offices in federal, state, and local governments to be ethical in carrying out their duties. In fact, Washington and state and local governments have gone to considerable length to ensure that the public's business is conducted properly. How? They have created ethics oversight commissions and adopted ethics laws, ordinances, rules, and codes to encourage ethical behavior. While these measures are useful and have a proper place, they are frequently insufficient. Following rules, regulations, and the law to stay out of trouble is important, but it is the moral minimum.

Perhaps the most important and largest challenge, however, is learning how to become ethically competent.

Becoming Ethically Competent

What knowledge, skills, and abilities does one need to be ethically competent? This is not an easy question to answer, as there is considerable debate about the matter. It is, of course, difficult to imagine that a public manager would be regarded as ethically competent if he had no knowledge of the profession's code of ethics, relevant ethics ordinances, or state ethics laws. Nor is it imaginable that one could become ethically competent without having the skills and ability to recognize an ethical issue and act appropriately to resolve it.

Another view of ethical competency is offered by James S. Bowman and his colleagues (2004). They contend that ethically competent administrators must understand and practice moral reasoning, be able to sort through competing values, and engage in prudent decision making. More specifically, they note that four abilities are needed: (a) principled moral reasoning, (b) recognition of ethics-related conflicts, (c) refusal to do something unethical, and (d) application of ethical theory.

As might be surmised, becoming ethically competent is not a simple or straightforward task. Yet, it is doable. And, it is imperative that men and women entering public service become ethically competent managers. An ethically competent manager must have an awareness of and sensitivity to ethical concerns in the organizational environment and must be able to differentiate between ethical and other management issues when circumstances warrant a distinction.

High on any list of competencies is the mandate to *serve the public interest.* In short, serving the public interest requires a government manager to place the public interest above his or her self-interests or the organization's self-interests. This is not an easy thing to do. As Kenneth Ashworth, an experienced public servant, puts it, "Working inside organizations, you will feel pressures to carry out orders you feel uneasy about, and, to get ahead, there will be temptations to compromise yourself and your principles or instincts" (2001, 162). This is not serving the public interest, is it? Of course, defining the public interest from the vantage point of government management is not always a straightforward matter. Still, it is incumbent on the ethically competent manager to make every effort to carry out his or her duties in a manner that is consistent with the public interest. The ethically competent manager must draw on his or her knowledge of the public interest and must possess the necessary skills and abilities to ensure that the public interest prevails.

Intertwined with serving the public interest is *respect for the law.* The rule of law is critical to democratic governance, and it is expected that those sworn to uphold the law will do just that, although there can be a place for legitimate, principled dissent. Public managers may not be elected officials who are charged with the responsibility to enact laws that govern the land. However, they are vital actors in energizing the law. The ethically competent public manager understands his or her role in a democracy and must act in a manner that is lawful and respectful of his or her elected bosses.

Other competencies place an emphasis on skills and abilities. One is the skill and ability to *recognize and differentiate between ethical issues and day-to-day management issues.* This is no trivial matter, as it can be difficult at times to discern which is which, and sometimes the two are undistinguishable. However, to mistake a management issue as an ethical issue or vice versa can result in mismanagement or improper intervention. Although it was asserted in a previous section that ethics can be managed from an organizational perspective, one should not conclude that all ethics issues can be subsumed as a type of management issue. Consider the matter of solicitations in the workplace. While this might be viewed as unethical issue, it can also be viewed as a management issue. Consider fund-raising efforts to support nonprofit organizations such as United Way. How employees are solicited can make the difference in determining whether it is an ethical issue or a management issue. Should employees feel pressured to "go along to get along," there would most likely be considerable anxiety and ethical angst.

Another competency, to *embrace ethical practices and behavior in the workplace,* also places an emphasis on skills and abilities. While most managers would find this meritorious, it is also the case that few managers actually do it. Why? Too often supervisors and top management fail to recognize the value in emphasizing ethical behavior until there is a serious issue or problem. There is a tendency to be reactive rather than proactive. Moreover, there is the possibility that higher-level managers may be unaware of misconduct at work. If employees do not report ethical problems, organizational managers may not recognize problems until a crisis is at hand.

Becoming an ethically competent manager also means having the ability to engage in *ethical reasoning,* an approach to resolving issues and dilemmas that can be taught and learned.

Ethical Reasoning

Public managers often approach "doing the right thing" from a utilitarian perspective. That is, they make decisions that benefit the greatest number of residents (or employees, when decisions apply only to the government workforce) while minimizing the potential harm. This "do no harm" approach is attractive because it is straightforward and on many occasions easy to understand. Still, there are times when these qualities are not sufficient. So what do administrators do when faced with especially difficult ethics moments? Some apply a blend of normative philosophies— utilitarianism, principles, and virtues—in what James H. Svara (1997) calls the "ethical triangle." Debra Stewart (1984, 20) adds that "most managers are neither pure deontologists, nor pure utilitarians, but rather operate according to a kind of ethical pluralism." Others apply ethical reasoning, which incorporates some aspects of the classic normative approaches but also emphasizes a decision-making logic and process. Carol W. Lewis (1991, 101–2) describes ethical reasoning as "a form of specialized problem solving . . . [that] . . . includes public service values, a systematic perspective, fact-finding, screening tools, and feedback devices and assessment tools."

Terry L. Cooper (2006) places ethical reasoning at the center of choice intended to resolve an ethical problem. Cooper's model "does not assume that ethical decisions are, can, or should be purely rational and principled" (29). Rather, human feelings are an inseparable part of our ethical life, he asserts. Values and judgments are at the crucible of the decision-making process to resolve an ethical problem. The individual must learn how to draw upon his or her moral imagination— acquire the ability to produce a movie in his or her mind, with realistic characters, a believable script, and clear imagery—to project probable consequences of the ethical choices the individual makes in given situation. Ethical reasoning emphasizes the dynamics and interplay between alternatives, values that might be derived from principles or virtues, and commonsense judgment to resolve a challenging ethical dilemma.

This section has discussed what it means to become ethically competent. In summary, it can be asserted that an ethically competent public manager is (1) committed to high standards of personal and professional behavior, (2) has knowledge of relevant ethics codes and laws, (3) has the ability to engage in ethical reasoning when confronted with challenging situations, (4) is able to identify and act upon public service ethics and values, and (5) promotes ethical practices and behavior in public agencies and organizations (Menzel 2010, 18).

FUTURE DIRECTIONS

Public service ethics and integrity are the topics of more than a half dozen new books. In 2005, H. George Frederickson and Richard K. Ghere edited the comprehensive review *Ethics in Public Management,* which covers topics such as leadership, organization, accountability, new managerialism, corruption, and globalization. Also appearing in 2005 was Carol W. Lewis and Stuart C. Gilman's second edition of Lewis's landmark book *The Ethics Challenge in Public Service,* appropriately subtitled *A Problem-Solving Guide.* In 2006, two additional books found their way into print. Jonathan P. West and Evan M. Berman in the edited volume *The Ethics Edge* (2006) focus attention on ethical issues in city management. The same year, Terry L. Cooper completed the fifth edition of *The Responsible Administrator,* underscoring once more the importance of responsibility and integrity in the management of administrative bodies. In 2007, three more books made their mark—Donald C. Menzel's *Ethics Management in Public Administration* offers guidance for those who not only want to more fully understand the dynamics of ethical and unethical behavior in the workplace but also are motivated to change the culture of their organization. James Svara added in *The Ethics Primer for Public Administrators in Government and Nonprofit Organizations* (2007) that managers must place ethics at the center of their work and build strong ethical cultures in their organizations. William L. Richter and Fran Burke produced a second edition of *Combating Corruption/Encouraging Ethics,* which offers practical guidance to management ethics. Breaking new ground in 2010 was Menzel's latest work, *Ethics Moments in Government: Cases and Controversies.* This book provides a framework and guidance for administrators in their quest for ethical competency.

Europeans have moved to center stage in investigating ethics issues as well. Transatlantic dialogues involving the Study Group on Ethics and Integrity of Governance of the European Group of Public Administration and the Section on Ethics of the American Society for Public Administration have been convened, one in Europe and the other in the United States. The dialogue in 2005 yielded the edited volume *Ethics and Integrity of Governance: Perspectives Across Frontiers* (Huberts, Maesschalck, and Jurkiewicz 2008). This volume has chapters on public service ethos, values, rationality and effectiveness of governance, and integrity management and instruments. A second dialogue, in 2007, resulted in another edited volume, *Ethics and Integrity in Public Service* (Cox 2009), which contains chapters on ethical foundations, management, leadership, and competency. This spate of books certainly acknowledges the rapidly growing interest in and need for new information and knowledge on ethics and integrity in public service worldwide. All recognize the need to view organizations as organic, living, and learning enterprises while at the same time placing the moral agency of the manager at the forefront of public life.

Terry L. Cooper (2004, 404) calls on ethics scholars to collaborate and focus on the "big" questions in administrative ethics:

1. What are the normative foundations for public administration ethics?
2. How do American administrative ethical norms fit into a global context?
3. How can organizations be designed to be supportive of ethical conduct?
4. When should people be treated equally in order to treat them fairly, and when should they be treated unequally?

As suggested in this chapter, studies of ethical decision making and moral development certainly contribute to a discussion of normative foundations for public administration ethics in that they raise fundamental issues about the role of administrators in exercising moral reasoning in democratic polities and societies transitioning from authoritarian regimes to more democratic regimes. When should managers "go along to get along," and when shouldn't they? What is a citizen administrator? What are the administrator's obligations to protecting constitutional values? Advancing the public interest? These questions are part and parcel of understanding ethical decision making and moral development.

Cooper raises the question of whether or not a global ethic is emerging and, if so, what the American experience has to contribute to a global ethic. Scholarship on ethics laws and regulations contributes to the discussion of American administrative norms in a global context. The research literature on American experiences illustrates both the diversity and the value added by commitment to the rule of law. Diversity in ethics laws and regulations in the U.S. provides little evidence of the imminent arrival of a universal governance ethic in the United States, not to mention the possibility of the global ethic that Cooper ponders. At the same time, greater global interdependence resulting from trade, travel, and technological advances in communication in combination with a growing emphasis on the rule of law might well suggest that a global ethic will evolve. Commitment to the rule of law presages the evolution of what Rohr (1989) calls a minimalist compliance conception of ethical behavior; that is, behavior that is legal is also ethical.

Perhaps most notable is what scholars laboring in the fields of organizational performance and ethics management have to say about the question, What can be done to design organizations to support ethical conduct? The short answer is as follows: Organizations can do and are doing a great deal, ranging from the development of codes of acceptable behavior to providing ethics training to conducting ethics audits and more. Still to come, however, are the identification and diffusion of best ethics management strategies and practices.

As Cooper aptly observes, the Progressive Age formula of treating everyone the same meant treating everyone fairly, but this is no longer the nostrum it once was. The age of standardization and the decline of patronage government were well suited for the belief in and practice that equal treatment for all is fair treatment for all. Postmodern societies along with ethnic, racial, gender, and age diversity have challenged elected officials and administrators around the world to rethink how to treat people unequally and yet be fair. Ethics scholars have probably contributed less to this discussion topic than to the other topics suggested by Cooper. Still, the studies that explore the ramifications of privatization are helpful in that they point to who benefits and who loses from an ethical perspective. One might also contend that studies of trust building within and between communities add to this discussion. It is hard to imagine how one might treat some unequally and some fairly without a high degree of trust among all involved. These are, indeed, big questions.

Still, the quest for ethical governance writ large is without end and ever more important in the twenty-first century. In this postmodernism age, will the ethical standards and traditions of years past be sustainable? Or is a new, emerging postmodern ethics on the horizon? These questions beg for answers that lie in the path of future research.

ACKNOWLEDGMENT

Some material in this chapter is adapted in part from Menzel 2005, 2007, and 2010.

REFERENCES

Ashworth, K. 2001. *Caught Between the Dog and the Fireplug or How to Survive Public Service.* Washington, DC: Georgetown University Press.

Barbaro, Michael. 2009. In New Jersey, ideal conditions for corruption. *New York Times,* July 27, A16.

Berman, Evan. 1996. "Restoring the bridges of trust: Attitudes of community leaders toward local government." *Public Integrity Annual* 1:31–49.

Bowman, James S., Jonathan P. West, Evan M. Berman, and Montgomery Van Wart. 2004. *The Professional Edge: Competencies in Public Service.* Armonk, NY: M.E. Sharpe.

Cooper, Terry L. 2004. Big questions in administrative ethics: A need for focused, collaborative effort. *Public Administration Review* 64 (July–August): 395–407.

———. 2006. *The Responsible Administrator.* 5th ed. San Francisco: Jossey-Bass.

Cox, Raymond W., ed. 2009. *Ethics and Integrity in Public Service: Concepts and Cases.* Armonk, NY: M.E. Sharpe.

Denhardt, Kathryn G., and Stuart C. Gilman. 2002. Extremism in the search for virtue: Why zero gift policies spawn unintended consequences. *Public Integrity* 4 (Winter): 75–80.

De Vries, Michiel S. 2002. Can you afford honesty? A comparative analysis of ethos and ethics in local government. *Administration and Society* 34 (July): 309–334.

Dobel, J. Patrick. 1999. *Public Integrity.* Baltimore, MD: Johns Hopkins University Press.

———. 2009. Value driven leading a management approach. The Electronic Hallway: Case Teaching Resources. www.hallway.org (accessed 23 July 2010).

Eimicke, William B., Steven Cohen, and Mauricio Perez Salazar. 2000. Ethical public entrepreneurship. *Public Integrity* 2 (Summer): 229–245.

Fain, Herbert. 2002. The case for a zero gift policy. *Public Integrity* 4 (Winter): 61–69.

Feldheim, Mary Ann, and Xiaohu Wang. 2003–4. Ethics and public trust: Results from a national survey. *Public Integrity* 6 (Winter): 63–75.

Frederickson, H. George, and Richard K. Ghere, eds. 2005. *Ethics in Public Management.* Armonk, NY: M.E. Sharpe.

Frederickson, H.G., and Meredith A. Newman. 2001. The patriotism of exit and voice: The case of Gloria Flora. *Public Integrity* 3 (Fall): 347–362.

Ghere, Richard K., 1996. Aligning the ethics of public-private partnership: The issue of local economic development. *Journal of Public Administration Research and Theory* 6 (4): 599–621.

———. 1999. Public integrity, privatization, and partnership: Where do ethics fit? *Public Integrity* 1 (Spring): 135–148.

Gibson, Pamela A. 2009. Examining the moral reasoning of the ethics adviser and counselor: The case of the federal designated agency ethics official. *Public Integrity* 11 (Spring): 105–120.

Gray, W. Robert. 2002. The four faces of affirmative action: Analysis and answers. *Public Integrity* 4 (Winter): 43–59.

Haines, David W. 2003–4. Fatal choices: The routinization of deceit, incompetence, and corruption. *Public Integrity* 6 (Winter): 5–23.

Hart, David K. 1992. The moral exemplar in an organizational society. In *Exemplary Public Administrators,* ed. Terry L. Cooper and N. Dale Wright, 9–29. San Francisco: Jossey-Bass.

Huberts, Leo W.J.C., Jeroen Maesschalck, and Carole L. Jurkiewicz, eds. 2008. *Ethics and Integrity of Governance: Perspectives Across Frontiers.* Northampton, MA: Edward Elgar.

International City/County Management Association (ICMA). 2008. Practices for effective local government management. http://icma.org/main/bc.asp?bcid=120&hsid=11&ssid1=2495&t=0 (point 17; accessed December 27, 2008).

Jurkiewicz, Carole L. and Roger G. Brown. 2000. Power does not corrupt absolutely: An empirical study. *Public Integrity,* 3:195–210.

Kohlberg, Lawrence. 1980. *The Meaning and Measurement of Moral Development.* Worcester, MA: Clark University Press.

Lewis, Carol W. 1991. *The Ethics Challenge in Public Service: A Problem-Solving Guide.* San Francisco: Jossey-Bass.

Lewis, Carol W., and Stuart C. Gilman. 2005. *The Ethics Challenge in Public Service: A Problem-Solving Guide.* 2d ed. San Francisco: Jossey-Bass.

Lovell, Alan. 2003. The enduring phenomenon of moral muteness: Suppressed whistleblowing. *Public Integrity* 5 (Summer): 187–204.

Marlowe, Justin. 2004. Part of the solution or cogs in the system: The origins and consequences of trust in public administrators. *Public Integrity* 6 (Spring): 93–113.

Menzel, Donald C. 2005. Research on ethics and integrity in governance: A review and assessment. *Public Integrity* 7 (Spring): 147–168,

———. 2007. *Ethics Management for Public Administrators: Building Organizations of Integrity.* Armonk, NY: M.E. Sharpe.

———. 2010. *Ethics Moments in Government: Cases and Controversies.* Boca Raton, FL: CRC Press.

Norden, James. Ethics (2009). ASPA online. www.aspaonline.org/ethicscommunity/definitions.htm (accessed July 29, 2009).

O'Leary, Rosemary. 2006. *The Ethics of Dissent: Managing Guerrilla Government.* Washington, DC: CQ Press.

Rest, James. 1986. *Moral Development: Advances in Research and Theory.* New York: Praeger.

Richter, William L. and Frances Burke. 2007. *Combating Corruption/Encouraging Ethics.* 2d ed. Lanham, MD: Rowman & Littlefield, Inc.

Rohr, John. 1989. *Ethics for Bureaucrats: An Essay on Law and Values.* 2d ed. New York: Marcel Dekker.

———. 2002. The ethical aftermath of privatization and contracting out: A constitutional analysis. *Public Integrity* 4 (Winter): 1–12.

Scheer, Robert. 1976. Interview with Jimmy Carter. *Playboy* 23 (11): 65–86. www.playboy.com/articles/jimmy-carter-interview/index.html (accessed December 27, 2008).

Schwartz, Robert. 2007–8. Regulatory ethics in theory and practice: Comparing two cases. *Public Integrity* 10 (Winter): 37–52.

Smith, Robert W. 2003a. Corporate ethics officers and government ethics administrators. *Administration and Society* 34 (January): 632–652.

———. 2003b. Enforcement or ethical capacity: Considering the role of state ethics commissions at the millennium. *Public Administration Review* 63 (May–June): 283–295.

Stewart, Debra. 1984. Managing competing claims: An ethical framework for human resource decision making. *Public Administration Review* 44 (January–February): 14–22.

Svara, James H. 1997. The ethical triangle: Synthesizing the bases of administrative ethics. *Public Integrity Annual* (1997): 33–41.

———. 2007. *The Ethics Primer for Public Administrators in Government and Nonprofit Organizations.* Sudbury, MA: Jones and Bartlett.

West, Jonathan P., and Evan M. Berman. 2003. Audit committees and accountability in local government: A national survey. *International Journal of Public Administration* 26:329–362.

———. 2004. Ethics training in U.S. cities: Content, pedagogy, and impact. *Public Integrity* 6 (Summer): 189–206.

———, eds. 2006. *The Ethics Edge.* 2d ed. Washington, DC: ICMA Press.

Wilson, Woodrow. 1887. The study of administration. Reprinted in *Political Science Quarterly* 56 (December 1941).

PART II

PUBLIC MANAGEMENT ISSUES

Management issues continue to be a salient aspect of scholarship in public administration. From Taylor and Fayol's early works on scientific principles through the turn to participatory and performance management, issues of how to better manage the delivery of public services pervade the literature. Work around these issues has been the impetus for a variety of innovations. Management by objectives, total quality management, collaborative management, and talent management are examples employed in the public sector. These innovations reflect evolving patterns and changing perspectives that are influencing the practice and study of public administration.

Contributors in Part II not only reflect the evolving patterns and changing perspectives but also advance theory and describe emerging management practices in the public sector. This begins with Norma M. Riccucci's chapter, "Human Resources Management: Current and Future Challenges," which discusses the diverse, dynamic, and extensive nature of the issues affecting the workforce in the public sector. Particular attention is given to four of the most notable, challenging, and enduring issues: affirmative action, labor-management relations, performance management, and succession planning. Responding to issues in these areas can be very costly. As Riccucci points out, governments at every level "continually experiment with programs and policies" to manage cost and improve performance.

Irene S. Rubin focuses on the instrument developed to manage cost and improve performance— public budgeting, which comported well with early management practices. However, as Rubin makes clear in "New Directions in Public Budgeting" it is no longer a purely technical activity, and has not been for some time. Budgeting is more dynamic than it used to be, and has more actors, tools, policy, programs, tensions, entitlements, and problems than ever before. Rubin concludes, "Budgeting is in need of a new wave of reform," and offers steps as to how this might be accomplished.

Judith R. Saidel examines the expanding role of not-for-profit organizations in the provision of public goods and services. Cross-sector relationships from this activity trend toward devolution and privatization and are formalized through a "contracting regime." Saidel uses "the proxy-partnership governance continuum" construct as a theoretical basis to advance understanding of complex government-nonprofit relationships, which help define elements of contemporary public administration. The continuum illustrates the range of cross-sector institutional relationships in the contracting regime and helps highlight the managerial challenges they represent for public administrators.

Accountability is the focus of Melvin J. Dubnick and Kaifeng Yang's chapter. They discuss management issues related to the extensive use of the concept in the public sector. This includes highlighting the various promises of accountability that make it so attractive to those seeking to improve governance and administration. However, as they observe, "The ubiquity of accountability . . . reflects its problems as much as its importance." Despite the status afforded accountability within managerial and political cultures, it has not resulted in enhanced governance as promised. For Dubnick and Yang, "As challenging as the pursuit of accountability has proven to be for students of public administration and governance, we do not have the luxury of abandoning our efforts to understand the concept and its use." They insist, "Our task is to continue to deal with the resulting theoretical and methodological challenges."

Stuart I. Bretschneider and Ines Mergel's chapter, "Technology and Public Management Information Systems: Where We Have Been and Where We Are Going," reviews theories of how technology changes relate to institutional, organizational, and procedural change. This includes a historical review of technology changes over the past fifty years and technology shifts and trends during this period. Bretschneider and Mergel also provide a series of propositional predictions of how these trends will work through preexisting government. The biggest challenge, according to Bretschneider and Mergel, "is not the technology itself, but the adaptation of technology within the given political and bureaucratic situation and institutional barriers."

The last chapter in part II, "Emergency and Crisis Management: Practice, Theory, and Profession," by William L. Waugh draws attention to management issues related to disasters. Reflecting on hurricane and tsunami disasters, Waugh chronicles emergency management's development as a profession and as "a distinct set of management practices worldwide." In addition to highlighting the progress the profession has achieved, Waugh also discusses areas that still need considerable attention. These include the need for proactive risk-reduction programs, which became a major international issue following the 2004 Indian Ocean tsunami, as well as the imperative to improve the international humanitarian assistance system, which was reaffirmed following the devastating Haiti and Chili earthquakes in early 2010.

CHAPTER 8

HUMAN RESOURCES MANAGEMENT

Current and Future Challenges

NORMA M. RICCUCCI

The field of human resources management (HRM) in the public sector is diverse, dynamic, and extensive. Sometimes referred to as public personnel, or more lately human capital management, it includes functions such as training and development; recruitment, testing, and hiring; promotion; position classification; compensation and retirement; and performance evaluation, human resources planning, and labor relations. While HRM and public personnel textbooks provide ample coverage of the mechanics of these and other HRM functions, there are a few topics that have lent themselves to more extensive coverage, given the political and legal ramifications surrounding their use and application in government settings. Those issues include, most prominently, affirmative action, labor relations, performance management, and succession planning. Additional concerns and issues around related topics in human resources include diversity, which is addressed in chapter 23 in this volume.

This chapter examines four of the most notable, challenging, and enduring issues that underlie the study and practice of public sector human resources management: affirmative action, labor-management relations, performance management, and succession planning. The chapter addresses why these topics have remained so significant, what theoretical and empirical advances have been made in each area over the past twenty years, and what the future holds for these critical areas of public sector human resources management.

AFFIRMATIVE ACTION

One of the most hotly debated, political, and grossly misunderstood issues in HRM is affirmative action. It continues to garner a good deal of attention because of its primary purpose: diversifying work and educational settings. Whenever human resources (HR) decisions consider such characteristics as race, ethnicity, and gender, the public is particularly circumspect, and those who feel adversely affected by the decisions become litigious, as the long history of common law illustrates. Evolving from equal employment opportunity (EEO) policies, programs, and law, which seek to eradicate employment discrimination, affirmative action is a proactive tool that seeks not only to end discriminatory HR decisions, but also to ensure diversity in the workplace so that organizations function more effectively and productively.

An important theoretical justification for affirmative action is representative bureaucracy, which holds that the social demographics of public bureaucracies ought to reflect the populations being served by those bureaucracies. Only then will the needs and interests of women and people of color be truly represented. A plethora of research has shown that governments at all levels have achieved passive representation, whereby the social composition of the bureaucracy mirrors that of the general population (see, for example, Rosenbloom and Featherstonhaugh 1977; Krislov and Rosenbloom 1981; Wise 1990; Guy 1992, 1993; Meier 1993; Naff 2001). Studies have also found that an active representativeness exists in a number of settings (see, for example, Meier 1975; Meier and Smith 1994; Keiser et al. 2002; Meier and Nicholson-Crotty 2006). Representative bureaucracy in the active sense indicates that women and people of color in the bureaucracy will actually push for the needs and interests of their counterparts in the general population. These studies warrant the use of affirmative action policies. Nevertheless, it is the courts that have determined the legal contours of its use.

Governments at every level as well as institutions of higher education began to develop affirmative action programs in large part to deflect potential discrimination suits filed by women and people of color. One of the earliest affirmative action decisions by the U.S. Supreme Court was the *Regents of the University of California v. Bakke* (1978), the landmark ruling upholding the use of affirmative action in admissions for the first time. Allan Bakke filed a "reverse discrimination" suit against UC Davis School of Medicine when, as he argued, students of color with lower standardized test scores were admitted over him. Although the High Court ruled in favor of Bakke in a 5–4 decision, the Court upheld the use of affirmative action providing it did not include numerical set-asides—erroneously referred to as "quotas" by the Court.

The decision was a major victory for affirmative action proponents. But the use of such concepts as "reverse discrimination" and "quotas" only served to obfuscate the issues and to create and foster opposition to affirmative action. *Reverse discrimination* is a play on words, and it has yet to be defined in any cogent, plausible, or credible way. Moreover, the concept of quotas has been greatly abused. Quotas are legal tools that are set by the courts after a finding of discrimination. It has been common, for example, for courts to set specific quotas around the hiring of women or people of color in the protective services after finding pervasive and systematic discrimination in such jobs as police officer, firefighter, or correctional guard. Courts will set a timeframe for the government agency to meet the quota; if it is not met, the court can impose a fine, hence the term *quota*. In practice, however, fines are rarely levied against the agency found guilty of continuing its discriminatory practices toward women or people of color, as long as it can demonstrate a good-faith effort toward fulfilling the quota.

Goals, in contrast, suggest a benchmark set voluntarily by agencies. If an agency is unable to meet its goals, it cannot or does not impose sanctions on itself. Unfortunately, the term *quota* has been conflated with *goals* and hence *affirmative action,* resulting in a stigma—not to mention incendiary reactions—when organizations set goals and timetables for diversifying their staffs or student bodies. The misuse of these terms and the conflagration surrounding them continue even today and fuel resistance to the use of affirmative action.

Although the *Bakke* decision involved university admissions, the ruling extends to the public workplace as well. After *Bakke,* the U.S. Supreme Court issued a number of favorable rulings to affirmative action, under both the U.S. Constitution and Title VII of the Civil Rights Act of 1964 as amended.[1] For example, in 1987, the Court issued a ruling in *Johnson v. Transportation Agency, Santa Clara County,* upholding, under Title VII, voluntarily developed affirmative action programs intended to correct gender imbalances in traditionally segregated job categories. Other favorable rulings under Title VII include, for example:

United Steelworkers of America v. Weber (1979). U.S. Supreme Court upholds the legality of voluntarily developed affirmative action plan under Title VII of the Civil Rights Act of 1964.

Fullilove v. Klutznick (1980). U.S. Supreme Court upholds constitutionality (under Fifth and Fourteenth Amendments) of federal set-aside programs enacted by the U.S. Congress.

Int'l Assoc. of Firefighters v. City of Cleveland (1986). U.S. Supreme Court upholds, under Title VII, affirmative action consent decree that provided for the use of race-conscious relief in promotion decisions.

U.S. v. Paradise (1987). U.S. Supreme Court upholds, under the Fourteenth Amendment to the U.S. Constitution, a court-ordered affirmative action plan aimed at remedying discrimination against African Americans in hiring and promotion decisions in Alabama Public Safety Department.

In 1989, however, the U.S. Supreme Court issued a number of regressive rulings not only to affirmative action, but also to equal employment opportunity precedents. For example, in *City of Richmond v. Croson* (1989) the U.S. Supreme Court struck down the constitutionality, under the Fourteenth Amendment, of a local government's set-aside program because it could not satisfy the criteria of the strict scrutiny test.[2] In addition, the Court in *Patterson v. McLean Credit Union* (1989), overturning a previous decision,[3] ruled that a Reconstruction-era civil rights statute— Section 1981 of the Civil Rights Act of 1866—could be used to protect people of color from hiring discrimination but not from other forms of bias on the job (e.g., harassment). In another decision, *Martin v. Wilks* (1989), the High Court allowed white firefighters to challenge, under Title VII, a consent decree, to which they were not a party, years after it had been approved by a lower court. Were it not for the Civil Rights Act of 1991, those decisions would have prevailed. Instead, the U.S. Congress, in a direct separation-of-powers challenge to those 1989 decisions, overturned every single negative Court ruling issued in 1989.

In 2003, in a long-awaited decision on the constitutionality of affirmative action, the U.S. Supreme Court reaffirmed its support for affirmative action with its ruling in *Grutter v. Bollinger* (2003). The Court majority ruled that the racial diversity of a study body can be a sufficiently compelling interest on the part of a state university to warrant the use of an admissions program that considered a variety of factors, including race, under the Equal Protection Clause of the Fourteenth Amendment to the U.S. Constitution.[4] The Court's decision offered definitive support for the widespread use of affirmative action, setting its *Bakke* decision on firmer ground.

Most recently, the Supreme Court issued a ruling in *Ricci v. DeStefano* (2009), which involved not affirmative action per se, but rather, more broadly, employment discrimination law. Because the ruling has implications for the goal of affirmative action—diversity—a brief discussion follows. In 2003, the New Haven, Connecticut, Fire Department administered a promotion exam for lieutenant and captain. Out of seventy-seven candidates taking the lieutenant exam, nineteen were African American and fifteen were Latino. Given that there were only eight vacancies for lieutenant, and based on the test scores, no African Americans or Latinos would be eligible for promotion. Forty-one applicants took the captain examination, of whom eight were African American and eight Latino. Because there were only seven captain vacancies, and based on the test scores, no African American and at most two Latinos would be eligible for promotion. The city determined that the exam had an adverse impact on the African American and Latino candidates and, fearing litigation, scrapped it. Seventeen white firefighters and one Latino firefighter filed suit against the city, alleging reverse discrimination under Title VII of the Civil Rights Act, and the Equal Protection Clause of the Fourteenth First Amendment to the U.S. Constitution. Both the federal district court and the U.S. Appeals Court for the Second Circuit ruled against *Ricci* and for the city. *Ricci* appealed to the High Court.

The Supreme Court reversed the lower court decisions and ruled for the white firefighters.

The 5–4 ruling, which revolved around Title VII and not the Constitution, stated, "Fear of litigation alone cannot justify the City's reliance on race to the detriment of individuals who passed the . . . examinations and qualified for promotions. Discarding the test results was impermissible under Title VII" (*Ricci v. DeStefano* 2009). The Court instead argued that there must be a "strong basis" in evidence for concluding that the tests might be vulnerable to a disparate impact claim. The statistical imbalance alone was not enough. According to the Court, without this showing, the city engaged in "express, race-based decision making," resulting in disparate treatment, which, along with disparate impact, is also prohibited by Title VII. It is interesting to note, as addressed above, that the High Court majority in *Grutter* upheld, under the Constitution, an admissions program relying on race as one of many factors for the purposes of diversifying the University of Michigan Law School. In the past, the Court had set a higher bar for the permissibility of race-based decision making under the Constitution as compared with Title VII cases. The composition of the Court in the *Grutter* case, however, was different. Justice Sandra Day O'Connor, an important swing vote in affirmative action cases, retired, thereby changing the balance of power on the *Ricci* Court.

The Court's *Ricci* decision, in effect, sets the two provisions of Title VII—disparate treatment and disparate impact—in an endless battle for primacy, which can only deter employers' efforts to promote equal opportunity and to end discriminatory practices. For example, according to the majority ruling, if the city could have demonstrated that the exams were not job related, the city may have prevailed. But subjecting the tests to validity studies would have been very costly to the city. Also, if the validity studies revealed that the tests were job related, the strong-basis-in-evidence standard created by the *Ricci* Court would have been satisfied, thereby clearing the way for the use of the promotional exams. But this would have defeated the city's express purpose of seeking to diversify the upper levels of its fire department.

A viable solution to this challenge in any government agency would be to provide a battery of tests for promotion to upper-level jobs. Oral exams, for example, are critical, and could be weighted more heavily than written exams. Other assessment tools such as computer simulations or group exercises might also be deemed more important than written exams. These types of arrangements may facilitate an employer's goal to diversify its upper echelons, while staving off possible litigation. Indeed, a recent study by the Merit Systems Protection Board (2009) found that, although not used extensively in the federal government, job simulations are associated with lower rates of adverse impact, have higher predictive ability, and are more likely to be perceived as fair and job-related among job candidates.

It is also worth noting the experiences in Bridgeport, Connecticut, as Justice Ginsberg offered in her dissenting opinion in the *Ricci* ruling. She pointed to evidence offered by Donald Day of the Northeast Region of the International Association of Black Professional Firefighters. Ginsberg wrote,

> Day contrasted New Haven's experience with that of nearby Bridgeport, where minority firefighters held one-third of lieutenant and captain positions. Bridgeport . . . had once used a testing process similar to New Haven's, with a written exam accounting for 70 percent of an applicant's score, an oral exam for 25 percent, and seniority for the remaining five percent. . . . Bridgeport recognized, however, that the oral component, more so than the written component, addressed the sort of "real-life scenarios" fire officers encounter on the job. . . . Accordingly, that city "changed the relative weights" to give primacy to the oral exam. . . . Since that time . . . Bridgeport had seen minorities "fairly represented" in its exam results (*Ricci v. DeStefano* 2009).

Today, scholars and practitioners of HRM continue to study the legal aspects of affirmative action, but also focus their energies on diversity or diversity management, addressed elsewhere in this volume. While diversity management is receiving considerable attention, there are some unaddressed aspects of diversity that still merit attention. For example, more studies systematically evaluating the effectiveness of diversity programs are needed.

LABOR RELATIONS IN THE PUBLIC SECTOR

Public employee unionism has grown considerably over the past twenty years compared to that in the private sector (see Table 8.1). Reasons for this growth range from the decline in private sector unionization (e.g., due to the shift in the economy from manufacturing to service, thus leading private sector unions to target public employees for unionization) to wage disparities between white-collar government workers and blue-collar workers in the private sector, the latter earning more than the former (see Riccucci 2007).

With the advent of state statutes providing government workers with the right to collectively bargain starting in 1959,[5] a surfeit of research began to appear in the field of HRM. A number of studies, particularly at the local level, examined the effects of labor unions on wages, finding that public employee unions have been effective in increasing the wages of their constituents (see Kearney 1979; Kearney and Morgan 1980; Methé and Perry 1980). Other studies examined the contours of the laws, focusing particularly on the provision and uses of impasse tools, such as mediation, fact-finding, and arbitration (Kearney 1984; Rosenbloom and Shafritz 1985). The use of these tools has been critical for public employees as, with a few exceptions,[6] states prohibit the right to strike.

At the federal level of government, after a number of executive orders, labor relations was placed on a statutory basis for the first time with Title VII of the Civil Service Reform Act of 1978, otherwise known as the Federal Service Labor-Management Relations Statute. With passage of this provision of the law, a number of studies began to examine the experiences of labor unions representing federal government workers (see, for example, Ingraham and Rosenbloom 1992; Rosenbloom and Shafritz 1985). Studies emphasized the fact that power is circumscribed at the federal level in that unions cannot negotiate over such fundamental issues as pay. At the state and local levels of government, unions generally have the statutory power to bargain over issues such as wages and terms and conditions of employment.

Research is waning in the area of public sector labor relations, as indicated by the paucity of studies generated in this compared to other areas of HRM over the past fifteen years or so. One of the reasons can be attributed to the ideographic approach to labor relations at the state and local levels of government. That is to say, each state has a unique statute governing public sector labor law. Unlike in the private sector, where there is a federal law—the National Labor Relations Act of 1935—that governs labor relations uniformly across the country for all private sector employees, whether you are employed in California or New York, each state enacts its own law or public policy to regulate public sector labor-management relations. This serves as a deterrent to broad-based studies of labor relations in all the fifty states. Thus, given the circumscribed set of conditions facing data collection, only case studies involving one or two states tend to be conducted.

At the federal level, Title VII governs labor relations for all federal employees across the country. However, the scope of that law is very narrow, and as noted, labor unions representing federal employees have very little power.[7] It would appear that research, especially on federal employee unionism, is spurred in part by executive or managerial efforts to change or restrict the unions',

Table 8.1

Percentage of Union Representation, Pubic and Private Sectors, 1992–2008 (in percent)

	1992	1996	2000	2004	2008
Private	12.7	11.2	9.8	8.6	8.4
Public	43.2	43.0	42.0	40.7	40.7
Federal	NA	38.9	36.7	35.0	33.0
State	NA	35.3	34.2	34.3	35.1
Local	NA	48.4	47.9	45.8	46.1

Source: U.S. Bureau of Labor Statistics, Archived news releases: Union members (annual), www.bls.gov/schedule/archives/all_nr.htm#UNION2 (accessed June 9, 2009).

and hence federal employees', powers and rights.[8] For example, a number of studies examined the provisions of Clinton's National Performance Review as they applied to labor unions, such as the creation in 1993 of the National Partnership Council (NPC), which promoted the use of labor-management cooperation in order to advise the president on labor matters (see, for example, Ban 1995; Suntrup and Barnum 1997; Kearney and Hays 1998; Masters and Albright 1998).

Studies have also traced the effects of George W. Bush's regulations on labor-management relations (see Bennett and Masters 2004; Masters 2004; Masters and Albright 2003). For example, Thompson (2007) in a cogent study looks broadly at labor-management reforms under the George W. Bush administration, especially at its adversarial stance toward labor unions—one of the first orders of the Bush administration was to issue Executive Order 13203, revoking Clinton's executive order establishing the National Partnership Council. Thompson asks whether the reforms are part of a management philosophy to improve governmental performance, or simply an effort to expand presidential control over the federal bureaucracy. Through a detailed analysis of Bush's labor reforms, Thompson (105) first points out that "President George W. Bush has taken a series of aggressive, antiunion actions, canceling an executive order issued by his predecessor that directed federal agencies to cooperate with union representatives in addressing common issues, withdrawing collective bargaining rights from multiple groups of federal employees based on national security considerations, and significantly narrowing the scope of issues over which unions in two of the largest federal departments are permitted to bargain." Thompson concludes that Bush's strategy was, ultimately, shortsighted, and that in the long run, his regulations will fail because the effects will be to lower employee morale and hence productivity.

More recently, there has been some research examining an important source of union power at the federal level: litigation. Federal employee unions are very apt to file lawsuits challenging the government's actions that seek to restrict their already beleaguered powers. For example, in the early part of his administration, President George W. Bush sought to deregulate HRM in the newly created Department of Homeland Security (DHS). Key provisions of his regulations, which Bush promised to apply to the entire federal workforce, would prove detrimental to labor unions. They would have provided the DHS with the authority to declare labor contracts void at any given time after the contracts had been successfully entered into. In effect, the DHS could unilaterally negate otherwise lawful collective bargaining contracts (Riccucci and Thompson 2008). In a series of lawsuits filed by federal employee unions (see *National Treasury Employees Union, et al. v. Chertoff* 2005a, 2005b, 2006), the Bush administration was blocked from implementing the regulations.

In sum, research on public sector labor relations has been sporadic and uneven, despite the fact that unions are more prevalent in the public than in the private sector, as indicated in Table 8.1. Certainly, much more research is needed at the state and local levels. There are challenges to data collection and many questions that have not been empirically answered. For example, what are the reasons and circumstances surrounding states' decisions to allow public employee unions some modified right to strike or to allow some public employees access to such tools as binding interest arbitration and others only to mediation? Also, cyberunions, which emphasize the growing importance and use of computer technology by unions, have become increasingly important in the private sector. To what extent have they captured the interests of HR specialists in the public sector? More broadly, how has the growing use of information technology changed the practices of unions in the public sector? These questions have not been addressed and would certainly contribute to greater theory building in the area of public sector labor relations.

Additional research is also needed on federal employee unions. Content analyses of court rulings or congressional committee hearings can further build the research base in federal employee labor relations. So too would interviews with congressional members and union officials on the power structures of unions. Ethnographic studies on the culture of labor relations would also be beneficial. For example, although the Bush administration revoked the formal basis of labor-management cooperation, did the National Partnership Council work to minimize adversarial relations between labor and management representatives in the federal government? Case studies or narratives would also help to build theory in public sector unionism. The key for generating greater interest in these and other questions may rest in the greater encouragement of graduate students in public administration and management to conduct research on public sector labor relations.

PERFORMANCE MANAGEMENT

Over the past decade or so, a good deal of attention has been placed on performance management in efforts to improve government performance. Interestingly, however, there is a glaring misconception around the use of the concept of *performance management.* As Risher and Fay (2007) point out, government employers have haphazardly conflated the terms *performance management* and *performance appraisal,* but the two refer to different functions. Performance appraisals are an HRM function, aimed at evaluating an individual employee's performance, generally once a year, to determine how well that employee is performing on the job. Based on the results, no action is taken, rewards are given, or disciplinary actions can be taken. In general, performance appraisal programs are aimed at past performance, not potential future employee performance.

In contrast, performance management is a broader, more comprehensive managerial process aimed at agency or departmental performance, and it is future oriented. It begins with performance planning discussions and focuses on the planned performance of a department or agency (not an individual), with a goal of improvement from the prior year. It has sought to promote the accountability of government agencies and programs. The Program Assessment Rating Tool, or PART, is an example of a tool aimed at evaluating and improving performance in the federal government in order to achieve better results. It is important to note that governments have not been able to develop methods of linking agency or department performance with individual employee performance.

Governments at every level have sought to motivate employees to improve their performance by offering merit pay raises or pay for performance (Bowman 1994, 2010). At the federal level, the Civil Service Reform Act of 1978 was one of the first major efforts that sought to link employee pay with performance. It contained two major provisions: merit pay for midlevel managers and merit pay for the Senior Executive Service (SES), the highest rungs of federal employment. James Perry in particular has written extensively on the former. Under this system, midlevel managers could be rewarded with pay increases for demonstrating "efficient" and "effective" behavior without having to promote them to a higher grade or salary step. As Perry (1986, 1991) and others (see, for example, Bowman 2010; Hays 2004, Kellough and Nigro 2002; Milkovich and Widgor 1991) found, efforts to link pay to performance were largely unsuccessful. First, there were problems with efforts to measure efficient and effective behavior. Second, merit pay was hampered by politics, whereby the most deserving employees were not being rewarded for their behaviors; favoritism played more into the decisions to reward employees than actual performance. In general, as Bowman (2010) has pointed out, "pay clearly matters. But as experience demonstrates, it is difficult to link compensation policies to desired results; good intentions are not necessarily assumed in a political environment, and in any event are simply not enough." Because of its failure to link pay with performance, this merit pay system was abolished in 1984.

The other provision of the Civil Service Reform Act sought to link pay to the performance of SESers. Here the top of the general schedule in the federal government was converted into "supergrades." As Ingraham (1987, 1993) has noted, this change was prompted more by the desire for managerial control over the bureaucracy whereby the most-senior-level workers could be transferred between and among federal agencies depending upon their performance. Also subject to the vagaries of politics, those SESers who performed well could receive one-time bonuses upward of $20,000, while those who were deemed underachievers by their political superiors were subject to transfer or dismissal from the SES. It would appear that merit pay programs were geared more toward attempting to control government employee behavior than toward genuinely seeking to reward good performers. Overall, these early efforts seeking to link employee performance to pay have failed.

Nevertheless, this has not prevented the government from continuing down this path (see Paarlberg, Perry, and Hondeghem 2008; Kellough and Lu 1993). One of the most recent efforts to link pay to performance was implemented under the George W. Bush administration. In early 2002 the DHS and the Department of Defense launched pay-for-performance systems. Interestingly, the pay increases would purportedly be linked to *organizational* outcomes, as measured by employee performance reviews. Objections to the plans by labor unions have created delays in the implementation of the new pay system at the DHS, resulting in its application only to *nonbargaining*-unit employees. As of this writing, it cannot be determined whether the plan is effective, but this presents an area ripe for research opportunities, particularly efforts to link individual performance with organizational outcomes, over which, for political reasons, employees may have little control.

The Department of Defense is experiencing similar delays, but a major challenge has been writing measurable job objectives or developing ways to link pay raises to performance. Efforts to move forward with the pay-for-performance plans persist, despite earlier failures in the federal government's experiences to link agency or department performance to individual employee performance.

Pay for performance is perhaps one of the most maligned areas in HRM. For one thing, appraisals tend to be subjective, impressionistic, and political, as the experience with the merit pay plan for midlevel managers as well as the SESers showed. Another problem with performance appraisal systems is that the preponderance of government work is not readily measurable in terms of outputs. The government is in the business of producing not products, but rather services. Measuring the quality of services is difficult because quality in government must take into account such factors as equity, justice, due process, accountability, and others that are not easily quantifiable. The government must pursue these values in the provision of services to American citizens. This is what distinguishes performance appraisal in the public sector from private enterprise, where goods as well as services may be more amenable to quantification, since values of equity, due process, and so forth are not at issue.

Bowman (2010) points out that "pay-for-performance programs may well have become an urban legend." Yet, despite the various challenges, performance appraisal systems, particularly those that seek to link pay with performance, are widely used. As a result, it is critical that future studies examine other variables that may lead to an improved or revitalized public service. For example, a number of other strategies such as training and development may be more viable, yet few studies exist for this topic. A number of studies examine the relationship between job satisfaction and job training (see Ritchie, Kirche, and Rubens 2006), but research needs to examine the potential linkage between job training and enhanced employee performance, since this is the subject matter that government institutions and perhaps the general public are most interested in.

SUCCESSION PLANNING

Human resources planning and, more recently, succession planning are key to an organization's overall strategic workforce planning efforts (U.S. Government Accountability Office 2005). Retirements, downsizing, outsourcing, and aging workers all create a need for effective succession planning in government, whereby key leadership and professional positions are filled. Yet, compared to the private sector, there is a dearth of research in this area, primarily because as Schall (1997) points out, governments across the country to do not readily engage in succession planning (also see Jarrell and Pewitt 2007; Pynes 2004; Kim 2002, 2003; Lynn 2001). Schall (1997, 4) argues that "succession planning is rarely used by public agencies because the executive's fortunes are generally tied to a particular administration." Another reason, she states, is because "leaders in the public sector have themselves not taken the issue of succession seriously" (6). Other reasons may relate to civil services rules regulating promotions, the use of seniority, and the burgeoning costs of succession planning, which would lead public sector officials to move it down the list of priorities, as they do with other vital HRM functions such as training and career development.

Nevertheless, succession planning is critical in the public sector, as government workforces continue to age, downsize, and outsource their labor (National Academy of Public Administration 1997). As Pynes (2004, 389–390) points out,

> Agency leaders need to understand how their workplaces will be affected by impending changes and prepare for the changes accordingly. Agency objectives should be formulated after relevant data on the quantity and potential of available human resources have been reviewed. Are there human resources available for short- and long-term objectives? To be competitive, organizations must be able to anticipate, influence and manage the forces that impact their ability to remain effective. In the service sector, this means they must be able to manage their human resource capabilities. All too often agencies have relied on short-term service requirements to direct their HRM practices. Little thought is often given to long-term implications. By invoking WFSP, agencies are better able to match their human resources requirements with the demands of the external environment and the needs of the organization. The human resources focus is not just an individual employee issue; it also focuses on integrating human resources into the organization's strategy. It becomes part of the visionary process. Strategic planning, budgeting and human resource planning are linked together.

Jarrell and Pewitt (2007) make the important point that succession planning is an ongoing process that not only involves the development of a succession plan, but maps out (1) how employees will be selected and staffed, (2) the sustainability of the program, and (3) the impact and evaluation of the program. Most important, as they and others argue, it must receive adequate funding at all stages.

Many have framed the issue of succession planning as a talent management issue (see Garrow and Hirsh 2008). For example, Dychtwaid and Baxter (2007, 325) state,

> We are heading toward a talent crisis of unparalleled proportions. In the latter decades of the 20th century, organizations enjoyed an abundance of young workers, fueled by the unprecedented baby boom that stretched from 1946 until 1964. In this century, the baby bust that followed the baby boom is creating a critical shortage of younger workers. At the same time, due to rising longevity and the aging of the baby boom generation, we are now experiencing an unprecedented growth in the numbers of mature workers. And yet, the vast majority of organizations persist in recruiting, training, engagement, and retention strategies that were created and designed for a youthful workforce.

Dychtwaid and Baxter (2007) also stress the need for succession planning to stave off a talent crisis in government workforces. Similarly, in the context of succession planning Calo (2008) argues that talent management is critical for the sake of knowledge transfer. He points out that "organizations must take steps to develop a strategy for successfully transferring the valuable knowledge that resides in their older workers to other members of their workforce. Denial, delay, or doing nothing may be appealing responses in the short term, especially when there is some evidence that older workers are working longer and that the supply of workers appears to be in balance with or exceeding demand" (404). But, he argues, in the long run, if governments do not engage in succession planning, they run the risk of being at a competitive disadvantage when competing for talent and intellectual capital.

The U.S. Government Accountability Office (GAO) has pointed out that succession planning is also an important practice for diversity management. In its 2005 report *Diversity Management: Expert-Identified Leading Practices and Agency Examples,* the GAO argues that succession planning "is tied to the federal government's opportunity to change the diversity of the executive corps through new appointments" (15). It goes on to say that

> the federal government faces large losses in its SES, primarily through retirement but also because of other normal attrition. The SES generally represents the most experienced and senior segment of the federal workforce. The expected loss of more than half of current career SES members through fiscal year 2007, as well as significant attrition in the GS-15 and GS-14 workforce—the key source for SES appointments—has important implications for federal agencies and underscores the need for effective succession planning. This presents the government with substantial challenges for ensuring an able management cadre and also presents opportunities to affect the composition of the SES.

A good deal of research is still needed on the use of succession planning in government agencies across the United States. There are some cases studies showing how successful it is in practice at the state and local levels (see, for example, Jarrell and Pewitt 2007; Pynes 2004; Holinsworth 2004; Kim 2002, 2003) and in federal agencies (see U.S. GAO 2005). Much more is needed, however. Additional case studies illustrating its successes may encourage greater use of succession planning in the public sector. As Pynes (2004, 402) concludes in her study, "Effective [succession planning] approaches serve as the foundation of any serious HRM initiative. They must be at the center of efforts to transform the cultures of agencies so that they become results-oriented and externally focused. To facilitate these changes, HRM personnel and department managers must acquire new competencies to be able to deliver HRM services and shift toward a more consultative role for HR staff."

THE NEED FOR FUTURE RESEARCH

As discussed previously, there are a number of areas in HRM that continue to demand attention. For example, in light of the U.S. Supreme Court decision in *Ricci* (2009), to what extent are cities and states across the country developing promotional exams that will effectively foster racial, ethnic, and gender diversity, without being vulnerable to "reverse discrimination" attacks? Are cities, as is the case with Bridgeport, Connecticut, described earlier, moving more toward favoring oral exams, given their relative success in fostering diversity, or is New Haven, Connecticut, more characteristic of the norm? Also, additional research is sorely needed on the efficacy of diversity programs. As Pitts and Wise (2010), point out, "Although arguments such as the business case for diversity are intuitively appealing and politically popular, there is little evidence that organizational diversity can be used to boost performance. Whether employee diversity improves organizational performance is an empirical question that has not been adequately tested in the public sector context."

Other areas ripe for research include public sector labor relations. In addition to the suggestions given in this chapter, there is very little comparative evidence on why, for example, some states have striking rights, while most others prohibit public sector unions from striking. Moreover, it is unclear whether the strike option is even used in those states, and if it is, how effective it has been for settling contract disputes. Additional comparative aspects of public sector labor relations that have not been studied include binding interest arbitration, scope of bargaining, and union organizing. Schools and departments of public administration across the country are not producing scholars who are studying this vital area of human resources management.

Although pay-for-performance programs will continue to be relied upon, despite the lack of evidence showing a linkage, other variables examining links with job performance could be explored. As noted, level of job satisfaction is one variable. Another is public service motivation (Perry 1996; Perry and Wise 1990). While it is widely believed that the level of public service motivation increases job performance, very little research has tested this question or hypothesis (see Bright 2007).

Finally, very little research exists on succession planning in the public sector. Because governments focus more on short- than on long-term planning, it is not as common as it is in the private sector. Nonetheless, as we have seen, some governments do rely on succession planning. An important first step might be to survey state and local governments as well as federal agencies to discover the extent to which it is actually being relied upon. Comparative case studies might then illustrate its benefits with respect to overall strategic planning in the public service.

CONCLUSION

Human resources management represents a vital field of public administration from the standpoint of both practice and theory. Governments at every level continually experiment with programs and policies to improve as well as control public employee behavior and performance. Affirmative action serves as a legal tool to diversify organizations, which enhances the overall productivity, not to mention democratic aspects of government institutions. Unions seek to protect the interests of public employees, but governments, particularly at the federal level, continue to promote reforms that can circumvent the goals of public employee unions. Of course, governments remain committed to improving employee performance and even linking it to overall organizational productivity. Yet, at the same time, governments may not be preparing for the future in that succession planning is not a staple of their HRM processes or strategies.

All these efforts provide rich opportunities for continual research in HRM. Case studies and best practices in particular help to build theory in HRM and more broadly in public management. They also serve as constructive examples for governments seeking to diversify their workplaces, genuinely work with unions to improve the working conditions of public employees, and ultimately improve their performance.

NOTES

1. It should be noted that the Supreme Court assesses the constitutionality of race-based affirmative action plans under the two-pronged strict-scrutiny test, which asks: (1) Is there a compelling government interest in the program or plan (e.g., to redress past discrimination) and (2) is it sufficiently narrowly tailored to meet its specified goals (i.e., is there an alternative plan or program that could be employed that does not classify people by race)? For gender, the Court applies the less exacting intermediate-scrutiny test, asking whether or not a governmental action is "substantially related" to an important or compelling government interest.

2. See Note 1.

3. *Runyon v. McCrary* (1976).

4. Compare to the Court's decision the same day in *Gratz v. Bollinger* (2003), in which the Court struck down the use of affirmative action by the University of Michigan's undergraduate programs. The Court found that the rating system employed by the university resembled a "quota" system because it granted points for a number of factors including "underrepresented" racial and ethnic status; thus, according to the Court it was unconstitutional under the Equal Protection Clause of the Fourteenth Amendment. The Court obviously favored the admissions program in *Grutter,* in which a point system was not used, and race was among a number of factors considered for admission to the law school.

5. Wisconsin was the first state to mandate collective bargaining for government workers in 1959. A number of other states soon followed suit (e.g., New York in 1967). Today, about forty states, in addition to the District of Columbia, have enacted laws mandating that governments at the state and local levels collectively bargain with employees' union representatives. As of this writing, there are eight states that do not have collective bargaining legislation covering public employees: Arizona, Arkansas, Colorado, Louisiana, Mississippi, North Carolina, South Carolina, and Virginia. For a discussion, see Kearney (2008).

6. As of this writing, the following thirteen states permit public employees some modified right to strike: Alaska, California, Hawaii, Idaho, Illinois, Minnesota, Montana, Ohio, Oregon, Pennsylvania, Rhode Island, Vermont, and Wisconsin (Kearney 2008).

7. The major source of union power in the federal government comes from sympathetic Democrats in Congress who tend to have large cohorts of federal employees in their districts. They serve as the primary watchdogs for federal employees' pay and conditions of employment.

8. Also see some of the studies following President Reagan's firing of air traffic controllers in 1981. See, for example, Beer and Spector (1982); Northrup (1984); and Perry (1985).

REFERENCES

Ban, Carolyn. 1995. Unions, management, and the NPR. In *Inside the Reinvention Machine: Appraising Governmental Reform,* ed. Donald F. Kettl and John J. DiIulio Jr., 131–151. Washington, DC: Brookings Institution.

Beer, Michael, and Bert A. Spector. 1982. Air traffic controllers. *Harvard Business School Cases* (May): 1–22.

Bennett, James T., and Marick F. Masters. 2004. The future of public sector labor-management relations: Part II—The federal sector. *Journal of Labor Research* 25 (1): 1–8.

Bowman, James S. 1994. At last, an alternative to performance appraisal: Total quality management. *Public Administration Review* 54 (2): 129–136.

————. 2010. The success of failure: The paradox of performance pay. *Review of Public Personnel Administration* 30 (1): 70–88.

Bright, Leonard. 2007. Does person-organization fit mediate the relationship between public service motivation and the job performance of public employees? *Review of Public Personnel Administration* 27 (4): 361–379.

Calo, Thomas J. 2008. Talent management in the era of the aging workforce: The critical role of knowledge transfer. *Public Personnel Management* 37 (4): 403–416.

City of Richmond v. Croson. 1989. 488 U.S. 469.

Dychtwaid, Ken, and David Baxter. 2007. Capitalizing on the new mature workforce. *Public Personnel Management* 36 (4): 325–334.

Fullilove v. Klutznick. 1980. 448 U.S. 448.

Garrow, Valerie, and Wendy Hirsh. 2008. Talent management: Issues of focus and fit. *Public Personnel Management* 37 (4): 389–402.

Gratz v. Bollinger. 2003. 123 S. Ct. 2411.

Grutter v. Bollinger. 2003. 123 S. Ct. 2325.

Guy, Mary E., ed. 1992. *Women and Men of the States: Public Administrators at the State Level.* Armonk, NY: M.E. Sharpe.

————. 1993. Three steps forward, two steps backward: The status of women's integration into public management. *Public Administration Review* 53 (4): 285–292.

Hays, Steven W. 2004. Trends and best practices in state and local human resource management. *Review of Public Personnel Administration* 24 (3): 256–275.

Holinsworth, Sheryn R. 2004. Case study: Henrico County, Virginia: Succession management: A developmental approach. *Public Personnel Management* 33 (4): 475–486.

Ingraham, Patricia W. 1987. Building bridges or burning them? The president, the appointees, and the bureaucracy. *Public Administration Review* 47 (5): 425–435.

————. 1993. Of pigs in pokes and policy diffusion: Another look at pay-for-performance. *Public Administration Review* 53 (4): 348–356.

Ingraham, Patricia W., and David H. Rosenbloom, eds. 1992. *The Promise and Paradox of Civil Service Reform.* Pittsburgh, PA: University of Pittsburgh Press.

Int'l Assoc. of Firefighters v. City of Cleveland. 1986. 478 U.S. 501.

Jarrell, Karen M., and Kyle Coby Pewitt. 2007. Succession planning in government: Case study of a medium-sized city. *Review of Public Personnel Administration* 27 (3): 297–309.

Johnson v. Transportation Agency of Santa Clara County. 1987. 480 U.S. 624.

Kearney, Richard C. 1979. The impact of police unionization on municipal budgetary outcomes. *International Journal of Public Administration* 1 (4): 361–379.

————. 1984. *Labor Relations in the Public Sector.* New York: Marcel Dekker.

————. 2008. *Labor Relations in the Public Sector.* 4th ed. New York: Taylor and Francis.

Kearney, Richard C., and Steven W. Hays. 1998. Reinventing government, the new public management and civil service systems in international perspective: The danger of throwing the baby out with the bathwater. *Review of Public Personnel Administration* 18 (4): 38–54.

Kearney, Richard C., and David R. Morgan. 1980. The impact of unionization on the compensation of municipal police. *Journal of Collective Negotiations* 9 (Spring): 361–379.

Keiser, Lael R., Vicky M. Wilkins, Kenneth J. Meier, and Catherine Holland. 2002. Lipstick and logarithms: Gender, institutional context, and representative bureaucracy. *American Political Science Review* 96 (3): 553–564.

Kellough, J. Edward, and Haoran Lu. 1993. The paradox of merit pay. *Review of Public Personnel Administration* 13 (2): 45–64.

Kellough, J. Edward, and Lloyd G. Nigro. 2002. Pay for performance in Georgia state government. *Review of Public Personnel Administration* 22 (2): 146–166.

Kim, Soonhee. 2002. Organizational support of career development and job satisfaction. *Review of Public Personnel Administration* 22 (4): 276–294.

————. 2003. Linking employee assessments to succession planning. *Public Personnel Management* 32 (4): 533–547.

Krislov, Samuel, and David H. Rosenbloom. 1981. *Representative Bureaucracy and the American Political System.* New York: Praeger.

Lynn, Dahlia Bradshaw. 2001. Succession management strategies in public sector organizations: Building leadership capital. *Review of Public Personnel Administration* 21 (2): 114–132.

Martin v. Wilks. 1989. 490 U.S. 755.

Masters, Marick F. 2004. Federal-sector unions: Current status and future directions. *Journal of Labor Research* 25 (1): 55–82.

Masters, Marick F., and Robert R. Albright. 1998. Federal managers and union representatives view partnership. *Public Manager* 27 (3): 33–36.

———. 2003. Labor relations in the Department of Homeland Security: Competing perspectives and future possibilities. *Labor Law Journal* 54 (1): 66–83.

Meier, Kenneth J. 1975. Representative bureaucracy: An empirical analysis. *American Political Science Review* 69 (2): 526–542.

———. 1993. Representative bureaucracy: A theoretical and empirical exposition. In *Research in Public Administration,* ed. James Perry, 1–35. Greenwich, CT: JAI Press.

Meier, Kenneth J., and Jill Nicholson-Crotty. 2006. Gender, representative bureaucracy, and law enforcement: The case of sexual assault. *Public Administration Review* 66 (6): 850–860.

Meier, Kenneth J., and Kevin B. Smith. 1994. Representative democracy and representative bureaucracy: Examining the top down and bottom up linkages. *Social Science Quarterly* 75 (4): 790–803.

Merit Systems Protection Board. 2009. *Job Simulations: Trying Out for a Federal Job.* Washington, DC: U.S. Merit Systems Protection Board.

Methé, David T., and James L. Perry. 1980. The impacts of collective bargaining on local government services: A review of research. *Public Administration Review* 40 (4): 359–371.

Milkovich, George T., and Alexandra K. Widgor, eds. 1991. *Pay for Performance: Evaluating Performance of Appraisal and Merit Pay.* Washington, DC: National Academy Press.

Naff, Katherine C. 2001. *To Look Like America: Dismantling Barriers for Women and Minorities in Government.* Boulder, CO: Westview Press.

National Academy of Public Administration. 1997. *Paths to Leadership: Executive Succession Planning in the Federal Government.* Washington, DC: National Academy of Public Administration.

National Treasury Employees Union, et al. v. Chertoff. 2005a. 385 F. Supp. 2d 1.

———. 2005b. 394 F. Supp. 2d 137. October.

———. 2006. 452 F.3d 839. D.C. Cir.

Northrup, Herbert R. 1984. The rise and demise of PATCO. *Industrial and Labor Relations Review* 37 (2): 167–184.

Paarlberg, Laurie E., James L. Perry, and Annie Hondeghem. 2008. From theory to practice: Strategies for applying public service motivation. In *Motivation in Public Management: The Call of Public Service,* ed. James L. Perry and Annie Hondeghem, 268–293. New York: Oxford University Press.

Patterson v. McLean Credit Union. 1989. 491 U.S. 164.

Perry, James L. 1985. The "old testament": A litany of beliefs about public sector labor. *Review of Public Personnel Administration* 5 (2): 1–4.

———. 1986. Merit pay in the public sector: The case for a failure of theory. *Review of Public Personnel Administration* 7 (1): 57–69.

———. 1991. Linking pay to performance: The controversy continues. In *Public Personnel Management: Current Concerns, Future Challenges,* ed. Carolyn Ban and Norma M. Riccucci, 73–86. White Plains, NY: Longman Press.

———. 1996. Measuring public service motivation: An assessment of construct reliability and validity. *Journal of Public Administration Research and Theory* 6 (1): 5–22.

Perry, James L., and Lois Recascino Wise. 1990. The motivational bases of public service. *Public Administration Review* 50 (3): 367–373.

Pitts, David W., and Lois Recascino Wise. 2010. Workforce diversity in the new millennium: Prospects for research. *Review of Public Personnel Administration* 30 (1): 44–69.

Pynes, Joan. 2004. The implementation of workforce and succession planning in the public sector. *Public Personnel Management* 33 (4): 389–404.

Regents of the University of California v. Bakke. 1978. 438 U.S. 265.

Ricci v. DeStefano. 2009. 2009 U.S. LEXIS 4945. June. www.lexisnexis.com.proxy.libraries.rutgers.edu/us/lnacademic/search/casessubmitForm.do (accessed June 30, 2009, and November 4, 2009).

Riccucci, Norma M. 2007. The changing face of public employee unionism. *Review of Public Personnel Administration* 27 (1): 71–78.

Riccucci, Norma M., and Frank J. Thompson. 2008. The new public management, Homeland Security, and the politics of civil service reform. *Public Administration Review* 68 (5): 877–890.

Risher, Howard, and Charles H. Fay. 2007. *Managing for Better Performance: Enhancing Federal Perfor-mance Management Practices.* Washington, DC: Center for the Business of Government.

Ritchie, William J., Elias Kirche, and Arthur J. Rubens. 2006. A process for development and validation of a customized scale to assess work environment in government organizations: A mixed method approach. *Review of Public Personnel Administration* 26 (4): 382–389.

Rosenbloom, David H., and Jeannette C. Featherstonhaugh. 1977. Passive and active representation in the federal service: A comparison of blacks and whites. *Social Science Quarterly* 57 (4): 873–882.

Rosenbloom, David H., and Jay M. Shafritz. 1985. *Essentials of Labor Relations.* Reston, VA: Reston Publishing.

Runyon v. McCrary. 1976. 427 U.S. 160.

Schall, Ellen. 1997. Public sector succession: A strategic approach to sustaining innovation. *Public Admin-istration Review* 57 (1): 4–10.

Suntrup, Edward L., and Darold T. Barnum. 1997. Reinventing the federal government: Forging new labor-management partnerships for the 1990s. In *Unions and Workplace Reorganizations,* ed. Bruce Nissen, 145–158. Detroit, MI: Wayne State University Press.

Thompson, James R. 2007. Federal labor-management relations reforms under Bush: Enlightened manage-ment or quest for control? *Review of Public Personnel Administration* 27 (2): 105–124.

United Steelworkers of America v. Weber. 1979. 443 U.S. 193.

U.S. v. Paradise. 1987. 480 U.S. 149.

U.S. Government Accountability Office (U.S. GAO). 2005. *Diversity Management: Expert-Identified Leading Practices and Agency Examples.* Washington, DC: U.S. General Accountability Office.

Wise, Lois R. 1990. Social equity in civil service systems. *Public Administration Review* 50 (5): 567–575.

CHAPTER 9

NEW DIRECTIONS IN PUBLIC BUDGETING

IRENE S. RUBIN

Public budgeting in the distant past was mostly a technical activity in which estimates of the next year's spending were gathered from departments and presented directly to the legislative body. Budgeting was legislatively dominated and highly decentralized. The scope of government activities was relatively limited. A small amount of new revenue might be available each year, which would be divided among existing programs, more or less in accordance with their proportion of the existing budget. There was little reprioritization and hence limited conflict over resources. This model of budgeting comported well with the idea that politics and administration could be separated from each other, with major policy decisions made by elected officials outside the administrative process. Famously described by Aaron Wildavsky as incrementalism, this budget model underlies many of the norms and rules of public budgeting.[1]

Public budgeting has changed enormously over time, with implications for both practitioners and academics. This chapter describes major issues and trends that have occurred since the 1921 Budget and Accounting Act, and outlines budget reforms that must occur to keep pace with these changes.

BUDGETING AND POLICY DEVELOPMENT

Budgeting has become much more policy laden and conflictual in recent years.[2] Policy and partisan conflicts often hold up the budget, sometimes past the start of the budget year. In 2009 alone, on Tuesday, June 30, just before the beginning of the new fiscal year, fourteen states lacked a final budget. Half resolved their problems in some way before midnight, but seven states began the new fiscal year without a signed budget. Pennsylvania has missed its June 30 deadline every year since 2003.[3]

Especially during times when the economy grows slowly and revenues fall behind estimates, cutbacks pose the possibility—and need—to reprioritize. These problems occur at all levels of government. Even small cities may have to decide how much they can afford for streets and sanitation, police and fire protection, and education. Unions, nonprofits dependent on the public budget, and program advocates sometimes round up supporters to sit in at council meetings where the budget is being decided. These decisions are controversial, often political, and clearly policy laden.

Not only is policy made through the budget and the budget made through policy decisions—as when a new drug benefit was added to Medicare—but the processes of making decisions themselves have become more policy laden and therefore more contestable. At the national level, in recent years, the term *budget process* has become oxymoronic, because a process suggests a list of rules, followed in sequence, known by the participants, and repeated from year to year. But the reality has been that the budget process has often been invented on the fly, during the year.

Part of the trend toward greater politicization of budgeting has to do with the increased scope of government and the different tools and program designs that are now in frequent use. Since the Great Depression, there has been an expansion of the use of and size of entitlement programs, which grant money directly to individuals or other levels of government when they meet certain requirements. Programs such as Social Security benefit huge numbers of people who form not so much an interest group as an interest class or sector of society—in this case, the aged. The political difficulty of reducing benefits of this sort to those who are dependent on them is evident in the description of Social Security as the third rail of politics—touch it and you die politically. Thus, the old model, which downplayed the public as a major budgetary actor, has been replaced by a different model.

NEW BUDGETING MODEL

Government at the national level and to some extent at the state level as well has taken on a greater role in the economy and in doing so has added a variety of new tools, including insurance, loans, loan guarantees, and even (temporary.) equity purchases. (Figure 9.1 highlights major differences among federal, state, and local budgeting.) Tax breaks for businesses or industries add to the mix, along with economic development tools, such as tax increment financing, that allow cities to spend money from other overlapping governments on economic development projects. These tools generate not only supporters outside of government but also potential conflict between governments in the same geographic area.

Many more actors get into the budget process than envisioned in the early models. One consequence is that some portions of the budget are protected by powerful interests. Rather than across-the-board cuts that seem on the surface fair to all, reductions in spending conform to what is politically acceptable. Moreover, one set of interests may push for spending increases while another argues for limits on taxation. To the extent that both are accommodated, the result is structural budget gaps, making deficits and their elimination a common feature of budgetary politics. Since people fight hard to keep what they have, efforts to rebalance the budget often are fought intensely; they are not a set of technical decisions quietly addressed by professional public administrators.

With much more at stake, the issue of who controls the budget has taken on more urgency. During the early 1900s, legislative controls shifted more to the executive. In New York, Illinois, and Maryland, the governor got nearly complete power over the budget. The 1921 Budget and Accounting Act at the national level shifted some power to the executive from the legislative branch, with the result that budget power was more evenly distributed between the two branches. This balance has not been stable or without controversy, however. When delegated powers were abused in the 1970s, Congress took back some of that delegated power by enacting the 1974 Congressional Budget and Impoundment Control Act.

At the state level, in those states in which the governor was granted a disproportionate amount of budgetary power, legislatures have fought for years to regain some influence.[4] In other states that were more legislatively dominated, power has shifted slowly more to the governor.

The tension between the executive and legislative branches over budgeting power has shown up even at the local level. Several large cities (e.g., St. Petersburg, Florida; San Diego, California; and Rochester, New York) have in recent years changed from a council manager

Figure 9.1   **Budgeting Differences Among Federal, State, and Local Governments**

1. The federal government can borrow to balance its budget, and it need not balance its budget each year. State and local governments, while they may borrow to close gaps sometimes, generally are required to balance their budgets each year. They do not always succeed, but they often try mightily to do so.

2. The national government has a much greater role in the economy than do state governments, and both have a larger role than local governments, which generally are too small and have borders too permeable to have much effect on the economy.

3. The national government and the states, sometimes in partnership, offer entitlements, the local governments much less so or not at all. Thus, the policy implications of entitlements affect local governments much less than they do national or state governments.

4. The national government and the states both have independent functions, the states are not technically speaking subordinates of the national government, but the local governments are creatures of the states and hence have much less autonomy. The states are also more responsible for the finances of the local governments.

5. Separation of the executive and legislative branches is much more clearly institutionalized at the state and national levels than at the local level, where the chief executive may be picked by and fired by the legislative body.

form to a strong mayor form, with an accompanying increase in executive budget control and enhanced veto power.

BUDGETING AS A POLITICAL EXERCISE

Budgeting is inherently political because it allocates to some purposes and not to others and benefits some at the greater expense of others. In addition to this inherent political content, the long-term trend is toward greater politicization and greater policy content. As this has occurred, the amount of conflict also has increased. The traditional techniques for keeping the level of conflict in control seem insufficient for the modern budget, sometimes bringing budgets into deficit—to appear to satisfy all claimants—and sometimes bringing the budget process to a standstill. Budget processes need to be able to deal with this increased scope, increased politicization, and increased conflict. The norms of budgeting, and the ways we describe budgeting, the concepts, have not necessarily kept up with this new reality, which requires new ways of thinking about balance, prioritization, participation, transparency, and accountability.

Budgeting has come a long way since its origins, with many waves of reform proposed and actually implemented—though the scholarly community has often focused on the reforms that did not seem to take hold rather than the ones that did.[5] But we seemed to have run out of reform proposals, calling on the old ones again and again, such as performance budgeting, or balanced budget amendments. The Federal Budget Concepts, created by a presidential commission in 1967, presents requirements for making the budget easily interpretable, and able to address simultaneously the needs of the economists and those of administrators. Although there has been some important work since 1967 on how to present loans in the budget, the budget concepts themselves have not been subject to a comprehensive review. As budgeting has evolved to include many different types of programs, including entitlements, loans, loan guarantees, and investments such as the purchase of equity shares, the concepts have not kept up.

Budgeting has continued to change in major ways, generating a new set of problems. It is time for some major reforms. Some of the research that needs to underlie such reforms has already been done, while other pieces are still to be carried out.

EXPANDING BUDGETING BEYOND INCREMENTAL ANNUAL COSTS

One of the major changes in budgeting has been the addition of different kinds of programs that do not have the characteristics of traditional budgeting, including entitlements, tax expenditures, grants, loans, loan guarantees, insurance, and equity shares.[6] Those who continue to consider public budgeting incremental have to focus on an increasingly small share of the budget, particularly at the national and state levels.

At the national level, so-called mandatory spending, for entitlements and interest on the debt, is about 60 percent of federal outlays; the traditional programs that were "controllable" through votes each year, and that grew a little each year, now occupy less than 40 percent of the outlays. By contrast, in the early 1960s, mandatory spending was about 32 percent of outlays.

It is difficult to summarize the state experience, but as at the national level, entitlements are taking a larger percentage of the budget. In Maryland, for example, two thirds of the general fund appropriation is mandatory spending.[7] For Medicaid alone, the most important entitlement program at the state level, Maine, Missouri, and Pennsylvania spent more than 30 percent of their budgets in 2007. The national average was at that time 14 percent.[8]

Recent efforts by the national government to bail out companies and prop up a failing economy highlight both the expanded scope of the government and the variety of resources and program structures that are used. The variety of these resources challenges traditional budgeting norms and concepts, such as annuality, balance, and consolidation, and introduces more risk and uncertainty than public budgeting has been used to. Many are not structured for annual review and funding; they may not last a full year, or they may go on indefinitely. Entitlements may be perpetual, and government bailout loans may be for months, rather than years.

It is not only the duration of different programs that varies; different jurisdictions dependent on each other may have different fiscal years, so that some revenue sources may be determined during instead of before the beginning of the budget year. This adds to the level of uncertainty in the budget. For example, at the state and local levels, if the donor government and the recipient government have different fiscal years, grants may have different fiscal years than the rest of the budget. In Michigan, the state fiscal year begins in October, while nearly all the local governments begin their budgets in July, with the result that the local governments have to guess at the state allocation, and then wait three months to see what the state actually does. Schools hire teachers they may have to lay off at midyear, while cities may hire police officers or firefighters they later find they cannot afford.[9] The state of Illinois begins its fiscal year in July—though it sometimes doesn't complete the budget on time—while many of the local governments in Illinois begin their fiscal years in April or May, well before they know how much the state will give them.

Some spending, such as for loan guarantees and insurance, is contingent, rather than actual, meaning that some unknown portion of it will end up as a government outlay. Even expenditures that are not contingent may be known or understood only within a range. Loan dollars going out the door are known, but what proportion of those loans will default, and hence the real costs of the program, remain unknown until the end of those loans. These numbers are thus estimates, spongy, accurate only within a range.

The variety of characteristics of each of these resources means that they do not add to each other in a meaningful way. For example, numbers that are more spongy should not be added to those that are more precise; estimates for tax expenditures do not add to each other, let alone to other spending figures. While budgets have always been estimates, on both the revenue and expenditure sides, the numbers in different parts of the budget have generally been comparable, so that adding them up across accounts and programs makes a kind of sense. The more different the resources, the less sense this process makes. One cannot meaningfully add a total of tax expenditures, which is itself not meaningful, to loan guarantees or other forms of insurance that are not direct outlays, to spending for stock purchases, which are themselves a form of money, but which have value that varies from day to day. That these different resources do not add up meaningfully and occur for different periods of time, rather than a single fiscal year, brings into question what balance means and how to calculate it.

BUDGETING AND ENTITLEMENTS

One of the main changes in budgeting over the years has been the creation and expansion of entitlement programs. The entitlements occupy the majority of the federal and large portions of state budgets. The characteristics of mandated spending are therefore critical not only to understanding budgeting as it has become, but also to highlighting current problems in public budgeting.

Entitlements merge program design and budget approval into one step, because the costs of the program are inherent in its design. Once the program has been approved, the costs of the program, the dollar outlays, are determined not by the legislature or the executive on an annual basis, but by the number of recipients who are eligible and the costs of delivering the service. This feature has a number of consequences.

One consequence is that budgeting for entitlements is either multiyear or so-called no year, which means it keeps on going; it does not need or indeed allow annual spending approval. This feature has led to the concept of "uncontrollables," which refers to spending that cannot be directly determined each year the way operating expenses are determined in the appropriations process. Entitlements are not actually uncontrollable but are difficult to control. The legislative committees that design these programs, which are not the appropriations committees, can alter who is eligible to receive benefits from these programs and how generous the benefits will be. Such changes may take years to agree on and more years before they take effect. Because these benefits are taken for granted and integrated into people's lives, and because so many people receive these benefits, entitlement programs can be politically difficult to reduce. They may grow automatically as costs rise, unless there is legislative intervention.

The multiyear and ongoing nature of the entitlements and the difficulty of cutting them back mean that entitlements challenge the concept of the annual budget, in which revenues and expenditures are determined for the following year, and balance is more or less assured. This concept of annual or biennial budget has been central to public budgeting but is not conceptually applicable to entitlements.

A second feature of entitlements is that they are automatic; they take priority in the budget. Other needs in the budget come after the entitlements have been covered. It is as if there were a permanent judgment that entitlements were the most important priorities of government, and other expenditures, for clean air or water, for public health, for safety, or for education were automatically of lower priority. Since entitlements are growing more rapidly than revenue, nonentitlement programs are being squeezed. Prioritization in the nonentitlement portion of the budget is increasingly limited to what to cut back or eliminate, not what to add, or what to emphasize. Entitlements thus force an intensification of competition between nonentitlement programs and simultaneously structure the process of prioritization, hijacking it in a budgetary sense, and changing the ground rules.

Entitlements challenge the traditional notion of budgetary balance. Their multiyear nature, the inability to control them during the annual appropriations cycle, and the interest group, class, and age-group pressures for expansion of benefits exacerbate the difficulty of achieving budgetary balance. When entitlements are structured as trust funds, with earmarked revenues, there is a connection between revenues, or income, and expenditures over time, but it is relatively easy for projected revenues to fall behind projected expenditures, as has happened for Social Security and Medicare. Balance, which in this case is balance over time, is conceptually possible but politically difficult to realize and maintain, since the consequences of not putting in enough revenue to cover promised benefits do not occur for a decade or more.

It is not necessary for an entitlement to be structured as a trust fund, and there may be no earmarked money to pay for it. When entitlements are paid from general revenues they put particular pressure on the nonentitlement budget. It is possible to design and pass an entitlement without specifying how it will be paid for, further obscuring the link between revenue and spending.

The challenge of entitlements to the traditional way of doing budgeting, and to the basic concepts that underlie the field, raise a number of fundamental questions for budgeting. The long-term nature of entitlements, their tendency to grow over time—such as with the aging of the population—faster than revenue, raise the question of sustainability. What does it mean when budgeters say that at the present rate of growth, entitlements will consume all the budget resources and there will be nothing left for any other purpose? What does it mean when budgeters or decision makers say that the Social Security trust fund will run out of money in such and such a year? Is it appropriate for entitlement spending to outrun revenues for a time, with the idea that there will be lower costs later, or more revenue? What does *balance* mean in the entitlement programs, and what does this definition mean for the rest of the budget, which has had to make room for the entitlements?

COPING WITH ENTITLEMENTS

One approach to addressing these knotty problems is to make the entitlements go away, at least from a budgetary, if not from a policy point of view. If the nature of the entitlements could be changed from a requirement for unlimited spending depending on the number of eligibles to spending up to a given ceiling, then the amount of spending on an annual basis would be controllable and predictable and would interfere less with the nonentitlement portion of the budget. The burden of uncertainty would be shifted to the recipients, who would not know whether they would get benefits or how much they would receive, because their benefits would be dependent on the number of applicants, which for many programs would not be totally predictable. The effect of a cap on spending would be to limit benefits, which biases the outcomes in the policy direction of reduced services. Thus, this solution has been controversial politically. At the same time, spending caps do not directly control cost increases. Costs may continue to increase while benefits do not, making programs increasingly ineffective at providing medical care, purchasing medicines, or whatever the goal of the program.

Putting a stopper in the bottle or transforming entitlement programs into grant programs, however desirable, puts budgetary logic ahead of programmatic needs. It would make more sense to try to control the sources of costs increases, where possible. If the cause of cost increases is an increased life expectancy, as it is for Social Security, the solution is probably not to reduce that life expectancy, but to put aside more money, to invest more now, so it will be there for a longer period of time, and possibly to adjust the age at which people become eligible for Social Security. Restructuring or redesigning the programs is thus one approach.

A second approach is to pay more attention to the interrelationship between entitlement programs and nonentitlement programs. Increased spending in the nonentitlement portion of the budget might well reduce costs in the entitlement portion, or at least control growth. Spending on public health, on clean water and clean air, can reduce costs for Medicare and Medicaid, for example. Maybe drug costs can be controlled if the government assumes the costs of invention and development of new medicines, which is one of the reasons why drug companies charge so much for drugs. Spending on particular programs in the nonentitlement portion, including regulatory programs, can help slow down the growth of entitlements and make them more affordable, and in the process reduce the pressure on the rest of the budget. Programs for identifying and either weeding out or reeducating doctors who make frequent or serious mistakes may reduce insurance costs and lawsuits.

More research needs to be done on the budgetary interdependence among programs, so that the effects of cuts in one place on other programs and other governmental units will be clearer, as well as the impacts of increases in one portion of the budget on reductions elsewhere. If increases in entitlements routinely push out spending on nonentitlements, a long-term negative cycle may be put in place.

ACHIEVING BUDGETARY BALANCE

While entitlements clearly violate the idea of an annual budget because they are multiyear or no year, they may be viewed over a given number of years, such as forty years or seventy-five years. Projections are made for this time period, in terms of likely number of beneficiaries and likely costs for each beneficiary. The point at which revenues fall below expenditures may be dozens of years off, and even though balance may be easier to achieve if done further in advance, the sense of urgency may not be sufficient to warrant legislative action. This has created a cottage industry of policy analysts designing various triggers to force action short of a catastrophe.

The concept of balance needs to be altered somewhat to fit long-term programs. They need to be dealt with in two phases, the first a projection over a given period of time, of revenues and expenditures, and the second a rematching of revenues and expenditures over that time period. The second step may be invoked if any of the underlying assumptions behind the projections changes in a given direction a given amount. The rematching should be based insofar as possible on what has caused the estimates to change. So if people are living longer, then perhaps the retirement age for benefits should be increased; if the costs of medicine are rising, then perhaps the government needs to bargain with the drug companies for bulk purchases, or engage in more testing of medicines or use more studies from abroad on what medicines deliver the most benefit, with the fewest side effects, rather than purchase whatever is newer and more expensive. If it is the cost of doctors that is rising, then perhaps insurance reform is in order or more control over incompetent doctors, and better record keeping from state to state.

What is needed here at the least is a transparent system for underscoring the assumptions underlying budget projections, so it will be clear to all where the assumptions were wrong, or the situation is changing, and hence where to attack the problems. If there is going to be more policy in the budget, then we need more policy analysis in the budget as well.

Long-term budgeting is by nature imprecise; one cannot budget for forty years as if one were budgeting for one. This problem has to be recognized and incorporated into the budget process, by engaging in tentative projections, identifying the underlying assumptions, and updating and making corrections as changes are known. This will create a decision process closer to an annual budget and improve the sense of control without capping or changing the nature of the entitlements. It introduces the notion of continual correction.

The idea of continual correction, of permanent budgeting, as opposed to permanent budgets, is particularly relevant where uncertainty is high, as it is in some entitlement programs, and as it is in loan, loan guarantee, and insurance programs, and more recently in various forms of government bailout funds. The costs to the government of loan programs depends on the rate of interest, and hence the degree of subsidy or below-market interest, and the rate of default. While market rates of interest at the time of the loans is knowable, in theory, it is more problematic in fact because the government gets involved only when commercial loans are either scarce or impossible to find. Moreover, the default rate is speculative, especially in new programs. Past experience in similar programs may provide a rough guide, but actual numbers will depend on future experience. The result is that cost estimates are uncertain and can be specified only within a range, and can be modified—the brackets for the range can narrow—over time as experience dictates. This combination of reliance on history and continual correction and ranges, rather than points, is actually the way loans are recorded at the federal level, but these techniques can also be applied to loan guarantees and insurance as well, at least in broad outline.

It is difficult to understand and easy to manipulate an estimate that is not based on precisely known costs, because these estimates are not disprovable or obviously wrong. Working with spongy numbers introduces a huge difficulty in the idea of balance. What does it mean to balance a loan program when the costs are given only within a range? What is the point of control? When do you know the program is failing, or that additional revenue should be added? If revenue estimates are given in points and expenditures as ranges, does balance mean that the revenue estimate falls within the range of expenditures? Might that not leave some expenditures uncovered? What attention needs to be given to trends, and the direction thereof? If the number of loan defaults increases during a recession, does that mean the cost of the program is increasing? Is the program unbalanced? When should that determination be made? The program might need constant monitoring, and close attention to trends and reversibility of those trends, and to segregating cyclical and secular trends.

As for insurance costs, or for possible loan defaults, these costs may never occur. The insured catastrophe may not happen, or payout may be within the revenue provided by premiums paid by policyholders; loan defaults may fall within the range of revenue provided by interest payments on functioning loans. Should one put in the budget costs that may not occur, and if so, what do they mean? If insurance is paid for through premiums, how should those premiums show up in the budget? If the government is guaranteeing loans, should it collect taxes to pay for probabilities of payouts over time? There are some conceptual problems here that need to be worked out.

The conceptual murk is deeper still in various bailout devices, as some of these involve loans that are for unknown periods of time, possibly short, possibly longer, and with an unknown failure rate. How much money is the government putting at risk since it is not a traditional loan or insurance program in which the risk is shared across a large number and where probabilities are based on averages with some successes and some failures. How does one measure risk or budget for it, when there is no prior history? While these problems in budgeting have been highlighted by antirecession measures at the national level, budgeting for contingent liability is a problem for all levels of government.

It is tempting here, as in the entitlement programs, to change the nature of the programs, to simply not record the possible spending and the loan repayment, but only the actual, as opposed to the projected, gap between them. In other words, wait until you know how much has actually been spent after loans have been paid back before recording them. Budgeting would look backward, to see how much was spent, rather than forward, to estimate how much will be spent. While this approach has the virtue of accuracy, it is not clear what the point of control would be or how one might ensure balance in such a model.

Another approach is to record the full amount of outgoing money as expenditure, and then record it as income as it comes in. This approach provides for possible control points but is likely to exaggerate costs substantially and create political pressure to make programs much smaller, possibly too small to handle the problems they are designed to deal with. The high up-front costs might discourage governments from trying them at all. This procedure does not really avoid the problem of spongy numbers, and it might have the consequence of persuading decision makers to ignore the numbers because the estimates are undoubtedly too high. In that case, this approach might well lead to deficits or at least make balance more elusive.

The third approach is to express costs that are not fully known as a range rather than a point. The range of costs for a bailout program or economic stimulus package can run the whole gamut from the government getting none of its money back to the government getting it all back with interest. While such a huge range may be a necessary starting point, presumably that range can be fairly quickly narrowed with experience. The result, however, would have to be constant budgeting and rebudgeting based on running estimates. The budget would have to show such loans or investments in terms of tranches, money loaned under a given program at a given time, and then watched and what happens recorded as it happens.

BUDGETING AS A DYNAMIC PROCESS

Budgeting is no longer a fixed process that once done stays done; there is much more uncertainty, much more risk, much more projection and estimate. The focus therefore has to be more on specifying the underlying assumptions, on short-term or continuous monitoring, and adjustment, done in real time as events change. We need to think in terms more of ranges than of points, which complicates not only the arithmetic but also the notion of balance, and, critically, when and how to rebalance when risk and exposure result in lower revenues or higher costs.

All these program types and structures are different from one another, in terms of the degree of uncertainty, the sponginess of estimates, and the time frame or duration. They do not meaningfully add up. You cannot add loan guarantee amounts to purchases of equity in a failing company, nor do either of these meaningfully add to outlays for Social Security. Social Security is legally separated from the rest of the budget, and its surpluses are earmarked for future recipients of Social Security benefits, but that has not stopped the misleading process of adding the Social Security balances to budget totals to offset deficits elsewhere, with the intent and result of making the deficit look smaller than it is. The traditional notion of the consolidated budget needs to be amended. This has begun to happen already, at the federal level, as various types of programs are recorded and described, but not merged into the rest of the budget. *Comprehensive* is still the operant term, but consolidation is becoming less relevant.

INCREASED AND DYSFUNCTIONAL CONFLICT

As budgeting has become more political and policy laden, and as the public and interest groups have found the pressure points to express sometimes contradictory views in law, the level of conflict has risen, sometimes to the point of collapse and failure. While failure seems a subjective term, most analysts would agree that a budget that routinely produced deficits, that was unable to prioritize or accommodate new needs, that was undemocratic, and that was routinely late—past the beginning of the fiscal year—was problematic. Struggles over closing budget gaps are sometimes so rancorous that government itself is closed down.[10] Failure to make decisions in a timely way may lead to stopgap measures that do not handle the finances of the government, but continue the previous year's budget unchanged, or short-term budgets that change spending levels from one week or month to the next.

The consequences of such uncertainty and failures include spending much public money on debt repayment, on interest costs, and reduced resources to solve collective problems. They include the costs of failure to prioritize expenditures. They include massive uncertainty of resource levels for those dependent on public funding. As the level of uncertainty rises, some nonprofits and other businesses dependent on government funding may close down or shrink in anticipation of budget cuts that might come late or never come at all. Uncertainty may prevent them from hiring or retaining existing staff. Organizations may hire temporary staff so that they have resources they can cut quickly if budget reductions come their way. Program administrators do not know how much money they will get; they cannot plan and so have to spend their time and energy fighting for resources.

Budget processes may fall victim to excess conflict, as contesting parties struggle to get their way in the budget, using the budget process as a tool, trying to shape it to their immediate needs. Legislators may not be given time to read budget proposals before they are asked to vote on them, decision processes may be closed to minority parties, and continual changes in decision making may leave participants in the dark as to how to influence the outcomes. To the extent that democracy lies in the process of decision making, it suffers from excessive conflict.

SOURCES OF CONFLICT

This intensification of conflict has many sources. Structural imbalances result from powerfully expressed contradictory demands for increased programmatic spending and tax reductions. At the state and local levels, the need to balance the budget annually may result in frequent bruising battles over cutbacks and tax increases. There may seem to be little middle ground, which exaggerates the policy standoff. With many program recipients actively supporting their programs and beneficiaries of tax breaks tightly holding on to them, cutback is politically fraught and difficult. Since there seem to be few political winners in such battles, politicians may shy away from them, which also results in late budgets. The growth in costs of entitlements also forces cuts in nonentitlement programs, enhancing the competition among the nonentitlements.

The scope of conflict is expanded as political actors fight for control of the budget process in order to influence the outcomes toward more spending or less taxes. Once such process changes are made, they may in turn exacerbate conflict, as they create winner-take-all structures, disempower the party out of power, or otherwise discourage compromise and bargaining. Building into the process features that favor one or another policy outcome not only makes the process a bone of contention, but also enhances the level of conflict. In California, for example, the budget process was changed so that a supermajority was required to pass the budget. The result is that minorities who oppose the agreements necessary to get the budget to pass can—and do—hold up the budget.

MANAGING CONFLICT IN THE BUDGET PROCESS

It is unlikely that the causes of this greater level of conflict will somehow disappear, that the clock can be turned back to a simpler time, when budgeting was less political and less policy laden. But conflict can—possibly—be managed, and the budget process can be made more resilient to policy conflict.

Some structural elements enhance conflict, and these can be remedied, at least in theory. If they cannot be changed in the governmental units in which they are most obvious, at least they can serve as a warning to other governmental units not to adopt these "reforms." While California has had a very difficult time eliminating the requirement for a supermajority to pass the budget, it has had a clearly detrimental effect in California. The policy outcome it seems to serve is better served by other requirements, such as supermajority requirements for tax increases; there is no need from a policy perspective to require a supermajority to pass the budget as well. This feature of the budget process empowers the minority party, which is understandably reluctant to give up this power, even though it leads to late budgets nearly every year.

Including policy in the budget process makes the budget process itself the subject of the controversy, and in the extreme case may result in the abandonment of the process. Processes should be as neutral to policy outcomes as possible and should be the result of regular consensus. Thus, efforts to build into the budget process a bias toward either growth or cutback are wrongheaded and likely to exacerbate the level of conflict. To the extent that they work, they can have serious implications for democracy. For example, Indiana's local budget laws built in a bias toward small government and low taxation, even when local citizens wanted more active government and were willing to be taxed to pay for it. These laws have changed only very slowly.[11]

Radical disempowerment of the legislature over the budget leads to legislatures holding up the budget in the hope of embarrassing the executive and forcing him or her to include some legislative priorities. When holding up the budget is the only power of the legislature, it is likely to use that power, to the detriment of timely decision making. Lack of real decision-making responsibility is likely to force the legislature to focus on earmarks or small projects they can point to for credit claiming, rather than focus on the overall budget, on balance, and on public priorities and problem solving. Battles between legislatures and executives may focus on the executive's power to control these earmarks, rather than on more substantive policy issues. Strong executive budget control to the exclusion of the legislative body sometimes leads to executives working to remove this one power of the legislature to hold up the budget, rather than to work toward more evenly balanced powers and responsibilities. These efforts may reinvigorate legislative attempts to change constitutions or revise the process to give legislators more say. In states where the balance of power is overwhelmingly in the hands of the governor, such as New York and Illinois, both of which have radically disempowered legislatures, the quality of public budgeting has been poor.

Illinois, for example, has routinely run deficits, though they have sometimes been hidden, and the state has been riddled with corrupt governors, who have sometimes used public spending for their own purposes. In New York, the state has routinely missed budget deadlines, and revenue estimates are often unrealistic, creating a sort of shadow play, where the actors are going through the motions but not actually making real budgetary decisions. The budget process is widely viewed as opaque.

Good government reformers need to give up the idea that more executive budget power is some kind of panacea for budgeting. Giving the executive more budget power was probably an improvement in the past, but it is possible to go too far; more and more is not necessarily better and better.

The budget process can be made part of the solution rather than part of the problem not only if it is relatively neutral in terms of policy outcomes and the result of consensus decision making, but also if it adapts well to conflict. Because winner-take-all formulations tend to exacerbate conflict, they should be avoided. More effort should be made to put more on the table, to create credit-claiming opportunities for minorities as well as majorities. More equal power sharing is likely to reduce the spiraling partisanship that results in bouts of vengeance for old budgetary war wounds when majority parties shift.

Budget processes that can deal with interruptions or missing information as one portion or another of the process is delayed due to conflict will work better in a climate of conflict. The so-called watchmaker model of stable assemblies fits here; that is, decision making should proceed in pieces that are each complete and that are assembled at the end, so that any interruption in one part allows work to go ahead in the other parts and does not force the parties to go back to the beginning.

Coming to agreement on priorities and rules for cutbacks in advance of a fiscal crisis can be helpful, so that when revenue drops below expectations, the cuts are routine and need not be fought out at that time. When the government is not facing actual cuts, the energy with which interest groups fight is much lower, making it more possible to make decisions on technical grounds.

Triggers too are likely to work better in prospect than in the present. That is, if there are automatic triggers for action to reduce the deficit in an entitlement fund, and if those triggers actually kick in several years down the road, there may be a political disconnect between the decision makers who created the trigger and the revenue-raising or cost-reduction action they mandated. In that case, the elected officials are less likely to be blamed for those decisions, and hence they are freer to make the kinds of decisions they feel they should; they can insulate themselves a little from political controversy.

The articulation of interests from all parties, public acknowledgment of how that testimony influenced decisions, and discussion of how the decisions were made—what information was used and had force—are likely to damp down competition and make everyone feel heard, even when all their demands are not met. If stakeholders understand that they had a chance to talk, and that someone else whose need was greater won the day, but the process was fair and open, they are less likely to build up resentment. There will be less antigovernment sentiment of the sort that results in the kind of handcuffing and closing off of alternatives found in some states—such as Colorado—through the referendum process. People tend to take government in their own hands, through direct democracy, when they feel they are not being listened to. The widely shared conclusion that government was deaf to the public was part of the motivation behind Proposition 13 tax limits in California. While it may be hard work to listen, and to explain why people cannot have everything they want, it is a better process than allowing disgruntled groups with opposite agendas to build contradictory requirements into laws and constitutions.

The public and interest groups are a real and ongoing part of public budgeting, especially perhaps at the national and state levels, but even at the local level. Incorporating citizen goals into budget planning can be helpful in curtailing the level of conflict between citizen and government over budget issues. This is a different set of skills than traditionally found in budgeting, but as budgets incorporate more policy and politics, the budget process has to include articulating and managing political demands and reporting back to the public in an understandable way that links to their demands.

Some governments are more active in soliciting public and interest group input and responding to it than others. It remains for research to examine this variation to see how it impacts the level of conflict, and what features of the budget process work best, not to suppress conflict, but to manage it.

LOOKING AHEAD

Budgeting has changed enormously, but because the changes have accumulated slowly and are greater at the national and state levels than at the local level, many academics have not fully appreciated the extent of the changes, the degree of politicization, the integration of policy into the budget and budget processes, and the level of conflict that often ensues. New program types, including entitlements, loans, loan guarantees, insurance, and equity investments, have introduced longer and shorter time spans, more uncertainty, and more risk. Budgeting has to catch up, to segregate portions of the budget with similar time horizons and degrees of uncertainty, to formulate new and relevant ways of measuring and achieving balance, and to manage uncertainty through frequent updates or continuous monitoring and ranges rather than point estimates.

Budgeting also has to catch up with the level of controversy inherent in the new budgeting. While it is tempting to say that the solution to citizen participation and demands is more secrecy, when citizens get fed up with government, they pass referenda; the differences among them, rather than being resolved, may be simultaneously expressed in law, creating an unworkable structure, feeding structural deficits, and contributing to the famous "train wrecks" of budgets that do not arrive in time and actually shut down government, in part or in whole. We cannot take for granted that budgeting will always work, that technical aspects of it will go on no matter what happens in the political or policy sphere. Budget processes sometimes collapse into adhocracy, which looks a lot like chaos, and fails the basic test of budgeting, prioritization.

There is much that needs to be done. Budgeting is in need of a new wave of reform. In some cases that means finishing up the reforms of the past, such as incorporating citizen priorities into the budget; in other cases it means not pushing reforms of the past to extremes. We also need new or modified budget concepts and norms that apply to the newer program types with different budgeting characteristics. Rebudgeting or continuous budgeting should become a norm in some parts of the budget; annuality should become less important; consolidation should be de-emphasized in favor of grouping similar structures and resources together. The definition of *balance* and ways of achieving balance may need to be rethought, and triggers that take effect in the future may need to become routine. We may need to learn to think with fuzzy numbers, with ranges instead of points.

For academics, teachers of public administration, these changes underscore the need to back off from the politics-administration dichotomy; at this point it is neither descriptive nor prescriptive. Moreover, these changes mean backing away from incrementalism in the classroom and in the textbooks, with the possible exception of some local governments, and even there, rather than assuming what one will or must see, it would be better to observe the extent to which the model still applies.

The integration of policy and budgeting means that training new budgeters needs to include more policy analysis, more ability to project and to specify the assumptions underlying those projections, and more ability to work with fuzzy or spongy numbers. Students of budgeting should learn more about conflict management and more about how to solicit and use public opinion, without unbalancing the budget, and without letting the level of conflict get out of hand.

For reformers, both academics and practitioners, the changes in public budgeting outlined in this chapter mean there is an urgent need to rethink the norms of budgeting, and even the definitions of key terms. *Annuality, consolidation,* and *balance* need to be reworked, to fit the range of program types. Budget processes may need to be redesigned, to withstand conflict without falling apart, to be more neutral, and to gain consensus. Budgeting norms need to include routine consultation with relevant publics, rather than isolation in a room with computers and software that estimates bond payback schedules. Budgeting is no longer a purely technical activity, and has not been for some time.

For practitioners the challenges are enormous: to accommodate to higher risk, more uncertainty, more public input, more conflict, and more policy. Budgeting is likely to be a more continuous activity, with constant monitoring and frequent adjustment. Public budgeting is more complicated than it used to be, but it is also more challenging and absorbing.

NOTES

1. Aaron Wildavsky, *The Politics of the Budgetary Process* (Boston: Little, Brown, 1964 and subsequent editions.)

2. There is a large literature on these topics. For conflict, see Irene Rubin, "Understanding the Role of Conflict in Budgeting," in *Handbook of Government Budgeting,* ed. Roy Meyers (San Francisco: Jossey-Bass, 1999); for one example of policy that focuses on the relationship between the decision-making process and policy outcomes, see Irene Rubin, "Budgeting," in *Handbook of Public Policy,* ed. B. Guy Peters and Jon Pierre (London: Sage, 2006). For many years, the Brookings Institution published an annual volume on the policy priorities in the federal budget, *Setting National Priorities.* After the end of that series, Brookings continued to publish on various aspects of policy in the budget. See, for example, Henry Aaron and Robert Reischauer, eds., *Setting National Priorities: The 2000 Election and Beyond* (Washington, DC: Brookings Institution Press, 1999), which discusses such issues as Medicare, Social Security, tax reform, and foreign policy spending.

3. Nicholas Riccardi and P.J. Huffstutter, "Budget Deadline Ticks Down for States," *Los Angeles Times,* July 1, 2009, http://articles.latimes.com/2009/jul/01/nation/na-shutdowns1 (accessed July 2, 2009); Michael McDonald and Terrence Dopp, "California, Illinois Fail to Meet Budget Deadline," *Bloomberg Report,* July 1, 2009, www.bloomberg.com/apps/news?pid=20601087&sid=aUBPQyZcuxPM. (Only four states do not begin their fiscal year July 1. They are Michigan and Alabama, October 1; New York, April 1; and Texas, September 1) (accessed April 15, 2010).

4. For some of this history in Maryland, see Roy T. Meyers and Thomas S. Pilkerton, "How Can Maryland's Budget Process Be Improved?" Maryland Institute for Policy Analysis and Research, September 2003, http://userpages.umbc.edu/~meyers/improveMD.pdf (accessed April 15, 2010). For recent history of this contention between legislative and executive branches over budgetary power, see chapter 4, box 1, in Irene Rubin, *The Politics of Public Budgeting,* 6th ed. (Washington, DC: CQ Press, 2009).

5. See, for example, Richard Rose, "Implementation and Evaporation: The Record of MBO," *Public Administration Review* 37, no. 1 (1977): 64–71; Allen Schick, "A Death in the Bureaucracy: The Demise of Federal PPB," *Public Administration Review* 33, no. 2 (1973): 146–156.

6. On the differences between traditional budgeting and budgeting for entitlements, see Joseph White, "Entitlement Budgeting v. Bureau Budgeting," *Public Administration Review* 32, no. 2 (1998): 510–528.

7. "Mandated Appropriations in the Maryland State Budget," Department of Legislative Services, Office of Policy Analysis, Annapolis, Maryland, September 2008, http://mlis.state.md.us/2008RS/misc/Mandates-InBudget.pdf (accessed April 15, 2010).

8. Center on Budget and Policy Priorities, "Policy Basics: Where Do Our State Tax Dollars Go?" April 13, 2009, http://www.cbpp.org/cms/index.cfm?fa=view&id=2783 (accessed April 15, 2010).

9. Ron Dzwonkowski, "Oct. 1 Is Too Late to Start Michigan's Fiscal Year," Freep.com, September 20, 2009, www.freep.com/article/20090920/COL32/909200500/Oct.-1-is-too-late-to-start-Michigan%5C-s-fiscal-year (accessed April 15, 2010).

10. Kathy Barks Hoffman, "Michigan Creeps Closer to 2nd Government Shutdown in 3 Years as Budget Deadline Nears," Breaking News 24/7, September 26, 2009, http://blog.taragana.com/n/michigan-creeps-closer-to-2nd-government-shutdown-in-3-years-as-budget-deadline-nears-179747/; William Selway and Ryan Flinn, "California IOUs Spurned as Schwarzenegger State Shutdowns Begin," July 10, 2009, www.bloomberg.com/apps/news?pid=20601110&sid=a0ma8jeg5jso (accessed April 15, 2010).

11. For more on Indiana's budget laws, see Irene Rubin, *Class, Tax and Power: Municipal Budgeting in the United States* (Chatham, NJ: Chatham House, 1998), 199–200.

CHAPTER 10

THE PROXY-PARTNERSHIP GOVERNANCE CONTINUUM

Implications for Nonprofit Management

JUDITH R. SAIDEL

During the 1980s and 1990s, cross-sector governance relationships between governmental and nongovernmental actors became increasingly common. Powerful and overlapping policy trends toward devolution, privatization, and the new public management movement underpinned this phenomenon, which had been under way since the Great Society programs of the 1960s. Norms and expectations shared by policy actors and organizations involved in legally based, formalized contracting relationships were sufficiently institutionalized by the mid-1990s to justify use of the term *contracting regime* to describe cross-sector governance interactions and related sector-specific practices (Smith and Lipsky 1993). At the same time, substantial theoretical progress occurred in identifying and interpreting the implications of these immense, evolutionary shifts in institutional relationships within public governance.

This chapter builds on two foundational constructs in the early literature on cross-sector governance—government by proxy (Kettl 1988) and the partnership paradigm (Salamon 1987). Modified slightly to *governance by proxy* and *governance by partnership*,[1] the constructs are identified in this analysis as opposite poles along a proxy-partnership governance continuum. The continuum is an integrative framework that captures the range of dynamic, cross-sector institutional relationships in the contracting regime and adds value to theory building on public governance in important ways explored in this chapter.

The next section examines the core ideas of government by proxy and the partnership paradigm and introduces the proxy-partnership governance continuum. Then a brief description of the size and scope of the contracting regime is provided and the proxy-partnership governance continuum is explained in more detail. The following section proposes a set of factors, or locational determinants, identified in the literature, that could account for the place of a cross-sector relationship on the continuum at a particular point in time. In the next section, the consequences of various locational positions are explored, as well as the challenges for nonprofit managers and potentially useful strategies to address issues associated with different positions along the continuum. The conclusion suggests promising directions for future research and some thoughts about the implications of the analysis for contracting policy.

FOUNDATIONAL ELEMENTS OF THE CONTINUUM

Two major contributors to theory building during these pioneering years were political scientists Donald Kettl and Lester Salamon, both of whom substantially expanded the frontiers of contracting and governance scholarship.[2] In the first edition of *Government by Proxy* (1988), Kettl quantified the extent of the federal government's reliance on outside parties for the production of goods and services, describing it as "one of the most complicated, difficult, and interesting phenomena of modern American Government" (5). He defined government by proxy as a kind of activity in which government relies on proxies or intermediaries to provide goods or services. Fourteen years later in *The Transformation of Governance: Public Administration for Twenty-first Century America,* Kettl expanded his analysis and embedded it in a broad theoretical treatment of the history of American public administration. He based the study on the underlying and organizing premise that "the way we think about and study public administration is out of sync with the way we practice it" (2002, xi).

Concurrently in the mid-1980s, Salamon directed the Nonprofit Sector Project at the Urban Institute. The project collected data from sixteen sites in the United States and documented for the first time the extensive flow of revenue from government at all levels to nonprofit organizations for the delivery of public programs. On the basis of these empirical studies, Salamon developed a new theory of government-nonprofit relations that placed the partnership construct at its core. His now classic analysis, "Partners in Public Service: The Scope and Theory of Government-Nonprofit Relations" (1987), was published in the first edition of the field-building Yale University Press volume, *The Nonprofit Sector: A Research Handbook.* Although the term *partnership* is not explicitly defined in the chapter, the implied definition is a relationship in which government revenues are exchanged for services delivered by nonprofit organizations.

Kettl's notion of nonprofits as proxies of government has not been widely adopted in the scholarly literature, and Salamon's partnership construct has not been operationalized very often by other researchers as a specific term for empirical testing. As argued in this chapter, both terms suffer connotation problems, perhaps because of their use in different contexts with different meanings. The term *proxy,* especially as applied to voting procedures, connotes an actor who carries out the will of the principal with no discretion exercised. According to common usage in American culture, the partnership idea implies a relationship of coequals characterized by shared goals and expectations. Both authors make clear in their extensive writings that these connotations do not capture the full scope of the phenomena they examine. Still, the terms hold these connotative implications.

Precisely because of these connotations, the terms *proxy* and *partnership* work well to anchor the opposite ends of a continuum of interdependent governance relationships that structure the contracting process. Collaborative public-private endeavors are not included in this construct, although important insights by scholars writing about collaborative governance inform the analysis. Following Gazley and Brudney, "Collaborations require voluntary, autonomous membership (partners retain their independent decision-making powers even when they agree to some common rules) [*sic*]" (2007, 390). At several points in the article, Gazley and Brudney explicitly exclude contractual relationships from the definition of collaboration. The authors cite Peters (1998), who observes that public-private partnerships, a term Gazley and Brudney use synonymously with collaboration, are based on principal-principal models, as differentiated from principal-agent relationships (2007, 391).

The proxy-partnership continuum is much needed as a theoretical basis to advance the understanding of the exceedingly complex government-nonprofit relationships that are a defining element of public administration today. In fact, underdeveloped theory related to these dynamic and interdependent institutional relationships constitutes a major challenge for both governance theory and the individuals and organizations that function as governance actors (Cho and Gillespie 2006).

In this chapter Kettl's phrase and Salamon's construct are modified slightly to *governance by proxy* and *governance by partnership,* respectively. The resulting array of interactions is labeled here as the *proxy-partnership governance continuum.*

VALUE ADDED AND LIMITATIONS OF THE CONTINUUM CONSTRUCT

A definitional feature of the continuum is the interdependent, even if asymmetric, nature of the government-nonprofit governance relationships (Saidel 1991, 1994) located at various points between its poles. Because it is constructed on the basis of reciprocal relationships, the continuum is relevant to both public administration and nonprofit management theory and, by extension, to the world of practice in which public administrators and nonprofit managers perform interdependent functions.

Second, the continuum illustrates the fundamental character of government-nonprofit relationships as dynamic and changing over time. Because many studies are cross-sectional in research design, the sometimes dramatic changes in the nature of multisector relationships are often obscured in the research literature. Two notable exceptions to this observation are Cho and Gillespie (2006) and Alexander and Nank (2009). Addressing the necessity of moving beyond static conceptualizations, Cho and Gillespie integrate systems dynamics and resource dependence theories into a model with multiple feedback loops that depicts changes over time in the quality of services delivered in a cross-sector system. Alexander and Rank utilize a ten-year longitudinal research design with three waves of qualitative data collection to study evolving relationships between a county department of children and family services and community-based nonprofit organizations.

A third and related benefit of the continuum is that it facilitates analysis of dramatically different management challenges that depend on where cross-sector relationships are located along its expanse at a particular point in history. Based on an understanding of the implications associated with various continuum locations, nonprofit managers will be better equipped to develop effective strategic responses.

Several limitations of the proxy-partnership governance continuum are acknowledged at the outset. One limitation is what might be called the black box problem. By characterizing a government-nonprofit relationship as unitary and therefore capable of being pinpointed on the continuum, the multilevel nature of both government and larger nonprofit organizations is masked. It is possible that within one institution, cross-sector relationships could be described differently depending on the program or even the individuals involved. Another limitation is that for-profit entities are not included in the framework, despite their current substantial participation in public governance.

THE CONTINUUM CONSTRUCT

In 2005, the most recent year for which data are available from *The Nonprofit Almanac* (Wing, Pollak, and Blackwood 2008), public charities reporting revenues and expenses to the Internal Revenue Service received about $103 million in government grants and just under $800 million in program service revenue, including government contracts and fees for service, such as Medicaid and Medicare fees.[3] These two sources of revenue constituted, on average, about 80 percent of all revenues raised by public charities (Wing, Pollak, and Blackwood 2008, 146). In some nonprofit subsectors, such as health, the average percentage of government-derived revenues is higher (90.8 percent) and in other subsectors, such as arts, culture, and humanities, the percentage is considerably lower (40.9 percent) (Wing, Pollak, and Blackwood 2008, 179, 167). For purposes of this chapter, however, the overwhelming phenomenon to note is the substantial dependence of public charities, or nonprofits classified as 501(c)(3) in the Internal Revenue Code, on government for revenues in one form or another.

Figure 10.1   **Proxy-Partnership Governance Continuum I**

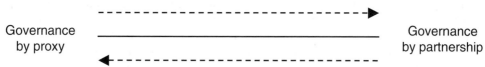

Governance   Governance
by proxy   by partnership

Between 1995 and 2005, the number of public benefit nonprofits increased 66 percent to about 311,000 entities (Wing, Pollak, and Blackwood 2008, 148). It is important to point out that not all of these nonprofits received revenues from government grants, contracts, or government-funded individual fees. Still, most of the larger entities across this continuously expanding array of nonprofit firms are engaged in funding relationships with government and, as a result, the challenges in public administration today for governance theory and for both public and nonprofit managers are formidable. The proxy-partnership continuum is a conceptual framework that meets the challenge, at least in part, by focusing on bilateral contracting relationships between nonprofit organizations and government agencies. Significant theoretical breakthroughs in public governance involving cross-sector institutional relationships have been achieved in network theory (e.g., Kickert, Klijn, and Koppenjan 1997; O'Toole 1997; Provan and Milward 1991, 1995; Milward and Provan 2000; Provan, Isett, and Milward 2004; Provan et al. 2005) and in collaborative public management or governance theory (cf. O'Leary, Bingham, and Gerard 2006). Still, writing as a preeminent network theorist in the *Public Administration Review* special issue, Agranoff argues, "One must remember that many local governments, nonprofits, and for-profits are bilaterally linked with state and federal agencies through grants, contracts, or cooperative agreements" and that networks "are not the be-all and end-all of collaborative management. They share a place—in many cases, a small place—alongside literally thousands of interagency agreements, grants, contracts, and even informal contacts" (2006, 57).

The proxy-partnership continuum depicted in Figure 10.1 offers a way to conceptualize the broad range of bilateral linkages. The broken arrows pointing in each direction illustrate the dynamic nature of the relationships along its expanse.

Governance by Proxy

In many ways, the form of governance by proxy, with no mitigating conditions that would push the relationship toward partnership, corresponds to the tenets of principal-agent theory derived from the discipline of economics; governance by partnership in its purest form is similar to stewardship theory, with roots in psychology and sociology (Davis, Schoorman, and Donaldson 1997, 24). Van Slyke (2006) provides a useful review of the two theories applied to government contracting with nonprofits in the social services arena. The primary characteristics of a principal-agent relationship are asymmetric information and divergent goals between the principal (government agency) and agent (nonprofit organization) that result in the principal's need to provide incentives or establish significant monitoring procedures to curb opportunistic behavior by the agent.

Applying the theory to government-nonprofit contracting relationships necessitates changing the level of analysis as established in the original formulation from relationships between individuals (Jensen and Meckling 1976) or, as formulated later, to relationships within organizations (Caers et al. 2006) to relationships between organizations in different sectors (Van Slyke 2006). A principal-agent cross-sector relationship that is highly formalized by means of a legally binding contract replete with regulatory, monitoring, and reporting enforcement provisions captures the essence of the governance-by-proxy pole on the continuum.

Although some implementation authority is necessarily shared or delegated, the principal re-tains through the contract mechanism considerable authority over the structure, scope, and pace of program delivery in order to "minimize the potential abuse of the delegation" (Jensen and Meckling 1976, cited in Davis, Schoorman, and Donaldson 1997, 23). This is especially true if relationships operate under the condition of performance contracting, in which final payment may be withheld until outcomes designated in the contract have been achieved. Writing about collab-orative capacity among multiple cross-sector actors, Weber, Lovrich, and Gaffney conceptualize this distribution of authority as a "vertical capacity dimension" (2007, 197). They highlight the hierarchical, compliance-focused nature of these relationships, anchored in goals set by govern-ment officials who rely on statutes and regulations as enforcement mechanisms.

Governance by Partnership

At the opposite end of the continuum, governance by partnership closely resembles principal-steward relationships in which the mission, values, and goals of both institutional parties are aligned and, therefore, governance structures are designed "to facilitate and empower rather than . . . monitor and control" (Davis, Schoorman, and Donaldson 1997, 26). Implementation authority is shared more broadly by government agencies with nonprofit partners because of an advanced level of trust that has developed between them (Davis, Schoorman, and Donaldson 1997; Van Slyke 2006). DeHoog and Salamon (2002) suggest that a more recent approach to contracting—the cooperative contracting process—is also aptly described as a partnership model in that govern-ment and contracting agency administrators engage jointly in developing contract terms, designing program design, and implementing changes over time.

A compelling example of governance by partnership is provided by Alexander and Nank (2009) in their longitudinal study of changing cross-sector relationships between a local department of children and family services and community-based neighborhood centers. Between 1998 and 2007, relationships evolved from predominantly adversarial in nature to remarkably collaborative. A primary, though not the only, driver of change was the development of trust between participants, facilitated by a combination of many influences. Evidence from the Alexander and Nank study of what is labeled here as governance by partnership includes authority sharing; work integration; and involvement of nonprofit leaders in government agency planning, hiring, and even promotional decisions (2009, 375).

Van Slyke (2006) also found that nonprofit organizations, perceived by government and self-defined as stewards, participate not only in implementation but at all points of the policy process, including problem definition, legitimation, implementation, and often assessment of program design outcomes in preparation for the next procurement cycle. This observation is considered further in the section on implications for nonprofit managers.

LOCATIONAL DETERMINANTS

What factors influence the location of bilateral government-nonprofit contracting relationships on the proxy-partnership continuum at a specific moment in history? Along with extensively cited scholars who have studied these relationships for many years (e.g. Gronbjerg 1993; Smith and Lipsky 1993; Salamon 1995; Smith 1994), this chapter argues that prevailing political and economic conditions explain more about the dynamics of cross-sector relationships than any other factor. Figure 10.2 illustrates the embeddedness of the proxy-partnership governance continuum in a political economy framework.

Figure 10.2 **Proxy-Partnership Governance Continuum II**

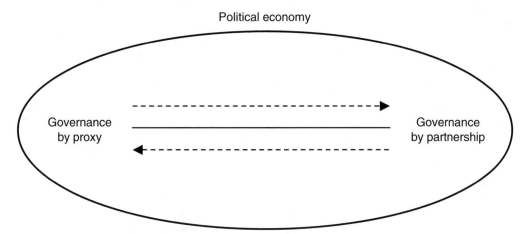

Based on observations before, during, and after the four most recent recessions, all occurring in periods of substantial nonprofit contracting activities by government and including the current "great recession" in the latter half of the twenty-first century's first decade, it seems clear that, during periods of highly constrained government revenues, most bilateral cross-sector contracting relationships are clustered at the governance-by-proxy end of the continuum. In a recent informal focus group with a handful of regional nonprofit CEOs, the response to a question about partnerships with government resulted in an emphatic consensus response: "Partnership? What partnership? The term is all rhetoric and no substance."[4] With almost all fifty states facing budget deficits in the 2010 fiscal year, state agency administrators focused on budget-cutting strategies that affect nonprofit contractors, often to the point of requiring givebacks of funds already allocated and distributed. Little or no official prior consultation with nonprofit managers occurred in these circumstances, in which public administrators felt severely constrained by fiscal realities and interacted with nonprofits as proxies.

On the other hand, during times of state budget surpluses and resources more widely available for nonprofit grants and contracts, many government-nonprofit relationships, especially those based on a long history and earned trust, will move toward the government-by-partnership end of the continuum. Van Slyke labels this dynamic an "evolved principal-agent relationship" (2006, 163).

In addition to economic circumstances, political and policy factors are important locational determinants. Alexander and Nank (2009) find that, when government dependence on community-based nonprofits is great because of their legitimacy in particular communities and government's need for legitimacy, cross-sector relationships characterized by shared decision making are located toward the governance-by-partnership end of the continuum.

Another example of a policy-related determinant occurs in periods when demands for accountability are reverberating loudly in the political atmosphere. Under this circumstance, public administrators are more likely to adhere to the strict regulatory, monitoring, and reporting requirements that characterize principal-agent relationships at the governance-by-proxy end of the continuum (Smith 2008). As Smith observed in an earlier piece, "Nonprofit management is now inextricably connected to the political process" (1994, 336). A major implication relevant to the proxy-partnership governance continuum construct is that nonprofit managers do not have the power entirely to control where their organization's relationship with a state agency is located along its expanse at any particular time. It should be noted, however, that nonprofit mismanagement or noncompliance can quickly push the relationship to the governance-by-proxy end of the continuum.

As mentioned earlier, the duration of a specific cross-sector partnership is another important locational determinant. The longer a contracting relationship that has produced acceptable results has been in effect, the deeper the ties of trust between government and nonprofit actors and the more likely the relationship is to be positioned toward the partnership end of the continuum. A reciprocal relationship of trust is often strengthened when key individuals in both sectors have been in office for a number of years and have worked together through tough program issues. This is especially true with respect to relationships at higher levels in nonprofit and government hierarchies between nonprofit CEOs and executive program directors and public sector contract managers and higher-level administrators.

Bureaucratic politics is relevant as well in that nonprofit managers and their influential board members may have advocated at important junctures in the budget or larger policy process on behalf of the state agency with other state government officials, such as members of the governor's executive staff, legislators, or staff members in the division of the budget (Saidel 1989). The political interdependence of state agencies and many nonprofit organizations is, by now, well documented (e.g., Saidel 1991, 1994; Smith 1994; Marwell 2004). In analyses of the dynamics of contracting, political favors performed by nonprofits must be taken into account in assessing the probable location of a contracting relationship on the proxy-partnership continuum.

LOCATIONAL CONSEQUENCES

A number of important consequences for nonprofit executives and leaders flow from the conceptualization of government-nonprofit contracting relationships as nonstatic and moving between the poles of governance by proxy and governance by partnership. These include persistent locational, resource, and administrative uncertainty; shifts in information availability and exchange; changes in authority shared and discretion permitted; increases and decreases in the frequency and intensity of monitoring; and enhanced or reduced access to bureaucratic policy making.

Persistent Uncertainty

Perhaps the most significant consequence is the omnipresent general condition of uncertainty about when, how extensively, and how suddenly shifts in location along the proxy-partnership continuum will occur. Movement of cross-sector relationships along the continuum happens for a variety of reasons and with very different warning signals. For instance, a commissioner or contract manager with whom a nonprofit executive has forged strong ties of trust and respect may announce a career change with no prior notification and no indication of the orientation toward provider relationships of her or his successor. On the other hand, a looming state budget crisis has a much longer warning period, and nonprofit managers with prior experience in such circumstances can anticipate the shifts in contracting relationships that are likely to occur. Still, the migration via contracting of fiscal instability from government to nonprofit service providers presents substantial managerial challenges (Smith 2008).

Locational uncertainty is a variant of the more pervasive uncertainty associated with the entire contracting process identified by scholars such as Gronbjerg (1993), Smith and Lipsky (1993), and Smith (1994). Smith, for example, focused specifically on cash flow, contract renewal, and negotiation issues as illustrative of the "profound uncertainties and management challenges for nonprofit agencies" related to contracting (2005, 375).

Shifts in Information Availability and Exchange

Variation in information exchange between governmental officials and nonprofit contractors is one of the specific consequences of different locational points on the proxy-partnership continuum. In an empirical study of social service contracting relationships in New York State, Van Slyke found that about two-thirds of public sector managers in a purposive sample utilized information sharing as a reward for nonprofit managers in whom they had a great deal of trust and information withholding as a sanction for those not so trusted (2006, 172). The information exchanged often had a "privileged" dimension in the sense that public administrators offered trusted providers suggestions about how to deal effectively with bureaucratic procedures and officials.

Several other consequences of location on the proxy-partnership continuum are closely related to information availability and exchange: the degree of authority shared and discretion permitted; the frequency and intensity of monitoring; and the extent of access to bureaucratic policy making. Each of these consequences is examined later in the chapter.

Changes in Authority Shared and Discretion Permitted

Early in his theory building, Salamon made the following critical observation: "The central characteristic of this pattern is the use of nongovernmental . . . entities to carry out governmental purposes, and the exercise by these entities of a substantial degree of discretion over the spending of public funds and the exercise of public authority" (1987, 110).

Specifying how much authority is shared and under what circumstances are questions unresolved in subsequent empirical studies. It is hypothesized here that cross-sector contracting relationships moving away from the proxy pole and toward the partnership end of the proxy-partnership continuum are associated with more authority sharing between government contract officials and nonprofit contractors. As a result, nonprofit managers are able to exercise more discretion in their interpretation of contract provisions and street-level programmatic decision making. This is consistent with Van Slyke's finding that trusted nonprofit providers were afforded more discretion in program innovation and implementation. The practice was specifically withdrawn by government officials when nonprofit contractors were no longer trusted (2006, 173). In the schema proposed here, a relationship in which trust has eroded and discretion exercised by the nonprofit contractor has been withdrawn could be understood as shifting toward the proxy end of the governance continuum.

In an in-depth analysis of accountability systems in government-nonprofit contracting, Whitaker, Altman-Sauer, and Henderson offer an alternative explanation for differences in discretion available to nonprofit contractors. Instead of trust as the determinant of discretion extended to nonprofit providers, the authors contend that variation in the "definition of expected performance" (2004, 120) by government contract writers results in more or less discretion and authority available to nonprofits. When government officials intend to change underlying conditions in the social economy, nonprofits will enjoy greater flexibility in programmatic decision making. In terms of the continuum construct proposed here, the contracting relationship will move toward the partnership pole. Conversely, according to Whitaker, Altman-Sauer, and Henderson (120), when the goals of government procurement officials are to have particular services or outputs provided, nonprofit discretion is more tightly circumscribed and the contracting relationship draws closer to the proxy end of the continuum.

Increases or Decreases in the Frequency and Intensity of Monitoring

Another consequence of location on the proxy-partnership continuum relates to monitoring practices and variation in the ways in which monitoring is implemented. In the context of the current public management norm of maintaining high levels of accountability in government practices, it can be conjectured that, in virtually all instances when the provisions of a legal contract are in place, a baseline level of formal monitoring such as an annual program audit and the review of periodic financial reports will occur. Confirming this likelihood, Van Slyke (2006) reports little variation in the level of oversight imposed through monitoring activities by public sector contract administrators, regardless of how much trust was invested in various nonprofit providers. He also found that agency and stewardship theories offer few clues about conditions under which the implementation and tone or style of monitoring will vary (181).

The proxy-partnership continuum construct provides a conceptual framework that can guide the formulation of some hypotheses about monitoring frequency and rigor. For instance, it is hypothesized that the location of a government-nonprofit contracting relationship on the proxy-partnership continuum will explain, to some extent, how formal and informal monitoring practices are actually experienced by nonprofit contractors. As an example, two CEOs of large and very large health and human service regional nonprofits recently commented that, in New York State's current condition of fiscal austerity, audits have taken on an entirely different character. Prior to the fiscal crisis, audits were conducted in a conciliatory way with the predominant communication mode of friendly negotiation based on the presumption of shared goals. By contrast, current audits are conducted in a highly formalized, "stick-to-every-minute-regulation" way with an adversarial communication mode and an implied sense of divergent goals.[5] These contrasting ways of carrying out monitoring functions correspond closely with a governance-by-partnership or principal-steward model in the first instance and a governance-by-proxy or principal-agent model in the latter example.

Enhanced or Reduced Access to Bureaucratic Policy Making

An additional consequence of location on the proxy-partnership continuum relates to policy access to bureaucratic decision making. In a recent empirical analysis of interest group influence on state agency policy making, Kelleher and Yackee find that contracting in general, regardless of whether the contractor is a for-profit or nonprofit entity, creates conditions under which contractors gain increased access to bureaucratic policy processes. "Yet, these exchanges also provide opportunities for contractors to convey their recommendations for policy change—be it shifts in programming, budgets, or policy priorities—to public managers" (2008, 2). The authors persuasively document through quantitative analysis of a large data set that contractors experience more access to agency decision processes than do other organized interests. The analysis is not extended to variations in access among contractors.

Some researchers have noted that government agency gatekeepers can at least partially open or close access on behalf of nonprofit contractors to bureaucratic policy making, especially to phases of the policy-making process other than implementation. In one study of resource interdependence between government agencies and nonprofits across four service areas (Saidel 1991) and another study of social service contracting relationships (Van Slyke 2006), evidence surfaced that, under certain conditions, nonprofit contractors were invited to participate in agency policy development and assessment of program outcomes. Van Slyke reports that, when contracting relationships are characterized by high trust, public managers are more likely to find ways for nonprofits to engage in the bureaucratic policy process. As reported earlier, research by Alexander and Nank (2009) finds similar results. In terms of the proxy-partnership continuum, one would expect that relationships closer to the partnership pole would involve higher levels of nonprofit participation in agency policy deliberations.

IMPLICATIONS FOR NONPROFIT MANAGERS

One of the most important recent advances in public management theory is the understanding that governance now simultaneously incorporates traditional, vertical, command-and-control relationships carried out within hierarchically structured public agencies and horizontal, more collaborative relationships that occur across complex, interorganizational, cross-sector linkages and networks of all kinds (Kettl 2002; Cooper 2003; Heinrich, Hill, and Lynn 2004; Agranoff 2006). For instance, Agranoff maintains that "although it is certainly true that mutual dependency is leading to an increasing number of horizontal relationships crossing many boundaries, lateral connections seem to overlay the hierarchy rather than act as a replacement for them" (57).

Citing Salamon's (2002) contributions to tools theory, Heinrich, Hill, and Lynn argue persuasively that "to ignore the role of hierarchical structures and management in network performance would be a primary error; command and control remain central to governance within a constitutional framework, albeit with a much expanded (in many ways more problematic) [sic] set of tools or instruments of policy and administration" (2004, 11).

Understanding the Complex Dynamics of Contemporary Governance

The relevance of this contention to nonprofit managers operating in the contracting regime is the implied guidance it offers for navigating the turbulent currents that surround the proxy-partnership continuum. By understanding the realities of the often simultaneous multilevel governance dynamics under which their government contracting counterparts operate, nonprofit managers can more easily anticipate probable changes in location of their contracting relationships along the continuum and the related consequences.

As an example, when governments confront significant budgetary shortfalls and government-nonprofit relationships move toward the proxy end of the continuum, nonprofit managers will recognize that the public managers with whom they interact will more often make decisions that are consistent with the vertical administrative dynamics that characterize government bureaucracies. Public contract managers will have less discretionary authority to share with providers and less opportunity to negotiate on matters such as waivers or exceptions to regulatory requirements. They may also be less able to encourage innovative program development initiatives advanced by nonprofit providers. They may involve even trusted nongovernmental actors less frequently in agency decision-making processes. Under these circumstances, regularly scheduled information meetings with providers may continue; however, the flow of information becomes primarily one way from government officials to nonprofit contractors.

Building and Sustaining Strong Information Networks

The importance of timely and accurate information is significantly heightened by the uncertainties inherent in current governance dynamics. Analysis of management challenges associated with reducing persistent uncertainty has a long history in private and public sector management literatures. Consistent with a major theme in most studies is the necessity of building strong information-gathering and environmental-scanning capacities that will yield signals about impending relationship changes, as well as suggestions about potential organizational repositioning strategies. Interestingly, the saliency of strong external information networks has a parallel in the heightened need for more sophisticated internal information systems that supply performance and outcome data to government and other contract overseers (Smith 2008).

Strengthening Political Acumen

The fundamental importance of highly honed political skills has long been recognized as a critical skill for nonprofit managers (Heimovics, Herman, and Jurkiewicz 1995). Skills such as bargaining, negotiation, and persuasion have been identified by a number of researchers as central to the contracting process, for both public and nonprofit actors (Kettl 1988, 2002; Salamon 2002; Smith 2008). In developing tools theory, Salamon (2002) makes the case for the necessity of public and other managers developing what he labels "enablement skills." He defines enablement skills as "the skills required to engage partners arranged horizontally in networks, to bring multiple stakeholders together for a common end in a situation of interdependence" (16). In addition to activation and orchestration competencies, Salamon adds modulation skills, which apply primarily to public contract managers inasmuch as they involve the distribution of "rewards and penalties" (16) to promote cooperation by third parties involved in governance relationships.

From the perspective of the proxy-partnership framework, it is suggested that modulation skills, defined differently, are also a key political skill that nonprofit managers should cultivate. These skills include the political savvy to modulate nonprofit strategies directed toward public sector counterparts. Under what circumstances is it appropriate to intensify or lessen advocacy pressures, a set of political skills that Smith (2008) finds are increasingly utilized? Under what circumstances should nonprofit managers lower expectations about the efficacy of bargaining and negotiation strategies and turn their strategic attention to alternative approaches? These choices may be fraught with peril, as different nonprofit stakeholder groups, including boards of directors, staff, service recipients, and large and small donors, interpret the exigencies of difficult governance dilemmas differently. At the same time, the importance of building and sustaining trust between contracting actors has been empirically demonstrated as critical to governance by partnership. The choice of modulation strategies by nonprofit managers that strengthen or diminish trust will likely have long-term ramifications.

Participating in Associations and Coalitions

A collective strategy that nonprofit contractors have increasingly adopted is participation in regional and statewide associations and coalitions (Gronbjerg 1993; Harlan and Saidel 1994; Smith 2005, 2008). Under conditions of environmental turbulence and uncertainty, nonprofit CEOs establish networks of information exchange to enhance their capacity to make sense of various fragments of environmental information. In addition, through the aggregation of voices, associations buffer individual nonprofit contractors from potential retribution when associations articulate positions that challenge prevailing agency policies. Describing a "changed political landscape," Smith (2008, S140) underscores the expanded presence and importance of associations and coalitions developed to influence state policy making. Alexander and Nank (2009, 380) note that, in an effort to limit the influence that a powerful county agency could exert over nonprofit contractors, social service nonprofits formed a collaborative to review and vote on all decisions related to the initiative they were implementing.

Developing Useful Interpretive Frameworks

Given the dramatic contrasts in these ways of carrying out governance functions, nonprofit executives are confronted with the "profound uncertainties and management challenges" noted by Smith (2005). How do they cope? How do they perform the central managerial function of interpreting environmental data and managing meaning for themselves and their organizations' internal and external stakeholders (Smircich and Stubbart 1985)?

One response to this question is a strategy derived from an empirical ethnographic study conducted more than twenty years ago that continues to ring true today. Based on eighteen in-depth interviews of nonprofit human services managers, Bernstein found that the dominant metaphor by which managers make sense of their experience in contracting is game playing. "Most managers make specific reference to game playing, and all use the language of games in their description of what they do and why" (1991, 21). Over and over, managers spoke of paradoxical circumstances in which part of the contracted agreement differed from the on-the-ground programs and services they operated. "In accepting these paradoxes, managers perceive their task as a game. This perception enables them to understand, get control of, and keep in perspective contracted services" (22).

Interestingly, when asked recently about how she experienced the contracting relationship with government, a human services nonprofit executive director immediately exclaimed, "Oh, it's a game that we all play!"[6] Apparently, the game metaphor is a powerful enabling strategy utilized by nonprofit managers to make sense of uncertain and occasionally unpredictable contracting relationships that vary between proxy and partnership dynamics.

Maintaining or Restoring Equilibrium

Another important strategy recently articulated by a nonprofit chief executive could be called an equilibrium approach. Interestingly, when introduced to the proxy-partnership continuum, this CEO of a more than $90 million health and human service nonprofit with almost total dependency on government contracts or third-party payments immediately defined the primary management implication for him as CEO as the search for leverage strategies that could counter the heavy hand of a powerful government funder and regulator. By doing so, the executive claimed, he could effectively push the government-nonprofit relationship away from the governance-by-proxy pole of the continuum and toward the partnership end.[7]

To accomplish this task, the nonprofit manager and his organization rely primarily on generating supplementary and alternative revenues through earned income in the market economy (cf. Hammack and Young 1993 for a comprehensive analysis of market-based strategies utilized by nonprofits). Finding alternative resources to reduce dependence on and, therefore, the power of one party over another in an exchange relationship is consistent with power-dependence theory formulated many years ago by sociologist Richard Emerson (1962) and utilized subsequently by researchers in many disciplines including the present author (Saidel 1991).

CONCLUSION

In this chapter, a new construct—the proxy-partnership governance continuum—is proposed to advance theory about the nonstatic character of government-nonprofit contracting relationships. Additionally, the conceptual framework is useful in enabling nonprofit managers to take into account the realities of the simultaneous multilevel governance dynamics under which their government contracting counterparts operate. As a result, they will be better positioned to make sense of and more effectively respond to changes over time in the character of contracting relationships.

Understanding the proxy-partnership continuum construct, locational determinants, and locational consequences facilitates action by nonprofit managers and others to address the long-recognized tensions in contracting between maintaining nonprofit autonomy and slipping into what Ralph Kramer (1981) labeled "vendorism" more than twenty-five years ago. If nonprofit managers and leaders can identify their organizations' location on the continuum and, to some extent, predict the probability of future shifts along its expanse, they may be able to maximize governance-by-partnership dynamics and buffer the negative effects of sudden or even gradual shifts toward governance by proxy. An important element of this leadership capacity is the enhanced ability to maintain the kind of nonprofit organizational mission clarity that many researchers have seen as imperiled by the contracting regime (Smith and Lipsky 1993; Kramer 1994; Alexander, Nank, and Stivers 1999).

Considerable room exists for future research to build on the solid base of empirical research literature in the area of bilateral and network contracting relationships. Further examination of the determinants and consequences of various locations on the proxy-partnership governance continuum would be fruitful. In these studies researchers could examine consequences such as information availability, authority sharing, discretion permitted, frequency and intensity of monitoring, and extent of access to bureaucratic policy making, as well as others that might surface.

Finally, the implications of shifting contracting relationships for service recipients and the service delivery system as a whole should be examined. Questions highly salient for practice should be raised, such as, Should policy efforts be made to diminish uncertainties associated with the current dynamic character of contracting relationships? Following an initiative in the United Kingdom, should state-level executive-branch policy makers undertake a study of the value of relational contracting (Dowds 2004)?

In a pathbreaking comparative study, Kramer (1981) argued that insufficient attention had been paid by scholars and policy makers to the consequences for the entire service delivery system of the rapidly expanding policy arrangement in which voluntary agencies play increasingly important roles in the delivery of publicly funded services. When applied to the dynamic character of uncertain contracting relationships developed over the ensuing decades, Kramer's concerns seem equally well-founded today.

NOTES

Susan Appe provided research assistance for this chapter. I acknowledge the valuable contributions made to this chapter by the editors and an anonymous reviewer.

1. Both scholars have also made major contributions to governance theory—Kettl in *The Transformation of Governance* (2002) and Salamon in *The Tools of Government: A Guide to the New Governance* (2002).

2. Kettl and Salamon worked together on a 1987 report for the National Academy of Public Administration titled "Third-Party Government and the Public Manager: The Changing Forms of Government Action."

3. The Internal Revenue Service Form 990, from which these data are derived, does not differentiate between levels of government in these two categories of revenues.

4. Focus group with five regional nonprofit chief executives, Nonprofit Executive Roundtable, Albany, NY, July 23, 2009.

5. Personal communication with the author, June 19, 2009.

6. Focus group with five regional nonprofit chief executives, Nonprofit Executive Roundtable, Albany, NY, July 23, 2009.

7. Personal communication with the author, June 19, 2009.

REFERENCES

Agranoff, Robert. 2006. Inside collaborative networks: Ten lessons for public managers. *Public Administration Review* 66 (S1): 66–75.

Alexander, Jennifer, and Renee Nank. 2009. Public nonprofit partnership: Realizing the new public service. *Administration and Society* 41 (3): 364–386.

Alexander, Jennifer, Renee Nank, and Camilla Stivers. 1999. Implications of welfare reform: Do nonprofit survival strategies threaten civil society? *Nonprofit and Voluntary Sector Quarterly* 28 (4): 452–475.

Bernstein, Susan R. 1991. *Managing Contracted Services in the Nonprofit Agency.* Philadelphia: Temple University Press.

Cho, Sungsook, and David F. Gillespie 2006. A conceptual model exploring the dynamics of government-nonprofit service delivery. *Nonprofit and Voluntary Sector Quarterly* 35 (3): 493–509.

Caers, Ralf, Cindy Du Bois, Marc Jegers, Sara De Gieter, Catherine Shepers, and Roland Pepermans. 2006. Principal-agent relationships on the stewardship-agency axis. *Nonprofit Management and Leadership* 17 (1): 25–47.

Cooper, Phillip J. 2003. *Governing by Contract, Challenges and Opportunities for Public Managers.* Washington, DC: CQ Press.

Davis, James H., David Schoorman, and Lex Donaldson. 1997. Toward a stewardship theory of management. *Academy of Management Review* 22 (1): 20–47.

Dowds, Brian. 2004. *Relational Contracting: A Study of Relational Contracting Applied to Homecare Services in the UK.* London: National Homecare Council.

DeHoog, Ruth H. and Lester M. Salamon 2002. Purchase-of-Service Contracting. In *The Tools of Government; A Guide to the New Governance,* ed. Lester M. Salamon. Oxford: Oxford University Press.

Emerson, Richard H. 1962. Power-dependence relations. *American Sociological Review* 27:31–41.

Gazley, Beth, and Jeffrey L. Brudney. 2007. The purpose (and perils) of government-nonprofit partnership. *Nonprofit and Voluntary Sector Quarterly* 36 (3): 389–415.

Gronbjerg, Kirsten A. 1993. *Understanding Nonprofit Funding.* San Francisco: Jossey-Bass.

Hammack, David C., and Dennis R. Young, eds. 1993. *Nonprofit Organizations in a Market Economy.* San Francisco: Jossey-Bass.

Harlan, Sharon L., and Judith R. Saidel. 1994. Board members' influence on the government-nonprofit relationship. *Nonprofit Management and Leadership* 5 (Winter): 173–196.

Heimovics, Richard D., Robert D. Herman, and Carole L. Jurkiewicz. 1995. The political dimension of effective nonprofit executive leadership. *Nonprofit Management and Leadership* 5 (Spring): 233–248.

Heinrich, Carolyn J., Carolyn J. Hill and Laurence E. Lynn Jr. 2004. Governance as an organizing theme for empirical research. In *The Art of Governance; Analyzing Management and Administration,* ed. Patricia W. Ingraham and Laurence E. Lynn, Jr. Washington, DC: Georgetown University Press.

Jensen, Michael C., and William H. Meckling. 1976. Theory of the firm: Managerial behavior, agency costs, and ownership structure. In *Firms, Organizations, and Contracts: A Reader in Industrial Organization,* ed. Peter J. Buckley and Jonathan Michie, 103–167. Oxford: Oxford University Press.

Kelleher, Christine A., and Susan W. Yackee. 2008. A political consequence of contracting: Organized interests and state agency decision making. *Journal of Public Administration Research and Theory* 19 (July): 1–24.

Kettl, Donald F. 1988. *Government by Proxy, (Mis?) Managing Federal Programs.* Washington, DC: Congressional Quarterly Press.

———. 2002. *The Transformation of Governance: Public Administration for Twenty-first Century America.* Baltimore, MD: Johns Hopkins University Press.

Kickert, Walter J.M., Erik-Hans Klijn, and Joop F.M. Koppenjan. 1997. Introduction: A management perspective on policy networks. In *Managing Complex Networks, Strategies for the Public Sector,* ed. W.J.M. Kickert, E. Klijn, and J.F.M. Koppenjan, 1–13. London: Sage.

Kramer, Ralph M. 1981. *Voluntary Agencies in the Welfare State.* Berkeley: University of California Press.

———. 1994. Voluntary agencies and the contract culture, "dream or nightmare?" *Social Service Review* (March): 33–60.

Marwell, Nicole P. 2004. Privatizing the welfare state: Nonprofit community-based organizations as political actors. *American Sociological Review* 69 (April): 265–291.

Milward, H. Brinton, and Keith G. Provan. 2000. Governing the hollow state. *Journal of Public Administration and Theory* 10 (2): 359–379.

O'Leary, Rosemary, Lisa B. Bingham, and Catherine Gerard. 2006. Special Issue on Collaborative Public Management. *Public Administration Review* 66 (supplement).

O'Toole, Lawrence J., Jr. 1997. Treating networks seriously: Practical and research-based agendas in public administration. *Public Administration Review* 57 (1): 45–52.

Peters, B. Guy. 1998. "With a little help from our friends": Public-private partnerships as institutions and instruments. In *Partnerships in Urban Governance,* ed. J. Pierre, 11–33. New York: St. Martin's Press.

Provan, Keith G., and Brinton H. Milward. 1991. Institutional-level norms and organizational involvement in a service-implementation network. *Journal of Public Administration Research and Theory* 1 (4): 391–417.

———. 1995. A preliminary theory of interorganizational effectiveness: A comparative study of four community mental health systems. *Administrative Science Quarterly* 40 (1): 1–33.

Provan, Keith G., Kimberly R. Isett, and Brinton H. Milward. 2004. Cooperation and compromise: A network response to conflicting institutional pressures in community mental health. *Nonprofit and Voluntary Sector Quarterly* 33 (3): 489–514.

Provan, Keith G., Mark A. Veazie, Lisa K. Staten, and Nicolette I. Teufel-Shone. 2005. The use of network analysis to strengthen community partnerships. *Public Administration Review* 65 (5): 603–613.

Saidel, Judith R. 1989. Dimensions of interdependence: The state–voluntary sector relationship. *Nonprofit and Voluntary Sector Quarterly* 18 (Winter): 335–347.

———. 1991. Resource interdependence: The relationship between state agencies and nonprofit organizations. *Public Administration Review* 51 (6): 543–551.

———. 1994. The dynamics of interdependence between public agencies and nonprofit organizations. In *Research in Public Administration,* vol. 3, ed. James L. Perry, 201–229. Greenwich, CT: JAI Press.

Salamon, Lester M. 1987. Partners in public service: The scope and theory of government-nonprofit relations. In *The Nonprofit Sector: A Research Handbook,* ed. Walter W. Powell, 99–117. New Haven, CT: Yale University Press.

———. 1995. *Partners in Public Service: Government-Nonprofit Relations in the Modern Welfare State.* Baltimore, MD: Johns Hopkins University Press.

———, ed. 2002. *The Tools of Government: A Guide to the New Governance.* Oxford: Oxford University Press.

Smircich, Linda, and Charles Stubbart. 1985. Strategic management in an enacted world. *Academy of Management Review* 10 (4): 724–738.

Smith, Steven R. 1994. Managing the challenges of government contracts. In *The Jossey-Bass Handbook of Nonprofit Leadership and Management,* ed. Robert D. Herman and Associates, 325–341. San Francisco: Jossey-Bass.

———. 2005. Managing the challenges of government contracts. In *The Jossey-Bass Handbook of Nonprofit Leadership and Management.* 2d ed., ed. Robert D. Herman and Associates, 371–390. San Francisco: Jossey-Bass.

———. 2008. The challenges of strengthening nonprofits and civil society. *Public Administration Review* 68 (December): S132–S145.

Smith, Steven R., and Michael Lipsky. 1993. *Nonprofits for Hire: The Welfare State in the Age of Contracting.* Cambridge, MA: Harvard University Press.

Van Slyke, David M. 2006. Agents or stewards: Using theory to understand the government-nonprofit social service contracting relationship. *Journal of Public Administration Research and Theory* 17 (September): 157–187.

Weber, Edward P., Nicholas P. Lovrich, and Michael J. Gaffney. 2007. Assessing collaborative capacity in a multidimensional world. *Administration and Society* 39 (2): 194–220.

Whitaker, Gordon P., Lydian Altman-Sauer, and Margaret Henderson. 2004. Mutual accountability between governments and nonprofits: Moving beyond "surveillance" to "service." *American Review of Public Administration* 34 (June): 115–133.

Wing, Kennard T., Thomas H. Pollak, and Amy Blackwood. 2008. *The Nonprofit Almanac 2008.* Washington, DC: Urban Institute Press.

CHAPTER 11

THE PURSUIT OF ACCOUNTABILITY

Promises, Problems, and Prospects

MELVIN J. DUBNICK AND KAIFENG YANG

Accountability is regarded as the hallmark of modern democratic governance and a central concept in public administration (Dubnick 2005). All major schools of thought in American public administration are arguably about accountability. For example, the new public administration (Frederickson 1980), the refounding movement (Wamsley et. al 1990), the new public management (NPM; Christensen and Laegreid 2002), and the new public service (Denhardt and Denhardt 2000) prescribe differently to what and whom public administrators should be held accountable. All major debates about recent government reforms are also related to accountability. NPM advocates insist that their performance-centered program improves government accountability, but opponents refute that the program hampers political accountability. Network believers claim that contracting and network-based delivery lead to better accountability, but other people caution that networks pose significant accountability challenges. The list can go on, and the truth is that accountability seems to be everywhere and on everybody's menu.

The ubiquity of accountability, however, reflects its problems as much as its importance. Because it is a normative standard of political and social life, its interpretation can be manipulated and its meaning is "murky" (Gormley), "ever expanding" (Mulgan), and "chameleon-like" (Sinclair) (see Behn 2001, p. 4). Public administration research on accountability has made significant progress in the past two decades, and we now know much about the nature, dimensions, methods, techniques, consequences, and dilemmas of accountability—more so in traditional bureaucracies than in nonprofits and partnerships (Bardach and Lesser 1996; Behn 2001; Jos and Tompkins 2004; Kearns 1996; Roberts 2002; Romzek and Dubnick 1987; Romzek and Ingraham 2000). Yet, it remains a problematic area conceptually, empirically, and theoretically. For researchers, the current framings (e.g., Romzek and Dubnick 1987; Kearns 1994, 1996; Bovens 1998; Koppell 2005), while establishing some common ground for analysis or a thread linking our fragmented endeavors, fall short in providing the much-needed commensurability required to generate a theoretically fruitful scholarship (see Dubnick 2002). For practitioners, it remains unclear how to deal with cross pressures of accountability and what to do with the often-conflicting prescriptions all claiming to improve accountability.

This chapter examines the status of the accountability research and practice. The various accountability promises are discussed and linked to major government reform initiatives. Its problems are then examined and prospects outlined.

PROMISES

In recent years the rise in the status of accountability within managerial and political cultures is rooted in its asserted benefits. This has been particularly the case over the past quarter century, when NPM was widely adopted in the public sector, but the promises of accountability can be traced far earlier in the history. Today, the desirability of accountability-focused solutions to governance problems has reached the level of fostering an almost indiscriminate reliance on the use of the instruments associated with the polymorphic accountability toolbox. It is from this view of its indiscriminate application that accountability can be considered "promiscuous." The use of the term *promiscuous* is meant generically here, but the authors of this chapter are not unaware of the sexual metaphor implied in its use, for accountability has recently attach itself to just about any reform agenda that happens to "stream" by.

Table 11.1 can help us comprehend just how pervasive the promiscuity is by framing the different "promises" implied in the application of accountability-based solutions to problems associated with the operations and governance of an organized effort. Each of the cells in the matrix can be regarded as a problematic situation defined by the stage in the effort at which it is perceived to occur (inputs, processes, outcomes) and the value the problem-solving agent assigns to the solution (i.e., is the accountability-based solution instrumentally valued as a means to an end, or is the solution itself intrinsically valued for its own sake?). The result is six major "promises of accountability" that tend to drive the adoption (and shape the implementation) of different accountability mechanisms.

At the input stage, accountability mechanisms are viewed (and valued) instrumentally as appropriate (i.e., "promising") solutions to issues requiring "control" in the broadest sense of the term. Public and nonprofit organizations require the effective (and perhaps efficient) use of scarce resources, and a common problem is how to structure, manage, and monitor the problematic situation that results (Ouchi 1979). Here the *promise of control* (cell A1) draws upon some of the most basic mechanisms associated with accountability—textbook approaches from the design of hierarchical and lateral reporting structures to establishing production metrics, record-keeping procedures, auditing standards and procedures, oversight and supervision protocols, communications networks, and so on. These mechanisms can be found in the classic management or bureaucracy literature (e.g., Taylor, Fayol, Weber, Gulick), as well as more recent writings on public productivity and input-based performance measurement.

The input stage is also the point at which accountability may be called upon to facilitate and foster responsible, trustworthy, and virtuous behavior—that is, to achieve the *promise of integrity* (B1). In the public sector, stories of "moral exemplars" and "unsung heroes" (Riccucci 1995) among public service professionals are complemented by laws, rules, and norms that serve to protect the integrity of their actions. Mechanisms as basic as ethics codes, civil service and whistleblower protections, human resources practices, and policies fostering professional commitment are designed, in part, to support the promise of integrity in public agencies. Market rules and legal regulations (e.g., Sarbanes-Oxley; Dubnick 2007) related to the behavior of high-level corporate executives and directors are intended to punish both malfeasance and misfeasance, as are mounting pressures emanating from both within and outside the firm for corporate social responsibility (Vogel 2005).

At first view, the *promise of ethics* (A2) seems redundant with that of integrity. After all, those who act with integrity are likely to be ethical by definition. There is, however, an important difference to be highlighted between behavior that is valued for its own sake ("doing the *right* thing," for which the label *integrity* is used) and behavior that is based on "doing

Table 11.1

The Six Promises of Accountability

	Accountability Solutions Valued	
Focus on	A. Instrumentally	B. Intrinsically
1. Inputs	A1. The promise of control	B1. The promise of integrity
2. Processes	A2. The promise of ethical behavior/choices	B2. The promise of legitimacy
3. Outcomes	A3. The promise of performance	B3. The promise of justice

the *correct* thing" as far as one's role or job in an organizational is concerned (Phillips and Margolis 1999). In regard to the latter, how does one ensure that those engaged in such an effort act (or decide) correctly or appropriately in an instrumental sense? This is the problem that was central to Chester Barnard's *The Functions of the Executive* ([1938] 1968) and was at the core of Herbert Simon's decision-focused view throughout his career ([1947] 1957). As a source of means for dealing with this set of problems, accountability has taken a variety of forms—from the articulation and sanctioning of standard operating procedures to the fostering of norms stressing rule following, loyalty, and other forms of organizational citizenship behaviors (Podsakoff et al. 2000). In the public sector, an example of a more direct link with ethics is found in the work of Rohr (1989) and Rosenbloom (1983; Rosenbloom, Carroll, and Carroll 2000), who call for the adoption and enforcement of regime values and the nurturing of constitutional competence among public administrators. While the ideal situation would involve recruiting individuals who come with a ready-made commitment to constitutional values (i.e., individuals with constitutional integrity), Rohr and Rosenbloom realize that competence in this must rely on training and oversight.

The *promise of legitimacy* (B2) is related to the widely held view that accountability is a core—if not defining—characteristic of democratic regimes (Held 2006; O'Donnell 2004). Just as divine designation or inspiration once determined the legitimacy of any governance arrangement, today "democraticness" is a requisite to any claim to govern in the public sphere (Buchanan 2002), and quite often in the private and third sectors as well. Given the identity of a range of accountability mechanisms with democraticness—from representation to election to transparency to participation—the application of these is regarded as intrinsically warranted. This is a perspective that underlies the "transparency agenda" pursued by government reformers at every level of governance (Hood and Heald 2006; Florini 2007; Fung, Graham, and Weil 2007). It is also central to the "democratic deficit" critique that has generated national and global calls for more accountability (Durant 1995) and effectively put the brakes on efforts to expand the authority and jurisdiction of the European Union (Dahl 1994; Majone 1998).

Perhaps more than any other types highlighted here, the *promise of performance* (A3) has had the greatest impact on the practice of public administration. Driven by the assumption that accountability is instrumentally linked to improved performance (see Dubnick 2005), this promise has had global impact and launched literally thousands of projects and programs designed to secure the hoped-for benefits. Long applied in the private sector as mechanisms designed as much for control purposes as for enhancing productivity, the approach has been advocated for third sector organizations (Kaplan 2001) and embraced by the public sector worldwide with an ideological fervor rarely seen. Assessments of these performance management efforts are starting to emerge (Radin 2006; Frederickson and Frederickson 2006), but for the moment it has the power of a movement that seems unstoppable.

The idea that the very act of "bringing to justice" is a form of justice itself is increasingly central to viewing accountability as the *promise of justice* (B3). This promise has deep roots in beliefs regarding the basic value of retribution and restitution in the law: holding one accountable for one's actions can range from eye-for-an-eye punishment (see Foucault 1977; Hibbert 2003) to contemporary applications of restorative approaches (Braithwaite 2006). But those are beliefs that would regard accountability as a means to the traditional ends of criminal or civil law. In those legal regimes that have established a high degree of legitimacy—that is, where most of the population assumes that the justice system is capable and likely to handle cases in a fair and just manner—the value of bringing someone to justice (to be held "accountable" in the juridical sense) becomes highly valued for its own sake.

Since at least the mid- to late 1980s, the role of accountability as the promise of justice has become a core issue in several of the most prominent cases involving "transitional justice" as regimes the world over "democratized" and sought to deal with past abuses of authority and human rights violations (Minow 1998; Bass 2000). The stark choices typically ranged from collective acquiescence (e.g., Portugal and post-Pinochet Chile) to harsh legal justice meted out by the victors (e.g., postinvasion Iraq, following what is known as the "Nuremberg paradigm") (Park 2001).

But in several jurisdictions both political realities and moral leadership resulted in the applications of alternative approaches, from "truth commissions" that focused on establishing a record of what took place under the prior regime, to various forms of reconciliation mechanisms that stopped short of juridical sanctions (e.g., the Garaca process in Rwanda), to combinations, such as the South African Truth and Reconciliation Commission, that offered amnesty in return for confessions of involvement. While few of these generated outcomes that proved satisfactory to victims and others seeking more severe punishments for violations of human rights and dignity, in most instances they did satisfy accountability's promise of justice in the sense described here (Roche 2005; Syring 2006). That is, the act of holding open hearings in which the past is acknowledged by both those who perpetrated and those who suffered is in fact the very definition of justice achieved.

The promises do not easily translate into realities, however. There are two types of problems. One type is inside each cell: The mechanisms underlying each cell are not well understood. In other words, each of the promises is often based on unfounded or untested assumptions. Dubnick (2005) demonstrates that the accountability-performance link (A3), the central idea behind NPM, has not been "proved" theoretically and empirically. What are the mechanisms, if any, that link account giving to individual and organizational performance? Indeed, scholars have questioned whether performance information will be honestly reported (Yang 2009), whether the information will be used effectively (Moynihan 2009), whether performance management fits the overall political institutional framework (Radin 2006), and ultimately, whether performance-reporting requirements improve government performance (Radin 2006).

Similarly, the promise of justice (B3) may not translate into real justice: Whether in fact accountability in this (or any) sense actually delivers real justice is an empirical question (perhaps an unanswerable one). This is the case locally as well as globally, for all firms and agencies (public and private) have developed a variety of mechanisms to foster the sense that misbehavior or malfeasance can be brought to account. The very existence of such mechanisms is often perceived as a measure of accountability, even in the absence of evidence that complaints and concerns are actually addressed. In fact, many citizens distrust government institutions not because there are no public hearings, independent audits, or performance reporting in place, but because when malfeasance is revealed via those techniques, nobody is actually held accountable. On the other hand, Kweit and Kweit (2006) show that the existence of public participation channels, rather than the outcome of participation, determines citizen trust in government. Overall, it is not clear how accountability techniques or forms affect the outcome distribution and individuals' sense of justice (e.g., procedural-outcome justice, justice-based need, capability, or "just desserts").

There are similar questions in other cells. For example, is transparency always good and preferable (B2)? Eisenberg and Witten (1987) state, "In organizations that are highly regulated or those in the public eye, communicative choices must be considered in light of how they will be interpreted by various publics" (424). Where should one place public managers' role in strategic communication in order to create a desirable environment (Meyer and Rowan 1977; Moore 1995)? Would standard operating procedures, conflict-of-interest rules, and financial-disclosure rules always produce ethical behavior (A2)? Does a code of ethics make a difference (B1)? Is political neutrality in civil service always preferable (B1)? Are control techniques sufficient to ensure the efficiency and effectiveness of resource allocation and utilization (A1)?

The second type of problems about the promises is that these promises often conflict with one another. For example, input-based accountabilities (A1) and process-based accountabilities (A2) are often associated with traditional public bureaucracies and considered as causes of bureaucratic pathologies. As a result, NPM advocates propose outcome-based accountabilities (A3) and "breaking through" or "reinventing" bureaucracies. However, NPM proposals are often criticized for damaging other accountabilities. Personnel flexibilities, pay for performance, and at-will employment, as prescribed by NPM, could reduce civil servants' political neutrality and governments' credible commitment, which ultimately make governments less accountable to public interests (B1). Entrepreneurship, risk taking, and efficiency first are often in tension with nonmission-based values such as transparency and due process (B2).

For individuals involved in the accountability relationships, different promises represent different accountability pressures. A large portion of the literature focuses on cross pressures of accountability and their potential negative consequences. For example:

- There are conflicts among pressures of accountability, and conflicts lead to problems such as disasters, crises, and mismanagement (Bardach and Lesser 1996; Dunn and Legge 2000; Koppell 2005; Romzek and Dubnick 1987; Romzek and Ingraham 2000).
- Overreliance on a particular type (or particular types) of accountability leads to problems: Production-oriented accountability leads to disaster and impedes change (Schwartz and Sulitzeanu-Kenan 2004); too much legal and hierarchical accountability damages professional and political accountabilities (Kim 2005); too much political and hierarchical accountability damages professional accountability (Romzek and Dubnick 1987); and formal procedural accountability exacerbates the limitations of political accountability (West 2004).
- There is no perfect model of accountability, and each may evolve into something unproductive or illegitimate (Jos and Tompkins 2004; Weber 1999).
- Accountability based on the classic principal-agent model or the market approach has serious limitations, especially in the context of contracting and privatization (Dicke 2002; Romzek and Jonhston 2005).
- Contracting, privatization, and hybrid organizations lead to great accountability challenges and require particular accountability capacities (Gilmour and Jensen 1998; Johnston and Romzek 1999; Klingner, Nalbandian, and Romzek 2002; Moe 2001; Romzek and Johnston 2005).
- Managerial reforms such as performance measurement, performance-based accountability, and reinvention have complications in traditional forms of accountability (Page 2006) and organizational performance (Benjamin 2008).

Yet, with notable exceptions (e.g., Kearns 1996; Moore 1995; Page 2004; Whitaker, Altman-Sauer, and Henderson 2004), much of the literature does not describe and explain empirically how actors of governance make sense and order of conflicting accountability pressures, nor does it *prescribe* what exactly managers should do to deal with the accountability dilemmas, offering limited actionable knowledge. A typical conclusion in the literature is that managers should balance different accountability sources (Dunn and Legge 2000). But how to balance? Balance is something that is easy to say but hard to do. Indeed, Romzek and Ingraham (2000) conclude that "sadly, it demonstrates that under the most intense pressures, the ability to make the right choices may not be present" (251). Koppell (2005) laments that "this is unlikely" (99). Roberts (2002) believes in the strength of dialogue-based accountability, but even so, she warns: Do it when other methods have failed.

PROBLEMS

As discussed previously, promiscuity is a significant problem in our pursuit of accountability. Despite its pervasive presence in almost any discussion of governance, the fact remains that a sense of what accountability entails is still lacking. It remains holographic, easy to see but impossible to grasp. Thus one is left with a central point somewhat similar to Wildavsky's commentary (1973) on planning: If accountability is the solution to everything, perhaps it is the solution to nothing. Both scholars and practitioners face a fundamental problem: There is not an overarching accountability theory that can help them understand the complex linkages or relationships among a diverse range of accountability promises and pressures. However, such an overarching theory is difficult to construct because of the multifunctional, polymorphic, and contingent nature of accountability.

Multifunctionality

An accountable relationship exists for a reason or purpose; that is, it has a "function" in the overall scheme of social relations that sustains it over time. While one might argue over the teleological premise that underpins functionalist views (see Pettit 1996), they do allow us to address the question of just what purpose accountability serves. And it is here where one runs into the first major obstacle to understanding the subject: As a social relationship, accountability is multifunctional. Applying Mahner and Bunge's (2001) logic of functionalism to account giving, one can identify at least five functions of accountability:

- "*Internal*" functionality: Accountability is perceived as a mechanism that constitutes or sustains, or both constitutes and sustains, the specific relationship between the parties. It is part of the normal internal workings of a specific, relatively closed (i.e., buffered from external interference) social relationship between at least two parties.
- "*External*" functionality: Accountability is a mechanism that defines its link to other entities in the task environment. It is a means for connecting the narrower relationship to its surroundings.
- "*Role*" functionality: Accountability constitutes a meaningful component of a more general organized effort; that is, it serves a constitutive or sustaining purpose in the overall system of relationships within which it is located.
- "*Value*" functionality: Accountability contributes in a positive or negative (i.e., dysfunctional) way to the performance of the organized effort; that is, it is treated in terms of the consequences it has for that overall system of relationships.

- "*Adaptive*" functionality: Accountability contributes to the continued viability of that system of relationships as an ongoing social endeavor; that is, it is an existential component of the more general organized endeavor of which it is a part.

In short, accountability as a simple social relationship can (and often does) perform different functions at different levels of social activity. For example, most of the literature on democratic governance would posit accountability as functionally adaptive, asserting that it would be difficult to imagine a democratic system that was not sustained by some effective form of accountability (e.g., Held 2006). But it is also clear that not all forms of accountability play a positive role in promoting democracy. In fact, some forms (e.g., bureaucratic) are often perceived as effectively dysfunctional in democratic settings (e.g., Scott 1998; Adams and Balfour 2004). Nevertheless, there is a substantial argument to be made for the necessity (i.e., role function) of seemingly non-democratic forms of accountability if democratic regimes are to succeed over time (e.g., Pollitt 1986; Richardson 2002). The literature is also replete with ironies and paradoxes (Michels 1999) that highlight the role played by oligarchic relationships and even slavery in the history of suppos-edly democratic organizations and regimes (in the case of ancient Athens; see Samons 2004).

The point here is not to question the possible link between democracy and accountability, but to highlight the analytic and empirical challenge posed by the multifunctional nature of account-giving behavior and relations. It is a challenge that can be resolved only through a process of defining and operationalization that focuses and narrows one's view of the object under study. As a result, in exchange for the ability to apply the tools of systematic thought and empirical analysis to an aspect of account-giving behavior, one knowingly (and necessarily) surrenders access to alternative views of accountability as well as the broader and more complex phenomena that make this aspect of governance so significant.

Polymorphism

The challenge posed by accountability's multifunctionality is magnified by the wide range of structural and operational forms associated with account-giving actions. These are so numerous, in fact, that any attempt to inventory them would prove fruitless. Consider, for example, the vast inventory of mechanisms (passive and active) associated with rendering an individual or organization accountable. From legal sanctions to monetary rewards, from detailed job descrip-tions to empowerment, from oversight to assessments, from audits to rankings, from instructions to management by objectives, from reporting to responding, from ethical constraints to broad grants of discretion—the list of mechanisms seems endless. The reality is that no particular mechanism or set of mechanisms defines accountability, not even the actions associated with the act of "accounting."

It is not surprising, therefore, that researchers often rely on typologies of such mechanisms based on some general characteristic. In some cases the mechanisms are associated with an arena of accountable action. Romzek and Dubnick (1987), for example, offer a scheme often used to sort mechanisms into four types depending on whether they are derived from legal, political, bu-reaucratic/organizational, or professional spheres. At other times it is the organizational and social context that provides the logic. Grant and Keohane (2005) set out seven types in their analysis of mechanisms relevant to global affairs, four based on the use of delegation (hierarchical, su-pervisory, fiscal, and legal) and three on forms of participation (market, peer, and reputational). Still others derive their categorization of mechanisms from observation of practices in specific arenas. Emanuel and Emanuel (1996), focusing on health care, provide a threefold typology of mechanisms at a very general level: professional, market, and political. Ebrahim (2003; cf. Kearns 1994) derives his five "categories of accountability mechanisms" (reports and disclosure statements, performance assessments and evaluations, participation, self-regulation, and social audits) from the observed practices of nongovernmental organizations.

Given the polymorphic nature of accountability—that is, its manifestation in a range of different "forms" and "mechanisms"—there is little choice for analysts but to cast conceptually porous typological nets on their subject matter. This is made necessary by the various "language games" involving the term *accountability,* something that becomes quite clear when one considers the various synonyms associated with it: *answerability, liability, responsibility, fidelity, responsiveness, obligation*—each frequently used interchangeably with *accountability,* and each linked directly to different forms of account-giving mechanisms (Dubnick 1998, 2002).

But there is a challenge here, for form can easily replace substance in the study of accountability, and in the process divert our attention to some of the more significant issues related to our subject. It is commonplace for a tautological logic to take hold and transform mechanisms of account giving from empirical examples into measures of accountability. Once on that slippery slope, the "measures" of accountability develop into the evaluative standards of just how "accountable" a government or official is—but in the process one loses sight of the more fundamental and unanswered questions about the nature and role of accountability in governance. Just as the study of democracy has been transformed into the comparative study of voting, deliberation, and various institutional forms, so the study of accountability has been narrowed to the examination of mechanisms that seem to ensure answerability, liability, control, and so on. One benefits from learning a good deal more about those mechanisms and their implementation, but that body of work does not advance the project of furthering the understanding of accountability.

Situatedness

Whatever the variation in form, accountability also varies by context. In that sense, accountability is not merely a "social" relationship. It is also cultural, temporal, and spatial. While one may reasonably develop generally applicable statements regarding the functions and forms of accountability from the studies, one can do so only contingently. In short, accountability is situated, and context matters.

Depending on one's research objective, this particular characteristic of accountability might be regarded as either problem or opportunity. On the problematic side, the contingent and embedded nature of accountability in governance (Bevir 2004; Fox and Miller 1995) will make generalizations and formal theory construction related to accountability challenging at best. On the positive side, the opportunity to create empirical strategies and innovative conceptual/theoretical approaches to contend with these challenges can be (and has been; see Simpson 2002) a driving force in the social sciences in general and in the study of accountability in particular.

Many scholars have proposed to study whether the patterns revealed in current studies hold in other settings (Romzek and Johnston 2005). Context affects accountability, including the form of government (Wang 2002), life stages of a partnership (Acar, Guo, and Yang 2008), different national cultures (Page 2006), historical times (Page 2006), policy systems (Kim 2005), organizational culture (Klingner, Nalbandian, and Romzek 2002), the accountability environment or organizational field (O'Connell 2006), and administrative reforms (Page 2006).

Situatedness also affects the choice of methodology—a great majority of the empirical accountability studies use qualitative designs, such as single case study and comparative case study (Koppell 2005; Romzek and Ingraham 2000; Schwartz and Sulitzeanu-Kenan 2004), interviews

(Acar, Guo, and Yang 2008), content analysis (Dicke and Ott 1999), or mixed methods but with strong qualitative emphasis (Dicke 2002). The use of qualitative designs is in line with those studies' purpose, which is to describe and understand the nature, change, process, and consequence of accountability relationships in a specific setting, not to quantitatively explain their correlates and determinants across settings.

Despite the importance of context, over time, accountability has lost its functional and structural ties to its origins. It is now less an identifiable institutional form rooted in specific legal and political traditions, and more a global cultural phenomenon—a worldwide icon of good governance (Dubnick 2002; Dubnick and Justice 2004). In many respects, accountability has become what some would classify as a keyword in our global culture (Williams 1985), one with a positive valence and universal appeal that is applied (casually—almost thoughtlessly) worldwide in the daily rhetoric of politicians of every ideological stripe as well as the mass media that covers them.

PROSPECTS

The promiscuity, multifunctionality, polymorphism, and situatedness of accountability make it one of the most elusive concepts in public administration. It would not be surprising if someone believes that accountability is merely an empty concept, an iconic symbol manipulated for both rhetorical and analytic purposes to help us rationalize or make some sense of our political world. It would not be surprising either if someone believes that an overarching accountability theory is impossible. Our belief is less pessimistic. Without predicting the exact future of accountability research, this chapter identifies several parameters of the future. This choice was made consciously not to pose specific research questions as core future issues, because accountability relates to nearly every topic of public administration, and choosing any set of questions would leave out many more other important ones. This chapter aims to offer general thoughts that will cut across various areas and topics.

Accountability: Metaproblem of Modern Governance

The concept of "metaproblem" is used in order to associate accountability with a small group of issues that have defined and shaped social theory and practice for centuries—a class of general problems often lurking in the background that continuously challenge the basic assumptions and institutional arrangements of social and political life at any particular time and place. By way of example, consider two such metaproblems—the "problem of evil" and the "problem of free will"—that have for centuries defined (and continue to define) issues and debates in fields as diverse as theology, philosophy, and the sciences.

In one sense, these metaproblems are the stuff of high-level philosophical analyses, the focus of analytic logic and scholasticist argumentation. In another sense, however, they are the grist for those engaged in reconciling ideas and ideals with realities and contingencies. Such metaproblems share three characteristics.

- First, they are historically transcendent or, in Michel Foucault's terms, historically a priori. While part of human history and subject to local and temporal variation (in the form of *problématiques,* or what Foucault [1997] terms "problematizations"), these metaproblems are not bounded by time and space.
- Second, metaproblems are ultimately intractable—they are dilemmas that cannot be "solved." Even when they are rendered more approachable when "problematized," there are no simple

or easy solutions, and those that are applied are likely to prove incomplete or ineffective in the long term.
*   Third, metaproblems and the problématiques they generate are "wicked" in the sense of being "messy" and often inviting solutions that require choices and actions that will themselves prove problematic or even make matters worse (see Rittel and Webber 1973).

Posited as a distinct metaproblem, the problem of accountability is transcendent in reflecting the centuries-old dilemma defined by the need to reconcile human potential for autonomy with the requirements of social order. Viewed in this light, both the history of political thought (e.g., from Plato's *Republic* to Rawls's *A Theory of Justice*—and beyond) and the analysis of political practice (through the historical examination of various governance arrangements) can be understood (and assessed) as efforts to specify ("problematize") and deal with the "intractable and wicked" metaproblem of accountability.

Accountability: The Duality of Agency and Structure

The metaproblem of modern governance boils down to this: the tension between "agencified" individuals and the structural order of the society, or between the human potential for autonomy and the requirements of social order. We believe that the current analytic approaches lack attention to human agency and its dynamic interaction with accountability structures. While a few studies have advanced accountability strategies that implicitly emphasize the role of human agency, proposing negotiated, anticipatory, or emergent accountabilities (Acar, Guo, and Yang 2008; Kearns 1994; O'Connell 2005; Roberts 2002; Whitaker, Altman-Sauer, and Henderson 2004), few of them examine how agents' strategic behavior is actually embedded in and constrained by current accountability structural forces and how the structural forces will respond to agents' new strategic behavior. The proactive steps taken by managers occur in a politicized environment, so how power, resources, legitimacy, and norms affect the steps and their impact is of great importance if one wants to understand the real process of accountability dynamics.

Anthony Giddens's (1984) structuration theory helps stress this point by establishing the structure-agency duality. Structuration means the interplay between structures and agency. Rather than conceptualizing structure as something given or external to individuals, Giddens (1984) argues that structure should not be taken as having some given or visible form external to people; it exists only in and through the activities of human agents: It is both an outcome and a medium of action. That is, "analyzing the structuration of social systems means studying the modes in which systems . . . are produced and reproduced in interaction" (25).

Applying Giddens's structuration theory, Yang (2008) considers accountability as structural properties of governance systems. Consistent with the ideal of the duality of structure, accountability is viewed as both the medium and the outcome of action. Accordingly, accountability is both means and ends, context specific, and emergent. Moreover, accountability as structures has aspects of legitimation, domination, and signification. This broader notion requires a focus that is beyond measuring and reporting inputs, outputs, and outcomes. It also indicates that accountability cannot be understood without considering power relations. Such a perspective opens some new questions, such as, Under what conditions can actors be transformative and policy learning be achieved? What are the social costs associated with accountability struggles? What new accountability forms can help us build an effective governance system to deal with emerging challenges? How can we explain the historical emergence and development of the constitutional and democratic forms of accountable governance that stand as our contemporary global ideal?

Accountability: Middle-Range Theories

In addition to efforts such as those using structuration theory to build a general framework, future studies of accountability may construct more middle-range theories to take "situatedness" of accountability seriously. As Perry (1991) asserts, a middle-range theory of administrative performance must be developed "within institutional contexts and structures characteristic of the public sector" (13). Accountability research should follow the same route. General typologies and frameworks are fine for certain purposes, but *credible* theories of accountability must of necessity be contingency theories. Accepting that fact will do much to shape the future of accountability studies, forcing researchers to design their empirical studies with care and analysts to qualify the conclusions they draw from observations of account-giving behavior.

In particular, mechanism-based theorizing can provide "an intermediary level of analysis in-between pure description and story-telling, on the one hand, and universal social laws, on the other" (Hedström and Swedberg 1998). A middle-range model with mechanism-based theorizing can shed light on the issue by revealing the linkages between the different forms and functions of accountability, as well as how they interact to influence performance. Yang (2008), for example, proposes the integration between an agency-based perspective of accountability and mainstream public management studies. The key is felt accountability—actors involved in the accountability relationship have their own perceptions about the relationship and its implication. From a managerial perspective, this suggests that one examines how actors of governance (both accountors and accountees) process the information and signals they receive and how they make decisions accordingly.

Accountability should be studied in connection with other management systems and literatures. As Wise and Freitag (2002) write, "[a]ccountability . . . cannot be considered in isolation. It affects and is affected by other important variables in the management context" (494). Based on the concept of felt accountability, Yang (2008) asks some new questions: How is felt accountability affected by organizational characteristics and individual characteristics? What are the mechanisms linking felt accountability with individual-level consequences and organizational performance? What are the contextual and environmental factors that provide the stage for public sector accountability mechanisms? How exactly do various government reform programs, such as contracting and managing for results, affect the accountability relationships? How would accountability evolve in networks and governance settings?

Methodology Diversity

As mentioned before, most accountability studies adopt qualitative research designs, which have many advantages. Future studies may expand the type of methodological choices. Dubnick (2005) stipulates that future research on accountability should learn from Tetlock's approach (1985, 1991), which uses experimental designs to study how perceived accountability pressures affect individuals' cognitive and emotional states, as well as how the relationship is moderated by variables such as timing, trust, and task environment. Dubnick further proposes that the individual-level Tetlock-type work should be placed in contextual settings such as systems of answerability and environments of blameworthiness.

To demonstrate the complexities of the interactions between actors and the reproduction of accountability structures, qualitative designs used in prior studies should be strengthened to better reveal the impact of context and embeddedness, as well as the process of changes. One alternative is a *process approach,* analyzing the sequence of events that shows how things change over time

(Pettigrew, Woodman, and Cameron 2001). Grounded theory, narrative, visual mapping, and temporal bracketing all have been used in other disciplines applying the structuration theory empirically (see Langley 1999). Pozzebon and Pinsonneault (2005), in particular, advocate for combining narrative and temporal bracketing, as the former helps recognize *when* and *how* changes are triggered and the latter helps explain *why*. Yang (2008) also proposes participatory action research as another alternative to generate actionable knowledge. Many empirical accountability studies rely on retrospective examination of past cases, but the most powerful empirical tests for knowledge are done not by simply describing it, but by making predictions about changing the universe (Argyris 2003).

Demonstrating the complexities of the interactions between actors and the reproduction of accountability structures can also be achieved via quantitative methods such as agent-based modeling (Yang 2008). In this computer-based approach, multiple actors act according to rules, in which utility optimization is but one of many possibilities, and complex social patterns emerge from the interactions among actors. As a result, agent-based modeling can show how collective phenomena occur and how the interaction of the actors leads to these phenomena. In addition, agent-based modeling can explore the impact of various institutional arrangements and paths of development on the collective result. A well-known case is Robert Axelrod's (1997) use of the method to study competition and collaboration.

If middle-range theories are to be constructed, even quantitative methods using survey research could be very useful. For example, survey data can be analyzed with structural equation modeling to assess the complex mediating relationships among accountability pressures or forms, organizational characteristics, individual attitudes or behaviors, and organizational performance. Interaction terms can be used in regression-type techniques to assess the interaction between accountability forms, or between accountability systems and other management systems, or between accountability structures and individual characteristics.

CONCLUSION

As challenging as the pursuit of accountability has proven to be for students of public administration and governance, we do not have the luxury of abandoning the efforts to understand the concept and its use. Unlike our colleagues in the "hard" sciences, who can (and have) moved on when a concept has proven too problematic (e.g., ether), we suffer the Sisyphean fate of philosophers who must deal with the problem of free will and determinism, or theologians who are cursed with the "problem of evil." The rhetorical and strategic uses of accountability have driven the research agenda and will continue to do so as long as the promises of accountability remain attractive to policy makers and the public they must satisfy. Our task is to continue to deal with the resulting theoretical and methodological challenges.

REFERENCES

Acar, Muhittin, Chao Guo, and Kaifeng Yang. 2008. Accountability when hierarchical authority is absent. *American Review of Public Administration* 38 (1): 3–23.
Adams, Guy, and Danny Balfour. 2004. *Unmasking Administrative Evil.* Armonk, NY: M.E. Sharpe.
Argyris, Chris. 2003. Actionable knowledge. In *The Oxford Handbook of Organization Theory,* ed. H. Tsoukas and C. Knudsen, 423–452. New York: Oxford University Press.
Axelrod, Robert. 1997. *The Complexity of Cooperation.* Princeton, NJ: Princeton University Press.
Bardach, Eugene, and Cara Lesser. 1996. Accountability in human services collaboratives. *Journal of Public Administration Research and Theory* 6 (2): 197–224.
Barnard, Chester I. [1938] 1968. *The Functions of the Executive.* Cambridge, MA: Harvard University Press.

Bass, Gary. 2000. *Stay the Hand of Vengeance.* Princeton, NJ: Princeton University Press.

Behn, Robert D. 2001. *Rethinking Democratic Accountability.* Washington, DC: Brookings Institution Press.

Benjamin, Lehn M. 2008. Bearing more risk for results: Performance accountability and nonprofit relational work. *Administration and Society* 39 (8): 959–983.

Bevir, Mark. 2004. Governance and interpretation. *Public Administration* 82 (3): 605–625.

Bovens, Mark. 1998. *The Quest for Responsibility.* New York: Cambridge University Press.

Braithwaite, John. 2006. Accountability and responsibility through restorative justice. In *Public Accountability,* ed. M.D. Dowdle, pp. 33–51. Cambridge: Cambridge University Press.

Buchanan, Allen. 2002. Political legitimacy and democracy. *Ethics* 112 (4): 689–719.

Christensen, Tom, and Per Laegreid. 2002. New public management: Puzzles of democracy and the influence of citizens. *Journal of Political Philosophy* 10 (3): 267–295.

Dahl, Robert. 1994. A democratic dilemma: System effectiveness versus citizen participation. *Political Science Quarterly* 109 (1): 23–34.

Denhardt, Robert, and Janet Denhardt. 2000. The new public service: Serving rather than steering. *Public Administration Review* 60 (6): 549–559.

Dicke, Lisa A. 2002. Ensuring accountability in human services contracting. *American Review of Public Administration* 32 (4): 455–470.

Dicke, Lisa A., and J. Steven Ott. 1999. Public agency accountability in human services contracting. *Public Performance and Management Review* 22 (4): 502–516.

Dubnick, Melvin. 1998. Clarifying accountability: An ethical theory framework. In *Public Sector Ethics: Finding and Implementing Values,* ed. Charles Sampford and N. Preston, pp. 68–81. Annandale, Australia: Federation Press/Routledge.

———. 2002. Seeking salvation for accountability. Paper read at American Political Science Association, Boston, MA, August 29–September 1.

———. 2005. Accountability and the promise of performance: In search of the mechanisms. *Public Performance and Management Review* 27 (3): 376–417.

———. 2007. Sarbanes-Oxley and the search for accountable corporate governance. In *Private Equity, Corporate Governance and the Dynamics of Capital Market Regulation,* ed. J. O'Brien. London: Imperial College Press.

Dubnick, Melvin, and Jonathan Justice. 2004. Accounting for accountability. Paper read at American Political Science Association, Chicago, IL, September 2–5.

Dunn, Delmer D., and Jerome S. Legge Jr. 2000. U.S. local government managers and the complexity of responsibility and accountability in democratic governance. *Journal of Public Administration Research and Theory* 11 (1): 73–88.

Durant, Robert F. 1995. The democratic deficit in America. *Political Science Quarterly* 110 (1): 25–47.

Ebrahim, Alnoor. 2003. Accountability in practice: Mechanisms for NGOs. *World Development* 31 (5): 813–829.

Eisenberg, Eric M., and Marsha G. Witten. 1987. "Reconsidering Openness in Organizational Communication." *The Academy of Management Review* 12 (3): 418–426.

Emanuel, Ezekiel J., and Linda L. Emanuel. 1996. What is accountability in health care? *Annals of Internal Medicine* 124 (2): 229–239.

Florini, Ann. 2007. *The Right to Know.* New York: Columbia University Press.

Foucault, Michel. 1977. *Discipline and Punish.* New York: Vintage Books.

———. 1997. Polemics, politics and problemizations: An interview with Michel Foucault (1984). In *Ethics: Subjectivity and Truth,* ed. P. Rabinow, 111–119. New York: New Press.

Fox, Charles, and Hugh Miller. 1995. *Postmodern Public Administration.* Thousand Oaks, CA: Sage.

Frederickson, David, and George Frederickson. 2006. *Measuring the Performance of the Hollow State.* Washington, DC: Georgetown University Press.

Frederickson, H. George. 1980. *New Public Administration.* University: University of Alabama Press.

Fung, Archon, Mary Graham, and David Weil. 2007. *Full Disclosure: The Perils and Promise of Transparency.* New York: Cambridge University Press.

Giddens, Anthony. 1984. *The Constitution of Society.* Berkeley: University of California Press.

Gilmour, Robert S., and Laura S. Jensen. 1998. Reinventing government accountability. *Public Administration Review* 58 (3): 247–258.

Grant, Ruth, and Robert O. Keohane. 2005. Accountability and abuses of power in world politics. *American Review of Public Administration* 99 (1): 29–43.

Hedström, Peter, and Richard Swedberg. 1998. Social mechanisms: An introductory essay. In *Social Mechanisms: An Analytical Approach to Social Theory,* ed. P. Hedström and R. Swedberg. Cambridge: Cambridge University Press.

Held, David. 2006. *Models of Democracy.* 3d ed. Malden, MA: Polity.

Hibbert, Christopher. 2003. *The Roots of Evil.* Stroud, UK: Sutton.

Hood, Christopher, and David Heald, eds. 2006. *Transparency: The Key to Better Governance?* Oxford: Oxford University Press.

Johnston, Jocelyn, and Barbara S. Romzek. 1999. Contracting and accountability in state Medicaid reform. *Public Administration Review* 59 (5): 383–399.

Jos, Philip H., and Mark E. Tompkins. 2004. The accountability paradox in an age of reinvention. *Administration and Society* 36 (3): 255–281.

Kaplan, Robert S. 2001. Strategic performance measurement and management in nonprofit organizations. *Nonprofit Management and Leadership* 11 (3): 353–370.

Kearns, Kevin P. 1994. The strategic management of accountability in nonprofit organizations. *Public Administration Review* 54 (2): 185–192.

———. 1996. *Managing for Accountability.* San Francisco: Jossey-Bass.

Kim, Seok-Eun. 2005. Balancing competing accountability requirements: Challenges in performance improvement of the nonprofit human services agency. *Public Performance and Management Review* 29 (2): 145–163.

Klingner, Donald E., John Nalbandian, and Barbara S. Romzek. 2002. Politics, administration, and markets: Conflicting expectations and accountability. *American Review of Public Administration* 32 (2): 117–144.

Koppell, Jonathan G.S. 2005. Pathologies of accountability: ICANN and the challenge of "multiple accountabilities disorder." *Public Administration Review* 65 (1): 94–108.

Kweit, Mary, and Robert Kweit. 2006. A tale of two disasters. *Publius* 36 (3): 375–392.

Langley, Ann. 1999. Strategies for theorizing from process data. *Academy of Management Review* 24 (4): 691–710.

Mahner, Martin, and Mario Bunge. 2001. Function and functionalism: A synthetic perspective. *Philosophy of Science* 68 (1): 75–94.

Majone, Giandomenico. 1998. Europe's "Democratic Deficit": The Question of Standards. *European Law Journal* 4 (1): 5–28.

Meyer, John W., and Brian Rowan. 1977. Institutionalized organizations: Formal structure as myth and ceremony. *American Journal of Sociology* 83 (2): 340–363.

Michels, Robert. 1999. *Political Parties: A Sociological Study of the Oligarchical Tendencies of Modern Democracy.* New Brunswick, NJ: Transaction Publishers.

Minow, Martha. 1998. *Between Vengeance and Forgiveness.* Boston: Beacon Press.

Moe, Ronald C. 2001. The emerging federal quasi government: Issues of management and accountability. *Public Administration Review* 61 (3): 290–312.

Moore, Mark. 1995. *Creating Public Value.* Cambridge, MA: Harvard University Press.

Moynihan, Donald. 2009. Through a glass, darkly: Understanding the effects of performance regimes. *Public Performance and Management Review* 32 (4): 586–598.

O'Connell, Lenahan. 2005. "Program Accountability as an Emergent Property: The Role of Stakeholders in a Program's Field." *Public Administration Review* 65 (1): 85–93.

———. 2006. Emergent accountability in state-local relations: Some lessons from solid waste policy in Kentucky. *Administration and Society* 38 (4): 500–513.

O'Donnell, Guillermo. 2004. Why the rule of law matters. *Journal of Democracy* 15 (4): 32–46.

Ouchi, William. 1979. A conceptual framework for the design of organizational control mechanisms. *Management Science* 25 (9): 833–848.

Podsakoff, Philip M., Scott B. MacKenzie, Julie Beth Paine, and Daniel G. Bachrach. 2000. "Organizational Citizenship Behaviors: A Critical Review of the Theoretical and Empirical Literature and Suggestions for Future Research." *Journal of Management* 26 (3): 513–563.

Page, Stephen. 2004. Measuring accountability for results in interagency collaboratives. *Public Administration Review* 64 (5): 591–606.

———. 2006. The web of managerial accountability: the impact of reinventing government. *Administration and Society* 38 (2): 166–197.

Park, Stephen Kim. 2001. Dictators in the dock: Retroactive justice in consolidating democracies. *Fletcher Forum of World Affairs* 25 (1): 127–142.

Perry, James. 1991. Strategies for building public administration theory. In *Research in Public Administration,* ed. J.L. Perry. Greenwich, CT: JAI Press.

Pettigrew, Andrew, Richard Woodman, and Kim Cameron. 2001. Studying organizational change and development. *Academy of Management Journal* 44 (4): 697–713.

Pettit, Philip. 1996. Functional explanation and virtual selection. *British Journal for the Philosophy of Science* 47 (2): 291–302.

Phillips, Robert A., and Joshua D. Margolis. 1999. Toward an ethics of organizations. *Business Ethics Quarterly* 9 (4): 619–638.

Pollitt, Christopher. 1986. Democracy and bureaucracy. In *New Forms of Democracy,* ed. D. Held and C. Pollitt. London: Sage.

Pozzebon, Marlei, and Alain Pinsonneault. 2005. Challenges in conducting empirical work using structuration theory. *Organization Studies* 26 (9): 1353–1376.

Radin, Beryl. 2006. *Challenging the Performance Movement.* Washington, DC: Georgetown University Press.

Riccucci, Norma. 1995. *Unsung Heroes.* Washington, DC: Georgetown University Press.

Richardson, Henry. 2002. *Democratic Autonomy.* New York: Oxford University Press.

Ring, Peter Smith, and James L. Perry. 1985. Strategic management in public and private organizations. *Academy of Management Review* 10 (2): 276–286.

Rittel, Horst W.J., and Melvin M. Webber. 1973. Dilemmas in a general theory of planning. *Policy Sciences* 4 (2): 155–169.

Roberts, Nancy. 2002. Keeping public officials accountable through dialogue: Resolving the accountability paradox. *Public Administration Review* 62 (6): 658–669.

Roche, Declan. 2005. Truth commission amnesties and the International Criminal Court. *British Journal of Criminology* 45 (4): 565–581.

Rohr, John A. 1989. *Ethics for Bureaucrats.* 2d ed. New York: Marcel Dekker.

Romzek, Barbara, and Melvin Dubnick. 1987. Accountability in the public sector: Lessons from the *Challenger* tragedy. *Public Administration Review* 47 (3): 227–238.

Romzek, Barbara, and Patricia Ingraham. 2000. Cross pressures of accountability: Initiative, command, and failure in the Ron Brown plane crash. *Public Administration Review* 60 (3): 240–253.

Romzek, Barbara, and Jocelyn Johnston. 2005. State social services contracting: Exploring the determinants of effective contract accountability. *Public Administration Review* 65 (4): 436–449.

Rosenbloom, David H. 1983. Public administrative theory and the separation of powers. *Public Administration Review* 43 (3): 219–227.

Rosenbloom, David H., James D. Carroll, and Jonathan D. Carroll. 2000. *Constitutional Competence for Public Managers.* Itasca, IL: F.E. Peacock.

Samons, Loren J. 2004. *What's Wrong with Democracy.* Berkeley: University of California Press.

Schwartz, Robert, and Raanan Sulitzeanu-Kenan. 2004. Managerial values and accountability pressures. *Journal of Public Administration Research and Theory* 14 (1): 79–102.

Scott, James C. 1998. *Seeing Like a State.* New Haven, CT: Yale University Press.

Simon, Herbert A. [1947] 1957. *Administrative Behavior.* 2d ed. New York: Free Press.

Simpson, David. 2002. *Situatedness, or Why We Keep Saying Where We're Coming From.* Durham, NC: Duke University Press.

Syring, Tom. 2006. Truth versus justice. *International Legal Theory* 12:143–210.

Tetlock, Philip E. 1985. Accountability: A social check on the fundamental attribution error. *Social Psychology Quarterly* 48 (3): 227–236.

———. 1991. An alternative metaphor in the study of judgment and choice: People as politicians. *Theory and Psychology* 1 (4): 451–475.

Vogel, David. 2005. *The Market for Virtue.* Washington, DC: Brookings Institution.

Wamsley, Gary L., Robert N. Bacher, Charles T. Goodsell, Philip S. Kronenberg, John A. Rohr, Camilla M. Stivers, Orion F. White, and James F. Wolf. 1990. *Refounding Public Administration.* Newbury Park CA: Sage.

Wang, Xiaohu. 2002. Assessing administrative accountability: Results from a national survey. *American Review of Public Administration* 32 (3): 350–370.

Weber, Edward. 1999. The question of accountability in historical perspective. *Administration and Society* 31 (4): 451–494.

West, William F. 2004. Formal procedures, informal processes, accountability, and responsiveness in bureaucratic policy making: An institutional policy analysis. *Public Administration Review* 64 (1): 66–80.

Whitaker, Gordon, Lydian Altman-Sauer, and Margaret Henderson. 2004. Mutual accountability between governments and nonprofits: Moving beyond "surveillance" to "service." *American Review of Public Administration* 34 (2): 115–133.

Wildavsky, Aaron. 1973. If planning is everything, maybe it's nothing. *Policy Sciences* 4 (2): 127–153.

Williams, Raymond. 1985. *Keywords: A Vocabulary of Culture and Society.* Rev. ed. New York: Oxford University Press.

Wise, Charles, and Christian Freitag. 2002. Balancing accountability and risk in program implementation: The case of national fire policy. *Journal of Public Administration Research and Theory* 12 (4): 493–523.

Yang, Kaifeng. 2008. Accountability in public organizations: A critical review and a preliminary map for future research. Paper presented at the Annual Conference of American Society for Public Administration, Dallas, TX.

———. 2009. Examining perceived honest performance reporting by public organizations. *Journal of Public Administration Research and Theory* 19 (1): 81–105.

CHAPTER 12

TECHNOLOGY AND PUBLIC MANAGEMENT INFORMATION SYSTEMS

Where We Have Been and Where We Are Going

STUART I. BRETSCHNEIDER AND INES MERGEL

Those who cannot remember the past are condemned to repeat it.
George Santayana, U.S. (Spanish-born) philosopher (1863–1952), in
The Life of Reason, vol. 1 (1905)

Over the past fifty years there have been huge changes in both information and telecommunication technology. With each major change, social scientists, management scholars, and public administration researchers have made a number of bold predictions about how each new technology would lead to sweeping changes in public organizations' structures and processes. Despite these claims, many of these predictions today remain unrealized. For example, in the 1950s many scholars suggested that new information technology (IT) would flatten organizational hierarchies and dramatically eliminate middle management (Leavitt and Whisler 1958). More than fifty years later, while we do see more diverse organizational structures, large hierarchical structures still persist and to some extent dominate, generally and particularly so in government.

In the 1980s scholars developed a more contingent perspective on the role of information technology in organizations. As one major textbook from the period notes, "Contemporary research also recognizes that organizations have a great deal of control over the impacts of systems on structure. Important groups in the organization determine, either consciously or unconsciously, what kinds of impacts on organizational structure will occur. Organizations can decide to centralize or decentralize power" (Loudon and Laudon 1988). This perspective suggested that technology does not ultimately drive the changes but rather enables new forms and approaches. Once enabled, these forms and processes are ultimately pushed into being through management action (King and Kraemer 1985; Stevens and LaPlante 1986; Kraemer, Dutton, and Northrup 1981).

Yet such lessons once learned are not always maintained. As the Internet began to dominate our experience, many again claimed that new technologies would lead us inevitably to new forms and processes. Terms such as *e-commerce* and *e-government* were coined along with claims that technology could enable direct democratic practices to replace representative institutions. Once again, ten years later we see change, but most large national governments still maintain large hierarchical structures, physical offices, and representative democratic institutions. We do not claim that new technology cannot lead to important changes but rather that the more reasoned models of management action, institutional forces, and the enacted-technology (Fountain 2001) perspective provide a better framework for prediction.

We proceed by first critically reviewing the various theories of how technology changes relate to institutional, organizational, and procedural change. This is followed by a historical review of changing technology over the past fifty years. This review identifies the major shifts and trends that have occurred with regard to both information and communication technology. The fourth section of the chapter provides a series of propositional predictions of how we see these trends working through preexisting government relationships based on preexisting institutions. We end the chapter by summarizing where we see the future potential of IT on both the structure of government organizations and management.

THEORETICAL FRAMEWORKS

As suggested in the introduction, there are a number of social science theories that attempt to explain the relationship between technological change and social, political, and economic institutions. We consider two broad groupings of theory. Diffusion and adoption theory form the basis for our understanding about mechanisms of technology transfer, which in turn help us to understand how new technology spreads and becomes visibly present. In the context of IT, these theoretical lenses help us to understand, for example, why new products and services, such as mobile phones, online purchasing, and entertainment services, or information services, such as Twitter, Google, and Wikipedia, quickly diffuse and become heavily used. The second broad set of theoretical lenses come mostly from sociology and consider how these new products and services work their way into institutional arrangements, organizational structures, and processes. We end this section with a discussion of how their models inform our understanding of information and communication technology's effect on government.

Adoption and Diffusion of New Technology

Two broad theories form the basis for most of our understanding of how new technology spreads. The first one, diffusion theory, describes aggregate phenomena and derives from the theory of contagion applied to disease process as early as the eighteenth century (Mahajan and Peterson 1985). The core explanation embedded here is that as individuals adopt something new (or contract a disease), when they come into contact with others, they communicate their experiences about the innovation (Coleman, Katz, and Menzel 1957; Strang and Soule 1998). This process of communication spreads the idea and increases the number of new adopters. The classic S-shaped curve used to explain cumulative adoption over time develops as the new idea spreads through a fixed population. Elements of the process that affect the speed of adoption typically include the nature of the innovation, the nature of the channels used to communicate the innovation, and characteristics of the members of the social system who consider individual adoption (Rogers and Shoemaker 1971; Rogers 2005). A number of enhancements to these models have also been considered that include economic variables such as price. These models have successfully explained numerous specific IT and telecommunication technology diffusions (Grajek and Kretschmer 2009) as well as aggregate diffusion of IT (Gurbaxanai and Mendelson 1990).

The second theoretical framework that informs our knowledge about technology transfer focuses on the decision-making process of individuals and groups with regard to new technology. Here, the unit of analysis switches from the aggregate number of adopters at a specific point in time to the individual or organization. Adoption models can be dynamic to look at the adoption process over time, though in many cases data are a simple cross section of cases at one point in time. These models typically focus on organizational and economic factors that affect adoption. Bretschneider and Wittmer (1993) applied this framework to explain greater adoption rates by public organizations than by private firms of comparable size, prior experience with computer technology, and overall investments in IT. Moon (2002) applied concepts from diffusion theory and organizational characteristics of local governments to explain adoption of e-government by U.S. local government. In a follow-up work by Norris and Moon (2005), the authors found that local governments were rapidly deploying e-government Web site applications, but in most cases these applications did not reflect any major organizational or procedural transformation in how local government conducted their operations.

The net result from applying diffusion and adoption models to each new wave of IT over the past forty years paints a somewhat consistent picture. Over time government organizations adopt new technology such that the pattern over time follows the classic S-shaped curve. The speed at which adoption occurs is affected by organizational characteristics but probably more so by general economic factors such as availability and price. Even small local governments make use of personal computers the way typewriters and filing cabinets systems were the core technology in use sixty years ago. A similar case can be made with regard to Internet and Web technology, though it is certainly not as ubiquitous across all levels or government as are personal computers. As with personal computing, cell phone technology and Web sites, diffusion through all levels of government is inevitable, but its form, level of use, and impact are not.

Models of Technological Change

Clearly, diffusion of technology is necessary but not sufficient for institutional and organizational change. Thus, we need to consider theories of how technological change affects organizational and institutional change. Garson (2006) summarizes four generic theories of how technology leads to change: technological determinism, reinforcement theory, sociotechnical theory, and systems theory. Technological determinism takes the view that technology is an "unstoppable" force that will refashion the world regardless of how human action manifests itself. Reinforcement theory, by contrast, focuses on preexisting institutions and organizations, which then shape and adjust how technology will manifest, typically in support of the status quo. Sociotechnical theory suggests that neither technology nor preexisting institutions matter, but that individuals may shape technological systems to their needs through design. Finally, the systems-theory approach transforms organizations through technocratic applications led by technicians.

Garson (2006) organizes these models into a factor-environment matrix to illustrate how each theory views the role of the environment on outcomes from the change process and the relative importance of technology versus human factors in producing the change (see Table 12.1).

The sociotechnical and reinforcement approaches tend to be human centered, with reinforcement theory suggesting that the preexisting environments into which the technologies emerge are overpowering forces. In a similar fashion, technological determinism views the environment as determining the outcome but in this context through the overpowering influence of the technology not the human institutions. Finally, systems theory, like sociotechnical theory, suggests that the environment does not determine the outcome but that technical expertise can refashion institutions and organizations. While Garson (2006) suggests that none of these models are an explanation, each contains an element of truth. The two competing dimensions of this analysis ask to what extent humans and technological forecasts drive change and to what extent these forecasts freely affect the nature of the changes produced. To some extent these dimensions parallel the ideas from structuration theory (Giddens 1984) and the role of structure and human agency. Work by DeSanctis and Poole (1994) and Orlikowski (2000) have adapted this framework to relationships

Table 12.1

The Factor-Environment Matrix

	Environmental Determinants	
Technology Factors	Unconstrained	Constrained
High-technology	Systems theory	Technological determinism
High-human	Sociotechnical	Reinforcement

Source: Based on Garson 2006: 7.

with IT. Finally, Fountain's (2001) technology enactment model also attempts to balance the role of structure and human agency to understand the process by which IT changes institutions and affects organizational outcomes.

The bottom line from this review is that the diffusion process spreads technology, but preexisting structure and human actions affect the final impacts and potential from these changes.

Once organizations have adopted a new technology, how it is used and its extent of use matter. In the private sector, the introduction of personal computing in the early eighties took at least a decade to begin to evidence economic gains (Dedrick, Gurbaxani, and Kraemer 2003). In the public sector, our ability to assess IT impact on final outcomes has been and continues to be significantly more difficult. Diffuse property rights, diffuse power and decision-making authority, and the use of political processes instead of markets lead to more complex decision processes with mixed incentives. Thus, the decisions to obtain new technology and to acquire consulting services to implement that technology are influenced by a complex mix of criteria. For example, Ni and Bretschneider (2007) found that U.S. state governments applied a complex mix of economic and political rationales in contracting out over a wide range of e-government services. Thus, economic gains in cost savings are not the only outcome associated with government investment in IT. The nature of the decision process in turn affects the potential use and impact of technology. Since economic gains are not the only expected outcome for adoption and use, different outcomes are expected and indeed occur. Other important decision criteria and concerns include but are not limited to equity of service, quality of service, and capacity to promote future economic development or business growth and to increase political participation.

The main conclusions from this analysis are twofold. First, normal adoption and diffusion processes push each new wave of technology into government. Clearly, organizational characteristics such as size and resources affect this process. Large, better-resourced governments tend to adopt earlier than small and poor ones. New technology and its diffusion through government provide the potential for simple, complex, minor, and major change in organizations and institutions, but they certainly do not guarantee them. Nevertheless, each new wave of technology penetrates and is then adapted to functional purposes within government. The second conclusion is that the process by which the adopted technology is adapted to government organizations involves a form of structuration process where preexisting structures and human agency interact to determine the form and use of the technology. Bozeman and Bretschneider (1986) provide a general framework for differentiation of public from private sector organizations in this regard, but certainly other important differentiating features are level and form of government, function, size, and culture. In order to develop a set of predictive propositions, though, we must examine the historical trends and impacts of technological change in both information and telecommunications.

HISTORICAL TRENDS IN INFORMATION AND TELECOMMUNICATIONS TECHNOLOGY

Over the past sixty years, organizations have experienced a number of changes in both information and communications technology. It is useful to organize these into a series of eras or waves around which central characteristics of the technology enabled different approaches to utilizing IT and communications systems in support of organizational operations. Table 12.2 attempts to organize these into five overlapping time periods and identifies six key characteristics around which clear trends emerge. It should be noted that while each of these five eras has a central ethos, many of the technologies and effects carry forward so that even today, large, complex, centralized computers are used, computerization of noncomputer processes is still a major focus for organizations, and e-mail is still a major form of communication.

The earliest introduction of computing into organizations is reflective of the preexisting structures and institutions and the nature of the technology itself. Large complex computers required specialized knowledge to operate and organization structure at the time reflected the principles of work specialization. Thus, analytic specialists in finance and human resources were the principle users of computer-generated information, and the systems to provide that information required specialized systems-analytic and computer technology skills. Most applications focused on converting paper systems into more automated versions. Communications systems remained separate from computing technology.

Two technical changes emerging in the late 1960s led to a new IT approach in the 1970s. First, smaller computers dubbed minicomputers were being developed. These smaller and less expensive machines in comparison to mainframes accelerated the diffusion process and led to more and more adoption and use of computer technology by smaller and smaller organizations. Second, the nature of the human interface with computer technology changed to what at the time was referred to as multiprogramming operating systems. These new operating systems, which eventually were applied to large mainframes as well, allowed direct terminal interaction of multiple users at the same time through one computer. Along with these changes, the level of technical expertise required to interact with computers was declining and training programs were reaching more and more people. This new arrangement broadened the base of end users to include substantive analysts and managers. It increased the variation in types of applications. Early types of data-analysis applications emerged that supported managerial decision making. During this era, the idea of database management systems emerged as a tool for unifying all data resources for an organization. Database management systems provide an instructive example of many of the points made earlier about diffusion and institutional change. Even today most organizations have not fully integrated database management systems as they were conceived of theoretically. The concept reemerged under a different name almost twenty years later, data warehousing, but continues to run into significant real organizational constraints in implementation. For example, compare Martin's (1976) definition of database management systems with Kimball and Ross's (2002) definition of data warehousing. Finally, the multiprogramming systems provided a critical new application, e-mail, which began the slow but continuing process of convergence between information and communication technology.

The advent of microcomputers in the 1980s was another major shift in computer technology. The development of local area networks and early wide area networks continued to accelerate the process of diffusion and adoption of computer technology by both organizations and individuals. Home computers, mostly for entertainment, further broadened the end-user base and diffusion of general knowledge on the nature of and use of IT. Within organizations, the dominant user group was more and more managers, and applications more and more served to support data analysis and managerial decision making. The research literature introduces concepts such as management information systems and decision support

Table 12.2

Historical Waves of Information and Communications Technology

Era	Central computer ethos	End user	Development process	Data/Data collection process	Effects	Communications
1950s–1960s	Central mainframe	Analysts	Professional system analysis	Transactions/File systems/Existing data collection systems	Automation	Mail, phone
1970s–1980s	Central timeshare	Analyst/managers	Professional systems analysis/End users	Transactions/File systems/Existing data collection systems	Automation	E-mail
1980s–1990s	Minicomputer, LANs	Managers	End-user development	Multiple data types/Database systems and GIS/New collection systems	Automation/Decision support/Organizational change/Personal computing in the home	E-mail
1990s–2000s	Internet	Managers/Citizens	End-user development	Multiple data types/DBS-GIS/Electronic sensing collection	Decision support/Organizational change/Citizen participation/Mobile computing	E-mail, cell phones, IM, listserves
2005 and beyond	Internet, Web 2.0, mobile devices	Citizens/Cross-organizations	End-user development	Citizen data entry/Inter- and Intra-agency data exchange	Citizen participation, Democratization/Transparency, Collaboration	Online social networking platforms

systems to support the idea that IT systems were for more than just automation. Many of the software systems available during this era permitted the end user to be the actual developer of the application. The broadening base of computers and growing access to networks further increased the use of e-mail. This was also the era when third-party network service providers emerged.

Interestingly, the fourth era was less about introducing any major new technology and more about increasing quality and performance and reducing cost for personal computing and network systems. The main changes in the 1990s were enhanced Internet systems with huge growth in bandwidth, reduced cost to personal home computing, and the rapid diffusion of mobile phones. All of these changes made e-mail almost ubiquitous across the work and home environments. They also permitted the development of n-way communication systems such as instant messaging. The further convergence of IT and communications technology led to the development of handheld phone-Internet-computing devices. One of the major outcomes from all these changes was the capacity of an organization to make use of IT through the Internet as a basic means of interacting with individuals. In the context of government organizations, this meant citizens who act as both indirect policy makers and direct service recipients. It was in this era that the concepts of e-government, e-democracy, and e-participation emerged. Looking at four of the categories identified in Table 12.2—computing, software, communications, and data—we can track under each a major change process or trend. Under computing we have moved from centralized blocks of computing capacity within organizations to an extremely decentralized computing environment.

The fifth era can be identified as an extension of the use of Internet within and across government and, more important, to its citizens. Using mostly free and open-source social networking platforms, government agencies are beginning to explore the use of so-called Web 2.0 tools (O'Reilly 2007). We define *Government 2.0* as the use of social media applications to increase participation, transparency, and interagency collaboration in the public sector. Prominent tools are, among others social networking platforms, content creation and sharing tools, Weblogs, and microblogging tools that allow for a bidirectional information exchange within governmental organizations and in governments' interactions with citizens. The main difference from previous e-government Web applications is a higher degree of interactivity as well as content production by both government and citizens (Cormode and Krishnamurthy 2008). These new technologies are being used both internally and externally to target Internet-savvy citizens and can reach users who are not using the traditional ways of interacting with government. The U.S. General Services Administration has signed prenegotiated agreements with social media providers, so that agencies can use the services for free to reach out to citizens (Aitoro 2009).

Even though the underlying technology itself is not new, the recent increase of social media applications can be attributed to their ability to support social networking needs of individuals whether they are citizens or public sector employees—people have the need to share success stories as well as report negative events in order to receive emotional support. The direct and quick feedback circles on social networking sites create a form of social justification that exists in the offline world typically through face-to-face interactions (Boyd and Ellison 2007; Joinson 2008). Younger employees also provide increased pressure for government to implement social media applications in the same way previous generations pushed for e-mail. Demographic shifts will change the makeup of the government workforce as baby boomers retire and are replaced by a younger generation with a high level of familiarity with these new technologies plus a lower threshold for exposing themselves on the Internet ("digital natives"; Liikanen, Stoneman, and Toivanen 2004; Palfrey and Gasser 2008). In addition to these psychological traits that support the use of social media applications, part of the current success of tools such as Twitter or Facebook can be attributed to a relatively high degree of technological literacy—so-called *slack capacity* within society to use social media applications for private purposes (e.g., sharing pictures or videos, writing Weblogs).

With most households operating one or more personal computers and the wide-scale use of mobile phones with direct access to the Internet, we expect a future where most individuals have immediate access to some computing capacity. Trends in software also make it possible for even relatively low-skilled individuals to create their own software applications and to make use of newly developed applications by others as they become available (see, for example, BlackBerry or iPhone applications for constant connectivity). In a world where each individual has computing capacity, has access to software applications, and is networked, mobile phones and the Internet allow individuals immediate communication to all other individuals and organizations. Similarly, this type of decentralized computing, access to software, and networked communications allow organizations to have immediate access to all relevant individuals and information sources. Finally, all of these trends also lead to major changes in both data capturing and data retrieval. Each individual (e.g., citizen) may now act as an input source of data about himself or herself, others, and their environment. We see this in the increasing ability of citizens to report events as they happen, including but not limited to fires, crimes, and traffic accidents (Ovide 2009; Gillmore 2006).

Embedded in each of these trends are some significant potential problems, particularly for government organizations. Problems of *standardization* and *integration* occur as market-driven diffusion of these technologies generates significant heterogeneity in hardware, software applications, and communication protocols. Unlike firms, government cannot target citizens but rather must typically deal with all individuals. Thus they will face higher variation than any business in just providing access or services. *Security* is a problem across all of these areas as well. Privacy issues faced by government are also more complex, as in most cases there exist statutes and rules not faced by business (Flaherty 1979). Another major problem faced by these new arrangements is best defined as increased *volatility in attitudes* and preferences of citizens. Constant and immediate access to information can lead to rapid but short-term changes in attitudes and behavior that can be problematic (Baird and Fisher 2005–6). The recent swine flu outbreak provides an example of how misinformation is spread as easily as information in this new environment (Morozov 2009; Sutter 2009; Wildstrom 2009). Such effects are well-known and systematically exploited to manipulate opinions and attitudes. Another problem that derives from this new environment is increased *fractionalization of groups* into smaller and smaller subdivisions with regard to preferences for public goods and services. This process increases the transaction costs required for generating equilibrium solutions over which public goods are to be provided. It also opens the Internet as a platform for mobilization and activism for even the smallest and most radical groups (such as terrorists; Chen, Thoms, and Fu 2008), as well as presidential campaigns (Noyes 2007).

Finally, and maybe most problematic, are issues of *aggregation of preferences*. Preferences for private goods and services are separable so that they are easily aggregated, but this is not true for preferences for public goods and services. An individual may highly value national defense and the environment but be faced with choices from a small set of political representatives whose preferences do not match those of the individual, leading to compromised decisions. Breaking individuals into smaller and smaller groups compounds the problems of political aggregation of preferences and makes equilibrium harder to find and less stable over time.

PREDICTIVE PROPOSITIONS FOR THE FUTURE DEVELOPMENT OF INFORMATION AND COMMUNICATION TECHNOLOGY IN GOVERNMENT

E-government is at an early stage of implementation and has not yet proven itself. Moreover, performance metrics to predict cost savings are difficult to evaluate (Moon 2002). According to West (2004,

2005), e-government initiatives have the possibility of enhancing democratic responsiveness and support the public belief that government is effective, although, at this point, it is unclear if investments in e-government have the potential to transform service delivery and public trust in government. While there are examples of very creative use of e-government applications in the public sector, there are also reports of failures, and we lack evidence to support the claim that the use of technology for service delivery truly results in less bureaucracy and increased service and information quality (Hazlett and Hill 2003). Clearly the current impacts are both uneven and not well understood. Nevertheless, in this section we provide some predictive propositions for the future development of technology use in the public sector and some of the conditions that support the trends we currently observe.

Proposition 1: Trends Will Force Major Changes to the Information-Sharing Paradigm of the Public Sector

As noted in our discussion of historic trends, new information and communication technology emphasizes improved communication through more diverse and broader channels of communications. This increases the potential for both individual and organizational communication across boundaries though a series of mechanisms. First, all types of costs are dramatically decreased: technology costs, human resource costs, and capital and operating costs. Second, greater contact with citizens increases demand for more integrated responses from any given government agency to include relevant information from other agencies. Dealing with the Social Security Administration often increases demand for information about taxes and health benefits, for example. The integration of the technology at the individual level, available 24/7, will continue to merge and blur personal and professional activities, creating even more demand for information sharing within and beyond government organizational boundaries.

A good example is found in current changes associated with homeland security. Supported by specific events, such as the 9/11 terror attacks, and a series of laws, government agencies have shifted from a need-to-know mentality of the cold war era to a need-to-share information paradigm. The urgency to improve information sharing before and after 9/11 resulted in laws and regulations, such as improvements to the Freedom of Information Act (U.S. Department of Justice 2008), the Information Sharing Strategy of the Intelligence Community (U.S. Office of the Director of National Intelligence 2008), or the Knowledge Management Act of the army (U.S. Army 2008). New technologies and the way that people have used the technology have forced government to rethink how to store and share information. While implementing some procedures and allowing social media tools to be applied within hierarchical and bureaucratic command-and-control organizations, government agencies will quickly bump up against various organizational boundaries and will have to be sensitive toward structural and institutional challenges as well as legal and cultural constraints.

Proposition 2: Increased Transparency and Accountability Lead to Political Authority

With the introduction of several new forms of sharing data created within government, we predict a higher degree of *transparency* and *accountability*. Currently citizens have had to file a Freedom of Information Act request to get access to information government agencies are producing. The Open Government Initiative of the Obama administration has led to several new transparency applications that include tracking of stimulus-package money on recovery.gov, as well as sharing of nonsensitive data produced in government agencies on data.gov. Citizens were asked to participate in online contests such as "Apps for Democracy" (iStrategyLabs 2008) in Washington, D.C., and "Apps for America" (Sunlight Foundation 2009) to create innovative social media applications using the data provided on both Web sites. Clearly a precondition for these approaches is direct access by citizens to government data. For example, one application under "Apps for Democracy" accessed city contracts and their dollar values to various vendors (iStrategyLabs 2008). These examples show the potential for increases in accountability that are possible, but more important, having more and more citizen access to information and communication technology at all times increases the demand for access to government held-data. Besides this positive development of sharing governmental data with the public, it seems necessary to move beyond the mere display of raw data in order to create an even higher degree of transparency. The general public probably doesn't have the tools and capabilities to fully understand and digest machine-readable data but needs easier-to-understand and more useful displays and visualizations of data along the lines of Google Flu Trends (Google 2008). Third parties such as Google, and other information service organizations, including NGOs, will also fuel this increased demand and help to track and report public information.

Proposition 3: Increased Width and Breadth of Communication Channels for Public Participation and Inclusion

Social media shows the potential to support increased *public participation* and *inclusion.* Citizens can now directly connect through a collection of diverse Web 2.0 applications to government agencies as outlined on USA.gov (U.S. Office of Citizen Services and Communications 2009), or submit their questions for the president to "Open for Questions" (White House 2009). Moreover, citizens can rate the submitted questions to highlight the urgency of a topic area, thereby potentially influencing the public agenda. The president addresses these questions, in Internet town hall meetings, blog posts, or weekly YouTube addresses. This two-step process of submission and rating has the property of creating a semi-automated ranking of the vast amounts of submitted questions, though it creates serious issues of selection and bias in the rankings. As opposed to the traditional condensed form of press releases, the social media content may be accessible to a broader and potentially different audience. Especially during crisis situations or public agenda–building processes, social media applications have shown their strength at mobilizing citizens: The Iranian election in 2009 showed that even when a government decides to block all news and communications channels, social-networking platforms and text messaging have the potential to supplement or even replace traditional news channels. Moreover, in situations such as natural disasters—the 2008 earthquake in China, for example—social-networking services gave citizens onsite reporting tools to broadcast their need for help live on YouTube, Facebook, and Twitter. Major news sites received their information through these channels instead of formal press releases or government information channels. In previous years, government officials needed days or weeks to understand and publicize disasters in distant and mostly disconnected parts of the country.

The more public officials use social networking technologies, the more they are also exposed to the public and at the same time change who is involved in the public agenda–building processes. For example, during the 2007–8 presidential campaign, then candidate Obama established a Web site, MyBarackObama.com, that offered supporters the opportunity to connect with one another and allowed the candidate to publish his position on specific topics. The interactive element of the Web site supported group building among citizens to add their opinions and exchange ideas with the candidate but, more important, with their peers. At the time, Obama promised to vote on the Foreign Intelligence Surveillance Act bill but changed his opinion over time (National Public Radio

2008). A wave of disapproval was published immediately on his Web site. Instead of taking the controversial issue off the platform, Obama responded to the criticism on the site and in the form of a press release, explaining his reasons for his voting decision. The opposing opinions of the audience were not controlled or dismissed, but convened and broadcasted, making the Internet a vehicle for a many-to-many platform instead of a unidirectional display of controlled information. The high degree of inclusiveness made the audience full participants instead of passive observers.

The demands for information sharing and peer production within traditional bureaucracies are emergent and are likely to challenge current organizational processes (Mergel, Schweik, and Fountain 2009). Another possible effect of higher degrees of inclusion and participation is increased uncertainty and variance in message content and the media used to transmit the message. This may create greater instability of all institutional forms, as the public demands more immediate reactions and responsiveness, leaving less time for deliberations and situational or contextual assessments.

Proposition 4: Increased Use of Interorganizational Collaboration Tools Will Lead to Increased Lateral Communications and Resource Sharing

Public organizations will continue to *increase lateral communications and resource sharing* both *within* and *across* organizational boundaries (see proposition 1). The example of Intellipedia within the intelligence community has shown that these changes will increase intra- and interorganizational *collaboration* with a simultaneous increase in coordination and governance efforts (Mergel 2010). Intellipedia—a wiki platform to share intelligence information across all sixteen intelligence agencies in the United States—was created to reduce the costs of parallel data processing and to break up knowledge silos that exist when information is stored and shared only within preselected e-mail lists, shared hard drives, or documents. The wiki platform—in accordance with the success of Wikipedia.org—allows authorized editors to upload information that others can edit, extend, and discuss, with the goal of creating controversies instead of unified opinions. The hope within the intelligence community is to reach better decisions based on conflicting information and conversations instead of unidirectional and single expert reports and opinions (Andrus 2005). Similar approaches now exist in other federal agencies, such as Techpedia (Department of Defense) or Diplopedia (Department of State). The prerequisite is to understand which agency is performing which tasks, and understand information needs as well as information creation at various levels of government. One downside to increases in lateral communication is the potential need for increased coordination and cultural adaptations in order to successfully share information across a governmental unit. These types of competing views of the data across agencies is also likely to lead to problems in policy formation and presentation, as political leaders try to use such data to push forward specific policies.

Proposition 5: Mission- and Target-Specific Information Sharing May Lead to Higher Effectiveness of Governmental Routines

We predict a potentially higher *effectiveness* of some governmental routines through an enhanced, broader, and more target-specific information dissemination. In 2009, the CDC used social media and networking tools during the swine flu outbreak and earlier during the salmonella contamination of peanut butter to reach citizens and endangered parts of society "where they are" (Centers for Disease Control 2009; Nagesh 2009). Tools such as Facebook pages and Twitter messages led to an enhanced immediacy and relevancy of information spread, while at the same time reaching specific target groups. The information channels used led to repostings of the messages in traditional news formats and were also supposed to create information ownership and prevent misinformation and rumors (Morozov 2009). What this example shows is the need for other institutions with a wider and in this case potentially worldwide reach, such as the World Health Organization, to take ownership of these new technologies. Moreover, applying mash-ups, such as healthmap.org/swineflu, where for example a Google Map is combined with government data about flu outbreaks, can help authorities track public perception—or, more important, misperceptions—to understand when to intervene and supply more relevant and mission-specific information.

Proposition 6: Information Overload Increases the Need for New Warranting Processes to Ensure Information Quality

The current examples of social software in Government 2.0 show some innovative and surprising side effects that might lead to procedural and organizational innovations (Kelman 2009). One major consequence of these changes is an increasing potential for problems associated with *information overload.* The standard response to information overload is to filter information, usually based on the individual's specific processes for assessing the accuracy and quality of the information. Consequently, some prefer news from the *New York Times* and others from Fox Broadcasting. In order to understand the quality and accuracy of the information created in different channels, which might then be replicated and reposted more broadly, government might have to create new warranting processes to ensure its own reputation and trustworthiness. This suggests that not only government, but society in general will need to develop new forms of *read and write literacy* for the vast amounts of information that are produced using social media in the public sector (DiMaio 2009). Citizens themselves need to learn to understand how to quality check information that is freely available on the Internet—not all information replicated and reposted on blogs is true. Mechanisms need to be developed to not only trust preferred sources but also verify online information. Besides reading ability, appropriate writing skills need to be developed: While some are carelessly publishing on social networking platforms, such as Facebook or Twitter, the personal warranting process needs to be refined to establish a writing literacy that protects individuals from future cost related to personal and professional reputation. These requirements are likely to change both the educational and socialization process of society.

Proposition 7: New Information-Sharing Possibilities Lead to Increased Volatility and the Need for More Specific Information Targeting

The new information-sharing possibilities also come with an *increased volatility in information and the need for more specific information targeting.* The swine flu example shows that there is an increased need for information warranting. The question is, therefore, Does government have to increase its role in setting standards, rules, and regulations? Government itself is more often held accountable and needs to lead by example, controlling the quality and standards of its information-sharing processes before it allows access to the public. We do acknowledge the apparent advantages of the current convergence of old and new information-sharing mechanisms (Giles 2005) but also need to take the potential downsides and unsolved issues into account.

CONCLUSIONS

It is difficult to predict future effects of new technology while living through a period of rapid changes in the technology itself. We do, however, see both benefits and problems deriving from the new technologies, as well as managerial and cultural challenges that public managers and chief technology officers are facing on all levels of government. It is important to evaluate the emerging applications on both their positive and negative dimensions. Moreover, what are missing at the moment are reliable evidence-based evaluation measures of current impacts.

The so-called Government 2.0 bundle of new information and communication technology applications has the potential to change the way government creates and shares information. They might also lead to an increased transparency and accountability of public authority. The broader range of communication and interaction channels resulting from these new information technologies may lead to increased inclusion and public participation. Responses, especially when it comes to mission-specific information, may therefore lead to an increased reaction speed and might enhance governmental effectiveness. As mentioned earlier, limited effectiveness and performance measures are available for the (now) traditional e-government applications, so that it is difficult to predict and evaluate the actual impact of new media tools. Specifically, very successful organizations using existing IT systems might see managerial and cultural challenges in adopting an additional Government 2.0 strategy. The current changes and innovations in IT can therefore create a more volatile (higher degrees of variation over time) political environment for organizations, which might threaten the status quo of the established information-sharing culture and organizational capacity. The bureaucratic organizational processes and existing infrastructure might have to be reevaluated to harness the power of social media in the public sector. Though such changes will be mediated by existing organizational and political environments, there is an increasing need for researchers to understand the managerial, cultural, and technological factors during the implementation and adoption phases.

The biggest challenge is not the technology itself, but the adaptation of technology within the given political and bureaucratic situation and institutional barriers (Federal Computer Week 2009). The bureaucratic top-down information-reporting strategies still exist but are now complemented and only partially replaced by a more vertical information-sharing approach—with unpredictable consequences. The resulting greater diversity in organizational structure to support the parallel set of new communication channels within and across government and with its citizens is enabled by the new technology but its ultimate impact will depend more on how they become embedded in the preexisting institutions.

Finally, we see a number of significant future challenges and issues that are unresolved when it comes to Government 2.0.

Cybersecurity, accountability, and *identity management* are open issues that deal with the question of how government data can be protected from unintended access, to whom government will allow access, and how government will warrant an individual identify. So far, mainly nonsensitive government data have been published on Web sites, such as data.gov, in the context of the transparency and open-government initiative of the Obama administration. Even though the actual use by the public is open, ownership rights remain an issue, especially when data are about citizens. These transparency efforts increase the likelihood of security breaches. Allowing public sector employees to post blog entries and to send out Twitter messages as representatives of their government organizations leads to two important accountability issues: To what extent are opinions published valid official governmental statements and to what extent should government be held accountable?

A topic currently being discussed but not yet fully implemented is the use of *cloud computing* and *shared services and resources.* This new model of computing involves outsourcing services and the access of computing capacity only when needed. Although this approach promises cost savings and enhanced efficiency, such proposed systems also might potentially remove flexibility and reduce organizational responsiveness. This type of contracted and multicentered computing service with a greater degree of decentralization is likely to lead to major problems of security and privacy. While this type of outsourcing of services is not an innovative practice in the public sector, it can lead to a diffusion of control and services with an overall loss of control. As soon as services are outsourced and moved beyond the organizational boundaries, the focal agency exerts only indirect control.

The *digital divide* among government organizations themselves needs to be mentioned as another unresolved issue: We do obverse unprecedented innovation on the federal government level when it comes to Web 2.0 applications (see, for example, Whitehouse.gov), with some spillover effects to the state level (see, for example, Utah.gov for a Web 2.0–style state portal designed with the help of the citizens). On the local and municipal levels, public managers are dealing with very different problems of capacity and resource limitations, which have led to voluntary collaborative governance initiatives, such as MuniGov2.0, to learn from each other without hiring expensive consultants and with minimal access to training opportunities. The digital divide also becomes evident in cases where government organizations either do not have Internet connections in their agencies or restrict Web access and publishing due to limited resources. As noted earlier, it is likely that eventually even the smallest government unit will have a Web presence and some applications, but capacity issues are likely to prevent most of these smaller governments to develop any meaningful applications involving two-way communication or social networking (West 2005).

As mentioned earlier, traditional e-service delivery performance research and evaluation have provided limited proof for the successful diffusion of e-government applications. It remains unclear the extent to which online services are improving responsiveness, reach, efficiency, and cost savings. The current Government 2.0 initiatives are driven less by conscious top-down strategies of the agencies themselves, but are mostly a response to successful use of social networking services outside of government. Cross-jurisdictional, hierarchical, and vertical studies are needed to understand this new phenomenon and its implications for managerial, cultural, procedural, and informational aspects of diffusion and their overall impacts (Mergel, Schweik, and Fountain 2009).

Also from a research perspective, these new technologies enable individuals to generate extensive amounts of data. In order to analyze these data and understand the impact of these new technologies, we suggest capturing more observations of passive behavioral data into e-government research (Lazer et al. 2009). This could include, for example, analyzing blog contents or the linkage structures of blogs. Future research should also include the use of pure experiments, natural experiments, and quasi-experiments to generate evidence-based prescriptions for alternative organizational structures and applications of technology to be able to gain deeper insights into the potentially sustainable changes we are observing.

REFERENCES

Aitoro, Jill R. 2009. GSA signs deals for agencies to use social networking sites. NextGov, March 25. www.nextgov.com/nextgov/ng_20090325_5490.php (accessed July 25, 2010).

Andrus, D. Calvin. 2005. Toward a complex adaptive intelligence community: The Wiki and the blog. *Studies in Intelligence* 49 (3). Available at www.cia.gov/library/center-for-the-study-of-intelligence/csi-publications/csi-studies/studies/v0149n03/html_files/Wik_and_%20Blog_7.htm.

Baird, Derek E., and Mercedes Fisher. 2005–6. Neomillenial user experience design strategies: Utilzing social-networking media to support "Always On" learning styles. *Journal of Educational Technology Systems* 34 (1): 5–32.

Boyd, D.M., and N.B. Ellison. 2007. Social network sites: Definition, history, and scholarship. *Journal of Computer-Mediated Communication* 13 (1). Available at http://jcmc.indiana.edu/v0113/issue1/boyd.ellison.html.

Bozeman, Barry, and Stuart Bretschneider. 1986. Public management information systems: Theory and prescription. *Public Administration Review* 46 (special issue): 475–487.

Bretschneider, Stuart, and Dennis Wittmer. 1993. Organizational adoption of microcomputer technology: The role of sector. *Information Systems Research* 4 (5): 88–108.

Centers for Disease Control and Prevention. 2009. Social media at CDC. Available at www.cdc.gov/social-media/ (accessed July 25, 2010).

Chen, Hsinchun, S. Thoms, and Tianjun Fu. 2008. Cyber extremism in Web 2.0: An exploratory study of international Jihadist groups. Paper present at the IEEE International Conference on Intelligence and Security Informatics, Taiwan, June 17–20, 98–103.

Coleman, J., E. Katz, and H. Menzel. 1957. The diffusion of an innovation among physicians. *Sociometry* 20 (4): 253–270.

Cormode, Graham, and Balachander Krishnamurthy. 2008. Key differences between Web 1.0 and Web 2.0. *First Monday* 13 (6). Available at http://firstmonday.org/htbin/cgiwrap/bin/ojs/index.php/fm/article/view/2125.

Dedrick, Jason, Vijay Gurbaxani, and Kenneth Kraemer. 2003. Information technology and economic performance: A critical review of the empirical literature. *ACM Computing Surveys* 35 (1): 1–23.

DeSanctis, G., and M.S. Poole. 1994. Capturing the complexity in advanced technology use: Adaptive structuration theory. *Organization Science* 5 (2): 121–147.

DiMaio, Andrea. 2009. Government 2.0 won't happen without Officer 2.0. Gartner Blog Network, May 30. Available at http://blogs.gartner.com/andrea_dimaio/2009/05/30/government-20-wont-happen-without-officer-20/ (accessed July 25, 2010).

Federal Computer Week. 2009. Social media apps defy government skeptics: Proponents hopeful they can sway federal agencies. *Federal Computer Week,* June 18. Available at http://fcw.com/Articles/2009/06/22/Buzz-social-media.aspx.

Flaherty, David. H. 1979. *Privacy and Government Data Banks.* Los Altos, CA: Mansell.

Fountain, Jane. 2001. *Building the Virtual State: Information Technology and Institutional Change.* Washington, DC: Brookings Institution Press.

Garson, G. David. 2006. *Public Information Technology and E-Governance: Managing the Virtual State.* Boston: Jones and Bartlett.

Giddens, Anthony. 1984. *The Constitution of Society: Outline of the Theory of Structuration.* Berkeley: University of California Press.

Giles, J. 2005. Internet encyclopedias go head to head. *Nature* 438 (December 1): 900–901. Available at www.nature.com/nature/journal/v438/n7070/full/438900a.html (accessed July 25, 2010).

Gillmore, D. 2006. *We the Media: Grassroots Journalism by the People, for the People.* Sebastopol, CA: O'Reilly Media (accessed July 25, 2010).

Google. 2008. Google Flu Trends. Google.org. Available at www.google.org/flutrends/ (accessed July 25, 2010).

Grajek, M., and T. Kretschmer. 2009. Usage and diffusion of cellular telephony, 1998–2004. *International Journal of Industrial Organization* 27 (2): 238–249.

Gurbaxanai, Vijay, and Haim Mendelson. 1990. An integrative model of information system spending growth. *Information Systems Research* 1 (1): 23–46.

Hazlett, Shirley-Ann, and Frances Hill. 2003. E-government: The realities of using IT to transform the public sector. *Managing Service Quality* 13 (6): 445–452.

iStrategyLabs. 2008. Apps for Democracy, Community Edition. Sponsored by iStrategyLabs and the District of Columbia's Office of the Chief Technology Officer. Available at www.appsfordemocracy.org/ (accessed July 25, 2010).

Joinson, Adam N. 2008. "Looking at," "looking up" or "keeping up with" people? Motives and uses of Facebook. In *Proceeding of the Twenty-sixth annual SIGCHI Conference on Human Factors in Computing Systems.* New York: ACM.

Kelman, S. 2009. Social networking technology—the unexpected uses. *Federal Computer Week,* March 25. Available at http://fcw.com/Blogs/Lectern/2009/03/Social-networking-technology-the-unexpected-uses.aspx (accessed July 25, 2010).

Kimball, Ralph, and Margy Ross. 2002. *The Data Warehouse Toolkit.* 2d ed. Hoboken, NJ: Wiley.

King, John L., and Kenneth L. Kraemer. 1985. *The Dynamics of Computing.* New York: Columbia University Press.

Kraemer, Kenneth L., William H. Dutton, and Alana Northrup. 1981. *The Management of Information Systems.* New York: Columbia University Press.

Kun, Huang, and Keith G. Provan. 2007. Resource tangibility and patterns of interaction in a publicly funded health and human services network. *Journal of Public Administration Research and Theory* 17 (3): 435–454.

Lazer, David, Alex Pentland, Lada Adamic, Sinan Aral, Albert-László Barabási, Devon Brewer, Nicholas Christakis et al. 2009. Computational social science. *Science* 323 (5915): 721–723.

Leavitt, Harold J., and Thomas L. Whisler. 1958. Management in the 1980s. *Harvard Business Review* 36 (November–December): 41–48.

Liikanen, J., P. Stoneman, and O. Toivanen. 2004. Intergenerational effects in the diffusion of new technology: The case of mobile phones. *International Journal of Industrial Organization* 22:1137–1154.

Loudon, Kenneth C., and Jane Price Laudon. 1988. *Management Information Systems: A Contemporary Perspective.* New York: Macmillan.

Mahajan, V., and Robert Peterson. 1985. *Model of Innovation and Diffusion.* Thousand Oaks, CA: Sage.

March, James G., and Herbert A. Simon. 1958. *Organizations.* New York: Wiley.

Martin, James. 1976. *Principles of Data-Base Management.* Englewood Cliffs, NJ: Prentice-Hall.

Mergel, I. 2010. The use of social media to dissolve knowledge silos in government. In *The Future of Public Administration Around the World,* ed. R. O'Leary, D. Van Slyke, and S. Kim. Washington, DC: Georgetown University Press.

Mergel, I., C. Schweik, and Jane Fountain. 2009. The transformational effect of Web 2.0 technologies on government. *Social Science Research Networks* (June 1). Available at http://papers.ssrn.com/s013/papers.cfm?abstract_id=1412796.

Moon, M. Jae. 2002. The evolution of e-government among municipalities: Rhetoric or reality? *Public Administration Review* 62 (4): 424–433.

Morozov, Evgeny. 2009. Swine flu: Twitter's power to misinform. *Foreign Policy* (April 25). Available at http://neteffect.foreignpolicy.com/posts/2009/04/25/swine_flu_twitters_power_to_misinform (accessed April 25, 2009).

Nagesh, Gautham. 2009. Agencies used social media to manage salmonella outbreak. Nextgov.com, February 9. Available at www.nextgov.com/nextgov/ng_20090209_7840.php (accessed July 25, 2010).

National Public Radio. 2008. Obama supporters rap their candidate on FISA. July 9. www.npr.org/templates/story/story.php?storyId=92357038 (accessed July 25, 2010).

Ni, Ya, and Stuart Bretschneider. 2007. The contracting out decision: A study of contracting for e-government services in state government. *Public Administration Review* 67:531–545.

Norris, Donald, and M. Jae Moon. 2005. Advancing e-government at the grassroots: Tortoise or hare? *Public Administration Review* 65 (1): 64–75.

Noyes, Katherine. 2007. Campaign 2.0, part 1: "Hillary 1984" is just the beginning. *TechNewsWorld* (April 4). Available at www.technewsworld.com/story/56682.html (accessed May 25, 2009).

O'Reilly, T. 2007. What is Web 2.0: Design patterns and business models for the next generation of software. *Communications and Strategies* 65 (1): 17–37.

Orlikowski, W.J. 2000. Using technology and constituting structures: A practice lens for studying technology in organizations. *Organization Science* 11 (4): 404–428.

Ovide, S. 2009. Twittering the USAirways plane crash. *The Wall Street Journal: Blogs,* January 15. Available at http://blogs.wsj.com/digits/2009/01/15/twittering-the-usairways-plane-crash/ (accessed July 25, 2010).

Palfrey, J., and U. Gasser. 2008. *Born Digital: Understanding the First Generation of Digital Natives.* New York: Basic Books.

Rogers, E.M. 2005. *Adoption of Innovation.* New York: Free Press.

Rogers, Everett, and F.F. Shoemaker. 1971. *Communication of Innovation: A Cross-Cultural Approach.* 2d ed. New York: Free Press.

Stevens, John M., and Josephine M. LaPlante. 1986. Factors associated with financial-decision support systems in state government: An empirical exploration. *Public Administration Review* 46 (November): 522–531.

Strang, D., and S.A. Soule. 1998. Diffusion in organizations and social movements: From hybrid corn to poison pills. *Annual Review of Sociology* 24:265–290.

Sunlight Foundation. 2009. Apps for America. http://sunlightlabs.com/contests/appsforamerica/.

Sutter, John. 2009. Swine flu creates controversy on Twitter. CNN, April 30. Available at www.cnn.com/2009/TECH/04/27/swine.flu.twitter/ (accessed April 30, 2009).

U.S. Army. 2008. Army Knowledge Management Principles. Available at http://www.army.mil/ciog6/docs/AKMPrinciples.pdf (accessed July 25, 2010).

U.S. Department of State. 2009. U.S. Department of State Freedom of Information Act. Available at www.state.gov/m/a/ips/.

U.S. Office of Citizen Services and Communications. 2009. Connect with government. Available at USA.gov. www.usa.gov/Topics/Multimedia.shtml (accessed May 25, 2009).

U.S. Office of the Director of National Intelligence. 2007. Intellipedia. www.intelink.gov/wiki.

———. 2008. United States Intelligence Community: Information Sharing Strategy. February 22. Available at www.dni.gov/reports/IC_Information_Sharing_Strategy.pdf (accessed July 25, 2010).

West, Darrell M. 2004. E-government and the transformation of service delivery and citizen attitudes. *Public Administration Review* 64 (1): 15–27.

———. 2005. *Digital Government: Technology and Public Sector Performance.* Princeton, NJ: Princeton University Press.

White House. 2009. Open for questions. Available at www.whitehouse.gov/OpenForQuestions (accessed May 25, 2009).

Wildstrom, Stephen. 2009. UPDATED: Twitter and swine flu: All noise, no signal. Bloomberg Business Week, April 28. Available at www.businessweek.com/the_thread/techbeat/archives/2009/04/twitter_swi9ne.html (accessed July 25, 2010).

CHAPTER 13

EMERGENCY AND CRISIS MANAGEMENT

Practice, Theory, and Profession

WILLIAM L. WAUGH

Emergency management has become an all-too-familiar function of government and increasingly a focus of nongovernmental and private sector action. The need for more effective emergency management capabilities became a national issue in the United States in the 1990s when the nation suffered a series of billion-dollar disasters. So too did the need for proactive risk-reduction programs, which became a major international issue following the 2004 Indian Ocean tsunami. Similarly, the imperative to improve the international humanitarian assistance system was reaffirmed when Haiti and Chili were devastated by earthquakes in early 2010. Emergency management has developed substantially as a profession and as a distinct set of management practices worldwide. This chapter examines the evolution of the profession and practice of emergency management and the development and impact of disaster policy and emergency management scholarship.

Emergency management is the term commonly used in the United States, Australia, Canada, and some other English-speaking nations. It is called *crisis management* in Europe and *disaster management* in India and within the United Nations and other international organizations. *Disaster risk reduction* is the focus of international efforts to mitigate hazards. There are significant differences in how emergency management is practiced in other parts of the world, particularly as regards the role of central governments, but there is increasing commonality in general approaches to managing hazards and disasters and increasing cooperation in the pursuit of solutions to emergency housing, communications, and other hazard mitigation and disaster issues.

THE EVOLVING PRACTICE OF EMERGENCY MANAGEMENT

Emergency management practitioners and scholars frequently use the stereotypical air raid warden or civil defense coordinator as a reference point in describing how far the profession and practice of emergency management have come in the last half century. During World War II and through the 1950s and 1960s, civil defense offices were responsible for local emergency planning, and their focus was almost solely on the threat of nuclear attack. Civil defense coordinators were frequently retired military who were untrained in emergencies other than nuclear attack, and the cultures of their organizations were decidedly command and control. After a series of major hurricanes and earthquakes in the late 1960s and 1970s, most notably Hurricane Camille in 1969, the National Governors Association lobbied for a reorganization of federal disaster relief agencies and programs. The result was the creation of the Federal Emergency Management Agency (FEMA) by President Carter in 1979. From the beginning, the agency adopted the comprehensive approach to emergency management. The approach is now the foundation of American emergency management. In essence, the comprehensive approach involves all hazards, all stakeholders, all impacts, and all phases or functions of emergency management.

All Hazards

The all-hazards approach is commonly referred to as the *multihazard* approach in other nations and in United Nations programs because it does not refer to literally all hazards. That is, programs typically focus on the broad range of known threats in the community and are flexible enough to adapt to unanticipated threats. Planners develop generic plans that can be adapted to specific disaster types, rather than having separate plans for each one. Mass evacuation, for example, is essentially the same for hurricanes as it is for other kinds of threats. Planners may develop annexes to deal with issues that are specific to only one disaster type, such as radiation exposure during nuclear accidents, or issues affecting one segment of the community, such as evacuating and sheltering special needs populations.

All Stakeholders

The involvement of all stakeholders means it is expected that hazard management and disaster operations will include public agencies, private firms, nongovernmental organizations, and, frequently, individual volunteers—all of whom might be called upon in a major disaster. For example, the state of California's manual for dealing with volunteers is titled *They Will Come,* and the expectation is that volunteers will come and should be put to work. In fact, the FEMA administrator, Craig Fugate (appointed in 2009), reminded a crowd of emergency management practitioners, scholars, and students in his opening plenary presentation at the 2009 National Conference of the International Association of Emergency Managers (IAEM) that 90 percent of search-and-rescue operations are conducted by neighbors, friends, and family members and that preparing the community to respond to disaster should be the priority rather than simply trying to get emergency responders to the scene a bit faster. A prepared community is much more resilient and can recover faster. Community resilience, including preparedness, is the new priority for emergency management programs.

Phases of Emergency Management

The phases or functions of emergency management are mitigation, preparedness, response, and recovery. Mitigation involves actions to prevent or reduce the impact of disasters, such as limiting development on floodplains or adopting building codes. Preparedness involves planning, training, exercising, stockpiling food and medical supplies, and other actions to ready for disasters. Response can involve firefighting, emergency medical treatment, evacuation, emergency sheltering, mass feeding, and other activities to save lives, property, and the environment. Recovery involves restoring lifelines, such as power and water, but is increasingly expanding to include redevelopment of the affected area and long-term treatment of the affected population. The phases overlap and are not always sequential. For example, covering damaged roofs with FEMA blue tarps is usually referred to as a response activity, but it is also a mitigation activity because it prevents or reduces damage to the interior of the structures. Predisaster recovery planning, a preparedness activity, might include stockpiling tarps and determining which organization will begin the process of covering roofs.

Professional emergency managers assume that their role involves an all-hazards approach, all stakeholders, all four phases or functions, and all impacts. The top professional credential, the

Certified Emergency Manager (CEM) designation, is based on that assumption, and candidates are tested on their knowledge of and experience in all of those aspects of emergency management. Failing to include all phases means failing the test.

THE EMERGENCY MANAGEMENT PROFESSION

The civil defense stereotype also provides a reference point for the changes in the profession of emergency management. The demographics of emergency management have been changing rapidly. Most of the old civil defense coordinators are long retired, and the retirement of baby boomers is opening the way for a new generation of personnel. That new cadre includes more women and more minorities and will have fewer retired military, although the U.S. Air Force has an emergency management job specialty and is encouraging its personnel to seek certified emergency manager certification and to engage with civilian emergency managers.

The increasing role of social media in disaster operations is only one of the many technological changes that are under way. Emergency management programs at all levels have Facebook pages, and officials use Twitter to pass along information to employees, clients, the public, and other stakeholders. Moreover, the emergency management profession is evolving, and demographic and technological changes are speeding that process. In many respects, demographic changes mirror those occurring elsewhere in American society and particularly the public service, which portend fundamental transformation in the values that underlie the emergency management profession. The "new" emergency management is transparent, participative, and collaborative and involves networks of public, private, and nongovernmental organizations, as well as unaffiliated volunteers.

EMERGENCY MANAGEMENT POLICY PRIORITIES

The civil defense stereotype is also a reference point for policy change. All-hazards plans may well include nuclear attack, but the threats have been redefined and, in some cases, changed fundamentally. Terrorism has been the focus of Homeland Security planning. Indeed, twelve of the fifteen planning scenarios that the Department of Homeland Security has used to design national exercises and to guide national planning are terrorism related—ranging from the detonation of a nuclear device to the use of biological agents. The three nonterrorism scenarios are a major earthquake, a major hurricane, and a pandemic. Floods, tornado outbreaks, tsunamis, wildfires, and other threats have not been part of the Homeland Security agenda, although changes are being made in planning assumptions under the Obama administration.

Mitigation clearly is a policy priority under the new administration, and investments are being made in federal funding programs to encourage mitigation planning and programs at the state and local levels. Mitigation was the centerpiece of the Clinton administration's emergency management effort. James Lee Witt, FEMA director during the "golden age" of FEMA in the 1990s, created Project Impact (the Building Disaster-Resistant Communities Program) to encourage and support mitigation efforts at the local level. The program was terminated in the early days of the George W. Bush administration despite evidence that it was effective in reducing the vulnerabilities of communities participating in the program. The mantra of Witt's FEMA was "one dollar spent on mitigation saves four dollars in recovery."

After 9/11, the focus was on response rather than mitigation and response to terrorism rather than response to natural and other man-made disasters. Hurricane Katrina was a reminder that the nation faces other risks, as well. The rejoinder to the observation that "the world changed on 9/11" is that the world changed again when Katrina made landfall. Restoring the nation's capacity to deal with large-scale natural disasters, as well as terrorism-related events, has been a federal priority since Hurricane Katrina in 2005.

LESSONS LEARNED

Seeking lessons learned is part of the emergency management culture. Preliminary assessments during disaster operations, called "hot washes," and after-action reports follow major operations. Strengths and weaknesses are noted, and in some cases, policies and programs are altered. However, communications interoperability, or the lack thereof, has been a major concern for decades. Many deaths in the World Trade Center towers on 9/11 could have been prevented if firefighters and police officers could have communicated with one another and with officials outside of the buildings. Communications failed again during the Katrina disaster. Emergency responders lacked the capability to talk with one another. A solution to the problem has been found in a few states, for example, Delaware and North Carolina, but not in many. Intergovernmental coordination has also been a problem in major disasters and in all of the Homeland Security TOPOFF (Top Officials) exercises. The same coordination and information-sharing issues were evident when the Homeland Security system failed to prevent the attempted bombing of the Northwest Airlines flight from Amsterdam to Detroit on Christmas Day 2009.

Emergency management is like other policy areas. Issues arise, often borne of crisis, and policies may change. The window of opportunity can be brief, even with a Katrina-scale disaster. Some issues find quick support. For example, because of media coverage of the Katrina disaster in New Orleans, Congress quickly passed the Pets Evacuation and Transportation Standards Act of 2006, sometimes referred to as the "no pet left behind act," to ensure that pets are taken care of in the next catastrophic disaster. Pet rescue and sheltering had been a subject of discussion within the professional emergency management community for years prior to Katrina, but little attention to that issue was evident in the Gulf response.

Special populations became a major concern because of Katrina, as well. Public health officials and medical responders to Hurricane Katrina were overwhelmed by the number of people with chronic conditions, such as heart disease, diabetes, and high blood pressure. Problems involving the evacuation of nursing homes and hospitals are also encouraging greater attention to their preparedness programs. Predisaster planning for FEMA trailer parks, transitional housing to move survivors from emergency shelters to permanent housing, partnerships with large retail firms such as Walmart for the provision of water, ice, and food, and predisaster negotiation of contracts for critical services such as roof repair and even the management of recovery operations are being implemented. Lessons were learned, and officials are trying to make sure that the nation is not embarrassed again by a poorly planned and executed disaster response.

There is still a long way to go in addressing known and unknown threats. The implications of climate change, for example, are only slowly being recognized. New York City is preparing for a rise in sea levels, increased precipitation and possible flooding, and temperature change that may result from climate change (New York City Panel on Climate Change 2009; New York City Office of Emergency Management 2009). Land-use planning and development are changing to ensure that the city is more sustainable, less vulnerable to natural disasters, more energy efficient, and "greener" in terms of reducing its global-warming emissions. Mitigation is linked to sustainability.

THE ORGANIZATION OF EMERGENCY MANAGEMENT

The civil defense coordinator stereotype yet again provides a convenient reference point for the evolution of emergency management organization and process. Civil defense received federal funding, but the system lacked strong organizational support. Local offices operated with minimal guidance from Washington and often with little connection to local and state agencies. In the early 1970s, the incident command system (ICS) was developed in California to manage responses to large wildfires that involved multiple jurisdictions and agencies. Because of the problem of coordinating multijurisdictional responsibilities during wildfires, Congress funded a study to identify and address the major organizational problems. The U.S. Forest Service and representatives of state and local fire departments participating in the FIRESCOPE (Fighting Resources of Southern California Organized for Potential Emergencies) Program developed ICS. The system identifies an incident commander with staff (safety, liaison, and public information) and line functions (operations, planning, logistics, and administration and finance). The ICS structure is flexible so that staff and line functions can be added as necessary. It provides unity of command, a clear hierarchy, and a common terminology. It is also based on the principles of management by objectives to ensure that the units follow a common set of objectives. The theory is that the first responder on the scene is the incident commander and command is transferred to more senior personnel as they arrive.

When the number of agencies grows larger, a multiagency command system (MACS) is implemented to facilitate coordination among the response agencies. The emergency operations center is the mechanism to coordinate efforts. Multiagency, multijurisdictional, intergovernmental, and intersector operations might necessitate creation of a unified command (UC) that provides for collective decision making and, at least in theory, consensus building. The incident management system (ICS, MACS, and UC) provides structures that are familiar and terminology that is common across jurisdictions, and thus multiple organizations can be integrated into the operations. While not universally understood and used, ICS is generally understood by emergency management and response agencies and by many private sector and nongovernmental organizations. ICS is also the foundation for the National Incident Management System developed after 9/11 to link local, state, and federal emergency management and Homeland Security resources. National Incident Management System compliance is now mandatory if agencies wish to receive federal funding.

ICS and the Standard Emergency Management System were common elements in California's programs. County governments were designated the "functional area" for emergency management, and regional support structures were created to coordinate the efforts of local and state agencies. The state also had a very-well-developed statewide training program and strong links to university-based research programs. Clearly, California was well ahead of other states in the development and professionalization of its emergency management system. The range of hazards in the state certainly encouraged the adoption of the all-hazards approach, and the necessity for multijurisdictional coordination encouraged the development of mechanisms to ensure that resources were available when needed.

EMERGENCY MANAGEMENT AND HOMELAND SECURITY

Finally, the civil defense stereotype has remained the symbol for nonprofessional, command-and-control, national security-focused emergency management. The forced marriage between emergency management and Homeland Security after 9/11 conjured up images of that past for many professional emergency managers. Conflicts over policy priorities, that is, terrorism versus natural disasters, became a struggle to preserve the core values of emergency management. Federal mandates are often met with resistance because they conflict with the more collaborative and cooperative processes that professional emergency managers have used for at least two decades, as well as conflict with local priorities. In California, the big threat is earthquakes, not terrorism.

In Florida, the focus is on hurricanes. Risk-based planning has become the tool for keeping attention focused on and resources ready for the most likely threats.

The George W. Bush administration also developed plans for "incidents of national significance" that increased federal authority to supplant state and local authority during catastrophic disasters (Derthick 2007). The Katrina disaster was not deemed an "incident of national significance," despite the perception that state capacities in Louisiana, including the capacities of the state executive, had been overwhelmed. The federalization of a major disaster would raise legal and practical issues, and the development of policies and procedures to deal with catastrophic disasters remains a priority.

The role of the U.S. Northern Command and other military assets is also being debated. The threats of terrorism, particularly bioterrorism, and pandemic have encouraged changes in law and practice to ensure greater executive control in emergencies. Authority to order quarantines, for example, has been clarified so that authorities can isolate infected populations should that become necessary to prevent the spread of disease. However, with few exceptions, so-called mandatory evacuations are not legally mandatory. Issues of authority are also addressed in both of the major sets of emergency management standards, the Emergency Management Accreditation Program (EMAP) and National Fire Protection Association (NFPA) standard 1600.

There has been a strong reaction from the nation's governors against efforts to give the federal government a lead role in catastrophic disasters. In fact, in 2004, when Florida suffered four hurricanes in quick succession, then governor Jeb Bush, brother of President Bush, declined direct federal involvement (Sylves 2008). Federal support was welcomed, but state authorities had the situation well in hand and did not need help in directing the disaster response. States now have added resources because they can borrow personnel and material through the Emergency Management Assistance Compact (EMAC).

EMAC was created as an agreement among southern states after Hurricane Andrew in 1992 and was opened to all states and territories in 1995 and chartered by Congress in 1996. The compact provides a mechanism for governors to request resources from other states. Resources, such as medical teams, are clearly defined, and states not affected by the disaster can offer to provide the resources at a negotiated price. During the Katrina and Rita disasters, almost sixty-six thousand personnel were deployed under EMAC. They included emergency managers, law enforcement officers, firefighters, medical personnel, building inspectors, public health officers, and other technical personnel. Equipment ranged from power generators to portable toilets (EMAC 2006). The availability of emergency management–trained personnel and related resources lessened the need for military personnel untrained in emergency operations. All states and territories were not members of EMAC when Katrina made landfall, but all were members soon after. More states adopted statewide mutual-aid agreements, as well, to facilitate the sharing of resources among communities.

Lastly, the Katrina disaster provided impetus for a reevaluation of the role and function of emergency managers. In 2006, Mike Selves, then president of IAEM, asked for FEMA assistance in assessing the state of the profession. His question was prompted by the evident lack of a correct understanding of emergency managers' roles—among public officials at all levels, the media, and the public—in response to the hurricane. Professional emergency managers were frustrated by poor decision making by officials, who knew little about emergency management. A working group was assembled in 2007 to develop a definition, mission statement, and vision for emergency management and to identify the basic principles that underlie its practice. The working group included representatives from IAEM, the National Emergency Management Association (the professional organization for state emergency managers), FEMA, the EMAP Commission (a standard-setting and accrediting body for state and local emergency management programs), the NFPA 1600 Committee (the standard-setting body for private emergency management and business continuity programs), the private sector, and the academic community (International Association of Emergency Managers, 2010). The group defined *emergency management* as "the managerial function charged with creating the framework within which communities reduce vulnerability to hazards and cope with disasters." The mission of emergency management was described in these terms: "to protect communities by coordinating and integrating all activities necessary to build, sustain, and improve the capability to mitigate against, prepare for, respond to, and recover from threatened or actual disasters, acts of terrorism, or other man-made disaster." The vision was defined as "safer, less vulnerable communities with the capacity to cope with hazards and disasters."

The eight "principles of emergency management" are:

1. Comprehensive
2. Progressive
3. Risk driven
4. Collaborative
5. Integrated
6. Coordinated
7. Flexible
8. Professional

The eight principles begin with comprehensive emergency management, that is, all hazards, all stakeholders, and so on. They also reaffirm that emergency management is collaborative and should be risk driven, clear messages that command-and-control approaches are inappropriate and ineffective and worst-case scenarios are not substitutes for good risk assessment. The products of the working group have been endorsed by the major stakeholders and are being integrated into FEMA's training programs.

RESEARCH ON DISASTER POLICY AND EMERGENCY MANAGEMENT

The objective here is to examine the state of the emergency and crisis management literature. Where did the literature come from, where is it now, and where is it likely to go in the near future? First, the terminology is important. Academic researchers in the United States and Europe most frequently simply refer to work in this area as *disaster research,* although some in political science and public administration now differentiate somewhat between *disaster policy research* and *emergency management research,* with the later being focused more closely on the operational side of the field.

As one might expect, disaster policy and emergency management research has followed the evolution of the profession and field, but it has also been driven by major disasters. The tributaries are many. "Focusing events," as Thomas Birkland (1997) has termed them, have drawn attention to problems and encouraged policy-relevant responses. However, there are also threads of research that have been sustained over decades and continue today on topics such as collective behavior in disasters, hazard mitigation, intergovernmental relations, warning systems, and evacuation. Through those sustained efforts, social science researchers have developed a fairly firm foundation for emergency management practitioners to operate on. In fact, to receive national certification as professional emergency managers, applicants have to be at least somewhat familiar with the social science literature on disasters and emergency management. The certified emergency manager reading list includes major scholarly works (International Association of Emergency Managers, 2010).

With a few exceptions, public administration scholars were late in joining the disaster research community. The broader social science disaster research community has been largely made up of sociologists. The research is applied for the most part but includes basic, theory-driven, empirical research. This context is important to an understanding of the public administration literature because the methodological foundation for the study of natural and technological hazards and disasters by social scientists has generally come from the sociologists. Fieldwork has been a mainstay (Stallings 2006; Rodriguez, Quarantelli, and Dynes 2007). Case studies are common although they have become much more theory- and data-driven.

Building Public Administration Research Capacity

Public administration scholars were actively recruited by FEMA in 1984. An agreement was signed between the National Association of Schools of Public Affairs and Administration (NASPAA) and FEMA to grow a research community within NASPAA member programs (FEMA 1985). Charles Bonser, then dean of the School of Public and Environmental Affairs at Indiana University, with the help of William Petak of the University of Southern California, organized a workshop to bring together disaster scholars. Thirty-four scholars were invited to the National Emergency Training Center as NASPAA/FEMA fellows in 1984 and given a broad overview of emergency management and social science disaster research over a two-week period (Bonser et al. 2010). The original intent was to continue building the community, but there was no follow-up to the initial workshop. Another product of the agreement was the 1985 *Public Administration Review (PAR)* special issue on emergency management. The issue served to introduce the broader public administration community to emergency management. About a dozen of the NASPAA/FEMA fellows are still active disaster researchers. The National Science Foundation has since funded projects to create a new generation of social science disaster researchers, including public administration and policy scholars, but it is still a relatively small community.

The second major contribution to the literature was the ICMA's green book on emergency management (Drabek and Hoetmer 1991), which included some of the same scholars and practitioners who participated in the 1985 special issue of *PAR*. Thomas Drabek has described the first green book as one of the major "bridge-building" efforts in disaster research (Drabek 2009). The volume became the handbook for local emergency managers and the basic textbook for students preparing for careers in the field. It is still a much-cited source of basic information on emergency management. The second edition (Waugh and Tierney 2007) summarizes the social science literature but is much more oriented toward public administration and the issues raised by the Katrina disaster.

The 9/11 attacks had a profound effect on the emergency and crisis management literature. The 2002 *PAR* special issue on 9/11 included a broader group of scholars and focused on democratic governance in the aftermath of the attacks. The emphases were the next steps in the "war on terrorism" and how they might change the environment in which public administrators and, indeed, the public work. Organizational and legal issues were paramount.

The 2007 *PAR* special issue "Administrative Failure in the Wake of Hurricane Katrina" was somewhat different. The perspective was more field oriented, including the argument that racism influenced the poor response, the ethical culture in Louisiana was an obstacle to effective action, the "big questions" concerning how to respond to events of such scale and intensity had not been resolved, and the failure to recognize and manage the risk reflected serious system flaws. There was consensus that the vulnerability of New Orleans should not have been a surprise to public officials.

The Research Threads

In 1984, FEMA was young and officials were still trying to define its mission. The mission boundaries included terrorism and other national security threats, as well as natural and technological disasters. The issues of the day were organizational and political. The dominant interests within FEMA were still national defense related. The emergency management research community in public administration was very small, but there were clear threads in the research, including, in particular, those of the scholars and practitioners who were focusing on the role of FEMA and the design of emergency management policy and those of the scholars and practitioners who were focusing on hazard mitigation. The threads of policy and mitigation research continued and, in fact, have since become intertwined (see, e.g., Godschalk et al. 2009).

The new threads in the literature are organizational issues, particularly relating to the emergency management networks, as well as presidential leadership, politics, and intergovernmental coordination: crisis leadership, collaborative leadership, and complex adaptive systems (see, e.g., Comfort, Ko, and Zagorecki 2004; Kapucu and Van Wart 2006). The principal research threads seem to be on collaboration and its essential elements, including communication and trust, and on the development of resilient organizations, communities, and nations (Comfort, Boin, and Demchak, 2010). Determining the preconditions for collaboration, whether derived from circumstances, organizational characteristics, or a particular leadership skill set, remains an unanswered question (Weber and Khademian 2008).

The social vulnerability thread is newer. The starkest pictures from the Gulf coast in 2005 were those of the elderly and children without food or adequate shelter. The poor disaster response was a national embarrassment, and increasing poverty in the United States and the increasing movement of population to vulnerable coastal areas portend more Katrina-like disasters in the near future. American society is becoming more rather than less vulnerable. The growing research focus on social vulnerability (Tierney 2006; Cutter and Emerich 2006) is understandable.

The intergovernmental, multiorganizational, and intersector coordination thread is many decades old. Coordination was a major problem during the Katrina response and recovery efforts. It was a major problem during the 1900 Galveston hurricane that killed six thousand to eight thousand people. It has always been a problem. What is new in the thread is the focus on organizational learning, communication, and collaboration. The thread is increasingly grounded in the collaboration and network management literature, and new methodologies are being brought to bear. (See chapter 17, "Collaborative Public Agencies in the Network Era," in this volume.) Michael McGuire (2009) has linked the development of the emergency management profession to collaborative activities and concluded that collaborative behaviors can be developed. There is a skill set that professional emergency managers can cultivate. He also concluded that emergency managers located in response agencies tend to collaborate less frequently because of the cultures of their organizations. Hierarchy and control are not conducive to open communication, flexibility, and collaboration and present particular problems when many participants are resistant to or unfamiliar with command-and-control structures (Waugh 2009a).

The incident command system may well reduce communication and interfere with collaboration, in other words. The skills of the official are critical, and success may well depend on the official's management style and collaborative experience. There are still fundamental questions concerning whether collaboration is related more closely to a leader's skills or to institutional mechanisms or circumstances. Conflicts over turf are not the only obstacles to coordination and collaboration. Different assumptions about leadership are also obstacles.

Another factor that may well facilitate collaboration is the development of standards for the practice of emergency management. Currently, EMAP sets standards for and accredits state and local emergency management programs. EMAP focuses on "programs," and that means all stakeholders who are involved in disaster responses, not just the public agency charged with protecting life and property. The necessity for collaboration is an assumption that underlies the standards, and the accreditation process seeks documentation of collaborative planning and decision making. To the extent that the standards affect organizational cultures and management styles, they will affect how emergency managers and agency personnel interact with outside groups (Waugh 2007).

The challenge of interorganizational coordination and collaboration has been a focus of considerable scholarship. Tensions created by the federal system of government, in which coordination is critical, have generated a range of arguments, from Donald Kettl's (2004) argument that government should be reorganized to address new challenges such as terrorism to Martha Derthick's (2009) questions concerning why the Bush administration failed to centralize its power in response to the challenge presented by catastrophic disasters. The showdown occurred during the 2004 hurricane season in Florida when Governor Jeb Bush declined federal aid. Governor Bush was point man in the National Governors Association's opposition to an expanded military role in disaster operations. Presidential disaster declarations are fraught with politics, and some presidents are more willing than others to use their authority to issue declarations for political purposes even for marginal disasters that could have been handled by state governments (Sylves 2008).

The literature is still coalescing around the issue of resilience. There is a research thread but still considerable debate over what is meant by *resilience*. Comfort, Boin, and Demchak (2010) go a long way toward sorting out its meaning and its many manifestations. The capacity to recover quickly is the usual interpretation, but the capacity to learn the correct lessons from past events, prepare for the next disaster, and be able to adapt effectively is very much a part of resilience. Organizational and community resilience increases with learning. Resilience is of particular importance because of the concerns about capabilities to deal with and recover quickly from catastrophic disaster. Disaster recovery used to mean restoration of lifelines and basic community functions, and now it may mean decades of redevelopment. The capacity to survive and recover from a category 5 hurricane, a magnitude 8 or higher earthquake, a great tsunami, a pandemic, an asteroid strike, or any other catastrophic event may well rest with individual communities. The Katrina disaster could have been worse. The Haitian earthquake in January 2010 demonstrated the need to address social vulnerability before the next disaster and may well test the capacity of that nation to recover despite the massive international effort to help. The Chilean earthquake and tsunami of February 2010 demonstrated the value of hazard mitigation in building national resilience. Chilean building codes and construction standards clearly saved lives and reduced property damage. The Haitian and Chilean disasters offer stark evidence of the need to build more resilient communities.

There is increasing attention to the emergency management profession itself (Blanchard 2009). On the one hand, the attention reflects changes in the demographics of the profession. It is the familiar story of baby boomers retiring and being replaced by people who are younger and better educated. The new generation of emergency managers includes more women and more minorities. On the other hand, there is greater appreciation for the skills and experience of current emergency managers. Many emergency management decisions made during the Katrina disaster were made by nonprofessionals. Fundamental errors were made in emergency planning and operations, not to mention in hazard mitigation, and it was a frustrating experience for those who knew better and had to watch from the sidelines (Waugh 2006). The successes have tended to be overlooked. For example, in most respects, the evacuations were remarkable in terms of the number of people moved out of harm's way (Derthick 2007). Developing a strategic view of emergency management to ensure that major policy choices are made before disaster strikes and to ensure less ad hoc response and recovery efforts is critical (Canton 2007). Effective emergency management programs require forethought and planning.

There are still important issues relative to the application of social science research to emergency management. Myths still influence policy design and program management, such as the myth that people will panic if given too much information or given an accurate picture of serious risks when, in fact, panic is more likely if too little information is provided and people do not understand what is happening. Emergency management is becoming a distinct profession, and there is greater attention to stress in disaster operations and the life cycle of relief operations from their heroic beginnings to their depressing conclusions, as well as to the generally mundane tasks of recruiting, retaining, and paying the workforce during crises.

Research on the emergency management profession is slowly developing (Blanchard 2009). Thomas Drabek's classic study, *The Professional Emergency Manager* (1987), concluded that interpersonal skills and the ability to interact effectively with other stakeholders are more important than technical skills. Today, he might well frame his conclusions in terms of collaboration and network management. Financial and human resource management concerns often overshadow disaster management concerns. Indeed, a 2003 National Science Foundation–funded workshop on the skills and competencies necessary for emergency management identified almost all of the core competencies required in master's of public administration programs, including an understanding of the social and political context, decision making, communication, leadership, analytical skills, budgeting, and human resources management (Thomas and Mileti 2003). What was not mentioned explicitly but was reflected in the inclusion of qualities such as empathy was the *public service ethic,* the desire to respond to public needs or simply *to do good.*

The Department of Homeland Security's relationship to FEMA and to the agency's state and local counterparts remains an issue even though the "FEMA in or FEMA out" debate appears to be over. Criticism of the department for its failure to maintain the emergency management capabilities developed during the Clinton administration likely encouraged President Obama to appoint an experienced emergency manager as FEMA administrator. Interestingly, the Obama's appointee, Craig Fugate, was the head of emergency management in the state of Florida and served under Governor Jeb Bush during the conflict with federal officials in 2004. He served in Republican and Democratic administrations in Florida and has broad experience the field. FEMA has had too few administrators with emergency management experience and expertise.

The big change in the emergency management literature has been new theoretical frameworks. There are better and evolving measures of risk, collaboration, change, and other variables. The case studies and field research that characterized early emergency management studies have been enriched with empirical data and modeled. Institutional analyses have similarly been brought up to current social science standards, and innovative modeling is being done. Legal analyses are still being conducted and, in fact, seem to be increasing after confusion over authority was evident during the Katrina response and issues such as quarantine authority have arisen because of the threat of pandemic, but the bar has been raised. Corrective action, including legislative reform, is being recommended.

The most significant contribution may be the use of network analysis. The sheer number and diversity of actors involved in hazard mitigation, disaster response, and disaster recovery efforts has encouraged researchers to adopt network analysis techniques to examine patterns of social interaction among the actors (Comfort, Ko, and Zagorecki 2004). The degree of centralization of authority, the nature and density of groups and subgroups, and the distance between actors are critical variables in understanding communication, coordination, integration, and collaboration.

The disaster literature has taken on a very international flavor as lessons are drawn from crisis experience around the world. Practitioners, too, are drawing upon the experience of professional colleagues in other countries. Some cross-fertilization is also due to the increased professionalization of emergency management and humanitarian assistance. Many issues are the same, particularly in regard to the development of an ethic regarding local economic, social, and political prerogatives, in other words, *community-driven development* in the humanitarian assistance vernacular and *local* or *community control* in domestic emergency management operations. Security for relief workers and those receiving aid is also a common concern. Sustainable assistance and the links between disaster recovery and development are growing issues in both. Transitioning from material aid to cash, both to stimulate the economy and to reduce logistical needs, is common to both. There is greater professionalism among nongovernmental, as well as governmental, actors in both domestic and international organizations. There is greater accountability for funds and greater accountability to donors for performance, be they philanthropic organizations, faith-based organizations, or public agencies (see, e.g., Harmer and Cotterrell 2005; Cahill 2007). The applicability of the Sphere Project's Humanitarian Charter and Minimum Standards for Disaster Response are issues that might be addressed by researchers. The Sphere Project is an international effort of nongovernmental organizations, United Nations agencies, and academic institutions to develop standards for food, housing, sanitation, water, health, and other essential services for refugee populations and disaster victims (Sphere Project 2010). The point is that there is cross-fertilization. Both the domestic and international disaster relief systems include public, private, and nongovernmental organizations, and domestic and international organizations may well collaborate in domestic or international operations. International relief organizations responded to the Katrina disaster and were integrated into operations. Firefighters from Mexico, Australia, and other nations frequently work wildfires in the western United States when fire season is over in their own jurisdictions. The practice of emergency management is internationalizing and the research is as well.

THE FUTURE OF EMERGENCY AND CRISIS MANAGEMENT

One axiom of emergency and crisis management is that major policy decisions follow major disasters or crises and all too frequently relate only to those events. There are exceptions, however. The Robert T. Stafford Disaster Relief and Assistance Act of 1988 provides a broad foundation for the nation's emergency response system, and the Disaster Mitigation Act of 2000, which amended the Stafford Act, mandates hazard mitigation planning as a condition for receiving disaster assistance. The Stafford Act and Disaster Mitigation Act of 2000 are all-hazards focused. The National Flood Insurance Program encourages mitigation efforts but has had limited success with reducing the risk of floods. By contrast, much of the legislation that followed the 9/11 attacks focused narrowly on securing the nation's borders and protecting civil aviation, the two major vulnerabilities revealed by the attacks, and comparatively little attention was paid to natural and technological hazards until Hurricane Katrina in 2005. The capabilities that FEMA and its state and local counterparts developed prior to 9/11 are now being rebuilt to ensure that the same mistakes will not be made in the next catastrophic disaster.

The lessons of 9/11 and Katrina are still driving emergency management policy and practice and disaster research. The major issues are how to deal with catastrophic disasters, what incentives will encourage hazard mitigation, how to reduce social vulnerability, and how to make intergovernmental and multiorganizational coordination more effective. The professional emergency management community is increasingly international and collaborative. The same is true of the disaster research community. Collaboration is increasing among planning, public administration, political science, sociology, geography, economics, and other scholars (see, e.g., Godschalk et al. 2009). Collaboration is being encouraged and facilitated by the Department of Homeland Security's centers of excellence and other research centers. Threads of research involving public administration scholars have been active for decades, and newer threads have developed since 9/11 and Katrina and other disasters. The hazard mitigation, network analysis, and social vulnerability threads are perhaps the most notable. There are other threads dealing with such issues as evacuation that include social scientists, but they seem to have greater momentum in other disciplines. Since 9/11 and the Katrina disaster, disaster research has gained some prominence in the public administration academic community and is having an impact on emergency management policy and practice in the professional community.

REFERENCES

Birkland, Thomas A. 1997. *After Disaster: Agenda Setting, Public Policy, and Focusing Events.* Washington, DC: Georgetown University Press.

Blanchard, B. Wayne. 2009. The FEMA higher education project. Twelfth Annual FEMA All-Hazards Higher Education Conference, National Emergency Training Center, June.

Bonser, Charles, Beverly A. Cigler, Louise K. Comfort, David R. Godschalk, Lenneal J. Henderson, Richard T. Sylves, and William L. Waugh, Jr. et al. 2010. The legacy of the FEMA/NASPAA public administration faculty workshop on emergency management after twenty-five years. Unpublished manuscript.

Cahill, Kevin M. 2007. *The Pulse of Humanitarian Assistance.* New York: Fordham University Press.

Canton, Lucien G. 2007. *Emergency Management: Concepts and Strategies for Effective Programs.* Hoboken, NJ: Wiley-InterScience.

Comfort, Louise K., Arjen Boin, and Chris Demchak. 2010. *Designing Resilience for Extreme Events: Sociotechnical Approaches.* Pittsburgh, PA: University of Pittsburgh Press.

Comfort, Louise K., Kilkon Ko, and Adam Zagorecki. 2004. Coordination in rapidly evolving response systems: The role of information. *American Behavioral Scientist* 48 (3): 295–313.

Cutter, Susan L., and Christopher T. Emrich. 2006. Moral hazard, social catastrophe: The changing face of vulnerability along the hurricane coasts. *Annals of the American Academy of Political and Social Science* 604:102–112.

Derthick, Martha. 2007. Where federalism didn't fail. *Public Administration Review* 67 (December): 36–47.

———. 2009. The transformation that fell short: Bush, federalism, and emergency management. Nelson Rockefeller Institute of Government, August. www.rockinst.org/pdf/disaster_recovery/gulfgov/gulfgov_reports/2009–08-Transformation_That_Fell.pdf (accessed September 2, 2009).

Drabek, Thomas. 1987. *The Professional Emergency Manager.* Boulder: Institute for Behavioral Science, University of Colorado.

———. 2009. Bridge-building within emergency management communities: Successes, pitfalls, and future challenges. *Journal of Emergency Management* (November): 1–3.

Drabek, Thomas, and Gerard Hoetmer. 1991. *Emergency Management: Principles and Practice for Local Government.* Washington, DC: International City/County Management Association.

Emergency Management Assistance Compact (EMAC). 2006. 2005 Hurricane season response: After action report. National Emergency Management Association/EMAC, September 19.

Federal Emergency Management Agency (FEMA). 1985. The FEMA/NASPAA public administration faculty workshop on emergency management: Conference report. Senior Executive Policy Center, Office of Programs and Academics, National Emergency Training Center, Federal Emergency Management Agency, January.

Godschalk, David R., Adam Rose, Elliott Mittler, Keith Porter, and Carol Taylor West. 2009. Estimating the value of foresight: Aggregate analysis of natural hazard mitigation benefits and costs. *Journal of Environmental Planning and Management* 52 (6): 739–756.

Harmer, Adele, and Lin Cotterrell. 2005. Diversity in donorship: The changing landscape of official humanitarian aid. HPG Research Briefing 20, September. London: Overseas Development Institute.

International Association of Emergency Managers. 2010. IAEM Homepage, www.iaem.com (accessed on August 5, 2010).

Kapucu, Naim, and Montgomery Van Wart. 2006. The evolving role of the public sector in managing cata-strophic disasters: Lessons learned. *Administration and Society* 38 (3): 279–308.

Kettl, Donald F. 2004. *System Under Stress: Homeland Security and American Politics.* Washington, DC: CQ Press.

McGuire, Michael. 2009. The new professionalism and collaborative activity in local emergency management. In *The Collaborative Public Manager: New Ideas for the Twenty-first Century,* ed. Rosemary O'Leary and Lisa Blomgren Bingham, 71–93. Washington, DC: Georgetown University Press.

New York City Office of Emergency Management. 2009. Planning for Emergencies: 2009 Hazard Mitigation Plan. http://nyc.gov/html/oem/html/about/planning_hazard_mitigation.shtml.

New York City Panel on Climate Change. 2009. Climate risk information. Report, February 17. www.nyc. gov/html/om/pdf/2009/NPCC_CRI.pdf.

Rodriguez, Havidán, E.L. Quarantelli, and Russell R. Dynes, eds. 2007. *Handbook of Disaster Research.* New York: Springer.

Sphere Project. 2010. Sphere Project Homepage, www.sphereproject.org (accessed on August 5, 2010).

Stallings, Robert, ed. 2006. *Methods of Disaster Research.* Philadelphia: Xlibris/International Research Committee on Disasters.

Sylves, Richard T. 2008. *Disaster Policy and Politics: Emergency Management and Homeland Security.* Washington, DC: CQ Press.

Tierney, Kathleen. 2006. Social inequality, hazards, and disasters. In *On Risk and Disaster: Lessons from Hurricane Katrina,* ed. Ronald J. Daniels, Donald F. Kettl, and Howard Kunreuther. Philadelphia: University of Pennsylvania Press.

Thomas, Deborah, and Dennis Mileti. 2003. Designing educational opportunities for the hazards manager of the 21st century. Report of the Workshop, Denver, Colorado, October 22–23.

Waugh, William L., Jr. 2006. The political costs of failure in the responses to hurricanes Katrina and Rita. In *Shelter from the Storm: Repairing the National Emergency Management System After Hurricane Katrina,* ed. William L. Waugh Jr., 10–25. Thousand Oaks, CA: Sage.

———. 2007. Local emergency management in the post-9/11 world. In *Emergency Management: Principles and Practice for Local Government.* 2d ed., ed. William L. Waugh Jr. and Kathleen Tierney. Washington, DC: ICMA.

———. 2009a. Mechanisms for collaboration in emergency management: ICS, NIMS, and the problem of command and control. In *The Collaborative Public Manager: New Ideas for the Twenty-first Century,* ed. Rosemary O'Leary and Lisa Blomgren Bingham, 157–175. Washington, DC: Georgetown University Press.

———. 2009b. FEMA in shambles. In *The Impact of 9/11: The Day That Changed Everything?* Vol. 1, ed. Matthew J. Morgan. New York: Palgrave Macmillan.

Waugh, William L., Jr., and Gregory Streib. 2006. Collaboration and leadership for effective emergency management. *Public Administration Review* 66 (December): 131–140.

Waugh, William L., Jr., and Kathleen Tierney, eds. 2007. *Emergency Management: Principles and Practice for Local Government.* 2d ed. Washington, DC: ICMA, 319–333.

Weber, Edward, and Anne M. Khademian. 2008. Managing collaborative processes: Common practices, uncommon circumstances. *Administration and Society* 40:431–464.

PART III

NETWORKING AND PARTNERSHIPS

Although the use of networks and partnerships has always been an aspect of public administration, the extensive use of these instruments for the provision of basic service is a contemporary phenomenon. Mutual-aid agreements between local governments were for emergencies; state compacts authorized by Congress were for very restricted purposes; and contracts with private and not-for-profit organizations were also very limited and for nonessential services. Self-sufficiency was the goal of each unit of government, and acquiring the necessary human, financial, and material resources was the objective. Governance was government.

As the authors in this section have discerned, governing by networks and partnership is rapidly becoming the new shape of the public sector. This trend in governing is driven by the realization that a unit of government alone, in an ever-changing and increasingly complex society, can no longer meet the needs of its citizens. Thus, public administration is transitioning from a focus on direct provision of services to the generation of public value. The four chapters in this section highlight this transition in governance that networking and partnerships are helping to facilitate.

Nowhere are networking and partnerships more evident than in the relationship between federal employees and contractors. Nicholas Henry's chapter, "Federal Contracting: Government's Dependency on Private Contractors," contains a thorough discussion of this relationship. It begins with a revisit to President Dwight D. Eisenhower's "Farewell Address to the Nation," which was devoted almost entirely to federal contracting. Henry cites the nearly 5.17 million private sector contract employees working indirectly for federal agencies to exemplify concerns raise by President Eisenhower and the administrative circumstances that make the federal government "contractor dependent." Moreover, what had been an arm's-length relationship between government employees and contractors is now a relationship in which the two groups are virtually indistinguishable. This leads Henry to conclude that "nowhere is the academic community more relevant to practicing public administrators than in clarifying the complexities of contracting."

Terry L. Cooper's chapter, "Citizen-Driven Administration: Civic Engagement in the United States," addresses recent innovations in civic engagement that impinge most directly on administration. It describes the historical context within which contemporary approaches to civic engagement in governance can be understood. It then puts forth the arguments that the most important new forms of citizen involvement have occurred at the local level and that local institutional reforms are the most significant recent innovations that actually drive administration. Cooper cites the Los Angeles neighborhood council system as an exemplar of new approaches to civic engagement.

The cutting edge of civic engagement for the foreseeable future, according to Cooper, will be in developing new institutional structures for engaging citizens in governance in a more continuous and sustained fashion. This will require creativity and work to design these new institutions in ways that are appropriate for each local context. It will also require those who lead to develop skills in the civic engagement processes that help shape the life of those institutions. Cooper asserts that the next major civic engagement challenge is to create new institutional structures that will link citizens to state and federal governments.

"Network Theory and Practice in Public Administration" is the focus of the third chapter in this section. Louise K. Comfort and her colleagues discuss interdependencies among governmental entities, nonprofit organizations, and private businesses in their shared service areas. They also examine the "network science" that is used to both facilitate and study these interdependencies and use Allegheny County, Pennsylvania, to illustrate the complexity of networks in urban regions. The emphasis is on how ineffective hierarchical structures are giving way to informal methods of addressing shared problems among multiple entities in metropolitan regions. These methods, as they point out, are leading to significant change in the administrative framework of urban regions. Comfort and her colleagues further suggest that network theory and practice may be used to develop resiliency in metropolitan governance.

Robert Agranoff's chapter, "Collaborative Public Agencies in the Network Era," concludes this section on networking and partnerships. The chapter begins with a look at conductive public agencies or networking bureaucracies, followed by a discussion of what collaborating public agencies look like in practice. Agranoff uses Metro High experimental school in Columbus, Ohio, as an example of a completely networked public organization. Attention is then given to leadership, organizing, and management challenges in the era of networking-oriented collaborative management.

As Agranoff argues, the field of public administration must pay considerably more attention to the changing external or conductive roles of public managers. For administrators in conductive agencies this means more than reading the rules and regulations, listening at hearings, engaging in information exchanges, dealing with advocates and adversaries, and reading project reports. It also involves working together to create knowledge-based public dialogue and to reach mutually arrived-at solutions to problems.

CHAPTER 14

FEDERAL CONTRACTING

Government's Dependency on Private Contractors

NICHOLAS HENRY

In 1961, President Dwight D. Eisenhower devoted his entire "Farewell Address to the Nation" to federal contracting. The topic was seemingly so eye glazing and mind-numbing that choosing it as the centerpiece of a major presidential message to the people appeared to verge on the weird.

It was far from that. In his nationally televised speech, the former Supreme Commander of Allied Forces in World War II and a pro-industry Republican coined the term *military-industrial complex,* warned Americans of its "grave implications," and stated that its "total influence— economic, political, even spiritual—is felt in every city, every State house, every office of the Federal government" (Eisenhower 1961, 2).

Ike's address not only was stunning in its implications for democratic governance, but also eerily prescient. "What had once been an 'arm's-length' relationship between government staff and contractors has become a relationship where these parties are virtually indistinguishable as they carry out agency missions" (Burman 2009, 65). The federal government itself now describes, ominously, its administrative circumstances as "a contractor-dependent environment" (U.S. Government Accountability Office 2006, 15)—and with reason. Nearly 5.17 million private sector workers, a number that is almost three times that of federal civilian employees, work indirectly for federal agencies through some 4 million "contract actions" (Federal Procurement Data System—Next Generation 2008, 1) let to more than 160,000 contractors each year (U.S. Government Accountability Office 2009c, "Highlights").

This chapter addresses the following features of federal procurement contracting: costs; policies and values; public agencies and personnel; inherently governmental functions versus commercial activities; public-private competitions; bidding practices; revolving doors; service contracts and the "shadow government" of consultants; contract management; corruption in contracting; the history and prospects of procurement reform; and current issues, trends, and opportunities for research.

PROCUREMENT: BUCKS, BUREAUCRACIES AND BUREAUCRATS

In the federal government, *procurement,* also known as *purchasing* and *acquisitions,* is government contracting with the private, independent, and public sectors to buy goods and services. Procurement is by far the dominant form of federal privatization. By contrast, state and local governments' predominant privatization type is to outsource their services for delivery to their citizens.

Listing largest expenditures first, federal procurement contracts are let for "other services," accounting for 44 percent of all contract dollars; supplies and equipment (42 percent); construction (7 percent);

automated data-processing services and equipment (5 percent); architecture and engineering (1 percent); and real property (1 percent) (Federal Procurement Data System—Next Generation 2008, 4).

The price of federal procurement is high, its procedures are convoluted, and its personnel overwhelmed.

Big Bucks: The Price of Procurement

From 2000 to 2008, federal contracting costs soared by 162 percent (Hiatt 2009; U.S. House of Representatives, Committee on Government Reform, Minority Staff, Special Investigations Division 2006, 3). This was a record rate that won contracting the title of "the fastest growing component of federal discretionary spending," burgeoning "twice as fast as other federal discretionary spending" (U.S. House of Representatives, Committee on Government Reform, Minority Staff, Special Investigations Division 2006, 1). Washington spent $532 billion per year on procurement in 2008 (Hiatt 2009). Federal contracts amounted to two-fifths of Washington's discretionary spending in 2005 (U.S. House of Representatives, Committee on Government Reform, Minority Staff, Special Investigations Division 2006, 3), up from less than a fourth just four years earlier (U.S. General Accounting Office 2003e, 8–10).

The Department of Defense, as the world's largest, richest bureaucracy, with a budget that exceeds the economies of all but a dozen nations, is Washington's Croesus of contracting. Nevertheless, with the end of the cold war, the Pentagon's share of acquisitions has slipped from 82 percent of all federal contract dollars in 1985 (U.S. General Accounting Office 2000, 2) to 72 percent today (Federal Procurement Data System—Next Generation 2008, 54). About three-quarters of all the remaining contract dollars are spent by just a half dozen civilian agencies (U.S. General Accounting Office 2002a, "Highlights").

Procuring Bureaucracies

Title 7 of the Civil Service Reform Act of 1978 authorizes administrators in all agencies to "make determinations with respect to contracting out" (U.S. General Accounting Office 1991, 19). The General Services Administration (GSA) assists agencies in purchasing and related projects with the goal of ensuring that the government gets good value for the dollar. The Office of Federal Procurement Policy, established by Congress in 1974 and placed in the Office of Management and Budget (OMB), is responsible for providing overall direction for government-wide procurement policies and procedures.

Procurement's Personnel: The Contracting Cadres

The primary purchasing personnel are an "acquisition workforce" that numbers over 61,400, the core of which is more than 28,400 contracting officers who are responsible for the business aspects of outsourcing (Federal Acquisition Institute 2008, 18). Regrettably, contracting officers may be ill equipped for these responsibilities. A fourth of them do not have a college degree (although this figure is shrinking), and they typically occupy midlevel supervisory positions (Federal Acquisition Institute 2008, 18). Yet, these administrators are responsible for managing a hugely complex system in the form of the Federal Acquisition Regulation, a document in excess of 1,600 pages, plus agency supplements amounting to another 2,900 pages. Moreover, the federal contracting workforce declined in size during the 1990s, led by the Pentagon, which lost nearly half of its contracting employees, and never recovered, even as the number of contracts and the dollars in them more than doubled (U.S. Government Accountability Office 2008a, 7, 1; U.S. Merit Systems Protection Board 2005, i).

PHILOSOPHIES OF FEDERAL CONTRACTING

Federal contracting is best understood as a normative system of values that change over time and are often expressed in administrative regulations.

OMB Circular A-95

The first of these regulations appeared in 1955, when what is now the Office of Management and Budget issued Bureau of the Budget Bulletin 55–4, which stated in a straightforward manner that the government would rely on the private sector for goods and services so that it would not be competing with business.

In 1966, OMB altered this philosophy. OMB Circular A-76, "Performance of Commercial Activities," reiterated that it is the government's policy "to rely on competitive private enterprise" to supply it with goods and services, but the government should itself perform those functions that "are inherently governmental in nature." The circular defined a *governmental function* as one "which is so intimately related to the public interest as to mandate administration by government employees."

Identifying "Inherently Governmental Activities"

All of this may sound crisp, clear, and concise, but, alas, it is not. Messiness emerges when the government tries to identify not its commercial activities, but, peculiarly, its governmental ones. Consider war. Most of us think that war, which constitutionally can be declared only by Congress, is about as "inherently governmental" as it gets, but the Constitution also empowers Congress to "grant Letters of Marque and Reprisal"—that is, to authorize privateers, usually ship owners, to make war on the nation's behalf. Congress used privateers extensively and effectively during the Revolution and the War of 1812, and, just as the fees that the federal government pays its contractors are taxed by the federal government, the booty that privateers looted also was taxed by Washington (Tabbarok 2007).

Today, we are witnessing a resurrection of privateering, or, at least, the privatization of war. At its height, Washington hired some 180,000 private contractors to assist with its military operations in Iraq, a number surpassing that of the troops there (Miller 2007). The Pentagon is quick to state that "we have issued no contract for any contractor to engage in combat" (Barstow 2004), and technically this is true.

In point of fact, however, private contractors ghosted into shadow soldiers. Civilian contractors were "working in and amongst the most hostile parts of a conflict" (Barstow 2004). At least 650 contractors have been killed in Iraq (Merle 2006), and some have even been awarded medals ostensibly reserved exclusively for soldiers (Cha and Merle 2004). "The line is getting blurred . . . and it is likely to get more blurred" (Barstow 2004). Blurred, indeed: A civilian contractor even wrote the Defense Department's policies for civilian contractors on the battlefield (Werve 2004)!

"Inherently governmental," in short, is subject to an infinitude of interpretations.

Identifying "Commercial" Activities

OMB Circular A-76 "appears to allow all functions not governmental in nature to be contracted out" (U.S. General Accounting Office 1991, 19), but, as with inherently governmental activities, the precise nature of those functions was left unsaid. To rectify this, President Ronald Reagan in

1987 issued Executive Order 12615, and Congress in 1998 passed the Federal Activities Inventory Reform Act (the FAIR Act), both of which, in conjunction with OMB Circular A-76, require OMB and the agencies to identify each year their *commercial activities,* or those functions that are more appropriately conducted by businesses (and which perhaps should be outsourced to them, rather than being retained by government).

In contrast to the amorphous and undefined inherently governmental activities, OMB now lists more than seven hundred specific commercial activities, and they are found throughout the federal hierarchy (U.S. Government Accountability Office 2008b, 8). Agencies annually identify those activities that are "competitive commercial." Typically, about a fourth of agencies' functions are so classified. Another quarter are "noncompetitive commercial," or functions that have been exempted from competition by statute or other means, and the remainder is governmental activities (U.S. General Accounting Office 2004, 6).

COSTING CONTRACTING THROUGH COMPETITIONS

More than nine out of ten Americans "do not believe that the [federal] government gets best value from its contractors" (Primavera Systems 2007, 1). Accordingly, gaining better value from privatization has increasingly concerned Washington's policy makers. For more than thirty years, federal officials have tried to ascertain whether government or nongovernmental organizations could conduct more cost-effective commercial activities by relying on *public-private competitions,* in which agencies select from their competitive commercial activities those that they wish to put out for bid. An agency's cost for performing these activities then is compared with the costs of its competitors. Whichever entity has the lowest cost, and still maintains standards, is awarded the contract. In theory, at least, these competitions maximize the competitive field, and, when an agency is underbid, they promote an internal examination of why the agency's costs are higher than its competitors' costs, thereby inducing future public efficiencies.

In 2003, federal officials recognized, for the first time, that public sector agencies were as legitimate competitors for federal contracts as were private and nonprofit sector organizations. This recognition was expressed in the first major revision in almost four decades of OMB Circular A-76, which listed ten "guiding principles" for federal privatization, including one that allows "public and private sources to participate in competition for work currently performed in-house . . . work currently contracted with the private sector, and new work" (U.S. General Accounting Office 2003b, "Highlights").

Have Competitions Worked?

Nearly three decades after federal agencies began public-private competitions, Congress tardily required all agencies to report annually on savings derived from their public-private competitions. Section 647(b) of the Transportation, Treasury, and Independent Agencies Appropriations Act of 2004 enacted this government-wide policy, known as the "Section 647 reporting requirement." In the first five years that data were collected, 1,375 public-private competitions were completed (U.S. Office of Management and Budget 2008, 1).

The question of whether public-private competitions have helped make federal acquisitions more efficient is increasingly controversial. At root, the controversy centers on how widely one defines its costs and benefits. At the narrower end of this spectrum, when analysts focus solely on fiscal facts, these competitions have a definite allure. Thanks to public-private competitions, according to OMB, the government saves more than a billion dollars each year. For every one dollar that Washington spends to conduct these competitions, it saves thirty dollars (U.S. Office of Management and Budget 2008, 1, 2, 11).

The rub in these impressive figures is one of numbers. Out of all the eligible positions, the feds have conducted public-private competitions for only 1.5 percent of them (U.S. Office of Management and Budget 2008, 1). Statistically, the competitions fail to provide "sufficient data" for determining whether the government saves or loses money by hiring contractors rather than using its own employees (U.S. Government Accountability Office 2008a, 11). Nevertheless, Congress has unearthed figures suggesting that the average annual cost of a federal contract employee ($250,000 in 2006 in selected agencies) may be almost twice that of a federal civil servant ($126,000) (O'Harrow and Higham 2007; O'Harrow 2007; Pincus and Barr 2007).

When the analytical scope is broadened to include factors other than fiscal savings, it is not at all clear that these competitions induce longer-term federal efficiencies. During the 1990s, when public-private competitions were at their lowest ebb (Gansler and Lucyshyn 2004, 9), the number of federal civilian employees sank by 11 percent, a record reduction (U.S. Bureau of the Census 2006, Table 481), reflecting the fulfillment of a prime objective of privatization, that of a leaner federal workforce, but one that seems not to be attributable to privatization. Even though public-private competitions have been conducted according to federal guidelines, their "full costs" are understated and result "in few job losses or salary reductions," but they do have "a negative impact on morale" (U.S. Government Accountability Office 2008b, "Highlights"). Public-private competitions are "a huge drain on management attention, deeply divisive, and stressful to the workforce, sucking up resources for minimal gain. . . . It is hard to find anyone inside or outside government who will privately say it's a good idea" (Wagner 2008, 51).

The Demise of Public-Private Competitions?

These concerns appear to have been heard. In 2008, the Office of Federal Procurement Policy introduced "commercial services management" noting that this new policy would "not ordinarily involve public-private competition or the potential conversion of work from the government to the private sector" (Johnson 2008, 1). The Clean Contracting Act of 2008 (Subtitle G of the Duncan Hunter National Defense Authorization Act for Fiscal Year 2009) overrode much of OMB Circular A-76 as it pertained to public-private competitions in the military services.

Section 324 of the National Defense Authorization Act for Fiscal Year 2008 and Section 736 of the Omnibus Appropriations Act of 2009 required the Pentagon and civilian agencies, respectively, to devise and implement in-sourcing guidelines that will ensure, on a regular basis, that consideration is given to using federal workers for new duties and duties performed by contractors.

"Many procurement analysts suspect" that public-private competitions "will tail off." In the words of a union member, "We could be the last guys with A-76" (Brodsky 2009).

BIDDING: RARELY OPEN

The enormous irony in public-private competitions, which have consumed so much time, money, and energy, is that there is very little competition in a far costlier aspect of contracting—federal bidding practices. Federal agencies select contractors for federal business by *full and open competition,* or soliciting competitive bids through widely distributed announcements; or by using various permutations of *negotiation,* which involves bargaining with a small number of preselected firms and, occasionally, some limited advertising; or by selecting a *sole source,* in which a contracting officer unilaterally selects a corporation that seems most qualified.

The central repository for federal procurement data maintains that two-thirds of all contracts, and half of all contract dollars, are let *without* "full and open competition" (Federal Procurement Data System—Next Generation 2008,1). These numbers appear to be defensively low (U.S. General Accounting Office, 2003c, 22–24; U.S. Government Accountability Office, 2004, 3).

How do agencies circumvent the bid procedure? Much of this circumvention is legal, if still questionable. Contracting officers have the power to waive bidding requirements, and they waive with gusto. Depending on the study, from about a third to nearly nine-tenths of all contracts are officially exempted from the "fair opportunity process" (U.S. General Accounting Office 2003c, 22–24; U.S. Government Accountability Office 2004, 3). In most cases, these waivers are granted without "fair and open competition," or with "unjustified exceptions" or "faulty justifications" (U.S. General Accounting Office 2003c, 22–23).

In addition, agencies are not above using guile when advertising projects for supposedly open bidding. For decades these deceptions have included the following: The agency miscodes a contract so that potential bidders cannot find it; it mentions a particular contractor in the solicitation for bids, thereby warning off potential competitors; or the agency mandates absurdly brief deadlines in the solicitation so that only preselected, and tipped-off, contractors can meet them ("Most Ads for Contractors Meaningless" 1980).

Even when contracts are let competitively, subterfuge and deceit remain. Contractors' initial estimated costs for hundreds of major projects built over nine decades in twenty countries, including the United States, on five continents were, on average, 28 percent short of their *actual* costs (Flyvberg, Holm, and Buhl 2002). This gap remained quite consistent over time; indeed, the current difference between the Pentagon's contractors' first estimates for weapon systems and their final costs is a remarkably similar average of 26 percent (U.S. Government Accountability Office 2008a, "Highlights"). The "overwhelming statistical significance" of these data is that "the cost estimates used to decide whether such projects should be built are highly and systematically misleading" and are "best explained by strategic misrepresentation, that is, lying" (Flyvberg, Holm, and Buhl 2002, 279).

If lowballing and lying may be commonplace among companies seeking agency contracts, it is a practice in which agencies are complicit. According to a federal "cost containment expert," prospective contractors know that if they tell administrators "how much something is really going to cost, they may scrub it. And they know that if they tell the Congress how much it's really going to cost, Congress may scrub it. So you start in with both sides knowing that it is going to cost more" (Proxmire 1970, 83). Although the quotation is dated, the reality that it reflects remains.

SPINNING THE REVOLVING DOOR

Who better to lobby government than those who know it from the inside? Thus, we enter the infamous revolving door. From the late 1990s to the mid-2000s, 12 percent of Washington's registered lobbyists were former federal officials (Brown 2006, 2). Today, almost one in three are former federal officials (Eggen and Kindy 2010).

Conversely, nearly a third, a plurality, of all upper-level federal hires who are hired from outside the government were working for a federal contractor when they were hired (U.S. Merit Systems Protection Board 2008,13). Administrators in the Department of Energy, which privatizes about 90 percent of its budget and is second only to Defense in the dollars that it contracts out, "bounce back and forth between government and industry just like Ping-Pong balls" (Neumann and Gup 1980). This is the essence of the revolving door.

The revolving door is hardly the exclusive aperture of the executive branch. About a fourth of members of Congress who leave office become lobbyists (up from a mere 3 percent in the 1970s), and similar patterns pertain for congressional staffers (Abramson 1998). Members of Congress who intend to voluntarily retire and become lobbyists sponsor significantly more legislation during their final term in office than do retiring members in their final term who do not expect to become lobbyists, suggesting that retiring members who become lobbyists may harbor "ambitions that potentially jeopardize the interest of the public" (Santos 2003, 62).

Federal officials who leave for the private sector are lured by greener pastures. Often, their salaries quadruple or even septuple (Abramson 1998; Baer 1996). But the real money is made by the special interests, which spent more than $3.24 billion in 2008 to lobby Washington, more than doubling their spending in just a decade (Center for Responsive Politics 2009). Former federal employees who lobby spend a fourth of all lobbying expenditures in Washington but more than compensate for their spendthrift ways by raking in two-thirds of all lobbying firms' fees (Brown 2006). More than half of all consulting contracts awarded by the Pentagon, virtually none of which are openly bid, go to former Pentagon employees. Significantly, 40 percent of these contracts are originally proposed by the contractor, a figure that appears to be about twice that of civilian agencies (U.S. General Accounting Office 1981).

Federal regulations that address the revolving door are laced with loopholes and are tepidly enforced. In 2000, just twenty-three days before he left office, President Bill Clinton issued Executive Order 13184, thereby revoking his own Executive Order 12834 of 1993 that required senior appointees to "pledge" that they would not lobby any federal agencies for five years after they left the federal employ, and never lobby for a foreign government or political party.

In 2007, Congress partially ameliorated Executive Order 13184 by enacting the Honest Leadership and Open Government Act, which bans Cabinet secretaries and other high-level administrators from lobbying their former agencies for two years following retirement. Congress was less forthcoming in slowing its own revolving door, although the act does apply the same prohibition on senators from lobbying Congress, lesser limitations on staffers, and none on representatives. All members and senior staffers, however, must disclose any current negotiations with prospective employers.

FEDERAL SERVICE CONTRACTS

A *federal service contract* is a legal agreement for the provision by the private sector of training, leasing, technical, professional, logistical, social, or managerial support to the federal government. Examples include computer programming, administrative assistance, and temporary labor. In 1985, service contracts amounted to only 23 percent of all federal contracting dollars (U.S. General Accounting Office 2000, 6). Today, they account for 60 percent (U.S. General Accounting Office 2003d, 1). As an indication of their growing importance, Congress in 2003 passed the Services Acquisition Reform Act, which creates incentives for performance-based service contracts and appoints in civilian agencies "chief acquisition officers" empowered to decide whether or not contracted programs may continue and force accountability among contractors and federal managers alike. Unfortunately, these officers have yet to meet expectations (Burman 2009, 65).

Costly Consultants

An extensive and expensive use of service contracts is the hiring of private consultants, who operate in a netherworld of dank and bureaucratic murk. Had the Departments of Energy and Defense used government employees instead of consultants, they would have saved significant sums—from more than a fourth to more than half (U.S. General Accounting Office 1994, Appendix 4).

More anecdotal, but revealing, evidence on the utility of the "Beltway bandits" abounds. Consider some statements by federal contracting officers (Neumann and Gup 1980):

- "The bottom line on contracts—pure paper studies. . . . The public gets . . . maybe 10 percent of their money's worth."
- Of one $250,000 study, described as "an unintelligible pile of papers," a federal administrator said, "Nothing was received and we paid thousands for it. It really is a lot of gobbledygook. . . . As a taxpayer, I'm sick" (Neumann and Gup 1980).
- "We're so busy trying to shovel money out the door, we don't have time to see what happens to it after it leaves. All the money could be stolen and I wouldn't know it. . . . The place is a madhouse" (Neumann and Gup 1980).

The waste (and the opportunity) is also recognized by the more enlightened consultants. A board member of the Institute of Management Consultants observes, "It's a game. . . . Government comes to us and wants help in identifying their problems, but they don't seem to be able to use the material. They could spend much less and get more for it" (Neumann and Gup 1980). "It looks like a conspiracy, but really it's chaos" (Guttman 1982). So stated one of the nation's leading experts on governing by contracting, and it is likely that he is accurate.

The Shadow Government

Chaotic incompetence is one thing. Policy manipulation, however, is another. A serious problem emerges when "advice" from private consultants waxes into policy executed by public administrators. The Government Accountability Office (GAO) has called Congress's attention to "contractors' influencing agencies' control of federal policies and programs" (U.S. General Accounting Office, 1981, 6), in reports dating from 1961. As a top GAO executive put it, "We've seen situations where an agency contracts out so much of its data gathering and policy analysis that it thinks it has control, but the consultant is, in effect, making the decision" ("Consultants: New Target for Budget Trimmers" 1981).

The question raised by these comments is fundamental. Who makes and implements public policy? Is policy made by representatives of the public interest or by representatives of private interests? The government first addressed these concerns in 1980 with OMB Circular A-120, which prohibited consultants from performing policy-related work that was "the direct responsibility of agency officials." The Office of Management and Budget replaced its circular in 1993 with OMB Policy Letter 93–1, which states, in even stronger language, that consultants' and other service contractors' "services are to be obtained and used in ways that ensure that the Government retains inherently governmental decision-making authority." A decade following the initial issuance of this policy, however, more than a fifth of federal contracts for consultants' services appeared to involve "inherently governmental functions" (U.S. General Accounting Office 1991, 5).

CONTRACTING IN INCOMPETENCE

Much federal contracting is a model of efficiency. The Pentagon, for example, pays less for some items than the private sector does because it is "already using commercial practices commonly followed by large firms" (Besselman, Arora, and Larkey 2000, 421). But much is not. For instance, at least a third of the American interrogators who were implicated in the severe mistreatment of prisoners in Iraq's infamous Abu Ghraib prison were not American soldiers, but private businesspeople. They were hired not by the Pentagon, as one might reasonably assume, but through a computer services contract overseen by a Department of the Interior's office in Arizona. In apparent violation of federal regulations, the contract was never opened for bid, and the contract itself was written by an employee of the firm that won the contract. The process was so convoluted that the army could not determine who wanted to hire private interrogators in the first place (Singer 2004a, 2004b).

How did this debacle happen? Unfortunately, it is an example of a far more pervasive problem of federal incompetence in privatizing. Time is money. Federal purchases of less than $100,000 take an average of three months to complete, compared with one to four weeks in the private sector, and buying information technology consumes more than four years, compared to thirteen months in the private sector, a practice that ensures permanent obsolescence (Gore 1993, 28, 1).

A lack of due diligence is money. Some federal contracts require that administrators assess the past performance of prospective contractors before awarding them contracts, but in seven out of ten of these contracts, contractors' previous performance is never assessed (U.S. Government Accountability Office 2009c, "Highlights").

Change is money. The Pentagon alters a whopping 63 percent of weapon systems requirements *after* their development has begun, and this dubious practice is associated with "significant program cost increases" (U.S. Government Accountability Office 2008a, "Highlights").

Unused leverage is money. Federal agencies miss "opportunities to leverage the government's buying power" by failing to use interagency contracts to purchase the same goods and services from common vendors. Although the data are dim, perhaps only a tenth of contract dollars are leveraged (U.S. Government Accountibility Office 2010, "Highlights").

Senseless rules are money. Federally imposed requirements tote up to 12 percent or more in additional contract costs (Gore 1993, 80).

Cost-reimbursement contracts are money. *Cost-reimbursement contracts* ask contractors to make a good-faith effort to meet estimated costs, but the government will (with some restrictions, depending on the contract) pay any costs exceeding that estimate. (The other two main types of federal contracts are *fixed cost,* in which the contractor is not reimbursed for expenses that surpass the agreed-upon cost, and *time and materials,* in which the government pays fixed, per-hour rates for all expenses within a preestablished ceiling.) A cost-reimbursement contract "involves high risk for the government because of the potential for cost escalation and because the government pays a contractor's costs of performance regardless whether the work is completed. . . . The complete picture of the government's use" of these contracts "is unclear," but it appears that they account for at least a fourth of all federal contract dollars (U.S. Government Accountability Office 2009a, "Highlights").

These poor practices have costly consequences.

CORRUPTION IN CONTRACTING

The feds' privatization procedures are meant to ensure, if not efficiency, then at least honesty. In this, they frequently fail. Between 1995 and 2007, seventy-one of the top one hundred federal contractors were fined more than $26 billion for 678 "instances of misconduct," including fraud, "defective pricing," poor performance, and violations of environmental, antitrust, health, ethics, tax, labor, and human rights laws, among many others types of misconduct (Project on Government Oversight 2009). In the Pentagon, America's biggest contractor, the Justice Department's

Operation Ill Wind exposed "America's biggest defense scandal." "No one will ever know how much the phony contracts and sweetheart deals really cost taxpayers," but it is known that they amounted to billions of dollars, and resulted in more than ninety convictions of contractors and federal executives for corruption (Pasztor 1995, 38).

The Structure and Culture of Contracting Corruption

Why does corruption in contracting continue unabated? In part, fraud flourishes because the structure of privatization itself is unusually corruptible. Of the twenty-five to thirty "high-risk" federal operations identified each year by the GAO as unduly vulnerable to "fraud, waste, abuse, and mismanagement" (U.S. Government Accountability Office 2005b, 3, 2), more than a third involve "large procurement operations or programs delivered mainly by third parties" (Goldsmith and Eggers 2005).

More deeply, the culture of contracting often places scant value on acquiring one's money's worth. Often, "the concept that the contracting officer's primary purpose is to acquire a contract that promises the highest quality at the lowest price is misleading if not false" (Cooper 1980, 462). The preeminent expectation by management, especially in the military, is that contracting officers produce the goods; keeping their costs down runs a distant second. As a former procurement officer put it, "It doesn't matter if you screw everything up, as long as you keep the dollars flowing" (Mitchell 1990).

Coming Back for More

In sum, Washington has a record of largely poor contract management; has built a privatization structure that allows an unusual level of corruption; and permits a contracting culture that places a greater stress on completion of the project than on honesty and cost-effectiveness. Worse, perhaps, Washington's enforcement of its own contracting regulations is negligible.

Even though the Federal Acquisition Regulation requires officials to do business only with "responsible sources" that have a "satisfactory record of integrity and business ethics," and even as federal contract costs more than doubled (Hiatt 2009; U.S. House of Representatives, Committee on Government Reform, Special Investigations Division 2006, 3), the number of "exclusions"—that is, *suspensions* (i.e., temporary exclusions pending investigations) and *debarments* (fixed-term exclusions, usually not exceeding three years)—issued by all federal agencies to contractors from 2003 to 2007 declined by 43 percent to fewer than forty-three hundred, an infinitesimal subfraction of federal contracts (President's Council on Integrity and Efficiency and Executive Council on Integrity and Efficiency 2008, Table 10).

Of far greater importance, large federal contractors are almost never suspended or debarred, despite long records of serious, including some criminal, violations. Not one of the twenty-five major corporations convicted of defrauding the federal government in the 1980s was banned from further contract work (Stevenson 1990). During the 1990s and 2000s, the top ten federal contractors shelled out almost $3 billion in fines and penalties for 280 instances of proven or alleged misconduct, but not one of them was excluded from further work (Amey 2005).

Why Does Washington Do It?

At least one reason why federal agencies keep contracting with these high-flying felons is practical. Few, if any, other contractors could take over some big, complex projects that these big, complex companies manage, so firing them may not be a realistic option. Another is technical. Various glitches may conceal from agencies an astounding 99 percent of the suspensions and debarments that other agencies have levied on their prospective contractors for past violations (U.S. Government Accountability Office 2005a, 2–3).

Yet another reason is managerial. Agencies sometimes fail to check the government's list of suspended and debarred companies; or the excluded companies change their identities; or, astonishingly, some agencies continue to contract with companies that they themselves excluded. Examples include the German contractor whom the army debarred because he tried to ship nuclear bomb parts to North Korea; nevertheless the army needlessly continued its contract with this "morally bankrupt individual" (to quote the army's own assessment) to the tune of another $4 million; or the corporation that the navy suspended because one of its employees had sabotaged repairs on an aircraft carrier that could have caused massive deaths—yet, "less than a month later, the Navy improperly awarded the company three new contracts" (U.S. Government Accountability Office 2009b, "Highlights").

But the main reason why the feds fire so few felonious firms is political. Canceling a government contract "drastically disrupts the careers of those associated with it," because the cancelation "hurts regional economies. What causes pain locally triggers congressional rescue activity" (Lambright 1976, 123). Bringing Congress into the act can be a federal administrator's worst nightmare, so "government contractual relationships may be more like treaties than contracts in that often no real separation occurs" (Cooper 1980, 462–463).

REFORMING FEDERAL CONTRACTING

Federal attempts to ensure honest dealing between the government and business date back to at least 1863, with the passage of "Lincoln's law," the False Claims Act. More contemporary federal efforts to reform contracting hearken back to the mid-twentieth century.

Early Efforts

Among the more important early legislative efforts to recast acquisitions are the Armed Services Procurement Act of 1949, which mandates advertised bidding for Defense and other agency contracts; the Truth-in-Negotiations Act of 1962, which requires contractors to support their bids with data; the Competition in Contracting Act of 1984, which established a bidding and appeals system that later was significantly simplified but still stands in principle; and the Procurement Integrity Act of 1988, which prohibits contract officers from discussing employment prospects with, and slipping inside information to, contractors with whom they are negotiating.

Congress also took an early interest in upgrading the contracting cadres, and in 1976 Congress created, as part of the General Services Administration (GSA), the Federal Acquisition Institute, designed to improve the professionalism of the civilian procurement workforce.

The Mixed Record of the 1990s

Congress renewed its commitment to deepening the professionalism of federal procurement personnel in the 1990s. In 1990, it enacted the Defense Acquisition Workforce Improvement Act, which ordered the Pentagon to establish a separate career path for its acquisitions specialists, and, in the following year, the Defense Acquisition University was founded as an equivalent to the prestigious National Defense University.

Four Serious Statutes

Also during the 1990s, Congress passed four laws designed to simplify privatization procedures. The Government Performance and Results Act of 1993 requires agencies to measure the performance of contractors. Washington still has some way to travel on this road, and it appears that only 11 percent of contracts meet performance-based criteria (U.S. General Accounting Office 2002b, 3).

The Federal Acquisition Streamlining Act of 1994 dramatically simplifies the buying of items costing less than $100,000, and the Information Technology Management Reform Act of 1996 is designed to shorten the time that it takes to buy information resources. The Federal Acquisition Reform Act of 1996 recasts the Federal Acquisition Regulation in terms of guidelines rather than rules; frees administrators from selecting only the lowest bidder; and simplifies the appeals process, reducing thirteen dispute-resolution boards to two.

Have the Statutes Worked?

Largely as a consequence of these laws, "the federal government is dramatically changing the way it purchases goods and services by relying more on judgment and initiative versus rigid rules for making purchasing decisions" (U.S. General Accounting Office 2003a, "Highlights"). Regrettably, however, judgment and initiative have not always had their intended effects.

In its zeal to streamline procurement, Congress significantly weakened the requirement, first established by the False Claims Act of 1863, that companies certify their prices as being the most favorable to the government; cut back contract audits; and authorized the General Services Administration, the feds' principal purchasing overseer, to collect "industrial funding fees"—that is, a percentage of the sales it handles—from vendors who sell to federal agencies. These changes amount to a set of incentives for GSA to overlook overcharges—the industrial funding fees alone cover GSA's budget—and the results are predictable. A decade following their passage, corporate sales to agencies that were conducted through the GSA's flagship program septupled, and "agencies have used the GSA to avoid true competition and steer work to preferred companies, resulting in cases of waste, fraud and increased cost to taxpayers" amounting to "hundreds of millions, if not billions," of dollars (O'Harrow and Higham 2007).

Trying Reform Again: Frustrations in the 2000s

During the 2000s, Congress tried again to gain a semblance of control over federal contracting. The Federal Funding Accountability and Transparency Act of 2006 (also known as the Obama-Coburn Act) required that all recipients of direct federal contracts, loans, and grants be listed, along with the money awarded, and that this information be made easily accessible to the general public.

The Services Acquisition Reform Act of 2003 and the National Defense Authorization Act for Fiscal Year 2004 authorized and created an Acquisition Advisory Panel. Its 474-page report, issued in 2007, provides a well-considered basis for reform, with systemic recommendations that stress improved definitions, requirements, coordination, and human capital, and more resources for contract management (U.S. Acquisition Advisory Panel 2007).

A result of this renewed thinking about procurement is new ethics rules, enacted by the Federal Acquisition Regulation Council in 2008 and added to the Federal Acquisition Regulation, that require mandatory disclosure when contractors violate particular laws, and expand the grounds for excluding contractors.

The Clean Contracting Act of 2008, mentioned earlier, not only exempted the Pentagon from much of OMB Circular A-76's requirements concerning commercial services, but also launched an extensive assessment of outsourced services, limited noncompetitive contracts, and began an effort to clarify just what "inherently governmental" should mean, with a goal of narrowing standards for what can be contracted out.

Despite these efforts, the same immense issues persist. Years after all the privatization reforms were in place, the comptroller general of the United States testified in 2008 that "we must engage in a fundamental reexamination of when and under what circumstances we should use contractors versus civil servants or military personnel . . . [and] we must address challenges . . . in assuring proper oversight." These problems demand "immediate attention" (U.S. Government Accountability Office 2008a, 13).

THE AUDACITY OF HOPE? A PRESIDENTIAL PRIORITY

Almost a half century following Eisenhower's farewell, the forty-fourth president, Barack Obama, on his forty-fourth day in office, delivered the second major presidential address on federal contracting, appropriately, in the Eisenhower Executive Office Building. Obama, who had long-standing concerns with contracting (as a senator, he had cosponsored the Federal Funding Accountability and Transparency Act), called for the reform of "our broken system of government contracting." He chided contractors who were "paid for services that were never performed, buildings that were never completed, companies that skimmed off the top," and who "have been allowed to get away with delay after delay after delay" (Obama 2009, 1, 2). Obama directed the Office of Management and Budget to identify wasteful and unneeded contracts, predicting that, "altogether, these reforms can save the American people up to $40 billion each year" (Obama 2009, 3), an impressive sum, but still a slender sliver—less than a tenth—of federal contracting costs.

Congress responded to the president's actions by passing three consequential bills that were promptly signed into law. One was the Weapon Systems Acquisition Reform Act of 2009, which received a unanimous vote in Congress, creating a new office for estimating program costs, reemphasized weapons testing before they entered production, and eased their termination.

The Fraud Enforcement and Recovery Act of 2009 dramatically expanded the risk for institutional recipients of federal funds by holding them potentially responsible for frauds perpetrated by their subcontractors; holds contractors liable for not returning overpayments; and eases whistleblowing.

The third law is the American Recovery and Reinvestment Act of 2009. Tucked away in this legislation that distributed $747 billion throughout an economy in crisis are the following clauses: a beefing up of whistle-blowing opportunities; the maximum possible use of competitively awarded, fixed-price contracts; and the establishment of a Recovery Accountability and Transparency Board, composed of inspectors general empowered to issue subpoenas.

Obama also issued three executive orders in 2009 that (1) denied reimbursement to contractors for expenses related to their resistance to, or encouragement of, unionization; (2) required postings about their workers' rights to unionize (or not); and (3) ensured job security for contracted employees when a new contractor took over an existing contract from a former contractor. In 2010, he signed an executive order barring agencies from issuing new contracts to tax scofflaws.

"Government contracting is plainly entering an era of . . . an unprecedented level of scrutiny . . . and significantly greater risk for contractors" (Vinson & Elkins LLP 2009). It is undeniably encouraging that, even though the federal government remains contractor dependent, an effort is being undertaken at the highest levels to liberate the government's dependency and to reassert its primacy in the implementation of public policy. Perhaps, however, the more potent cure for contracting woes is the likelihood of its shrinking use in the future. It is projected that, due to squeezed budgets resulting from significant deficit spending, federal contracting costs will grow at a compound annual rate of just 2 percent, "a very, very slow growth rate," from 2008 to 2014 (Castelli 2009). This glacial growth rate may be the single best prospect for gaining greater control of federal procurement.

ISSUES, TRENDS, AND NEEDED KNOWLEDGE

For the first time in six decades, the nation has a president, and perhaps a Congress, that recognize that reform must be undertaken. It might be anticipated that both the White House and the Capitol will continue to push for greater transparency, firmer enforcement, and better management in federal contracting. These efforts have begun with the Pentagon, but, given the quarter-century trend of procurement spending lowering in Defense, and its corresponding rise in civilian agencies, the president's focus probably will expand to include the whole of government.

It is, however, difficult to overstate the private sector's resistance to acquisitions reform. As a direct result of the accelerating revolving door, Washington's lobbyists have grown in number, sophistication, and clout, and all signs suggest that these trends will continue their steady expansion, and that lobbyists will challenge any changes that threaten their slurping at the federal trough.

The scholarly community can help federal administrators deal with these realities. Among questions that need answering are:

- How can the term "inherently governmental function" be made more clear and operational?
- What more needs to be done to slow the revolving door?
- In administering the occluded world of federal outsourcing, how can public administrators increase transparency, enforcement, and accountability?

Nowhere is the academic community more relevant to practicing public administrators than in clarifying the complexities of contracting. And no practice so fully expresses the intellectual roots of public administration as does federal acquisitions. Collaboration, competition, corruption, reform, management, and the public interest—it's all there.

NOTE

Portions of this chapter are adapted from Nicholas Henry's *Public Administration and Public Affairs,* 11th ed. (New York: Longman, 2010).

REFERENCES

Abramson, Jill. 1998.The business of persuasion thrives in the nation's capitol. *New York Times,* September 29.

Amey, Scott. 2005. Suspension and disbarment: The record shows that the system is broken. *Federal Times,* March 21. www.federaltimes.com (accessed May 22, 2005).

Baer, Susan. 1996. "Revolving door" spins fast as ever for ex-Clintonites. *Baltimore Sun,* December 1.

Barstow, David. 2004. Security companies: Shadow soldiers in Iraq. *New York Times,* April 19.

Besselman, Joseph, Ashish Arora, and Patrick Larkey. 2000. Buying in a businesslike fashion—and paying more. *Public Administration Review* 16 (5): 421–434.

Brodsky, Robert. 2009. Legislators ask defense agency to rethink public-private competition. Government-Executive.com, February 2. www.govexec.com/dailyfed/0209/020209rb1.htm (accessed March 4, 2009).

Brown, Elizabeth. 2006. *More Than 2,000 Spin Through Revolving Door.* Washington, DC: Center for Public Integrity.

Burman, Allan V. 2009. Six practical steps to improve contracting. *Business of Government* (Spring): 62–66.

Castelli, Elise. 2009. Contract spending expected to flatten. FederalTimes.com, June 8. www.federaltimes.com/article/20090608/ACQUISITION03/906080301/1034/IT04.

Center for Responsive Politics. 2009. Lobbying database. OpenSecrets.org. www.opensecrets.org/lobbyists/.

Cha, Ariana Eunjung, and Renae Merle. 2004. Line increasingly blurred between soldiers and civilian contractors. *Washington Post,* May 13.

Consultants: New target for budget trimmers. 1981. *U.S. News and World Report,* December 1, 40.

Cooper, Phillip J. 1980. Government contracts in public administration: The role and environment of the contracting officer. *Public Administration Review* 40 (5): 459–468.

Eggen, Dan, and Kimberly Kindy. 2010. Three of every four oil and gas lobbyists worked for federal government. *Washington Post* (July 22).

Eisenhower, Dwight D. 1961. *Farewell Address to the Nation.* Washington, DC: U.S. Government Printing Office.

Federal Acquisition Institute. 2008. *Annual Report on the Federal Acquisition Workforce, FY 2007.* Washington, DC: U.S. Government Printing Office.

Federal Procurement Data System—Next Generation. 2008. *Federal Procurement Report, FY 2007,* Section 3: Agency views. Washington, DC: U.S. Government Printing Office.

Flyvberg, Bent, Mette Skamris Holm, and Soren Buhl. 2002. Underestimating costs in public works projects: Error or lie? *Journal of the American Planning Association* 68 (3): 279–295.

Gansler, Jacques, and William Lucyshyn. 2004. *Competitive Sourcing: What Happens to Federal Employees?* Washington, DC: IBM Center for the Business of Government.

Goldsmith, Stephen, and William D. Eggers. 2005. Government for hire. *New York Times,* February 21.

Gore, Al. 1993. *From Red Tape to Results: Creating a Government That Works Better and Costs Less, Reinventing Federal Procurement.* Washington, DC: U.S. Government Printing Office.

Guttman, Daniel. 1982. *60 Minutes.* New York: CBS Television Network (November 30).

Hiatt, Fred. 2009. 600,000 bad hires? *Washington Post,* April 27.

Johnson, Clay, III. 2008. *Memorandum for the President's Management Council: Subject, Plans for Commercial Services Management.* Washington, DC: U.S. Office of Management and Budget, July 11.

Lambright, W. Henry. 1976. *Governing Science and Technology.* New York: Oxford University Press.

Light, Paul C. 2003. *Fact Sheet on the New True Size of Government.* Washington, DC: Brookings Institution.

Merle, Renae. 2006. Census counts 100,000 contractors in Iraq. *Washington Post,* December 5.

Miller, Christian. 2007. More contractors than troops in Iraq. *Los Angeles Times,* July 14.

Mitchell, Russell. 1990. It was Mr. Fixit vs. the Pentagon—and the Pentagon won. *Business Week* (December 24): 52.

Most ads for contractors meaningless. 1980. *Washington Post,* June 25.

Neumann, Jonathan, and Ted Gup. 1980. An epidemic of waste in U.S. consulting research. *Washington Post,* July 22.

Obama, Barack. 2009. *Remarks by the President on Procurement.* Washington, DC: White House.

O'Harrow, Robert, Jr. 2007. Costs skyrocket as DHS runs up no-bid contracts. *Washington Post,* June 28.

O'Harrow, Robert, Jr., and Scott Higham. 2007. Changes spurred buying, abuses. *Washington Post,* June 8.

Pasztor, Andy. 1995. *When the Pentagon Was for Sale: Inside America's Biggest Defense Scandal.* New York: Scribner.

Pincus, Walter, and Stephen Barr. 2007. CIA plans cutbacks, limits on contractor staffing. *Washington Post,* June 11.

President's Council on Integrity and Efficiency and Executive Council on Integrity and Efficiency. 2008. *A Progress Report to the President, Fiscal Year 2007.* Washington, DC: U.S. Government Printing Office.

Primavera Systems. 2007. *America, Inc.—Annual Shareholder Management Report.* Crystal City, VA: Primavera Systems.

Project on Government Oversight. 2009. Federal Contractor Misconduct Database. Washington, DC: Project on Government Oversight. http://www.contractormisconduct.org/ (accessed January 15, 2010).

Proxmire, William. 1970. *Report from the Wasteland: America's Military Industrial Complex.* New York: Praeger.

Santos, Adolfo. 2003. Post-congressional lobbying and legislative sponsorship: Do members of Congress reward their future employers? *LBJ Journal of Public Affairs* 16 (4): 56–64.

Singer, P.W. 2004a. A contract the U.S. military needs to break. *Washington Post,* September 12.

———. 2004b. Nation builders and low bidders in Iraq. *New York Times,* June 15.

Stevenson, Richard W. 1990. Many caught but few are hurt for arms contract fraud in U.S. *Washington Post,* November 12.

Tabbarok, Alexander. 2007. The rise, fall, and rise again of privateers. *Independent Review* 11 (4): 565–578.

U.S. Acquisition Advisory Panel. 2007. *Report of the Acquisition Advisory Panel to the Office of Federal Procurement Policy and the United States Congress.* Washington, DC: U.S. Government Printing Office.

U.S. Bureau of the Census. 2006. *Statistical Abstract of the United States, 2006,* 125th ed. Washington, DC: U.S. Government Printing Office.

U.S. General Accounting Office. 1981. *Civil Servants and Contract Employees: Who Should Do What for the Federal Government?* FPCD-81–43. Washington, DC: U.S. Government Printing Office.

———. 1991. *Government Contractors: Are Service Contractors Performing Inherently Governmental Functions?* GAO/GGD-92–11. Washington, DC: U.S. Government Printing Office.

———. 1994. *Government Contractors: Measuring Costs of Service Contractors Versus Federal Employees,* GGD-94–95. Washington, DC: U.S. Government Printing Office.

———. 2000. *Federal Acquisition: Trends, Reforms, and Challenges.* GAO-T-OCG-00–7. Washington, DC: U.S. Government Printing Office.

———. 2002a. *Acquisition Workforce: Status of Agency Efforts to Address Future Needs.* GAO-03–55. Washington, DC: U.S. Government Printing Office.

———. 2002b. *Contract Management: Guidance Needed for Using Performance-Based Service Contracting.* GAO-02–1049. Washington, DC: U.S. Government Printing Office.

———. 2003a. *Acquisition Management: Agencies Can Improve Training on New Initiatives.* GAO-03–281. Washington, DC: U.S. Government Printing Office.

———. 2003b. *Competitive Sourcing: Implementation Will Be Key to Success of New Circular A-76.* GAO-03–943T. Washington, DC: U.S. Government Printing Office.

———. 2003c. *Contract Management: Civilian Agency Compliance with Revised Task and Delivery Order Regulations.* GAO-03–983. Washington, DC: U.S. Government Printing Office.

———. 2003d. *Contract Management: Comments on Proposed Services Acquisition Reform Act.* GAO-03–716T. Washington, DC: U.S. Government Printing Office.

———. 2003e. *Federal Procurement: Spending and Workforce Trends.* GAO-03–443. Washington, DC: U.S. Government Printing Office.

———. 2004. *Competitive Sourcing: Greater Emphasis Needed on Increasing Efficiency and Improving Performance.* GAO-04–367. Washington, DC: U.S. Government Printing Office.

U.S. Government Accountability Office. 2004. *Contract Management: Guidance Needed to Promote Competition for Defense Task Orders.* GAO-04–874. Washington, DC: U.S. Government Printing Office.

———. 2005a. *Federal Procurement: Additional Data Reporting Could Improve the Suspension and Debarment Process.* GAO-05–479. Washington, DC: U.S. Government Printing Office.

———. 2005b. *GAO's 2005 High-Risk Update.* GAO-05–350T. Washington, DC: U.S. Government Printing Office.

———. 2006. *Federal Acquisition Challenges and Opportunities in the 21st Century.* GAO-07–45SP. Washington, DC: U.S. Government Printing Office.

———. 2008a. *Defense Acquisitions: DOD's Increased Reliance on Service Contractors Exacerbates Longstanding Challenges.* GAO-08–621T. Washington, DC: U.S. Government Printing Office.

———. 2008b. *Department of Labor: Better Cost Assessments and Departmentwide Performance Tracking Are Needed to Effectively Manage Competitive Sourcing Program.* GAO-09–14. Washington, DC: U.S. Government Printing Office.

———. 2009a. *Contract Management: Extent of Federal Spending Under Cost-Reimbursement Contracts Unclear and Key Controls Not Always Used.* GAO-09–921. Washington, DC: U.S. Government Printing Office.

———. 2009b. *Excluded Parties List System: Suspended and Debarred Businesses and Individuals Improperly Receive Federal Funds.* GAO-09–174. Washington, DC: U.S. Government Printing Office.

———. 2009c. *Federal Contractors: Better Performance Information Needed to Support Agency Contract Award Decisions.* GAO-09–374. Washington, DC: U.S. Government Printing Office.

———. 2010. *Contracting Strategies: Data and Oversight Problems Hamper Opportunities to Leverage Value of Interagency and Enterprisewide Contracts,* GAO-10–367. Washington, DC: U.S. Government Printing Office.

U.S. House of Representatives, Committee on Government Reform, Minority Staff, Special Investigations Division. 2006. *Dollars, Not Sense: Government Contracting Under the Bush Administration.* Washington, DC: U.S Government Printing Office.

U.S. Merit Systems Protection Board. 2005. *Contracting Officer Representatives: Managing the Government's Technical Experts to Achieve Positive Contract Outcomes.* Washington, DC: U.S. Government Printing Office.

———. 2008. *In Search of Highly Skilled Workers: A Study on the Hiring of Upper Level Employees from Outside the Federal Government.* Washington, DC: U.S. Government Printing Office.

U.S. Office of Management and Budget. 2008. *Competitive Sourcing: Report on Competitive Sourcing Results, Fiscal Year 2007.* Washington, DC: U.S. Government Printing Office.

Vinson & Elkins LLP. 2009. Recovery act includes unprecedented accountability and transparency provisions. V&E Litigation Update (February 17). http://www.vinson-elkins.com (accessed June 10, 2009).

Wagner, G. Martin. 2008. Words from the wise: What senior public managers are saying about acquisition. *Business of Government* (Spring): 50–52.

Werve, Jonathan. 2004. Contractors write the rules. Washington, DC: Center for Public Integrity. http//:projects. publicintegrity,wow/org/report.aspx?ais-334 (accessed December 14, 2004).

CHAPTER 15

CITIZEN-DRIVEN ADMINISTRATION

Civic Engagement in the United States

TERRY L. COOPER

This chapter addresses recent innovations in civic engagement that impinge most directly on administration, hence the title, "Citizen-Driven Administration." It develops an argument that the most important new forms of citizen involvement have occurred at the local level. The chapter first describes the historical context within which contemporary approaches to civic engagement in governance can be understood. It then adopts what may be a controversial position, by identifying local institutional reforms as the most significant recent innovations that actually drive administration, and presents the Los Angeles neighborhood council system as a major case study of these new approaches.

These institutional reforms are viewed as reflecting "citizen-centered" civic engagement. Particular engagement techniques that facilitate deliberation, either face-to-face or electronic in form, and collaboration of various kinds, are then viewed as necessary instruments for the effective implementation of local institutional reforms, but of lesser importance when used in isolation in an episodic fashion.[1] The chapter concludes with recommendations for moving forward with the next step in civic engagement development by linking local governance with state and federal government agencies. It intentionally avoids a more obvious approach of presenting an introductory overview of citizen participation or developing a "catalogue" of current techniques for deliberation and collaboration, but instead identifies three particularly innovative ones that may have relevance for advancing the effectiveness of citizen-centered civic engagement through the new institutional reforms at the local level.[2]

CITIZENS, GOVERNANCE, AND THE CONSTITUTION

The United States was founded with two minds with respect to the role of the citizenry in governance.[3] The perspective that gained dominance initially was that advanced by the Federalists and embodied in the U.S. Constitution. It provided for minimal direct participation by ordinary people in the formation of public policy, allowing the popular direct election of only one member of the House of Representatives. The Federalist position was based on a largely negative view of human nature summed up well in *Federalist Paper* 10. There humans are characterized as driven by passions, conflict, and self-interest. The Federalists argued that, given this kind of human nature, the likely result of direct participation by the mass of citizens would be the formation of destructive factions that would make governance difficult if not impossible. Consequently, the process of governing had to be buffered from direct influence by the citizenry.

The other mind with respect to civic engagement that was operative during the founding era was that of the Anti-Federalists, who held a very different view of human nature as being capable of civic virtue, cooperation, and rational deliberation. From their orientation, citizens should be as directly involved in governance as possible since participation was seen as the way citizens were developed in terms of both skills and regard for the larger civic good. Thus, the Anti-Federalists argued for the importance of keeping government local and close to the citizenry, where participation could occur more naturally and frequently.

The Federalists carried the day in the constitutional struggle, but not without concessions to the Anti-Federalist concern over centralized government removed from direct popular control. The first ten amendments to the Constitution, the Bill of Rights, were adopted to appease Anti-Federalist concerns. These two broad perspectives have remained with us throughout our history. The continuing interaction that has occurred during the past two hundred years between these two views of human nature and the role of the people in governance has had the effect of democratizing our Constitution and governance process. It has done so mainly by increasing the breadth of electoral participation to include African American men, women, and people eighteen years of age and older. Along with greater electoral inclusiveness we have gained the direct election of the U.S. Senate by the citizenry and the abolishment of the poll tax, which presented an impediment to low-income voters, especially African Americans in the South.

However, beneath the formal participation structures of government, which were focused almost exclusively on voting, there have been since the colonial era ongoing processes of direct self-government at the local levels. Alexis de Tocqueville (2007) described a web of voluntary associations that was a mechanism for combining the relative weakness of individuals in an egalitarian society into aggregations of power that could effectively solve problems, assert needs and preferences, and engage government. Tocqueville noted that these associations were the training grounds for citizenship and civic competence. In them, people learned how to associate their interests with those of others and to cooperate to achieve common goals, either through mutual self-help or by petitioning government. From the colonial era to the present, there have been myriad other self-organizing efforts including the committees of correspondence through which the Revolutionary War was organized, the Underground Railroad, which aided the escape of slaves from the South, militia organizations, communal societies, religious organizations, crime-prevention associations, good-government organizations, volunteer fire departments, and labor unions, among others.

Impetus for this kind of civil society participation in governance came not only from the Anti-Federalist impulses that were kept alive among us, but also from similar perspectives reflected in the democratic practices of Puritan communities that evolved into the New England town meetings, our tradition of voluntary associations noted by Tocqueville that were particularly necessary in frontier settlements, and the stream of ideas that constitute the Jeffersonian tradition of self-governance.

CITIZEN ENGAGEMENT AND PROGRESSIVE REFORM

The watershed changes for these forms and traditions of civic engagement came at the end of the nineteenth century and in the early decades of the twentieth century. During that era, the American Progressive reform movement began the pivotal process of radically transforming the administrative institutions of government based on the norms of professionalism, efficiency, scientific management, and administrative management. The Progressives also accomplished constructive reforms of the electoral process that established the referendum, recall, and initiative in many states. One result was the creation of more opportunities for citizens to influence the electoral process, but nothing beyond it that addressed the growing influence of the administrative agencies of government in the lives of the people.

In fact, a direct result of the Progressive institutional reforms was the creation of barriers against the influence of the citizenry on the day-to-day administration of government. In the Progressive program of reform, citizens were expected to vote for representatives, use the three new mechanisms for changing laws and elected representatives, but otherwise leave the administration of government services to the professional experts and their "scientific" methods. At a time when the de facto power of the bureaucracy was increasing dramatically, citizens were increasingly confronted by a technical professional role definition of the administrator that precluded the need for their lay input. Coupled with an emphasis on the "scientific" design of bureaucratic administrative organizations, this professionalization of administration established formidable barriers to anything like sustained civic engagement. There were countercurrents throughout this era moving toward more direct citizen engagement, particularly reflected in the work of Mary Parker Follett, most specifically in *The New State* ([1918] 1965), but they were unable to overcome the strong tide of Progressive reform.

CITIZENS AND THE PROFESSIONAL ADMINISTRATIVE STATE

By the 1960s, it had become obvious to many people in our increasingly diverse American society that their interests were not being addressed adequately, either by the professional experts or by elected officials. Interest groups had been identified by American pluralist thought in the early twentieth century as the best way to channel the interests of citizens to government in a complex, large-scale society such as the United States (Bentley 1908; Truman 1951). However, by the 1960s, Theodore Lowi (1969) and others (Parenti 1974) began to critique this thesis for its lack of support from the research on interest groups. By that time, the trend was toward single-interest groups with very narrow foci representing an elite with the power and financial resources to create effective lobbying organizations. During the 1960s and 1970s, the diverse interests in American society became more and more assertive—even aggressive—in relation to government at all levels, especially the federal government. The result was that the Progressive legacy of the professionalized administrative state came under fire.

Within the academy, the Progressive approach to the administrative role was also challenged by a series of authors beginning in the 1940s and with considerable force by the New Public Administration, which emerged during the late 1960s and early 1970s (Frederickson 1971; Marini 1971). The notion that a science of administration was possible was largely dismissed, and the assumption that administration could operate free of politics and value commitments was aggressively challenged. Also, the myth of the public administrator as simply following orders from the political policy makers was dispelled. It became increasingly clear that public administrators were exercising considerable discretion through their policy proposals, through participation in the policy-formation process, and most of all in the implementation of policy (Aberbach 1981).

As citizens experienced an inability to understand and influence the professionalized bureaucracy in the 1960s, frustration boiled over into action. Having been indoctrinated into thinking they lived in a democracy that provided government of, by, and for the people, citizens began to realize that what scholars were calling the "administrative state" was anything but democratic (Waldo 1948). Demonstrations, protests, civil disorder (sometimes involving widespread violence), and litigation combined to create a turbulent and uncertain environment in cities across the nation.[4]

The mass-based community organization movement launched by Saul Alinsky of the Industrial Areas Foundation in Chicago during the 1940s found fertile ground for its approach to civic engagement in the turmoil of the 1960s and 1970s. Alinsky's approach involved the use of conflict to create change in government, almost exclusively at the local level (Alinsky 1969, 1971). He worked mainly with the poor and dispossessed using money that came largely from churches. Alinsky sought to identify communities that had little economic or political power and help them mobilize around the latent conflict between themselves and the power structure of society at all levels. His strategy was to raise latent conflict to the surface and focus explicitly on the adversarial relationship between low-income people and specific leaders in government, including both politicians and public administrators. He assumed that cooperation with government was not desirable because poor people would always be co-opted in the process. Behind Alinsky's approach was his experience in the labor movement. Having written a biography of United Mine Workers leader John L. Lewis (1949), Alinsky was attempting to apply a labor-organizing model to low-income communities.

This adversarial or conflict-based approach to engaging government typified much of the civic engagement action and theory during the 1960s and 1970s. Regardless of whether it followed Alinsky's theory, strategies, and tactics, the dominant view of civic engagement during this era was that power was a zero-sum game. For the citizenry to have more power, government would have to have less. It was assumed that government would never willingly relinquish power, so aggressive adversarial advocacy was believed to be necessary. This was true of the civil rights movement, the anti–Vietnam War movement, the student movement, the women's movement, and the environmental movement, as well as the community organization movement. The adversarial orientation of this time period can be clearly seen in Sherry Arnstein's (1969) classic article, "A Ladder of Citizen Participation," which became one of the central reference documents for many pursuing the study of civic engagement during these years. In that essay, Arnstein presents a ladder model of citizen participation that comprises eight rungs, with "manipulation" and "therapy" at the bottom characterized as "nonparticipation." "Citizen control" and "delegated power" are at the top and identified as "degrees of citizen power" (217). The assumption clearly and starkly laid out by Arnstein, both in her model and in the accompanying text, was that power is an equation in which government loses power when citizens gain power.

The community organizing of the kind typified by Alinsky began to reveal its limits during the 1970s. Neighborhoods were small cells in the body politic and had limited power when they confronted citywide interests. One might well organize a neighborhood effectively and still lose over and over again in the contest for political power in the large urban centers of America. Poor people were always in the minority and regularly lost when confronting majority interests and power. Adversarial tactics might yield limited results for particular communities, but for anything involving larger scales when the interests of the poor and the affluent collided, the poor tended to lose.[5]

During the 1970s, a shift became evident that had begun during the later years of the War on Poverty of the 1960s: the increased adoption of legislative mandates for citizen participation at the local level, mostly embedded in federal statutes. The response of federal elected officials to growing and more aggressive demands for participation, at all levels of government, was to divert political pressure away from themselves and onto public administrators. They accomplished this strategy by writing into legislation specific mandates for the inclusion of citizens in the implementation of federal programs. Politicians were able to tell the activists that they had responded to their demands by adopting 155 federal mandates for citizen participation by the end of the Carter administration (Advisory Commission on Intergovernmental Relations 1979). It was up to local public administrators receiving federal money to carry out those requirements.

These government-initiated, largely unfunded mandates worked with varying degrees of effectiveness. All suffered from a lack of resources for their implementation, and administrators' logical response was to comply at the minimally required level so as not to drain resources otherwise allocated for the operation of their programs. Administrators were put in a bind in which their most reasonable way out was to do just enough to comply with the legal mandates but not enough to make them work well (Cooper 1979).

CITIZEN ENGAGEMENT IN THE 1980S

The 1980s reflected yet another shift, marked by the election of Ronald Reagan to the presidency. The noise in the streets had died down, the war in Vietnam had ended after the United States and its allies in South Vietnam were defeated in 1975, and the nation had been lulled into a more passive mode. Reagan appeared to care little for citizen participation beyond the voting booth and moved quickly to disarm those few in Washington, D.C., who were making serious efforts to carry out the legal mandates established during the Carter years. Creighton (1995), for example, describes how the Interagency Council on Citizen Participation was summarily shut down and its files seized by federal agents.

One finds a relative hiatus in the literature on citizen participation throughout the 1980s. It is not that nothing was written on the subject during this decade, but the diminution in the flow of literature and federal government activity is noteworthy (Creighton 1995). The action shifted during these years back to neighborhoods, self-help, and local government. Boyte's (1980) "backyard revolution" revealed a lot of nearly invisible activity at the small scale of neighborhoods in the form of mutual self-help, beautification, arts, and recreation organizations.

FROM GOVERNMENT TO GOVERNANCE: INSTITUTIONAL REFORMS FOR CIVIC ENGAGEMENT

A sea change in approaches to civic engagement emerged about twenty years ago and launched what remains the major innovation through institutional reform at the local level. The numerous new techniques of deliberation and collaboration since that time may be seen as providing support in its development and implementation. Toward the end of the 1980s, one began to hear an occasional voice that referred to governance as differentiated from government. Among the earliest of those voices was that of Harlan Cleveland, who argued that what we need more of is governance, not government (Cleveland 1988). Within the United States and in the international arena, this distinction was articulated with increasing clarity, arguing that the process of governing should no longer be understood as the sole business of government but as involving the interaction of government, business, and the nonprofit (or nongovernmental) sectors. The term *collaborative governance* is now one of the prominent topics in the public administration literature.[6]

Reflecting the governance approach, during these years new experiments in institutional innovation began to occur here and there across the nation between cities and their neighborhoods. The power of focusing on institutional design, clearly demonstrated by the Progressive reformers, was being redirected into the hands of citizens rather than operating exclusively under the control of professional experts (Cooper 1984). Officially recognized neighborhood council organizations emerged during the late 1980s and early 1990s in places such as Portland, Oregon; Minneapolis and St. Paul, Minnesota; Dayton, Ohio; and Birmingham, Alabama. This general approach to institutional innovation was first articulated in Milton Kotler's (1969) *Neighborhood Government: The Local Foundations of Political Life*. In that work, Kotler called for the creation of legal jurisdictions at the neighborhood level that would function as units of government with certain specified authority and powers. Prompted by the current interest in similar approaches to reconnecting citizens with governance in a more formal manner, Kotler's book was reissued in 2005 (see Cooper 2005).

Berry, Portney, and Thomson's (1993) *The Rebirth of Urban Democracy* documents and evaluates some of these innovative governance experiments in a piece of exemplary social science research carried out over several years. The authors studied five cities that have neighborhood council systems: Portland, Oregon; Dayton, Ohio; St. Paul, Minnesota; Birmingham, Alabama; and San Antonio, Texas. These were matched with ten control cities (two cities each) that did not have neighborhood council systems. Data were gathered on all of these cities using multiple rounds of surveys, interviews, and observation. The key measurement tool employed for comparison was an "index of community participation" (ICP), which the authors constructed from five indicators of participation.

Rebirth reports extraordinarily rich findings from Berry, Portney, and Thomson's thorough and systematic research. They note that much of the research on citizen participation in governance has had a pessimistic tone that generally blames citizens for not really being interested in participation and denigrates their potential contributions. Berry and coauthors suggest that "social scientists have largely given up on participatory democracy" (212). Contrary to that negative posture, these researchers argue that their data "show that when administrators make a good-faith effort to make citizen participation work rather than trying to undermine it, the performance of public involvement programs is dramatically different from that described in the literature" (212). Contrary to conventional wisdom in the social sciences, these neighborhood council systems do not increase conflict, but actually reduce it. Particularly relevant to the general trend of growing distrust and alienation from government, the authors maintain that these "neighborhood associations defuse hostility rather than create it." Further, "both regular and marginal participants in neighborhood associations actually had higher feelings of efficacy than did comparable populations of activists in conventional community groups." Also, it is of crucial significance that although a large proportion of administrators observed that this kind of citizen participation did cause delay, "they overwhelmingly felt that the benefits outweighed the costs" (213). Specific statistical findings from this research indicate that greater tolerance for others is positively correlated with greater participation. This is largely attributed to the learning that occurs through participation that increases "the attitudes necessary to maintain a strong democracy" (231). One of the strongest positive relationships found was between participation and the development of a sense of community that was independent of socioeconomic status.

Assuming people are more likely to act in the governance process if they believe it will make a difference, Berry, Portney, and Thomson's findings on efficacy are of great importance. They studied both internal and external efficacy, the internal form having to do with *feeling* efficacious and the external with *objective* accomplishments. Their data show a clear and significant relationship between participation in the neighborhood councils and both forms of efficacy. Relevant to knowing how to act in order to be efficacious, these authors found "that participation in face-to-face activities is highly associated with increased knowledge of local governance" (274).

Finally, consistent with the importance of the new institutional innovations represented by neighborhood councils, the authors found that "the correlations between knowledge and the level of community participation are consistently higher in the more structured than in the less structured participation cities" (275). The establishment of new institutional structures for participation at the neighborhood level is of crucial importance since they appear to yield greater participation, which, in turn, reduces destructive conflict and produces greater efficacy and political knowledge. There appears to be no similar evidence for any innovations at the state and federal levels that have had such significant salutary effects.

This kind of civic institutional innovation has now spread to a number of American cities, including Seattle, Washington; Columbus and Dayton, Ohio; New York City; Portland, Oregon; Minneapolis and St. Paul, Minnesota; Birmingham, Alabama; Los Angeles, California; and a number of others.[7]

THE CASE OF LOS ANGELES: A GRAND EXPERIMENT IN INSTITUTIONAL REFORM

An extended treatment of Los Angeles is included here because the governance reforms adopted there in a new city charter in 1999 represented a major step in the development of these neighborhood-level civic engagement institutions to larger-scale urban areas. The system established there was the first in a major metropolis that attempted to create formal links to communities intended primarily for participation in governance rather than the decentralized delivery of services. This innovation was inspired by the work of Berry, Portney, and Thomson and represents one of those relatively rare instances of social science scholarship leading directly to major changes in government.[8] Los Angeles had experienced growing sentiment for secession from the city by the San Fernando Valley, which was subsequently joined by Hollywood, and the Los Angeles harbor area that included San Pedro and Wilmington. These subareas of Los Angeles had felt for years that the city had gladly accepted their tax money but very reluctantly provided needed public services. They felt alienated from the distant city hall government and distrustful of its leaders. The idea of neighborhood councils that seemed to have worked well in the medium-sized cities studied by Berry and colleagues emerged in the hearings on creating a new city charter as the item that attracted the most intense and widespread interest among residents of the city. Members of the charter reform commissions and the city council saw the creation of neighborhood councils as a way to head off the secession movements.

With broad support, a new charter was adopted by the voters in June 1999 mandating that a citywide system of neighborhood councils be organized from the grass roots up, allowing for considerable variation in form, structure, and size of the councils. People in each community were required to identify their own boundaries, design their own bylaws, adopt their own systems of financial accountability, and then request certification from the city Board of Neighborhood Commissioners. This appears to be the most formalized experiment in providing civic engagement at the grass roots that has been officially connected to the governance process. One requirement imposed from above is that each of the eighty-nine neighborhood councils must include all stakeholders within its community—that is, those who live, work, or own property within the specified area.[9] Each council initially received $50,000 annually to help support its work; that has now been lowered to $45,000 under the pressure of the current financial crisis.[10]

The Los Angeles neighborhood council system reflects the governance perspective of the late 1980s up to the present. This current institutional innovation orientation of civic engagement in the United States is still playing out, and it is unclear where it will lead. Berry, Portney, and Thomson (1993) have demonstrated the general effectiveness of these experiments in facilitating civic engagement in small to medium-sized cities. However, the results are not yet clear with respect to how this approach will work in large metropolitan complexes such as New York and Los Angeles. The research on the Los Angeles system shows mixed results. Some neighborhood councils are well organized and function reasonably, well while others are less successful. The major problems faced by the councils include difficulty in recruiting the participation of immigrants, renters, and young people. They vary considerably in the extent to which they reflect the composition of their constituents in the community and, therefore, in the extent to which they are perceived as legitimate representative bodies. Many of the councils need help in building their capacity to deal with city administrative agencies and legislative processes.

The Civic Engagement Initiative (CEI), originally named the Neighborhood Participation Project, at the University of Southern California School of Policy, Planning, and Development conducted extensive research on the Los Angeles neighborhood council system for ten years (1996–2006) as it was debated, established in the 1999 charter, and developed through its first seven years of implementation. More than twenty scholarly journal articles, two PhD dissertations, and a series of policy briefs have been published on this research. (See the CEI Web site at www.usc-cei.org for a listing of these publications.) The main summative evaluation, available on the Web site, has been published as a policy brief by the CEI under the auspices of the Urban Initiative at the University of Southern California. It is titled, "Toward Community Engagement in City Governance: Evaluating Neighborhood Council Reform in Los Angeles" (Musso et al. 2007). The major findings at that point in 2006 were the following:

1. A citywide system of operating neighborhood councils had been successfully established during the five years since the Los Angeles Department of Neighborhood Empowerment was fully functioning under the new charter provision, with an implementing ordinance, and a specific plan in place. That was attributable to the enormous outpouring of energy and time by the people of Los Angeles, who volunteered countless hours doing the hard work of organizing their neighborhoods and preparing the required certification documents. Contrary to the myth that the people are apathetic and uninterested in participation, the residents of Los Angeles were eager to engage in the difficult process of organizing neighborhood councils even before they were approved. Unfortunately, the city was much less forthcoming with its support, staff and funding to assist those volunteers in accomplishing such an enormous task. More than eighty neighborhood councils had been certified by that time, seventy-four of which had accomplished the difficult task of electing boards and beginning the work of representing their communities to the city. Although there was substantial variation among the councils, the average number of constituents was thirty-eight thousand and the average board consisted of twenty-one members, most holding monthly meetings with committee work going on between full board meetings.

2. Based on surveys of the boards, it is clear that most of those participating in the organizing process are not newcomers to civic activity but people who have been relatively active in community and political life in their areas and the city. The board members are "more likely than neighborhood residents to be white, wealthy, highly educated, and homeowners" (Musso et al. 2007, 7). This was not unexpected given the resources, time, and commitment necessary to accomplish the required organizing. However, it does mean that the council boards may not reflect the demographic profiles of their communities and may not accurately reflect the views of their constituents. The CEI report cautions against focusing too narrowly on the inadequate degree of this kind of descriptive representation by the councils. Deficiencies of this kind in the composition of council boards do not necessarily indicate their inability to act on behalf of their communities. Berry, Portney, and Thomson found that the existence of neighborhood councils in the cities they studied increased trust in the municipal governance process even among those who did not participate but knew the councils existed.

3. The focus on the complex certification and board election processes may have drained energy away from outreach to the communities the councils represent, thus producing the lack of adequate representation identified in item 2. From the beginning of the organizing process there was a tendency to confuse outreach with organizing. Outreach involves the distribution of information through flyers, e-mail, posters in prominent locations, notices in community newspapers, and similar means of notifying people of the new councils. Organizing requires personal contact

in addition to the dissemination of information to persuade people to participate and to create social capital by establishing bonds of trust. In the early years there was insufficient organizing and too much reliance on outreach, perhaps due to the drain of resources devoted to the certification process. In some cases this has created a deficit in social capital that can be invested in the governance process.

4. It was assumed by the political leadership of the city that the creation of the councils would be a way of more effectively connecting the people to the governance process, thereby heading off secession by reducing distrust of government. However, during the early years the anticipated interaction between the neighborhood councils and city officials was slow getting started. This was mainly because the city was slow initiating some of the mechanisms that would encourage this interaction, such as the early notification system to let people know of planned city activity in their communities and the participatory budget mechanisms to involve citizens in the development of the annual city budget. Also, some elected officials had not fully embraced the neighborhood councils and tended to keep them at arm's length. The CEI study of the development of contacts between city officials and neighborhood councils showed that it "remained stagnant between our 2003 and 2006 surveys" (8). With respect to engagement with the city bureaucracy, most of those agencies were still dominated by personnel with the old Progressive-era technical professional role identities. They tended to see the new councils not as assets, but rather as annoying distractions from their main work.

5. The people of Los Angeles appear to have felt empowered by the creation of the neighborhood council system within a relatively short time, even though the city's performance had actually changed little. The CEI study reports that "the good news is that compared to 1998—the year before Charter reform was adopted—Angelenos feel better about the direction of the City and, in particular, the direction of their neighborhoods" (12). The subjectivity of this "feeling" of empowerment should not be dismissed lightly since it appears to be motivating people to continue pursuing more responsive engagement with the city.

Overall, the neighborhood councils seem to be developing the capacity to engage the city more actively and effectively since those early years, but there is considerable variation among them. During the charter hearing process, the Neighborhood Participation Project offered consistent advice to all parties that a "grand experiment" of this magnitude would take many years of work and development to create a neighborhood council system that could be expected to work well. At this point it is not clear how effectively the majority are engaging the city, but from time to time in recent years the councils have flexed their collective muscles in ways that suggest they are making considerable progress. The current mayor, Antonio Villaraigosa, has not offered strong support for the neighborhood councils, and when he tried to reduce the annual budget allocation to each council of $45,000 by about 75 percent as a way of dealing with the city's 2009 budget crisis, he learned quickly that the councils were able to muster strong support from across the city very quickly for retaining their allocations intact. The mayor backed down rapidly in the face of citywide opposition. Two similar citywide actions by the councils have concerned rate setting by the Los Angeles Department of Water and Power and an attempt by the Los Angeles Police Department to begin charging fees for their responses to burglar alarms.

Several formal and informal elements of the system have emerged that have helped in building the capacity of the councils for collective action, sharing of information, and engaging the administrative agencies of the city. Regional and citywide networks have developed over recent years that serve the purposes of information sharing and collective action. The CEI report cites the existence of a "Citywide Alliance of Neighborhood Councils" (www.allncs.org) that meets regularly with city officials; "the Los Angeles Neighborhood Council Congress, the Valley,

Harbor and Northeast Alliances, and other issue- or identity-oriented networks." The report concludes that "these various neighborhood networks have increased the flow of information among community activists in the city's many sub-regions" (7). Since that report was published, "the Citywide Issues Group" that is oriented toward collective action has emerged (http://www.lancissues.org). A newsletter published by neighborhood council leaders that began in hard copy during the charter reform process as *Charter Watch* is now widely distributed in digital form as *CityWatch* and provides a regular flow of information about city and neighborhood council activities (www.citywatchla.com).

GOVERNANCE AND THE ADMINISTRATIVE STATE

In addition to institutional innovations, effective and sustained civic governance currently requires processes for engaging the administrative state. In the medium-sized cities studied by Berry, Portney, and Thomson, this is worked out neighborhood by neighborhood as the need arises. That approach is much less effective in larger metropolitan complexes since the administrative agencies are so large and therefore tend to be more insular. In cities like Los Angeles that were heavily influenced by the Progressive reform movement, these bureaucracies have been left to their own professional technical devices for decades and have become nearly impenetrable. Opening them up to diverse communities with different needs and preferences—in effect democratizing the administrative state—is not easy.

As the neighborhood councils came online in significant numbers in the early 2000s and got beyond the certification and board election steps, they turned their attention to service-delivery problems, and thus to the city departments and agencies. With a few notable exceptions, they encountered disinterest and resistance from the city bureaucracy. The CEI launched the Collaborative Learning Project (CLP) in 2003 to develop processes for establishing neighborhood council–city department working relationships.[11] The intention was to test the viability of collaborative, as opposed to earlier adversarial, approaches to these relationships. A process called "Learning and Design Forums" (L&D) was developed with the following key features:

1. One or more neighborhood councils and a single city department are selected to participate in a deliberative process over a period of several months concerning how public services will be delivered to meet the needs and preferences of the council area(s).
2. The selected council(s) and department are recruited through meetings with top management and council board members to explain the L&D process and gain formal commitment to participate.
3. The council(s) and department select participants as official representatives of their organizations.
4. Each group of participants meets to develop a statement about their experience over recent years in working with the other.
5. Three half-day sessions approximately one month apart are convened with the participants to deliberate over the contents of a written memo of understanding about service delivery as the key product of the sessions. The first session begins with presentations of the statements from step 4 above.
6. Each session is led by a professional facilitator with the main objective of developing a memo of understanding, but the ability and freedom to work with the required flexibility to assist each group of participants through the steps appropriate for its style and needs. This allows the action research team to sit on the sidelines, observe, and take notes.

7. Homework is agreed to by both agency and neighborhood council representatives at the end of each L&D session. This often takes the form of research, drafting proposals for the memo, seeking advice from constituents, and similar tasks. Sometimes this is done separately and at other times in joint task committees.

8. Surveys are administered before the first session and between sessions to assess the participants' views of the other side, including their responsiveness, trustworthiness, and willingness to work collaboratively. Participants are also asked to assess the performance of the facilitator and the overall progress of the sessions. A transcript of the notes on the overall flow of each session is sent out to participants between sessions for comment and correction.

9. Each session is debriefed with the facilitator and the research team immediately following its conclusion to determine strategy for the next session and any other interventions that may be needed.

The experience has been that this is a useful and effective model for moving toward opening up and democratizing the way administrative agencies work with people in communities. However, it was found that several elements are necessary to make the process successful:

1. A professional facilitator who has no vested interest beyond a successful working relationship between councils and agencies is essential. Considerable skill is required to break through the role definitions people bring to the sessions, resolve conflict, and maintain a focus.

2. The process works best when groups of three or four geographically continuous councils work together with one administrative agency. This provides a more diverse range of participants and establishes a geographic area of sufficient size to be more practical for an agency to address.

3. The inclusion of elected officials or their representatives is essential. Both neighborhood council and city department representatives appear to take the process more seriously when city council and mayoral staff members are present as observers. Also, it is important that elected officials not view the L&D process as something that might be threatening to or subversive of their authority, but constructive and collaborative with them.

4. A written memo of understanding to be signed by both sides provides a working focus for a product to be created by the end of the L&D process. It is a way of clarifying in a sustainable way what has been agreed to by both parties, who will take on particular tasks and determine how they will be done, deadlines for reports and meetings, changes in service delivery modes and types, and any other details that are part of the outcome of the L&D process.

FROM TECHNIQUES AND AD HOC PROJECTS TO CITIZEN-CENTERED CIVIC ENGAGEMENT

This institutional reform approach at the local level reflects well what is being called "citizen-centered" civic engagement. In a seminal study led by Cynthia Gibson in 2006, entitled "Citizens at the Center: A New Approach to Civic Engagement,"[12] the author argues that there is a shift toward a new approach to civic engagement that needs further development. This new emphasis is away from particular participatory techniques, specific projects, and particular problems to a citizen-centered approach to civic engagement. Citizen-centered civic engagement focuses primarily on the following:[13]

1. Cultural change instead of short-term solutions and outcomes. Gibson argues that the lack of a deeply rooted culture of civic engagement is the most fundamental problem rather than helping citizens influence the outcome of some particular policy issue or learn some new participatory technique. There are numerous techniques but an inadequate culture of engagement to sustain and effectively employ them.

2. Providing opportunities for "people to form and promote their own decisions, build capacities for self-government, and promote open-ended civic processes." Gibson maintains that this approach is contrasted with offering specific focused opportunities for citizens to "plug into" projects, events, techniques, and exercises "driven by outside experts, professionals, organizations, or those external to the community."

3. Approaches that are "pluralistic and nonpartisan." Building a culture of engagement requires interaction with diverse people holding a variety of beliefs and political perspectives. Deliberation using an array of techniques to create collaboration across partisan philosophical commitments and oriented toward some greater good is required to ground a culture of engagement that transcends attachment to some partisan viewpoint. Practice at that kind of collaboration can support all kinds of problem solving.

4. Transcending ideological silos. One of the things that repels citizens from collaborative participation is suspicion that some partisan political perspective is behind an engagement effort. Citizen-centered civic engagement is oriented toward the needs and concerns of citizens rather than the advancement of a partisan agenda. It is driven by problems and needs rather than political commitments.

5. Going beyond "the perennial and wearisome debate over which is more important or lacking—'service or politics'—that tends to dominate public discussions about civic engagement in the United States." Gibson argues that this is a false dichotomy that offers a simplistic choice. She maintains that there is a very large and complex territory between the two that connects them into a continuum that bridges volunteering at one end and voting at the other.

6. Doing more than just talking. The tendency to romanticize deliberation as the main element in democratic civic engagement, according to Gibson, may cause us to ignore the importance of achieving outcomes. Deliberation is an important part of the democratic self-governing process, but process sometimes overcomes product. People need to see that deliberating will lead to tangible results. Assuming that all problems can be addressed through talk seems "naïve, elitist, or simply unfeasible."

7. Understanding that citizen-centered approaches "do not replace politics or other democratic processes." They are not a substitute for government and political institutions. Gibson quotes David Mathews, president of the Kettering Foundation, as asserting that "organic, citizen-based democracy is not an alternative form of politics like direct democracy; it is the foundation for democratic institutions and representative government." Civic engagement at the grass roots provides a basis for connecting individual citizens to the process of representative democracy. It is the way citizens form collective opinions that can make representation work.

DELIBERATIVE PROCESSES FOR CIVIC ENGAGEMENT INSTITUTIONS

The new institutional reforms that have created ongoing permanent mechanisms for self-organized and self-directed civic engagement seem to best exemplify this citizen-centered civic engagement. These neighborhood-level citizen institutions represent a very significant shift away from episodic citizen participation provided and controlled by public officials and government agencies often referred to in the past as "citizen participation." Efforts at institutional reform have attempted to move civic engagement from the ad hoc adversarial struggle of the 1960s and the government-initiated mandated participation of the 1970s to sustained participation in the governance process that seeks collaboration, even if there is conflict from time to time in the midst of officially sustained participation.

This is not the only form of contemporary civic engagement, but it is the most significant new dimension of the process. However, once these new systems are created, they need to make use of an increasingly wide array of options for techniques for deliberation and collaboration. Taken in isolation from sustained and embedded civic engagement channels, these methods amount to little more than tools for political and administrative dominance. However, employed by these new citizen-driven institutions, they may be seen as instruments for citizen empowerment. They are important parts of systemic approaches to civic engagement. New institutional structures alone are not sufficient to create effective civic engagement; processes for deliberation toward resolving conflict, reaching consensus, and making decisions are required.

The L&D process developed by the CLP has been discussed here as one example of techniques for deliberation and consensus building. There are many other specific techniques that represent innovations in the governance *process* that could effectively complement the innovations in governance *structure*, most of which are well-known among civic engagement specialists. These include the Kettering Foundation's National Issues Forum approach, the work of the National Policy Consensus Center, Choice Work Dialogues, Citizens Juries, Consensus Conferences, Study Circles, Deliberative Polling, and Citizen Assemblies. (See Lukensmeyer and Torres, 2006 for detailed review and discussions of these techniques and processes.) There are also electronic media such as Web sites, blogs, and social networking systems that can be effectively used within civic engagement institutions. For purposes of this chapter, three particularly promising approaches that could be employed effectively in the new local government institutions are reviewed briefly. The first is widely known in the United States, but the second two are less known here and taken from international experience.

1. America Speaks

This is the largest-scale and best-developed of the new approaches. America Speaks (AS), founded by Carolyn Lukensmeyer in 1995 as a nonprofit organization, conducts deliberation events that range in size from those with fewer than a hundred participants to some that involve thousands. These deliberations sometimes focus on specific local concerns and on other occasions engage broad national policy issues. The key to the approach employed by AS is that it "integrates state-of-the-art technology with small-group, face-to-face dialogue to allow thousands of people to deliberate simultaneously about important issues and come to shared priorities" (Lukensmeyer 2008, p. 1). Using combinations of multiple facilitated small groups in one or several locations, each member of which has a laptop linked to others at the table and to a central server, with theme managers who circulate among the tables and post information on large central video screens, information is exchanged and issues debated. AS has available more than four thousand trained facilitators who skillfully lead discussion and feed the ongoing viewpoints and information into a central system for ordering and display to the entire body of participants.

The AS approach blends together a combination of face-to-face discussion with anonymous information exchange similar to that which occurs in the Delphi technique developed at the Rand Corporation several decades ago. The value of face-to-face discussion is that it includes all of the nonverbal elements of that kind of deliberation, such as expressions of emotional intensity and of opposition or support; the value of anonymous exchange of information is that it excludes the kind of "noise" or emotional distraction that occurs in face-to-face discussion due to personal attributes that may create attractions, aversions, or biases and may block or distort communication (Helmer-Hirschberg 1966; Helmer-Hirschberg and Rescher 1960).

AS has successfully conducted deliberation events dealing with a wide range of topics and in a variety of settings. It has conducted annual sessions to engage hundreds of citizens from the local elected councils in the development of the Washington, D.C. budget. AS provided a deliberative process for approximately five thousand participants in one large hall focused on how to redevelop the site of the World Trade Center in New York City, which was destroyed in the terrorist attacks on September 11, 2001. In 2008, AS produced twenty different deliberation projects across the nation ranging from fifty members in the Grantmakers for Children, Youth and Families Summit in Washington, D.C., to four hundred in New Mexico's Children Cabinet Town Hall Meeting in Albuquerque, New Mexico, to two thousand participants in the National Performing Arts Convention in Denver, to twelve thousand people involved in a deliberation for Equal Voice for America's Families in Birmingham, Chicago, and Los Angeles. Thus, there is a great deal of flexibility and adaptability in the AS process (Lukensmeyer 2008). It employs technology, human facilitators, feedback processes from table groups to the full assembly, and opportunities for conflicting views to be identified and examined. AS designs its deliberative events to fit particular local situations and problems using the appropriate combinations of various types of resources.

Other uses of electronic communication media are also emerging but are still of secondary importance and have complementary roles to play similar to those of the other engagement processes mentioned earlier. The Obama campaign, and its use of Web sites, blogs, e-mail, and social networking sites, is often offered as an example of the effectiveness of these tools. They are useful for disseminating information, mobilizing people for events and actions, and to a limited extent sharing opinions about policy; however, since this chapter focuses on citizen-driven administration these techniques are most effectively used to complement the processes of local civic engagement institutions. The Obama campaign clearly saw the value of linking these process tools to their organizations on the ground, state by state and city by city nationwide. Community organization strategies that utilize these tools can be powerful. However, electronic process tools may be useful in stimulating movements and actions, as in the case of Iran following the questionable presidential election of 2009 with its use of Twitter and Facebook, but institutions are required for governance using these and other process techniques. Otherwise, they are more appropriately understood as election campaign techniques rather than instruments of civic engagement.

2. Participatory Videography

Sometimes approaches developed in one setting can be effectively adapted for use in others that are very different. That is the case with participatory production of videos by communities. The use of self-images that are created and controlled by members of a community through digital videography can be a powerful technique for generating deliberation, building support for certain policies or policy changes, and communicating with administrative agencies. It can be used effectively by any community, but especially those without strong resources in written communication.

The American Refugee Committee (ARC), an international nonprofit organization, has been employing participatory videography in refugee communities in Rwanda, Uganda, South Sudan, Liberia, and Thailand for four years with considerable success. ARC has been conducting programs dealing with sexually transmitted diseases, and gender-based violence in refugee camps since 2004. In 2006 ARC began working in partnership with Communication for Change (C4C), a nonprofit community video-production organization, to build video production capacity into refugee communities.[14] Named "Through Our Eyes," the project was intended to empower refugees by giving them the skill, through two weeks of training, to be able to produce their own videos. With self-produced video images they have been able to depict the problems of violence against women and girls through their own eyes as they experience them. Women tell their own stories about the abuse to which they are frequently subjected, and men talk about how they view those practices. These compelling videos, with legitimacy grounded in their own experience by their own people, are then employed by their own refugee leaders to generate deliberation about these problems, surface and address conflicts, and talk about behavior changes that are required. These videos also have become a means of projecting to organizations such as the U.S. Agency for International Development how the refugees themselves define their problems and the resources needed to resolve them. This is citizen-oriented civic engagement in a deeply compelling form.

The same videographic techniques might be used by communities within the United States, to communicate first with their own residents, but also with their own city governments about their problems and needs. Digital videography equipment has made it relatively easy and inexpensive to capture compelling images of everything from traffic congestion to housing dilapidation, to gang graffiti, to potholes in the streets, to trees that need trimming, to eyesores and empty spaces that call for attention. Videos can vividly depict both problems and opportunities. People who will never read a written report may watch a video. Since the participation of young people is lacking in neighborhood councils and similar organizations, this kind of image communication may be one way to stimulate their interest and engage their skills. Participatory videos have great untapped potential for enhancing citizen-centered civic engagement at the local level in the United States. One can imagine a municipal Web site on which videos from neighborhoods throughout the city might be found depicting through the eyes of the residents how they view the needs for city services, their perspectives on the built environment and the resident population, as well as planning alternatives. These videos could be accessed by city agencies and other communities to better understand the needs and viewpoints around the city. These could be easily updated annually, or even more often.

3. Participatory Mapping

This technique, also developed originally for use with nonurban populations in other parts of the world, involves the creation and control of self-images of communities by their own members, similar to participatory videography, but requiring no special equipment.[15] In this case, the technology is much simpler and involves the making of maps by communities to depict their own relationship to the space in which they live, again as seen through their own eyes. Kevin Lynch ([1960] 1965) used cognitive mapping techniques in cities as a research tool to identify the most significant elements of the built environment of cities as seen through the eyes of their residents.[16] Participatory mapping is used currently with communities in developing countries as an engagement or advocacy tool. Instead of relying on experts to define a community's map, residents do it for themselves. Residents meet together to talk about what important features of their community should be represented symbolically on a map they produce together as a way of asserting how they view their community. Both assets, such as groves of trees, parks, schools, businesses, libraries, and hospitals, and problems, such as toxic sites, illegal dumping areas, areas of high crime, failing roads, nuisance businesses, and unsafe intersections, might be included in a community's assessment of its situation. Creating the maps and getting reactions to them stimulate discussion among members of a community about how they view themselves.

For example, it might be richly enlightening, both to the neighborhood councils and to the city agencies involved in the CLP mentioned earlier, if each side created maps that represent how they view the participating communities. Exchanging these symbolic representations might well generate discussion indirectly that would be too sensitive to articulate directly in verbal descriptions. A new map reflecting collaboration in planning public service delivery might be another useful product of the CLP negotiations to accompany a memo of understanding. Discussion and negotiation around symbolic representations such as maps may have the power to engage people with greater intensity and imagination than words alone. A combination of participatory videos, participatory maps, and the kind of technological tools employed by America Speaks could increase interest among a broader range of the population than is now typically represented in civic engagement institutions such as neighborhood councils.

CONCLUSIONS

The cutting edge of civic engagement for the foreseeable future will be in developing new institutional structures for engaging citizens in governance in a more continuous and sustained fashion. That will require creativity and work to design these new institutions in ways that are appropriate for each local context. Those who lead them will need also to develop skills in the civic engagement processes that help shape the life of those institutions. Structure and processes must complement each other. Beyond the local level, the next major challenge is to create new institutional structures that will link citizens to state and federal governments.

President Barack Obama has called upon civic engagement organizations around the nation to offer recommendations about what his administration should do to encourage civic participation. Based on the line of argument developed in this chapter, it is suggested that the following elements be included in a national strategy on civic engagement.

1. A White House Office on Public Engagement has already been established by President Obama on May 11, 2009 (White House, Office of the Press Secretary 2009). That office needs to be enhanced with direct linkages to state-level liaison people, and in some cases key people in the major metropolitan areas of the nation, especially those responsible for civic engagement institutions such as neighborhood councils and similar structures. The challenge for the administration is to develop civic engagement institutions appropriate for federal governance that are the equivalents of those emerging at the local level.

2. National leadership by the White House Office on Public Engagement is needed to help with capacity building and consultation among citizens, elected officials, and administrative agencies if representative democracy is to be opened to more direct engagement with the people, and the administrative state is to be democratized along the lines suggested in the discussion of the Collaborative Learning Project. Elected officials need to learn to work with citizens beyond election campaigns. Public bureaucracies will have to do business differently by reaching out to include the citizenry rather than resisting their participation. This will require federal grants and training opportunities to develop civic engagement skills and new national civic participation institutions.

3. The White House Office on Public Engagement should begin by sponsoring a series of large-scale deliberation events around major national policy initiatives to involve citizens in the policy development process rather than after policy is approaching final form. Nothing is so transparently a sham than calling for public comment with great fanfare after elected officials, administrative agencies, and interest groups (sometimes called the "policy iron triangle") have already been working together on a legislative proposal for months or years. The means for conducting these deliberation events is already well developed and working. The new institutions that ought to be linked to these processes exist at the local level in some places, but need to be created where they do not. New institutional forms need to be designed for connecting local engagement institutions with various federal policy initiatives.

4. Incentives should be provided by offering priority points in federal grant making for cities that have created institutions such as neighborhood councils to engage citizens in communities in collaborative governance. Continuing to funnel federal grants into existing institutions of representative government will do less to encourage more direct civic engagement than if there are direct participation systems in place. If money is not connected to new ways of running our democracy, little is likely to change.

Significant progress in democratizing the administrative state through citizen-driven public administration is now within our grasp. The groundswell of interest in collaborative governance provides the larger context within which institutional reforms that turn the table on the Progressives may be possible. It is essential that we keep our eyes at that level of change in civic engagement, reaching for robust and sustained engagement of our people that will fulfill the promise of democratic governance for our time. Techniques come and go, but institutions abide and empower.

NOTES

1. Much of this material was used directly or adapted from portions of Terry L. Cooper, Thomas A. Bryer, and Jack W. Meek, "Citizen-Centered Collaborative Public Management," special issue, *Public Administration Review* 66 (2006): 76–88. Permission was granted by the editor in chief of *Public Administration Review* and my coauthors.

2. For a good introductory text, see James Creighton's *The Public Participation Handbook* (2005). Another recent how-to manual is Bob Graham's *America, The Owner's Manual* (2010).

3. This argument about these two perspectives has been developed in detail in Terry L. Cooper, *An Ethic of Citizenship for Public Administration* (1991).

4. See, for example, the treatment of alienation among the citizenry in chapters 1–2 of Cheryl King and Camilla Stivers, *Government Is Us* (1998).

5. I experienced this problem personally during my years as a community organizer for the United Methodist Church in the mid- to late 1960s in East Harlem, New York, and the Pico-Union neighborhood of Los Angeles. In Los Angeles, the low-income areas of the city were represented by no more than five members of the fifteen-member city council. Anytime their interests were at odds with the rest of the city, they lost.

6. The recent work by C. Sirianni, *Investing in Democracy: Engaging Citizens in Collaborative Governance* (2009), is one major example. A new comparative work on collaborative governance is Jung, Mazmanian, and Tang, eds., *Collaborative Governance in the United States and Korea* (2009).

7. Unfortunately, there are no comparative evaluations of neighborhood council systems across the United States that would provide a basis for identifying the best institutional forms for this approach. A problem in carrying out such a study is the importance of context in determining "best practices" in particular settings. *The Rebirth of Urban Democracy* (Berry et al. 1993) comes closest but focuses on neighborhood councils in only five medium-sized cities and was not intended to do that kind of analysis.

8. *The Rebirth of Urban Democracy* was read by a city council chief deputy who began to circulate it to others in the Los Angeles city government, including his boss and other city council staff members.

9. This means that one might be a stakeholder in more than one neighborhood council and that all residents, whether U.S. citizens, legal residents, or undocumented people, are eligible.

10. The 1999 charter provisions, the implementing ordinance, the plan for the system, and other information about the Department of Neighborhood Empowerment, the Board of Neighborhood Commissioners, specific councils, and other related matters can be found at the Department of Neighborhood Empowerment Web site: http://www.lacityneighborhoods.com/.

11. Terry L. Cooper and Thomas A. Bryer, "Collaboration Between Los Angeles City Departments and Neighborhood Councils: Findings and Recommendations from the Collaborative Learning Project" (policy brief published and distributed to neighborhood council leaders, city agency heads, elected officials, and interested scholars by the University of Southern California Urban Initiative, 2007). This policy brief is available online at http://www.usc-cei.org/?url=cbp.php. The full findings of the CLP to date are summarized on page 3 of that document. More detailed analysis and findings can be found in the articles by Cooper,

Bryer, Meek, and Kathi in various combinations as coauthors and authors in the reference list at the end of this chapter. The CLP was funded by the Hewlett Foundation, the James Irvine Foundation, and the USC Urban Initiative.

12. This report is based on interviews with "scores of leaders in the service/civic engagement field, as well as those outside this domain; culling the findings of scholarly research; and synthesizing numerous mainstream articles, websites, and publications" (Gibson 2006, 1).

13. The quotations from this section are drawn from pages 9–11 of the report.

14. See the articles by Lowen (2008), Molony, Konie, and Goodsmith (2007), and Cooper and Ward (2009).

15. See, for example, International Fund for Agricultural Development, "Good Practices in Participatory Mapping" (2009).

16. His best-known work, *Image of the City,* was based on cognitive mapping exercises in three major U.S. cities: Los Angeles, Boston, and Jersey City.

REFERENCES

Aberbach, J.D. 1981. *Bureaucrats and Politicians in Western Democracies.* Cambridge, MA: Harvard University Press.

Advisory Commission on Intergovernmental Relations. 1979. *Citizen Participation in the American Federal System.* Washington, DC: Advisory Commission on Intergovernmental Relations.

Alinsky, S.D. 1949. *John L. Lewis: An Unauthorized Biography.* New York: Putnam.

———. 1969. *Reveille for Radicals.* New York: Vintage Books.

———. 1971. *Rules for Radicals: A Practical Primer for Realistic Radicals.* New York: Vintage Books.

Arnstein, S. 1969. A ladder of citizen participation. *Journal of the American Institute of Planners* 35 (4): 216–224.

Bentley, A.F. 1908. *The Process of Government: A Study of Social Pressures.* Chicago: University of Chicago Press.

Berry, J.M., K.E. Portney, and K. Thomson. 1993. *The Rebirth of Urban Democracy.* Washington, DC: Brookings Institution Press.

Boyte, H.C. 1980. *The Backyard Revolution: Understanding the New Citizen Movement.* Philadelphia: Temple University Press.

Bryer, T., and T.L. Cooper. 2007. Challenges in enhancing responsiveness in neighborhood governance. *Public Performance and Management Review* 31 (2): 191–214.

Cleveland, H. 1988. Theses of a new reformation: The social fallout of science 300 years after Newton. *Public Administration Review* 48 (3): 681–686.

Cooper, C., and L. Ward. 2009. Partnerships for change. *Monday Developments* (April): 28.

Cooper, T.L. 1979. The hidden price tag: Participation costs and health planning. *American Journal of Public Health* 69 (4): 368–374.

———. 1984. Citizenship and professionalism in public administration. *Public Administration Review* 44 (special issue): 143–151.

———. 1991. *An Ethic of Citizenship for Public Administration.* Englewood Cliffs, NJ: Prentice Hall.

———. 2005. Introduction. In *Neighborhood Government: The Local Foundations of Political Life,* by Milton Kotler. Lanham, MD: Lexington Books.

Cooper, T.L., and T.A. Bryer. 2007. William Robertson: Exemplar of politics and public management rightly understood. *Public Administration Review* 67 (5): 816–823.

Cooper, T.L., T.A. Bryer, and J.W. Meek. 2005. *The Public Participation Handbook: Making Better Decisions Through Citizen Involvement.* San Francisco: Wiley.

———. 2006. Citizen-centered collaborative public management. *Public Administration Review* 66 (special issue): 76–88.

———. 2008. Outcomes achieved through citizen-centered collaborative public management. In *Big Ideas in Collaborative Public Management,* ed. R. O'Leary and L. Bingham, 211–229. Armonk, NY: M.E. Sharpe.

Creighton, J.L. 1995. Trends in the field of public participation in the United States. *Interact: The Journal of Public Participation* 1 (1): 7–23.

———. 2005. *The Public Participation Handbook.* San Francisco: Jossey-Bass.

Follett, M.P. [1918] 1965. *The New State: Group Organization, the Solution of Popular Government.* Gloucester, MA: Peter Smith.

Frederickson, H.G. 1971. Toward a new public administration. In *Toward a New Public Administration: The Minnowbrook Perspective,* ed. F. Marini, 309–331. Scranton, PA: Chandler.

Gibson, C.M. 2006. Citizens at the center: A new approach to civic engagement. Paper, Case Foundation, Washington, D.C.

Graham, B. 2010. *America, The Owner's Manual: Making Government Work for You.* Washington, DC: CQ Press.

Helmer-Hirschberg, O. 1966. *The Delphi Method for Systematizing Judgments About the Future.* Los Angeles: Institute of Government and Public Affairs, University of California.

Helmer-Hirschberg, O., and N.H. Rescher. 1960. *On the Epistemology of the Inexact Sciences.* Santa Monica, CA: Rand Corporation.

International Fund for Agricultural Development. 2009. Good practices in participatory mapping. A review prepared for the International Fund for Agricultural Development (IFAD). www.ifad.org/pub/map/PM_web.pdf (accessed August 20, 2010).

Jung, Y.D., D.A. Mazmanian, and S.Y. Tang, eds. 2009. *Collaborative Governance in the United States and Korea.* Seoul, Korea: Seoul National University Press.

Kathi, P.C., and Cooper, T.L. 2005. Democratizing the administrative state: Connecting neighborhood councils and city agencies. *Public Administration Review* 65 (5): 559–567.

———. 2008. Connecting neighborhood councils and city agencies: Trust building through the learning and design forum process. *Journal of Public Affairs Education* 13:617–630.

King, C.S., and C. Stivers. 1998. *Government Is Us: Public Administration in an Anti-Government Era.* Thousand Oaks, CA: Sage.

Kotler, M. 1969. *Neighborhood Government: The Local Foundations of Political Life.* New York: Bobbs-Merrill.

———. 2005. *Neighborhood Government: The Local Foundations of Political Life.* Rev. ed. Lanham, MD: Lexington Books.

Lowen, J.T. 2008. Through their eyes: Victims of gender-based violence fight back with video. *Utne Reader* (May–June): 34–35.

Lowi, T.J. 1969. *The End of Liberalism; Ideology, Policy, and the Crisis of Public Authority.* New York: W.W. Norton.

Lukensmeyer, C.J. 2008. *Transforming Governance Through Innovation: 2008 Program Report.* www.americaspeaks.org/_data/n_0001/resources/live/AS_Report_08.pdf.

Lukensmeyer, C.J., and H.T. Torres. 2006. *Public Deliberation: A Manager's Guide to Public Deliberation.* Washington, DC: IBM Center for the Business of Government.

Lynch, K. [1960] 1965. *Image of the City.* Cambridge, MA: MIT Press.

Marini, F., ed. 1971. *Toward a New Public Administration: The Minnowbrook Perspective.* Scranton, PA: Chandler.

Molony, T., Z. Konie, and L. Goodsmith. 2007. Through our eyes: Participatory video in West Africa. *Forced Migration Review* 27:26–27.

Musso, J., C. Weare, M. Elliott, A. Kitsuse, and E. Shiau. 2007. Toward community engagement in city governance: Evaluating neighborhood council reform in Los Angeles. Urban Policy Brief. Los Angeles: Civic Engagement Initiative, University of Southern California.

Parenti, M. 1974. *Democracy for the Few.* New York: St. Martin's Press.

Sirianni, C. 2009. *Investing in Democracy: Engaging Citizens in Collaborative Governance.* Washington, DC: Brookings Institution.

Tocqueville, de A. 2007. *Democracy in America.* New York: Norton.

Truman, D.B. 1951. *The Governmental Process: Political Interests and Public Opinion.* New York: Alfred A. Knopf.

Waldo, D. 1948. *The Administrative State.* New York: Ronald Press.

White House, Office of the Press Secretary. 2009. President Obama Launches Office of Public Engagement: A New Name, Mission for White House Liaison Office. Press release, May 11. www.whitehouse.gov/the_press_office/President-Obama-Launches-Office-of-Public-Engagement/.

CHAPTER 16

NETWORK THEORY AND PRACTICE IN PUBLIC ADMINISTRATION

Designing Resilience for Metropolitan Regions

LOUISE K. COMFORT, CLAYTON WUKICH, STEVE SCHEINERT, AND LEONARD J. HUGGINS

Metropolitan regions are undergoing significant changes that create greater interdependencies among governmental entities, nonprofit organizations, and private businesses in their shared service areas (Miller 2002; Rusk 2003). As populations in these regions have sought to increase regional economic development by spreading to suburbs, these policies have resulted in a concentration of low-income households in depressed neighborhoods in central cities (Downs 1994). The resulting shift in economic development has led to increased unemployment, impoverishment, crime and violence in the central cities, as well as a diminishing tax base, declining quality in public education, aging infrastructure, and an increased demand for governmental services to counter deteriorating social and economic conditions for the urban population (Downs 1994; Leavitt and Kiefer 2006). Yet, *perceived inefficiency* and *growing distrust* of governmental services (Barzelay 2001) have resulted in the reluctance of citizens to raise taxes needed to fund public services.

In older industrial regions, such as Allegheny County, Pennsylvania, population is decreasing, but *demand for services is still increasing,* due to high rates of unemployment, aging populations, and a declining tax base that funds urban services. Given these conditions, urban regions are becoming increasingly vulnerable to a range of threats (Cutter, Boruff, and Shirley 2003) that require innovative strategies in the design, delivery, and management of public services.

The consequence of these social, economic, infrastructural, and demographic changes is an evolution in administrative structures of urban regions. Where traditional administrative hierarchy had focused primarily on maintaining control over personnel and resources to ensure reasonable equity and accountability in managing public funds (Behn 1998), increasing demands for public services are requiring public agencies to find new ways of getting the work done (Behn 2001; Kettl 1993). Traditional administrative practice led to orderly performance in stable societies, but largely failed to adapt to changing conditions. In practice, ineffective hierarchical structures are giving way to informal methods of addressing shared problems among multiple entities in metropolitan regions (Bryson 2004; Frederickson and Smith 2003). These methods are leading to significant change in the administrative framework of urban regions. This chapter explores an approach to network theory and practice that may be used to develop resiliency in metropolitan governance.

DESIGNING RESILIENCE FOR METROPOLITAN REGIONS

Much of the professional debate regarding networks has centered on their capacity to absorb shocks and adapt to changing conditions more readily than hierarchical administrative structures. This capacity, termed *resilience,* has generated an outpouring of research and exploration to determine exactly what factors contribute to it and whether it can be developed systematically in complex environments exposed to risk. A working definition of resilience (Boin, Comfort, and Demchak (2010, chapter 2) is stated as follows: "Resilience is the capacity of a social system (e.g., an organization, city, or society) to proactively adapt to, and recover from, disturbances that are perceived within the system to fall outside the range of normal and expected disturbances."

Metropolitan regions are intrinsically complex. The scope and frequency of daily interactions among physical, engineered, social, and economic systems generate risk. In such environments, vulnerability in operational structures and processes may be reversed through self-organization, networked communication and collaboration, and continuous monitoring and review by experienced managers. In these complex settings, facilitating the search, exchange, and feedback processes characteristic of distributed cognition creates a productive working strategy for managing the interdependence of public, private, and nonprofit organizations (Comfort 2008). Risk reduction on a regional scale is fundamentally a governance process.

INFORMAL NETWORKS

Changes in administrative structure can be observed directly in the informal networks of action that have emerged among public, private, and nonprofit organizations (Feiock and Scholz 2010) to reduce urban risk and manage threats to public health and safety (Comfort, Mosse, and Znati 2009). These networks of action cross jurisdictional and disciplinary boundaries as communities search for effective mechanisms to mitigate shared exposure to risk, but are limited in resources and personnel. As expanding populations move into regions previously deemed unsafe (e.g., coastal zones, flood plains, canyons prone to wildland fires) or critical infrastructure deteriorates under heavy use and lack of maintenance, the demand for emergency services outstrips the capacity of particular communities to protect their populations (Morrow 1999). This situation creates a dilemma of increasing demand but diminishing capacity that compels public organizations to search for new means of engaging their communities in managing risk (Nakagawa and Shaw 2004). Ironically, the crucible of shared risk often compels disparate organizations to search for, and find, a common interest in public safety that allows them to overcome narrow interests and forge more collaborative means of providing essential public services for their communities (Dynes 2006).

The cumulative pattern of change in the economic, social, and political conditions of metropolitan regions over the last fifty years has created urban environments characterized by complex organizational and jurisdictional interactions, uncertainty in the outcomes of prescribed policies, and scarcity of resources to meet mounting public problems. These deteriorating conditions have fostered a lively and vigorous debate regarding the need for change in the design, delivery, and management of public services. If indeed change is needed, it also requires new methods of monitoring, measurement, and calibration of resources and attention to adapt policy and practice to the interdependent demands of urban regions.

NETWORK THEORY AND DEBATE

Multiple threads of theory and analysis weave through the debate on urban problems that are nested in the structure of intergovernmental policy and practice. A key thread is recognition of the declining capacity of government to manage effectively the growing complexity in the design and delivery of public services at any level of operation (Milward and Provan 1998). Milward and Provan term this decline the "hollow state" and provocatively acknowledge the decreasing capacity of government to cope with the growing demands of difficult, interdependent, and expensive issues in public administration. The option of contracting services to private or nonprofit agencies places government personnel at a deep disadvantage, if this decision is not informed by seasoned expertise and careful oversight. This option becomes even more problematic as these same public agencies face declining budgets and diminished ranks in personnel (Kettl 1993).

The disadvantages of contracting out governmental services can be countered, DiIulio (1994) argues, by developing strong principal/agent relationships that provide a coping mechanism for public agencies facing increased demands. Such relationships largely shift the burden of oversight and authority to the federal level. This practice has had the undesirable consequence of weakening subnational governments still further, as these agencies bear the brunt of increased demand for services without the personnel or expertise to manage them effectively (Bryson 2004).

The debate continued with a vigorous set of claims for addressing the seemingly intractable issues of managing the complex design and delivery of public services at multiple levels of jurisdictional operation and geographic location (Barzelay 2001). These claims led to the rise of new public management (NPM), which increased emphasis on monitoring and measurement of performance in the set of agencies involved in service delivery. The focus of management then shifted to tracking the information processes used by a lengthening chain of agencies (Pollitt 2003). In important but unexpected ways, the NPM approach created the basis for developing a focus on networked management of services that crossed sectoral boundaries.

The shift in focus to intersectoral networks, public/private partnerships, and joined-up government represents different approaches for coping with the realities of heterogeneous populations in urban regions. These realities include: increased access to information by citizens regarding governmental performance; conflicting goals among community groups; and the instabilities of economic performance in democratic societies (Schneider and Ingram 2005). Although the values of individual rights, social equity, and civic participation remain strong, the challenges of achieving this vision of a democratic society—in a highly differentiated, resource-constrained, public environment that is subject to random fluctuations caused by extreme events—are significant. Public agencies may choose strategies of action to cope with declining resources, such as postponing repair of basic infrastructure, but the random occurrence of a natural disaster may compel an entirely different allocation of budget and personnel in practice, with serious consequences for the community. The long-developing deterioration of a complex set of levees and pumps in the city of New Orleans foreshadowed the ensuing catastrophe of Hurricane Katrina and illustrates this dilemma. It is this tension between choice and randomness (Kauffman 1993) in managing public affairs that creates a context in which networked forms of organization that provide essential public services offer singular advantages in facilitating adaptation to changing conditions.

The central task of managing change, given the interaction between choice and randomness in the public arena, spurs the generation of complex forms of organization to meet public needs. For example, the spontaneous organization of community groups to rebuild damaged communities after disaster builds partnerships among affected residents that did not exist prior to the event (Phillips 2009). In these evolving settings, the capacity of one organization to serve as the intermediary among many organizations in transmitting information, resources, or expertise required to solve a specific problem will create a base of knowledge and experience for that organization that represents soft power, or centrality, in the network. The organization is, essentially, filling a 'structural hole' or gap in the network of organizations (Burt 1992) that may carry over into other areas of community practice long after the recovery from the initial event has stabilized.

Other threads in the debate include the tension between leadership and frontline personnel in generating change (Kelman 2005; Radin 2006). The focus on social capital as a means of overcoming the inherent uncertainty attendant in efforts to manage change has likely been romanticized rather than rigorously evaluated in most instances of social action. Social capital may indeed bridge gaps in understanding and experience among unlikely actors in unexpected situations and forge bonds of commitment among newfound partners to achieve a shared goal of civil security, but the measurement of its reliability and robustness over time remains questionable in dynamic environments.

The debate regarding strategies for managing change summarizes a set of conditions that acknowledges a shifting balance in authority and expertise among public, private, and nonprofit organizations. No longer do governmental agencies play the commanding role in terms of resources and expertise. Given the legal responsibility for the protection of lives, property, and continuity of operations in civil society as implied in the preamble of the U.S. Constitution (Tribe 1988, xxxi) public agencies are compelled to innovate and explore more effective forms of interaction with other actors in organized society. This dynamic has driven the public search for partnerships with other organizations, exemplified by George H.W. Bush (1988) in his call for a "thousand points of light" to support public service.

CHANGING THE INFORMATION INFRASTRUCTURE TO SUPPORT COORDINATED ACTION

The dynamics driving social, economic, and political change have had different degrees of impact on different population groups within metropolitan regions, creating gaps in equity and access to public services that generate social needs. Yet, significant advances in computational power, telecommunications, and the design of technical infrastructure have created the capacity for individuals and organizations to search for, and exchange, information over wide distances and diverse loci of operations to support coordinated action to meet those needs (Coakes, Willis, and Clarke 2002). These technical advances in communications that enable the timely exchange of information have altered irrevocably the organizational world. Public administration is based fundamentally on processes of decision making (Simon 1997), and assumes accurate, timely information as a basis for decision. Without access to timely, accurate information, public agencies are constrained in the actions they can reasonably take and limited by the cognitive capacity of human managers (Miller 1956), despite their good intentions or commitment to public values.

These technical advances do not diminish the political context of decision making in changing, uncertain environments (Boin et al. 2005), but they do make it easier to update and store information, disseminate information more widely, and trace decision processes over time. The changes in technical infrastructure are nonetheless related to the economic costs and benefits of implementing public policy. Benefits gained from reducing paperwork and time involved in communication and coordination by using information management and communication processes were touted by the Clinton administration in the 1990s as a major force in their *Reinventing Government* campaign (Kettl 1994). This campaign, established as a major priority in the Clinton administration and led by then vice president Al Gore, was designed in part to respond to the public reluctance to pay taxes for perceived inefficiencies in governmental practice. By incorporating effective uses of information technology into its management functions, the Reinventing Government program sought to increase efficiency, decrease costs, and improve performance in the administration of public programs. While considerable public attention was focused on this effort, the Clinton administration learned from experience that introducing information technology effectively into administrative processes involved more than buying computers and software. Rather, it meant redesigning the organizational processes by which agency personnel determined what data to collect, where and how it should be stored, who had access to it and when, as well as creating a staff of sociotechnical experts who understood the organizational functions of the agency sufficiently to design appropriate technical support for the staff (DiIulio and Kettl 1995).

The bold hopes of the Clinton administration to offset the costs of public administration by increasing the efficiency and timeliness of a diminished public service (U.S. Senate 1993) were largely not met, but this national experiment demonstrated the potential for reconsidering government as a sociotechnical system. While the tools approach advanced by Salamon (2002) and his coauthors focused largely on the financial instruments used to enact public programs and bring together public, private, and nonprofit organizations in the common enterprise of public service, Reinventing Government substantially shifted the administrative change effort to managing information needed for timely, efficient decision making. In so doing, the program strengthened the technical and conceptual basis for designing networks of action to address public sector problems.

Social media are increasingly triggering changes in the technical infrastructure of urban regions to enable faster and more efficient information exchange. Advanced information and communication technologies such as Twitter, Facebook, and other Web 2.0 technologies are revolutionizing how people interact with public administrators and share information with one another as well as other organizations, energizing an innovative form of networked governance. "Twitterers," for example, have emerged as the new first responders for information dissemination from crime scenes, disasters, and even normal daily operations that affect people, places, and policies. Policy makers receive a range of information and significant detail in real time and near real time, which can prompt quicker, more instantaneous decision making. Essentially, the emergence of Web 2.0 technologies has further challenged the shortcomings of rational choice theories (Buchanan and Tullock 1999), but has enhanced the collective action approach proposed by Ostrom (2005) and others. Increased access to multiple means of communication for a wider group of participants raises the rate of citizen engagement in coordinated action. Yet, administrators need to balance organizational communication processes with the changing technology, and design institutions that are capable of evolution, learning, and adaptation (Goodin 1996). The challenge for urban governments is to support, utilize, and manage these Web 2.0 information technologies to improve networked governance, a task that entails minimizing disruption of the governing process while maximizing its productivity.

THE EMERGENCE OF NETWORKS IN PUBLIC ADMINISTRATION

Although the concept of networks in public administration is not new, the preceding review of different forms of informal, reciprocal interaction among organizations from different sectors, disciplines, and jurisdictions creates a distinct knowledge base to support inquiry into more advanced forms of networks capable of managing more challenging sets of policy problems (Ostrom 2005). Informal communication processes to link information to action have been recognized as part of the political process since Brutus betrayed Caesar, but the types of networks that are drawing attention in current public administration have a different profile (Barabási 2002; Watts

2003). These networks are focused on action and are formed to achieve a specific goal (Churchman 1979). Their components are intelligent in that they seek, store, and exchange information to support decision making in reference to a shared goal. The goal is directed toward achieving the public good, as defined by the set of participating actors, not the limited benefit of specific actors for particular ends. The networks, further, are cognizant of their own actions, errors, and accomplishments, and interactions among members of the networks constitute a self-correcting, self-organizing dynamic to maintain their focus on inquiry. While the goals of some networks may be disputed by other actors in the society (Sageman 2004), the organization of the network depends on, first, its clear articulation of a shared goal, and second, the flow of information among its members to achieve that goal. The third characteristic of this type of network, used for either constructive or destructive purposes, is its ability to monitor its own actions and to update, correct, and synthesize information collected by its members to support the group's continued effort to achieve its stated goal.

INTELLIGENT NETWORKS

Known as *intelligent networks,* this form includes any actor that can send, receive, store, and process information. Such networks include individuals, groups, organizations, computers, and institutions as actors (Breiger, Carley, and Pattison 2003), each operating at its own level of capacity and contributing to the shared knowledge base for the whole system. Information search and exchange processes drive the formation and adaptation of these networks, and the impact of the network on its immediate environment relies on the asymmetry of information generated by the density of interactions within the network in contrast to the more dispersed transactions among other actors in the wider environment. Theorists examining such networks, explored also as potential instruments for disrupting enemy actions in military environments (Alberts and Papp 2000), acknowledge the neutrality of networks as an organizational form. The impact of the network is defined by its goal, and the value of the goal is assigned by the designers of the network. Such networks may be used to achieve either positive or negative results, as declared by members of the network in contrast to the wider society (Raab and Milward 2003). Intelligent networks are, foremost, social instruments designed to mobilize collective action, and their sustainability is measured by outcomes achieved against their defined goals.

What all networks demonstrate, positive and negative alike, is that the communications patterns, both among members within the network and between the network and its external environment, change the organizational structure of the network. Tracing the information flow among the members within the network identifies which members influence the actions of other members under what conditions and at what times. Further, tracing the information flow between the network and other actors in its operating environment reveals the degree of influence that the network is able to exert in the service of its goal. Understanding the dynamics of networks as vehicles for mobilizing public action compels managers in metropolitan regions to think more creatively about what options are available to them for managing change.

The task of managing change in metropolitan regions under uncertain conditions presents a particular challenge for public administration. The articulation of governance as a mode of management that integrates resources and personnel from public, private, and nonprofit organizations (Salamon 2002; Kettl 2009) offers a framework, albeit a temporary one, for action in complex, dynamic environments. The basis for mobilizing action is shared knowledge, and while this knowledge is distributed (Hutchins 1995), the process of information search and exchange stimulates a learning process among the participants that guides the action in real time. This is especially important in dynamic conditions in which the capacity to adapt quickly is vital to sustaining the shared goal of the community. In this process, the relationships among public, private, and nonprofit actors are realigned to create a better fit with the demands of the changing environment, as the participating actors update and adapt their actions to balance efficiency, equity, and effectiveness in daily practice more appropriately.

THE SCIENCE OF NETWORKS

Albert Barabási selected *The New Science of Networks* as the subtitle for his 2002 book, *Linked*. In doing so, he acknowledges the primary weaknesses of networks as they have been adopted, applied, and identified in much of the literature in public administration and management. In practice, networks of communication and exchange are easily recognized, yet they are documented, characterized, and measured with much greater difficulty. In part, this difficulty stems from the continual flux of social interaction in which action networks operate. Yet, a larger part of the difficulty derives from the time and systematic effort required to gather, code, collate, and analyze data on network performance. This cost in time and effort is especially characteristic of the kinds of multilevel, multiorganizational, multisector networks that operate in the public arena.

In an effort to address the theoretical and analytical problems of understanding institutional diversity, Elinor Ostrom (2005) proposed a framework to examine the analysis and development of organizations operating in different action situations in different public arenas. Her institutional analysis and development (IAD) framework links actors involved in specific action situations to the larger issues that animate the public arena. In doing so, Ostrom offers a means of identifying interdependencies among actors operating at different levels of action and authority. This analytical framework is particularly useful for the kinds of intergovernmental networks characteristic of public administration.

The measurement of performance in interdependent networks remains a critical factor in assessing their impact in public affairs. Such networks represent relationships among actors that form, dissolve, reform, and adapt to changing conditions (Axelrod and Cohen 1999). The dynamic characteristics of networks attracted the interest and attention of mathematicians, physicists, and computer scientists. A wide-ranging group of researchers focused on devising means to measure and model the changing impact of networks, both on their members and on the environments in which they operated (Carrington, Scott, and Wasserman 2005). Many shared a background of research on complex, adaptive systems, and recognized networks of public policy and administration as a subset of this larger domain. John Holland (1995), a computer scientist interested in the dynamic exchange of information among diverse actors, offered a conceptual framework for the development of complex systems. His argument, that complex systems emerge out of an inherent search for order among organizations interacting in unstructured environments, captures one dimension of this dynamic. The opposite dimension, the equally powerful tendency for systems to disintegrate without a continual influx of fresh energy, or entropy (Fermi 1956; Tong 2008), represents the counterforce in this dynamic process.

Efforts to characterize and measure the changing dynamics of networks were facilitated by the rapid advance of computational theory during the nineties. Although sociologists had earlier recognized the importance of networks, their focus was largely limited to small groups and single organizations (Doreian and Hummon 1976). With the advent of increased access to computational power, researchers in business organizations (Nohria and Eccles 1992) and public organizations (Axelrod 1984) developed methods to simulate organizational behavior under different sets of conditions. These efforts cumulated in a coherent approach termed *computational organizational theory*

(Prietula, Carley, and Gasser 1998). Using computational methods, these researchers successfully demonstrated the merits of conditional exploration of different strategies of action undertaken by different sets of actors under different initial conditions of resources, knowledge, communication, and time (Carley 2000). Complemented by parallel explorations of network structure, dynamics, and measurement among mathematicians, sociologists, economists, and other modelers (Wasserman and Faust 1994; Watts 1999), the systematic development of a science of networks began to shape the understanding of networks, their design, and their functions in the public arena. Applying these methods to actual policy problems and testing them for validity and reliability in the world of practice have become the focus for a distinguished set of policy and management researchers (Newman, Barabási, and Watts 2006). This expanding group of researchers has developed a new set of tools and computational programs to advance the design and management of networks operating as large-scale systems in the public arena.

NETWORKS AND THE MANAGEMENT OF LARGE-SCALE SOCIOTECHNICAL SYSTEMS

For public administrators concerned with the management of large-scale sociotechnical systems providing public services, the concepts proposed by the network analysts offered fresh ways of thinking about intergovernmental and intersectoral problems. Network analysis bridges the study of organizational systems that manage public services with the management of technical systems, such as telecommunications, transportation, water, power, and wastewater distribution systems, that provide these services. Both sets of systems—organizational and technical—are geographically distributed, and maintaining effective performance between the two types of operating systems at multiple levels of operation is essential to the efficient delivery of public services. For example, the concept of "scale-free networks" that draw resources, knowledge, and participants from multiple levels of operation by choice as well as random events (Barabási 2009) to address a particular policy problem, such as shelter after a storm, clarifies the phenomenon of preferential attachment in networks of action that often stymies public managers seeking to balance equity with efficiency by introducing legal requirements through public policy.

Given the developments in theory and method over the last twenty years, social network analysis has emerged as a leading technique for studying the emergent and rapidly changing environments that characterize the complex adaptive systems that public managers so frequently encounter. Rather than focusing on the characteristics of the actors involved in the situation under study, social network analysis (SNA) examines the ties that exist between these actors. The analysis includes the relative characteristics of each interaction, but it focuses on the observed set of interactions, the distribution and patterns of the interactions, and the content of the interactions, including directionality. Such analytical methods provide a more accurate means of assessing rapidly changing situations by examining both the constituent parts and the whole of the operating systems. SNA examines actor and network performance by assessing the resources of each actor as well as their patterns of distribution and utilization.

For example, SNA will readily show when needed resources are present in a system, but cannot reach the actors who need them or who would otherwise use them, by showing the lack of connection between the actors. It can also explain network performance in rapidly deteriorating situations by providing models of the network and system resilience that are necessary for effective intervention. It is this combination of tools that makes SNA an effective method for the study of complex adaptive systems.

Simon and Feiock (2008) summarize the basic network measures, including density, which calculates a ratio of the number of observed connections to the number of possible connections in the network. They also explain several methods for identifying the key actors, that is, the most central actors, of a network and describe small world networks. This frequently observed phenomenon can be measured mathematically to determine how information can be transmitted rapidly to a large number of agents by a small set of key actors, each of whom has a wide set of interactions in a given domain or region. By identifying central actors, analysts can also assess which organizations would face the heaviest workloads under urgent stress. Managers can then use these results to determine whether the organization that has formal authority in a given situation actually performs the functions expected by that authority in practice.

Density, in contrast, measures the frequency of interactions among actors in the network regarding a specific task or problem occurring in a given location at a particular time. Measures of density also reveal when interactions among agents are constricted or controlled due to "structural holes," or gaps in the pattern of connections among actors in the network (Simon and Feiock 2008). Wasserman and Faust (1994) compare different types of networks operating at different levels of interaction, focusing on the identification of subgroups or cliques in the performance of different functions within the network. They also discuss the measurement of qualitative concepts, such as the prestige or social capital of an actor. When paired with network maps that visually depict the network's structure (Borgatti, Everett and Freeman 2002), this set of analytic methods provides an informed profile of an action network.

The focus on structure and process allows network researchers to analyze complex adaptive systems more effectively than other methods. By charting interactions, SNA not only shows their frequency among members of a network, but also measures the robustness and reliability of the network's performance. When the content of interactions among members is coded, network analysis can be used to characterize access to information and other resources within the system and provide a measure of resilience for a system under stress. For example, Comfort and her coauthors (Comfort and Haase 2006; Comfort, Oh, and Ertan 2009) analyzed the networks of organizations engaged in response operations following the 2005 and 2008 hurricanes on the Gulf Coast. These analyses identified differences in practice by emergency service agencies mobilized in response to similar urgent events. While standard after-action reports create a useful dialogue regarding the effectiveness of multiorganizational actions taken in reference to specific disasters, social network methods additionally provide measures of strength or weakness in interagency performance that can assist managers in planning to reduce risk in future extreme events.

The contribution of network analysis to public administration and theory lies in its measurement of dynamic interactions among individuals and organizations in relation to the changing conditions of their operational environment. Building on the analytical framework of network analysis, computational simulation of organizational action has emerged as an important method of assessing possible strategies of action in environments that are too large or too dangerous or too extreme to study in actual practice. Simulation is developing as a powerful method for investigating alternative strategies of organized action in extreme situations, such as battlefield environments, earthquake disasters, or breakdowns of large-scale technical systems such as nuclear plants. This method has increased in utility as computers have become more powerful and accessible. Accordingly, researchers have become more innovative in adapting simulation to explore relationships among variables identified in their studies.

As researchers have applied simulation techniques to real-world policy problems, they have communicated their findings to wider audiences of practicing managers as well as other interested researchers in the social sciences (Gilbert and Troitzsch 2005). Through continued development, simulation has advanced research on complex systems, drawing from theories of nonlinear dynamics, distributed cognition, artificial intelligence, and dynamic aspects of change (Conte and Castelfranchi 1995). Social scientists doing simulation research often work in conjunction with computer scientists (Lin and Carley 2003) or information scientists (Zagorecki, Ko, and Comfort 2010) to integrate social concepts with technical skills in the development of a new class of sociotechnical models that explore complex administrative systems in practice.

As methods of inquiry into administrative practice, social network analysis and simulation modeling have distinct limits in representing complex environments. Standard network analysis assumes that relationships among actors are dichotomous. Yet, the depiction of a dichotomous relationship indicating a random interaction between just two actors may not represent accurately an action system or event. Many, if not most, interactions include more than two actors. Observed interactions include at least three actors, and often more. This lack of specificity in defining interaction gives these techniques flexibility in application, but also adds complexity to the interpretation of findings from these methods. For example, many interactions exhibit what network analysts refer to as multiplexity, that is, the existence of multiple ties between two actors (Isett and Provan 2005).

GISCIENCE

Capturing the context of social networks and their actors goes beyond the usual identification of structure and process in network analysis. Not new, but increasingly used in the analysis of interdependent functions in metropolitan regions, geographic information science represents a useful means to explore spatial dynamic processes (Gimblett 2002). Developing a geographic information system (GIS) enables an analyst to capture, store, manipulate, analyze, and display geographic information using digital computation. Using GIS software, an analyst can generate a map of spatially located relationships. For example, comparative network studies of nested systems that are typical of regional or metropolitan analysis may represent social interactions at different spatial scales (Chase-Dunn and Hall 1997). Traditional network analysis does not explicitly consider space, yet networks are inherently spatial. GIS enables the modeling of interactions among actors, physical locations, and available resources. Successful incorporation of social science data into a GIS knowledge base and the construction of spatially explicit models from these data remain inconsistent and somewhat pedantic. The inherently static data used in GIS analysis often limit its capacity to model dynamic processes (Goodchild, Parks, and Steyaert 1993). Not only do social scientists use GIS to overlay data and conduct complex spatial analyses, but over the past decade, researchers have explored ways to integrate social networks and GIS (Butts 2009). This method allows analysts to isolate and characterize segments of the networks by attributes, which not only improves visualization, but also reveals the dynamic structure of the network.

GIScience is used to analyze, forecast, and visualize spatial interactions across networks. Visualizing how distance affects relationships increases the merit of network analysis. For example, one can estimate how a disease might spread in a population through the integration of the sociospatial processes of GIS in network analysis, and thus improve estimation and governance of rates of spread of the disease in metropolitan regions. GIS enables network analysts to construct visualizations of how networks have changed their spatial scale over time. In fact, incorporating spatial dimensions into networks may reveal that some networks are not as scale free as suggested by Barabási (2002). Geographic distance and location may limit some networks. GIS can therefore enable network analysts to test further complex causal models over time and space, which would then provide evidence and strategies for improved governance and information flow. Analyzing spatial movement in networks can influence how networks are managed or interpreted as they cross organizational boundaries or traverse different jurisdictional and spatial scales.

The cumulative set of concepts, methods, and metrics that form the basis of the new science of networks makes a substantive contribution to the field of public administration. This science acknowledges the technical dimension in large-scale organized systems that characterize metropolitan regions, and provides a means of measuring the interaction between the technical systems of transportation, communications, electrical power, gas, water, and wastewater distribution and the organizations that operate them. In addition to instruments of financial management advocated by Salamon (2002) and his coauthors as a means of facilitating governance, the set of network analytic methods and models enables managers from both organizational and technical agencies to create a common knowledge base to support informed decision making for their given metropolitan region. Such a common knowledge base may be accessed by public, private, and nonprofit managers who operate interdependent systems, thereby informing their concurrent decisions in terms of meeting regional needs.

SOCIOTECHNICAL SYSTEMS

The distinguishing characteristic of metropolitan regions is the interdependence of their technical and organizational systems, as indicated previously. This interdependence has given rise to a model of governance that is based not just on shared financial responsibility among public, private, and nonprofit organizations, but also on the shared knowledge and critical expertise required to manage these large-scale systems effectively. For example, if the mayor of a city, often trained in law, does not understand the vulnerabilities posed to the transportation system by the region's aging engineered structures, she or he may not recognize the risk generated for the wider community by delaying needed maintenance of key bridges for budgetary reasons. The collapse of the I-35W bridge in Minneapolis on August 1, 2007, even as the bridge was being repaired, illustrates this risk. The need is not for an omniscient mayor, but rather for shared recognition that the knowledge needed to manage metropolitan regions is distributed (Hutchins 1995). That is, no single official or agency has all the information that is needed to make informed decisions on the wide range of issues that current public managers confront on a daily basis. In contrast, different organizations, and different managers within those organizations, have partial knowledge needed to balance risk of malfunction against resources of funds, attention, and personnel time to maintain continuity of operations. The challenge is to pool the shared knowledge in a timely, valid way and make it accessible to each manager who participates in decisions regarding management of the system under review.

Essential services for a metropolitan region, such as water and power distribution, human resources, and financial management, need collaborative management in order to maintain continuity of operations over time. Collaborative management in complex regional settings requires an information infrastructure sufficient to support the timely search and exchange of valid information regarding the status and performance of sociotechnical systems (Comfort and Haase 2006).

FUTURE RESEARCH

In a continuing effort to understand the rapidly changing environments of metropolitan regions, maintaining research on current issues is critical. While many problems in this interdependent policy environment deserve attention and action, four are basic to creating the learning environment that is essential for professional administrators. First, the need to enhance processes for rapid feedback, updating information, and organizational learning is central to effective management of public issues in a dynamic environment. Current technologies for information exchange, such as Twitter, Facebook, and instant messaging, speed the flow of information rapidly across large numbers of people in spontaneous and undirected ways. Understanding these dynamic information processes and how they influence civic engagement in, or resistance to, governmental action is critical to maintaining an open, responsible, democratic society.

Second, and related to the first issue, is the task of building and maintaining current knowledge bases regarding complex public issues that are interdisciplinary, but accessible to interested citizens as well as relevant agencies, officials, and managers. The benefit of constructing current databases, especially on contested or controversial problems, is that of providing a neutral source of information to foster individual and organizational learning on both sides of the debate. Determining how to engage multiple actors in this task and creating an open, transparent, public knowledge base sets an example of informed participation by citizens and officials that enhances governance structures and processes.

Third, reviewing, designing, and advancing the methods and metrics for assessing risk in the interdependent functions of metropolitan regions is a key area needed for improving public management in metro regions. It is not only the municipal level of operation that needs exploration, but also county, state, and federal arenas of action and the interdependencies among them that constitute key areas for future research.

Finally, exploring ways to strengthen the scientific expertise required to manage increasingly complex and difficult public issues, such as climate change, energy production and distribution, and public health threats, is basic to improving shared governance among agencies and organizations operating in metropolitan regions.

CONCLUSIONS

In this brief review of network theory and practice in public administration, we draw four primary conclusions. First, network science offers a disciplined approach to monitoring and measuring the interdependent set of policy issues and practice that characterize metropolitan regions. The current concepts of governance, while insightful, lack the rigorous measurement of dynamic interactions among public, private, and nonprofit organizations that lead to policy change. Without such measurement, it is difficult for policy makers to craft viable strategies to manage the uncertainty generated by dynamic interactions among public, private, and nonprofit organizations in the daily operations of a metro region.

Second, network science is based fundamentally on an understanding of networks as systems of action. In these action systems, the participants—individuals, groups, organizations, computers, institutions—search for and exchange information as a basis for their respective actions in reference to actions taken by others. Consequently, identifying the relationships that link one actor to another under what conditions and to what degree becomes a primary step in assessing the degrees of independence, dependence, and interdependence in the complex set of administrative relationships that characterize metropolitan regions. Only when the underlying structure of relationships among actors is understood and mapped for particular administrative or policy issues can effective change be achieved in practice.

Third, effective decision making in interdependent environments, such as metropolitan regions, depends upon timely, valid processes of information search and exchange. This basic requirement for collaborative decision making can be facilitated by a well-designed decision support system (Comfort, Mosse, and Znati 2009). Designing and implementing decision support systems (DSS) to enhance institutional capacity and performance at local, state, and federal levels of operation represent key steps for strengthening governance in practice. A DSS uses improved communications processes and computation to gather, store, analyze, and exchange data that show the current state of the sociotechnical systems that operate in metropolitan regions. It provides that information quickly and efficiently to those who need it.

Finally, the concepts, analytical techniques and models presented by social network analysis, GIScience, and computational simulation provide public managers with an increased ability to anticipate risk in dynamic environments, calibrate different patterns of response to uncertain events, and assess the interdependencies among operating systems identified by other methods and measures. The emerging science of networks offers the conceptual and analytical tools to enable public managers to function more efficiently and effectively in the complex, dynamic environments characteristic of metropolitan regions. Linked to decision processes within and among organizations, network science offers a powerful method of improving administrative practice in more nuanced, calibrated ways. As decision makers learn and apply these methods in practice, they will enable metropolitan regions to become more resilient in managing risk and random events.

REFERENCES

Alberts, D.S., and D.S. Papp. 2000. *The Information Age Anthology.* Washington, DC: Institute for National Strategic Studies, National Defense University.

Axelrod, R.M. 1984. *The Evolution of Cooperation.* New York: Basic Books.

Axelrod, R.M., and M.D. Cohen. 1999. *Harnessing Complexity: Organizational Implications of a Scientific Frontier.* New York: Free Press.

Barabási, A.-L. 2002. *Linked: The New Science of Networks.* Cambridge, MA: Perseus.

———. 2009. Scale-free networks: A decade and beyond. *Science* 325:412–413.

Barzelay, M. 2001. *The New Public Management: Improving Research and Policy Dialogue.* Berkeley: University of California Press.

Behn, R.D. 1998. The new public management paradigm and the search for democratic accountability. *International Public Management Journal* 1 (2): 131–164.

———. 2001. *Rethinking Democratic Accountability.* Washington, DC: Brookings Institution Press.

Boin, A., L.K. Comfort, and C. Demchak. 2010. The rise of resilience: Concepts, questions and theoretical approaches. In *Designing Resilience:Preparedness for Extreme Events,* ed. L.K. Comfort, A. Boin, and C. Demchak. Pittsburgh: University of Pittsburgh Press.

Boin, A., P. t'Hart, E. Stern, and B. Sundelius. 2005. *The Politics of Crisis Management: Public Leadership Under Pressure.* New York: Cambridge University Press.

Borgatti, S.P., M.G. Everett, and L.C. Freeman. 2002. *UCINET for Windows: Software for Social Network Analysis.* Harvard, MA: Analytic Technologies.

Breiger, R., K.M. Carley, and P. Pattison, eds. 2003. Dynamic social network modeling and analysis: Workshop summary and papers. Committee on Human Factors, Board on Behavioral, Cognitive, and Sensory Sciences. Washington, DC: National Academy Press.

Bryson, J.M. 2004. *Strategic Planning for Public and Nonprofit Organizations: A Guide to Strengthening and Sustaining Organizational Achievement.* San Francisco: Jossey-Bass.

Buchanan, J., and Tullock, G. 1999. *The Calculus of Consent: Logical Foundations of Constitutional Democracy.* Indianapolis: Liberty Fund.

Burt, R.S. 1992. *Structural Holes: The Social Structure of Competition.* Cambridge, MA: Harvard University Press.

Bush, G.H.W. 1988. 1988 Republican national convention acceptance address. American Rhetoric. www.americanrhetoric.com/speeches/georgehbush1988rnc.htm (accessed January 16, 2010).

Butts, C.T. 2009. Revisiting the foundations of network analysis. *Science* 325:414–416.

Carley, Kathleen. 2000. Computational analysis of social and organizational systems. *Organizational Science* 34 (2): 4–10.

Carrington, P.J., J. Scott, and S. Wasserman, eds. 2005. *Models and Methods in Social Network Analysis.* Cambridge: Cambridge University Press.

Chase-Dunn, C., and T.D. Hall. 1997. *Rise and Demise: Comparing World Systems.* Boulder, CO: Westview Press.

Churchman, C.W. 1979. *The Systems Approach and Its Enemies.* New York: Basic Books.

Coakes, E., D. Willis, and S. Clarke. 2002. *Knowledge Management in the Sociotechnical World.* London: Springer Verlag.

Comfort, L.K. 2008. Distributed cognition: The basis for coordinated action in dynamic environments. Paper presented at the workshop Exploring Innovative and Sustainable Approaches to Improve Community Resilience in Disaster Prevention and Response, Davos, Switzerland, August 29–30.

Comfort, L.K., and T.W. Haase. 2006. Communication, coherence, and collective action: The impact of hurricane Katrina on communications infrastructure. *Public Works Management and Policy* 11 (1): 1–16.

Comfort, L.K., D. Mosse, and T. Znati. 2009. Managing risk in real time: Integrating information technology into disaster risk reduction and response. *Commonwealth: A Journal of Political Science* 15:27–46.

Comfort, L.K., N. Oh, and G. Ertan. 2009. The dynamics of disaster recovery: Resilience and entropy in hurricane response systems 2005–2008. *Public Organization Review* 9: 309–323.

Conte, R., and C. Castelfranchi. 1995. Understanding the functions of norms in social groups. In *Artificial Societies: The Computer Simulation of Social Life,* ed. N. Gilbert and R. Conte, 252–267. London: UCL Press.

Cutter, S.L., B.J. Boruff, and W.L. Shirley. 2003. Social vulnerability to environmental hazards. *Social Science Quarterly* 84:242–261.

DiIulio, J.J. 1994. *Deregulating the Public Service: Can Government Be Improved.* Washington, DC: Brookings Institution.

DiIulio, J.J., and D.F. Kettl. 1995. *Fine Print: The Contract with America, Devolution, and the Administrative Realities of American Federalism.* Washington, DC: Center for Public Management, Brookings Institution.

Doreian, P., and N. Hummon. 1976. *Modeling Social Processes.* New York: Elsevier North-Holland.

Downs, A. 1994. *New Visions for Metropolitan America.* Washington, DC: Brookings Institution.

Dynes, R.R. 2006. Social capital: Dealing with community emergencies. *Homeland Security Affairs* 2 (2): 1–26.

Feiock, R.C., and J. Scholz, eds. 2010. *Self-Organizing Federalism.* Cambridge: Cambridge University Press.

Fermi, E. 1956. *Thermodynamics.* New York: Dover Publications.

Frederickson, H.G., and K.B. Smith. 2003. *The Public Administration Theory Primer.* Boulder, CO: Westview Press.

Gilbert, N., and K.G. Troitzsch. 2005. *Simulation for the Social Scientist.* 2d ed. Philadelphia: Open University Press.

Gimblett, R. 2002. *Integrating Geographic Information Systems and Agent-Based Modeling: Techniques for Simulating Social and Ecological Processes.* New York: Oxford University Press.

Goodchild, M., B.O. Parks, and L.T. Steyaert, eds. 1993. *Environmental Modeling with GIS.* Oxford: Oxford University Press.

Goodin, R. 1996. Institutions and their design. In *The Theory of Institutional Design,* ed. R. Goodin. Cambridge: Cambridge University Press.

Holland, J.H. 1995. *Hidden Order: How Adaptation Builds Complexity.* Reading, MA: Addison-Wesley.

Hutchins, E. 1995. *Cognition in the Wild.* Cambridge, MA: MIT Press.

Isett, K.R., and K.G. Provan. 2005. The evolution of dyadic interorganizational relationships in a network of publicly funded nonprofit agencies. *Journal of Public Administration Research and Theory* 15:149–165.

Kauffman, S.A. 1993. *The Origins of Order: Self-Organization and Selection in Evolution.* New York: Oxford University Press.

Kelman, S. 2005. *Unleashing Change: A Study of Organizational Renewal in Government.* Washington, DC: Brookings Institution Press.

Kettl, D.F. 1993. *Sharing Power: Public Governance and Private Markets.* Washington, DC: Brookings Institution.

———. 1994. *Reinventing Government? Appraising the National Performance Review.* Washington, DC: Center for Public Management, Brookings Institution.

———. 2009. *The Next Government of the United States: Why Our Institutions Fail and How to Fix Them.* New York: W.W. Norton.

Leavitt, W.M., and J.J. Kiefer. 2006. Infrastructure interdependency and the creation of a normal disaster: The case of hurricane Katrina and the city of New Orleans. *Public Works Management Policy* 10:306–314.

Lin, Z., and K.M. Carley. 2003. *Designing Stress Resistant Organizations: Computational Theorizing and Crisis Applications.* Boston: Kluwer Academic Publishers.

Miller, D.Y. 2002. *The Regional Governing of Metropolitan America.* Boulder, CO: Westview.

Miller, George A. 1956. The magical number seven, plus or minus two: Some limits on our capacity for processing information. *Psychological Review* 63:81–97.

Milward, H.B., and K.G. Provan. 1998. Principles for controlling agents: The political economy of network structure. *Journal of Public Administration Research and Theory* 8:203–219.

Morrow, B.H. 1999. Identifying and mapping community vulnerability. *Disasters* 23:1–18.

Nakagawa, Y., and R. Shaw. 2004. Social capital: A missing link to disaster recovery. *International Journal of Mass Emergencies and Disasters* 22:5–34.

Newman, M.E.J., A.-L. Barabási, and D.J. Watts. 2006. *The Structure and Dynamics of Networks.* Princeton, NJ: Princeton University Press.

Nohria, N., and R.G. Eccles. 1992. *Networks and Organizations: Structure, Form and Action.* Boston, MA: Harvard Business School Press.

Ostrom, E. 2005. *Understanding Institutional Diversity.* Princeton, NJ: Princeton University Press.

Phillips, B. 2009. *Disaster Recovery.* New York: Auerbach Publications.

Pollitt, C. 2003. *The Essential Public Manager.* Philadelphia: Open University Press/McGraw Hill.

Prietula, M.J., K.M. Carley, and L.G. Gasser. 1998. *Simulating Organizations: Computational Models of Institutions and Groups.* Menlo Park, CA: AAAI Press/MIT Press.

Raab, J., and H.B. Milward. 2003. Dark networks as problems. *Journal of Public Administration Research and Theory* 13:413–439.

Radin, B. 2006. *Challenging the Performance Movement: Accountability, Complexity and Democratic Values.* Washington, DC: Georgetown University Press.

Rusk, D. 2003. *Cities Without Suburbs: A Census 2000 Update.* 3d ed. Washington, DC: Woodrow Wilson Center Press.

Sageman, M. 2004. *Understanding Terror Networks.* Philadelphia: University of Pennsylvania Press.

Salamon, L.M. ed. 2002. *The Tools of Government: A Guide to the New Governance.* New York: Oxford University Press.

Schneider, A.L., and H.M. Ingram. 2005. *Deserving and Entitled: Social Constructions and Public Policy.* Albany: State University of New York.

Simon, A.A., and R.C. Feiock. 2008. Methods of network analysis. In *Handbook of Research Methods in Public Administration.* 2d ed., ed. Y. Kaifeng and G.J. Miller. Boca Raton, FL: Auerbach Publications.

Simon, H.A. 1997. *The Sciences of the Artificial.* 3d ed. Cambridge, MA: MIT Press.

Tong, Ming. 2008. Entropy: A New Perspective of Risk and Crisis Management Studies. Paper presented at the International Conference on Risk, Crisis, and Public Management, Nanjing University, Nanjing, China, September 26–27. (2008). Trans. by Wen Jiun Wang. Pittsburgh, PA: University of Pittsburgh.

Tribe, L., ed. 1988. *American Constitutional Law.* 2d ed. Mineola, NY: Foundation Press.

U.S. Senate. 1993. Government Performance and Results Act of 1993. Calendar No. 96, Report 103–58. Washington, DC: Senate Committee on Governmental Affairs.

Wasserman, S., and K. Faust. 1994. *Social Network Analysis: Methods and Applications.* New York: Cambridge University Press.

Watts, D.J. 1999. *Small Worlds: The Dynamics of Networks Between Order and Randomness.* Princeton, NJ: Princeton University Press.

———. 2003. *Six Degrees: The Science of a Connected Age.* New York: W.W. Norton.

Zagorecki, Adam, Kilkon Ko, and Louise K. Comfort. 2010. Interorganizational Information Exchange and Efficiency: Organizational Performance in Emergency Environments. *Journal of Artificial Societies and Social Simulation* 13 (3) 3. Available at http://jasss.soc.surrey.ac.uk/13/3/3.html (accessed August 20, 2010).

CHAPTER 17

COLLABORATIVE PUBLIC AGENCIES IN THE NETWORK ERA

ROBERT AGRANOFF

This chapter is an attempt to account for how public agencies are "catching up" in the policy and management portfolio as they face the challenges of engaging with a host of nongovernmental organizations (NGOs) in various forms of networked activities. *NGO* refers to U.S. and international nonprofit and for-profit organizations that are not enabled by some government entity. This movement has made public agencies more conductive; that is, they work with a series of interlocutors, along with performing their more traditional planning, staffing, financing, and regulating functions. Rather than hollowing out or somehow abdicating its functions to NGOs, government can be seen as changing by rapid externalization. These changes predominantly involve linkage, partnering, and networking activities with NGOs, and emergent forms of collaborative leadership.

Over the twentieth century, governments in many countries, including the United States, shifted from entities that primarily offered direct services (e.g., postal, welfare, state institutions, fire, police, universities) to entities that initially added grants to other governments and private organizations, then included regulation of other governments, along with loans and loan guarantees, fees and charges, cash payments, vouchers, and purchase-of-services contracting with NGOs. Now governments are adding joint ventures, that is, programming in partnership with NGOs (Agranoff 2008). As a result, the managerial dramas of federalism, intergovernmental relations, and intergovernmental management are now being played out in terms of collaboration and networks (see chapter 18, "Historic Relevance Confronting Contemporary Obsolescence?" in this volume), new forms of governance. As Kooiman (2004, 3) indicates, "Governance of and in modern societies is a mix of all kinds of governing efforts by all manner of sociopolitical actors, public as well as private; occurring between them at different levels, in different governance modes and orders." While this diffusion over various actors is constantly changing, it is moving toward a system where government increasingly is a facilitator and cooperating partner. "As such, it is more appropriate to speak of shifting rather than shrinking roles of the state" (3).

Transacting among these various mechanisms involves interactive processes (Agranoff and McGuire 2003) and employment of various "tools" of governance. According to Salamon (2002, 14–15), the latter involves reducing the division between the public and private spheres, looking for management models other than command and control, and rejecting the idea that these tools are self-administering. They require aggressive management. It is these concerns that are addressed here. How is contemporary public management organized to manage across sectors? How does one manage within networks involving the legitimacy and authority of the state and its NGO partner executants?

The chapter begins with a definition of the conductive public agency, today's networking bureaucracy. That is followed by a demonstration of what these collaborating public agencies look like in practice, through a set of hypothetical but demonstrative examples, as the relationship between these agencies and their partners are explored. The chapter next looks at a real-world example of a postmodern completely networked public organization, an experimental science and mathematics school in Columbus, Ohio: Metro High School. Then, after looking at Metro and the other conductive agencies, some emergent features of collaborative organizing that differ from standard management practices are demonstrated. The last substantive section of the chapter presents eleven leadership, organizing, and management challenges in the era of networking-oriented collaborative management. The concluding observations offer extant challenges of cross-sector management.

THE CONDUCTIVE ORGANIZATION

Today's bureaucracies at all levels and types appear less like those organizations in the days of the emerging bureaucratic organization, what was once known as Weberian, Taylorist, or mass-production-like Fordist. Within, organizational structures have become more flexible and permeable over the twentieth century (Clegg 1990, 181). This has two important implications for public management in the network era. First, public administrators and program specialists who work in public agencies are more attuned to internal organizational experiences that are less rigid, cross divisional boundaries of their own structures, reach out to other agencies of their government, and involve an increasing number of cross-sector and intergovernmental experiences. Second, this exposure and experience, with a changing hierarchical paradigm, has brought on certain levels of comfort with those emergent cross-boundary transactions.

The postbureaucratic, open-boundaried flexible understanding of organizing is considered to be beyond twentieth-century organizing. The latter refers to observers like Max Weber (1946) who defined bureaucracy in his classic essay, written in the early twentieth century, as a hallmark of modernism, as opposed to charismatic and traditional models. These models, as is well-known, stress the importance of hierarchy, rules, divided tasks, specified procedures, and the like. On the contrary, as Figure 17.1 illustrates, Clegg (1990, 11) leads with the idea that he calls *postmodern organizing,* which involves structuring more generalized or de-differentiated tasks. Yet there is much more; it involves opening the boundaries of organizations, with a problem rather than rule-based orientation, and with a methodological focus on what people do, how they discover ideas, and how they adapt to different practices from elsewhere. To Clegg, this is post-Weberism, where models of organizing are understood without orthodoxy and are likely to present a variety of approaches, without previous forms of standardization or "one best way." The organization is not a machine but an adaptive entity capable of being captured rhetorically, symbolically, or both.

Public agencies and organizations need postmodern tools as they increasingly operate "outside," often with a similar extent of effort as they use "inside," as they connectively engage other organizations or representatives of other organizations. This phenomenon has been captured by a number of observers, most cogently by Saint-Onge and Armstrong (2004) in *The Conductive Organization,* where the importance of partnerships is at the core: "The capability to effectively manage complex partnerships is growing in importance as organizations are reconfigured. Organizations are becoming more and more involved in complex value-creation networks, where the boundaries between one organization and another become blurred and functions are integrated. Being able to create and leverage participation in network-designed and -delivered solutions is becoming a critical organizational and leadership capability. Trust fosters this commitment and cements the network partnership. By forming value-creation networks focused on fulfilling customer requirements, true customer calibration can be accomplished" (26).

Figure 17.1   **Clegg's Tenets of Modern/Postmodern Organization and Management**

Modern Organizing	Postmodern Organizing
Differentiation of tasks	De-differentiation
Individual skill sets/tasks	Teams of quasi specialists/generalists
Boundaried organizations	Boundaryless organizing
Structured hierarchies	Open, networked organizing
Rules of operation	Problem-solving procedures
Meta-narratives, e.g., contingency determination by size, transactions costs	What agents actually do in accomplishing constitutive work
Rules of managing, e.g., span of control	Understanding what is being managed
People at the top/managers know best	People and agencies in and around organizations also know what is in their interests
Policies and procedures manuals	Engagement in actions based on practical interest
Culturally constrained adaptation of management practices	Adaptation of practices from other cultures

Source: Adapted from Clegg 1990, 10–13.

Obviously pitched to business, public agencies have become increasingly conductive as well through such partnerships. Saint-Onge and Armstrong (2004) define the conductive organization as "an organization that continuously generates and renews capabilities to achieve breakthrough performance by enhancing the quality and the flow of knowledge and by calibrating its strategy, culture, structure and systems to the needs of its customers and the marketplace" (179).

To Saint-Onge and Armstrong, the conductive organization operates through a balanced organizational structure, working both horizontally and vertically. It has a cohesive culture, systems, structures, and strategies that support a constructive leadership context. It seeks high-quality internal and external relationships, feeding the creation, management, and use of knowledge. Its capabilities are enhanced as an inherent part of resolving issues and meeting challenges (2004, 16). Leadership is key in the conductive organization:

> Leaders articulate the common objectives and values to which the network commits and around which it can coalesce. Control must be replaced by empowerment through self-initiation, with the network members being given the freedom to find the most appropriate route to achieve project goals.
> The network will be held accountable for delivering its objectives. Leadership's responsibility is to ensure that systems and structures are in place that enable the members of the network to collaborate, learn, share knowledge, and execute their responsibilities. The network's output is the generation of capabilities. (191)

Thus, in cross-organizational endeavors, leaders are key, particularly "champions," who sustain organizational commitment, and "alliance managers," who enable people to work together efficiently and role model trust and collaboration (Holbeche 2005, 179). Leaders, then, are responsible for generation of capacities, promoting the flow of knowledge within the organization and with the organization and other entities, synchronization of the key collaborating organizations, examining mutual capabilities, and calibrating internal organizing structures to external needs.

In this chapter the aim is to reach deeper into how public agency structure and process are changing as a result of increasing conductivity. The conductive public agency represents a new generative metaphor that helps us to understand the permeable bureaucracy in the sense that Schön (1979) calls for means of capturing emergent thought and action.

THE CONDUCTIVE PUBLIC AGENCY

The "state" is externalizing rather than emptying out. Indiana state government, one of the more notable examples of employing the NGO sector, retains a notable state presence. One of its smallest departments, Administration, employs more than two hundred people to oversee state purchasing, the state vehicle and aviation fleet, real estate transactions, and the Government Center campus in downtown Indianapolis. The state's largest agency, Family and Social Services Administration, is highly externalized but nevertheless employs more than forty-eight hundred staff, who do everything from basic service eligibility to quality and standards control, service contract management and program oversight, information and evaluation, and policy analysis. In order to understand how public administrative work has become outside as well as inside, two hypothetical diagrams of conductive agencies are considered, one that continues to deliver its services through its hierarchy but nevertheless engages in a set of linkages that support its core mission, the other that primarily externalizes its direct services essentially by contracting. Each demonstrates how public organizations engage in numerous external transactions.

The agency depicted in Figure 17.2 is in appearance like many other federal, state, or local agencies. It models the U.S. Department of Agriculture/Rural Development, which provides grant, loan, technical assistance, and other programs through its state offices, with most of its loan services offered in direct service delivery, but in partnership with other NGOs, and with leading institutions (banks, savings and loans) plus state and local governments. (For ease of identification it is called USDA/RD Office in this chapter.) At the state level, it could also represent a welfare department, where the core eligibility, case management, and income payments functions continue to operate on a direct services basis, in-house with state employees, but a host of support programs and training, child care, health care, and food stamps operate on more of an external basis. At the local level, the figure could resemble a department of planning, building, or economic development, where permitting and inspections operate inside but most of the development functions are external in some NGO or other department.

As shown in the diagram (from the twelve o'clock position), (b1) the USDA/RD Office involves contractual relations with a series of NGOs, for example, banks and supply cooperatives; (b2) the department regularly consults with a small number of allied federal departments, that is, the Department of Housing and Urban Development, the Department of Health and Human Services, and this includes some formal interagency agreements; (b3) the agency is also in coordination with other (for example, state and local) governments, and through these other governments with NGOs; (b4) it has grant, regulatory contract, procurement, and related legally defined connections with recipient small local governments (and indirectly with NGOs); (b5) it is also involved in one or more chartered or nonchartered agriculture product development and value-added networks, including some that are legally established (e.g., economic development council); (b6) it engages in formal partnerships with a series of NGOs; (b7) it contracts for audit and other support services; and (b8) the agency also engages in other external relations with state rural development advisory boards, and has formal contacts with the rural trade associations in the state. This is not an unusual situation, as the typical state USDA/RD Office is heavily engaged outside of its internal grant and loan bureaucratic boundaries and procedures, connecting with the major state and local

Figure 17.2 **A Moderately Conductive Public Agency: United States Department of Agriculture/Rural Development (USDA/RD) Office**

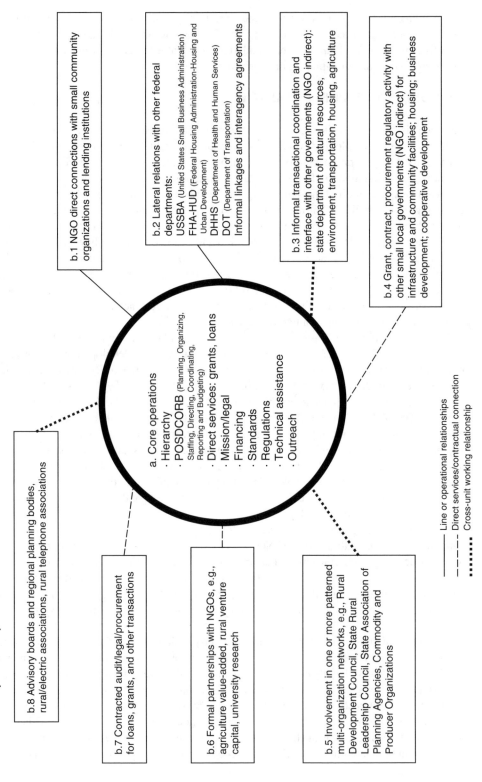

b.1 NGO direct connections with small community organizations and lending institutions

b.2 Lateral relations with other federal departments:
USSBA (United States Small Business Administration)
FHA-HUD (Federal Housing Administration-Housing and Urban Development)
DHHS (Department of Health and Human Services)
DOT (Department of Transportation)
Informal linkages and interagency agreements

b.3 Informal transactional coordination and interface with other governments (NGO indirect): state department of natural resources, environment, transportation, housing, agriculture

b.4 Grant, contract, procurement regulatory activity with other small local governments (NGO indirect) for infrastructure and community facilities; housing; business development; cooperative development

a. Core operations
· Hierarchy
· POSDCORB (Planning, Organizing, Staffing, Directing, Coordinating, Reporting and Budgeting)
· Direct services: grants, loans
· Mission/legal
· Financing
· Standards
· Regulations
· Technical assistance
· Outreach

b.8 Advisory boards and regional planning bodies, rural/electric associations, rural telephone associations

b.7 Contracted audit/legal/procurement for loans, grants, and other transactions

b.6 Formal partnerships with NGOs, e.g., agriculture value-added, rural venture capital, university research

b.5 Involvement in one or more patterned multi-organization networks, e.g., Rural Development Council, State Rural Leadership Council, State Association of Planning Agencies, Commodity and Producer Organizations

——— Line or operational relationships
– – – Direct services/contractual connection
········· Cross-unit working relationship

rural players. All of this makes the USDA/RD Office an example of one agency that continues to deliver its core services internally while remaining highly involved externally.

Those public agencies that externalize all or mostly all of their core services are exponentially conductive. The example in Figure 17.3 is hypothetical but targets particular human services functions, aging, intellectual and developmental disabilities (ID/DD), and vocational rehabilitation services, where all direct services functions are delivered externally, mostly through purchase-of-services contracting. Again, for ease of identification the agency is called State Human Services.

First, within the core operations (a) there is a line called "program units," from which four programs operate: Program a.1 (aging) offers federally financed grants in the form of contracts to thirteen area agencies on aging (nine nonprofit NGOs, two in city government, and two in regional planning agencies) that do planning and organizing of services that are purchased by the agencies on aging from hundreds of food, nursing, activity, transportation, and other vendors, some of whom further subcontract. Program a.2 (rehabilitation) operates with some fifty-five state employee counselors/case managers who in turn contract federal- and state-funded direct services in habilitation, medical, training, counseling, and education from various NGO vendors. Program a.3 (residential) is for persons who need complete residential services, for example, nonprofit or for-profit nursing homes (this state operates no state intellectual disabilities/developmental disabilities institutions, having closed the last one in 2006), mostly funded by federal and state Medicaid. Program a.4 (noninstitutional ID/DD services) is federally and state funded through a single for-profit case-management contract and then by purchased services from some eighty-three dispersed (for-profit or nonprofit) rehabilitation centers, which in turn subcontract certain day, medical, dental, and support services. Note that only the externalized direct services picture has been portrayed to this point.

From the twelve o'clock position in Figure 17.3, at b.1 is the important State Human Services Medicaid Policy Office, which oversees standards, payments, performance indicators, and the like; at b.2 are university research, demonstration, and training affiliations; at b.3 is a series of program external advisory boards; at b.4 are quasi-state (comprised of state employees and external experts) licensing boards and regional and national accreditation bodies; at b.5 are state (federally funded) planning councils and study groups; at b.6 are contracted and client information firms, those that engage in client costing and other information services; at b.7 is the office of the departmental secretary; at b.8 is the state health board, responsible for facility inspection, standards, and enforcing Medicaid-based client rights (e.g., neglect and abuse); and at b.9 are the federal government offices in the U.S. Department of Health and Human Services (e.g., Office of Aging, Centers for Medicaid/Medicare, Rehabilitation Services Administration). All of these contacts for both externalized direct services and all of the other contacts make State Human Services highly conductive in the postmodern sense.

These extensive external connections, one would say bureaucracy in the era of governance, are not unusual for an increasing number of public agencies. Some would argue that to have external relations is not really new, and that is true. The concept of "boundary spanning" (Thompson 1967) and interorganizational relations (Galbraith 1977) reaches back for decades. That is not the point. It is now not only the existence of linkages but the degree and intensity of such conductivity that is relevant. It is the interactive demands to manage together that make contemporary operations challenging and requires management to take new approaches.

Leading-Edge Organizing: Metro's Network Structure

Innovative collaborative-based organizing can be better illustrated by focus on a networked public agency, a real-world science and math high school that appears to have eschewed the lines and

278

Figure 17.3 **A Highly Conductive Public Agency: State Human Services**

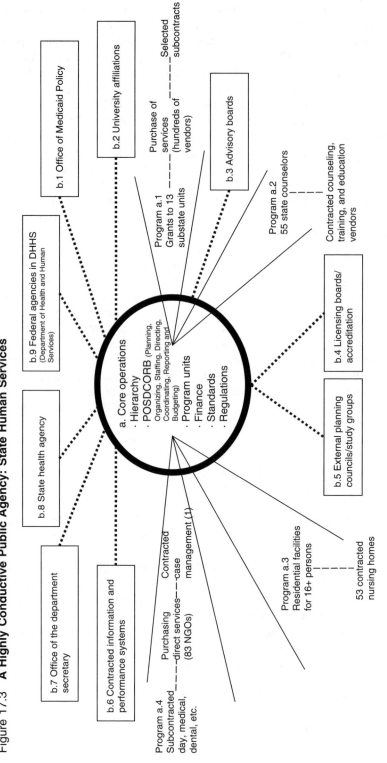

boxes of hierarchy. It is a quintessentially conductive agency that reveals many of the key emergent features of public agency management across boundaries.

Metro High School, in Columbus, Ohio, is an accelerated science, technology, engineering, and math (STEM) undertaking that is uniquely operated by a set of public and private agencies. In this case it extends the USDA/RD and State Human Services models by externalizing all but the traditional core classroom operations, supported by highly conductive learning models. Metro's major learning partners include the Educational Council (superintendents of sixteen of Franklin County's school districts), Ohio State University (OSU), national and state Coalitions for Essential Schools (CES), that is, Knowledge Works in Ohio, and Battelle Corporation, a research and development private sector organization. In addition, other nonpartners are involved: learning sites where students experience internships, projects, field placements, and classes; the PAST Foundation, which organizes research, field learning, and dissemination of STEM learning to the sixteen school districts; nonacademic contractual arrangements with OSU for library and student counseling; OSU volunteer leadership and educational resources; and other community resources such as industry/educator curricula task forces.

Metro's governance is a multifaceted combination, including Educational Council (EC) policy agreement, advice by a steering group, Metropolitan Partnership Group (MPG), and and is administered by the Metro school administration (which is very flat in organization) and the EC staff. The school admits about one hundred students for each class, by interview and lottery; students are ratioed and then apportioned by school population among the sixteen districts. The school operates on an accelerated basis and by subject mastery. Students must master the eighteen subject-related credits required for Ohio high school graduation, normally in their first two years, after which they attend classes at OSU for credit. In addition to the network that undergirds the operation of the school, a community of students, teachers, and parents is involved in many aspects of the school experience (Hunter et al. 2008).

The Metro structure depicted in Figure 17.4 does not look anything like a traditional hierarchy. It is represented by lines and a circle to indicate networked inputs, which are represented by the boxes with organizations that conductively operate Metro. It is actually less complicated than it appears at first look. Legally, Metro is not a school, but an entity that is officially a project of the EC, which is its official governing body. The EC ratifies official decisions normally worked out by the interagency Metropolitan Partnership Group, which explores options and strategies and ultimately formulation of policies and holds the entity together. It is the most involved with school oversight as well, except for fiscal and budget matters, which are handled by the EC executive director and staff.

As shown in Figure 17.4, there is close interaction with the sixteen school districts, the responsible entities for enforcing Ohio high school graduation requirements and career counseling for the Metro students they send. Then there is the consultation/coaching work of Knowledge Works, a commitment of more than $1.1 million during the first four years of the school's existence. OSU also provides Metro with more than $1 million per year in space contributions, and three colleges allocate nearly $1 million each to support up to ten graduate students who are assigned to Metro. The other major partner, Battelle, a large research laboratory, provides seed money, is a major learning partner for STEM, and provides major field learning sites. In addition, there are contractual agreements with OSU for student psychological counseling and for library use. The PAST Foundation plays an important role in transmitting STEM and small school learning to the school districts, and has worked with a research team sponsored by the Battelle Center for Science and Math Education at OSU. Then there are the learning centers, where students apply their knowledge and build mastery portfolios that lead to credit. Also supporting the school's work

280

Figure 17.4 **Metro—Super-Conductive Public Program**

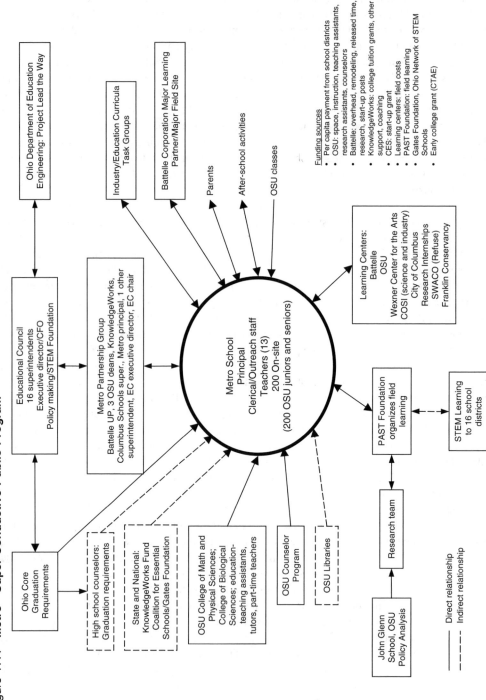

Figure 17.5 **Eight Emergent Organizational Features of Metro**

1. A conductive, open boundaries entity
2. Substantial investments in maintaining connectivity
3. Continuous feedback and redirection
4. Interpartner articulation of important processes
5. Lateral links into policy making from a variety of stakeholders
6. Decision making by consensus that floats into process and ultimately upward
7. Enlistment of real and in-kind financial and learning resources from multiple sources
8. Adaptable, nonhierarchical structure

are OSU classes, after-school activities (journalism, engineering clubs), parent involvement, and a series of industry/educator curricular task forces.

The eight features that distinguish Metro as a different kind of public organization are identified in Figure 17.5. First and foremost, it is a conductive organization. A STEM school like Metro does not have to be organized as a network; it could be a charter school, a special unit of local government, or some other special unit carved out as a school district. It adapted into the network model because it needed open boundaries to build working relationships and to access multiple learning resources and sites. The founders clearly wanted to be independent of any single school district, and they did not want to create a new school district, with an accompanying hierarchy and bureaucracy. They wanted to maximize organizational flexibility. However cumbersome in appearance, this particular structure was reported as suited to Metro's founders' needs for high connectivity.

Second, it is an entity that invests heavily in human and material resources that maintain these connections, including key personnel to maintain collaborative, curricular, and learning-site linkages. For example, one Battelle professional is assigned to the school for linking in scientific learning experiences at Battelle laboratories and other sites. A professional education administrator is involved in school and curricular liaison with the state education agency, the sixteen school districts, and mixed-source curricular task forces. Part of this connectivity also involves infrastructure maintenance through continuing partner dedication of key resources, for example, space, equipment, access to programs, and the like. But there is more. One would also have to point to heavy involvement of students and parents in developing the learning culture of the school, the outreach to the real world through student projects, and the attempt to "export" STEM learning to the sixteen school districts as connective endeavors.

Third, Metro's structure is designed for continuous feedback regarding its organizing, operations, achievements, and culture. Input is regularly provided laterally by key partner representatives, learning-site coordinators, consultants, and coaches, as well as from administrators, teachers, students, and parents. One very important operational example is the building of curricula by task groups that include experienced teachers, university professors, representatives of industry and government, and others. Learning modules are under constant revision, staying as close to the state of the art as possible.

Fourth, resource links are reinforced by participants who have learned that the "devil can be in the details." Issues such as mastery portfolios, pedagogical methods, learning milestones, and individual student pacing are articulated by Metro, learning sites, and the school districts. While these, among other issues, bring heavy transaction costs across organizations, they are conductive maintenance costs that must be borne. These details require routine interorganizational contact—way beyond the old "coordination" at the point of service.

Fifth, operating and support personnel—teachers, learning-site coordinators, parents, supporting associations, curricular task force members—all play a role in the development of operating policies and procedures. Together, they are attempting to find their way into a STEM education that will fit into Metro's mastery model and that is potentially exportable. Developmental work leads to the creation of operating knowledge, which then finds its way to the administration and ultimately to the governance bodies. It is the process of collaborative exploration that leads to knowledge development, which is neither top-down nor bottom-up—but sideways or in all directions. After creation, this operating knowledge works its way invariably into the administrative and governance structures rather than waiting for some form of hierarchical approval.

Sixth, more essential than a hierarchical structure are the partnership affiliations, in this case for STEM education, by learning sites and the support of industry representatives. This structurally requires flexibility that allows for rapid input of information, knowledge, and resource potential, and the ability to make or defer decisions "on the fly." Moreover, it is a decision style that follows a partnership-oriented mode, by consensus. Rather than adopting a long-range plan or plans, as issues arise they are approached on an individual basis, and agreements are reached and rapidly implemented.

Seventh, resources—financial support and learning—real dollars, organizational dollar commitments, and in-kind contributions are found wherever they may lie. Metro does not have a single budget handed down from a higher authority or from the sixteen districts collectively. It is not even clear that it has a budget in the traditional public management sense. A per capita dollar flow roughly equivalent to the annualized state aid formula is agreed upon by the EC, but this amount is generally between 20 and 25 percent of Metro's costs. The remainder is from grants, donations, and in-kind contributions. Other funding sources come and go, as do learning sites and project opportunities in the community. Resource issues are then forced to be "collaboratively fungible." Financing is a problem-oriented "pay as you go and as you can" challenge. The summary in the lower right of Figure 17.4 lists major 2006–8 multiple resource support.

Eighth, and finally, not only is the structure nonhierarchical, but it was built to suit the challenges as they were faced and to accommodate the collaborative nature of the undertaking. It is designed to promote partnering mind-sets and instill trust and a will to collaborate, as Saint-Onge and Armstrong (2004, 16) maintain. The structure, with the exception of a formal (EC) and informal (Metropolitan Partnership Group) governance structure, is more accurately illustrated in the Figure 17.4 depiction of partner, learning resource, and support relationships than in a hierarchically oriented table of organization.

It is therefore difficult to label or identify Metro as an organization in the standard, hierarchical sense. It is an organized undertaking that has unusual public agency standing. Metro was initially made possible by the dedicated energies of key champions and of community leaders. As the school broadens its operations, layers of area teachers, learning-site representatives, and support personnel from OSU expand the network beyond its original and core alliance partners. Metro stands as an example of postbureaucratic organizing by network.

Emergent Conductive Organization Features

An entity like Metro is one alternative to a single-organization hierarchy, even those that have opened up, like the USDA/RD Office and State Human Services. Unlike a true hierarchy, Metro includes a multiagency governing body (EC) and a governance and advisory structure (Metro Partnership Group and administrators); it is not *divisionalized* or specialized. The network is structured by overlays of students, parents, teachers, administrators, learning-site representatives, and learning partners. Instead of command and control, Metro as a network features consensus-based decision models. Its participants experience role differentiation in an overlapping fashion but operate with a fluid participatory agreement-seeking orientation. Authority is in many places. In the case of the two hypothetical examples identified in Figures 17.2 and 17.3, one sees hierarchies moving in this direction. In particular, the highly externalized structure in State Human Services is coming to resemble Metro in many important aspects. Organizationally, "boundaries" are opening up to systems of comanagement at both the operating policy and services delivery levels. Theoretically, this makes conductive agencies very different from standard hierarchies. An additional series of features, beyond the conductive USDA/RD Office, State Human Services, and Metro characteristics already identified, appear to be hallmarks of conductive organizing as they appear to be emerging in similar organizing situations.

Like Metro, many conductive organizations will be nonhierarchical to one degree or another, with networklike highly *flexible collaborarchies*. A study (Agranoff 2007) of fourteen networks defined them as self-managed bodies of officials who employ self-imposed rules that use consensus to develop collaborative capacity (Bardach 1998), instigating exchanges and developing cooperative dispositions and mutual understandings among the individuals trying to work together on common tasks (307). The Metro study demonstrates that the principle of "soft guidance" by the multiple focal nodes is an accurate description of the way decisions are made and actions are taken (Windhoff-Héntier 1992). Such guidance is the collaborative or network equivalent of direct supervision in hierarchical organizations. The most central administrators in Figure 17.3 (State Human Services), the top-level departmental secretary and the administrators of the divisions and the three operating program heads (b.7, a, a.1, a.2, a.3), are significant for information flow and planning, but they do not dominate the operations of the network. The division head and the program heads are indeed the center of the service operation universe, but there is substantial evidence from previous network research that suggests that a focal hub or hubs between the service planner and deliverers can be critical to network success (Meier and O'Toole 2003). Although the classical approach views networks as being flat, self-organizing, completely interdependent entities (Powell 1990), it has been found that, in practice, a network center is not uncommon. Case studies of community mental health networks, for example, demonstrate that the effectiveness of the networks was based in part on the extent to which the network was coordinated centrally through a core agency (Provan and Milward 1995). The key is that in flexible collaborarchies there may be an operational hub in the government agency, but other nodes have been, and remain, indispensable to a conductive unit's operation.

Another principle of collaborative organizing appears to be legal authority by *transferred governance*. In order to avoid a state of complete anarchy, partnerships, networks, and related collaborative bodies need to have some body of legitimate authority to make agreements and for operational rule making. Given their interorganizational nature, legally based hierarchical executive authority is not a good fit. Rather, these bodies are more comfortable with the transformation of partial authority from the hierarchical organizations they represent to a collegial body that takes in input from "below," seeks consensus, and decides (McGuire 2002). The Metro EC operates very much in this fashion. It has some overlapping representation on the Metro Partnership Group, including the key superintendent (who sends almost 60 percent of the students) but listens on most policy issues to the Metro Partnership Group, which in turn overlaps with the administration, which relies on multiple lateral inputs. In a similar sense, governance in conductive public agencies like USDA/RD Office is based on the ability of key partners with legal authority to shift (minor) portions of their legally based hierarchical authority to the collaborative structure or to those agencies down the line that carry out programs or offer services. This would clearly be the case with regard to their grants and loans to small communities.

Another experience is that conductive organization planning and organizing is problem focused. It normally is flexible and springs from multiparty agreements that are *interactive, discursive,* and *sequential.* The extensive Metro network of contacts, contracts, grants, and partnerships depicted in Figure 17.4 was built piece by piece, not as an externally created, finely tuned machine that was completely ready to operate from the outset with a five-year plan. Conductive agencies meet their challenges as they emerge, almost on a case-by-case, one-by-one basis. For example, an agency like State Human Services could spend from three to four years coming to agreement with the eighty-three rehabilitation agencies regarding reimbursement costs for day and for residential-based services. It will involve information systems, cost models, reporting data, task force studies, multiple meetings, starts and stops, failed vendor contracts, and perhaps legislator inquiries. Clearly, the experience is a protracted process. As needs arise, plans follow to meet a particular challenge. This nonlinear mode appears to be a characteristic of flexible organizing.

In a similar fashion to most conductive organizations, Metro and State Human Services (Figure 17.3) experience relatively *complex operations,* with series upon series of multinetworked interactions and transactions. A succession sequence of problem emergence–problem delay–problem solution at Metro demonstrates how adaptive structures need to anticipate challenges but often delay solving them until they have put together the multiple agreements and resources required for earlier, more pressing concerns. The space issue at Metro is an example. Metro first had to find a space, with the prime cooperation of Battelle and OSU. When the students arrived, Metro had to find learning sites outside of the school. In the third year, the first class was about to enter OSU, and a new space issue arose: where classes would be held besides at OSU because the original site is limited to two hundred students. Like many other networks, small and large problems are solved as they need to be faced, by collaborative agreement, not when they are uncovered (Agranoff 2007). In the case of State Human Services, every time a new Medicaid order or standard is changed, it sends reverberations and new challenges through the agency and its working partners.

In turn, the key network or conductive agency strategic interactions are regularized or patterned into *sets of joint strategies* that are the interorganizational equivalent of interdepartmental agreements or decisions that affect operations in bureaucracies. They are approached as negotiations-adjustments-accommodations-decisions by partners between major participating organizations. It is not unusual in an extended services department like that of State Human Services to engage in a series of agreements between the government agency and interlocutors (NGOs) over payment rates and reimbursement mechanisms, billing forms and formats, required program and fiscal reporting, standards of services quality, professional qualifications of client contact personnel, and performance indicators. These major issues normally become multiparty operating policies but are built one by one between the impacted organizations on a more or less consensus basis, not by mandate, and form one important set of conductive operational "rubrics."

An additional set of key organizational concerns, particularly with purchase-of-services contracting in the State Human Services example, is at the core of interorganizational conductivity: the constant demand for more detailed, articulation-based interoperability (Jenkins 2006, 321). This collaborative management practice is a means of bridging organizations or operations at a more detailed level. It has been defined as "reciprocal communication and accommodation in order to reach interactive operating policy and programming forthcoming. In an externalized services agency, the work of one contractor often must fit with the work of others who are serving the same client. The Metro process of awarding each student credit for work done in the classroom and in the field or laboratory fits this process, as the Metro curriculum coordinator or principal and a school district professional look at records and portfolios and come to agreement on what constitutes the classroom equivalent of a given project. Likewise, the agency in Figure 17.2 (USDA/RD Office) will have to develop working understandings between its financial and procurement procedures (a) and contractees (b.1) and grantees (b.4) so that external agents follow accepted funding and audit procedures. Interoperability involves considerably more than the standard "bargaining and negotiation," often gratuitously thrown around in the literature on coordination. The process follows a sequence something like this: joint agreement on core principles, interactive planning, reaching key understandings, program articulation routines, reciprocal decision operationalization, and feedback and correction. Interoperability is a quintessential boundary-spanning activity that will draw increasing administrative interest as organizations of the future accelerate their interdependencies (Agranoff and McGuire, in progress).

Moving more externally, any conductive organization that operates outside of traditional government boundaries like the Metro network or State Human Services faces *multiple performance accountability* points. In this case it is to the partners, to external stakeholders in industry and business, to the scientific community, to public agencies, and to the small schools movement and to students and their families (for Metro). Esmark (2007, 283, 287, 293–294) suggests that there are three challenges in network accountability, which appear to be relevant for conductive agency or partner endeavors. First, networks need to be considered as representative forums, to be inclusive in scope and to be concerned with relevant stakeholders outside of the formal membership of the network. Second, networks need to institutionalize procedures of publicly assuming responsibility and giving explanations according to basic standards of communication to the stakeholders or moral constituency outside of the network. Third, in networks, accountability means that recognition must be given internally to different types of mandates or sanctions from participating representative organizations at the same time that they pay attention to nonorganized stakeholders. This is a challenging order for multiorganizational entities, and it makes the performance quotient quite difficult. As Robert Behn (2001, 77) concludes, collaborative operations mean that "the one-bill, one policy, one organization, one accountability holdee principle doesn't work for performance."

Finally, in any situation where a public agency is involved in working with multiple partners, these entities will have to work hard to *build their own joint-venture legitimacy*. As partners rather than bureaus, they will rarely have the kind of "automatic" legislative authorization that modern bureaucracies have experienced to enable their existence. Even with a legal charter, the networked entity will still have to prove its mettle, as various pieces of the "public trust" are contracted out to NGOs, which now also have a role in program development. How a network or collaborative structure grows and evolves into public acceptance is an important question (Human and Provan 2000) that requires considerable study in the future. Maintaining the legitimacy of the Metro network as a recognizable entity, particularly to outsiders, became one mechanism for growth and acceptance. The founders understood that building legitimacy means that internal network participants need to find public value in their membership and continue to provide resources and support (Moore 1995). In the Metro study, a great deal of collaborative capacity was built among the major partners, but the social network analyses and the interviews with teachers and parents reveal a marked gap in the degree of connectivity with the learning partners (Hunter et al. 2008). Metro is now finding a way for these potentially influential entities to become viable participants in the network's processes in order to enhance legitimacy.

CHALLENGES IN MANAGING CONDUCTIVE AGENCIES

The case is being made for government action that extends beyond the unilateral actions of government officials. They now are called upon to develop more involved external working contacts.

It therefore entails the induced interactive multilateral actions involving NGOs operating *with* public agencies. This involves, as Frederickson (1999, 703) has indicated, changing tasks of administration as jurisdiction and management become increasingly separated. Eleven emergent collaborative management functions for those working in and with conductive agencies appear to be at the core of the public management challenge.

1. Executive Leadership in External Mobilization

First and foremost are challenges related to involving people from disparate venues to engage in policy and entrepreneurial leadership. This is actually an internal and an external task. Internally, it is important that collaborative managers receive the proper leadership signals and support, and this is a primary function of the collaborative "champion." Without such top-level support, the internal natural bureaucratic resistances and turf-protection behaviors (of which there are many) can flourish. This champion role also includes support by agency executives, such as department heads. Empowerment is also critical. Leaders must go beyond lip service; they must facilitate an internal atmosphere that generates program-level participation, sharing of information, joint learning, and participative decision making. In many ways this model of empowerment of staff to work outside the agency is a contemporary extension of more traditional executive leadership functions.

Externally, targets involve convincing or working with critically important organizations outside government—the regulated, competing businesses, alternative service deliverers, and advocacy groups—to participate in a collaborative endeavor. This normally requires initial enlistment of a series of top NGO executives, industry and trade associations, and advocacy groups, after which technical and managerial people can be brought into the collaborative enterprise for the detailed negotiations. These tasks are more nontraditional, convincing sets of external parties to enter into new working relationships *with* government (Agranoff 2003; Bryson and Crosby 1992).

2. Network Promotion

A related conductive role for the public manager involves the need for public agencies to reinvent themselves by encouraging the creation and flow of information across public agencies and outside of government. Clearly, the existing deep involvement of public managers as alliance managers in generating partnerships, networks, challenge grants, venture capital pools, and contracts-for-services programs, as well as electronic information networks, underscores this role. Partners do not automatically come together, but they can be leveraged. Public managers are in pivotal positions to perform such convening actions. As a result, bureaucrats cannot wait to read about networks of agencies in the latest trade publication or journal or for NGOs to seek them out. They need to look for and include potential stakeholders that can transform human capital into live systems of problem identification and solution (Bryson and Crosby 1992).

3. Brokering the Collaborative

Yet another challenge relates to the employment of early government intervention policies. In order to achieve results, the public manager cannot wait for ideas to come forward from outside of government but must discover and create potential opportunities for action, linking scarce public resources with external resources, ideas, and investments. This is the brokering role that not only brings the parties together but makes timely public investments and moves collaborative groups along.

But more is necessary. The public manager cannot sit back and watch these programs develop outside of government, because too much is at stake. Managers need to broker by bringing different actors to the table, activating and facilitating them. This is very different behavior from handing out a grant or a loan or monitoring a contract. Brokering involves a whole set of human capital skills in negotiation and creation of a culture of joint problem solving that values equality, adaptability, discretion, and a focus on results (Agranoff 2003; Bardach 1998; McGuire 2000). This type of team building is not new, but working at it across organizations requires somewhat different considerations than apply in the case of the hierarchical organization (Agranoff and McGuire 2001).

4. Mutual Learning Models

Deliberative work under these circumstances involves a different kind of process than consultation or reacting to proposals. It involves growing and learning together. As Forester (1999, 62) suggests, in deliberative work, citizens (in this case participants) integrate the worlds of "is" and "ought" as well as "science" and "ethics" as they learn how to get something done and what ought to be done in new and unique situations. "Connecting governance and dispute resolution, politics and ethics, deliberative practice involves the most intellectually intriguing issues . . . how can we learn not only about technique but about value; how can we change our minds about what is important, change our appreciation of what matters, and, more, change our practical sense about what we can do together too." The administrator in the conductive agency cannot sit back and react but must become a part of this process of looking for and helping respond to concern and need by forging the new and possible.

5. Internal and External Organizing

Calibrating the organization to be able to work with external groups, needs, and interests goes well beyond the normal tenets of organizational design, including the standard building of teams (Provan and Kenis 2008). The key is not divisional realignment or more and more teams but opening these functions to organized agency clientele through constant processes that inform the agency's thinking, actions, and relationships through constant knowledge flow, that is, intimate understanding of its external working interlocutors. This can invoke a number of mutual actions, such as continuing work with stakeholders, codeveloped solutions, accepting input on shaping rules, cross-functional integration (e.g., joint production), integration with external agency or external organization operating systems, developing solutions based on externally perceived value, and strategic partnerships (Saint-Onge and Armstrong 2004, 57). Clearly, these practices have become part of the new organizational design, a set of lateral overlays on the enduring hierarchical structure.

6. Information Beyond the Walls

The conductive agency administrator will increasingly need to capture the information-based nature of the agency. Deliberation works better when the parties engaged in joint undertakings are better informed. Networks find it hard to settle the most nettlesome problems that they face unless they combine existing information bases into decision-ready knowledge (Agranoff 2007, chapter 7). Information strategies definitely make the quality of deliberation easier, and that is why conductive administrators invest increasing resources of database collections and new information systems, along with planning and skill building, community leadership, needs analysis, action planning, education, and training, as well as program impact studies.

7. Conductive Public-Serving Staff

In these times, knowledge employees are wanted. The conductive organization needs a knowledge-oriented administrator base. As information is converted into knowledge that is transacted and modified through deliberation, the agency needs to capture those invisible assets that reside largely in the minds of humans, requiring less strict supervision and with worker and manager working side by side. The rules of supervision for knowledge workers are different. According to Davenport (2005, 192–201) they entail (1) participation by managers in the work instead of overseeing work; (2) changing from organizing hierarchies to organizing communities; (3) retaining workers rather than hiring and firing them; (4) building knowledge skills rather than manual skills; (5) assessing invisible knowledge achievements instead of evaluating visible job performance; (6) building knowledge-friendly cultures instead of ignoring culture; (7) fending off bureaucracy rather than supporting it; (8) relying on a variety of human resources, wherever they may be located, instead of relying on internal personnel. These principles of human resources management clearly apply to those public agency employees who are working out of the organization with others on joint resolution of issues and problems.

8. The Core Function of Building Communities

Building high-quality relationships comes in part through establishing communities of problem solvers. It is common practice for conductive agencies to deliberate through the building of communities of practice and taking advantage of epistemic communities. Communities of practice are self-organizing systems that share the capacity to create and use knowledge through informal learning and mutual engagement (Wenger 2000). Most communities are self-organized and bring in new knowledge bearers when needed, from wherever they can be found. Maintenance of communities of practice requires effort to keep different types of knowledge bearers in, by challenging busy people with solving important public problems and by calling on their experience and know-how in an interdisciplinary manner.

Community can be facilitated by mobilizing a multiagency group of professionals from different disciplines who share common outlooks and similar solution orientations. Haas (1992, 3) suggests that these persons can represent a variety of disciplines and share normative and principled beliefs, which provide a value-based rationale for social action. They also tend to share causal beliefs, notions of validity, and a common policy enterprise. An epistemic community normally produces consensual knowledge. Even in the face of anomalous data, the community may suspend judgment in order to maintain its scientific legitimacy, maintaining for the moment its power resource (Hass 1990, 55). Even though epistemic community members may not constitute the most powerful decision makers, they "are well situated to provide a driving logic for cooperation" (Thomas 2003, 41).

9. Knowledge Agencies

Among the new core activities that agencies pursue can be a knowledge strategy. It has been suggested that the conductive organization enhances value by interacting with organized external clientele in collaboration, particularly through communities. A conductive organization can then capture intangible assets through the exchange of knowledge. According to Saint-Onge and Armstrong (2004, 38), value creation involves the managed interaction among (1) the human capital of the agency, (2) the structural or organizational capabilities, and (3) interacting external agents and partners. All three need to be developed in a knowledge strategy on an integrated basis. Many activities are involved in the process of knowledge management (Davenport and Prusak 2000), a process that entails identifying, extracting, and capturing fluid mixes of framed experiences, values, contextual information, and expert insight that constitute the assets of any undertaking. In the case of public conductive organizations, knowledge is derived on a highly interactive basis and is geared to adding some form of public value (Agranoff 2007, chapters 7 and 8).

Conductive agencies might pursue one or more of many knowledge management activities. Working with organized clientele, they can begin by surveying the universe of data and information among those involved in a project or program. They can also search for external databases of potential internal use. Extant data can then be used to develop "own source" explicit (codified) knowledge, through such means as libraries, map inventories, strategic plans, fact sheets and policy guides, focused studies, surveys, conferences and workshops, electronic bulletin boards, process reviews, long-range plans, models and simulations, and market studies. Although tacit (noncodified) knowledge is harder to deal with, it can be approached through stakeholder consultations, best practices or benchmark exchanges, work groups as "communities of practice," study-project report panels, expert presentations, specialized workshops, (strengths, weaknesses, opportunities, and threats) or SWOT workshops, hands-on technical assistance, community leadership development sessions, forums on "what works," direct agency outreach, "help desks," and public hearings. The agency can then work at the explicit/tacit interface through informal feedback on the myriad of activities it engages, usually through informal postproject assessment. Finally, some of the knowledge needs of partner agencies can be served through formal reports, responses for data requests, supplying modeling and planning data, circulating policy reports, sponsoring in-agency forums and report sessions, providing technical expert linkages, and possibly providing agency-requested studies.

10. Conductive Electronic Communication

It follows that agencies need to establish conductive support through electronic communication. It will come as no surprise that all of these knowledge activities are now supported by the use of different types of information and communications technology: e-mail, teleconferencing, Web-based geographic information systems, decision-support software, and the like. These are essential tools since partners are situated in disparate organizational locations. However, because of the collaborative nature of their tasks, they are not a substitute for face-to-face meetings, but a parallel mode of collaborative work. In the same way that organizations seek structured predictability, organized collaborative actions require the use of open-ended processes of coordinating purposeful individuals who can apply their unique skills and experiences to particular problems confronting the collaborative undertaking at hand. They are part of the distributed knowledge systems that are created across boundaries, possessing somewhat fewer constraints or rule-bounded actions. Often at the center of such relationships, the conductive agency needs to foster information and communication technology links along with the more direct community of practice building mentioned above.

11. Assessing Conductivity's Value Adding

Public managers should not, as Bardach suggests, be impressed by the idea of collaboration per se, but only if it produces better organizational performance or lower costs than its alternatives

(1998, 17). The rationale for investment in a network or other forms of collaborative management normally entails more than collective public purpose, vaguely understood; it also includes those advantages collaboration can bring to each partner's mission and operations and to the specialists and managers as professionals. Thus, value adding can be accounted for from the perspective of the administrator or specialist, participating organization, network process, and network outcomes. This value adding helps to bridge the gap of difficult-to-measure outcomes by shifting the ground to intermediate ones (Wye 2002, 27).

The value added from network participation for managers and specialists is not well understood. An exception is Thomas's (2003, 41) study of interagency collaboration in biodiversity preservation, which demonstrates the epistemic interactions among program specialists who naturally cooperate. To the professional manager, the interagency process provides for a broadened "expansion of possibilities" in both technical and interactive ways and thus brings self-development benefits. Closely related are benefits to the network participants' home organizations. The literature on networking points to the importance of expanding information and access to expertise of other organizations, pooling and accessing financial and other resources, sharing risks and innovation investments, managing uncertainty, fulfilling the need for flexibility in operation and response time, and accessing other adaptive efficiencies (Alter and Hage 1993; Powell 1990). All of these functions potentially are channeled through critical problem-solving or program-adjustment processes, which bring potential to add value to an organization.

The collaborative process itself provides potential value in both process and tangible ways. From a process standpoint, collective—rather than authority-based—organizing, decision making, and programming prevail but follow group dynamics similar to those of single organizations (Agranoff 2003; McGuire 2002). Managing a collaborative enterprise involves formal or informal benchmarking of joint "steering" of interaction processes that sequence activation, guided mediation, finding strategic consensus, joint problem solving, and the activities of maintenance, implementation, and adjustment (Kickert and Koppenjan 1997, 47–51). These actions contribute to productive collaborative products. Tangible outcomes vary considerably by collaborative undertaking, but specific products of networks include Web sites, service agreements, mutual referrals, joint investment projects, incidents of NGO assistance, loans arranged, grants facilitated, investments leveraged, and so on. Another set of tangible results includes end stages of collaborative processes: adapted policies, new target populations served, joint or collaborative databases, exchanged resources, new program interfaces, mutually adapted technologies, and enhanced interagency knowledge infrastructures (Agranoff and McGuire 2001; Kickert and Koppenjan 1997; O'Toole 1997). Collaborative performance management is thus eminently assessable along four dimensions: professional, organizational, process, and product.

EXTENDING THE CONDUCTIVE AGENDA

These practices are not part of an idealistic managerial agenda but reflect the real work of public managers in the network era (Agranoff 2007; McGuire 2009; Edelenbos, Klijn, and Steijn 2009; Meier and O'Toole 2003). The public manager is also a network operative. The prior agenda suggests that more needs to be known about the emergent interactivity of public agencies. Most agencies today are involved heavily in both intergovernmental and interorganizational webs of relationships that are a product of the state moving from more of a provider role to one that "enables" a series of social and economic activities (Loughlin 2000).

One core concern is where the boundaries of the state might lie. Hirst (2000) indicates that only government can pull together the various strands because it continues to distribute powers and responsibilities, remains the focus of political identity, and is the main institution of democratic legitimacy; as a result, other entities view its decisions and commitments as reliable. Nevertheless, government continues to externalize its functions, even such quasi-legal functions as public auditing, child welfare intake and referral, welfare case management, the operation of public roads, prisons, and correctional facilities, and many more. Questions about these activities need to be continually asked, as Berry and Brower (2005, 11) indicate: "We should ask who creates the goals of these activities and how desirable outcomes are identified and disseminated."

If one accepts the idea that the state has not hollowed out (Milward, Provan, and Else 1993) but has shifted its role, we must know more of what the state is doing and how that differs from its prior role of providing direct-services delivery activities. For example, regarding ID/DD in many states, where the running of institutions was the core activity (and budget eater), externalized services have now given way to Medicaid policy and Medicaid program specialists, quality control and community care outcomes specialists, planning and information specialists, facility inspectors, case managers, and contract managers. Other than the thousands of displaced direct-care and first-level middle-management personnel at state institutions, some small number but substantial core of state workers appear to be at work doing different things and are deployed in new units. Moreover, some states (e.g., North Carolina, Ohio) have decentralized the direct services management and oversight functions to local government units or special multicounty units, casting doubtful shadows on privatization. Meanwhile, managers in the NGOs who have departed government now run nonprofit programs that are 90 to 95 percent publicly funded. All of this makes the hollow state seem somewhat less hollow. More must be learned about these nondirect-service public agency roles, who fills them, how staff are educated and trained, what kind of work they do, how are they supervised, and most important, what kind of operational roles they play within networks and in managing conductivity.

Research in these arenas can help to define that important middle ground between government and agent or partner. Although we are able to offer some clues here (see also Smith and Lipsky 1993) about how parties—NGO and government—work interactively, more needs to be known about how public agencies and their NGOs reach important agreements. One documented incident suggests years of protracted interactions, trade-offs, counterproposals, and at-the-table interactive collaborative agreements among network partners who now guide Indiana ID/DD services (IN-ARF 2009). Their long-term aim, to develop a uniform methodology for purchase of services, is an example of the movement in contracting toward some form of interactive process (Van Slyke 2007), but more needs to be known about how programs are shaped between service-delivery agents and government.

Related are the complicated processes of how citizen representatives, scientists and engineers, public agency program administrators, and interest group trade associations sit at the table and solve the most nettlesome of shared power and responsibility policy problems. This, of course is one of the reasons why networks are formed (O'Toole 1997), as are other collaborative bodies (Agranoff and McGuire 2001). Cases exist in the literature that describe such processes (Agranoff 2007; Imperial 2004; McGuire 2009). Generally, they involve some blending of the various legal, political, technical, and financial considerations (Agranoff 1986) as the parties try to fit together a puzzle of interests, constraints, experiences, and knowledge. More needs to be known about how networks of actors sit down to solve problems since so many issues are multisector, multiprogram, and multiagent in nature.

A final knowledge gap is that of understanding the linkages from clients receiving services to the policies and programs that enable these services. This is a particularly acute issue when government contracts client contact and intake functions. In some U.S. states, for example, Texas and Indiana, attempts have been made to remove intake for welfare payments, that is, assistance under Temporary Assistance for Needy Families (TANF), food stamps, and Medicaid eligibility, from state employee caseworkers in the field and turned over to private information or customer service firms. In other situations the first-step case-management or gate-keeping function has been contracted out to private, for-profit firms. Clients' first contact can be with a telephone call center or a computer terminal, not a person. A lot has been written in local newspapers about various service fallouts in these situations. That is not the issue here. The concern is if one "backward maps" (Elmore 1985) from client-service provider up the line to intermediate (e.g., state government) service principal to policy-enabling bodies (e.g., federal government), what is it doing to program structure? Moreover, whom does the program serve, those in need or those who administer the program? Finally, and most important from a public management standpoint, what have these arrangements done to public programming? Public administration as a field has yet to answer these questions surrounding purchase of direct-services contracting.

CONCLUSION

More than the public agencies illustrated are conductive. Thousands of city and county governments not only engage in community and economic development activities, but work externally with services-oriented citizen boards, contract for services, and partner with other governments and nongovernmental entities (Agranoff and McGuire 2003). At the state level, most highway construction is by contracting by state transportation agencies, and highway planning is shared with networks of metropolitan planning organizations. State environmental management agencies administer federal legislation through local governments and regulated industries and organizations. At the federal level, more and more agencies, for example, Department of Housing and Urban Development housing programs, Community Development Block Grants, Economic Development Administration, Commerce–Small Business Administration, Health and Human Services (e.g., Medicaid and Older Americans Act), all operate by intergovernmental contract with grant intermediaries at the first stage and beyond, making them equally conductive. In various ways they all have to connectively engage, and in most cases, with emergent forms of deliberative engagement.

Bureaucracy thus continues to play important roles. As functions have been added to it, it has not been diminished so much as changed. Johan Olsen (2006) concludes that bureaucracy is still with us, embedded in democratic-constitutive principles and procedural rationality, coexisting with market and network forms. Bureaucracy faces "different challenges, command[s] different resources and [is] embedded in different political and administrative traditions" (18). Bureaucracy, in this sense, needs to come to grips with externalization; it must adapt to increased operation between markets and networks.

As a result, the field of public administration must pay considerably more attention to the changing external or conductive role of public manager. For the administrator in the conductive agency, it means more than reading the rules and regulations, listening at hearings, engaging in information exchanges, dealing with advocates and adversaries, or reading project reports. It involves working together to create knowledge-based public dialogue and to reach mutually arrived at solutions to problems of mutual concern. Calibration of external information, concerns, and needs is now part of a regularized connectivity through interactive joint problem-resolution processes. Conductive public agencies work primarily with NGO administrators on calibration, knowledge, strategy, and implementation—all collaborative processes. This is the emergent role for the public administrator or program professional in the public agency.

REFERENCES

Agranoff, Robert. 1986. *Intergovernmental Management: Human Services Problem-Solving in Six Metropolitan Areas.* Albany: State University of New York Press.

———. 2003. *Leveraging Networks: A Guide for Public Managers Working Across Organizations.* Arlington, VA: IBM Endowment for the Business of Government.

———. 2007. *Managing Within Networks: Adding Value to Public Organizations.* Washington, DC: Georgetown University Press.

———. 2008. Conductive public organizations in networks. In *Civic Engagement in a Networked Society,* ed., Eric Bergrud and Kaifeng Yang, 85—108. Charlotte, NC: Information Age.

Agranoff, Robert, and Michael McGuire. 2001. Big questions in public network management research. *Journal of Public Administration Research and Theory* 11 (July): 295–326.

———. 2003. *Collaborative Public Management: New Strategies for Local Governments.* Washington, DC: Georgetown University Press.

———. In progress. *Interoperability: Managing Public Agency Interfaces.*

Alter, Catherine, and Jerald Hage. 1993. *Organizations Working Together.* Beverly Hills, CA: Sage.

Bardach, Eugene. 1998. *Getting Agencies to Work Together.* Washington, DC: Brookings Institution Press.

Behn, Robert. 2001. *Rethinking Democratic Accountability.* Washington, DC: Brookings Institution Press.

Berry, Frances Stokes, and Ralph S. Brower. 2005. Intergovernmental and intersectoral management: Weaving, networking, contracting out and management rules into third party government. *Public Performance and Management Review* 24 (1): 7–17.

Bryson, John, and Barbara Crosby. 1992. *Leadership for the Common Good.* San Francisco: Jossey-Bass.

Clegg, Stewart R. 1990. *Modern Organizations: Organization Studies in the Postmodern World.* London: Sage.

Davenport, Thomas H. 2005. *Thinking for a Living: How to Get a Better Performance and Results from Knowledge Workers.* Boston: Harvard Business School Press.

Davenport, Thomas H., and Larry Prusak. 2000. *Working Knowledge: How Organizations Manage What They Know.* Boston: Harvard Business School Press.

Edelenbos, Jurian, Erik-Hans Klijn, and Bram Steijn. 2009. Network managers in governance networks: What they do and how effective are they? Paper presented at the Tenth Public Management Research Conference, Columbus, Ohio, October 1–3.

Elmore, Richard F. 1985. Forward and backward mapping: Reversible logic in the study of public policy. In *Policy Implementation in Federal and Unitary Systems,* ed. Kenneth Hanf and Theo A.J. Toonen. Dordrecht, Netherlands: Martinus Nijhoff.

Esmark, Anders. 2007. Democratic accountability and network governance. In *Theories of Democratic Network Governance,* ed. Eva Sorensen and Jacob Torfung. Houndsmills, Basingstoke, UK: Palgrave Macmillan.

Forester, John. 1999. *The Deliberative Practitioner: Encouraging Participatory Planning Processes.* Cambridge, MA: MIT Press.

Frederickson, H. George. 1999. The repositioning of American public administration. *PS: Political Science and Politics* 32 (4): 701–711.

Galbraith, Jay. 1977. *Organization Design.* Reading, MA: Addison-Wesley.

Haas, Peter M. 1990. *Saving the Mediterranean: The Politics of International Environmental Cooperation.* New York: Columbia University Press.

———. 1992. Introduction: Epistemic communities and international policy coordination. *International Organization* 46 (1): 1–35.

Hirst, Paul. 2000. Democracy and governance. In *Debating Governance,* ed. Jon Pierre, 13—35. Oxford: Oxford University Press.

Holbeche, Linda. 2005. *The High Performance Organization.* Amsterdam: Elsevier.

Human, Shirley E., and Keith G. Provan. 2000. Legitimacy building in the evolution of small-firm multilateral networks: A comparative study of success and demise. *Administrative Science Quarterly* 45 (2): 327–365.

Hunter, Monica, Robert Agranoff, Michael McGuire, Jill Greenbaum, Janice Morrison, Maria Cohen, and Jing Liu. 2008. *Metro High School: An Emerging STEM Community.* Grant 420038AC-07, 31. Columbus, OH: PAST Foundation/Battelle Center for Mathematics and Science Education Policy.

Imperial, Mark. 2004. *Collaboration and Performance Management in Network Settings: Lessons from Three Watershed Governance Efforts.* Washington, DC: IBM Center for the Business of Government.

INARF. 2009. Reimbursement reform update. E-mail from Indiana Association of Rehabilitation Facilities to INARF and Arc members, August 6.

Jenkins, William O. 2006. Collaboration over adaptation: The case for interoperable communications in homeland security. *Public Administration Review* 66 (3): 319–322.

Kickert, Walter J.M., and Joop Koppenjan. 1997. Public management and network management. In *Managing Complex Networks,* ed., Walter J.M. Kickert, Erik-Hans Klijn, and Joop Koppenjan, 35–61. London: Sage.

Kooiman, Jan. 2004. *Governing as Governance.* London: Sage.

Loughlin, John. 2000. Regional autonomy and state paradigm shifts. *Regional and Federal Studies* 10 (2): 10–34.

McGuire, Michael. 2000. Collaborative policy making and administration: The operations demands for local economic development. *Economic Development Quarterly* 14 (3): 276–291.

———. 2002. Managing networks: Propositions on what managers do and why they do it. *Public Administration Review* 62 (5): 426–433.

———. 2009. The new professionalism and collaborative activity in local emergency management. In *The Collaborative Public Manager,* ed. Rosemary O'Leary and Lisa B. Bingham. Washington, DC: Georgetown University Press.

Meier, Kenneth J., and Laurence J. O'Toole Jr. 2003. Public management and educational performance: The impact of managerial networking. *Public Administration Review* 63 (6): 689–699.

Milward, H. Brinton, Keith Provan, and Barbara Else. 1993. What does the "hollow state" look like? In *Public Management: The State of the Art,* ed. B. Bozeman. San Francisco: Jossey-Bass.

Moore, Mark. 1995. *Creating Public Value: Strategic Management in Government.* Cambridge, MA: Harvard University Press.

Olsen, Johan P. 2006. Maybe it is time to rediscover bureaucracy. *Journal of Public Administration Research and Theory* 16 (January): 1–24.

O'Toole, Laurence J. 1997. Treating networks seriously: Practical and research-based agenda in public administration. *Public Administration Review* 57 (1): 45–52.

Powell, Walter W. 1990. Neither market or hierarchy: Network forms of organization. *Research in Organizational Behavior* 12 (1): 295–336.

Provan, Keith G., and Patrick Kenis. 2008. Modes of network governance: Structure, management, and effectiveness. *Journal of Public Administration Research and Theory* 18 (2): 224–352.

Provan, Keith G., and H. Brent Milward. 1995. A preliminary theory of interorganizational effectiveness: A comparative study of four community mental health systems. *Administrative Science Quarterly* 40 (1): 1–33.

Saint-Onge, Hubert, and Charles Armstrong. 2004. *The Conductive Organization.* Amsterdam: Elsevier.

Salamon, Lester M. 2002. The new governance and the tools of public action. In *The Tools of Government,* ed. Lester M. Salamon, 1–47. New York: Oxford University Press.

Schön, Donald A. 1979. Generative metaphor: A perspective on problem setting in social policy. In *Metaphor and Thought,* ed. Andrew Ortony. Cambridge: Cambridge University Press.

Smith, Steven R., and Michael Lipsky. 1993. *Nonprofits for Hire: The Welfare State in the Age of Contracting.* Cambridge, MA: Harvard University Press.

Thomas, Craig W. 2003. *Bureaucratic Landscape: Interagency Cooperation and the Preservation of Biodiversity.* Cambridge, MA: MIT Press.

Thompson, James D. 1967. *Organizations in Action.* New York: McGraw-Hill.

Van Slyke, David. 2007. Agents or stewards: Government nonprofit social service contracting relationships. *Journal of Public Administration Research and Theory* 17 (2): 157–187.

Weber, Max. 1946. *From Max Weber: Essays in Sociology.* Trans. and ed. H.H. Gerth and C. Wright Mills. New York: Oxford University Press.

Wenger, Etienne. 2000. Communities of practice: The key to knowledge strategy. In *Knowledge and Communities,* ed. Eric L. Lesser, Michael A. Fontaine, and Jason A. Slusher. Boston: Butterworth-Heinemann.

Windhoff-Héntier, Andriene. 1992. The internationalization of domestic policy: A motor of decentralization. Paper prepared for European Consortium for Political Research Joint Sessions, Limerick, Ireland, March 12–16.

Wye, Chris. 2002. *Performance Management: A "Start Where You Are Use What You Have" Guide.* Arlington, VA: IBM Endowment for the Business of Government.

PART IV

GOVERNANCE AND REFORM

Governance and *reform* have become common expressions in the public administration vernacular. There is disagreement, however, on what the terms mean. More precisely, they often have relative meanings. For some in the profession, *governance* is what governments do. For others it is intersector, interorganizational collaboration; some see it as citizen-driven administration. *Reform* also has many connotations. It is used to refer to political, legislative, and administrative processes. What is consistent about governance and reform is they both serve to reinvigorate discussions, which often yield new prospects, proposals, and vision for improving the provision of public services.

The works in this section fall in this category. Deil S. Wright, Carl W. Stenberg, and Chung-Lae Cho's chapter, "Historic Relevance Confronting Contemporary Obsolescence? Federalism, Intergovernmental Relations, and Intergovernmental Management" explores the use of governance in the context of "federalism and its legacy concepts, intergovernmental relations and intergovernmental management." The authors point out that these are "the antecedents and foundation stones on which the triumvirate of collaboration-networking-governance is erected" and that have framed governance and management thinking for decades.

Beverly A. Cigler's chapter, "Neglected Aspects of Intergovernmental Relations and Federalism," also addresses issues of governance in the U.S. federal system. It examines interstate relationships, state-local relations, intermunicipal relations, and the increasing internationalization of states and local governments. As Cigler observes, "the state of the discipline" and the "state of the practice" often proceed at different paces, emphasizing different activities, which can suggest research gaps in the field. A major point Cigler makes through this chapter is that these are neglected areas in need of the attention of public administration scholars. Cigler also suggests that "less discussion about government and more about governance " would be helpful in this regard.

In "Politics, Bureaucratic Dynamics, and Public Policy," Robert F. Durant and John Marvel argue for a more robust, practical, and theoretical understanding of the dynamics of policy, politics, and administration (PPA). They contend that this is needed to break from deference to dominant ideas, epistemologies, and methodologies that stymie progress in appreciating the dynamic nature of administrative phenomena. The authors review research in several fields to foster understanding of PPA dynamics and examine three theoretical approaches for potential to take the study of PPA to the next level of explanatory and predictive power. Durant and Marvel's conclusion is that traditional public administration methods and analytical frameworks "have reached as far as they can go alone in explanatory and predictive power, given their mismatch with the empirical realities" and emerging governance models, and, hence, the need for PPA dynamics.

Stephen E. Condrey and Jonathan P. West explore the contemporary state of civil service reform in the United States in their chapter, "Civil Service Reform: Past as Prologue?" Particular attention is given to broad-based reforms that aimed to fundamentally change the nature of the public service. The chapter begins with a brief history of the foundations and evolution of merit-based civil service. It then focuses on specific cases: state reform initiatives in Georgia and Florida, local government reform activities in Jefferson County, Alabama, and reform efforts in the U.S.

Department of Homeland Security. The chapter also provides a set of implications for the future of civil service in the United States. Condrey and West conclude, "There is obviously no 'one best way' to organize the provision of human resources management services to local, state, and federal government," and tensions between "need for managerial flexibility" and "requirement of a neutrally competent bureaucratic corps" will endure.

David H. Rosenbloom's chapter, "Public Administration's Legal Dimension: Three Models," reviews the status of law in the contemporary field of public administration. Legal dimensions of public administration in the United States are explained in terms of the Madisonian, the 1946 legislative-centered, and the judicial models for infusing constitutional rights into public administrative practice. Several explanations are considered for why law is given such dire coverage in public administration. None was found to be valid. Rosenbloom concludes that all three models will persist into the foreseeable future but questions whether public administration's legal dimensions will be fully integrated into public administration theory, research, scholarship, and pedagogy.

"Governance in the Midst of Diversity: Issues and Challenges" concludes this section on governance and reform. In this chapter, Harvey L. White explores the various dimensions of diversity and their effects on the administration of public services. A brief review of classical, modern, and postmodern theory is provided to emphasize that "diversity is both old and new; it transcends time." White notes that ideals put forth by governance theorists constitute the intellectual foundation for discussions of race, age, gender, disability, sexual preferences, ethnicity, and multiculturalism that pervade the literature in public administration and allied fields. White's conclusion is that while issues surrounding diversity represent significant challenges, the dynamics they generate continue to be an important source of energy for sustaining, invigorating, and expanding effective governance.

CHAPTER 18

HISTORIC RELEVANCE CONFRONTING CONTEMPORARY OBSOLESCENCE?

Federalism, Intergovernmental Relations, and Intergovernmental Management

DEIL S. WRIGHT, CARL W. STENBERG, AND CHUNG-LAE CHO

Collaborative public management, managing across boundaries, leveraging networks, and governance through networking are contemporary concepts that characterize a near tsunami sweeping across recent public administration literature. These novel and creative formulations describe, analyze, and prescribe complex modes of management for the current practicing public administrator. In retrospect Rhodes (1996, 658) was prescient in claiming, "governance is about managing networks."

The significance and relevance of the "collaboration-networking-governance movement" cannot be denied (Robinson 2006; Bingham and O'Leary 2008; O'Leary 2009). This chapter does not challenge or question the promising paths charted in that literature. Rather, it explores the antecedents and foundation stones on which the triumvirate of collaboration-networking-governance is erected. Those building-block components are represented by federalism and its legacy concepts, intergovernmental relations and intergovernmental management, concepts that have framed governance and management thinking for decades.

PUBLIC ADMINISTRATION AND FEDERALISM

Federalism was an idea as well as a set of formal legal governance arrangements present and prominent in the founding of the Republic. Its nature and controversial character energized the constitutional framers at Philadelphia in 1787 and pervaded the classic essays known as *The Federalist Papers*. Agranoff and McGuire (2001, 671) observed that "public administration and the processes of federalism have merged to a nearly indistinguishable point." Across more than two centuries the character and operational meaning of federalism has been shaped and reshaped. Whichever singular, combination, or convergent usage of the terms *federalism* (FED), *intergovernmental relations* (IGR), and *intergovernmental management* (IGM) is employed, their relevance has been central to practice, research, and teaching.

The purpose of this chapter is not to review the historic origins and transformations of the three concepts. Instead, the intent is to extract the prominent and pertinent themes and features of FED, IGR, and IGM embedded in more than 350 issues over nearly seven decades of the *Public Administration Review (PAR)*. The time frame (starting in 1940) and focus mean that *PAR* solidly anchors the subject matter as defined and refined by contributing authors.[1]

The approach taken here might be labeled a reverse conceptual-chronological analysis. The focus is successively on the three main concepts in reverse order: IGM, IGR, and FED. Within each the prominent issues and institutional features are traced in chronological fashion. Figure 18.1 depicts the temporal and conceptual scheme that frames the discussion. These periods set in motion and culminate in the current features of collaborative public management and the multiple nuances associated with governance through networking.

CONCEPTUAL SCOPE AND SIGNIFICANCE

Electronic methodology enables us to trace the presence of these concepts as they appeared in the titles, abstracts, or texts of articles from 1940 through 2007. IGM did not emerge until the 1970s and is the least frequently used term, with a total of 52 appearances. IGR occurred most frequently (a total of 447 appearances), was present in the earliest issues, and reached peak usage in the 1970s. With a total of 438 appearances, FED likewise peaked in the 1970s, but somewhat surprisingly, exceeded the usage of IGR from the 1980s onward.

Frequency alone, of course, does not confirm significance. Yet it is difficult to discount the extent to which the three concepts bulk large in the literature. More than seven hundred articles incorporated one or more of the three terms across seven decades, or nearly 25 percent of the three thousand articles appearing in the journal. Clearly, IGM, IGR, and FED have formed important conceptual pillars for the field of public administration.

Linkages between FED, IGR, and IGM and the current concepts of governance, collaboration, and networking are informative and instructive. The total number of appearances of governance was 718, compared with 701 for networking and 453 for collaboration. Governance actually appeared in a small number of articles in the three earliest decades. Since the 1970s, however, its usage has accelerated. From 73 in the 1970s its appearance climbed to the 100–200 range in the 1980s and 1990s but soared to 308 (of nearly 500 articles) during 2001–2007.

Collaboration usage presents a rather different pattern. In the six decades from 1940 to 2000, the concept appeared in an average of 40 to 50 articles in each period. Since 2000, collaboration has escalated fourfold to occurrences in 176 articles.

The last concept, networking, illustrates a third trend. Its usage doubled from the first two decades to the third decade. It doubled again from 51 to more than 100 in the three following decades. From an average of 116 across three decades (1970s–1990s) it more than doubled (to 252 articles) in the most recent decade.

One common feature connects the three contrasting trends. This is the sharp and dramatic rise in the presence of governance, collaboration, and networking in the current decade when compared to usage in any prior decade. Clearly, these three concepts have pervaded the parlance of twenty-first-century public administration literature in an unprecedented fashion.

The connections of IGM, IGR, and FED to the cluster of the three latter concepts can be explored further by examining the overlapping that occurs in the simultaneous use of the first cluster of three terms with the second cluster. (The article overlap analysis is feasible only with JSTOR for volumes 1–60. Our review of *PAR* issues published from 2001 through 2007 was less amenable to computer technology.) Usage of IGM, IGR, and FED is accompanied by the simultaneous presence of one or more of the other three concepts in articles, respectively, 83 percent, 49 percent, and 58 percent of the time. In other words, whenever IGM, IGR, or FED appeared in a *PAR* article, there is a 50 to 80 percent likelihood that governance, collaboration, or networking accompanies that usage.

The converse direction of the relationship is not as strong between the contemporary three-

Figure 18.1 **Historical Patterns and Phases: FED, IGR, and IGM**

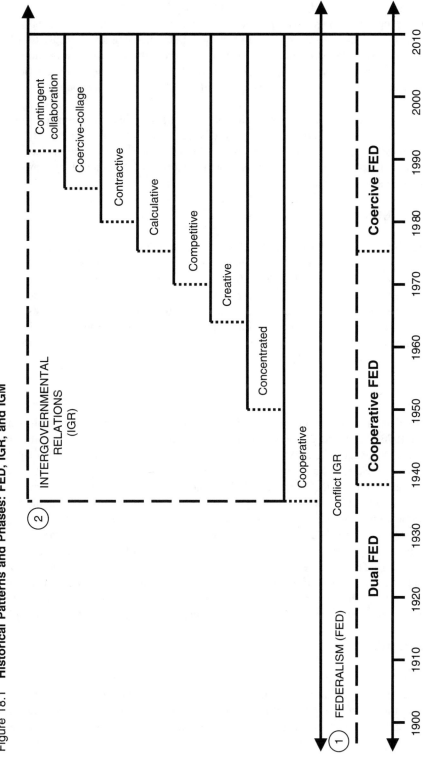

concept cluster and the three focal concepts of this essay. That is, IGM, IGR, and FED have lower appearance proportions in articles where governance, collaboration, and networking occur. When governance is used, nearly half (45 percent) of the articles also employ IGM, IGR, or FED. For articles employing collaboration and networking, the proportions using one or more of the focal concepts are lower (respectively, 36 percent and 38 percent). In the aggregate, however, the extent of overlap and simultaneous usage across these dual three-concept clusters is striking if not remarkable.

To set the stage for the further exploration of those relationships, the presence and pertinence of how IGM, IGR, and FED have been employed is assessed since 1940. Two sets of observations drawn from the period are offered. The first is a broad-brush sketch of the landscape depicted by the focal concepts as they were used in prominent articles. The other set captures prominent topical themes across the decades.

INTERGOVERNMENTAL MANAGEMENT

Figure 18.1 identifies two IGM periods differentiated during the four decades since the concept originated and gained currency. IGM appears in ten articles in the 1970s, twenty in the 1980s, twelve in the 1990s, and ten in the 2001–2007 period. Despite its recent and modest appearance, IGM represented notable refinements over FED and IGR. One focus included varied national administrative practices, while the second constituted a predominant local emphasis framing the shift to the present prominence of collaborative public management. Among key terms employed in giving robustness to IGM were *problem solving, nonhierarchical networking, constructive coping strategies,* and *intersectoral administration.*

Top-Down IGM

While practicing public administrators undoubtedly performed intergovernmental management before the 1970s, the concept did not enter formal discourse until the Study Committee on Policy Management Assistance (SCOPMA) in 1974–75. This national U.S. Office of Management and Budget–National Science Foundation initiative produced numerous papers, reports, and videos, and a special issue of *PAR* (December 1975). Schick was explicit about the top-down focus of IGM: "The Study Committee took it for granted that the federal government should have a lead role in stimulating management improvement by states and localities" (1975, 722).

The top-down approach left a hierarchical legacy that produced subsequent analyses aimed at shaping interjurisdictional relationships into what Sundquist earlier called the "centralization of objective-setting" (1969, 3). He argued for "responsibility for guiding the whole system of federal-state-local relations, viewed for the first time as a *single* system" (246; italics in original). While no single, unitary, or hierarchical approach was approximated much less achieved, the presence of national supremacy in policy management and implementation impacted the 1980s and beyond.

Bottom-Up IGM

Elazar (1962, 1984), Grodzins (1966), and other observers highlighted the strength of local and state center(s) of power, authority, and influence in the American political system. In place of decentralization, Elazar emphasized the noncentralized character of FED and IGR. It was not surprising, then, that the top-down aspects of IGM were soon challenged and largely overridden by bottom-up practices and analyses.

Among the earliest to challenge hierarchical predispositions was Lovell (1979). She found that coordination within and among local governments was "highly effective" and the result of three key strategies: (1) orchestration by jurisdiction leaders; (2) self-linking among functional specialists; and (3) meshing by community-based organizations. By the 1980s implementation studies appeared in a wide variety of sources, with a prime example by Agranoff and Lindsay (1983) titled "Human Services Problem Solving at the Local Level."

By the 1990s, the "devolution revolution" cemented attention to IGM at the state-local levels. Agranoff (1991) revisited human services delivery and stressed the need for service integration by placing emphasis on organizations with structures that produced "transorganizational management." Illustrative of the "reform decade" (Hebert, Brudney, and Wright 1999) was an emphasis on achieving results—whether through reinventing government, managing for results, or performance measurement.

The Middle Way

Attention to and exposition of the two contrasting periods of IGM over four decades are not as simple or polarized as the top-down and bottom-up discussions suggest. Throughout this time frame, several balanced or middle-way essays appeared that clarified and informed various aspects of IGM.

An explicit middle way was applied to IGM (as well as FED and IGR) by Derthick (1987) in her essay "Madison's Middle Ground in the 1980s." Madison's idea of "dual supremacy" left intact state and local governments with substantial authority for major domestic purposes and programs relatively free from national administrative supervision. Derthick noted that "Madison was correct in supposing that the national government would not be well suited to the entire tasks of governing a vast country" (66).

Several other middle-way essays were published in 1990. Wise (1990) applied organization design issues to public service agencies in the "Post-Privatization Era." He reinforced early theorizing about IGM that incorporated private and nonprofit entities as integral parts of public service-delivery configurations. Paired with Wise was an essay by Wright (1990), who offered a matrix that specified and compared six features of IGM with those of IGR and FED. Illustrative criteria and IGM features were: (1) leading actors—program policy professionals; (2) authority relations—nonhierarchical networks; (3) entities involved—mixtures of public, private, and nonprofit entities. In short, IGM by the 1990s had emerged as a concept that encompassed both theory and practices quite distinct from those of IGR and FED.

INTERGOVERNMENTAL RELATIONS

The concept of IGR first appeared in print in 1937 (Snider 1937), but the most widely recognized originator and promoter of the term was William Anderson. Despite his leadership in creating, defining, and extending use of the concept, he seldom employed the term in *PAR* articles. It fell to followers, who relied on the concept in the 1940s with a frequency equal to that of FED.

Wartime (1941–45) prompted the expanded use of IGR. The wartime mood of IGR was aptly captured by a renowned scholar of local administration (Bromage 1943, 35): "Cooperative government by federal-state-local authorities has become a byword in the prodigious effort to administer civilian defense, rationing, and other wartime programs. . . . Intergovernmental administration, while it is part of all levels of government, is turning into something quite distinct from them all."

In a rare IGR article focused on state-local relationships, Weidner (1944) examined state administrative supervision of local government (counties) in Minnesota. He found that "state agencies are restricted to an important degree in their supervisory activities by the inability or the unwillingness of local officials to see or agree with their points of view" (233). Weidner further noted, "The central thesis in this study . . . is that local governments, by means of their influence in the legislature and in other ways, exert important power in the formulation of state policies."

Usage of IGR through the 1950s and 1960s expanded to cover an extensive and varied array of topics, issues, and problems. Regardless of the range or types of topics, the 1950s was a legitimating decade for the term. In 1953 Congress gave IGR statutory status by creating the temporary (two-year) Commission on Intergovernmental Relations (PL 82–105). The commission delivered its report in 1955 and multiple subsidiary documents (Gaus 1956). Further legitimacy of IGR came in 1959 with the statute (PL 86–390) creating the Advisory Commission on Intergovernmental Relations (ACIR). Wright (1965) subsequently explored the ACIR's creation, unique features, and policy orientation, while Roberts (1989) examined the creation, roles, and impacts of state-level counterparts of the national ACIR. Decades later, Conlan (2006) reviewed a half century of IGR (and FED) in addressing the contributions by as well as the abolition of the ACIR.

The Great Society policies and programs from the 1960s left a residue of IGR issues examined fiscally and functionally for more than a decade. Harman (1970) assessed the first block grant program (Safe Streets Act of 1968). Lieber (1970) discussed environmental quality in the context of Earth Day, while Kennedy (1972) considered the "Law of Appropriateness" for IGR actions. Citizen participation in intergovernmental program implementation was a featured topic carried over from the "maximum feasible participation" mandate associated with the War on Poverty in the 1960s. Nearly a dozen articles looked at facets of public participation. The further significance of civic involvement was recognized in a full-fledged special issue of *PAR* edited by Strange (1972), with the eight articles summarized under the broad title, "The Impact of Citizen Participation on Public Administration."

The 1970s constituted a high-water mark in the use of IGR, perhaps traceable to the prominence of urban and fiscal policy issues. The 1980s, however, did not lag far behind. Two intergovernmental themes were prominent in the early part of the decade. One was cutback management and fiscal stress at the state and local levels (Levine 1978; Stenberg 1981). A second and closely related theme was devolution, a topic prompted largely by the Reagan administration's "New Federalism" initiatives involving block grants.

A symposium in *PAR* (January 1981) provided an array of articles on the impact of resource scarcity on urban public finance. Clearly associated with fiscal strictures and stresses was an early essay on national and state mandates (Lovell and Tobin 1981). Kettl (1981) focused on local-level block grant implementation as the "fourth face" of FED and IGR through the use of numerous noncity (nonprofit) agencies. Managing conflict and resolving IGR disputes gained considerable attention as stress across jurisdictional boundaries went well beyond apparent zero-sum games and forced fiscal trade-offs. Fiscal austerity contributed to the problems of "dispensing disappointment," when federal grant applications had to be rejected because of limited funds (Sunshine 1982), and encouraging grantsmanship games (Lorenz 1982).

Conflict on a number of IGR topics persisted through the latter part of the 1980s. One major venue for resolving IGR conflict was the judiciary, especially the U.S. Supreme Court. Cases coming before the Court involved fair labor standards as applied to state and local functions, municipal government violations of antitrust laws, state government advocacy before the Supreme Court, and interstate conflicts over water rights.

Near the close of the decade, dual synthesis-type essays provided useful reflections on two institutional issues. Berman and Martin (1988) reviewed state-local relations from the standpoint of local discretion. In one respect the analysis was representative of a secular shift away from national-state relations to IGR at the state and local levels. This was reinforced by Schneider and Park (1989), who reported the rapid rise from the 1970s through the 1980s in the significance of counties as major service-delivery agents in metropolitan areas. Finances and functionalism appeared as dominant themes in the 1980s. The presence of courts and counties as important actors, however, served as a reminder of the significance of institutional entities in the resolution of policy conflicts and respective role responsibilities in IGR.

The frequency of IGR articles in the 1990s was somewhat lower than in the two previous decades, a pattern that followed the reduced use of FED. Four major themes can be identified among essays linked to IGR in the 1990s: (1) fiscal issues; (2) courts, mandates, and regulatory problems; (3) administrative leadership; and (4) the institutional significance of American counties. Only illustrative aspects of these themes can be mentioned.

In the opening issue of the decade, Bland and Chen (1990) assessed the impact of the 1986 Tax Reform Act on taxable municipal bonds. When the Supreme Court (*South Carolina v. Baker*) decided that interest paid on state and local bonds was not constitutionally exempt from the federal income tax, the authors concluded that currently exempt bonds would require an additional $441 million in interest payments (in 1988 only) and more than $6 billion during the life of the bonds. Watson and Vocino (1990) also analyzed the 1986 Tax Reform Act and concluded more generally that it further reduced state and local governments to an essentially subservient fiscal position.

Legal issues that connected courts, mandates, and regulations insinuated themselves throughout the decade. O'Leary and Wise (1991) explored the "new partnership" between judges and administrators (raised earlier by Rosenbloom 1987) when the latter are operating under court orders involving schools, prisons, and other state and local functions. In a companion piece, Wise and O'Leary (1992) provided an overview of court decisions that, on balance, did not clearly favor either the national or the state governments.

Leadership by generalist administrators, especially at the state and local levels, in the intergovernmental arena came to the forefront more clearly in the 1990s than in any prior decade. The role of leaders and leadership in an IGR context has seldom been addressed in a direct or systematic manner. This was especially the case when the focus involved generalist executives, whether elected or appointed. A few articles highlighted but failed to fill this gap.

Cigler (1990) explored how "The Paradox of Professionalism" contributed to tensions between policy program professionals and administrative generalists in an IGR context. Bullard and Wright (1993) found that women increasingly broke the glass ceiling to lead newer or younger state agencies that were created in response to national policies. Yoo and Wright (1994) examined empirically the intergovernmental perspectives of top-level state executives. Generalist education (in public administration) combined with organizational position to explain the perceived extent of national influence exerted on state agencies through the receipt of federal aid. Morgan and Watson (1992) compared the policy leadership roles of mayors and managers and concluded that their external (intergovernmental) roles were notably different. Near the end of the decade, Bowling and Wright (1998) offered an overview of administrative leadership at the state level. The diversity and professionalism of state agency heads fostered greater effectiveness in both horizontal and vertical networks.

County government, long criticized as the "dark continent" of American governance, came out of the shadows in varied ways during the 1990s. Menzel and colleagues (1992) provided an assessment of past and prospective research on county government across the twentieth century, including performance, leadership, professional management, responsiveness, democratic institutions, and county roles in intergovernmental systems. Cigler (1994), in a nationwide study, surveyed county-state relationships with special attention to the state-level lobbying efforts of county associations. Waugh (1994) assembled multiple arguments for why emergency management agencies should be situated in county governments. Morgan and Kickham (1999) tested the relationship between county governance forms and the fiscal behavior of matched sets of counties. No difference existed in policy patterns or services between traditional fragmented structures and appointed (or elected) executive forms.

In summary, what might be said of IGR as it rose to prominence and persisted in usage across six decades? First and foremost, IGR acquired legitimacy and increased usage during the 1940s and 1950s. Second, that usage escalated substantially during the 1960s and 1970s when urban, fiscal, and functional policy issues were near the top of local, state, and national public agendas. Third, finances and functionalism persisted in prominence through the 1980s and 1990s. Fourth, these last two decades also reflected important institutional elements and accountability aspects of IGR as courts, counties, and leadership themes gained prominence.

FEDERALISM

Historical as well as contemporary links between public administration and FED are seldom "merged" and "indistinguishable" as Agranoff and McGuire suggest (2001, 671). Waldo in *The Administrative State* (1948, 128) noted that "there is a close similarity between the rigid politics-administration viewpoint and that philosophy of federalism that pictured state and nation moving noiselessly and without friction each in its separate sphere." Just as the politics-administration dichotomy was attacked and shelved, so was the layer-cake or "dual federalism" description of national-state relations on the path toward oblivion (Grodzins 1966). During the initial decade, however, the usage of FED matched the frequency of IGR occurrences.

While IGR originated in the cooperative federalism era, FED did not decline or fall into disuse for at least two reasons. One was its historical, legal, constitutional, and political significance. A second reason was the tendency to attach an array of adjectives or metaphors to the term. Adjectival and metaphoric FED was so prolific by the 1980s that one persistent researcher counted "497 literal as well as figurative representations of various models, metaphors, conceptions, and types of federalism" (Stewart 1982, 239). This pattern was so rampant, according to Davis (1978, ix), that "the subject [federalism] has indeed fallen on hard times."

The lead article in the first issue of *PAR* during World War II was by Frank Bane, whose own career was the epitome of FED and IGR. He served as the first commissioner of the Social Security Administration, later as longtime executive director of the Council of State Governments, and as the first chairman (1960–66) of the ACIR. His essay "Cooperative Government in Wartime" described the rapid implementation of rubber and sugar rationing. They were implemented within two *months* after Pearl Harbor! Bane noted that one consequence is "a new type of federalism that can be adapted readily to the changing demands of the modern world" (1942, 102).

FED appeared in a small but diverse set of articles through the 1940s and 1950s. Almost without exception they fit the mold of cooperative or collaborative national-state relationships. By the 1960s the changing dynamics of politics, policy, and finances brought to the forefront a bevy of issues. The most distinctive feature of topics discussed under FED in the 1960s and 1970s was the extensive overlap with IGR. Several articles simultaneously use IGR and FED in the discourse about wide-ranging subjects, including water resources, the metropolitan desk, national-state metropolitan policies, the creation of the Department of Housing and Urban Development, urban affairs, cities in partnerships, urban information systems, nationally promoted citizen participation, and transportation policies.

The overlapping usage of IGR and FED during the 1960s and 1970s tended to cluster around the node of national-local relationships involving urban fiscal issues. The role of state government(s), seemingly bypassed, was not totally ignored. Reeves (1968, 1970) and Olson (1975) emphasized key roles and responsibilities that the states fulfilled in the federal system. Olson, for example, assessed the management strategies of governors in "Changing the Equilibrium of the Federal System."

The transition from cooperative to coercive (or regulatory) FED did not occur in any clear or precise fashion. Instead, it was a gradual accretion marked by incremental accumulations. The commerce, taxing, spending, and supremacy provisions in the Constitution had always been available for use, subject to court interpretations. By the 1970s, however, the onset of environmental and other regulatory legislation such as the Occupational Safety and Health Act and the Surface Mining Control and Reclamation Act infused coercive aspects more prominently into national-state relations. Lovell addressed "nearly a thousand mandates" that were "an exploding issue" (1981, 318).

The robust legal and coercive dimensions of FED were prominent and sometimes dominant streams flowing through the 1980s and 1990s. There were, of course, many rivulets covering topics such as energy, emergency management, fishery resources, and water basin and Great Lakes environmental conflicts. Other conflicts clustered around community development, privatization, revenue-sharing termination, disaster responses, Aid to Families with Dependent Children and Medicaid policies, and hazardous waste regulatory reforms. The tone and tenor of these topics displayed the increased tensions derived from command-and-control tendencies embedded in national legislation and administrative regulations (Stoker and Wilson 1998; Cho and Wright 2001).

Two broad themes covered the breadth and depth of FED in the 1990s. One theme, consistent with the coercive trend toward national dominance, revolved around the Supreme Court. The second addressed prominent political dynamics involving an "unbalanced" federal system.

No less than six significant articles on the Court and FED appeared during the 1990s. O'Leary and Wise (1991) assessed the implications of *Missouri v. Jenkins* (1990), in which a "new triumvirate" emerged involving local administrators, legislative bodies, and the courts. The authors concluded that the federal courts were clearly the senior partners. A year later Wise and O'Leary (1992) asked, "Is Federalism Dead or Alive in the Supreme Court?" The authors declared that its presumed death was mistaken.

Wise and O'Leary (1997) as well as Emerson and Wise (1997) revisited the Court's role a half decade later in two different issue areas: environmental regulation and state and local exercise of the "takings" clause. In both instances the Supreme Court did not send clear signals about national-state roles and relationships. Yet when Wise (1998) pursued a reassessment less than a year later, he found that the Court was selectively intervening to protect state sovereignty. Within a year of the Wise analysis, Jensen (1999) concluded that the Supreme Court seemed destined to operate as an irregular and unpredictable umpire in the unending effort to call "balls and strikes" in the federalism "game."

Legal and political actions in the 1990s revealed the Supreme Court to be a significant but selective umpire on the field of FED. At the top of the batting order, however, were the president, the Congress, and often the states. Three essays assessing these multiple players focused on how to maintain balance in the federal system. Rivlin (1992a,b) offered a "new vision" of changed relationships between the national government and the states. Summarizing the argument in her book *Reviving the American Dream,* she proposed a well-defined division of roles and responsibilities between the states and national government. The changes, she contended, would improve economic policy as well as revitalize governmental performance at all levels. Kee and Shannon

(1992) emphasized fiscal imbalances from both explanatory and normative standpoints. In some respects, Rivlin and Kee and Shannon presaged the "New Federalism" contained in the Republican Party's Contract with America, which precipitated the political turnabout in the 1994 congressional elections. Walker accurately captured for the 1990s the status of what he called "New Federalism III." His phrase for FED and the conflicts over rebalancing an unbalanced system was, "the advent of ambiguous federalism" (Walker 1996, 271).

No single or simple set of statements about FED can fully capture the complex patterns, major periods, and substantive trends of FED. What can be said, however, is that the attention devoted to FED across six decades is a representative reflection of its implications for and impact on public administrators in the American political system. FED is unlikely to be merged with or appear indistinguishable from public administration. Nevertheless, the theory and practices of public administration cannot be insulated or isolated from federalism as a fundamental feature framing the functioning of the American republic.

WHAT MAY HAVE BEEN MISSED: 1940–2000

Before completing an assessment of the implications of this analysis it is relevant to identify gaps in coverage of FED, IGR, and IGM over the years. They are: (1) state and local institutional capacity; (2) horizontal interjurisdictional cooperation; (3) regionalism; (4) functional (programmatic) topics; and (5) intergovernmental implementation issues.

Particularly noticeable is the paucity of articles covering the resurgence and transformation of state governments. This oversight persists even as debates have continued over the devolution revolution, unfunded mandates, innovation diffusion, and state responses to natural and other disasters (Bowman and Kearney 1986; Teaford 2002). Selected attention was given to state administrators in articles appearing in the 1990s, but little treatment was given to the states as laboratories of democracy after the mid-1980s (Stenberg 1985). Responses to the Katrina disaster brought to the forefront lingering questions about state capacity, coordination, and leadership (Ink 2006; Derthick 2007).

A second gap involves horizontal federalism or the joint actions by states (or by localities) to address problems that transcend boundaries and require lateral multijurisdictional planning, policy development, and administrative arrangements. (See also chapter 19, "Neglected Aspects of Intergovernmental Relations and Federalism," in this volume for additional commentary.) Over several decades only minor attention was given to interagency dimensions of federal field administration. Examples include federal regional councils and multistate bodies such as the Appalachian Regional Commission. While there has been robust growth in published research on interstate relationships, this field has not been well represented. Similarly, interlocal relationships received sparse treatment, especially the rise, retrenchment, and rebirth of councils of governments as well as national- and state-authorized (or mandated) areawide planning and coordinating bodies. Interstate compacts and interlocal contracts and agreements are among the oldest and most popular approaches to collaborative governance. Yet these institutional arrangements have received relatively little attention from contributors.

Another coverage gap is functional federalism—the services delivered by public agencies through the intergovernmental system. The span of functions covered by authors is impressive, including welfare, health, water resources, emergency management, environmental quality, manpower and employee training, human services, natural hazards, and energy. Among missing core services are K–12 public education, higher education, law enforcement, transportation and infrastructure, and economic and rural development.

Associated with the above gaps is an implementation perspective. Substantial attention during the 1970s was devoted to subnational capacity building consistent with the top-down orientation of IGM. Two decades later a few articles addressed the performance measurement movement of the 1990s, for example, National Performance Review, Government Performance and Results Act (GPRA), and Program Assessment Rating Tool (PART), the President's Management Agenda, and regulatory federalism. These articles focused almost exclusively on national-level initiatives and directives. Relatively little attention was given to issues associated with state and local implementation of and accountability for national policies, program goals, and performance requirements as they filtered through state, regional, and local agencies to produce results, outcomes, or impacts.

DIVERSE THEMES: 2001–7

World and national events have provided critical contexts for FED, IGR, and IGM since 2000. First, in the wake of the September 11 (2001) terrorist attacks and the Katrina disaster (2005), numerous articles were published dealing with terrorism, homeland security, natural disasters, and emergency management. Often these featured a melding of IGR and IGM with collaboration and networking. Second, other articles during this period addressed the impacts of globalization using governance and IGR frameworks.

There has been increased scholarly attention to subjects neglected during previous decades. (See chapter 19, "Neglected Aspects of Intergovernmental Relations and Federalism," in this volume for additional commentary.) Noteworthy are an increased number of articles on regional and interlocal collaboration. These articles include topics on contracts and agreements, city-county consolidation, economic development, public authorities, and local and metropolitan government reinvention. Several articles addressed local leadership challenges that required working across jurisdictional and sectoral boundaries.

A second topic of mounting interest was state governance. Findings from surveys of American state administrators conducted over the previous four decades continued to appear (Bowling, Cho, and Wright 2004; Bowling et al. 2006), joined by assessments of the states' reinvention progress (Thompson 2002; Brudney and Wright 2002). The states' performance in managing budget and policy processes and fiscal affairs gained visibility (Clingermayer 2002; Cornia, Nelson, and Wilko 2004), as did state roles in disaster responses, welfare, ethics, and environmental policy.

Third, K–12 education surfaced in *PAR* from 2001 onward. Topics covered were perspectives on school district funding (Moser and Rubenstein 2002), the legacies of the fiftieth anniversary of *Brown v. Board of Education* (Henderson 2004), and the role of networks in education policy implementation (Meier and O'Toole 2003). One essay posed the key question "Why has public administration ignored public education and does it matter?" (Raffel 2007).

THE CONTEMPORARY SCENE: ARE IGM, IGR, AND FED OBSOLETE?

Agranoff and McGuire identified and described four models in "American Federalism and the Search for Models of Management" (2001). One indication of the broader import, scope, and consequence is that that essay prefigures two book-length empirically based publications (Agranoff and McGuire 2003; Agranoff 2007). The contents and interpretations found in those two volumes indirectly and perhaps unintentionally reveal the evident decline of FED, IGR, and IGM. Both books bypass the traditional trinity and emphasize almost exclusively the fourth model, collaborative network management.[2] Agranoff and McGuire defined collaborative public management as "a concept that describes the process of facilitating and operating in multiorganizational arrangements to solve problems that cannot be solved or easily solved by single organizations" (2003, 4).

FED, IGR, and IGM remained central to a wide-ranging essay by Conlan (2006). Titled "From Cooperative to Opportunistic Federalism," it is both a period piece (but not time bound) as well as an institutional and interpretive analysis. More than any other essay encountered in the current era, Conlan's piece explored and elaborated the patterns, problems, and prospects impinging on FED, IGR, and IGM.[3] In the context of the questions raised about the future utility of the three terms, the Conlan essay offers a promising platform for discussion and guidance.

In a paired essay, McGuire (2006) responded to the Conlan article. With IGM as a springboard, McGuire adopted a bottom-up approach in viewing operations of the diverse and noncentralized character of the American system. Where Conlan focused attention on national policies and changing institutional patterns, McGuire identified and emphasized the extensive collaboration occurring at local, regional, and state levels. McGuire (677) noted Conlan's "predominantly negative view of opportunism from the top." He offered a more a positive perspective about intergovernmental operations when viewed from the bottom. He concluded, "As collaborative intergovernmental and interorganizational networks develop in many policy areas, the opportunities for assertive and regional actions are both prominent and encouraging" (679).

The essays by Agranoff and McGuire (2001), Conlan (2006), and McGuire (2006) provide virtual bookends for a shelf of articles and themes that permeated *PAR* from 2001 through 2007. FED, IGR, and IGM clearly retained selective usage. But the greater presence and prominence of collaboration, networking, and governance were clear for all to see. Indeed, the latter terms have taken off like rockets from a launchpad in the current decade, while IGM, IGR, and FED have declined sharply in usage over the past three decades.

Have the two contrasting trends signaled a sea change in the relevance and utility of IGM, IGR, and FED? Are these long-standing concepts not only dispensable but perhaps already obsolete? To what extent do they retain utility and value in the new worlds of terrorism, homeland security, natural disasters, and emergency management? Have governance, collaboration, and networking diminished if not replaced IGM, IGR, and FED?

It would be a welcome and worthwhile achievement to offer definitive answers to these queries. Consistent with the long-term perspectives guiding this chapter, however, the answers to these questions require a later and longer time frame from which to offer responses. What can be provided are propositions and related questions that merit careful and constructive pursuit at a later date.

PROPOSITIONS ABOUT FED, IGR, AND IGM

Eight basic propositions are offered about the significance of these three conceptual pillars on which the contemporary edifice of American public administration is firmly founded. First and foremost, it is nearly impossible to understand adequately the character and content of governance in the United States without a substantial grasp of the theory and practice of federalism. Nor is it feasible to understand how public policy is made and implemented without an informed awareness of the meaning and application of the concepts of intergovernmental relations and intergovernmental management.

Second, from a public policy standpoint, many major domestic turning points, seismic shifts, or punctuated equilibria involving political and policy change in the United States can be analyzed and understood better from the standpoint of FED, IGR, and IGM. FED references the constitutional, institutional, and legal framework on which policy decisions are grounded. IGR points to the prominence of key actors whose attributes, actions, and attitudes give specific shape to important policy choices. IGM incorporates domains of networking, coping, and problem solving that are inherent in program implementation processes (Agranoff 1986; Wright 1990).

Third, the multilevel and multisectoral systems of governance and administration in the United States contain very few continuous or near-perfect harmonious interjurisdictional relationships. Most constitutional, institutional, political, organizational, and policy-making interactions reflect regular tensions, conflicts, and cleavages. This dimension is critical for three reasons. One is the existence of more than eighty-nine thousand local governmental jurisdictions. These political entities populate the profuse landscapes of urban and rural governance. A second and allied horizontal feature is the presence of more than five hundred thousand popularly elected local officials who govern these thousands of public entities. A third "horizontal" feature is the presence and active participation of hundreds of thousands of nonprofit NGOs. Given these challenging and complex conditions, how, then, are public policies formulated, enacted, and implemented? The short but problematic answer is: Only with great difficulty!

Fourth, the difficulties involved in formulating and implementing public policies and programs place a premium on the boundary-spanning abilities of all public officials. The boundaries between and among the three major sectors—governmental, nonprofit, and profit making—are blurred at best and border on the indistinguishable at worst. They add several magnitudes of complexity and uncertainty to public policies and to interjurisdictional relationships. Moreover, they contribute to citizen confusion about the allocation of responsibility for providing services and making taxing and spending decisions. IGM, IGR, and FED are near-indispensable lenses or prisms for viewing the roles of generalists and of specialists in the conduct of governance in the United States (Wright 1990).

Fifth, tension exists between FED, with its legacy concepts of IGR and IGM, and the governance-collaboration-networking movement embedded in the broader comparative literature on multilevel governance (see chapter 17, "Collaborative Public Agencies in the Network Era," in this volume). A central theme in multilevel governance analyses is the gravitation or reallocation of powers both upward (from or beyond) the nation-state toward supranational entities, and also downward toward subnational jurisdictions. What emerges from the migration or drift of power is what Rhodes (1996, 1997) noted—the absence of sovereign authority because of network autonomy. Under these circumstances, where is democratic accountability located and how are institutional responsibilities assigned?

Sixth, network autonomy and the multiple stakeholders involved in making and implementing public policy can create ambiguous or ambivalent responses to the question, Who is accountable? The growing scope and complexity of IGM, IGR, and FED have been overlaid by a myriad of nonprofit and for-profit organizations, private contractors, and individual citizens. But the many faces of government and the weblike design of governance may become confusing to those outside the numerous collaborative systems and networks. One net effect is the increased opportunity for blame shifting.

Seventh, the world of multilevel and multisectoral governance poses a further fundamental question: To make effective public policy and implement it, how, where, when, and which governments (and officials) matter? The fit between jurisdictions and networks may be unclear. Nevertheless, governments, their elected officials, and public administrators are held responsible for making the final decisions (Agranoff and McGuire 2001). The role of governments may be shifting from direct to indirect service provision and from a single to a multijurisdictional focus. But the scope of the public sector does not appear to be shrinking. If anything, the public sector continues to expand. The growth of collaboration and networks with nongovernmental actors has produced transactions and arrangements that still account for only a modest fraction of the public's business (Agranoff 2006). The end result is more a complement to than a challenge of governmental authority.

Finally, Peters and Pierre (2004) view the issue of democratic accountability as a "Faustian bargain" in which democracy is a trade-off with multilevel governance. They note that "most of the analytic models and interpretations of multilevel governance that we have seen so far have fallen into the same trap as some analyses of governance, that is, a previously state-centric and constitutional perspective has been almost completely replaced by an image of governing in which institutions are largely irrelevant" (75). The authors extend their critique by arguing, "The novelty of governance is the emphasis on process over institutions," in which "multilevel governance has become a popular model of intergovernmental relationships partly because it draws on informal and inclusive ideals of decision making and partly because it appears to be a cozy, consensual, and accommodating process" (76).

Peters and Pierre have a valid point, which we acknowledge and share to some degree. At the same time, our approach in this chapter has been to recognize, retain, and reinforce the integrity of institutional arrangements in the American setting. We emphasize and promote the prominence of institutions, especially those associated with FED. In a simultaneous and complementary manner, we incorporate process elements that are regularly derived from IGM and IGR analyses. In short, responsive public management through collaboration and networking occurs in a framework of responsible democratic governance.

CONCLUSION

This multidecade analysis has probed the scope and depth of an immense volume and a rich variety of research in which IGM, IGR, FED, as well as governance, collaboration, and networking appeared in the featured journal of public administration. A firm foundation of research relating to all six concepts has been established. The former three have a solid and significant heritage in the subject matter addressed since 1940. It remains to be determined whether the recent surge of interest in the latter three terms represents more than "old wine in new bottles."

As scholars and practitioners continue to explore and experience the lineage and linkages between these key sets of terms, two questions raised during this chapter call for urgent attention. First, governance, collaboration, and networking stress processes. Where do institutional capacity, democratic accountability, and performance responsibility fit in? Second, intergovernmental and multilevel approaches stress cooperation and lean toward bottom-up approaches. Yet, contemporary IGR has been characterized as coercive federalism that features regulations, unfunded mandates, and preemptions of a top-down nature. Where is the intersection of and balance between devolution and centralization? This query is all the more relevant because, as Cleveland (2000) argued, "the future is uncentralized." The added relevance and importance of administration (and administrators) was noted by Cleveland: "They [the best public administrators] will help all of us, the sovereign 'public,' get used to the idea that no one can possibly be in general charge, so we are all partly in charge" (297).

It has taken several decades to clarify, incorporate, and operationally employ the trinity of FED, IGR, and IGM. How long will it take to clarify, confirm, standardize, and systematically employ governance, collaboration, and networking as valuable operational concepts? And how will the latter triumvirate of terms constructively connect with the former trinity?

The search for conceptual handles that effectively codify the range of administrative experience and practice remains a continuing challenge. We have charted the reefs and crosscurrents traversed by evolving concepts across nearly seven decades. The course and destinations ahead promise even more turbulent waters.

How the current credit, financial, and housing crises and the employment and stock market declines will impact FED, IGR and IGM raise a host of additional navigational challenges. Components of the American Reinvestment and Recovery Act of 2009 contain numerous implications for the interjurisdictional relationships and the balance of power between national and subnational governments. Prominent policies focus on public infrastructure investments, elementary and secondary education spending, and Medicaid relief.

The form, shape, and operational content of these and related intergovernmental policies will go a long way toward defining and refining the nature of FED, IGR, and IGM over the next decade. Whatever the focus—teaching, research, or practice—and regardless of the method employed— institutional or behavioral—these concepts offer a promising, not an obsolete, framework for continued attention and utility in the field of public administration.

ACKNOWLEDGMENTS

We were superbly assisted in this endeavor by master of public administration research assistants enrolled at the University of North Carolina. K.C. Tydgat skillfully tracked, evaluated, assembled, and edited the references both in and beyond *PAR*. Victoria Cunningham (dual-degree master of public administration and information science) made an otherwise impenetrable and unmanageable search engine workable for the 2001–7 years of *PAR*. Ingrid Rosiuta made invaluable contributions to editing successive revisions of the text and references in preparing the final draft of this chapter. The text is a substantially revised and condensed version of a longer and differently configured essay in the Public Administration Foundation Series commissioned under the auspices of *Public Administration Review*. For an exposition and analysis of the use of FDR, IGR, and IGM in *Public Administration Review* from 1940 through 2007, see Deil S. Wright, Carl W. Stenberg, and Chung-Lae Cho, Aspanet Public Administration Foundation Series, http://www.aspanet/org/ scriptcontent/index_par_foundationsseries.cfm.

NOTES

1. JSTOR enabled us to track article usage of FED, IGR, and IGM from 1940 through 2000 (vols. 1–60). Frequencies for the present decade (vols. 61–67) were identified using the Blackwell-Synergy search engine. The electronic search processes excluded use of the concepts in tables, figures, references, endnotes, or author's biographic information. It also excluded book reviews and book notes as well as specialized sections and commentaries, for example, editorials and TOPs (Those Other Publications). In a somewhat ironic if not curious twist of tallying articles in *PAR* by subject matter, the number of articles classified as focusing on IGM, IGR, or FED from 2000 to 2005 was zero (0)! See Terry 2005 ("Reflections and Assessment"). For an earlier review and interpretation of articles on FED and IGR appearing in *PAR* for vols. 1–43 (1940–1983), see Wright and White), 1984. In those 43 volumes, approximately 300 articles relevant to IGR and FED were identified.

2. The first volume (2003) referenced FED as covering the top-down and donor-recipient models. IGR was notably absent in the text and index. In the second volume (2007), a discussion of FED is bypassed (not indexed), while IGR and IGM are summarized in a two-page overview. The near-exclusive themes in the two volumes are collaboration and networking. Does this signify a paradigm shift away from the trinity concepts (FED, IGR, IGM)?

3. A simple count of the usage frequency does not alone justify the strength of Conlan's essay. It is notable, however, that the numbers of occurrences of FED, IGR, and IGM are, respectively, 44, 32, and 24.

REFERENCES

Note: FED, IGR, or IGM following the reference indicates the relevance of the item to the concept.

Agranoff, Robert. 1986. *Intergovernmental Management: Human Services Problem-Solving in Six Metropolitan Areas.* Albany: State University of New York Press. (IGR, IGM)
———. 1991. Human services integration: Past and present challenges in public administration. *Public Administration Review* 51 (6): 533–542. (IGM, IGR)
———. 2006. Inside collaborative networks: Ten lessons for public managers. *Public Administration Review* 66 (s1): 56–65. (IGM)
———. 2007. *Managing Within Networks: Adding Value to Public Organizations.* Washington, DC: Georgetown University Press. (IGM)
Agranoff, Robert, and Valerie A. Lindsay. 1983. Intergovernmental management: Perspectives from human services problem solving at the local level. *Public Administration Review* 43 (3): 227–237. (IGM)
Agranoff, Robert, and Michael McGuire. 2001. American Federalism and the Search for Models of Management. *Public Administration Review* 61:671–681. (IGM, IGR, FED).
———. 2003. *Collaborative Public Management: New Strategies for Local Governments.* Washington, DC: Georgetown University Press. (IGM)
Bane, Frank. 1942. Cooperative government in wartime. *Public Administration Review* 2 (2): 95–103. (FED)
Berman, David R., and Lawrence L. Martin. 1988. State-local relations: An examination of local discretion. *Public Administration Review* 48 (2): 649–660. (IGR)
Bingham, Lisa Blomgren, and Rosemary O'Leary, eds. 2008. *Big Ideas in Collaborative Public Management.* Armonk, NY: M.E. Sharpe. (IGM)
Bland, Robert L., and Li-Khan Chen. 1990. Taxable municipal bonds: State and local governments confront the tax-exempt limitation movement. *Public Administration Review* 50 (1): 42–48. (IGR, FED)
Bowling, Cynthia J., and Deil S. Wright. 1998. Change and continuity in state administration: Administrative leadership across four decades. *Public Administration Review* 58 (5): 429–444. (IGM, IGR, FED)
Bowling, Cynthia J., Chung-Lae Cho, and Deil S. Wright. 2004. Establishing a continuum from minimizing to maximizing bureaucrats: State agency head preferences for governmental expansion—a typology of administrative growth pastures, 1964–1998. *Public Administration Review* 64 (4): 489–499. (IGR)
Bowling, Cynthia J., Christine A. Kelleher, Jennifer Jones, and Deil S. Wright. 2006. Cracked ceilings, firmer floors, and weakening walls: Trends and patterns in leading american state agencies, 1970–2000. *Public Administration Review* 66 (6): 823–836. (IGR)
Bowman, Ann O.M., and Richard Kearney. 1986. *The Resurgence of the States.* Englewood Cliffs, NJ: Prentice-Hall. (IGR, FED)
Bromage, Arthur W. 1943. Federal-state-local relations. *American Political Science Review* 37:35–48. (IGR)
Brudney, Jeffrey L., and Deil S. Wright. 2002. Revisiting administrative reform in the American states: The status of reinventing government during the 1990s. *Public Administration Review* 62 (3): 353–361. (IGR)
Bullard, Angela M., and Deil S. Wright. 1993. Circumventing the glass ceiling: Women executives in American state governments. *Public Administration Review* 53 (3): 189–202. (IGR)
Cho, Chung-Lae, and Deil S. Wright. 2001. Managing carrots and sticks: Changes in state administrators' perceptions of cooperative and coercive federalism during the 1990s. *Publius: The Journal of Federalism* 31 (1): 57–80. (IGR, FED)
Cigler, Beverly A. 1990. Public administration and the paradox of professionalization. *Public Administration Review* 50 (6): 637–653. (IGR, IGM, FED)
———. 1994. The county-state connection: A national study of associations of counties. *Public Administration Review* 54 (1): 3–11. (IGR)
Cleveland, Harlan. 2000. The future is uncentralized. *Public Administration Review* 60 (4): 293–297. (IGM)
Clingermayer, James C. 2002. Dollars and decisions: Fiscal policy and administration in the American states. *Public Administration Review* 62 (6): 736–739. (IGR)
Conlan, Tim. 2006. From cooperative to opportunistic federalism: Reflections on the half-century of the commission on intergovernmental relations. *Public Administration Review* 66 (5): 663–679. (IGR, FED)

Cornia, Gary C., Ray D. Nelson, and Andrea Wilco. 2004. Fiscal planning, budgeting, and rebudgeting using revenue semaphores. *Public Administration Review* 64 (2): 164–179. (IGR)

Davis, S. Rufus. 1978. *The Federal Principle: A Journey Through Time in Quest of Meaning.* Berkeley: University of California Press. (FED)

Derthick, Martha. 1987. American federalism: Madison's middle ground in the 1980s. *Public Administration Review* 47 (1): 66–74. (IGM, FED)

———. 2007. Where federalism didn't fail. *Public Administration Review* 67 (s1): 36–47. (IGM, FED)

Elazar, Daniel J. 1962. *The American Partnership: Intergovernmental Partnership in the 19th Century United States.* Chicago: University of Chicago Press. (IGR, FED)

———. 1984. *American Federalism: A View from the States.* 3rd ed. New York: Harper and Row. (IGR, FED)

Emerson, Kirk, and Charles R. Wise. 1997. Statutory approaches to regulatory takings: State property rights legislation issues and implications for public administration. *Public Administration Review* 57 (5): 411–422. (FED)

Gaus, John. 1956. Federalism and intergovernmental relations. *Public Administration Review* 16 (2): 102–109. (IGR, FED)

Grodzins, Morton. 1966. *The American System: A New View of Government in the United States.* Chicago: Rand McNally. (IGR, FED)

Harman, B. Douglas. 1970. The bloc grant: Readings from a first experiment. *Public Administration Review* 30 (2): 141–153. (IGR, FED)

Henderson, Lenneal J., Jr. 2004. *Brown v Board of Education* at 50: The multiple legacies for policy and administration. *Public Administration Review* 64 (3): 270–274. (IGR, FED)

Herbert, F. Ted, Jeffrey L. Brudney, and Deil S. Wright. 1999. Reinventing government in the American states: Measuring and explaining administrative reform. *Public Administration Review* 59 (1): 19–30. (IGR)

Ink, Dwight A. 2006. An analysis of the House Select Committee and White House reports on Hurricane Katrina. *Public Administration Review* 66 (6): 800–807. (IGM, IGR)

Jensen, Laura S. 1999. Federal authority vs. state autonomy: The Supreme Court's role revisited. *Public Administration Review* 59 (2): 97–99. (FED)

Kee, James Edwin, and John Shannon. 1992. The crisis and anti-crisis dynamic: Rebalancing the American federal system. *Public Administration Review* 52 (4): 321–329. (FED)

Kennedy, David J. 1972. The law of appropriateness: An approach to a general theory of intergovernmental relations. *Public Administration Review* 32 (2): 135–143. (IGR, FED)

Kettl, Donald F. 1981. The fourth face of federalism. *Public Administration Review* 41 (3): 366–371. (IGR, FED)

Lieber, Harvey. 1970. Public administration and environmental quality. *Public Administration Review* 30 (3): 277–286. (IGR)

Levine, Charles H. 1978. Organizational decline and cutback management. *Public Administration Review* 38 (4): 316–325. (IGR)

Lorenz, Patsy Hashey. 1982. The politics of fund raising through grantsmanship in human services. *Public Administration Review* 42 (3): 244–251. (IGM, IGR)

Lovell, Catherine H. 1979. Coordinating federal grants from below. *Public Administration Review* 39 (5): 432–439. (IGM, IGR, FED)

———. 1981. Evolving local government dependency. *Public Administration Review* 41:189–202. (IGR, IGM, FED)

Lovell, Catherine H., and Charles Tobin. 1981. The mandate issue. *Public Administration Review* 41 (3): 318–331. (IGR, FED)

McGuire, Michael. 2006. Intergovernmental management: A view from the bottom. *Public Administration Review* 66 (5): 677–679. (IGM)

Meier, Kenneth J., and Laurence J. O'Toole Jr. 2003. Public management and educational performance: The impact of managerial networking. *Public Administration Review* 63 (6): 689–699. (IGM, IGR)

Menzel, Donald C., Vincent L. Marando, Roger B. Parks, William L. Waugh, Jr., Beverly A. Cigler, James H. Svara, Mavis Mann Reeves, J. Edwin Benton, Robert D. Thomas, Gregory Streib, and Mark Schneider. 1992. Setting a research agenda for the study of the American county. *Public Administration Review* 52 (2): 173–182. (IGR, FED)

Morgan, David R., and Kenneth Kickham. 1999. Changing the form of county government: Effects on revenue and expenditure policy. *Public Administration Review* 59 (4): 315–324. (IGR)

Morgan, David R., and Sheilah S. Watson. 1992. Policy leadership in council-manager cities: Comparing mayor and manager. *Public Administration Review* 52 (5): 438–446. (IGR)

Moser, Michele, and Ross Rubenstein. 2002. The equality of public school district funding in the United States: A national status report. *Public Administration Review* 62 (1): 63–72. (IGR, FED)

O'Leary, Rosemary. 2009. *The Collaborative Public Manager.* Washington, DC: Georgetown University Press. (IGM)

O'Leary, Rosemary, and Charles R. Wise. 1991. Public managers, judges, and legislators: Redefining the "new partnership." *Public Administration Review* 51 (4): 316–327. (IGR, FED)

Olson, Kenneth C. 1975. The state, governors, and policy management: Changing the equilibrium of the federal system. *Public Administration Review* 35:764–770. (IGR, FED)

Peters, B. Guy, and Jon Pierre. 2004. Multi-level governance and democracy: A Faustian bargain? In *Multi-Level Governance,* ed. Ian Bache and Matthew Flinders, 75–89. New York: Oxford University Press. (IGR)

Raffel, Jeffrey A. 2007. Why has public administration ignored public education and does it matter? *Public Administration Review* 67 (1): 135–151. (IGR, FED)

Reeves, H. Clyde. 1968. Role of state governments in our intergovernmental system. *Public Administration Review* 28 (3): 267–270. (IGR, FED)

———. 1970. Have state policies produced the current urban problems? *Public Administration Review* 30 (2): 155–160. (IGR, FED)

Rhodes, Roderick S.W. 1996. The new governance: Governing without governance. *Political Studies* 4 (4): 652–667. (IGR, IGM)

———. 1997. *Understanding Governance: Policy Networks, Governance, Reflexivity, and Accountability.* Berkshire, UK: Open University Press. (IGM, IGR)

Rivlin, Alice M. 1992a. A new vision of American federalism. *Public Administration Review* 52 (4): 315–320. (FED)

———. 1992b. *Reviving the American Dream: The Economy, the States & the Federal Government.* Washington, DC: The Brookings Institution.

Roberts, Deborah D. 1989. Carving out their niche: State advisory commissions on intergovernmental relations. *Public Administration Review* 49 (6): 576–580. (IGR)

Robinson, Scott E. 2006. A decade of treating networks seriously. *Policy Studies Journal* 34 (4): 589–599. (IGM)

Rosenbloom, David H. 1987. Public administrators and the judiciary: The "new partnership." *Public Administration Review* 47 (1): 75–83. (FED)

Schick, Allen. 1975. The intergovernmental thicket: The questions still are better than the answers. *Public Administration Review* 35:717–722. (IGM, IGR)

Schneider, Mark, and Kee Ok Park. 1989. Metropolitan counties as service delivery agents: The still forgotten governments. *Public Administration Review* 49 (4): 345–352. (IGR)

Snider, Clyde F. 1937. County and township government in 1935–36. *American Political Science Review* 31:894–898. (IGR)

Stenberg, Carl W. 1981. Beyond the days of wine and roses: Intergovernmental management in a cutback environment. *Public Administration Review* 41 (1): 10–20. (IGM, IGR, FED)

———. 1985. States under the spotlight: An intergovernmental view. *Public Administration Review* 45 (2): 319–326. (IGR, FED)

Stewart, William H. 1982. Metaphors and models and the development of federal theory. *Publius: The Journal of Federalism* 12 (1): 5–24. (FED)

Stoker, Robert P., and Laura A. Wilson. 1998. Verifying compliance: Social regulation and welfare reform. *Public Administration Review* 58 (5): 395–405. (IGR, FED)

Strange, John H. 1972. Citizen participation in community action and model cities programs. *Public Administration Review* 32 (6): 655–669. (IGR)

Sundquist, James L. 1969. *Making Federalism Work: A Study of Program Coordination at the Community Level.* Washington, DC: Brookings Institution Press. (IGR, FED)

Sunshine, Eugene S. 1982. Minimizing the disappointment of unsuccessful applicants in grant programs. *Public Administration Review* 42 (5): 479–483. (IGM, IGR)

Teaford, Jon E. 2002. *The Rise of the States: Evolution of the American State Government.* Baltimore, MD: Johns Hopkins University Press. (FED, IGR)

Terry, Larry D. 2005. Reflections and assessment: Public administration review, 2000–05. *Public Administration Review* 65 (6): 643–645.

Thompson, Frank J. 2002. Reinvention in the states: Ripple or ride? *Public Administration Review* 62 (3): 353–361. (IGR)

Walker, David B. 1996. The advent of an ambiguous federalism and the emergence of new federalism III. *Public Administration Review* 56 (3): 271–280. (FED)

Waldo, Dwight. 1948. *The Administrative State: A Study of the Political Theory of American Public Administration.* New York: Ronald Press. (FED)

Watson, Douglas J., and Thomas Vocino. 1990. Changing intergovernmental fiscal relationships: Impact of the 1986 tax reform act on state and local governments. *Public Administration Review* 50 (4): 427–434. (IGR, FED)

Waugh, William L., Jr. 1994. Regionalizing emergency management: Counties as state and local government. *Public Administration Review* 54 (3): 253–258. (IGR)

Weidner, Edward W. 1944. State supervision of local government in Minnesota. *Public Administration Review* 4 (3): 226–233. (IGR)

Wise, Charles R. 1990. Public service configurations and public organizations: Public organization design in the post-privatization era. *Public Administration Review* 50 (2): 141–155. (IGM, IGR)

———. 1998. Judicial federalism: The resurgence of the Supreme Court's role in the protection of state sovereignty. *Public Administration Review* 58 (2): 95–98. (FED)

Wise, Charles R., and Rosemary O'Leary. 1992. Is federalism dead or alive in the Supreme Court? Implications for public administrators. *Public Administration Review* 52 (6): 559–572. (IGR, FED)

———. 1997. Intergovernmental relations and federalism in environmental management and policy: The role of the courts. *Public Administration Review* 57 (2): 150–159. (IGM, IGR, FED)

Wright, Deil S. 1965. The advisory commission on intergovernmental relations: Unique features and policy orientation. *Public Administration Review* 25 (3): 193–202. (IGR, FED)

———. 1990. Federalism, intergovernmental relations, and intergovernmental management: Historical reflections and conceptual comparisons. *Public Administration Review* 50 (2): 168–178. (IGM, IGR, FED)

Wright, Deil S. and Harvey L. White, eds. 1984. *Federalism and Intergovernmental Relations.* Washington, DC: American Society for Public Administration.

Yoo Jae-Won and Deil S. Wright. 1994. Public administration education and formal administrative position: Do they make a difference? A note on Pope's proposition and Miles' law in an intergovernmental context. *Public Administration Review* 54 (4): 357–363. (IGR)

CHAPTER 19

NEGLECTED ASPECTS OF INTERGOVERNMENTAL RELATIONS AND FEDERALISM

BEVERLY A. CIGLER

The preponderance of intergovernmental relations, intergovernmental management, and federalism scholarship examines vertical relationships connecting the U.S. national government, the fifty states, and the more than eighty-nine thousand local governments of all types. Money, mandates, preemption, and the relative power of the states and the national government are the key research foci. This chapter, instead, examines interstate relationships, a horizontal dimension of federalism and intergovernmental relations; state-local relations, a vertical dimension; intermunicipal relations, a horizontal dimension taking place within the confines of state-local relations; and the increasing internationalization of states and local governments, another horizontal topic. Relatively neglected research emphases are noted. (See chapter 18, "Historic Relevance Confronting Contemporary Obsolescence? Federalism, Intergovernmental Relations, and Intergovernmental Management," in this volume for additional commentary.)

The "state of the discipline" and the "state of the practice" often proceed at different paces, emphasizing different activities. Practice can suggest gaps in scholarly research and can help shape an emergent research agenda. The topics reviewed here have research linkages to other disciplines, but the focus is on the public administration literature. A primary objective is to uncover research gaps by highlighting promising conceptualizations, typologies, and refinements to various research traditions that focus on individual governments but also on governance and all sectors.

INTERSTATE RELATIONS

Theorists of horizontal federalism, or, more broadly, interstate relations, approach the topic in much the same way as theorists of vertical federalism or nation-state relations have done. They examine competitive relationships (Dye 1990; Kenyon and Kincaid 1991). States are economic competitors—for federal funds (Berch 1992; McKinnon and Nechyba 1997), higher-income residents, tourists, and new businesses offering high salaries. The competition may be facilitated by the national government's policies, such as its ability to pick "winners and losers" in awarding grants, economic stimulus funds, and even taxation policies.

On the other hand, state political boundaries often do not coincide with economic, cultural, or other realities, making some level of cooperation essential and even routine. Each state has the same status with the federal government, or what Watts (1999) calls de jure symmetry. State officials interact informally and formally with one another without the approval of the national government in most cases and develop an array of arrangements administered by managers working across state boundaries. These horizontal linkages are examples of cross-jurisdictional collaborative management, so prominent in public administration (see chapter 17, "Collaborative Public Agencies in the Network Era," in this volume; Agranoff and McGuire 2003), that can result in win-win outcomes for efficient and effective service delivery and policy making.

Benefits and costs of interstate cooperation and competition have been studied (Kenyon and Kincaid 1991), but definitive conclusions are unsettled. Competition may offer residents more choice, forcing a state to be more efficient in service provision and improving allocative efficiency (Tiebout 1956). Boehmke and Witmer (2004) found that economic competition leads to policy innovation and expansion. Rom, Peterson, and Scheve (1998) found that state sensitivity to other states' welfare policies motivated a state to examine and then adopt changes. The adoption of innovative health maintenance organization legislation was in part explained by the proportion of contiguous states previously enacting similar legislation (Balla 2001).

Some potential benefits and costs of service provision are enhanced by economies of scale that cannot be realized without cooperation. Competitive federalism through interstate competition can also have negative consequences. The rent-seeking behavior of states in competing for federal resources and industry can lead to unfavorable outcomes (Zimmerman 1994). When states compete for the same end, the outcomes for individual states tend toward zero-sum, although the federal system as a whole may benefit.

Highly competitive interactions among and between the states may spur cooperation when the losing states conclude that collaboration may lead to success. Cooperative efforts can be relatively informal or can create alliances that require new administrative agreements or management structures. An example of a broad-ranging cooperative effort is the ongoing work of the Multi-State Streamlined Sales Tax Commission, which helps states agree on how to tax online purchases. The Emergency Management Assistance Compact is also widely regarded as one of the administrative successes of the response to the Katrina tragedy.

MULTISTATE LEGAL ACTION: NEGLECTED ISSUE

Interstate compacts (U.S. Constitution, article 1, section 10) require congressional consent, but the purpose of the provision was not to inhibit the ability of states to act in concert with one another but to protect the preeminence of the new national government by preventing states' infringement on federal authority or altering the federal balance of power by compact. Only compacts that affect a power delegated to the federal government or that alter the political balance within the federal system require congressional consent today. If a water-basin agreement among states affects the water rights of a nonparty state, it needs congressional approval. A compact that threatens to interfere with federal preemption likely needs congressional approval. Most compacts are in areas in which state authority is clearly preeminent, such as education. Congressional consent, when needed, is generally not burdensome and is usually a resolution since the Constitution does not specify the means or timing of consent. Interstate compacts are used heavily in the regulatory arena and are examples of a cooperative horizontal federalism approach.

COORDINATED INITIATIVES: NEGLECTED ISSUE

Cooperation among and between states includes joint multistate legal action and optional enactment of uniform laws (Florestano 1994; Nice 1984; Bowman 2004), with each type of interstate cooperation involving different levels of engagement. Multistate legal action (Bowman 2004) may not involve long-term or involved administrative commitment since staff work occurs in the early stages and is handled by the initiating state. The sparse existing work by scholars studying state attorneys general is important (Clayton 1994; Zimmerman 1998; Bolleyer 2006). State attorneys general have worked together to fight the tobacco companies and Wall Street. Through the National Association of Attorneys General, policy guidelines are developed in such areas as consumer protection, civil rights, energy and environmental issues, cyberspace law, Medicaid fraud, health care, Amber Alert, and antitrust. Policies are adopted on those issues, and the association has ties to similar organizations worldwide.

Other interstate cooperative action relates to conformity across states (Nice 1984). By matching its law to that of a peer-established norm, a state is in a cooperative venture but implements its own uniform laws. The nonprofit, unincorporated National Conference of Commissioners on Uniform State Law in the United States works with counterpart international organizations, and also drafts laws to be adopted through voluntary state action.

Increasing in popularity are coordinated initiatives that could also become multistate executive orders and other informal administrative agreements (Bowman 2004). Mediated through the Constitution's Full Faith and Credit Clause (article 4, section 1, in which U.S. states have to respect the "public acts, records, and judicial proceedings" of other states); the Dormant Commerce Clause (inferred from the Commerce Clause, article 1, prohibiting a state from passing legislation that improperly burdens or discriminates against interstate commerce); and the Fourteenth Amendment's Equal Protection Clause, in which "no state shall . . . deny to any person within its jurisdiction protection of the laws," states work together on issues such as the treatment of criminal offenders after incarceration and marriage laws, simply because people and goods travel. Interstate compacts are the most comprehensive since they result from sustained interaction and require the development of administrative management structures and continuing engagement beyond the date of enactment. The compacts are powerful lawmaking tools in that they are basically contracts among and between states entered into through state legislation. Interstate compacts increase the power of the states at the expense of the federal government because, once approved by Congress, they have the full force and supremacy of federal law, although the terms of a compact can be enforced in federal court to prevent states from ignoring their compact responsibilities.

COOPERATIVE HORIZONTAL FEDERALISM: NEGLECTED ISSUE

Heinmiller's (2007) review of a proposed Great Lakes–St. Lawrence River Basin Water Resources Compact suggests a novel constitutional mechanism for states to bind themselves to common substantive and procedural environmental protection standards, implemented individually with regional resources and enforcement. A compact might involve the joint development by a group of states of common minimum substantive or procedural legal standards to manage a shared resource, water, but leave individual states the flexibility and autonomy to administer the standards under state law. In the context of Great Lakes water management, the states could craft regional minimum standards to govern water withdrawals, while allowing individual states to develop programs tailored to their specific needs and preferences. Discretion is not absolute, due to programmatic reviews and enforcement by peers. However, the regulatory standards, programmatic obligations, and enforcement mechanisms come from the states' obligations to one another, not from a congressional mandate.

The cooperative horizontal federalism approach is a novel way to make policy. Common minimum standards are developed jointly by the states and incorporated into state law and then individually implemented. Individual state efforts are not undermined in a "race to the bottom," and flexibility to shape policies best suited to specific needs and preferences in each state is permitted. Federal environmental protection is still needed, but this "third way" is distinct from the traditional state-versus-federal debate. For environmental policy, the model borrows features from traditional environmental federalism, that is, cooperative vertical federalism, and existing interstate water management compacts, or horizontal federalism. The common minimum standards are developed by the collective states, which serve the function typically held by the federal government. The interstate compact mechanism establishes the standards and programmatic enforcement.

The next two sections of the chapter examine state-local relations and intermunicipal relations. The first, a vertical dimension of federalism, is important in its own right but is necessary to understand horizontal intermunicipal relations since local governments are "creatures of the states."

STATE-LOCAL RELATIONS: NEGLECTED ISSUE

State-local relations are an important and much neglected area of intergovernmental relations that span constitutional, political, and fiscal ties that bind states and localities, as well as the complex interactions among and between them in delivering public goods and services. Cooperative models of federalism are prominent in understanding state-local relations. Constitutionally, local governments are creatures of state government; however, states depend on local governments to provide essential goods and services. This downplays solely command-and-control policy making. State legislators are elected locally, and many enter the legislature after holding positions at the local level. Municipal and county associations are powerful legislative lobbies (Nice 1998; Cigler 1995).

Some of the first states formed as federations of local government, suggesting the controversial notion that local governments are not constitutionally inferior to state government and rejecting the characterization of states as unitary political systems. Local charters provide a legal basis for local control, as does home rule, which increases local autonomy. Recognizing their interdependence, Elazar (1998) regarded states as unions of their civil communities.

Suggesting that less emphasis be placed on any single government, Cigler (1998) argued that it is the system of government that is most important. Less discussion about government and more about governance, and less emphasis on intergovernmental, but more on intersector relations are both essential. She conducted interviews with six state officials in each state who worked primarily on local issues. Trends that affect state-local relations were deciphered and set in the backdrop of enormously complex and intertwined problems related to demographic changes, technological development, economic trends, citizen demands, resource scarcity, and other factors. Twelve principles that guide cooperative state-local relations for the twenty-first century were developed, defining both practice and goals and suggesting research agenda topics (Table 19.1).

Osborne and Gaebler's book *Reinventing Government* (1992) was the inspiration for "State-Local Relations: A Need for Reinvention?" (Cigler 1993), which suggests a research agenda. Four broad categories of state-local interaction were developed using a typology put forth in Richard Elmore's policy research (1987). Table 19.2 presents the typology, which is used to organize the discussion that follows. States use one activity or a combination of activities within each category targeted to change the behavior and actions of local governments.

Mandates

Mandates are regulations or court orders. Unfunded legislative mandates are a significant source of friction between the states and local governments, spanning many areas such as the environ-

---

Table 19.1

Principles Guiding Cooperative State-Local Relations

- A focus on alternatives to monopoly government, such as contracting and public competition
- Government as facilitator, enabler, information generator and disseminator
- Holistic approaches to problem solving
- Regional approaches to service delivery and policy making
- Community-level service provision
- Concentrated resources and more individual and governmental self-reliance
- Balancing of citizen rights and responsibilities
- Mandate, regulatory, and fiscal flexibility
- Accountability for performance
- Citizen engagement
- Experimentation, risk-taking, innovation
- A focus on prevention

Table 19.2

Typology of State-Local Interactions

- Mandates
- Inducements
- Capacity building
- System changing

---

ment, health, and employee pensions. Court decisions, such as those related to school finance systems or the constitutionality of certain taxes, are important to state-local relations. States are very active in trying to find ways to help local governments comply with mandates. A bundle of legislative procedural options—program monitoring, fiscal notes, sunset and sunrise programs—increase levels of legislative scrutiny for reducing the negative financial effects of mandates for localities and attempt to improve legislative decision making. Another option for dealing with mandates is reimbursement, the legislative provision of funding to pay for new mandates through appropriations, taxes, or fees. Currently, state and local governments appear to be struggling most with mandates for employee health insurance, pension costs, local government procurement, and care of prisoners.

Inducements

Since the mid-1990s, *incentivizing* is the word that has been used to refer to positive inducements that states make to nudge local governments to engage in cooperative behavior. More points are given in grant competitions for local jurisdictions that cooperate with one another. Shared services are promoted, although states also offer financial inducements for mergers and consolidations. Another type of inducement is provision of negotiation and mediation assistance to resolve local disputes.

Capacity Building

This category of state-local interaction (Table 19.2) spans a range of state activities geared toward increasing local governments' abilities in the managerial, technical, financial, and collaborative skills realms, as well as their political will to make difficult governance decisions. State technical assistance to local governments is capacity building, as is the provision of revenue flexibility. Honadle (1981) defined capacity building as the ability to anticipate and influence change, make informed, intelligent decisions about policy, develop programs to implement policy, attract and absorb resources, manage resources, and evaluate current activities to guide future actions. Simply put, capacity is the ability to do what is needed and wanted, and states play a central role in helping to build local capacity, including building collaborative skills for intermunicipal interactions.

The provision of revenue flexibility to local governments by a state (Nice and Fredericksen 1995) builds local capacity. A local government's fiscal flexibility depends on the appropriateness, variety, and productivity of its revenue sources. Having authority over sources of significant revenue potential results in flexibility to adapt to changing demands for services and new circumstances. If local governments must rely on the extensive use of earmarked sources, flexibility is diminished (Cigler 1993, 1996; Pagano and Johnston 2000). Cigler (1996) reviewed the literature on state-local fiscal options and developed five broad categories that states can draw on to increase the revenue flexibility of their local governments (Table 19.3). The last category consists of system-changing activities. States must also be concerned with newer ways that local governments obtain revenue, through financing tools related to the activities of special authorities and other entities that are entrepreneurial in leveraging public and private funds (Weber 2003).

Home rule usually refers to a state providing structural options for its local government, but it can apply to local finance (Krane 2001), and fiscal flexibility may be more important than structural flexibility. Many states struggle with how to modernize and rationalize taxation and finance powers of the state and its local governments. This means reconsideration of constitutional provisions applying to taxes, property tax limits or abolishment of the property tax, debt limits, the roles of public authorities and special districts in financing, and overhauling nonproperty taxes. This area of state-local relations is among the most contentious since devolution has shifted more responsibilities to local governments, often without increased funding (unfunded mandates) or enhanced ability to raise revenues.

A significant capacity-building activity is state monitoring of fiscal stress, that is, a community's financial condition. Beth Honadle (2003) and Kloha, Weissert, and Kleine (2005a, 2005b) document that the state roles in forecasting, mitigating, and averting local government fiscal crises are expanding. Local governments experience financial difficulty from many sources: declining revenues due to less sales tax, property tax, or intergovernmental revenues; increased liabilities; high levels of debt; problems stemming from salary and fringe benefit costs or public safety; and a variety of operating gaps. In their book, Honadle, Costa, and Cigler (2004) provide an introduction to and applications of widely used measures of fiscal stress.

Still another capacity-building activity is state provision of technical assistance to local governments. Assistance is often combined with inducements to get local governments to change how they work together, use various revenue options, or other perform activities. Many states offer "schools" for newly elected officials through their departments of community affairs, municipal associations, or universities, and some states (e.g., Georgia) mandate training for newly elected officials.

System Changing

The greatest likelihood for reinventing state-local relations may be in restructuring local government, which usually requires state action. Annexation, tax-base sharing, transfer of powers

Table 19.3

Ways That States Increase Local Revenue Flexibility

- Changing the level or pattern of intergovernmental assistance
- Altering local tax options
- Revising property tax laws and administration
- Altering user charges or fees
- Encouraging or mandating a fundamental restructuring of the system of local governance

among governments, and city-county consolidation are examples, as is state or city takeover of the schools. Currently, functional consolidations of a specific service—police, fire, schools, solid waste—are more popular than consolidations of governments in a region. Maryland, Virginia, and other southern states have countywide school districts, and their model has attracted attention from other states. System-changing options often involve intermunicipal relations.

INTERMUNICIPAL RELATIONS

Roscoe Martin (1963) was the first scholar to develop a continuum of the ways to organize services in a metropolitan area or region. His classification system was flexible so that others could incorporate new practices, which was done by David B. Walker (1987, 1995) and Patricia Atkins (1998). Walker highlighted seventeen alternative arrangements, and Atkins provided twenty-five. The classifications begin with options that require none or very little loss of autonomy or intermunicipal interaction, such as the use of informal agreements. The different ways to organize and deliver services mostly involve increased intermunicipal or state-local interactions and a relative loss of autonomy. Examples are formal interlocal agreements, interlocal service contracts, privatization, multicommunity partnerships, regional councils, special-purpose districts, transfers of functions, annexation, tax-base sharing, functional service consolidations, regional authorities, consolidated or merged governments, and metropolitan government. The typologies related to intermunicipal service delivery are useful both for heuristic purposes and for targeting specific options for research study. Indeed, entire bodies of literature now focus on topics such as special districts; privatization, especially contracting out and public-private partnerships; and city-county consolidations.

The theoretical underpinning about the options can be divided into several "schools." Ostrom, Tiebout and Warren (1961) utilized the field of public goods economic theory (Tiebout 1956), which characterized the pattern of local governments in metropolitan areas as polycentric, and used that interpretation to explain the organization of governments for the delivery of services. They carefully distinguished between the *provision* and the *production* of local services. A local government could provide services to its residents or choose to let residents provide the services themselves. If a service was provided, there were options for its production, including in-house, contracting out to another government or to a private vendor, or the use of volunteers or vouchers (ACIR 1973, 1987).

The polycentric theory of local public economies, at the time of its development, stood in sharp contrast to a model of metropolitan governance that has a metropolitan structure intended to capture economies of scale in service provision. Advocates of consolidating existing jurisdictions claimed that a fragmented governmental system with multiple and overlapping governments was incapable of cooperation to resolve problems that cross jurisdictional boundaries and that competition among and between local governments was a wasteful duplication of services.

Since the 1960s, the polycentric theory, or the "public choice" school, was developed further (Ostrom 1973) and tested by empirical research (e.g., Ostrom, Parks, and Whitaker 1978; ACIR 1987; Ostrom, Bish, and Ostrom 1988). Most research, however, has emphasized the value of efficiency (Bish 1971), to the neglect of equity, effectiveness, accountability, or other values. Much of the early research compared the unit costs of in-house versus contracted production and found private producers to be more efficient than public producers of the same services (Savas 1982, 1987; ACIR 1987). That research, however, focused on a few local services such as solid waste collection.

City-County Consolidations

The research on city-county consolidations is representative of findings on government structure at the end of the Martin (1963), Walker (1987, 1995) and Atkins (1998) classifications—those options that are most difficult to enact and that represent the greatest challenges to local autonomy. Carr and Feiock (2004) and Leland and Thurmaier (2004) provided recent book-length assessments of city-county consolidation. Staley and colleagues (2005) reviewed nearly three dozen recent peer-reviewed studies of city-county consolidations for the Indiana General Assembly. They drew five conclusions: significant gains in efficiency are unlikely; significant gains in perceived service quality are more likely but not ensured; modest changes to city governance, such as some functional consolidations, are unlikely to have a major impact on economic development; morale problems are a major obstacle to consolidation; and context matters, with research results mixed and done on a case-by-case analysis.

Boyd (2008) reviewed city-county merger studies nationwide for a New York commission, and his findings dovetailed with the Indiana study. He considered ways for local jurisdictions to be dissolved or merged and the transfer of functions to counties. In additional to the Indiana study, Boyd located seven other recent academic and nonacademic literature reviews of the topic. Other comparative analyses of consolidations were published by the Pennsylvania Economy League of Southwestern Pennsylvania (2007) and Ball State University's Center for Business and Economic Research (Faulk and Hicks 2009), which focused on the costs of consolidation. Laura Reese (2004) also provided a thorough review of the metropolitan reorganization literature.

There continues to be some support for the consolidation and simplification of local government structures in urban areas, but that support lies primarily outside of academia—pushed by civic groups and newspapers. Proponents still draw on the progressive reform tradition of the early twentieth century, with its belief in centralizing authority to take power away from old-style political machines. Olberding (2002) notes that nearly 80 percent of city-county consolidation proposals in the United States have been rejected by voters. She also explains that the emphasis on centralized regional governments promoted in the 1960s to enhance efficiencies and maximize economies of scale, sometimes backed by federal funding, also lost popularity during the 1980s. Only a few large city-county consolidations have occurred in the last forty years. Widely studied is the Indianapolis UniGov system, created by the legislature in 1969. Rosentraub's research on UniGov offers positive and negative lessons learned and is important because UniGov did not eliminate all other local governments. It is basically a multilayered system with five cities, nine townships, eleven school districts, and seven police departments that has attributes of regional cooperation but preserves local control of other basic municipal services (Rosentraub 2000). School district consolidations are still popular for study, but not often implemented (Duncombe and Yinger 2001).

Shared Services: Neglected Issue

The most discussed and evaluated intermunicipal option "in practice" is the sharing of services on a voluntary basis. There are thousands of shared service agreements among local governments across the states, and there is an extensive literature on the topic, mostly produced by state agencies, legislative commissions, and local governments, especially counties and regional organizations. There is less peer-reviewed academic research, although academics have produced reports for government agencies and legislatures. Cigler (2001) conducted baseline research in Pennsylvania on intermunicipal organizations—councils of government—and service delivery.

Other Pennsylvania research is reported in Honadle, Costa, Cigler (2004) from interviews with local officials to ascertain perceived barriers to intermunicipal cooperation, in general, and formal intergovernmental agreements, in particular, including how to overcome those barriers. A lack of information about available options, not unwillingness to change, proved to be a major barrier to change. State government's role in providing financial incentives and capacity building by developing model agreements, collaborative skills-building training, and other factors was explored, based on information gathered from published reports in forty-three states. Skelly's (1997) criteria for evaluating the impact of various service-delivery options and Hirsch's (1991) definitions of options such as intergovernmental agreements were used to examine alternatives on efficiency, effectiveness, accountability, and equity criteria.

Handbooks on alternative service-delivery options, most involving intermunicipal interactions, were developed by Armington and Ellis (1984) and Eggers (1997). Innovative databases and inventories exist on intermunicipal cooperation, such as those at the University of Albany and the Institute for Local Governance and Regional Growth at the University of Buffalo. These are largely untapped by academics for peer-reviewed publications. Before there can be shared services or other intermunicipal cooperation, it is often the case that state laws must be changed, a topic of substantial interest across the states, which generally have outdated municipal classification systems and powers. If counties and municipalities do not have the same functions in a state, for example, cooperation is more difficult (Cigler 1994).

Some states (New York, Pennsylvania, New Jersey) have formal shared municipal service incentive grant programs based on competition. In New York, the state's shared services program uses relatively small amounts of resources to encourage significant amounts of collaborative thinking among small, rural governments, but the funds available are for areas in which sharing is already common. Significant changes do not occur for the more challenging functional areas, as communities are prone to buy things together more than to do things together (New York State Commission on Local Government Efficiency and Competitiveness 2008).

State capacity building to promote intermunicipal cooperation includes reviewing statutes governing cooperation, identifying options, conducting feasibility analyses for interested communities, providing seed funding for collaboration, and helping to negotiate agreements and to maintain completed agreements. Much of the research by "pracademics" has shifted from concentration on and advocacy for one option or another to answering questions about how a given option will work (Warner and Hebdon 2001).

Lamothe, Lamothe, and Feiock (2008) reviewed the literature that draws on the influences of transaction costs, markets, and a limited number of jurisdictional factors to focus primarily on production mechanisms. The jurisdictional factors they consider are management capacity, management structure, and market position. Similarly, Andrew (2009) provided an overview of interjurisdictional agreements and how they operate, as well as their patterns of use, based on recent literature. The literature used for the assessments does not consider some useful findings from case

Figure 19.1   **The Continuum of Multicommunity Collaboration** (MC^2)

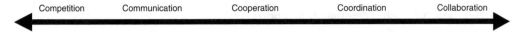

studies, especially the role of capacity building and provision of information about options. Many recent studies overlook the basic notion that the characteristics of a service dictate, in large part, what types of tools and approaches are most useful for delivering a service and what the outcomes are likely to be in terms of efficiency, effectiveness, equity, and accountability (Skelly 1997).

Regional Economic Collaboration: Neglected Issue

Transaction costs theory, collective action, and network theory concepts were used for field research in six rural regions of the United States and one Canadian province. The field study communities were selected using a snowball technique based on national telephone interviews with state and province officials familiar with clusters of communities with long-term collaborations in regional economic development and service delivery. The multidisciplinary research team represented planning, sociology, economics, and public administration. Findings and typologies developed by the public administration member focused on "multicommunity collaboration" (MC^2)—alliances among multiple communities and across sectors (Cigler 1992, 1999, 2001). A continuum of types of collaboration among the study communities was developed, ranging from conflict, to networking or communication, cooperation, coordination, to truly collaborative relationships in which actors recognized their "shared destiny" (Figure 19.1). Significantly, the organizations studied had themselves evolved along such a continuum of partnership over many years.

Successful alliances began with partnerships on relatively small projects in less contentious service and policy areas (e.g., arts festivals) and then made slow, steady progress over many years, using measurable results to snowball successes further along the continuum. The findings and continuum have been used and refined by other researchers studying collaboration, including Keast et al. (2004) and Guo and Acar (2005).

Key obstacles to the multicommunity efforts were related to allocation of costs, policy-making structures, conflict resolution, contract specifics and length, project administration, and selection of services. These were circumvented by leadership quality and removal of legal and statutory impediments, real or perceived, on a host of issues: general- versus limited-purpose governments, differing county and municipal authority, collective bargaining, and revenue and financing issues. When parties to an alliance saw mutual benefits and mutual powers, with no transfer of sovereign powers, chances of acceptance increased.

From the case study research a set of nine "preconditions" that help explain the emergence of multicommunity collaborative organizations was developed (Table 19.4). Whether a particular precondition is "necessary and/or sufficient" for complex collaborations to occur was not established; that is, the exploratory comparative case studies were not used to posit a causal theory. Instead, the preconditions highlight aspects of emergent multiorganizational, multisector, and multicommunity collaboration in need of scrutiny before serious theory development can occur. Practical strategies of facilitating partnership formation are also derived from the preconditions, which also suggest categories of research needs for studying intermunicipal collaboration.

Overall, visionary leadership by a local champion, informed capacity building including financial and technical assistance, especially training in collaborative skills development, were especially important to the areas studied.

Table 19.4

Preconditions for Multicommunity Collaboration (MC^2)

- A disaster occurrence
- Fiscal stress or perceived stress
- A political constituency for cooperation
- Supportive capacity-building from state government, municipal associations, or foundations
- Early and continued support of local elected officials
- A clear demonstration of advantages
- The presence of a policy entrepreneur
- An early focus on visible, effective strategies
- An emphasis on collaborative skills-building to create win-win solutions

Large-Scale Regional Collaboration: Neglected Issue

The "big options" for rejuvenating metropolitan-area competitiveness in a global economy involve large-scale regional collaboration. Governance today takes place amid ecosystems, watersheds, laborsheds, commutersheds, and other boundary-spanning descriptions. Since twenty-first-century challenges cross jurisdictional boundaries, so must governance systems. Cooperative intergovernmental relations, both interstate and intermunicipal, are but one part of the governance system that must meld public, private, and nonprofit interactions. Cooperative ventures by states can be induced or mandated or encouraged by the national government, as is the case with metropolitan transportation planning and, increasingly, workforce investment policy.

Interstate and intermunicipal relations research provides some insight for understanding current policy challenges. However, research on intergovernmental relations that focuses on governments, which are geography bound without borders that necessarily coincide with either problems or potential solutions, is limited. In the melding of a governance system involving all sectors, in addition, government may be the weak actor, so placing it center stage for analysis may not be as useful as other approaches. A state's lack of capacity building for its local governments, weak finances, or any number of other factors may explain "government as weak actor," but the key point here is that studying the entire governance system with all its sectors—public, private, nonprofit—and civil society may be most fruitful for research.

Collective action theory and hypotheses regarding cooperation—among and between individuals, associations, agencies, governments—is proving to be a useful approach to understanding the big challenges in a metropolitan region. Susan Mason (2008) points out that collective action can solve problems that no one individual can solve alone and that the collective action literature describes circumstances that inhibit cooperation, such as transaction costs and the free-rider problem. Collective action theory offers ways to overcome collective action problems to improve cooperation, such as social institutions and self-governing authority. Social institutions are not necessarily governments; instead, they can be neighborhood organizations, nonprofits, economic development organizations, or other entities. Self-governing authority allows organization members to create their own contractual relations, which lowers transaction costs of establishing and monitoring new institutions, reduces the free-rider problems, and fosters communication. Using collective action theory and hypotheses, Mason was able to draw more insights about ways to obtain regional cooperation in employment and training policy. This was because key actors were not in government and the cooperation problems were not confined to the government sector.

The focus in the public administration and political science literature is on horizontally and vertically linked organizations that centralize regional efforts through coordinated interlocal collaboration (Lowery 2000; Feiock 2004, 2007). The work is grounded in collective action theory and methods that Richard Feiock has coined as "institutional collective action." His and other institutional-collective-action-oriented studies envision regionalism occurring through voluntary intergovernmental contracts and other agreements and exchanges that achieve collective benefits. This literature is important and growing in volume—too much to be given full consideration here. The positive conclusion is that much of what is being found through research has been known in practice for some time (e.g., Wisconsin Policy Research Institute 2002). Important is that earlier research that did not use the institutional collective action terminology had similar conclusions. Government agencies, legislative commissions, and municipal associations, as well as individual governments, are increasingly receptive to fact-based analysis, comparative reviews of how services are currently delivered, and available options, including financial, technical, and information-based inducements.

Special Purpose Authorities and Megaprojects: Neglected Issue

The power of special authorities (Caro 1975) has been known and viewed by reform advocates in a pejorative way due to being "hidden" or "shadow" governments that may lack accountability and increase local government fragmentation. On the other hand, these entities have grown in importance because they can bypass the constraints faced by municipal governments that lack fiscal, technical, and managerial capacity—and legal authority. Deal making by public officials bypasses the public and highlights a need for scrutiny and accountability, but the resulting large-scale public-private ventures largely shape regional economic development (Fainstein 2001).

Altshuler and Luberoff (2003) explain that the megaprojects are not created and implemented by municipal governments, which provide basic allocational services (Peterson 1981). Instead, the projects are the result of state agencies and regional entities that leverage public and private funds. Special authorities are largely independent in their operations from municipal governments and work across metropolitan areas. An area's transportation infrastructure, that is, its network of highways, roads, bridges, tunnels, mass transit, airports, seaports, and harbors, as well as its water, wastewater, and solid waste disposal systems are likely run by networks of special authorities that manage and finance them (Graham and Marvin 2001). The specialized networks help to create authorities to finance and manage tourism and entertainment facilities such as sports stadiums and convention centers. These special-purpose entities operate locally and globally, not just with general-purpose governments, but with entire industries—infrastructure, sports, and entertainment.

In the twenty-first century, special authorities are not simply financing and administrative mechanisms. They are powerful political forces that shape the nature of metropolitan areas and regions, and, thus, they shape intermunicipal, state-local, and interstate relations, but also interactions among and between sectors. They challenge scholarship that focuses solely or primarily on governments and highlight the need for injecting more concern about accountability into scholarship on metropolitan areas. Mullin (2009) examined the capacity of special districts for engaging in responsive and collaborative decision making for promoting the sustainable use of water resources. She concluded that specialization was most beneficial for less severe policy problems.

Cigler (2001) put forth a research agenda for studying multiorganizational, multisector, and multicommunity organizations by public administration scholars. It includes topics such as the effects on accountability when government is the "weak sector" within a collaboration; the basis for legitimacy for organizations not possessing traditional government authority; the representativeness of the new organizations guiding economic development; government's role in the new types of organizations; and questions related to boundary, such as, Who's in charge? and Who does what?

Can there be regional governance through collaboration, not regional government? The most significant work "in practice" is in the area of land-use planning and growth management, topics not generally researched by public administration's intergovernmental scholars. Dale Krane (1993) argued that intergovernmental research needs to be more closely integrated with public policy research. Studying what is occurring within the growth management policy arena can be helpful in understanding intermunicipal and regional collaboration. Around the nation, groups of municipalities and counties, with the capacity-building help of state agencies, are using what can be called regional-cooperative (Staley 1992) models that avoid formal regional agencies, one-size-fits-all orientations, and tampering with local autonomy. Cost sharing, not revenue sharing, is promoted. New sources of revenue, generally some forms of development levies, are tapped. Negotiation, mediation, and arbitration processes are used, rather than cumbersome, more costly judicial remedies. The goal is to achieve sustainability and resiliency for regions. Cooperative agreements are pursued among local governments when a service to be delivered or a policy to be decided merits joint solution. States are strengthening their laws that guide intermunicipal cooperation and are providing more assistance, both financial and technical. Indeed, Frug and Barron (2008) argue that state law that determines what local governments can and cannot do with revenue, land use, schools, and more stifles urban innovation. The academic literature examining structural versus networked approaches to metropolitan areas in terms of their ability to reduce disparities between cities and suburbs and to enhance a region's ability to compete in the global economy supports collaboration (Savitch and Vogel 2000).

The study of the networks for policy making and service delivery in large American metropolitan areas and their edge cities has moved beyond regionalism to examination of megaregions, which will contain two-thirds of the U.S. population by 2050 (Ankner and Meyer 2009). These economic drivers are networks of metropolitan centers, and their surrounding areas are connected by existing environmental, economic, cultural, and infrastructure relationships. Research already suggests that there may be as many as ten U.S. megaregions that cross municipal, state, and even country borders. To understand, explain, and perhaps influence their development, public administration's intergovernmental scholars must go well beyond their current understanding of intermunicipal and interstate relations. Planning on an interjurisdictional level will become more important, with infrastructure planning and financing serving as the skeleton that links jurisdictions and regions. The European Union is the most advanced model of regional governance, and it has attracted the attention of an increasing number of researchers (Kirkham and Cardwell 2006). France, Britain, Germany, and Italy now work together on many fronts, including having the same currency and despite having different cultures, resources, and languages. The European Union model is basically a three-part regional government system: a metropolitan commission to deal with the regional scale, a regional legislature comprised of elected representatives, and a council of mayors and supervisors.

INTERNATIONALIZING FEDERALISM: NEGLECTED ISSUE

States and local governments are engaging in matters formerly considered national. Forty-four U.S. cities, eighteen counties, and sixteen states passed or considered legislation related to the Convention on the Elimination of All Forms of Discrimination Against Women, or CEDAW, signed by President Carter in 1980 but not ratified by the Senate. Some have formally advocated that the

United States ratify CEDAW. Some, most notably San Francisco, integrated CEDAW principles into their operations. Some individuals opposing the Kyoto Protocol, signed by President Clinton, based their arguments on power and process. Using the acronym COMPASS to suggest the importance of place, the Committee to Preserve American Security and Sovereignty (1998) claimed that decisions usually classified as domestic in U.S. law and politics, not foreign, gave power to the president at the expense of Congress, local governments, and private groups.

When President George W. Bush withdrew U.S. support for the Kyoto Protocol, cities such as Seattle and Salt Lake City enacted ordinances targeting to Kyoto utility emissions guidelines. In spring 2005, nine U.S. mayors agreed to their own climate protection program, approved by the U.S. Conference of Mayors and, by fall 2008, 884 mayors who represent more than 81 million people endorsed the program. The mayors pledged to cut greenhouse gas emissions 7 percent below 1990 levels by 2012, which meets the U.S. target in the Kyoto Protocol. The horizontal interaction extends worldwide through the Large Cities Climate Leadership Group, renamed C40, which includes more than thirty-five of the world's largest cities, including some in the United States. These efforts attempt to reduce emissions, promote technological development, spur the adoption of climate regulation by the U.S. Congress, and promote international climate regulatory cooperation. A number of U.S. states cooperate with some Canadian provinces and a number of European countries on "cap and trade" issues (The International Carbon Action Partnership, www.icap.carbonaction.com).

What previously were viewed only as nation-to-nation issues—the Kyoto Protocol, CEDAW, human rights issues, food safety, and toy safety—are increasingly considered to be translocal governance issues as a result of interactions among local and state governments, facilitated by their networks, most notably the state and local associations. Other examples of state and local interactions in the traditionally international realm are initiatives taken to alter the conduct of the Vietnam and Gulf wars as well as the current conflict in Iraq. Conflict in Northern Ireland and the Middle East, nuclear-free zones, divestment or selective purchasing, the sanctuary movement, and efforts to promote nuclear disarmament and to protect against land mines, to end apartheid in South Africa, and to provide restitution for holocaust victims all saw interstate and intermunicipal interactions. States consider divestment against Sudan, often in consultation with other states with measures already enacted (Hobbs 1994; Fry 1998).

There is a growing legal literature on this topic (Resnik 2008). Ahdieh (2008) makes a key point: The dynamic part of subnational, national, and international coordination today is not the national coordination of subnational actors in the service of international needs; instead, state and local governments are increasingly engaged with foreign authorities and international questions. These interactions suggest yet another "third way" in emergent American federalism, a system in which interdependence and overlap foster the potential for recurrent engagement, learning, and coordination. Substates' horizontal coordination leads to international agreements and law.

Conlan, Dudley, and Clark titled their 2004 article "Taking on the World: The International Activities of American State Legislatures." They examined state legislation in 2001–2 and found hundreds of bills focused not just on promoting tourism and trade, but also on globalization, immigration, human rights, and climate control. Policy activists working through networks and organizations link legislators across state boundaries, helping to diffuse policy innovations. Johnson (2005) asserts that subnational governments and their professional associations enter into agreements and interact with one another and their counterparts in other countries in ways that are beyond the control, supervision, or even monitoring of the national government. That includes developing policy agendas that produce resolutions and lobbying either horizontally or vertically. By 2000, for example, twenty-six municipalities and four states had enacted economic sanction laws aimed at Myanmar (Burma), Nigeria, and other nations (Guay 2000). Borut (1998) provides examples of local governments adopting an international agenda.

SUMMARY

Horizontal dimensions of intergovernmental relations, intergovernmental management, and federalism are examined in this chapter by focusing on interstate and intermunicipal issues. This focuses particular attention on legal relationships among subnational governments in the federal system. Research gaps, such as multistate actions less formal than interstate compacts—joint legal action, coordinated initiatives, and policy making through flexible, collaborative agreements across states—are important areas for future research as states shape nationally relevant policies. How, and in what other ways, are states reshaping our understanding of federalism? Intermunicipal relations are addressed, in part, by using a governance approach to incorporate the roles and interactions of all sectors. What challenges face researchers in designing local governance research? Should traditional notions of dual federalism be reconceptualized, in addition, due to the growing activism by states and local governments in the international arena, guided by cooperation and interdependence?

The areas of state-local relations and intermunicipal relations present opportunities to highlight promising conceptualizations, typologies, and refinement to some long-standing research traditions. Four broad categories of state-local interaction—mandates, inducements, capacity building, and systemic change—frame the discussion. Promising ways to study intermunicipal issues—collective action theory, case study research, and crossing municipal boundaries by studying regional special authorities and megaregions—offer research gaps in understanding rural, metropolitan, and regional economic development in the global context. Especially emphasized is the need to use more case study research to uncover key variables to incorporate into empirical studies.

The literature reviewed shows that academic researchers continue to emphasize topics that the practitioner community has abandoned, for example, structural government consolidation. How can public administration research be more attuned to significant trends in practice? The continuum of types of collaboration and the set of preconditions for the emergence of collaborative organizations offer an expanded research agenda to help answer questions about regional governance through collaborative, not structural, change. The chapter's focus on contemporary and emerging issues of "practice" that currently outpace scholarly research output demonstrate that the state of the practice can help shape future academic research in federalism and intergovernmental relations, areas of fundamental importance to the American system of governance.

REFERENCES

Advisory Commission on Intergovernmental Relations (ACIR). 1973. *Substate Regionalism and the Federal System.* Vol. 1, *Regional Decision Making: New Strategies for Substate Districts.* Washington, DC: U.S. Government Printing Office.
———. 1987. *The Organization of Local Public Economies.* Washington, DC: U.S. Government Printing Office.
Agranoff, Robert, and Michael McGuire. 2003. *Collaborative Public Management: New Strategies for Local Government.* Washington, DC: Georgetown University Press.
Ahdieh, Robert B. 2008. Foreign affairs, international law, and the new federalism: Lessons from coordination. *Missouri Law Review* 73: 1185–1245.
Altshuler, Alan, and David Luberoff. 2003. *Mega-Projects: The Changing Politics of Urban Public Investment.* Washington, DC, and Cambridge, MA: Brookings Institution Press and Lincoln Institute of Land Policy.

Andrew, Simon A. 2009. Recent developments in the study of interjurisdictional agreements: An overview and assessment. *State and Local Government Review* 41 (2): 133–142.

Ankner, William D., and Michael Meyer. 2009. Investing in megaregion transportation systems: Institutional challenges and opportunities. In *Megaregions: Planning for Global Competitiveness,* ed. Catherine Ross, 166–190. Washington, DC: Island Press.

Armington, R.Q., and W.D. Ellis, eds. 1984. *This Way Up: The Local Official's Handbook for Privatization and Contracting out.* Chicago: Regnery Gateway.

Atkins, Patricia S. 1998. Regionalism. In *International Encyclopedia of Public Policy and Administration.* Vol. 4, ed. Jay M. Shafritz, 1935–1943. Boulder, CO: Westview Press.

Balla, Steven J. 2001. Interstate professional associations and the diffusion of policy innovations. *American Politics Research* 29 (3): 221–245.

Berch, Neil. 1992. Why do some states play the federal aid game better than others? *American Politics Quarterly* 20 (3): 366–377.

Boehmke, Frederick J., and Richard Witmer. 2004. Disentangling diffusion: The effects of social learning and economic competition on state policy innovation and expansion. *Political Research Quarterly* 57 (1): 39–51.

Bish, Robert L. 1971. *The Public Economy of Metropolitan Areas.* Chicago: Markham Publishing.

Bolleyer, Nicole. 2006. Federal dynamics in Canada, the United States, and Switzerland: How substates' internal organization affects intergovernmental relations. *Publius: The Journal of Federalism* 36 (4): 471–502.

Borut, Donald J. 1998. Stepping up to the international agenda. *Nation's Cities Weekly,* January 19.

Bowman, Ann O'M. 2004. Horizontal federalism: Exploring interstate interactions. *Journal of Public Administration Research and Theory* 14 (4): 535–546.

Boyd, Donald. 2008. Layering of local governments and city-county mergers. A Report to the New York State Commission on Local Government Efficiency and Competitiveness, March 21.

Caro, Robert A. 1975. *The Power Broker.* New York: Vintage Books.

Carr, Jered B., and Richard C. Feiock, eds. 2004. *City-County Consolidation and Its Alternatives: Reshaping the Local Government Landscape.* Armonk, NY: M.E. Sharpe.

Cigler, Beverly A. 1991. Intermunicipal Organizations. Center for Rural Pennsylvania, a Legislative Agency, Harrisburg, PA.

———. 1992. Pre-conditions for multicommunity collaboration. In *Multicommunity Collaboration: An Evolving Rural Revitalization Strategy,* ed. Peter F. Korsching, Timothy O. Borich, and Julie Stewart, 53–74. Ames, IA: Northwest Central Regional Center for Rural Development.

———. 1993. State-local relations: A need for reinvention? *Intergovernmental Perspective* 19 (1): 15–18.

———. 1994. The county-state connection: A national study of associations of counties. *Public Administration Review* 54 (1): 3–11.

———. 1995. Not just another special interest: The intergovernmental lobby. In *Interest Group Politics.* 4th ed., ed. Allan J. Cigler and Burdett Loomis, 131–153. Washington, DC: Congressional Quarterly Press.

———. 1996. Revenue diversification among American counties. In *The American County: Frontiers of Knowledge,* ed. Donald C. Menzel, 166–183. Tuscaloosa: University of Alabama Press.

———. 1998. Emerging trends in state-local relations. In *Governing Partners: State-Local Relations in the U.S.,* ed. Russell L. Hanson, 53–74. Boulder, CO: Westview Press.

———. 1999. Pre-conditions for the emergence of multicommunity collaborative organizations. *Policy Studies Review* 16 (1): 86–102.

———. 2001. Multiorganization, multisector, and multicommunity organizations: Setting the research agenda. In *Getting Results Through Collaboration: Networks and Network Structures for Public Policy and Management,* ed. Myrna P. Mandell, 71–85. Westport, CT: Quorum Books.

Clayton, Cornell W. 1994. Law, politics and the new federalism: State attorneys general as national policymakers. *Review of Politics* 56 (3): 525–553.

Committee to Preserve American Security and Sovereignty (COMPASS). 1998. Treaties, national sovereignty, and executive power: A report on the Kyoto Protocol. Presented at the U.S. Chamber of Commerce Conference: American Sovereignty and Security at Risk, Alexandria, VA, May 18. http://jamesvdelong. com/articles/environmental/kyoto.html (accessed September 19, 2009).

Conlan, Timothy J., Robert L. Dudley, and Joel F. Clark. 2004. Taking on the world: The international activities of American state legislatures. *Publius: The Journal of Federalism* 34 (3): 183–200.

Duncombe, William, and John Yinger. 2001. Does school district consolidation cut costs? Working Paper No. 33, Center for Policy Research, Maxwell School of Citizenship and Public Affairs, Syracuse, NY.

Dye, Thomas R. 1990. *American Federalism: Competition among Governments.* Lexington, MA: Lexington Books.

Eggers, William. 1997. *Performance-Based Contracting: Designing State-of-the-Art Contract Administration and Monitoring Systems.* Los Angeles, CA: Reason Foundation.

Elazar, Daniel J. 1998. State-local relations: Union and home rule. In *Governing Partners: State-Local Relations in the U.S.,* ed. Russell L. Hanson, 37–52. Boulder, CO: Westview Press.

Elmore, Richard F. 1987. Instruments and strategy in public policy. *Policy Studies Review* 7 (1): 174–186.

Fainstein, Susan S. 2001. *The City Builders.* Lawrence: University Press of Kansas.

Faulk, Dagney, and Michael Hicks. 2009. *Local Government Reform in Indiana.* Muncie, IN: Center for Business and Economic Research, Miller College of Business, Ball State University.

Feiock, Richard C. 2004. Introduction: Regionalism and institutional collective action. In *Metropolitan Governance: Conflict, Competition, and Cooperation,* ed. Richard C. Feiock, 8–26. Washington, DC: Georgetown University Press.

———. 2007. Rational choice and regional governance. *Journal of Urban Affairs* 29:47–62.

Florestano, Patricia S. 1994. Past and present utilization of interstate compacts in the United States. *Publius: The Journal of Federalism* 24 (4): 13–25.

Frug, Gerald E., and David J. Barron. 2008. *City Bound: How States Stifle Urban Innovation.* Ithaca, NY: Cornell University Press.

Fry, Earl H. 1998. *The Expanding Role of State and Local Governments in U.S. Foreign Affairs.* Washington, DC: Council on Foreign Relations.

Graham, Stephen, and Simon Marvin. 2001. *Splintering Urbanism: Networked Infrastructures, Technological Mobilities, and the Urban Condition.* New York: Routledge.

Guay, Terrence. 2000. Local government and global politics: The implications of Massachusetts' "Burma law." *Political Science Quarterly* 115 (3): 353–376.

Guo, Chao, and Muhittin Acar. 2005. Understanding collaboration among nonprofit organizations: Combining resource dependency, institutional, and network perspectives. *Nonprofit and Voluntary Sector Quarterly* 34 (3): 340–361.

Heinmiller, B. Timothy. 2007. Do intergovernmental institutions matter? The case of water diversion regulation in the Great Lakes Basin. *Governance* 20 (4): 655–674.

Hirsch, Walter Z. 1991. *Privatizing Government Services: An Economic Analysis of Contracting Out by Local Governments.* Monograph and Research Series 54. Los Angeles: Institute of Industry, UCLA.

Hobbs, Heidi. 1994. *City Hall Goes Abroad: The Foreign Policy of Local Politics.* Thousand Oaks, CA: Sage.

Honadle, Beth Walter. 1981. A capacity-building framework: A search for concept and purpose. *Public Administration Review* 41 (5): 575–580.

———. 2003. The state's role in U.S. local government fiscal crises: A theoretical model and results of a national survey. *International Journal of Public Administration* 26 (13): 1431–1472.

Honadle, Beth Walter, James M. Costa, and Beverly A. Cigler. 2004. *Fiscal Health for Local Governments: An Introduction to Concepts, Practical Analysis, and Strategies.* New York: Elsevier.

Johnson, Bertram. 2005. Associated municipalities: Collective action and the formation of state leagues of cities. *Social Science History* 29:549–558.

Keast, Robyn, Myrna P. Mandell, Kerry Brown, and Geoffrey Woolcock. 2004. Network structures: Working differently and changing expectations. *Public Administration Review* 64 (3): 363–371.

Kenyon, Daphne A., and John Kincaid. 1991. Introduction. In *Competition Among States and Local Governments,* ed. Daphne A. Kenyon and John Kincaid, 1–33. Washington, DC: Urban Institute Press.

Kirkham, Richard, and Paul James Cardwell. 2006. *The European Union: A Role Model for Regional Governance?* Aspen, CO: Aspen Publishers.

Kloha, Philip, Carol Weissert, and Robert Kleine. 2005a. Someone to watch over me: State practices in monitoring local fiscal conditions. *American Review of Public Administration* 35 (3): 236–255.

———. 2005b. Developing and testing a new composite model to predict local fiscal distress. *Public Administration Review* 65 (3): 278–288.

Krane, Dale. 1993. American federalism, state governments, and public policy: Weaving together loose theoretical threads. *PS: Political Science and Politics* 26 (2): 186–190.

———, ed. 2001. *Home Rule in America.* Washington, DC: Congressional Quarterly Press, 356–366.

Lamothe, Scott, Meeyoung Lamothe, and Richard C. Feiock. 2008. Examining local government service delivery arrangements over time. *Urban Affairs Review* 44 (1): 27–56.

Leland, Suzanne M., and Kurt Thurmaier, eds. 2004. *Case Studies of City-County Consolidation.* Armonk, NY: M.E. Sharpe.

Lowery, David. 2000. A transaction costs model of metropolitan governance: Allocation versus redistribution in urban America. *Journal of Public Administration Research and Theory* 10 (1): 49–78.

Martin, Roscoe C. 1963. *Metropolis in Transition: Local Government Adaptation to Changing Urban Needs.* Washington, DC: U.S. Government Printing Office, Housing and Home Finance Agency.

Mason, Susan G. 2008. Regional cooperation in employment and training policy: A matter of collective action or intergovernmental relations? *Community Development: Journal of the Community Development Society* 39 (4): 1–16.

McKinnon, Ronald, and Thomas Nechyba. 1997. Competition in federal systems: The role of political and financial constraints. In *The New Federalism: Can the States Be Trusted?* ed. John Ferejohn and Barry R. Weingast, 3–61. Stanford, CA: Stanford University Press.

Mullin, Megan. 2009. *Governing the Tap: Special District Governance and the New Local Politics of Water.* Cambridge, MA: MIT Press.

New York State Commission on Local Government Efficiency & Competitiveness (2008). Twenty-first Century Local Government. New York: Albany (April) (www.nyslocalgov.org).

Nice, David C. 1984. Cooperation and conformity among the states. *Polity* 16 (Spring): 494–505.

Nice, David C. 1998. The intergovernmental setting of state-local relations. In *Governing Partners: State-Local Relations in the U.S.,* ed. Russell L. Hanson, 17–36. Boulder, CO: Westview Press.

Nice, David, and Patricia Fredericksen. 1995. Fiscal federalism. In *The Politics of Intergovernmental Relations.* 2d ed., ed. David C. Nice and Patricia Fredericksen, 49–82. Chicago: Nelson-Hall.

Olberding, Julie C. 2002. Foes regionalism beget regionalism? The relationship between norms and regional partnerships for economic development. *Public Administration Review* 62:480–491.

Osborne, David, and Ted Gaebler. 1992. *Reinventing Government.* Reading, MA: Addison Wesley.

Ostrom, Vincent. 1973. *The Intellectual Crisis in Public Administration.* Tuscaloosa: University of Alabama Press.

Ostrom, Vincent, Robert Bish, and Elinor Ostrom. 1988. *Local Government in the United States.* San Francisco: Institute for Contemporary Studies.

Ostrom, Vincent, Robert B. Parks, and Gordon P. Whitaker. 1978. *Patterns of Metropolitan Policy.* Cambridge, MA: Ballinger.

Ostrom, Vincent, Charles M. Tiebout, and Robert Warren. 1961. The organization of government in metropolitan areas: A theoretical inquiry. *American Political Science Review* 55:831–842.

Pagano, Michael, and Jocelyn Johnston. 2000. Life at the bottom of the fiscal food chain: Examining city and county revenue decisions. *Publius: The Journal of Federalism* 30 (1): 159–170.

Pennsylvania Economy League of Southwestern Pennsylvania. 2007. A comparative analysis of city/county consolidations. Pittsburgh, PA, February 7. www.alleghenyconference.org/PEL/PDFs/CityCountyConsolidationsComparativeAnalysis.pdf.

Peterson, Paul E. 1981. *City Limits.* Chicago: University of Chicago Press.

Reese, Laura A. 2004. Same governance, different day: Does metropolitan reorganization make a difference? *Review of Policy Research* 21 (4): 595–611.

Resnik, Judith. 2008. The internationalism of American federalism: Missouri and Holland, the Earl F. Nelson lecture. *Missouri Law Review* 73 (4): 1105–1147.

Rom, Mark Caro, Paul E. Peterson, and Kenneth F. Scheve Jr. 1998. Interstate competition and welfare policy. *Publius: The Journal of Federalism* 28 (3):17–37.

Rosentraub, Mark S. 2000. City-county consolidation and the rebuilding of image: The fiscal lessons from Indianapolis's UniGov program. *State and Local Government Review* 85 (2): 180–191.

Savas, E.S. 1982. *How to Shrink Government: Privatizing the Public Sector.* Chatham, NJ: Chatham House Publishing.

———. 1987. *Privatization: The Key to Better Government.* Chatham, NJ: Chatham House Publishers.

Savitch, Hank V., and Ronald K. Vogel. 2000. Metropolitan consolidation versus metropolitan governance in Louisville. *State and Local Government Review* 32 (3): 198–212.

Skelly, M.J. 1997. *Alternative Service Delivery in Canadian Municipalities.* Toronto, Ontario: Intergovernmental Committee on Urban and Regional Research.

Staley, Sam. 1992. *Bigger Is Not Better—The Virtues of Decentralized Local Government.* Cato Policy Analysis 166. Washington, DC: Cato Institute.

Staley, Samuel R., Dagney Faulk, Suzanne M. Leland, and D. Eric Schansberg. 2005. The effects of city-county consolidation: A review of the recent academic literature. A report prepared for the Indiana Policy Review Foundation for the Marion County Consolidation Study Commission, Indiana General Assembly, November 16. www.in.gov/legislative/interim/committee/2005/committees/prelim/MCCC02.pdf.

Tiebout, Charles. 1956. A pure theory of local expenditures. *Journal of Political Economy* 64:416–424.

Walker, David B. 1987. Snow White and the 17 dwarfs: From metro cooperation to governance. *National Civic Review* 76 (1): 14–28.

———. 1995. *The Rebirth of Federalism.* Chatham, NJ: Chatham House Publishers.

Warner, Mildred, and Robert Hebdon. 2001. Local government restructuring: Privatization and its alternatives. *Journal of Policy Analysis and Management* 20 (2): 315–336.

Watts, Ronald L. 1999. The theoretical and practical implications of asymmetrical federalism. In *Accommodating Diversity: Asymmetry in Federal States,* ed. Robert Agranoff. Baden-Baden, Germany: Nomos Verlagsgesellschaft.

Weber, Rachel. 2003. Equity and entrepreneurialism: The impact of tax increment financing on school finance. *Urban Affairs Review* 38 (5): 619–644.

Wisconsin Policy Research Institute. 2002. *Cooperation, Not Consolidation: The Answer for Milwaukee Governance.* Wisconsin Policy Research Institute Report. Vol. 15 (8). Thiensville: Wisconsin Policy Research Institute.

Zimmerman, Joseph F. 1994. Introduction: Dimensions of interstate relations. *Publius: The Journal of Federalism* 24 (4): 1–11.

———. 1998. Interstate cooperation: The roles of the state attorneys general. *Publius: The Journal of Federalism* 28 (1): 71–89.

CHAPTER 20

POLITICS, BUREAUCRATIC DYNAMICS, AND PUBLIC POLICY

ROBERT F. DURANT AND JOHN MARVEL

The eminent philosopher of science Karl Popper once wrote, "If our civilization is to survive, we must break with the habit of deference to great men" (1966, vii). The same can be said of disciplinary needs to break from deference to dominant ideas, epistemologies, and methodologies that stymie progress in appreciating the dynamic nature of administrative phenomena. In this essay, we contend that the same applies if we are to acquire a more robust practical and theoretical understanding of the dynamics of the policy, politics, and administration (PPA) nexus as they have evolved over the past half century.

The premises of our argument are threefold. First, scholarship in public administration related to the PPA nexus has significantly improved our understanding of its dynamics, but scholars have not sufficiently incorporated recent developments in cognate fields, including political science, cognitive psychology, and evolutionary biology. Second, even were this to happen, the evolution of governance in the United States toward networks requires researchers to expand the locus (where PPA takes place) and focus (what to examine) of their research if understanding and theory building are to proceed profitably. Third, the methodological approaches and epistemologies that now dominate the study of PPA dynamics have reached the limits of their explanatory power because they have minimized the interactive and reciprocal effects of time (history), timing (context), and time sensitivity (contingency) in their research designs and because they have focused too heavily in theory building and administrative reform on advancing a "rationality project" (Stone 2001) in the field.

We begin by reviewing our understanding of PPA dynamics from a sample of major research findings in public administration, policy sciences, political science, and public management. Illustrated is how an increasing gap developed between ordinary citizens and policymaking. Next, we review and critically assess three major theoretical approaches falling under the general rubric of the new institutionalism—rational choice, sociological, and historical institutionalism—and their potential for taking the study of the PPA nexus to the next level of explanatory and predictive power. The chapter concludes by examining the implications of these theoretical developments for future research on the dynamic relationship between policy and administration—as well as other topics—in the study of American bureaucracy.

THE PPA NEXUS: CONVENTIONAL PERSPECTIVES ON AN ENDURING PROBLEMATIC

Our understanding of PPA dynamics has changed over the past quarter century in important and positive ways. It is useful to organize this multidisciplinary and far-ranging literature in terms of (1) the conflating of the politics-administration dichotomy into the policy-administration dichotomy; (2) the blurring of this dichotomy by scholars; and (3) the return to a policy-administration dichotomy by some administrative reformers associated with the new public management (NPM).

Separating Policy and Administration?

Among the most famous issue-framing words written in American public administration are those of Woodrow Wilson urging the United States as a late-nineteenth-century democratic republic to adapt administrative principles derived from historically authoritarian European nations: "If I see a murderous fellow sharpening a knife cleverly, I can borrow his way of sharpening the knife without borrowing his probable intention to commit murder with it" (1887, 200). While not the originator of the politics-administration dichotomy, his rationale for it was simple: Politics took place among elected officials in legislatures, and administrators applying objective principles of administration should merely carry them out in an effective, efficient, and economical manner. They would do so as neutrally competent agents applying the principles of administration and scientific management to society's problems.

It was not long, however, before the *politics*-administration dichotomy was conflated into a *policy*-administration dichotomy (Rosenbloom 2008). For the dominant majority in the late-nineteenth- and early-twentieth-century Progressive reform movement (1877–1920) in America, the focus became one of establishing societal order through planning that was informed by techno-scientific rationality and fostered by creating public agencies staffed by public interest–oriented experts making policy (Kolko 1963). The sources of disorder and irrationality for these reformers were corrupt political machines fueled by rising numbers of immigrants, as well as legislative dominance of policymaking.

During the Progressive Era, small businesses, corporate interests (the Rockefeller and Carnegie families), and rising middle-class professionals took a leading role in shaping the emerging administrative state, as well as in shifting scholarly focus from legal to management concerns about its operations. In the process, what typically were seen as Progressive anticorruption administrative reform efforts that reduced the power of business often increased their power in policymaking. Independent regulatory commissions such as the Interstate Commerce Commission and the Chemistry Bureau (charged with implementing the Pure Food and Drug Act of 1906) were actually lobbied for by industry associations (Kolko 1963). Kolko chronicles, for example, how "any measure of importance in the Progressive era was not merely endorsed by key representatives of businesses involved; rather, such bills were first proposed by them" (283).

Amid all this, the avatar of policy and administrative progress was the burgeoning profession of engineers that tripled in the United States between 1880 and 1930 (from approximately 7,000 to 226,000). So giddy were engineers about their ability to plan societies on engineering principles that economist Thorstein Veblen spoke of a "directorate" of engineers that would lead a revolution for a "more competent management of the country's industrial system" to replace an older political order that "has most significantly fallen short" (Barry 1997, 266). Opined the leader of one important engineering association: "The golden rule will be put into practice by the slide rule of the engineer" and coordinated by executive branch experts (Barry 1997, 265). At the local and state government levels, efforts to depoliticize the PPA nexus came packaged during the first two decades of the twentieth century in, among other things, the city manager movement. Then, as the Depression persisted, the attraction of centralized planning by administrative experts became even more alluring to Progressives, with the models being Mussolini's Italy and both Lenin's and Stalin's Soviet Union (Shlaes 2007). This fascination is reflected in 365 articles and eighty-one books on this topic published between 1920 and 1931, with the U.S. press intensely following Mussolini's model throughout the 1930s (Shlaes 2007, 116).

Some worried about the ascendancy of experts in policymaking and the information asymmetry they presumably held over political officials, as well as the marginalization of citizens who lacked the expertise to participate. Settlement women such as Jane Addams and African American activists such as Mary McLeod Bethune, for instance, lamented citizens' impact on democracy, fearing that they—and especially low-income and minority citizens—would become estranged from government (McCluskey and Smith 1999; Stivers 2000). Still others, such as Herbert Hoover, joined in the associationalist movement in worrying about the policy innovation–stifling nature of centralized bureaucracies (Durant 2009).

Associationalists offered a so-called third way between the nation's historical reliance on laissez-faire individualism, citizen estrangement from government, and the rising allure of European-style centralized planning. They saw the role of federal agencies as "stimulat[ing] the private sector to *organize and govern itself*" in the public interest (George Nash as quoted in Clements 2000, 128). "Decentralization, voluntarism, and localism" was the mantra of these activists in the Harding and Coolidge administrations (Clements 2000, 96). Moreover, associationalists counted on pressure from a public opinion tutored by national conferences highlighting the findings of federal agency research as key to progress, in contrast to conventional Progressives, who saw it as "meddlesome."

Putting Them Back Together Again in the Administrative State

While some heterodoxy—including the associationalists'—existed prior to and during the "golden age" of public administration in the 1930s (see Lynn 2006), the mid- to late 1940s witnessed the evisceration among academics and politicians of the policy-administration dichotomy. In enacting the Administrative Procedure Act of 1946, Congress acknowledged that agencies were policy makers exercising discretion that members of Congress had delegated to them (Rosenbloom 2000). To many, their New Deal and war-related experiences demonstrated that separating policy from administration was descriptively, normatively, and instrumentally wrong (Gaus 1947; Long 1949; Waldo 1984).

What *could* be separated, some argued, were facts from values in agency decision making (Simon 1947). But could the PPA nexus really be parsed in this fashion? Public administration, political science, and policy scholars soon concluded that it could not and began to focus on the study of bureaucratic politics as the driver of agency policymaking. This commenced in the 1950s (Truman 1951) and continued in the 1960s with a conceptualization of the PPA nexus at all levels of government as one driven, variously, by cozy triangles, whirlpools, or iron triangles (Lowi 1969; Redford 1969). While Truman saw pluralism at work in policymaking in New Haven in the 1950s, for instance, other elite theorists saw business elites dominating the policy process in legislative and bureaucratic settings across the United States (also see Stone 2001 for the same conclusion in recent decades). At the federal level, scholars saw policy bubbling up from closed, cozy relationships among interest groups, agencies, and congressional oversight committees. Interest groups attempted to influence the inevitable discretion that agencies were exercising, agencies were amenable to capture because they needed interest group electoral support and information, and legislative oversight committees needed interest group contributions and information to counter agency information asymmetries.

Partly in response to these arguments, the 1950s and early 1960s also saw the emergence of the policy studies movement. In Lasswell's (1951) vision, policy science was to address present gaps in the study of PPA dynamics, including the absence of a problem-focused, multidisciplinary, and methodologically sophisticated (emphasizing welfare economics and cost-benefit analysis) discipline privileging democratic values. Ironically, however, policy analysis joined public administration's founders in marginalizing laypersons in the PPA nexus. Favored again was a faith in specialized technocratic expertise to reflect the democratic values Lasswell sought in policy processes, not citizen participation in agency deliberative processes. Meanwhile, in public administration, administrative reform efforts turned repeatedly during the 1960s and 1970s to favoring "responsive competence" to executives and away from "neutral competence" in the PPA nexus. Whether the planning, programming, and budgeting system of the Lyndon Johnson era, management by objectives during the Richard Nixon presidency, or zero-based budgeting during the Jimmy Carter years, each of these rational-comprehensive decision-making efforts disappointed proponents and advantaged experts over laypersons.

Concerns about agency capture still prompted political science and public administration scholars such as Lowi, Redford, Frederickson, and Ostrom to call for more politically oriented reforms to revive democratic constitutional values in agency policymaking. Lowi (1969) argued for the limitation of congressional delegation to agencies absent clear standards set by Congress (juridical democracy); Redford (1969), for understanding the moral dimensions of agency decision making (democratic morality); Frederickson (1971), for abandoning technocratic rationales and for giving primacy to social equity in agency policymaking; and Ostrom (1973), for abandoning public administration's embrace of centralized government as ill suited to the U.S. Constitution's focus on decentralized policymaking.

Ostrom's public choice perspective was grounded in the now-familiar imperialistic incursions of economics into public administration, political science, and public policy (Buchanan and Tullock 1962). In their own way, public choice theorists called for "bringing citizens back in" to the PPA nexus but as individual consumers (rather than as citizens) devoid of any sense of common purpose or public interest. They portrayed PPA dynamics as dominated by agency bureaucrats who were monopoly providers of services because of the information asymmetries they enjoyed over elected officials.

This focus on direct or implicit incorporation of citizens as consumers into the PPA nexus carried over into economists' prescriptions for local government administration. Here, policymaking and service delivery were adduced more efficient and responsive if citizens could "shop around" a competitive metropolitan marketplace populated by duplicative and overlapping service providers, whether operationalized as the citizenry as a whole (Tiebout 1956) or as subsets of citizens who have the most to gain from knowledge of particular policies or services. From these, others (including governments) would take their policy cues (Teske et al. 1993).

Yet beginning in the late 1970s and continuing over the next two decades, empirical support began waning for the iron triangle as a driver of both policy-administration dynamics and public choice. Heclo (1977) described the iron triangle as "disastrously incomplete." More accurate, he claimed, were "issue networks" of actors on various sides of policy issues who were motivated less by material stakes and more by normative or purposive concerns. Issue networks were also conceptualized as less structured, characterized by fluid participation of actors, and having access based on expertise in any given policy domain.

Thus, consistent with earlier public administration and policy perspectives, Heclo saw "technopols" dominating the PPA nexus. He was joined subsequently in the 1980s and 1990s by policy analysts who stressed the power of ideas, ideology, and knowledge in organizing enduring networks of interacting interest groups, agency bureaucrats, and the media. Proponents of such "advocacy coalitions" (Sabatier and Jenkins-Smith 1993) were joined by intergovernmental relations scholars who saw the PPA nexus metaphorically as a "picket fence": vertical functional subsystems of actors organized around programs and driving policymaking in a professional/bureaucratic-dominated complex (Beer 1978).

To this were added so-called first and second generations of policy implementation scholarship (Goggin et al. 1990) that claimed to fill a gap in public administration research by linking administration to policies and policies to outcomes (Mazmanian and Sabatier 1989; Pressman and Wildavsky 1973). These researchers identified a more complex PPA nexus than even Heclo discerned. Units of analysis combined vertical (intergovernmental) "macroimplementation" structures with horizontal (intragovernmental and cross-sectoral) "microimplementation" structures. Critiquing notions of federal control, researchers wrote about policy implementation as mutual adaptation and "learning what to prefer" among federal, state, and local actors (Pressman and Wildavsky 1973).

Still, as in the professional/bureaucratic complex, laypersons remained marginalized from policy decisions unless they joined groups or filed court suits. Bargaining took place, but it occurred largely among structured associations of governments (e.g., the National Conference of Mayors and the National Governors Association), professional experts in agencies, and interest groups with stakes in agency decisions. Moreover, the more prescriptive implementation literature of the first two generations labeled citizen participation positively (ensure access to supportive actors), negatively (too much complexity of joint action foiled implementation), and contingently (it all depends on the situation and support for policy aims). Only in more recent times have implementation scholars in the postmodernist tradition placed layperson participation as the primary goal of implementation (deLeon and deLeon 2002).

Ironically, the tendency for agencies to marginalize citizen participation in policymaking was partly a function of the aforementioned federal Administrative Procedure Act and its progeny at the state level ("little APAs"). The administrative rulemaking process afforded greater access and influence to well-organized interests with technocratic, business, and legal skills. In the process, court suits became the only redress for citizens excluded from agency deliberations. Dubbed the "procedural republic" (Sandel 1984), this situation only further fostered fragmentation and judicialization of rulemaking and adjudicatory processes, a dynamic that again disadvantaged unorganized interests even more in agency policymaking.

These trends were exacerbated further by the exponential rise of professional advocacy groups in Washington that began in the 1960s and continued throughout the twentieth century. The more crowded the policy space, noted Heclo (1977), the greater the number of interest groups. This occurs as policies overlap, disagreements among original coalitions develop, and subsequent policies create winners and losers. Amid this growth, a decided tilt ensued toward professionally led rather than mass-mobilization interest groups involved in issue networks and advocacy coalitions (Skocpol 2007). Partly to cope with this growth, efforts began in the federal government to centralize policymaking in the White House and agency rulemaking in the Office of Information and Regulatory Affairs in the Office of Management and Budget. This, too, increased the opacity of policymaking and rulemaking to average citizens, a development paralleled by increasing cynicism about government as agency rulemaking became ever more "conflictual, contingent, and reversible" (Klyza and Sousa 2008). At the same time, the so-called rights revolution (Teles 2007) also began to depoliticize issues during the last quarter of the twentieth century, turning them over to courts and agencies to interpret and apply. Once something is proclaimed a "right" (e.g., children's rights), legislative discussions on it are possible only on the margins and then only in courts.

Many court suits had direct effects on federal agencies, as well as state and local governments, especially in the policy arenas of schools, prisons, and mental institutions (O'Leary 1993). This new PPA nexus of courts and agencies wrought profound budget and operational consequences for agencies at all levels of government. Within agencies, researchers found that (at least in the short term) attorneys gained in relative power over program bureaucrats, court suits advantaged litigated programs over others in the budget process, and court suits could occasion risk-averse behavior by program managers (O'Leary 1993). But they also could gain legitimacy, input, and enhanced power for disadvantaged citizens (at least classes of citizens) and programs within the otherwise opaque PPA nexus (Melnick 2005).

The Quest to Recreate the Policy-Administration Dichotomy in an Era of Networked Governance

By the mid-1980s and 1990s, the realpolitik of fiscal stress, downward pressures on the size of governments due to market globalization, and political advantage also meant that presidents and members of Congress faced perverse incentives to enact or expand policies without increasing the visible size of the federal government's workforce. Regnant since has been the allure to policy makers of a "neoadministrative state" (Durant 2000) that, despite claims for shrinking government, has actually increased its size to approximately 16 million employees if one counts the public, private, and nonprofit actors performing formerly federal functions (Light 1999). With this development have come new PPA dynamics that public managers and researchers are still trying to fathom.

As it has evolved thus far, this neoadministrative state of networked governance consists of pushing some federal responsibilities and the authority to make policy on behalf of national societies upward to international agencies (e.g., the World Trade Organization), downward to state and local government agencies, and outward to private and nonprofit organizations. By 2002, more than 5 million contractor positions supplemented 1.7 million federal civil servants and 1.5 million military personnel (Light 2006). At that time, contract employees comprised 62 percent of combined contracting, civil service, and military positions. Furthermore, an increasing tendency existed to contract core government functions to nongovernmental actors, including the design of policy and the monitoring of contract performance, even in inherently governmental functions such as national security (Durant, Girth, and Johnston 2009).

The PPA nexus thus now takes place within and across parts of agencies (e.g., various program offices), across sectors, and in ever more crowded and overlapping policy spaces. Nor are the efforts of the Obama administration to rebuild agency capacity and to "contract-back-in" (Chen 2009) likely to stymie these trends appreciably. Much of Congress's economic stimulus package (the American Recovery and Reinvestment Act), for example, involved pass-through funding to states and localities and private sector subsidies, albeit with line items budgeted for some capacity rebuilding in the federal government. Relatedly, Treasury secretary Timothy Geithner's plan to address the banking crisis relied on public-private partnerships to buy up toxic bank assets. Finally, it takes time for contracts to expire, delays in federal hiring are notorious, and agencies have grown dependent on contractors for technical skills.

Unchanged and compelling for the PPA nexus, however, is Waldo's (1984) advice to embed efficiency within a broader context of values. Nevertheless, a narrow one-size-fits-all market-oriented prescription for administrative reform animated management reform agendas prior to the Obama administration. This NPM philosophy sought a return to the policy-administration dichotomy. As embraced by minimal state proponents, the NPM accorded no special role for public service or the public interest in policymaking, aside from what market forces dictated.

Importantly, others not attuned to NPM prescriptions also pointed to emerging "wicked" policy problems (Rittel and Webber 1973) in the pre-Obama era as requiring networking and partnering as key components of governance. Wicked problems are those (e.g., drug abuse, teenage pregnancy, and terrorism) with no accepted definition. Moreover, one problem is interrelated with others, cross-sectoral (public-private-nonprofit) collaboration is essential for success, and solutions are precarious and controversial. Wicked problems also are multi-attribute in nature; solutions to them require the balancing of a variety of values rather than the predominance of any one value.

While some have called these networks a "hollow state" (Milward and Provan 2000), public agencies remain the only partners operating with the sovereign authority of the state. Prior research also suggests that agencies working with networked programs often remain principal sources of funding. Consequently, agencies still have strong bargaining and legal levers with other partners in networks (Agranoff and McGuire 2003). A boundaryless agency's policy success also seems to require appointees who know how to build a strong sense of common purpose among network members with diverse goals. Research also suggests that agencies view budgets, personnel actions, and decision rules as tools for coaxing cooperation from others, for deregulating operations, and for leveraging resources with other organizations to advance policy purposes. As with the tendency of issue networks and advocacy coalitions to marginalize the disorganized and laypersons, however, evidence is mixed that a dark side of networks is also emerging. In this networked state, some find that experts operating within these networks will hold asymmetric information, power, and access (Frederickson 1999).

SOME OTHER ROADS LESS TAKEN: THE PPA NEXUS AND THE NEW INSTITUTIONALISM

The preceding review of a sample of findings from conventional quantitative and qualitative studies of the PPA nexus has illustrated the richness of major findings to date. Absent in the public administration and policy literature, however, is a high level of theoretical development. In this section, we go beyond these literatures to assess three neoinstitutionalist approaches to the study of American bureaucracy that have not gained as much traction among public administration or policy scholars but that can enrich our understanding of the PPA nexus and offer the promise of greater theoretical advancement. The three approaches are rational choice institutionalism, sociological institutionalism, and historical institutionalism.

Rational Choice Institutionalism

Despite devastating critiques of their efforts on both empirical and normative grounds (Meier and O'Toole 2006), American political scientists have applied rational choice institutionalism (RCI) perspectives borrowed from economics as a theoretical framework for studying the PPA nexus. The "calculus approach" of RCI assumes that individuals are purposive utility maximizers. That is, individuals know exactly what they want (they have ordered preferences) and choose, through a series of probabilistic calculations, the course of action that will secure it for them. RCI then emphasizes how institutions (rules, regulations, and norms) structure strategic interaction among self-interested individuals in policymaking. Institutions thus provide strategic actors with the "rules of the game" (e.g., penalties for defection from an agreement, number of rounds in the game) that shape behavior, which then leads to policymaking (and vice versa). Consequently, while sharing the top-down perspective of classical theorists, RCI envisions a different PPA nexus from early public administration's emphasis on subordinates as either neutrally competent or cogs in a wheel uncritically taking orders from superiors. In their place are created strategic actors who are influenced by and who influence institutional constraints on their behavior.

RCI scholars have also advanced our understanding of the relationship linking politics, policy, and administrative structures. This relationship has long been known as less about effective policymaking and more about politics, position, and power (Seidman 1998). But RCI scholars have taken this insight to new theoretical levels by invoking principal-agent theory, transaction-cost analysis, and theories of agency discretion and legislative delegation. Especially relevant from this robust body of research is that winning legislative coalitions use structures, procedures, and processes to increase the political and administrative transaction costs for opponents seeking to change policy or organizational behavior in the future. Put more technically, winning coalitions fear that "coalitional drift," "bureaucratic drift," or unsympathetic presidents using the tools of the administrative presidency (Durant 1992; Nathan 1983) will try to change their original intent. Consequently, they impose administrative structures, processes, and procedures on agencies that they hope will make significant policy changes difficult.

They also do so by making the agency an independent commission, by manipulating the agency's leadership structure (e.g., longer terms for agency leaders to insulate them from political takeover), or by vesting the agency with a high level of budgetary autonomy (e.g., multiyear budget authorizations rather than annual authorizations) (Wood and Bohte 2004). Also effective in delimiting policy change is setting agency policymaking on autopilot (e.g., granting little discretion to agencies and reducing congressional monitoring costs), increasing transaction costs for those seeking to intervene judicially (e.g., limiting standing to sue and the timing of lawsuits), and stacking the deck (e.g., ensuring that members of the winning coalition have access to agency decision making by creating advisory councils). Importantly, even as enacting coalitions seek to insulate pet agencies or programs, they also must make compromises with opposing coalitions that want "room to enhance their future power, access, and influence in program operations and decision making" to tilt decisions their way (Durant 2006, 472).

Also consistent with RCI assumptions and the rationality project more broadly, presidents (as well as governors and mayors) have tried to gain "responsive competence" in the PPA nexus from agencies by using performance measures (e.g., the Program Assessment Rating Tool during the George W. Bush administration). Legislatures have adopted similar approaches (e.g., the Government Performance and Results Act of 1993). Prior research suggests that efforts at centralized performance measurement can advance presidential and legislative agendas effectively (Moynihan 2008), but it also illustrates how elected officials can politicize performance measures, thus calling into question their inherently technocratic qualities (Lewis 2008). They also impose opportunity costs on agencies in terms of data collection, even though scant evidence exists that information asked for is useful to agency managers (Radin 2006). Nor do agency or program-centric performance measurement systems adequately accommodate the PPA dynamics in networks. Performance measures may even produce goal suboptimization if not done correctly (Durant 1999).

RCI's top-down, principal-agent assumptions also fly in the face of recent research by public administrationists. These scholars find that street-level bureaucrats adopt "citizen-agent" policymaking roles as they categorize clients as needy and worthy to work with, as opposed to "state-agent" roles where they treat clients by the book (i.e., through top-down rule promulgation) (Maynard-Moody and Musheno 2000). In the process, they set policies (Lipsky 1980). Nor do RCI's hierarchical assumptions and single-agency focus comport well with today's nonhierarchical networked governance (and, hence, policymaking) models.

Sociological Institutionalism

Neither does the RCI model adequately explain or predict PPA dynamics when another major variant of neoinstitutionalism is considered: sociological institutionalism (SI). This "cultural" approach draws on Simon's (1947) original insight that individuals are boundedly rational satisfi-cers, as opposed to unfailing utility maximizers, when it comes to their decision-making behavior in organizations. Individuals have preferences and would like to satisfy them, but because they are fallible human beings and not calculating automatons, they are not always able to choose the policy that would objectively be "best" in a given situation (Simon 1985, 294). Instead, they "turn to established routines and familiar patterns of behavior to attain their purposes" (Hall and Taylor 1996, 939). As a result, SI sees institutions as having a profound effect on all individual behavior in agencies, including policymaking: "Institutions provide moral or cognitive templates for interpretation and action. The individual is seen as an entity deeply embedded in a world of institutions, composed of symbols, scripts and routines. These provide the filters for interpreta-tion, of both the situation and oneself, out of which a course of action is constructed" (Hall and Taylor 1996, 939).

Yet another insight into the PPA nexus is the relationship offered by sociological institutional-ists between structures and legitimacy—an important yet underappreciated ingredient to successful agency policy formulation, implementation, and evaluation. DiMaggio and Powell (1983), for example, suggest that organizations within a given field (e.g., welfare offices or universities) tend to adopt certain institutional arrangements and policies because of pressure from the government or from other organizations upon which they are dependent, as a response to uncertainty, or to comport with professional norms. In general, according to this line of reasoning, organizations in a given field come to resemble one another in policies, programs, and structures through a process of "institutional isomorphism." Organizations become copycats. A "logic of appropriateness" rather than a logic of consequences (means-ends concerns) drives agency structures and, hence, policymaking within and between organizations. This makes the logic of appropriateness definitely applicable to the study of an emergent networked state (March and Olsen 1989) and offers a theoretical grounding for behaviors witnessed in cases of either successful or unsuccessful implementation.

The logic of appropriateness applied to the study of PPA dynamics, in turn, both accommodates and finds its own theoretical grounding in cognitive, evolutionary biology, and neuroscientific theories. For instance, prior research consistently finds careerists responsive to the administrative presidency, at least in terms of their collective outputs (e.g., issuing fewer mine-safety violations) (Golden 2000; Wood and Waterman 1994). Likewise, one important comparative case analysis of policy reorientation by Reagan appointees in four agencies suggests that loyalty (i.e., following presidential agendas) was the default option of careerists in most instances (i.e., their appropriate role in a constitutional system) (Golden 2000). Research also suggests that appeals to careerists' calling to public service (e.g., a desire to serve others) can be an effective motivational approach that presidential appointees too often overlook (e.g., Perry and Hondeghem 2008).

Challenged, too, by cognitive theory, evolutionary psychology, sociobiology, and neurosci-ence are many of the rationality assumptions underlying RCI, welfare economics, and public choice approaches to understanding decision making in the PPA nexus. They also offer theoretical grounding for the importance of policy image framing, deceit, and peer pressure in explaining and predicting behavior in that nexus. LeDoux (2002), for instance, finds that our brains are hardwired for emotions to affect, and frequently to override, conscious rational processes. Others such as McDermott (2004) find that "emotional rationality" not only affects but drives and improves decision making.

Still others find that people in deliberation situations have different kinds of "utilities" to maximize, including a reputational utility that can override their rationally calculated preference (Kuran 1995). For evolutionary reasons, people tend to be hypersensitive to others' impressions of them. Relatedly, while the aforementioned "bounded rationality" of decision makers in the PPA nexus has long been recognized by public administrationists and policy scientists as prompting shortcuts or heuristics, evolutionary psychologists trace the source of this behavior to evolutionary pressures for survival. Decision makers resort to heuristics as a legacy from our species' hunter-gatherer ancestors, who had to make quick assessments of situations and people in order to protect themselves from others (Cosmides and Tooby 1992).

Evolutionary psychologists also offer theoretical grounding for understanding stovepiping and turf protection as prominent features of the PPA nexus, while simultaneously attesting to the self-interested nature of cooperative behavior. Stovepiping and turf protection are evolutionarily "selected" behaviors attributable to the value our hunter-gatherer ancestors placed on identifying with their group in the face of food, shelter, and other shortages. Yet they also predisposed our ancestors to engage in cooperative behavior with others in their tribe in order to encourage sharing when resources were scarce. The idea of "wary collaborators" (Alford and Hibbing 2004) has also been applied as a theoretical basis for explaining, among other things, persons fearing free riders off of their labors. These theories—and their link to the logic of appropriateness—illustrate how important institutional embeddedness is to understanding contemporary behavior. They also combine with other elements of SI more generally to show the poverty of the rationality approach as a sole basis for understanding the dynamics of the PPA nexus, as well as the contribution of rules, norms, ideas, ideology, and emotion to those dynamics and for future theory building.

Historical Institutionalism

Historical institutionalists often borrow RCI and SI assumptions about individual behavior, about how institutions affect behavior (including how institutions are defined), and about processes of institutional origin and change. But historical institutionalism (HI) is unique in its own right. As two of its leading proponents summarize (Pierson and Skocpol 2007), HI departs from standard social science conventions by taking the "long view" (283) in the study of political and administrative phenomena that "separates the study of 'the present' from the study of 'the past.'" Pierson and Skocpol write, "A long view allows us to identify and appreciate features of the political environment that shift only slowly. Never dramatic enough at any particular moment to call attention to themselves, these slow-moving shifts may nonetheless . . . represent important changes that cry out for explanation, or they may constitute important sources of other shifts that are [too] easily attributed instead to more proximate but superficial events" (283).

HI scholars thus especially question the logic of standard cross-sectional quantitative research, in particular standard regression analyses, although their critique also applies to poorly crafted qualitative research. Pierson (2004) argues that cross-sectional and short-term statistical analyses dominate journals, but they are useful solely for explaining or predicting one type of PPA dynamic: the "tornado" effect (short-term cause and short-term effect). Yet PPA dynamics are often better explained by "cumulative" effects (e.g., Sunbelt in-migration and Republican political dominance of the South), by triggering once certain thresholds are reached in the interaction of variables (e.g., white flight from schools or global warming), or by "causal chains" of factors (e.g., suburbanization leading to jobs moving to the suburbs and away from central cities, thus resulting in reduced tax revenues at any point in time) that cross-sectional analyses miss (also see Raadschelders 2010 for similar arguments).

To measure any one variable at any given time may miss these kinds of long-term secular effects because they have not yet materialized. Relatedly, proximate variables may have immediate measurable effects, but they may not be the real explanation for the PPA dynamics of interest. Carpenter's (2001) historical analysis, for example, decimated the congressional dominance theory of policymaking by showing how it was actually "bureaucratic dominance" of Congress at work. Thus, the "independent" variables in any cross-sectional analysis may simply be the most visible and proximate manifestations of prior events and trends (e.g., demographic or representational shifts in Congress). And while conceding that longitudinal analyses and game theory approaches to understanding phenomena are possible, insufficient numbers of data points or gaps typically weaken longitudinal statistical analyses.

HI scholars thus eschew the pursuit of general laws of social behavior. They argue instead that a "very small number of *causal mechanisms and processes* recur throughout the whole range of collective [behavior]—with different initial conditions, combinations, and sequences producing systematic variation from time to time and setting to setting" (Tilly 2003, xi; emphasis added). Differentiating their approach from purely descriptive historical research that focuses on the uniqueness of PPA dynamics, HI scholars thus strive for theoretical parsimony by identifying common causal mechanisms. As Pierson (2004) observes, it is not just what happens to affect given social outcomes but also when it happens. Those events coming earlier in time shape, amplify, and constrain the path that subsequent reforms take; they also are infinitely more difficult to dislodge later because of the constellation of political forces that coalesce around them. Thus, especially useful for adding value to our practical and theoretical understanding of PPA dynamics is HI's focus on such causal mechanisms as path dependency; feedback; sequencing, ordering, and crucial junctures of events; the constitutive effects of policy and administration over time; the intercurrence of authority regimes; and venue shifting.

Perhaps the most basic of these causal mechanisms are "feedback" (or "amplification") and "constitutive" effects that produce path dependency. The former are instances where policies mobilize interest groups or modify bureaucratic capacities in ways that alter the future trajectories of these and other policies. Recognizing these feedbacks, historical institutionalists do not view the causal relationships between politics and policy, politics and administration, or policy and administration as one-way streets. Rather, policy influences politics and administration influences both. In effect, they have constitutive features. Public policy can influence, or feed back into, politics by giving latent interest groups incentives to coalesce around newly created benefits and to lobby for their continuation and expansion (Pierson 1993). Thus, while conventional analyses of proximate variables assume that interest groups spark politics, policy, and administration, a longer view sees that policies and administration actually create interest groups, advantaging some and disadvantaging others over time. As two leading HI scholars put it, "Institutions and interests don't align at a given point in time, they push and pull each other through time" (Orren and Skowronek 2004, 94).

Once a benefit exists, so do beneficiaries—beneficiaries who will be loath to surrender the "spoils" generated by policy and whose advantage is perpetuated by administrative structures that ensure their access and influence in the future (Pierson 1993, 599). Consider, for instance, New York City's rent control laws, which were instituted in 1943. Originally intended to be a temporary check on inflation, these rent controls are still around today. They are still around because those who benefit have an incentive to advocate for their continuance, as well as institutionalized agency access to do so. Skocpol's (1992) work documents a similar phenomenon with respect to Civil War pensions. She shows that once veterans began receiving these pensions, they were spurred on to "demand ever improved benefits" from agencies to which they had access (59).

That policies create interest groups is hardly a revelation to public administrationists studying the PPA nexus, as our review of the literature in the previous section documents. What is different, however, is how the longitudinal perspective taken reveals that policies also have constitutive effects in permanently marginalizing groups not included originally as beneficiaries in subsequent rounds of negotiations. HI scholars also advance theory by noting that changes in context can alter constitutive effects, bringing in previously marginalized or disadvantaged groups. These include major shocks to the political system (e.g., the end of the Cold War); a re-valencing of actors involved in the issues (e.g., nuclear power going from positive to negative valence in the 1960s); issue redefinition; morphing of policies into other types over time (e.g., from benign distributive into conflictual redistributive policies); and boundary effects (i.e., where events in one area of politics affect related areas) (Baumgartner and Jones 1993). Absent these effects, however, one can offer theoretical grounding for incremental policy change.

Administrative capacities are important not only because they restrict or expand future policy formation and implementation options in the PPA nexus but also because "bureaucrats themselves are politically relevant" (Pierson 1994, 36). As we have chronicled in the previous section of this chapter, it is common knowledge that bureaucrats possess discretion and that this discretion inevitably affects the manner in which policies are implemented. The political relevance of bureaucrats for historical institutionalists, however, goes beyond this standard picture. As Pierson notes, "Administrators are sometimes energetic policy entrepreneurs, devoting careers to the construction of political coalitions that can further their policy ambitions" (36). Moreover, because bureaucrats possess information and expertise that politicians do not, they "can credibly claim to know what the government can and cannot do, what will work and what will not" (36). In short, bureaucrats can alter the policy options available to politicians.

Yet another concept with resonance for understanding PPA dynamics is what HI scholarship calls "intercurrence" of authority regimes. This happens because one administrative regime or "order of authority" (Thelen 1999) is not replaced by another set of authority relationships when policy or administrative reforms occur. Produced are "multiple, asymmetric" orderings of authority that are not "created or recreated all at once, in accordance with a single ordering principle" (Orren and Skowronek 2004, 182). This leads to conflict and bargaining among representatives of earlier and later regimes over how much authority will shift as a result of policy change or reform, with the amplifying effects of sequencing, path dependency, and constitutive properties advantaging the interests benefiting from earlier policies (Orren and Skowronek 2004). As Klyza and Sousa (2008) illustrate, for example, natural resource management statutes implemented by today's agencies frequently find their efforts in conflict because pro-development statutes (e.g., the Mining Act) from earlier eras that are assigned to them are layered among resource conservation statutes (e.g., the Endangered Species Act) in their own departments or in other agencies (e.g., the Environmental Protection Agency).

HI scholars also note how the interaction effects of different institutions (also known as "institutional coupling") can drive change through venue shifting and the creation of parallel institutions that are intended to alter PPA dynamics (Jones and Baumgartner 2005). For instance, congressional political stalemate since the early 1980s has not produced policy stalemate. Produced instead has been significant venue changing, with legislative battles shifted (as noted earlier) to agency rulemaking (e.g., centralizing rule clearance in the Office of Management and Budget), the use of unilateral tools of the presidency (e.g., executive orders and presidential signing statements), and the courts. The unilateral tools of the administrative presidency allegedly give presidents what economists call "first-mover" advantages; presidents can move quickly and below the radar without congressional approval to advance their agendas by issuing executive orders, presidential proclamations, presidential bill signing statements, executive agreements (rather than treaties), and national security directives (but see Durant and Resh 2009).

Also made more attractive to legislators because of political paralysis in the PPA nexus are the use of indirect policy tools (e.g., tax expenditures, subsidies, and loan guarantees) and the creation of parallel institutions (Clemens 2006; Teles 2007). The latter become especially attractive when policy spaces are crowded, when existing regimes prove impervious to reform, or when opponents try to circumvent or head off more stringent regulatory authority structures. Yet HI scholars have identified "interpretive effects" of such policies—effects that undermine support for pure governmental as opposed to nongovernmental or quasigovernmental solutions to public problems. As such, they offer theoretical grounding for the persistent move toward agency downsizing, contracting out, and network governance (Durant 2009).

As Mettler (2005) documents, the tools used by government to advance public purposes can affect levels of civic engagement and perceptions of government. When citizens see direct links (or "traceability") between government action and the betterment of their lives (as did recipients of the GI Bill), they tend to value government more highly. In contrast, indirect and market-based tools of government, such as tax subsidies and third-party government, obfuscate those links, making it appear that government is "receding" from citizens' lives. In the process, citizens' support for government solutions to societal problems wanes, as does their concern for supporting broad (rather than targeted) capacity building in public agencies—a keystone of effective agency involvement in the PPA nexus.

CONCLUSION

Our aim in this essay has been to illustrate the strengths, gaps, and major alternatives for advancing a practical and theoretical understanding of the PPA nexus. Our point in highlighting the potential contributions of RCI, SI, and HI—and their accompanying insights from cognitive science, evolutionary psychology, and neuroscience—to the study of PPA dynamics is not to denigrate conventional approaches or to disparage their impressive findings. Nor has it been to advocate that RCI, SI, and HI replace traditional analyses. Rather, we argue that public administrationists should use them to supplement their traditional approaches, recognizing that each, in turn, has strengths and weaknesses. Traditional methods and analytical frameworks have reached as far as they can go alone in explanatory and predictive power, given their mismatch with the empirical realities of traditional and emerging governance models (and, hence, PPA dynamics) in America. It is difficult for us to imagine how understanding and theory building on the PPA nexus can profitably advance without taking these developments in cognate subfields and disciplines into consideration in future research.

REFERENCES

Agranoff, Robert, and Michael McGuire. 2003. *Collaborative Public Management: New Strategies for Local Governments.* Washington, DC: Georgetown University Press.

Alford, John R., and John R. Hibbing. 2004. The origin of politics: An evolutionary theory of political behavior. *Perspectives on Politics* 2 (4): 707–723.

Barry, John M. 1997. *Rising Tide: The Great Mississippi Flood of 1927 and How It Changed America.* New York: Simon & Schuster.

Baumgartner, Frank R., and Bryan D. Jones. 1993. *Agendas and Instability in American Politics.* Chicago: University of Chicago Press.

Beer, Samuel H. 1978. Federalism, nationalism, and democracy in America. *American Political Science Review* 72 (1): 9–21.

Buchanan, James M., and Gordon Tullock. 1962. *The Calculus of Consent: Logical Foundations of Constitutional Democracy.* Ann Arbor: University of Michigan Press.

Carpenter, Daniel P. 2001. *The Forging of Bureaucratic Autonomy: Reputations, Networks, and Policy Innovation in Executive Agencies, 1862–1928.* Princeton, NJ: Princeton University Press.

Chen, Chung-An. 2009. Antecedents of contracting-back-in: A view beyond the academic paradigm. *Administration and Society* 41 (1): 101–126.

Clemens, Elisabeth S. 2006. Lineages of the Rube Goldberg state: Building and blurring public programs, 1900–1940. In *Rethinking Political Institutions: The Art of the State,* ed. Ian Shapiro, Stephen Skowronek, and Daniel Galvin, 187–215. New York: New York University Press.

Clements, Kendrick A. 2000. *Hoover, Conservation, and Consumerism: Engineering the Good Life.* Lawrence: University Press of Kansas.

Cosmides, Leda, and John Tooby. 1992. Cognitive adaptations for social exchange. In *The Adapted Mind,* ed. Jerome H. Barkow, Leda Cosmides, and John Tooby, 163–228. Oxford: Oxford University Press.

deLeon, Peter, and Linda deLeon. 2002. What ever happened to policy implementation? An alternative approach. *Journal of Public Administration Research and Theory* 12 (4): 467–492.

DiMaggio, Paul J., and Walter W. Powell. 1983. The iron cage revisited: Institutional isomorphism and collective rationality in organizational fields. *American Sociological Review* 48 (2): 147–160.

Durant, Robert F. 1992. *The Administrative Presidency Revisited: Public Lands, the BLM, and the Reagan Revolution.* Albany: State University of New York Press.

———. 1999. The political economy of results-oriented management in the "neoadministrative state": Lessons learned from the MCDHHS experience. *American Review of Public Administration* 29 (4): 1–16.

———. 2000. Whither the neoadministrative state? Toward a polity-centered theory of administrative reform. *Journal of Public Administration Research and Theory* 10 (1): 79–109.

———. 2006. Agency evolution, the new institutionalism, and "hybrid" policy domains: Lessons from the "greening" of the U.S. military. *Policy Studies Journal* 34 (4): 469–490.

———. 2009. Theory building, administrative reform movements, and the perdurability of Herbert Hoover. *American Review of Public Administration* 39 (4): 327–351.

Durant, Robert F., Amanda Girth, and Jocelyn Johnston. 2009. American exceptionalism, human resource management, and the contract state. *Review of Public Personnel Administration* 29 (3): 207–229.

Durant, Robert F., and William G. Resh. 2009. Presidential agendas, administrative strategies, and the bureaucracy. In *Oxford Handbook of the American Presidency,* ed. George C. Edwards III and William G. Howell, 577–600. New York: Oxford University Press.

Frederickson, H. George. 1971. Organization theory and new public administration. In *Toward a New Public Administration: The Minnowbrook Perspective,* ed. Frank Marini, 309–331. Scranton, PA: Chandler Press.

———. 1999. The John Gaus lecture: The repositioning of American public administration. *PS: Political Science & Politics* 32 (4): 701–711.

Gaus, John M. 1947. *Reflections on Public Administration.* Birmingham: University of Alabama Press.

Goggin, Malcolm L., Ann O. Bowman, James P. Lester, and Laurence J. O'Toole, Jr. 1990. *Implementation Theory and Practice: Toward a Third Generation.* Glenview, IL: Scott, Foresman, and Little, Brown.

Golden, Marissa Martino. 2000. *What Motivates Bureaucrats? Politics and Administration During the Reagan Years.* New York: Columbia University Press.

Hall, Peter A., and Rosemary C.R. Taylor. 1996. Political science and the three new institutionalisms. *Political Studies* 44:936–957.

Heclo, Hugh. 1977. *A Government of Strangers: Executive Politics in Washington.* Washington, DC: Brookings Institution Press.

Jones, Bryan D., and Frank R. Baumgartner. 2005. *The Politics of Attention: How Government Prioritizes Problems.* Chicago: University of Chicago Press.

Klyza, Christopher M., and David Sousa. 2008. *American Environmental Policy, 1990–2006: Beyond Gridlock.* Cambridge, MA: MIT Press.

Kolko, Gabriel. 1963. *The Triumph of Conservatism: A Reinterpretation of American History, 1900–1916.* New York: Free Press.

Kuran, Timur. 1995. *Private Truths, Public Lies: The Social Consequences of Preference Falsification.* Cambridge, MA: Harvard University Press.

Lasswell, Harold. 1951. The immediate future of research policy and method in political science. *American Political Science Review* 45 (March): 133–142.

LeDoux, Joseph. 2002. *Synaptic Self: How Our Brains Become Who We Are.* New York: Penguin Books.

Lewis, David E. 2008. *The Politics of Presidential Appointments: Political Control and Bureaucratic Performance.* Princeton, NJ: Princeton University Press.

Light, Paul C. 1999. *The True Size of Government.* Washington, DC: Brookings Institution Press.

———. 2006. The tides of reform revisited: Patterns in making government work, 1945–2002. *Public Administration Review* 66 (1): 6–19.

Lipsky, Michael. 1980. *Street-Level Bureaucracy: Dilemmas of the Individual in Public Services.* New York: Russell Sage Foundation.

Long, Norton. 1949. Power and administration. *Public Administration Review* 9 (4): 257–264.

Lowi, Theodore J. 1969. *The End of Liberalism: The Second Republic of the United States.* New York: W.W. Norton.

Lynn, Laurence E., Jr. 2006. *Public Management: Old and New.* New York: Routledge.

March, James G., and Johan P. Olsen. 1989. *Rediscovering Institutions: The Organizational Basis of Politics.* New York: Free Press.

Maynard-Moody, Steven, and Michael Musheno. 2000. State-agent or citizen-agent: Two narratives of discretion. *Journal of Public Administration Research and Theory* 10 (2): 329–359.

Mazmanian, Daniel A., and Paul A. Sabatier. 1989. *Implementation and Public Policy.* Lanham, MD: University Press of America.

McCluskey, Audrey Thomas, and Elaine M. Smith. 1999. *Mary McLeod Bethune: Building a Better World.* Bloomington: Indiana University Press.

McDermott, Rose. 2004. The feeling of rationality: The meaning of neuroscientific advances for political science. *Perspectives on Politics* 2 (4): 691–706.

Meier, Kenneth J., and Laurence J. O'Toole, Jr. 2006. *Bureaucracy in a Democratic State: A Governance Perspective.* Baltimore, MD: Johns Hopkins University Press.

Melnick, R. Shep. 2005. The politics of partnership. In *Public Administration and Law,* ed. Julia Beckett and Heidi O. Koenig, 84–95. Armonk, NY: M.E. Sharpe.

Mettler, Suzanne. 2005. *Soldiers to Citizens: The G.I. Bill and the Making of the Greatest Generation.* New York: Oxford University Press.

Milward, H. Brinton, and Keith G. Provan. 2000. Governing the hollow state. *Journal of Public Administration Research and Theory* 10 (2): 359–380.

Moynihan, Donald P. 2008. *The Dynamics of Performance Management: Constructing Information and Reform.* Washington, DC: Georgetown University Press.

Nathan, Richard. 1983. *The Administrative Presidency.* New York: John Wiley.

O'Leary, Rosemary. 1993. *Environmental Change: Federal Courts and the EPA.* Philadelphia: Temple University Press.

Orren, Karen, and Stephen Skowronek. 2004. *The Search for American Political Development.* New York: Cambridge University Press.

Ostrom, Vincent. 1973. *The Intellectual Crisis in American Public Administration.* Tuscaloosa: University of Alabama Press.

Perry, James L., and Annie Hondeghem. 2008. *Motivation in Public Management: The Call of Public Service.* Oxford: Oxford University Press.

Pierson, Paul. 1993. When effect becomes cause: Policy feedback and political change. *World Politics* 45 (4): 595–628.

———. 1994. *Dismantling the Welfare State? Reagan, Thatcher, and the Politics of Retrenchment.* Cambridge: Cambridge University Press.

———. 2004. *Politics in Time: History, Institutions, and Social Analysis.* Princeton, NJ: Princeton University Press.

Pierson, Paul, and Theda Skocpol. 2007. *The Transformation of American Politics: Activist Government and the Rise of Conservatism.* Princeton, NJ: Princeton University Press.

Popper, Sir Karl Raimund. 1966. *The Open Society and Its Enemies.* 5th ed. Princeton, NJ: Princeton University Press.

Pressman, Jeffrey, and Aaron Wildavsky. 1973. *Implementation: How Great Expectations in Washington Are Dashed in Oakland.* Berkeley: University of California Press.

Raadschelders, Jos C.N. 2010. Is American public administration detached from historical context? *American Review of Public Administration* 40 (3): 235–260.

Radin, Beryl A. 2006. *Challenging the Performance Movement: Accountability, Complexity, and Democratic Values.* Washington, DC: Georgetown University Press.

Redford, Emmette S. 1969. *Democracy in the Administrative State.* New York: Oxford University Press.

Rittel, Horst W.J., and Melvin M. Webber. 1973. Dilemmas in a general theory of planning. *Policy Sciences* 4 (2): 155–169.

Rosenbloom, David H. 2000. *Building a Legislative-Centered Public Administration: Congress and the Administrative State, 1946–1999.* Tuscaloosa: University of Alabama Press.

————. 2008. The politics-administration dichotomy in U.S. historical context. *Public Administration Review* 68 (1): 57–60.

Sabatier, Paul A., and Hank C. Jenkins-Smith. 1993. *Policy Change and Learning: An Advocacy Coalition Approach.* Boulder, CO: Westview Press.

Sandel, Michael J. 1984. The procedural republic and the unencumbered self. *Political Theory* 12 (1): 81–96.

Seidman, Harold. 1998. *Politics, Position, and Power: The Dynamics of Federal Organization.* 5th ed. New York: Oxford University Press.

Shlaes, Amity. 2007. *The Forgotten Man: A New History of the Great Depression.* New York: HarperCollins.

Simon, Herbert A. 1947. *Administrative Behavior.* New York: Free Press.

————. 1985. Human nature in politics: The dialogue of psychology with political science. *American Political Science Review* 79 (2): 293–304.

Skocpol, Theda. 1992. *Protecting Soldiers and Mothers: The Political Origins of Social Policy in the United States.* Cambridge, MA: Belknap Press.

————. 2007. Government activism and the reorganization of American civic democracy. In *The Transformation of American Politics: Activist Government and the Rise of Conservatism,* ed. Paul Pierson and Theda Skocpol, 39–67. Princeton, NJ: Princeton University Press.

Stivers, Camilla. 2000. *Bureau Men, Settlement Women: Constructing Public Administration in the Progressive Era.* Lawrence: University Press of Kansas.

Stone, Deborah. 2001. *Policy Paradox: The Art of Political Decision Making.* New York: W.W. Norton.

Teles, Steven M. 2007. Conservative mobilization against entrenched liberalism. In *The Transformation of American Politics: Activist Government and the Rise of Conservatism,* ed. Paul Pierson and Theda Skocpol, 160–188. Princeton, NJ: Princeton University Press.

Teske, Paul, Mark Schneider, Michael Mintrom, and Samuel Best. 1993. Establishing the micro foundations of a macro theory: Information, movers, and the competitive local market for public goods. *American Political Science Review* 87 (3): 702–713.

Thelen, Kathleen. 1999. Historical institutionalism in comparative politics. *Annual Review of Political Science* 2: 369–404.

Tiebout, Charles. 1956. A pure theory of local public expenditures. *Journal of Political Economy* 64 (5): 416–424.

Tilly, Charles. 2003. *The Politics of Collective Violence.* Cambridge: Cambridge University Press.

Truman, David B. 1951. *The Governmental Process: Political Interests and Public Opinion.* New York: Knopf.

Waldo, Dwight. 1984. *The Administrative State: A Study of the Political Theory of American Public Administration.* 2d ed. New York: Holmes and Meier.

Wilson, Woodrow. 1887. The study of administration. *Political Science Quarterly* 2 (2): 197–222.

Wood, B. Dan, and John Bohte. 2004. Political transaction costs and the politics of administrative design. *Journal of Politics* 66 (1): 176–202.

Wood, B. Dan, and Richard W. Waterman. 1994. *Bureaucratic Dynamics: The Role of Bureaucracy in a Democracy.* Boulder, CO: Westview Press.

CHAPTER 21

CIVIL SERVICE REFORM

Past as Prologue?

STEPHEN E. CONDREY AND JONATHAN P. WEST

Civil service systems have traditionally undergirded public management structures in the United States. Job security, protection from outside political influence, and a solid and progressive career ladder were once universal expectations for public servants. In most, if not all cases, these expectations were a direct benefit of civil service protections. However, civil service protections in many jurisdictions have eroded. The intention of civil service was to create a cadre of career public servants who would be protected from undue political influence in the management of the public's business. In essence, civil service systems would assist in the creation of a "neutrally competent" bureaucracy. As with all public policy, the creation of civil service systems has resulted in unintended consequences. In some cases, it has resulted in insulated and isolated bureaucratic actors who are seemingly unresponsive to the legitimate demands of elected leaders. As a direct reaction to this phenomenon, civil service systems have been under sustained attack by elected and appointed officials for the past two decades. Thus, the history of civil service and civil service reform can be defined by the competing and sometimes mutually exclusive demands of neutral competence and political responsiveness.

This chapter explores the contemporary state of civil service reform in the United States. As discussed here, broad-based civil service reform aims to fundamentally change the nature of the public service. The chapter begins with a brief history of the foundations and evolution of merit-based civil service. The chapter then focuses on specific cases. The first two cases spotlight civil service reforms in the American states, with a particular emphasis on Georgia and Florida and their recent move to abolish or significantly alter civil service protections for state employees. The chapter then highlights the case of Jefferson County, Alabama, and that jurisdiction's efforts to modernize its civil service system under the watchful eye of a federal judge. The fourth case focuses on the U.S. Department of Homeland Security and its dabbling with different reform initiatives. The chapter concludes with a set of implications for the future of civil service in the United States.

CIVIL SERVICE AND PUBLIC MANAGEMENT

Ever since the passage of the Pendleton Act of 1883, governments have struggled with the need for a neutrally competent bureaucracy and the simultaneous need for the same bureaucratic actors to be responsive to the needs of political and appointed officials as the conduit of the public will (see chapter 2, "The Profession of Public Administration: Promise, Problems, and Prospects," in this volume). The Pendleton Act sought to minimize the use of spoils as the basis for the system by replacing it with other values such as merit, protectionism, and political neutrality. The Civil Service Reform Act of 1978 modified structural characteristics of the system by creating the Office of Personnel Management, the Merit System Protection Board, and the Federal Labor Relations Authority in place of the abolished U.S. Civil Service Commission. Other reforms have been less sweeping and more incremental in nature. Civil service reform occurs at the state and local levels as well.

As suggested previously, constant, persistent tension between neutral competency and political responsiveness has been the defining theme in the civil service literature. Kellough and Nigro state it well: "The challenge has always been to find a way to temper the control and flexibility that are required with appropriate levels of protection for public employees" (2006, 2). Van Riper (1958) and Schultz and Maranto (1998) trace the history of the federal civil service in the United States. Condrey and Maranto (2001) examine the trend at all levels of government to dilute the once sacred civil service value of employee job protection from undue political influence. This move to "radical reform" of civil service systems is occurring not only in the federal government but in state and local governments as well. These "reforms" are in direct reaction to the reforms of 1883 and the subsequent diffusion and strengthening of civil service protections throughout the last century. Radical reform, in the vein of new public management,[1] seeks to "let managers manage," unfettered by the constraints of civil service protections.

Proponents of radical reform contend that a nineteenth-century solution to the problems of spoils politics and inefficiency is indeed insufficient to address the complex problems that face public bureaucracies in the early twenty-first century. Hence the issue, much as Mosher (1968) posited forty years ago: How can civil service systems be designed that yield a professional workforce that is protected from elective and managerial abuse while allowing elected and appointed officials to exercise sufficient power over bureaucratic actors and actions? The following four cases—two from state government and one each from local and federal governments—address this enduring problem in a different fashion and thus make excellent examples to explore the complexity and promise of civil service reform.

STATE OF GEORGIA

The term *radical reform* has become almost synonymous with the state of Georgia. Georgia was "ground zero" for radical civil service reform. In 1996, then governor Zell Miller successfully sought passage of legislation that abolished civil service protections for state employees hired after July 1, 1996. The bill also contained a provision that would remove civil service protections from employees as they accepted promotions within the state, thus becoming "at will." By early 2008, almost 83 percent of the state's 80,313 employees were considered "unclassified" or "at will" (see Table 21.1).

The Georgia experience has been described as a perfect storm when it comes to radical reform (Condrey 2002). Georgia has long been a right-to-work state with weak public employee unions. Also, Governor Miller had done his homework—he had the state's legislative and bureaucratic leadership on his side as well as strong editorial support from the state's largest-circulation newspaper. Furthermore, the State Merit System (essentially the state's personnel agency) had a reputation as a rule-bound bureaucracy, more inclined to serve its own interests than those of the agencies it represented.

J. Edward Kellough and Lloyd Nigro note that the 1996 Georgia reform also decentralized human resources management, removing it from a central personnel agency and diffusing the responsibility to the various departments. The authors note that such an arrangement was "along lines suggested by influential reform groups, such as the Winter Commission (1993) and the

Table 21.1

Percentage of Unclassified Versus Classified Employees, State of Georgia, 1999–2008

	Classified		Unclassified		
December 31	Number	Percentage of total	Number	Percentage of total	Total
1999	39,716	51.34	37,641	48.66	77,357
2000	34,906	44.78	43,047	55.22	77,953
2001	31,132	39.08	48,524	60.92	79,656
2002	28,116	34.49	53,393	65.51	81,509
2003	25,349	31.37	55,465	68.63	80,814
2004	22,445	27.88	58,068	72.12	80,513
2005	19,861	24.30	61,877	75.70	81,738
2006*	17,830	21.67	64,452	78.33	82,282
2007*	15,769	19.22	66,266	80.78	82,035
2008*	13,818	17.21	66,495	82.79	80,313

Source: Georgia State Merit System (personal correspondence, March 13, 2009).

Note: Headcount totals for full-time equivalent full-time employees for each year were pulled as available from PeopleSoft HR System as they existed on March 11, 2009. For purposes of consistency from year to year, FTE employees are defined as all regular, benefit-eligible employees on nontemporary pay plans.

*Records for 2006 and forward are under current review by state personnel as some may have been affected by the most recent PeopleSoft upgrade.

federal National Performance Review"[2] (Kellough and Nigro 2006, 118). Thus, civil service in Georgia had sustained a two-pronged attack—it had lost its ability to serve as a protector of merit and also as a central organizing mechanism for human resources in the state. What has been the result of these reforms? Did they live up to the promise anticipated by supporters? The Kellough and Nigro (2006) survey of state of Georgia employees points to the "long-term consequences of human resources policy and management in the state." They describe any perceived performance improvement resulting from the reforms as "marginal" (142). Battaglio and Condrey (2009) also surveyed Georgia human resources professionals, who are in a unique position to view civil service reforms and assess their broader impact beyond more than just one or more specific cases. The Battaglio and Condrey survey reinforces Kellough and Nigro's findings. The more salient results of the survey are shown in Tables 21.2 and 21.3.

Table 21.2 displays human resources professionals' experience with employment-at-will. As such, it concentrates on the "proper" or intended use of employment at will—keeping the workforce aligned with strategic objectives. Almost half of the respondents indicate that at-will employment has been used to (a) trim workforces to keep them in line with overarching managerial objectives (41 percent), (b) meet agency budget shortfalls (46 percent), and (c) achieve downsizing targets (47 percent). While it is a normative statement that these are desirable uses, they are, nonetheless, part of the intended reforms that the Winter Commission and others have espoused over the past several decades. It is also in keeping with the neomanagerialist philosophy of new public management (Bowman and West 2007b).

Just as proponents of at-will and decentralized employment tout its managerial advantages, opponents warn that its misuse can have serious adverse consequences for public organizations. Table 21.3 sheds light on these possibilities in the context of the Georgia reforms.

Table 21.3 reports that almost one-third (30 percent) of responding Georgia human resources professionals believed that at-will employment is used in some instances to fire competent em-

Table 21.2

Georgia Human Resources Professionals' Experience with Misuse of Employment-at-Will

	Percentage Who Agree/Disagree	Mean
EAW is sometimes used to fire competent employees so other people with friends or connections to government can be hired	30.2/49.5	2.61
I know of a case where a competent employee was fired at-will so that another person with friends or connections to government could be hired	10.3/74.1	1.91
Employees have been terminated at-will because of personality conflicts with management	32.4/46.7	2.71

Cronbach's Alpha = .802

Source: Battaglio and Condrey 2009.
Note: Respondents were asked to indicate their agreement or disagreement with survey statements related to employment at-will using the following scale: 1 = "Strongly Disagree"; 2 = "Disagree"; 3 = "Neither Agree/Disagree"; 4 = "Agree"; and 5 = "Strongly Agree." Percentages reported in the table do not sum to 100 percent due to rounding and omission of "Neither Agree/Disagree" responses.

Table 21.3

Georgia Human Resources Professionals' Experience with Employment-at-Will

	Percentage Who Agree/Disagree	Mean
Employees have been terminated at-will because of changing managerial priorities/objectives	40.7/35.0	3.02
Employees have been terminated at-will in order to meet agency budget shortfalls	46.0/37.2	3.09
Employees have been terminated at-will in order to meet agency downsizing goals	47.3/35.9	3.14

Cronbach's Alpha = .842

Source: Battaglio and Condrey 2009.
Note: Respondents were asked to indicate their agreement or disagreement with survey statements related to employment at-will using the following scale: 1 = "Strongly Disagree"; 2 = "Disagree"; 3 = "Neither Agree/Disagree"; 4 = "Agree"; and 5 = "Strongly Agree." Percentages reported in the table do not sum to 100 percent due to rounding and omission of "Neither Agree/Disagree" responses.

ployees so that people with friends or political connections can be employed, with 10 percent able to name a specific case of such an incidence. Thus, the return of spoils politics to employment in Georgia appears to have been aided by the 1996 "reforms." Furthermore, while civil service was intended to thwart the influence of electoral politics in the workplace, it also had the effect of protecting employees from the damaging effect of personality conflicts with management. A perhaps unintended consequence of the Georgia reform is that almost one-third (32 percent) of the responding human resources professionals know of a case where an employee had been terminated at will because of "personality conflicts with management."

These findings bring into question whether an at-will, decentralized employment environment can foster an open and trusting environment that is essential to a healthy workplace. Battaglio and Condrey's findings suggest just the opposite through the use of ordered logistic regression of the impact of employment-at-will experience on organizational trust: "The study findings indicate that EAW [employment-at-will] systems may have a fundamental flaw in that they may undermine trusting workplace relationships necessary for effective public management" (2009, 689). Implementation of reformers' objectives in Georgia was more complex than originally envisioned and appears to have fostered adverse unintended consequences.

STATE OF FLORIDA

Five years after Georgia instituted its 1996 reforms, then governor Jeb Bush of Florida declared his intent to modify the state's civil service system, shifting emphasis from "protection to performance." Promising businesslike efficiency gains, despite the absence of convincing data of inefficiency (e.g., showing that poor performance results when state workers are protected from arbitrary management decisions), the governor favored a private sector approach to personnel practices that would cut costs, improve productivity, and enhance flexibility. He thought change was needed to relieve managers from cumbersome, stultifying personnel policies and thereby afford them more discretion to improve government performance.

In addition to Governor Bush, the main advocates for the reforms were Florida business leaders (Council of 100), Republican state legislators, and taxpayer groups. Public employees, unions, Democratic legislators, appointees (e.g., "the efficiency czar"), and a special master (a labor mediator mandated by Florida law to provide advice to lawmakers when collective negotiations reach an impasse) opposed the reform initiatives (see West and Bowman 2004 for discussion of stakeholders and their interests). Editorial opinions in the state's largest newspapers were divided. The public was largely uninformed and at best offered tepid support to reform. Ultimately, the bill was approved quickly in the Republican-controlled House of Representatives on a party-line vote and the state Senate passed it along party lines as well. Service First was signed into law in May 2001.

While the new legislation modified the state's classification and compensation system by simplifying job titles and pay (broadbanding)[3] and eliminated the notion of seniority throughout the state personnel system (except for police, fire, and nurses), the most sweeping reform was the conversion of sixteen thousand supervisory positions in the state employment system to at-will status. This case deals primarily with the most contentious feature of reform: removal of civil service job protections in state government and implementation of at-will employment (for a discussion of other elements in Service First, see West 2002; Walters 2002; and Bowman, West, and Gertz 2006).

One year after the implementation of Service First, James Bowman and his colleagues (2003) surveyed state employees whose jobs were converted from Florida's tenured Career Service to unprotected Selected Exempt Service. General findings suggested that many in the Selected Exempt Service group lacked complete information about the law's provisions, and characterized the reform as a move to downsize government and enhance managerial discretion. Respondents were skeptical that the law would enhance hiring processes or responsiveness, and nearly half contended that the reform would lead to reduced productivity.

In 2006, West and Bowman surveyed Florida human resources professionals. Their research paralleled that of Battaglio and Condrey (2009) in that they viewed human resources managers as pivotal in assessing the impact of reforms. The 2005 survey findings confirmed many observations made by Bowman and his colleagues after the first year of operation under Service First, and they are very similar to the findings from Georgia.

Table 21.4 reports Florida human resources professionals' experience with employment at will. Replicas of the questions in the Georgia survey were used in Florida; the focus is on the strategic purpose behind the use of at-will employment. Half of the respondents indicated that at-will employment is used to meet agency downsizing goals, with fewer agreeing that it is used to implement managerial priorities (43.8 percent) and meet agency budget shortfalls (41.3 percent). Here again, findings indicate alignment between managerial strategy and employment at will: These results closely mirror the Georgia survey findings and are consistent with new public management philosophy, the Winter Commission recommendations, and some of the promises made by reform proponents (Bowman and West 2008).

While these purported advantages associated with at-will employment are voiced by reformers seeking to enhance managerial discretion and flexibility, opponents fear the adverse consequences from potential abuse of such discretion, so evident historically during the spoils era.[4] Table 21.5 highlights the concerns in the Florida setting.

Table 21.5 examines misuse of at-will employment. Florida's human resources professionals are less likely than Georgia managers to identify instances where employment at will has been used to fire competent employees so other people with friends or connections to government can be hired (18.8 percent). Nonetheless, nearly one in five Florida human resources professionals report knowledge of spoilslike termination decisions and, as in Georgia, one in ten has firsthand knowledge of such a case. Findings from Florida are also similar to those in Georgia in that nearly three out of ten human resources professionals know of employees who have been terminated at will because of personality conflicts with management. These findings suggest the Janus face of at-will employment and the complexity of implementing the concept without negative consequences (see West and Bowman 2006; Bowman and West 2007a).

In an attempt to validate the perceptions of human resources professionals and compare them with others, Bowman and West (2007b) conducted semistructured telephone interviews with more than fifty staff members who converted from Florida's Career Service to Selected Exempt Service in the central and district Departments of Transportation, Environmental Protection, and Children and Families and eight human resources managers in these departments. Not surprisingly, the views of the human resources professionals tended to be more sanguine regarding the purpose and impact of Service First than were those whose status had been converted to Selected Exempt Service, who would be losing their job protection. Human resources professionals in these three departments saw the key purposes of Service First as providing greater managerial flexibility, discretion, and benefits, and as coinciding with the governor's intent to "refresh" the workforce and push for privatization. They cite improvements in timely recruitment but acknowledge mixed results on employee morale and loyalty. They opine that political accountability and responsiveness are largely unchanged. In general, they had mixed views on whether Service First represented a successful application of the business model to government and on whether employees were viewed more as a cost than an asset.

Table 21.6 reports in summary form the results of interviews with those employees converted from Career Service to Selected Exempt Service in these Florida departments. This group is more critical or guarded in their assessments of Service First. They more frequently cite the negative effects of the reform measures with respect to the reform goals themselves and the impacts on recruitment, morale and loyalty, pay, nonpartisan service, and public sector employment appeal. They think that public employees are more frequently thought of as a cost to be borne rather than an asset deserving of investment and that the application of the business

Table 21.4

Florida Human Resources Professionals' Experience with Employment-at-Will

	Percentage Who Agree/Disagree	Mean
EAW is sometimes used to fire competent employees so other people with friends or connections to government can be hired	18.8/51.6	2.38
I know of a case where a competent employee was fired at-will so that another person with friends or connections to government could be hired	11.1/76.2	1.87
Employees have been terminated at-will because of personality conflicts with management	29.7/48.4	2.64

Cronbach's Alpha = .950

Source: West and Bowman 2006.
Note: Respondents were asked to indicate their agreement or disagreement with survey statements related to employment at-will using the following scale: 1 = "Strongly Disagree"; 2 = "Disagree"; 3 = "Neither Agree/Disagree"; 4 = "Agree"; and 5 = "Strongly Agree." Percentages reported in the table do not sum to 100 percent due to rounding and omission of "Neither Agree/Disagree" responses.

Table 21.5

Florida Human Resources Professionals' Experience Use of At-Will Employment

	Percentage Who Agree/Disagree	Mean
Employees have been terminated at-will because of changing managerial priorities/ objectives	43.8/28.1	3.13
Employees have been terminated at-will in order to meet agency budget shortfalls	41.3/42.9	3.00
Employees have been terminated at-will in order to meet agency downsizing goals	50.8/31.8	3.25

Cronbach's Alpha = .963

Source: West and Bowman 2006.
Note: Respondents were asked to indicate their agreement or disagreement with survey statements related to employment at-will using the following scale: 1 = "Strongly Disagree"; 2 = "Disagree"; 3 = "Neither Agree/Disagree"; 4 = "Agree"; and 5 = "Strongly Agree." Percentages reported in the table do not sum to 100 percent due to rounding and omission of "Neither Agree/Disagree" responses.

model to government was unsuccessful. They more frequently identify "no change" resulting from Service First when it comes to service provision, responsiveness, and productivity. Thus, while Florida has undertaken "radical" reform, the results on balance are mixed at best, with the preponderance of opinion being negative among those most directly affected. Reformers in other states are cautioned that patterning their reforms on the Florida experience may not yield the desired results they envision (see Bowman 2002). Lessons from Florida suggest the need for careful consideration of the pros and especially the cons of reform in advance of dismantling civil service protection.

Table 21.6

Predominant Views on Service First (*n* = 51 SES officials)

Reform dimension	Department of Transportation			Department of Environmental Protection			Department of Children and Families		
	Positive	Negative	No change	Positive	Negative	No change	Positive	Negative	No change
Reform goals	X				X			X	X
Recruitment			X		X			X	X
Service provision			X			X		X	X
Responsiveness			X			X	X		X
Productivity			X			X	X		X
Morale and loyalty		X			X			X	
Pay		X	X		X	X		X	
Nonpartisan service		X			X			X	
Employment appeal		X	X		X			X	
Cost or asset		Cost			Cost			Cost	
Business model		Unsuccessful			Unsuccessful			Unsuccessful	

Source: Adapted from Bowman and West (2007b).

DIFFUSION TO OTHER STATES

Has Georgia and Florida's decentralized, at-will approach diffused to other states? The most recent study of this phenomenon was conducted by Steve Hays and Jessica Sowa (2006). This comprehensive survey of the fifty states examines human resources practices related to the expansion of at-will employment, the diminution of employee rights, and the decentralization of the state personnel function. Table 21.7 displays a summary of the Hays and Sowa findings. The results of the survey are astounding and signal that a quiet revolution related to civil service reform is in full motion in the American states. The survey reveals that only eight of the fifty states (16 percent) retain a fully centralized personnel system; twenty-eight of fifty (56 percent) report an expansion of at-will employment; and thirty-one of fifty (62 percent) report a "decline in job security."

Hays and Sowa characterize the above findings as "sobering" (112) because reform initiatives were much more common than expected. Following are several examples of comments from the state personnel officials interviewed in each state:

- "Our perception of job security has changed drastically in the last five years. The politicians want us to 'do more with less.' Soon we'll be 'doing everything with nothing.'" (Minnesota)
- "The uncovering of positions is being done quietly. Old notions of job security are changing. We've seen more and more agency heads come in from the private sector bringing the private sector mentality. They're much more inclined to terminate workers. As the older generation of career employees retires, they're being replaced by outsiders with a different—almost antigovernment—attitude." (Vermont)
- "Politicians in the state continually argue that the merit system hinders performance and efficiency. It [the merit system] is probably doomed." (Nebraska)
- "There is no longer any such thing as job security. 'Just cause' dismissals are seriously threatened." (Rhode Island) (Hays and Sowa 2006, 14–15)

There is little question that civil service reform has spread among the American states. Bowman and West (2007b) believe that these reforms have been driven by a blind trust in the private sector model and its supposed easy transfer to public sector organizations, something they term a "powerful illusion" (142). It remains, however, unclear whether the at-will, decentralization movement that started in Georgia will continue to diffuse among the states. The financial meltdown of Wall Street and recession of 2008–10 have most probably diminished the luster of applying private sector models to public agencies. Furthermore, the private sector fervor may be tempered by the call to public service that President Obama has put forward.

While no crystal ball is in hand, it is a safe bet that the Georgia and Florida experiences with at-will, decentralized human resources management will continue to influence the field. We turn next to an example of how a civil service system was rebuilt, rather than abolished.

PERSONNEL BOARD OF JEFFERSON COUNTY, ALABAMA

Founded in 1935, the Personnel Board of Jefferson County, Alabama, is an example of a traditional, centralized civil service system. The agency is administered by a three-member board that is appointed by a citizen's panel; members of the board may hold elective office. The Personnel Board administers the hiring and compensation programs for the city of Birmingham, Jefferson County, Jefferson County Health Department, and approximately nineteen other cities within Jefferson County. By design, the Personnel Board seeks to separate political influence from the hiring and

Table 21.7

General Summary of Interview Findings: Snapshot of Current Conditions in the States' Personnel Systems

State	Level of Human Resources Decentralization	Expansion of At-Will Employees	Range of Grievable Issues	Activist Governor	"Decline in Job Security"
Alabama	Partial	No	Agency specific	No	Yes
Alaska	Centralized	No	Restricted	Yes	No
Arizona	Partial	Yes	Restricted	Yes	Yes
Arkansas	Significant	Yes	Restricted, agency specific	No	Yes
California	Partial	No	Expansive	Yes	Yes
Colorado	Significant	Yes	Restricted	Yes	Yes
Connecticut	Partial	No	Expansive	No	No
Delaware	Partial	Yes	Expansive	No	No
Florida	Significant	Yes	Restricted	Yes	Yes
Georgia	Significant	Yes	Restricted	No	Yes
Hawaii	Centralized	No	Expansive	No	No
Idaho	Partial	Yes	Agency specific	No	Yes
Illinois	Partial	No	Expansive	No	Yes
Indiana	Recentralizing	Yes	Restrictive	Yes	Yes
Iowa	Significant	Yes	Expansive	No	No
Kansas	Significant	Yes	Expansive, agency specific	Yes	Yes
Kentucky	Centralized	Yes	Expansive	Yes	No
Louisiana	Partial	No	Restricted	No	Yes
Maine	Recentralizing	No	Expansive	Yes	Yes
Maryland	Partial	No	Expansive	No	No
Massachusetts	Partial	Yes	Expansive	Yes	Yes
Michigan	Partial	No	Expansive	No	Yes
Minnesota	Partial	No	Expansive	No	Yes
Mississippi	Partial	Yes	Restricted	Yes	Yes
Missouri	Significant	Yes	Agency specific	Yes	Yes
Montana	Partial	No	Restricted	No	No
Nebraska	Centralized	Yes	Restricted	No	Yes
Nevada	Partial	No	Expansive	No	No
New Hampshire	Partial	No	Expansive	No	No
New Jersey	Partial	Yes	Expansive	No	Yes
New Mexico	Centralized	No	Expansive	No	No
New York	Partial	No	Expansive	No	No
North Carolina	Significant	Yes	Restricted	No	Yes
North Dakota	Significant	No	Restricted	No	No
Ohio	Partial	Yes	Restricted	No	No
Oklahoma	Significant	Yes	Restricted	No	Yes
Oregon	Partial	Yes	Expansive	Yes	Yes
Pennsylvania	Significant	No	Expansive	No	No
Rhode Island	Centralized	Yes	Expansive, but not utilized	Yes	Yes
South Carolina	Significant	Yes	Restricted	No	Yes
South Dakota	Centralized	No	Expansive	No	No
Tennessee	Centralized	No	Restricted	No	No
Texas	Complete	Yes	Not applicable	No	Yes
Utah	Partial	Yes	Expansive	Yes	No
Vermont	Significant	Yes	Restricted	Yes	Yes
Virginia	Significant	No	Restricted	No	Yes
Washington	Significant	Yes	Restricted	Yes	Yes
West Virginia	Partial	Yes	Restricted	Yes	Yes
Wisconsin	Partial	No	Expansive	Yes	Yes
Wyoming	Partial	Yes	Restricted	No	No

Source: Hays and Sowa 2006.

discipline of employees of its member jurisdictions. In practice, it has been a lightening rod for political intrigue, lawsuits, and controversy extending over the past five decades.

As the protector of "merit," the Personnel Board has designed tests for initial employment and promotion within its covered jurisdictions. The NAACP along with other parties sued the Personnel Board in the 1970s over its employment practices, which it deemed discriminatory and in violation of the Equal Employment Opportunity Act of 1972. A consent decree was entered into in 1981, with the agency charged with improving its employment practices and creating nondiscriminatory selection instruments (Battaglio and Condrey 2007).

However, this was to be a long rather than a short story, with various suits and countersuits claiming both discrimination and reverse discrimination. In 2002, the presiding federal court judge found the Personnel Board in contempt of court and appointed a receiver to serve as the sole board member and administrator of the Personnel Board. This is the only instance that could be documented of a federal court placing a personnel system under receivership (Battaglio and Condrey 2007; Sims 2009).

The receiver, Dr. Ronald Sims, a management professor at the College of William and Mary, states that the long history of federal reporting and oversight had become standard operating procedure with the Personnel Board, but unacceptable to the federal judge in charge of monitoring the consent decree: "While the former leadership of the PBJC [Personnel Board of Jefferson County] may have viewed this situation as tolerable, the federal court clearly did not" (Sims 2009). Additionally, the legal costs for the Personnel Board alone exceeded $10 million, an amount that presiding U.S. District Court Judge Lynwood Smith described as "staggering and mounting by the hour" (Stock 2008, 1A). These fees were eventually negotiated to about one-quarter of that amount (Stock 2009, 2B) but demonstrate the long and involved legal battle all parties endured.

As receiver, Sims was given extraordinary power by the court to design an effective system of human resources management. Here the emphasis was on strengthening testing, classification, and compensation, and the underlying information technology system. This is in contrast to Georgia and Florida, where the emphasis was on decentralization and lending more power and influence to management. Sims found an agency mired in the past with little human or electronic infrastructure to carry out its task to administer the human resources system for more than twelve thousand employees: "The staff was generally not computer literate. Few desktop computers existed in the organization. In short, the Receiver believed that the lack of infrastructure contributed to PBJC's [the Personnel Board's] struggling to execute its basic statutory responsibilities" (Sims 2009). Following is a partial listing of Sims' accomplishments as the court's receiver:

- Conducted a classification and compensation study
- Assessed the skills of Personnel Board staff, replacing and retraining as deemed appropriate
- Engaged a skilled consultant to revamp public safety hiring procedures
- Recruited a professional examination development team
- Instituted professional development activities for Personnel Board staff
- Revised the organization's rules and regulations
- Renovated the physical offices of the Personnel Board
- Implemented a state-of-the-art human resources information system (Sims 2009)

As a result of Sims' promising efforts, the Personnel Board was released from court supervision in November 2008 (Walton and Stock 2008).

Riccucci and Naff state that the structural arrangement the Personnel Board utilizes is contrary to the trend for other local government organizations. The two authors note similar trends for local governments comparable to what was discussed earlier for the states: "Put simply, independent agencies of a regulatory nature were having great difficulty in serving the needs of elected executives and public managers. They became viewed as obstacles to efficiency and effectiveness and were often seen as unduly influenced by pressure groups" (2008, 38).

So what is the final result of the court-ordered modernization of the Personnel Board of Jefferson County, Alabama? Can a revamped 1935 civil service system that isolates human resource policy decisions from management and elected leaders be effective in the twenty-first century? The jury is still out, but the Personnel Board is in fact better able to serve its clients than it was prior to receivership. However, problems still exist concerning complex relationships with the elected leadership of the jurisdictions it serves. The mayor of Birmingham has been engaged in an ongoing struggle with the Personnel Board over the hiring of a public works director, and Jefferson County continues to seek release from court supervision. Is the Personnel Board simply a rebuilt 1935 Cadillac ready for action in today's fast-paced human resources management environment?

To put this case in perspective, the 1935 act establishing the Personnel Board was an attempt to modernize and professionalize government from the bottom up. It is a logical conclusion that the civil service system was established to help create a professional workforce for these governmental bodies. However, one can speculate about what would have been the result if the 1935 legislation had instead dealt with the top of the organization—an approach that would have created or encouraged city and county manager forms of government—and in turn whether this would have led to the increased professionalization of the respective workforces. Because the city and county lacked professional top-level leadership, the civil service system became a way to protect employees from the vagaries of the various elected officials that would occupy offices of power. However, civil service protection alone has done little to provide the city of Birmingham and Jefferson County citizens with healthy and functioning governments. As of this writing, the mayor of Birmingham (who was formerly the county commission chair) has been convicted in federal court on sixty counts of bribery, four former county commissioners have been convicted of accepting bribes, and the county faces possible bankruptcy over sewer bond payments (Hubbard 2009, 1; Wright 2009, 1).

DEPARTMENT OF HOMELAND SECURITY

The federal government's Department of Homeland Security is another interesting example of civil service reform. The tragic and traumatic events of September 11, 2001, gave rise to the largest reorganization of the federal government since World War II with the creation of the Department of Homeland Security (DHS). Kingdon (1995) describes such periods of time as a "policy window," an unusual convergence of circumstances and ideas allowing for a major policy shift. As Stivers and Hummel note, "Change through crisis has been an ongoing theme in American government. In a system designed to move hesitantly and incrementally, emergencies, not grand theory, are what often spark the energy for significant action" (2007, 1011).

Part of the Bush reorganization plan for DHS was a lessening of civil service rules allowing for more flexibility with labor relations, compensation, and a denial of property rights to some employees of the newly formed agency, namely those employees of the Transportation Security Administration (Naff and Newman 2004; Underhill and Oman 2007).

Kay Coles James, Office of Personnel Management director under the second President Bush, outlined the proposed DHS reforms in congressional testimony:

- A pay-for-performance system in which high performance is expected and rewarded, to an extent not permitted under the General Schedule; that streamlines and modernizes job classifications and pay levels; and that takes into account both national and local rates aid by employees in the private sector in setting pay for the Department's key occupational groups.
- A labor relations system that permits the Department to act quickly in situations where flexibility and swift implementation are most critical to achieving its mission (for example, in the deployment of personnel or introduction of new technology); that provides for the swift and fair resolution of labor disputes by a newly established and independent DHS Labor Relations Board; and that preserves the right of employees and their unions to bargain collectively over important working conditions.
- A streamlined mechanism for handling major disciplinary actions and employee appeals that preserves due process and retains intact all existing employee protections against reprisal, retaliation, and other prohibited personnel practices. It is important to note that the proposed regulations on employee appeals are the result of extensive and constructive consultation with the Merit Systems Protection Board, as required by the statute. (U.S. Congress 2004)

If there is a lesson to be learned from the DHS/Transportation Security Administration experience it is that public human resources management, as Frank Thompson observed more than thirty years ago, is necessarily "political" (Thompson and Oakland Project 1975). The creation of DHS in October 2001 reverberated in the elections of 2002. Triple-amputee Senator Max Cleland, who helped lead the fight to preserve the employment rights of Homeland Security employees, was painted as a terrorist sympathizer by his political opponents and lost his bid for reelection in Georgia. Norma Riccucci and Frank Thompson observe: "In sum, the election results of 2002 suggest that the Bush administration effectively reframed the debate over the human resource system in the DHS from an issue of management flexibility versus employee rights to an issue of national security versus self-interested union power" (2008, 879). However, as the political winds changed, DHS announced in early 2008 that it would "abandon its efforts to revise the labor relations component of the personnel reform, and it also pledged to proceed more slowly in its efforts to implant [a] pay-for-performance personnel system" (Riccucci and Thompson 2008, 884).

As with the Georgia and Florida cases (and contrary to the Jefferson County experience) the DHS example is a case of "reform" being driven for the purposes of increased managerial flexibility through decentralization of the human resources management function. James Thompson terms this "disaggregation." Commenting on the Department of Defense as well as the Department of Homeland Security, Thompson observes that "a direct consequence of these new systems, however, is the disaggregation of the federal personnel system into multiple, agency-specific systems. Disaggregation, in turn, represents a fundamental threat to an institution whose viability is contingent on its inherently collective nature" (2006, 497).

One significant difference in comparing the attempted DHS reforms with the reforms in Georgia, Florida, and the Jefferson County Personnel Board is the complicating presence of unions at the federal level. As mentioned earlier, Georgia and Florida are both right-to-work states with ineffectual union representation. The same could be said for the Jefferson County Personnel Board, with the exception being that employee "organizations" (with no collective bargaining rights) have exerted considerable influence on the state legislature to keep the Personnel Board intact in spite of being on opposite sides of the consent decree that spurred judicial oversight.

In DHS, the National Treasury Employees Union played an important part in mitigating the Bush administration's efforts to exert increased managerial control over the agency (Riccucci and

Thompson 2008). As evidenced by the Clinton experience, unions do not always oppose management when they perceive that mutual interests are involved. The National Partnership Council, created by Clinton's Executive Order 12871, "required federal agency heads to attempt to forge partnerships with federal employee unions." Riccucci and Thompson note that such mandated cooperative efforts took place while "other measures of the Clinton administration sought to enhance managerial discretion over human resources" (2008, 878).

Robert Tobias, a professor at American University and a former president of the National Treasury Employees Union, notes the Bush administration's quick reversal from the Clinton administration's overtures for a cooperative partnership between labor and management. Tobias states that unlike other chief executives, Clinton recognized "that labor and management each have interests that can be satisfied only with the cooperation of the other" (2005, 360).

It is a safe bet that Bush's personnel-related DHS reforms were largely unsuccessful due not only to their managerialist tendencies but also to the chilled relationship with key unions. While the Homeland Security Act promised increased "managerial discretion" in instituting pay for performance and administering collective bargaining relationships, implementation proved to be difficult, with little of a substantive nature accomplished by the end of Bush's second term (Riccucci and Thompson 2008, 880).

A quote from the congressional testimony of AFL-CIO's Robert Ault sums up the attitude of union officials about the DHS reforms: "The National Security Personnel System is not about security: it is about control. As you know, the blueprint for NSPS was written not in the Pentagon, but at the Heritage Foundation. It was embraced by the White House within the first few days after the inauguration of President Bush—a full nine months before 9–11. It was not proposed as a tool of national security but as a means for "controlling the bureaucracy." 9–11 was not the reason for NSPS: it was the excuse" (U.S. Congress 2005).

COMPARING THE CASES

James Thompson (2007, 250) notes in describing Bush's proposed DHS reforms that "although it [was] not 'employment-at-will,' it represented a class movement toward providing managers with greater control over the workplace." In this manner, the case of DHS is very similar to the experience in Georgia, Florida, and other states that are incrementally dismantling employee rights and protections built up over the past three-quarters of a century. In the case of DHS, it remains to be seen what President Obama's management philosophy will entail. However, it is sure to somewhat thaw the chilled relations with federal employee unions.

While the Georgia case presents an extreme example of civil service reform (abolition), it also signals an increased desire for managerial discretion in governing. However, the reported chilling effect that at-will employment has on building trusting workplace relationships should give even radical reformers pause. Without an administrative infrastructure that is based on trust and mutual respect, it is hard to fathom how complex government bureaucracies can function effectively.

Florida's reform is as radical as Georgia's in its thrust, if not its reach, by eliminating vested property rights of sixteen thousand career employees. Prompted by those who wanted to apply a business model to government, reformers eliminated job security for these workers and instituted the private sector at-will employment concept. As in Georgia, there was little consideration for the resulting adverse consequences of such a change for workforce morale, trust, and commitment to the public service ethos.

The Personnel Board of Jefferson County case reminds us of the potential (and largely untapped) power the courts can have in influencing the reform (and modernization) of civil service systems. It will be interesting to see how and if this modernized version of a centralized civil service authority will adapt to the needs of twenty-first-century organizations.

In each of the four cases, reformers promised that performance would improve if civil service systems were modified. Some reforms did bear positive fruit, but the complexities of implementing the reforms and unanticipated consequences have limited their success in each instance.

CONCLUSION: PAST AS PROLOGUE?

There is obviously no "one best way" to organize the provision of human resources management services to local, state, and federal government. There are, however, enduring tensions—primarily the tension between the need for managerial flexibility and the requirement of a neutrally competent bureaucratic corps.

There are lessons to be learned from all four cases. The state of Georgia case points to the fact that unbridled elected and bureaucratic power will most certainly prevail in organizations with weak employee unions and little support from external actors. The result is a weakened or nonexistent civil service and ultimately a less readily qualified corps of employees to provide necessary governmental services.

The lessons from Florida are that ideology and political ambition can prompt reform in spite of the absence of persuasive evidence that government is performing poorly or that the corporate model can be easily applied to a government setting. Florida's civil service reform is a classic example of addressing the wrong problem with a "solution" that has resulted in few constructive performance improvements and has had adverse consequences for the state workforce.

The Personnel Board of Jefferson County case points to the fact that the federal courts have an enormous untapped potential to reform civil service systems. As such, it would behoove elected and appointed officials to get their own houses in order or risk intervention from the federal courts, whose only guidelines are laws, not the most current human resources or public administration text.

The Department of Homeland Security example illustrates the necessary lesson that in a union environment, civil service reform will be successful only in an organizational milieu conducive to trust, respect, and mutuality.

In summary, the tension between neutral competence and political responsiveness will continue to influence how civil service systems are managed, reformed, modernized, and modified. As organizations seek a proper balance between employee rights and managerial flexibility, it is hoped that effective government service will be the guiding principle. Our overall assessment is that the state of civil service reform in the United States is in a period of transition. The possibility of encroaching spoils and cronyism looms on the horizon, as political and bureaucratic actors seek to add avenues for managerial flexibility to civil service systems. In pursuing "reform" of civil service systems, these leaders should be cognizant of why these civil service systems were initially formed—to professionalize government service, as well as to provide continuity of governance. If in the haste to reform civil service systems officials lose sight of this fact, we may well see the current penchant for radical reform providing a return to the unprofessional human resources practices of the past.

NOTES

The authors are grateful to Christine Ledvinka, Martha Medina, Linda Seagraves, and Alex Daman for their research assistance in preparing this chapter.

1. New public management refers to a business-oriented approach to public administration that emphasizes decentralization, marketization, restructuring, and modernizing to enhance management rights and reduce government size.

2. The Winter Commission issued a report under the auspices of the National Commission on the State and Local Public Service. Among other things it recommended a more flexible personnel system, decentralization, greater managerial discretion, less emphasis on seniority, fewer job classifications, streamlined procedures, portable pensions, and pay for performance. The National Performance Review (later renamed National Partnership for Reinventing Government) refers to a Clinton administration initiative that sought to cut red tape, improve government performance, and hold public employees responsible for program results.

3. Broadbanding exists when several grades are combined, creating a broader salary range for a position. It allows more discretion at the agency level, offers more organizational flexibility, and provides incentives for long-term development. However, it may create problems in ensuring equal pay for equal work.

4. The spoils era refers to a historical period (1826–86) when appointment to government jobs was viewed as spoils of office (similar to spoils of battle) to those active in a victorious campaign.

REFERENCES

Battaglio, P.R., and S.E. Condrey. 2007. Framing civil service innovations: Assessing state and local government reforms. In *American Public Service: Radical Reform and the Merit System,* ed. J.S. Bowman and J.P. West, 25–46. Boca Raton, FL: CRC Press.

———. 2009. Reforming public management: Analyzing the impact of public service reform on organizational and managerial trust. *Journal of Public Administration Research and Theory* 19 (4): 689–708.

Bowman, J.S. 2002. At-will employment in Florida government: A naked formula to corrupt public service. *WorkingUSA* 6 (2): 90–102.

Bowman, J.S., M. Gertz, S. Gertz, and R. Williams. 2003. Civil service reform in Florida: State employee attitudes one year later. *Review of Public Personnel Administration* 23 (4): 286–304.

Bowman, J.S., and J.P. West. 2007a. Lord Acton and employment doctrines: Absolute power and spread of at-will employment. *Journal of Business Ethics* 74:119–130.

———. 2007b. Ending civil service protections in Florida government: Experiences in state agencies. In *American Public Service: Radical Reform and the Merit System,* ed. J.S. Bowman and J.P. West, 123–150. New York: Taylor and Francis.

———. 2008. Removing employee protections: A "see no evil" approach to civil service reform. In *Ethics and Integrity of Governance: Perspectives Across Frontiers,* ed. W.J.C. Huberts, J. Maesschalck, and C. Jurkiewicz, 181–196. Cheltenham, UK: Edward Elgar.

Bowman, J.S., J.P. West, and S. Gertz. 2006. Florida's service first: Radical reform in the sunshine state. In *Civil Service Reform in the States,* ed. J.E. Kellough and L. Nigro, 145–170. Albany: State University of New York Press.

Condrey, S.E. 2002. Reinventing state civil service systems: The Georgia experience. *Review of Public Personnel Administration* 22 (2): 114–124.

Condrey, S.E., and R. Maranto. 2001. *Radical Reform of the Civil Service.* Lanham, MD: Lexington Books.

Hays, S.W., and J.E. Sowa. 2006. A broader look at the "accountability" movement: Some grim realities in state civil service systems. *Review of Public Personnel Administration* 26 (2): 102–117.

Hubbard, Russell. 2009. Langford guilty: Mayor convicted on all 60 counts. *Birmingham News,* October 29, 1, 6A.

Kellough, J.E., and L.G. Nigro. 2006. *Civil Service Reform in the States: Personnel Policy and Politics at the Subnational Level.* Albany: State University of New York Press.

Kingdon, J.W. 1995. *Agendas, Alternatives, and Public Policies.* 2d ed. New York: HarperCollins College Publishers.

Mosher, F.C. 1968. *Democracy and the Public Service.* New York: Oxford University Press.

Naff, K.C., and M.A. Newman. 2004. Symposium: Federal civil service reform: Another legacy of 9/11? *Review of Public Personnel Administration* 24 (3): 191–201.

Riccucci, N., and K.C. Naff. 2008. *Personnel Management in Government: Politics and Process.* 6th ed. Boca Raton, FL: CRC Press.

Riccucci, N.M., and F.J. Thompson. 2008. The new public management, homeland security, and the politics of civil service reform. *Public Administration Review* 68 (5): 877–890.

Schultz, D.A., and R. Maranto. 1998. *The Politics of Civil Service Reform.* New York: P. Lang.

Sims, R.R. 2009. Civil service reform in action: The case of the personnel board of Jefferson County, Alabama. *Review of Public Personnel Administration* 29 (4): 382–401.

Stivers, C., and R.P. Hummel. 2007. Personnel management: Politics, administration, and a passion for anonymity. *Public Administration Review* 67 (6): 1010–1017.

Stock, E. 2008. Personnel suit fees exceed $10 million: Some fear expense may cripple cities. *Birmingham News,* November 17, 1A–4A.

———. 2009. Judge to evaluate payment plan to New York City law firm. *Birmingham News,* May 13, 2B.

Thompson, F.J., and Oakland Project. 1975. *Personnel Policy in the City: The Politics of Jobs in Oakland.* Berkeley: University of California Press.

Thompson, J.R. 2006. The federal civil service: The demise of an institution. *Public Administration Review* 66 (4): 496–503.

———. 2007. Federal labor-management relations under George W. Bush: Enlightened management or political retribution. In *American Public Service: Radical Reform and the Merit System,* ed. J.S. Bowman and J.P. West, 233–254. Boca Raton, FL: CRC Press.

Tobias, R.M. 2005. Employee unions and the human resource management function. In *Handbook of Human Resource Management in Government.* 2d ed., ed. S.E. Condrey, 351–373. San Francisco: Jossey Bass.

Underhill, J., and R. Oman. 2007. A critical review of the sweeping federal civil service changes: The case of the departments of homeland security and defense. *Review of Public Personnel Administration* 27 (4): 401–420.

U.S. Congress. 2004. Senate. Committee on Homeland Security and Governmental Affairs. *Joint Hearing: The Key to Homeland Security: The New Human Resources System.* 108th Cong., 2d sess. Testimony of the Honorable Kay Coles James. http://hsgac.senate.gov/public/index.cfm?FuseAction=Hearings. Hearing&Hearing_id=a4d2f798-ba55–4847–8ff3-cae70371cd73.

———. 2005. Senate. Committee on Homeland Security and Governmental Affairs. *From Proposed to Final: Evaluating Regulations for the National Security Personnel System.* 109th Cong., 1st sess. Testimony of Ronald Ault. http://hsgac.senate.gov/public/index.cfm?FuseAction=Hearings.Hearing&Hearing_ID=0d9bf9f5–2ebe-4b73–9a96–96bd81eb0f51.

Van Riper, P.P. 1958. *History of the United States Civil Service.* Evanston, IL: Row, Peterson.

Walters, J. 2002. *Life After Civil Service Reform: The Texas, Georgia, and Florida Experiences.* Arlington, VA: IBM Endowment for the Business of Government.

Walton, V., and E. Stock. 2008. Personnel board freed from decree: Bias case duties met, court says. *Birmingham News,* November 21, 1A–6A.

West, J.P. 2002. Georgia on the mind of radical civil service reformers. *Review of Public Personnel Administration* 22 (2): 79–93.

West, J.P., and J.S. Bowman. 2004. Stakeholder analysis of civil service reform in Florida: A descriptive, instrumental, normative human resource management perspective. *State and Local Government Review* 36 (1): 20–34.

———. 2006. The Janus face of at-will employment. Paper presented at the Western Political Science Association annual meeting in Albuquerque, New Mexico, March.

Wright, Barnett. 2009. Corrupt culture kills trust. *Birmingham News,* November 2, 1, 3A.

CHAPTER 22

PUBLIC ADMINISTRATION'S LEGAL DIMENSIONS

Three Models

DAVID H. ROSENBLOOM

Public administration in the United States has at least three highly developed legal dimensions: the constitutional separation of powers; administrative law; and individual constitutional rights. Respectively, these can be conveniently referred to as the "Madisonian model," based on James Madison's writings on the separation of powers in the *Federalist;* the "1946 legislative-centered model for administrative law," reflecting Congress's effort in 1946 to develop a framework for exercising greater control over federal administration; and the "judicial model for infusing constitutional rights into public administrative practice." In this chapter, consideration is given first to the relationship of law to U.S. public administration, followed by review of the origins, structure, and scope of each model as well as their collective impacts on public administration.

PUBLIC ADMINISTRATION AS A FIELD OF STUDY AND LAW IN THE UNITED STATES

As a self-conscious enterprise, U.S. public administration began as a field of management and science rather than an endeavor based on legal principles. It developed out of the confluence of the civil service reform movement of the 1870s–90s, which insisted that politics should be separate from administration, and the Progressive (1890–1924) and scientific management movements (1911–30s), which sought further depoliticization and the building of a science of administration. With management and science as its pillars, law was considered of secondary or even lesser importance to administration. Leonard White's *Introduction to the Study of Public Administration* (1926), the first U.S. textbook on the subject, affirmed that "the study of administration should start from the base of management rather than the foundation of law, and is therefore more absorbed in the affairs of the American Management Association than in the decisions of the courts" (White 1926, vii–viii). By 1937, Luther Gulick and Lyndall Urwick could present public administration as a science in their highly influential volume, *Papers on the Science of Administration.* In Gulick's view, this science treated efficiency as "axiom number one in [its] . . . value scale" (Gulick 1937, 192).

These early works and movements contributed to the public administration "orthodoxy" that had fully emerged by the late 1930s. The orthodoxy's claims of being both scientific and apolitical were debunked in the 1940s by a number of extraordinary works. Herbert Simon's *Administrative Behavior* (1947) and article "The Proverbs of Public Administration" (1946) convincingly demonstrated that although the orthodoxy may have contained a lot of common sense, it was not scientific. Its prescriptions for organizational design and administrative behavior were, like proverbs, contradictory. In *The Administrative State* (1948), Dwight Waldo added to the attack on the orthodoxy by exposing its latent—and nondemocratic—political theory. In 1949, Paul Appleby, a leader in the field, referred to public administration as a "political process" in his book *Policy and Administration* (Appleby 1949).

Having lost what was as close to a dominant paradigm as modern U.S. public administration has ever had, in the late 1940s and 1950s the field turned to case studies as a means of rebuilding its body of knowledge. Many of the casebooks produced during this period highlighted public administration's political dimensions (Rosenbloom 1995). As the case study movement declined in the 1960s, "bureaucratic politics" became a major focus of the field. This coincided with the rise of logical positivism in political science, which strengthened the view promoted by Simon and others that public administration could and should be scientific. Not everyone agreed, and the field entered a prolonged period of epistemological pluralism and subject matter heterodoxy, with a variety of methodological approaches, intellectual currents, and subfields operating largely independently of one another. A major effort to reframe the field in the late 1960s, the new public administration, fell short, and it was not until the rise of the new public management and reinventing government movements of the 1980s and 1990s that the prospect of developing a dominant paradigm seemed plausible (Marini 1971; Kettl 2002).

Law stood largely on the sidelines through all this intellectual development and turmoil. It never came close to being center stage. Beginning in 1940, several administrative law texts designed for use in master of public administration (MPA) programs became available (Rosenbloom 1995). However, administrative law was never integrated into public administration's mainstream, and one would be hard-pressed to conclude that it constitutes even a subfield. Using Jay Shafritz and Albert Hyde's sixth edition of the *Classics of Public Administration* (2007) as a marker of high-impact works, it can be noted that from the 1950s forward the field produced excellent research and scholarship that skirted around law in dealing with federalism, intergovernmental relations, and ethics. However, much of the field was oblivious to the importance of law in public administration. Even the *Classics'* selection "Watergate: Implications for Responsible Government," a product of the elite National Academy of Public Administration, neglected to include adherence to the rule of law among its prescriptions for ethical political and administrative behavior. The only piece in *Classics* that presents law as a central component of public administration is Rosenbloom's "Public Administrative Theory and the Separation of Powers," first published in 1983.

A more systematic recent examination, "The Status of Law in Contemporary Public Administrative Literature, Education, and Practice," concludes that law is prominent neither in the contemporary public administration literature nor in MPA pedagogy (Rosenbloom and Naff, forthcoming). Reporting on Zeger van der Wal's research on public administrative values, it noted that lawfulness ranked near the bottom—twenty-first—on a list of thirty value clusters derived mostly from the U.S. public administration literature on ethics (van der Wal 2008). A survey jointly conducted by Katherine Naff and David Rosenbloom with the National Association of Schools of Public Affairs and Administration in 2008 found that although 88 percent of U.S. MPA programs accredited by the National Association of Schools of Public Affairs and Administration offer at least one law course, in about 60 percent of the MPA programs a student can receive a degree without taking a single law-oriented course. Most of the law courses offered emphasize administrative law (84 percent), constitutional law (45 percent), and personnel/human resources management law (36 percent), with the remainder focusing on environmental law, housing and community development, local government, collective bargaining, health, elections, nonprofit, and tax law (Rosenbloom and Naff, forthcoming). The survey results indicate that a majority of MPA students do not take any law course (Rosenbloom and Naff, forthcoming).

Why is law not more central to U.S. public administration? One possible explanation could be that law is irrelevant to public administrative practice. However, multiple sources of evidence strongly suggest that this is not the case. For example, van der Wal found that "lawfulness" ranks very high in the value scale of Dutch administrators (van der Wal 2008, 70, 73, 74). Three decades ago, Marshall Dimock, a leading contributor to the field of public administration, observed, "To the public administrator, law is something very positive and concrete. It is his authority. . . . It does three things: tells him what the legislature expects him to accomplish, fixes limits to his authority, and sets forth the substantive and procedural rights of the individual and group" (Dimock 1980, 31). Steven Maynard-Moody and Michael Musheno's study *Cops, Teachers, Counselors* (2003) also finds that law is very salient to street-level administrators. In some areas of public administration, including environmental protection, litigation is frequent enough to be a normal part of the administrative process (O'Leary 1993). It should also be noted that in 2008, an American Society for Public Administration Task Force on Educating for Excellence in the MPA Degree called for MPA education in the United States to be anchored in the Constitution. It emphasized the need to teach students to use public authority "lawfully" (2008, 21).

If law is relevant to public administrative practice, then what else can explain its tangential status in public administrative literature and pedagogy? Perhaps part of the answer is that law should be left to the lawyers. This begs the question. Public administration is comprised of several subfields that could similarly be left to expert professionals: budgeting and finance (economists and accountants); organizational behavior (sociologists); personnel (human resources management specialists); (some) methodologies (statisticians); general management (MBAs and managerial consultants). Public administration is a distinctive academic field precisely because it combines several subfields in which others might claim greater expertise into a public sector context that studies and seeks to guide the behavior of millions of public servants.

Another possible explanation is that as a field of study, U.S. public administration remains captured by its origins in management and aspirations to become scientific. Managerial values are often at odds with legal values. Due process is not necessarily efficient process. Distributive issues are likely to be decided differently according to marginal costs than within the framework of the constitutional requirement of equal protection of the laws.

Law and science are also an uneasy fit. One can study many aspects of law scientifically—judicial and street-level enforcement behavior, compliance, the impact of legal liability, and much more. However, law has a fundamental normative component that does not seem amenable to scientific inquiry or resolution. U.S. courts are quite candid about making normative judgments. For instance, in a case involving the doctrine of state action, the Supreme Court noted, "What is fairly attributable [to the state] is a matter of normative judgment, and the criteria lack rigid simplicity" (*Brentwood Academy v. Tennessee Secondary School Athletic Association* 2001, 295). In another case, the Court reasoned that the cruel and unusual punishments clause of the Eighth Amendment "must draw its meaning from the evolving standards of decency that mark the progress of a maturing society" (*Rhodes v. Chapman* 1981, 346). More complexly, many legislative and judicial decisions involve normative trade-offs. For instance, which of the following should be valued more when conflicts arise: free exercise of religion or the prohibition against government establishment of religion; freedom of speech or a quiet neighborhood; individual privacy or public safety? Anyone who has read many Supreme Court constitutional law decisions can attest that the normative quality of law sometimes makes both the majority and dissenting opinions convincing.

On a deeper level, public administration and law incorporate different mind-sets that act to frustrate their integration. U.S. constitutional law tends to be contractarian in outlook, whereas public administration is utilitarian (benefit-cost) and instrumental (cost-effectiveness). The Declaration of Independence succinctly (and famously) captures the contractarian roots of the constitutional order: "We hold these Truths to be self-evident, that all Men are created equal, that they are endowed by their Creator with certain unalienable Rights, that among these are Life, Liberty, and the Pursuit of Happiness—That to secure these Rights, Governments are instituted among Men, deriving their just Powers from the Consent of the Governed." Contractarianism has two features that are salient here. First, government is established by the consent of the governed. It is "we the people" who by mutual agreement created the U.S. federal government for the purposes set out in the Constitution's preamble. Government is contractually bound, in a sense, to fulfill or at least not undermine those ends. Second, individual rights are natural rights that predate government rather than owe their existence to it. This is most clearly expressed by the Ninth Amendment: "The enumeration in the Constitution, of certain rights, shall not be construed to deny or disparage others retained by the people." The First, Second, and Fourth Amendment references to "the right of the people" similarly assumes that the rights they protect preexist the Constitution and the government it creates. The listing of these rights has nothing to do with their origins—it simply identifies them. Theoretically, these rights would be protected by the Ninth Amendment—and just as strongly—even if they were not enumerated.   Contractarianism is not absolute, but it makes benefit-cost and cost-effectiveness irrelevant or of secondary concern. This is epitomized by the Fifth Amendment's "takings clause": "nor shall private property be taken for public use without just compensation." No matter how much the polity might benefit from taking someone's land for a road, dam, bridge, missile site, or other public good, government cannot take private land if it cannot afford, or is unwilling to pay, a just price for it. Contractarian property rights trump utilitarian calculations. Extrapolating from private property, the clause reflects the principle that public goods should not be produced by unshared private burdens. This principle militates against abridging individual rights because they are costly to protect or for the sake of administrative convenience. In a jail reform case, a federal district court explained, "Inadequate resources can never be an adequate justification for the state's depriving any person of his constitutional rights. If the state cannot obtain the resources to detain persons awaiting trial in accordance with minimum constitutional standards, then the state simply will not be permitted to detain such persons" (*Hamilton v. Love* 1971, 1194). In an equal protection case, the Supreme Court similarly reasoned that "the fact that the implementation of a program capable of providing individualized consideration [of each applicant to the University of Michigan College of Literature, Science, and the Arts] might present administrative challenges does not render constitutional an otherwise problematic system" (*Gratz v. Bollinger* 2003, 275).

More generally, constitutional law requires that when some rights are abridged, the incursion on them be by the means that are least restrictive of the exercise of those rights or narrowly tailored so that abridgments closely fit the achievement of the government's purpose. The least restrictive alternative and narrow tailoring requirements may make public policies and administrative actions more expensive without increasing the intended benefits. However, contractarianism demands that when individuals are compelled to sacrifice their rights for the common good, the loss should be minimized.

These aspects of contractarianism are clearly at odds with a great deal of public administrative interest in maximizing benefit-cost ratios and achieving high levels of cost-effectiveness. Perhaps the best—but certainly not the only—example is in budgeting. The core idea of modern public budget theory was explained by Vern Lewis in 1952: "Budget decisions must be made on the basis of relative values. . . . The results must be more valuable than they would be if the money were used for any other purpose," and "the results must be worth their cost in terms of alternative results foregone or displaced" (Lewis 1952, 213–214, 215). In order to see where this logic can lead if unchecked by contractarian constitutional law, one has to look only as far as the treatment of prisoners before the Eighth Amendment was first applied to the conditions of their confinement in the late 1960s, or to residential public mental health facilities before involuntarily confined patients gained a right to treatment in the 1970s, or to a broad range of litigation dealing with public administrative violations of individual rights in the 1950s and 1960s (see Rosenbloom and O'Leary 1997; Rosenbloom, O'Leary, and Chanin 2010).

In the U.S. Madisonian system of checks and balances, it was virtually certain that once the modern administrative state developed, it would be retrofitted into the constitutional separation of powers and made to comport with constitutional values. To a substantial extent, the nation accomplished this from the mid-twentieth century forward. Retrofitting contributed mightily to public administration's contemporary legal dimensions. However, it came from outside public administration into it rather than from inside administrative doctrine and practice. Not being a creation of public administration, these dimensions are easily viewed negatively as unnecessarily complicating theory, practice, and education in the field. The next three sections explain the field's legal dimensions in terms of the models mentioned earlier with the intent of making law more accessible and central to public administrative thought.

THE MADISONIAN MODEL: THE SEPARATION OF POWERS

The Madisonian model for the separation of powers is an overarching legal dimension of U.S. public administration (see Bertelli and Lynn 2006; Rosenbloom 1983). It is familiar to students of U.S. government and is a leading framework for analyzing the impact of the Constitution on federal administration. The model rests on the assumption that the constitutional separation of powers and system of checks and balances promote incentives for both Congress and the presidency to control administrative agencies. In Madison's words, "the great security against a gradual concentration of the several powers in the same department, consists in giving to those who administer each department, the necessary constitutional means, and personal motives, to resist encroachments of the others" (*Federalist* 51, 268). This can be achieved by connecting "[t]he interest of the man . . . with the constitutional rights of the place" so that "ambition [is] made to counteract ambition" (268).

Madison emphatically rejected the notion that the three branches of government should be completely separate from one another: "it is not require[d] that the legislative, executive, and judiciary departments, should be wholly unconnected with each other"; rather, they should "be so far connected and blended as to give each a constitutional control over the others" (*Federalist* 48, 256). Nevertheless, researchers looking through the Madisonian lens tend to view the relationship between Congress and the presidency as zero-sum. For instance, after assessing 141 post–World War II federal administrative reforms, Paul Light concluded that "69 *shift* power toward the president, 37 toward Congress" (1997, 205; emphasis added). Similarly, several researchers spawned a substantial debate over whether there is presidential or congressional dominance of federal agencies (among others, see McCubbins and Schwartz 1984; McCubbins, Noll, and Weingast 1989; Katzmann 1994; Wood and Waterman 1994; Weingast and Moran 1983; Calvert, McCubbins, and Weingast 1989; Vogler 1993).

Madison foresaw the zero-sum potential and had a "remedy" for the "inconveniency" that "in republican government, the legislative authority necessarily predominates." Bicameralism, in his view, would keep the legislature in check by dividing it "into different branches; and to render them, by different modes of election, and different principles of action, as little connected with each other, as the nature of their common functions, and their common dependence on the society, will admit" (*Federalist* 51, 269).

It remains a moot point whether the constitutional design anticipates a large role for Congress in federal administration. The Constitution gives Congress a great deal of authority over administrative matters: All offices must be established and all money drawn from the treasury by law. Congressional action is necessary to create, empower, structure, staff, house, and fund federal agencies. Theoretically, Congress holds the ultimate trump card with respect to administration. By *inaction* in the annual federal budget cycle, it can fail to fund agencies. No funds, no agency— which is a weapon too powerful to use except in highly unusual circumstances. However, it is also one that can be used to reduce agency budgets through calibrated legislative action. For these reasons, W.F. Willoughby, a leading public administration scholar in the 1920s and 1930s, considered Congress to be "the source" and "possessor of all administrative authority" (Willoughby 1927, 11; 1934, 115, 157).

As Madison anticipated, however, fragmented congressional structure makes coordination difficult. Light (1997, 206) noted that "Congress was still quite capable of loaning the keys to administrative reform to the presidency" with respect to paperwork reduction. But what else could it do? Its committee structure makes it impossible to coordinate all the forms federal agencies use to obtain information from the general public. Congress gave this project to the Office of Management and Budget in the Executive Office of the President, which potentially has the wherewithal to coordinate agency action and thereby reduce the staggering paperwork burden generated by federal agencies.[1]

Also writing in *The Federalist,* Alexander Hamilton picks up on Madison's point regarding fragmentation with specific regard to administration. Hamilton noted, "The administration of government, in its largest sense, comprehends all the operations of the body politic, whether legislative, executive, or judiciary; but in its most usual, and perhaps its most precise signification, it is limited to executive details, and falls peculiarly within the province of the executive department" (*Federalist* 72, 374). Hamilton thought that despite Congress's far-reaching constitutional powers, federal administration would of necessity be dominated by the president. He contended that an energetic executive is "essential to the steady administration of the laws" (*Federalist* 70, 362). Energy and the unity of the presidential office went together because "decision, activity, secrecy, and dispatch, will generally characterize the proceedings of one man, in a much more eminent degree than the proceedings of any greater number; and in proportion as the number is increased, these qualities will be diminished" (*Federalist* 70, 363).

The Constitution's vagueness with respect to presidential power can be used both to strengthen and to weaken Hamilton's view of the president as the primary force behind effective administration. Article 2 of the Constitution vests "the executive power" in the president but does not specify its content or scope. Article 2 also authorizes the president "to take care that the laws be faithfully executed." Some presidents and analysts have read these clauses as conveying broad inherent and implied powers over administration. Others read them more narrowly. With respect to domestic matters, the Supreme Court has generally taken the latter approach. Historical research is inconclusive, leaving presidential power and the presidency to be largely what presidents make of the office (Neustadt 1991; Skowronek 1997).

Following the zero-sum approach, Hamiltonian thinking often leads to prescribing a diminished role for Congress in federal administration. The 1937 President's Committee on Administrative Management, whose work eventually led to creation of the Executive Office of the President, sought to establish clear presidential dominance of federal administration. The legislative package it generated was denounced in Congress as the "dictator bill," and one senator seemed to sum up the disgust of others in declaring that "no member of that committee had any real belief in Congress or any real use for the legislative department of government" (Karl 1963, 24; Polenberg 1966, 127; see Rosenbloom 2000, 16–20, for more context). The committee maintained that the president should have "final authority to determine the uses of appropriations, conditions of [federal government] employment, the letting of contracts, and the control over administrative decisions, as well as the prescribing of accounting procedures" (President's Committee on Administrative Management 1937, 22). Congress's role was essentially to fund agencies and get out of the way: "[O]nce the Congress has made an appropriation, an appropriation which it is free to withhold, the responsibility for the administration of the expenditures under that appropriation is and should be solely upon the Executive" (President's Committee on Administrative Management 1937, 49–50). Importantly, the committee explicitly admonished Congress not to impose "upon the Executive in too great detail minute requirements for the organization and operation of the administrative machinery" which absolve "the President . . . from part of his executive responsibility" (President's Committee on Administrative Management 1937, 49). Although the committee averred that Congress had a legitimate constitutional role in overseeing federal administration, it blamed legislative disorganization for failure to do so effectively. Several of these themes are reflected in subsequent calls for federal administrative reform, most recently by the National Performance Review (Arnold 1986; Gore 1993, 17, 20, 34).

As explained in the next section, in 1946 Congress developed a legislative-centered approach to federal administration in an effort to restore its coequality with the outsized post–New Deal, post–World War II presidency. Having achieved considerable success by the 1970s, a growing consensus held that federal administration is under the "joint custody" of Congress and the president (Rourke 1993). Rather than one branch dominating, the kind of blending favored by Madison enabled the two branches to share influence over administration on different levels and in overlapping ways.

Joint Custody of Federal Administration

Joint custody is manifested in statutes such as the Inspector General Act (1978) and the Government Performance and Results Act (1993). Inspectors general are executive appointments who report to Congress. The president can dismiss them at will but must supply the reasons to Congress. They are likened to "congressional 'moles' within their agencies" (Moore and Gates 1986, 10; Gore 1993, 31). The Government Performance and Results Act requires agencies to consult with Congress (read committees and subcommittees) when engaging in mandatory periodic strategic planning. Although Congress has not consistently used this feature of the act to strengthen its influence over the agencies, it remains a tool that can be employed to enable (sub)committees to provide greater definition to the statutory missions and delegated legislative authority that empower agencies.

Constitutional interpretation by the Supreme Court also supports joint custody. In *Morrison v. Olson* (1988), the Court made it clear that federal administration is subordinate to all three branches of government. The decision upheld the constitutionality of the independent counsel provisions of the 1978 Ethics in Government Act. The act provided that when requested by the attorney general, a court called the Special Division would appoint an independent counsel. The independent counsel had the "full power and independent authority to exercise all investigative and prosecutorial functions and powers of the Department of Justice, the Attorney General, and any other officer or employee of the Department of Justice" (*Morrison v. Olson* 1988, 663). Armed with this authority, independence was also ensured by the provision that the independent counsel could be dismissed "by the personal action of the Attorney General . . . only for good cause, physical disability, mental incapacity, or any other condition that substantially impairs the performance" of his or her duties (*Morrison v. Olson* 1988, 663). The Special Division was authorized to terminate the independent counsels upon completion of their missions. The statute specifically gave Congress oversight of the independent counsel's performance.

From a *separation* of powers perspective, the statute was extraordinary. Using its statutory and constitutional authority, Congress provided for a court to appoint an individual to a core executive post in which he or she could exercise the powers of the Department of Justice and yet was subject to dismissal only by the attorney general for limited causes. In upholding the statute, the Court reasoned that the independent counsel was an inferior officer whose appointment did not require Senate confirmation and that the appointment, termination, and related duties it thrust on the Special Division did not violate article 3 of Constitution, which limits the judicial power to deciding cases and controversies. The core of the Court's holding was that nothing in the act "sufficiently deprives the President of control over the independent counsel to interfere impermissibly with his constitutional obligation to ensure the faithful execution of the laws" (*Morrison v. Olson* 1988, 693). Looking for clearer boundaries among the three branches a lone dissenting Justice Antonin Scalia was incredulous at the majority's decision: "There are now no lines. If the removal of a prosecutor, the virtual embodiment of the [president's] power to 'take care that the laws be faithfully executed,' can be restricted, what officer's removal cannot?" (*Morrison v. Olson* 1988, 726).

Morrison interpreted the Madisonian model to provide for separate institutions sharing power over administration. The Supreme Court read the Constitution to provide the president with something far less than exclusive authority over the agencies and officers of the national government. Its ruling is in keeping with the Supreme Court's 1838 decision in *Kendall v. U.S.,* which remains good law today: "It would be an alarming doctrine that congress [*sic*] cannot impose upon any executive officer any duty they may think proper, which is not repugnant to any rights secured and protected by the constitution [*sic*]; and in such cases, the duty and responsibility grow out of and are subject to the control of the law, and not the direction of the President" (*Kendall v. U.S.* 1838, 610).

By 1988, then, it seemed settled that, constitutionally, the executive branch was subject to joint custody or, more accurately as the judicial model for infusion of constitutional rights into public administrative practice explains, tripartite control. However, President George W. Bush's administration had a different perspective and pushed the Madisonian model away from shared and blended control toward a more rigid separation of powers in which the executive branch would overwhelmingly be the domain of the president.

Unitary Executive Branch Theory

The Bush-Cheney administration interpreted executive power under the Constitution very broadly, reflecting a version of the theory that the executive branch is unitary. Christopher Yoo, Steven Calabresi, Anthony Coangelo, and Laurence Nee prominently developed this theory in a series of law review articles covering interbranch conflicts from the founding to 2004. It holds that "all three branches of the federal government have the power and duty to interpret the Constitution and the meaning of the Constitution is determined through the dynamic interaction of all three branches" (Yoo, Calabresi, and Colangelo 2005, 606). This power and duty cannot be left to the Supreme Court alone "[b]ecause the Supreme Court is often an interested party in separation of powers disputes [and] permitting it to act as the final arbiter would contravene the jurisprudential rule against permitting parties from being judges in their own cases" (Yoo, Calabresi, and Nee

2004, 6). The theory maintains that the president has unfettered power to "remove subordinate policy-making officials at will," "to direct the manner in which subordinate officials exercise discretionary executive power," and to "veto or nullify such officials' exercises of discretionary executive power" (Yoo, Calabresi, and Colangelo 2005, 607).

As developed by these authors, it is obvious that the unitary executive branch theory is at odds with Supreme Court rulings such as *Morrison* and *Kendall* as well as a great deal of historical and contemporary practice. Anticipating this criticism, Yoo, Calabresi, and Colangelo (2005, 607) "do not claim that there is a consensus among all three branches of government as to the president's control of the removal power and of the powers to direct and nullify. Rather [they] claim only that there is no consistent, three-branch custom, tradition, or practice to which presidents have acquiesced permitting congressionally imposed limits on the president's sole power to execute the law."

Taken to its logical conclusion, this theory would go a long way toward placing the executive branch solely under the president and preventing Congress from prescribing administrative procedures for rule making, adjudication, transparency, human resources management, and other activities. To the extent that Congress did vest discretionary authority in executive branch officials, the theory would permit the president to exercise it personally regardless of where the law placed it. For instance, regardless of the president's level of expertise in environmental science and policy, he could directly exercise a congressional delegation of legislative authority to the Environmental Protection Agency to make rules for clean air or any other matter. Indeed, he could personally take over the rule-making authority of any or all executive branch agencies.[2] Presumably, following the President's Committee on Administrative Management, it would also mean that once Congress appropriates money to the executive branch, it is up to the president to determine how it should be spent. If implemented, the theory would dramatically strengthen the president's and weaken Congress's role in federal administration.

President George W. Bush made it clear in a series of signing statements that he subscribed to a version of the theory of a unitary executive branch. Signing statements are "official pronouncements" that a president may make upon signing a legislative bill into law (Halstead 2006, 1). These statements may include general comments about the law, the president's interpretation of it, how he proposes to administer it, and any constitutional or other objections he may have to one or more of its provisions (Halstead 2006, 1). Signing statements reach back to the presidency of James Monroe (1817–25). Relative to historic practice, Bush's signing statements were much more apt to assert that the laws being signed encroached on presidential power and would be implemented "in a manner consistent with the President's constitutional authority to supervise the unitary executive branch" (Halstead 2006, 9; Van Bergen 2006, 3; American Bar Association 2006, 15; Rosenbloom 2010). This or similar language was used by Bush upon signing the USA Patriot Improvement and Reauthorization Act (2005), McCain Detainee Amendment (2005), and a variety of laws dealing with reporting and military matters. Collectively, Bush's statements add up to the proposition that because the president is constitutionally bound to protect the article 2 powers and functions of the presidential office, he is required to assess the constitutionality of statutory provisions and to ignore those he deems unconstitutional.

As the Madisonian model predicts, Bush's reliance on this formulation of the unitary executive branch theory generated substantial pushback. The American Bar Association Task Force on Presidential Signing Statements and the Separation of Powers Doctrine concluded that it is "contrary to the rule of law and our constitutional system of separation of powers" for a president "to claim the authority or state the intention to disregard or decline to enforce all or part of a law he has signed, or to interpret such a law in a manner inconsistent with the clear intent of Congress"

(American Bar Association 2006, 5; see also Pfiffner 2008). Critics maintain that if the president believes parts of a bill are unconstitutional, the oath of office requires him to veto it. During the run up to the 2008 presidential election, Republican candidate John McCain expressed this position, saying he would "[n]ever, never, never, never" issue signing statements because "[i]f I disagree with a law that passed, I'll veto it" (Abramowits 2008).

The future of unitary executive branch theory is uncertain. As a candidate, President Barack Obama was critical of Bush's signing statements. Nevertheless, in March 2009, he issued one of his own claiming that several provisions of the Omnibus Appropriations Act encroached on his constitutional authority and would be treated as nonbinding (Obama 2009a). However, in so doing, Obama did not rely on unitary executive branch theory.

What is more certain is that the Madisonian model will continue to beget interbranch conflicts and tensions over control of federal administration. The question of the relative roles of the president and Congress in federal administration was raised in the earliest days of the Republic by the "Decision of 1789,"[3] and as Madison predicted, it remains for presidents and congresses to find workable answers for the conditions of the nation during their times. This dynamic interplay between the president and Congress forms U.S. public administration's longest recurring legal dimension.

THE 1946 LEGISLATIVE-CENTERED MODEL FOR ADMINISTRATIVE LAW

The 1946 legislative-centered model rests on three pillars: (1) Congress treats federal agencies as its adjuncts for performing legislative functions and regulates them through administrative law; (2) it supervises its adjuncts; and, (3) Congress and its members intercede in agency decision making regarding district-oriented spending and constituency service. The model was developed by Congress in 1946 out of concern that it might "lose its constitutional place in the Federal scheme" due to the vast growth of federal administration and presidential power during the New Deal and World War II (La Follette 1946, 11). By 1946, the scope of federal administration was so vast that any legislative effort to regain coequality in the separation of powers would necessarily require gaining greater control and influence over the agencies. For Congress, 1946 was very largely about strengthening its own operations and capacity rather than reining in or checking presidential power. In a very real sense, the exercise was one of "refounding" itself in response to the development of the administrative state (Rosenbloom 2000). Piecemeal efforts had been under way earlier, but putting all the pieces together had to wait until the conclusion of World War II.

ADMINISTRATIVE LAW

Regulating Federal Agencies as Adjuncts of Congress for Legislative Functions

By 1946, members of Congress realized that "as the country has grown and its activities have become more diversified and complex," they necessarily had to delegate more of their legislative authority to the agencies (U.S. Congress 1946, 5659). As Congressman Francis Walter explained: "There are the legislative functions of administrative agencies, where they issue general or particular regulations which in form or effect are like the statutes of the Congress. . . . Congress—if it had the time, the staff, and the organization—might itself prescribe these things. Because Congress does not do so itself and yet desires that these things be done, the legislative power to do them has been conferred upon administrative officers and agencies" (U.S. Congress 1946, 5648). For Congress in the 1930s, the question was about the propriety of delegation; by 1946, it was how to regulate and oversee its use (Rosenbloom 2000, 30–35). The Administrative Procedure Act (APA) of 1946 provided one part of the initial answer; the Legislative Reorganization Act of 1946, the other.

The APA treats administrative agencies as legislative adjuncts primarily through its rule-making provisions. It bases these on the straightforward premise that insofar as feasible, agency rule making should mimic legislative lawmaking. In Walter's words, "Day by day Congress takes account of the interests and desires of the people in framing legislation; and there is no reason why administrative agencies should not do so when they exercise legislative functions which the Congress has delegated to them" (U.S. Congress 1946, 5756).

The APA's original provisions for rule making are relatively straightforward. Judicial decisions, executive orders, and additional statutes have added great complexity over time. There are three general types of rules: legislative (substantive), procedural, and interpretive (or "interpretative," as written in the APA). Agencies are required to publish final rules in the *Federal Register,* but the APA establishes procedural requirements only for the enactment of legislative rules. These procedures are too complicated to discuss in detail here (see Rosenbloom 2003; Lubbers 2006). Essentially, as rule making has evolved, informal rule making requires the agency to publish a notice of proposed rule making, accept and consider comments from the public, issue a final rule, and allow at least thirty days for affected entities to begin conformance. Formal rule making involves quasi-judicial hearings and processes. It is used far less frequently than informal rule making, may be presided over by an administrative law judge, and requires final rules to be supported by substantial evidence on the record as a whole. Direct final rules are published in the *Federal Register* and go into effect at a specified future date unless adverse comments are filed. Interim final rules are immediately effective upon publication and may be withdrawn after comments are received. Hybrid rule making allows an agency to combine informal and formal rule-making formats by grafting hearings or other types of input sessions onto notice and comment procedures. In negotiated rule making, agencies negotiate rules with committees of stakeholders. A good-cause exception allows agencies to make rules without a specified procedure other than publication in the *Federal Register* when normal requirements would be "impracticable, unnecessary, or contrary to the public interest" (APA 1946, section 553[a][3][b]).

Today, rule making is far more complex than originally required by the APA. Judicial decisions compel agencies to be able to defend the procedures and logic used to develop final rules. Rules can be rejected by courts because the notice of proposed rule making was inadequate, the relationship between it and the final rule was too attenuated, procedures were irregular, the agency failed to respond adequately to comments, the final rule is not supported by the record or logic, the agency failed to comply with a statute, and more. Executive orders give the Office of Management and Budget's Office of Information and Regulatory Affairs a large role in overseeing agencies' rule-making activity and the content of the rules they seek to propose. The substantive requirements of these orders change over time. However, they may require cost-benefit analysis and impact statements on a number of concerns such as inflation, vibrant federalism, family viability, and environmental justice. Additional legislation also requires a variety of impact assessments or statements as well, including consideration of how rules will affect small businesses and other entities. The Congressional Review Act (1996) creates an expedited procedure by which Congress may nullify major legislative rules before they go into effect.[4] Although Madisonian blending is certainly present with respect to rule making, overall, Congress has succeeded in regulating agencies' use of the legislative authority it delegates to them.

In the 1930s and 1940s, one of the complaints against federal administrative processes, including rule making, was that they were secretive. The Constitution requires each house of Congress to "keep a Journal of its Proceedings" for publication "from time to time" (article 1, section 5).

Following the idea that agencies should emulate legislative processes, the APA provided that they should release "matters of official record" to "persons properly and directly concerned" unless there were "good cause" or a statutory basis for not doing so (section 3[c]). "Properly and directly concerned" was interpreted as a standing requirement and became a basis for withholding information. Congress eventually tried to fix this problem through the Freedom of Information Act of 1966 and the Government in the Sunshine Act of 1976 (see Rosenbloom 2003, 119–133). Both acts view disclosure of agency records as the norm, and neither includes a general standing requirement. The Freedom of Information Act covers written records; the Sunshine Act covers multiheaded federal boards and commissions and brings transparency to their meetings. The 2007 Openness Promotes Effectiveness in our National Government Act (OPEN Government Act) strengthens the administration of freedom of information and extends it to some records generated by contractors.

The other two features of the 1946 legislative-centered model increase congressional control and influence over federal administration. They helped to make the model coherent and contributed to its institutionalization. However, they are given only cursory review here because they are tangential to federal administration's legal dimensions (for a fuller analysis, see Rosenbloom 2000).

Supervising the Agencies

From a Madisonian perspective, it is axiomatic that if agencies function as legislative adjuncts, Congress will supervise them. As Senator Robert La Follette Jr., a chief sponsor of the Legislative Reorganization Act of 1946, explained, having "delegated its rule-making power to" the agencies, Congress needed to establish "regular arrangements for follow-up in order to assure itself that administrative rules and regulations are in accord with the intent of the law" (La Follette 1946, 45).

The Legislative Reorganization Act was designed to improve Congress's capacity to legislate and oversee federal administration. It reduced the unwieldy number of standing committees in both houses, charged them with exercising "continuous watchfulness" of the agencies under their jurisdiction, and revamped their configuration so that their organization would be parallel in each chamber *and* the overall structure would be coordinated "with the pattern of the administrative branch" (U.S. Congress 1946, 10054). It also provided for each committee to hire professional staff to help with legislation and oversight. In addition, it contained several provisions intended to strengthen Congress's role in federal budgeting.

The Legislative Reorganization Act of 1970 strengthened Congress's oversight mission by calling on the standing committees more actively to "review and study, on a continuing basis, the application, administration, and execution of those laws, or parts of laws" under their jurisdiction (section 118). It also reorganized the Legislative Reference Service into the Congressional Research Service in an effort to provide Congress with a modern-style "think tank," which can enhance its capacity to steer federal administration. As mentioned earlier, the Government Performance and Results Act (1993) goes further by involving Congress in agency strategic planning. It also requires annual performance reporting, which can improve congressional monitoring of the agencies.

Interceding for Districts and Constituents

The Legislative Reorganization Act of 1946 established a retirement system for members of Congress. Its provision for "continuous watchfulness" anticipated that the members would have sufficient expertise to supervise the agencies, which requires long tenure. Whether intentional or coincidental, the 1946 legislative-centered model helped to generate the "career Congress" (Hibbing 1991). Morris Fiorina's 1977 and 1989 analyses of the decline in competitive congressional seats identify three main elements, each connected to 1946. First, the members quickly saw electoral advantage in delegating controversial policy matters to the agencies and then criticizing administrative action when it was unpopular with the voters back home. Second, casework, and third, district oriented public works spending "are basically pure profit" in terms of incumbency (Fiorina 1977, 45). Each of the latter two was facilitated by actions taken in 1946.

The Legislative Reorganization bill contained a provision for the members of Congress to hire additional personal staff. One member called it "the single, most valuable part of the bill, from the standpoint of the Congressman's work" because staffers could "take responsibility, especially in handling matters with the executive departments, thereby freeing us for our primary responsibility, namely, to study national problems and devise and enact wise legislation to deal with them" (U.S. Congress 1946, 10084). The provision was defeated in the House, but beginning in 1947 the senators began hiring personal staff for casework and other purposes and the House members eventually followed suit. Starting from a base of about two thousand personal staff in both houses combined in 1947, the number reached almost twelve thousand by the 1990s, of which about 47 percent were stationed in the home districts and states rather than in Washington, DC (Ornstein, Mann, and Malbin 1996, 127, 131, 133, 135).

District-oriented public works spending, often called "pork barrel," goes back to the Rivers and Harbors legislation of 1824 (Fitzgerald and Lipson 1984, viii). During the New Deal, federal public works were a major strategy for economic recovery. In the economic emergency, Congress lost much of its traditional control of where the money went. The Employment Act of 1946 is best known for ratifying Keynesian fiscal policy and creating the Council of Economic Advisers. However, rationalizing public works spending and making it wholly dependent on Congress were also among its core purposes. The idea behind this part of the act was for Congress to develop a prioritized list of public works for federal funding and to authorize their undertaking based on the level of economic stimulus necessary to reduce unemployment. From the members' standpoint, a key feature of the act was that "it all depends on Congress" and "does not authorize the Executive to spend a dime" (U.S. Congress 1945, 8954, 8959, 9055).

As noted earlier, the importance of casework and public works spending to public administration's legal dimensions lies primarily in their contribution to the legislators' incumbency, which helped institutionalize the 1946 legislative-centered model for administrative law.

THE JUDICIAL MODEL FOR INFUSING CONSTITUTIONAL RIGHTS INTO PUBLIC ADMINISTRATIVE PRACTICE

The federal judiciary began to infuse constitutional rights into public administrative practice in the early 1950s. By 1975, this infusion crystallized into a systematic model that remains the framework for defining constitutional rights in the context of U.S. public administration. Like the 1946 legislative-centered model, the judicial constitutional rights infusion model is coherent in that its individual features are mutually supportive. However, it developed incrementally in a variety of court decisions rather than according to an overall plan or "refounding." The underlying concern was that the rise of the administrative state, coupled with public administrative doctrine and practice, threatened to undermine individuals' constitutional rights and freedoms. Disquiet with administrative power was expressed in many judicial quarters, but perhaps nowhere more strenuously and consistently than by Supreme Court Justice William Douglas. In three cases in the early 1970s, he admonished his colleagues that "the bureaucracy of modern government is not only slow, lumbering, and oppressive; it is omnipresent"; "today's mounting bureaucracy, both at the state and federal levels, promises to be suffocating and repressive unless it is put into the harness of procedural due process"; and "the sovereign of this Nation is the people, not the bureaucracy" (*Wyman v. James* 1971, 335; *Spady v. Mount Vernon* 1974, 985; *U.S. v. Richardson* 1974, 201).

The judicial constitutional rights infusion model has two main components: (1) establishing previously undeclared constitutional rights for individuals in their encounters with public administration as clients and customers, public employees, inmates in prison, involuntarily confined patients in public mental health facilities, contractors, and subjects in street-level regulatory interactions; and (2) facilitating the enforcement of these rights. Enforcement, in turn, has three subcomponents: (a) relaxing the requirements of standing to sue government; (b) developing remedial law; and (c) making most public employees potentially personally liable in civil suits for money damages if they violate "clearly established statutory or constitutional rights of which a reasonable person would have known" (*Harlow v. Fitzgerald* 1982, 818). These are analyzed at length elsewhere and need only be outlined here (see Rosenbloom and O'Leary 1997; Rosenbloom, O'Leary, and Chanin, 2010).

Constitutional Rights in Administrative Encounters

Historically, clients, customers, and public employees lacked constitutional rights in their encounters with public administration due to a judicial construction called the "doctrine of privilege." It held that benefits and jobs conveyed by the government were privileges rather than rights and, therefore, one who voluntarily received them could not contest the conditions on which they were offered. Although somewhat illogical, the doctrine extended to the distribution of privileges, making discrimination largely safe from challenge under the Fourteenth Amendment's equal protection clause. The doctrine of privilege led to abridgments of clients,' customers,' and public employees' substantive, privacy, procedural due process, and equal protection rights. The Supreme Court began to replace the doctrine in the 1950s and by 1972 declared that it had "fully and finally rejected the wooden distinction between 'rights' and 'privileges' that once seemed to govern the applicability of procedural due process rights" (*Board of Regents v. Roth* 1972, 571). It was replaced by three doctrinal approaches that developed more or less simultaneously: new property, unconstitutional conditions, and modern equal protection of the laws.

New property doctrine redefined civil service employment and government benefits, such as welfare, contracts, and occupational and other licenses, as a form of property (see Reich 1964). In treating them as new property, the federal courts applied procedural due process to their deprivation and termination.[5] Procedural due process typically requires judges to balance the potential harm to an individual, the constitutional interest in correct decision making to prevent arbitrary governmental action, and the government's interest in avoiding administratively cumbersome, time-consuming, and expensive decision-making procedures. Depending on the circumstances, it can require agencies to hold elaborate hearings before terminating what were once considered privileges not subject to constitutional protection. New property doctrine has substantial impacts in many areas of administration, particularly welfare and public sector human resources management.

Unconstitutional conditions doctrine protects substantive rights, including freedom of speech, religion, and association, and privacy. It regulates the conditions government may attach to the benefits and jobs it supplies. Conditions that significantly impinge on the exercise of constitutional rights are likely to be unconstitutional unless the government has a compelling interest in making them part of the administrative scheme (see Baker 1990; Rosenbloom and O'Leary 1997, 134–138).

Modern equal protection doctrine controls the distribution of government benefits and jobs. It has a three-tier structure. Administrative and public policy classifications based on race or ethnicity are considered "suspect," as are classifications based on citizenship at the state and local governmental levels, but not at the federal level.[6] Suspect classifications are subject to strict scrutiny, meaning that the reviewing court will not be deferential to the government's claims. The government is required to demonstrate that it has a compelling interest for employing the classification and that its use is narrowly tailored to closely fit the achievement of that interest. In the context of affirmative action policies, which may serve a compelling governmental interest, narrow tailoring is fairly well defined. It requires (1) assessing the efficacy of alternative policies that do not use suspect classifications; (2) a fixed stopping point; (3) individualized consideration of each applicant; (4) a waiver provision so that adequate staffing is never foreclosed; (5) that individuals who are not members of the affirmative action target groups are not made significantly worse off in an objective sense;[7] and (6) proportionality in terms of the relevant population (*Gratz v. Bollinger* 2003; *Grutter v. Bollinger* 2003).

Classifications based on factors such as residency, wealth, and age are nonsuspect. The burden of persuasion is on the challenger to show that they are not rationally related to a legitimate governmental purpose. Classifications based on sex (male/female) are subject to intermediate scrutiny. The government must be exceedingly persuasive in demonstrating that they are substantially related to the achievement of an important governmental purpose (*U.S. v. Virginia* 1996).

In addition to these doctrinal developments, in the late 1960s and early 1970s, Eighth Amendment protection was expanded to cover the conditions of confinement (see *Rhodes v. Chapman* 1981). Involuntarily confined public mental health patients received a substantive due process right to treatment and habilitation (*Wyatt v. Stickney* 1971; *Youngberg v. Romeo* 1982). In the 1990s, the free speech rights of contractors and entities involved in noncontractual preexisting commercial relationships with government were interpreted to parallel those of public employees (*Board of County Commissioners, Wabaunsee County v. Umber* 1996; see also *O'Hare Truck Service v. City of Northlake* 1996).

Turning to enforcement, standing to sue was relaxed to the point that "one who is hurt by governmental action has standing to challenge it" (Davis 1975, 72). Standing requires an individual injury (or imminent injury) that is concrete and particularized, attributable to government action, and subject to redress through a judicial decision. Historically, "concrete" was generally interpreted narrowly. However, by the 1970s it could include injuries to aesthetic, recreational, and other somewhat intangible interests. Standing is flexible, and some post-1990 cases seem to make it more difficult to obtain, whereas others do not (see *Lujan v. Defenders of Wildlife* 1992; *Massachusetts v. Environmental Protection Agency* 2007).

The courts developed remedial law in cases dealing with public school desegregation and prison and public mental health reform. The essence of the remedial law case is that the remedy extends well beyond the original plaintiffs and requires the court to oversee the implementation of thoroughgoing institutional reforms that may take a decade or more to complete. By the late 1970s, remedial law was a well-established means of vindicating equal protection rights in public school and government personnel systems, as well as Eighth Amendment rights in prisons.

Finally, by 1975, public employees' historic absolute immunity from constitutional tort suits was redefined as qualified immunity only. This was the capstone of the judicial constitutional rights infusion model because it created a strong incentive for public employees to know and respect the clearly established constitutional rights of the individuals upon whom they act. Local governments face constitutional tort liability if their policies, including failure to train, lead directly to violations of individuals' constitutional rights (*City of Canton v. Harris* 1989; *Pembaur v. City of Cincinnati* 1986). State and federal agencies cannot be sued for money damages in this type of litigation. Qualified immunity transcends retrospective enforcement. Because constitutional rights are what the courts declare they are, qualified immunity provides the judiciary with proactive leverage over public administrative behavior. When the courts rule that a customer, client, prisoner, or other individual has procedural due process, equal protection, or other constitutional rights, knowledge of these rights and the duty to protect them become a matter of job competence for public administrators (Rosenbloom and O'Leary 1997, 301–323).

As developed by 1975, the judicial constitutional rights infusion model remains in place, notwithstanding an almost complete change in the composition of the Supreme Court (Justice John Paul Stevens being the only holdover as of this writing). The Court has expanded rights in some areas (property under the takings clause and contractors' free speech rights), reduced them in others (aspects of public employees' freedom of speech and Fourth Amendment rights generally), provided greater equal protection when public policy classifications are based on sex, and, depending on one's interpretation, either expanded or contracted equal protection rights in the context of affirmative action-like policies in public employment, government contracting, and public university education (expanded if one thinks equal protection should be color-blind, contracted if color conscious).[8] The Supreme Court never displayed great enthusiasm for remedial law, which is typically a product of the federal district courts, and it may be even less inclined to support it now than previously (*Parents Involved in Community Schools v. Seattle School District No. 1* and *Meredith v. Jefferson County Board of Education* 2007 [decided together]). The Court also declined to extend constitutional tort liability to federal agencies and contractors (*Federal Deposit Insurance Corporation v. Meyer* 1994; *Correctional Services Corp. v. Malesko* 2001). However, none of the components of the judicial constitutional rights infusion model has been substantially changed, and public administration remains infused with constitutional rights.

THE FUTURE: THE PERDURABILITY OF PUBLIC ADMINISTRATION'S LEGAL DIMENSIONS

U.S. public administration's contemporary legal dimensions are highly likely to persist into the foreseeable future. The Madisonian model has defined some aspects of federal administration since the founding. Within its overall framework, the presidency and Congress share joint custody over federal administration. Depending on political, economic, and security circumstances, one institution or the other *or both* may expand control. Presidential influence over the agencies increased dramatically during the New Deal and World War II. Using the 1946 legislative-centered model, Congress imposed its values on federal administration in the immediate post-Watergate period by enacting the Federal Advisory Committee Act (1972), Privacy Act (1974), major amendments to the Freedom of Information Act (1974), Congressional Budget and Impoundment Control Act (1974), Government in the Sunshine Act (1976), Ethics in Government Act (1978), and Inspector General Act (1978). During the prolonged security threat brought home by the terrorist attacks of September 11, 2001, President Bush pushed the limits of executive power with considerable success. However, limits remain. As the Supreme Court's plurality emphasized in *Hamdi v. Rumsfeld* (2004, 535–536), "We have long since made clear that a state of war is not a blank check for the President when it comes to the rights of the Nation's citizens." Two days into his administration, on January 22, 2009, President Obama issued an executive order mandating closure of the terrorist detention facilities at the U.S. naval base at Guantánamo Bay (Obama 2009b). In May, Congress refused to fund the closure (see Murray 2009). The constitutional system of checks and balances continues to function as "A Machine That Would Go of Itself," as it has for 220 years, with the Civil War its only major breakdown (see Kamen 1987).

The 1946 legislative-centered model and the judicial model for infusing constitutional rights into public administrative practice are also institutionally well entrenched. The legislative-centered model has been in place for more than sixty years. It is well established and requires only sporadic maintenance, tinkering, and upgrading. It serves both Congress's interest in regulating and supervising federal administration as well as its members' desire for incumbency. The judicial model for the infusion of constitutional rights into administrative practice may be more fragile. A reversal of qualified immunity doctrine, a return to something like the doctrine of privilege, or a clear rejection of remedial law would seriously damage it and probably cause its demise. However, fully in place since 1975, it provides the federal courts with considerable retrospective and prospective leverage over administrative behavior affecting constitutional rights. It serves politically conservative members of the bench who may be inclined to protect property rights more and free speech rights less and to interpret the equal protection clause as a barrier to affirmative action policies, as well as liberal members disposed to expand substantive due process and other rights and to promote equality through race-conscious measures. From an institutional perspective, it is difficult to imagine why the judiciary would want to lose its leverage over public administration or what would impel the courts to surrender it.

What is far less certain is whether these legal dimensions—the separation of powers, administrative law, and constitutional law—will be fully integrated into public administrative theory, research, scholarship, and pedagogy. The academic field of public administration tends to be executive centered. To some extent, the movement toward redefinition of public administration as public management reinforces this tendency. Neither approach—an executive-centered nor a narrow public-management focus—bodes well for bringing law into the mainstream. An executive-centered lens will often see law as an interference with cost-beneficial and cost-effective administration. A public-management lens tends to focus on tools, techniques, and practices more than on political and legal contexts. The irony is that public managers in the executive branch are acutely aware of public administration's legal dimensions (Ban 1995; Bertelli and Lynn 2006). Perhaps by turning more attention to how public administrators actually do their jobs, as Maynard-Moody and Musheno (2003) did with police, teachers, and counselors at the street level, the field can gain a better understanding and appreciation of its legal dimensions.

NOTES

1. In 1994, before passage of the second Paperwork Reduction Act (1995), the annual paperwork burden was estimated to be 6.5 billion hours and to consume 9 percent of the GDP (Strauss et al. 1995, 872).

2. It is not clear whether the unitary executive branch theory would encompass the independent regulatory agencies, which as a matter of constitutional law are not considered part of the executive branch (see Moreno 1994).

3. The Decision of 1789 was to allow dismissal of the secretary of the Department of Foreign Affairs by the president without the Senate's concurrence. (See Rosenbloom 1971, 26–33, for an analysis.)

4. Major rules are defined as those expected to have an economic impact of $100 million annually or substantial effects on costs, prices, productivity, employment, or other key economic concerns.

5. Procedural due process applies to the termination of a benefit during the term for which it was offered, but not to its expiration.

6. This is because the federal government has comprehensive authority over immigration and naturalization.

7. A harsh burden should not be placed on so-called innocent third parties (i.e., nonminorities). Truncating their horizons by not offering promotion or training is not considered unduly harsh because, objectively, it leaves them in the same position they already occupy. Dismissal or demotion to make room for affirmative action eligibles would generally violate narrow tailoring.

8. For examples, see among many others *Dolan v. City of Tigard* 1994; *Lucas v. South Carolina*

Coastal Council 1992; *Board of County Commissioners, Wabaunsee County v. Umber* 1996; *O'Hare Truck Service v. City of Northlake* 1996; *Garcetti v. Ceballos* 2006; *Atwater v. City of Lago Vista* 2001; *Ricci v. DeStefano* 2009; *U.S. v. Virginia* 1996; *Adarand Constructors v. Pena* 1995; *Gratz v. Bollinger* 2003; *Grutter v. Bollinger* 2003.

REFERENCES

Abramowitz, Michael. 2008. On signing statements McCain says "never," Obama and Clinton, "sometimes." *Washington Post,* February 25, A13. www.washingtonpost.com/wp-dyn/content/article/2008/02/24/AR2008022401995.html.

Adarand Constructors v. Pena. 1995. 515 U.S. 200.

Administrative Procedure Act (APA). 1946. PL 79–404. 60 Stat. 237.

American Bar Association. 2006. Task force on presidential signing statements and the separation of powers doctrine: Report. www.abanet.org/op/signingstatements/aba_final_signing_statements_recommendation-report_7–24–06.pdf.

American Society for Public Administration Task Force on Educating for Excellence in the MPA Degree. 2008. Excellence in PA report, part 2. *PA Times* 31 (6): 21.

Appleby, Paul. 1949. *Policy and Administration.* University: University of Alabama Press.

Arnold, Peri. 1986. *Making the Managerial Presidency.* Princeton, NJ: Princeton University Press.

Atwater v. City of Lago Vista. 2001. 532 U.S. 318.

Baker, Lynn. 1990. The prices of rights. *Cornell University Law Review* 75:1185–1257.

Ban, Carolyn. 1995. *How Do Public Managers Manage?* San Francisco: Jossey-Bass.

Bertelli, Anthony, and Laurence Lynn Jr. 2006. *Madison's Managers.* Baltimore, MD: Johns Hopkins University Press.

Board of County Commissioners, Wabaunsee County v. Umber. 1996. 518 U.S. 668.

Board of Regents v. Roth. 1972. 408 U.S. 564.

Brentwood Academy v. Tennessee Secondary School Athletic Association. 2001. 531 U.S. 288.

Calvert, Randall, Mathew McCubbins, and Barry Weingast. 1989. A theory of political control of agency discretion. *American Journal of Political Science* 33 (August): 588–611.

City of Canton v. Harris. 1989. 489 U.S. 378.

Correctional Services Corp. v. Malesko. 2001. 534 U.S. 61.

Davis, Kenneth. 1975. *Administrative Law and Government.* St. Paul, MN: West.

Dimock, Marshall. 1980. *Law and Dynamic Administration.* New York: Praeger.

Dolan v. City of Tigard. 1994. 512 U.S. 374.

Federal Deposit Insurance Corporation v. Meyer. 1994. 510 U.S. 471.

Federalist, The. 2001. Ed. George Carey and James McClellan. Indianapolis: Liberty Fund. Originally published in 1787–1788.

Fiorina, Morris. 1977. *Congress: Keystone of the Washington Establishment.* New Haven, CT: Yale University Press.

———. 1989. *Congress: Keystone of the Washington Establishment.* 2d ed. New Haven, CT: Yale University Press.

Fitzgerald, Randall, and Gerald Lipson. 1984. *Porkbarrel.* Washington, DC: Cato Institute.

Garcetti v. Ceballos. 2006. 547 U.S. 410.

Gore, Al. 1993. *From Red Tape to Results: Creating a Government That Works Better and Costs Less.* Washington, DC: U.S. Government Printing Office.

Gratz v. Bollinger. 2003. 539 U.S. 244.

Grutter v. Bollinger. 2003. 539 U.S. 306.

Gulick, Luther. 1937. Science, values, and public administration. In *Papers on the Science of Administration,* ed. Luther Gulick and L. Urwick, 189–202. New York: Institute of Public Administration.

Gulick, Luther, and L. Urwick, eds. 1937. *Papers on the Science of Administration.* New York: Institute of Public Administration.

Halstead, T.J. 2006. *Presidential Signing Statements.* Washington, DC: Congressional Research Service.

Hamdi v. Rumsfeld. 2004. 542 U.S. 507.

Hamilton v. Love. 1971. 328 F. Supp. 1182.

Harlow v. Fitzgerald. 1982. 457 U.S. 800.

Hibbing, John. 1991. *Congressional Careers.* Chapel Hill, NC: University of North Carolina Press.

Kamen, Michael. 1987. *A Machine That Would Go of Itself.* New York, NY: Knopf.

Karl, Barry. 1963. *Executive Reorganization and Reform in the New Deal.* Cambridge, MA: Harvard University Press.

Katzmann, Robert. 1994. Explaining agency decision-making. In *Handbook of Regulation and Administrative Law,* ed. David Rosenbloom and Richard Schwartz, 325–341. New York: Marcel Dekker.

Kendall v. U.S. 1838. 37 U.S. 524.

Kettl, Donald. 2002. *The Transformation of Governance.* Baltimore, MD: Johns Hopkins University Press.

La Follette, Robert. 1946. Congress wins a victory over Congress. *New York Times Magazine,* August 4, 11ff.

Legislative Reorganization Act. 1946. PL 79–601. 60 Stat. 812.

———. 1970. PL 91–510. 84 Stat. 1140.

Lewis, Vern. 1952. Toward a theory of budgeting. In *Classics of Public Administration.* 2d ed., ed. Jay Shafritz and Albert Hyde, 213–229. Chicago: Dorsey Press.

Light, Paul. 1997. *The Tides of Reform.* New Haven, CT: Yale University Press.

Lubbers, Jeffrey. 2006. *A Guide to Federal Agency Rulemaking.* 4th ed. Chicago: American Bar Association.

Lucas v. South Carolina Coastal Council. 1992. 505 U.S. 1003.

Lujan v. Defenders of Wildlife. 1992. 504 U.S. 555.

Marini, Frank, ed. 1971. *Toward a New Public Administration: The Minnowbrook Perspective.* Scranton, PA: Chandler.

Massachusetts v. Environmental Protection Agency. 2007. 549 U.S. 497.

Maynard-Moody, Steven, and Michael Musheno. 2003. *Cops, Teachers, Counselors.* Ann Arbor: University of Michigan Press.

McCubbins, Mathew, Roger Noll, and Barry Weingast. 1989. Structure and process; politics and policy. *Virginia Law Review* 75 (2): 431–482.

McCubbins, Mathew, and Thomas Schwartz. 1984. Congressional oversight overlooked. *American Journal of Political Science* 28 (February): 165–179.

Moore, Mark, and Margaret Gates. 1986. *The Inspectors General.* New York: Russell Sage Foundation.

Moreno, Angel. 1994. Presidential coordination of the independent regulatory process. *Administrative Law Journal* 8:461–516.

Morrison v. Olson. 1988. 487 U.S. 654.

Murray, Shailagh. 2009. Senate demands plan for detainees. *Washington Post,* May 20. www.washingtonpost.com/wp-dyn/content/article/2009/05/19/AR2009051903615.html.

Neustadt, Richard. 1991. *Presidential Power and the Modern Presidents.* New York: Free Press.

Obama, Barack. 2009a. Statement by the President. Washington, DC: White House, March 11. www.whitehouse.gov/the_press_office/Statement-from-the-President-on-the-signing-of-HR-1105/.

———. 2009b. Executive order 1392 review and disposition of individuals detained at the Guantánamo Bay Naval Base and closure of detention. Washington, DC: White House, January 22. www.whitehouse.gov/the_press_office/closureofguantanamodetentionfacilities/.

O'Hare Truck Service v. City of Northlake. 1996. 518 U.S. 712.

O'Leary, Rosemary. 1993. *Environmental Change.* Philadelphia: Temple University Press.

Ornstein, Norman, Thomas Mann, and Michael Malbin. 1996. *Vital Statistics on Congress, 1995–1996.* Washington, DC: Congressional Quarterly.

Parents Involved in Community Schools v. Seattle School District No. 1; Meredith v. Jefferson County Board of Education. 2007. 551 U.S. 701 (decided together).

Pembaur v. City of Cincinnati. 1986. 475 U.S. 469.

Pfiffner, James. 2008. *Power Play.* Washington, DC: Brookings Institution.

Polenberg, Richard. 1966. *Reorganizing Roosevelt's Government.* Cambridge, MA: Harvard University Press.

President's Committee on Administrative Management. 1937. *Report of the committee.* Washington, DC: U.S. Government Printing Office.

Reich, Charles. 1964. The new property. *Yale Law Journal* 73 (5): 733–787.

Rhodes v. Chapman. 1981. 452 U.S. 337.

Ricci v. DeStefano. 2009. 557 U.S.; 129 S.Ct. 2658 (2009).

Rosenbloom, David H. 1971. *Federal Service and the Constitution.* Ithaca, NY: Cornell University Press.

———. 1983. Public administrative theory and the separation of powers. *Public Administration Review* 43 (3): 219–227.

———. 1995. The use of case studies in public administrative education in the U.S. *Journal of Management History* 1 (1): 33–46.

———. 2000. *Building a Legislative-Centered Public Administration: Congress and the Administrative State, 1946–1999.* Tuscaloosa: University of Alabama Press.

———. 2003. *Administrative Law for Public Managers.* Boulder, CO: Westview.

———. 2010. Reevaluating executive centered public administration. In *Oxford Handbook of American Bureaucracy,* ed. Robert Durant. New York: Oxford University Press.

Rosenbloom, David H., and Katherine Naff. Forthcoming. The status of law in contemporary public administrative literature, education, and practice. In *The Future of Public Administration, Public Management and Public Service Around the World: The Minnowbrook Perspective,* ed. Rosemary O'Leary, David Van Slyke, and Soonhee Kim. Washington, DC: Georgetown University Press.

Rosenbloom, David H., and Rosemary O'Leary. 1997. *Public Administration and Law.* 2d ed. New York: Marcel Dekker.

Rosenbloom, David H., Rosemary O'Leary, and Joshua Chanin. 2010. *Public Administration and Law.* 3rd ed. Boca Raton, FL: Taylor and Francis.

Rourke, Francis. 1993. Whose bureaucracy is this anyway? Congress, the president, and public administration. *PS: Political Science and Politics* 26 (4): 687–692.

Shafritz, Jay, and Albert Hyde, eds. 2007. *Classics of Public Administration.* 6th ed. Belmont, CA: Thomson/Wadsworth.

Simon, Herbert. 1946. The proverbs of administration. In *Classics of Public Administration.* 6th ed., ed. Jay Shafritz and Albert Hyde, 124–137. Belmont, CA: Thomson/Wadsworth, 2007.

———. 1947. *Administrative Behavior.* New York: Free Press.

Skowronek, Stephen. 1997. *The Politics Presidents Make.* Cambridge, MA: Belknap Press of Harvard University.

Spady v. Mount Vernon. 1974. 419 U.S. 983.

Strauss, Peter, Todd Rakoff, Roy Schotland, and Cynthia Farina. 1995. *Gellhorn and Byse's Administrative Law.* 9th ed. Westbury, NY: Foundation Press.

U.S. Congress. 1945. Congressional Record. Vol. 91, 79th Cong., 1st sess. Washington, DC: U.S. Government Printing Office.

———. 1946. Congressional Record. Vol. 92, 79th Cong., 2nd sess. Washington, DC: U.S. Government Printing Office.

U.S. v. Richardson. 1974. 418 U.S. 166.

U.S. v. Virginia. 1996. 518 U.S. 515.

Van Bergen, Jennifer. 2006. The unitary executive. Findlaw, January 9. http://writ.news.findlaw.com/commentary/20060109_bergen.html.

van der Wal, Zeger. 2008. Value solidity. Doctoral diss. Vrije University, Amsterdam, Netherlands.

Vogler, David. 1993. *The Politics of Congress.* 6th ed. Madison, WI: Brown and Benchmark.

Waldo, Dwight. 1948. *The Administrative State.* New York: Ronald Press.

Weingast, Barry, and Mark Moran. 1983. Bureaucratic discretion or congressional control? *Journal of Political Economy* 91 (3): 765–800.

White, Leonard. 1926. *Introduction to the Study of Public Administration.* New York: Macmillan.

Willoughby, W.F. 1927. *Principles of Public Administration.* Washington, DC: Brookings Institution.

———. 1934. *Principles of Legislative Organization and Administration.* Washington, DC: Brookings Institution.

Wood, B. Dan, and Richard Waterman. 1994. *Bureaucratic Dynamics.* Boulder, CO: Westview.

Wyatt v. Stickney. 1971. 325 F. Supp. 781; 334 F. Supp. 1341.

Wyman v. James. 1971. 400 U.S. 309.

Yoo, Christopher, Steven Calabresi, and Anthony Colangelo. 2005. The unitary executive in the modern era, 1945–2004. *Iowa Law Review* 90 (2): 601–731.

Yoo, Christopher, Steven Calabresi, and Laurence Nee. 2004. The unitary executive in the third half-century, 1899–1945. *Notre Dame Law Review* 80 (1): 1–110.

Youngberg v. Romeo. 1982. 457 U.S. 307.

CHAPTER 23

GOVERNANCE IN THE MIDST OF DIVERSITY

Issues and Challenges

HARVEY L. WHITE

Diversity represents significant challenges for effective public management and service provision at all levels of governance and in each sector of society. It also constitutes new opportunities to rethink and expand the capacity of public service and help support human advancement in a variety of endeavors. Many challenges and opportunities emanate from rapidly changing demographics that are transforming society and affecting delivery of and demand for public goods and services. Others are by-products of emerging social and culture values. The mosaic of language, racial, cultural, ethnic, age, economic, gender, and sexual groups with demands on public resources necessitates not only a more diverse set of services but a variety of management strategies, techniques, and technologies for providing them as well. Moreover, an examination of diversity should not only consider the composition of the public workforce and recipients of public services but also focus attention on when, where, and how services are delivered and the technologies employed.

This chapter addresses an array of diversity issues and challenges and their effects on the administration of public services. It also gives attention to technologies that are enhancing the capacity of public administrators to promote good governance. First, the chapter provides an overview of diversity as a governance concept in political and administrative theory literature. This is followed by an overview of select human difference issues such as multiculturalism, same-sex marriage, and generation preferences. Consideration is then given to diverse technologies and the expanding range of services government must provide. The chapter concludes with a discussion of management challenges confronting public service professionals.

DIVERSITY AS A CONCEPT IN GOVERNANCE

Diversity as a concept in governance is well grounded in political and administrative theory. The literature in these areas is replete with discussions on class and social divisions, representativeness, culture, religion, gender, race, ethnicity, and other ways humans differ. This includes work by classical, modern, and postmodern theorists.

As Arlene Saxonhouse (1992) points out in her work, *Fear of Diversity,* early theorists such as Socrates, Plato, and Aristotle addressed the role of diversity in achieving good governance. Socrates, for instance, began his philosophical work by abandoning astronomy and focusing his attention on differences humans bring to the agora, or marketplace (Meagher 2008). Plato stresses diversity in his work as the main characteristic that enables a city to survive and that is also essential for it to thrive (Reader 2005). Not only does Aristotle, in Plato's *Republic*, argue for diversity but warns,

"It is clear that if the process of unification advances beyond a certain point, the city will not be a city at all" (Rackham's translation 1932, 71).

Theorists as different as Adam Smith, Karl Marx, and Emile Durkheim give attention to human difference in their work. While these scholars typically focused on the material or class-conflict aspects of diversity, they recognize its governance implications as well. As Hartmann and Gerteis (2005) point out, there are gestures in these scholars' work toward the impact and value of diversity in "modern societies." Adam Smith emphasizes the rights of individuals to pursue self-interest through which both individuals and their nations would prosper. Marx recognizes diverse class interests in society, which he believes necessitate new governance arrangements. And Durkheim stresses different social conditions that allow individuals to distinguish themselves and require the use of government to prevent structural inequalities or class monopolies. Jean-Jacques Rousseau, Immanuel Kant, Georg W.F. Hegel, and other modern theorists also gave consideration to diversity and governance. For these theorists, human difference is an aspect of the values that govern society, even though it was not the primary consideration in their work (Hartmann and Gerteis 2005). Religion, forms of government, natural rights, dialectics, and other factors were the principal focus of their attention. This is not the case for many contemporary and postmodern scholars, particularly those with a focus on administrative theory.

Twentieth-century theorist John Rawls's (1993) criticism of utilitarian administrative politics was influential in this regard. He calls for a society that permits people with diverse values and different ways of life to live in peace with mutual respect for one another's basic rights in a system of political liberalism. Rawls's work continues to influence the embrace of social equity initiatives in public administration (Frederickson 1997). Similarly, Charles Taylor's (1983) vision in his work for a "politics of difference" is very influential in contemporary discussions of diversity and governance. In this politics, government would find ways to support racial or ethnic groups seeking to retain their unique identities. Taylor's concept is widely used, in Canada and to some extent in Africa, to advocate for inclusive approaches to governance.

Public administration scholars draw upon the work of these and other theorists to address a variety of differences that affect the delivery of public goods and services (Hoffman and Graham 2009). The governance ideals theorists put forth constitute the intellectual foundation for discussions of race, age, gender, disability, sexual preferences, ethnicity, and multiculturalism that pervade the literature in public administration and allied fields.

Herbert Simon (1976) initiated work on decision making in his acclaimed book, *Administrative Behavior,* by referring to the "pursuits among philosophers." He then moves to a subtle consideration of human differences through a discussion of "group versus individual alternatives." As he explains, "Hence, the alternatives available to the group must be carefully distinguished from the set of alternatives available to the individual" (Simon 1976, 105). His views of diversity were enhanced in his effort to understand and value multiple perspectives to problem solving. Economist Scott Page (2007) uses Simon's work in his highly acclaimed book on the value of human difference to illustrate how groups that display a range of perspectives outperform groups of like-minded experts.

A parallel to Simon's work that continues to have a tremendous impact on diversity literature in public administration is Donald Kingsley's (1944) early scholarship on public service. Kingsley draws upon the work of modern political theorists in his writings on the British civil service, in which he coined the term "representative bureaucracy." He argues that ". . . bureaucracies, to be democratic, must be representative of the groups they serve" (Kingsley, 1944, 305). A large number of public administration scholars utilized the representative bureaucracy concept to address diversity and governance issues (Long 1952; Van Riper, 1958, Mosher 1982; Riccucci and Saidel 1997; Grissom, Nicholson-Crotty, and Nicholson-Crotty 2009).

RACE AND ETHNICITY

An early focus of representative bureaucracy was on the low levels of racial and ethnic inclusion in the civil service (Riccucci 1987; White and Rice 2010). In this regard, public administration scholars point out that to be truly representative, the public service must be inclusive of diverse racial and ethnic groups. They spell out specific governance enhancements that result from a more racially inclusive bureaucracy (Kranz 1976; Pitts 2009). These include:

- More democratic decision making and better decisions by expanding the number and diversity of views brought to bear on policy making;
- Improved bureaucratic operations and outputs from decisions and services that are more responsive to the needs of all citizens, particularly members of minority groups;
- Better human talent development and management decisions;
- An increase, both symbolically and actually, in the legitimacy of public service and other governance institutions; and
- Elevation of social equity and justice to prime administrative values on par with other values in public administration paradigms (Kranz 1976; White and Rice 2010).

As representative bureaucracy scholars have come to realize, racial and ethnic groups possess distinct cultural values and perspectives that can enhance governance (Kranz 1976). Numerous studies have confirmed racially differentiated perspectives on an assortment of governance and public service–related issues (Gabbidon and Higgins 2009; Rushefsky 2002; Lipset and Schneider 1983). Bringing diverse perspectives to bear on deliberations is also shown to improve outcomes (Page 2007; Linstone 1984; Linstone 1999). Demographics suggest that the challenges and opportunities for achieving a more representative bureaucracy are expanding in the United States.

If current trends continue, the demographic profile of the United States will change dramatically by the middle of this century (Kinder and Sanders 1996). Population projections by the Pew Research Center indicate that nearly one in five Americans (19 percent) will be foreign-born in 2050, well above the 2005 level of 12 percent, and also surpassing the historic peak immigrant population percentages of 14.8 percent in 1890 and 14.7 percent in 1910 (Figure 23.1) By 2050, the racial and ethnic mix will be quite different as well. Non-Hispanic whites, who made up 67 percent of the population in 2005, are projected to decrease to 47 percent. Hispanics will rise from 14 percent of the population in 2005 to 29 percent in 2050. African Americans will continue to make up 13 percent of the population (Passel and Cohn 2008).

Although racial and ethnic inclusion in the civil service has been enhanced, most minority groups are still underrepresented at all levels of government in the United States, particularly in management and leadership positions. Not only does the quest continue for a more racially representative bureaucracy; it has also gradually expanded to embrace other differences. This includes the focus on gender representation in the civil service.

GENDER REPRESENTATIVENESS IN CIVIL SERVICE

Gender scholars are using representative bureaucracy to focus attention on the proverbial glass ceiling which prevents the advancement of women and minorities to higher levels of management. Many public administration scholars also address issues of "gender representativeness" in public service. Riccucci's (1986, 1987, 1990) research addresses women's employment and other protected groups at all levels of government and within not-for-profit organizations. Naff's

Figure 23.1   **Population By Race and Ethnicity, Actual and Projected: 1960, 2005, and 2050** (percent of total)

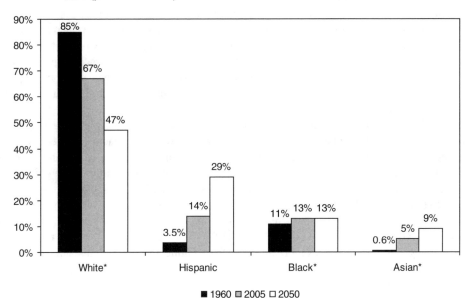

■ 1960 ▨ 2005 ☐ 2050

Source: Pew Research Center (2008).

Note: *All races modified and not Hispanic; American Indian/Alaska Native not shown. See "Methodology." Projections for 2050 indicated by white bars.

(1994) work on the glass ceiling draws attention to gender inequity in upper-level management at the state and federal levels of government. Strivers' (2002) work applies a gender lens to the field of public administration by looking at issues of status, power, leadership, legitimacy, and change. Guy (2002) focuses on the difference that gender makes in policy development and implementation. These and a variety of other gender scholars continue to highlight the need for a more representative bureaucracy and attention to women's contributions for the advancement of public service and effective governance.

MULTICULTURALISM AS DIFFERENCES

Advocates of multiculturalism draw upon theories of representative bureaucracy as well as political liberalism to justify the embrace of cultural differences in public administration. This entails two basic arguments. First is Rawls's liberal premise that a fully human existence entails the freedom to live according to one's cultural traditions (Hoffman and Graham 2009). The second asserts that an understanding of cultural behaviors of individuals and communities served is a requisite for effective public administration (White and Rice 2005). Victoria Antonova's discussion of diversity management and concepts of multiculturalism in Russia draws upon both of these arguments. From a pluralistic perspective, Antonova (2007, 8) notes, "If multiculturalism's principles are within the very fabric of the civil service this would indicate that multicultural principles are highly valued by public administration and the state—which, in turn, would make it possible to assume that such principles are shared by both citizens and government." Antonova (2007, 5) makes an equally persuasive argument for a more representative public service: "If multiculturalism actually works within the civil service (which is the centre of public administration) it could be said that civil society and government institutions will benefit from multiculturalism—and that multiculturalism should thus be developed within a diverse society, and within the civil service, which would enable the latter to demonstrate and increase its ability to achieve its own goals."

Antonova is only one of many scholars who use multiculturalism to challenge and expand public administration. Her uniqueness, however, is not only the linkage of her work to the two main arguments for multiculturalism in public administration, but the emphasis placed on governance as well. As she points out, "Another important issue related to the governance level is the role played by the civil service when forming multicultural policies and putting forward antidiscrimination legislation" (Antonova, 2007, 7).

Antonova's observations on governance and multiculturalism deserve particular notice. It is important, in this regard, to not confuse the authority to govern with the capacity to govern. Although achieving a political majority is extremely important in a democracy, majority-centered politics does not ensure effective governance. Achieving a majority enhances authority to govern, but, as the emerging body of work on multiculturalism makes clear, achieving inclusiveness enhances capacity to govern. Whether moral majorities, silent majorities, ethnic majorities, or racial majorities, the lack of inclusiveness has hindered effective governance (Sheeran 1983; Makanza 2008; Schiesinger 2009). Clarification of both subtle and often major distinctions between majority rule and effective governance deserves more attention from public administration scholars.

VALUING DIFFERENCES

Walter Broadnax (2000) contends that the desired state of inclusiveness suggested by multiculturalism can be achieved by shifting the current focus on rights to "valuing differences." Similarly, Lani Guinier describes the valuing of difference as a strength to be built upon to enhance several aspects of governance that are crucial features of democratic societies. According to Guinier (1994, 175), "Decision making that values diversity multiplies the points of access to government, disperses power, and struggles to ensure a full and developed rational dialogue."

Building on this premise, Jong Jun argues in the *Social Construction of Public Administration* that there is a very special role for public administrators in fostering an atmosphere for valuing differences. For Jun (2006, 199), "the perplexing questions are about how public administrators in a multicultural society can help citizens see diversity as a strength to be built upon and how public administrators can provide opportunities to develop intergroup discourse for dialogue and sharing for mutual concerns in the community."

The concept of a "representative bureaucracy" has helped sensitize public administration scholars and practitioners to the need for a more inclusive public service. It continues to serve as a conceptual framework for advancing a variety of diversity issues. Although widely embraced, the concept has not diminished diversity as a challenge for governance.

DIVERSITY AS A CHALLENGE FOR GOVERNANCE

The diversity challenge for governance is long-standing and the source of many societal tensions. These tensions continue to manifest themselves in race and gender legacy debates around taxation, representation, employment, career advancement, and suffrage. They are also present in census activity, immigration, educational opportunity, rights and citizenship privileges for same-sex couples, access to public facilities, and many other social issues. Essentially, the tension is about the rights afforded members of a society and whether there will be limits on the access to these rights for a subset of members because of their differences (Walzer 1995). That is, will the concept of diversity continue to expand and value differences manifesting themselves in contemporary society?

If the expansive nature of diversity developed through various governance initiatives reflects society's capacity to become more inclusive, the answer to the question posed above may be yes. There are also strong tensions that suggest otherwise as well. The progression of initiatives to address racial and ethnic disparities, prevent religious persecution, enhance opportunities for racial minorities, provide access for the disabled, and advance gender equity is indicative of how encompassing diversity has become. Added to this mantle are diverse groups that have been given protected class status against discrimination and harassment (i.e., national origin, skin color, age, familial status, sexual orientation, disability, veteran, and genetic information nondiscrimination).

Even though the expanding nature of diversity has resulted in a succession of challenging and contentious issues, governance has effectively ameliorated emanating tensions with new laws, policies, programs, and administrative procedures. An emerging group of complex differences, however, are far more challenging, and there are few generally acceptable governance mechanisms available to address them. These include issues relating to citizenship rights and privileges of same-sex couples, and recognition of multiracial and generational group differences.

Citizenship Rights and Privileges of Same-Sex Couples

Same-sex couples are demanding spousal privileges, benefits, and marital and parental rights available to other couples. These demands have sparked contentious debates in the United States and other parts of the world. Same-sex couples argue that they should not be denied the rights and privileges afforded others couples simply because of their same-sex difference.

The complexity of this difference is that it may conflict with values important to other groups, religious communities, and traditional families. Deciding what constitutes a marriage and subsequently a family, as well as who has the right to make this determination, is not clear. Legislation, court decisions, referendums, and religious edicts have not given clarity to these issues. Even religious communities themselves are deeply divided over same-sex marriage.

The Catholic Church and most Evangelical Christian churches are actively opposed to gay marriage. Gays and lesbians are fully accepted in some but not all Protestant denominations. Several denominations are grappling with whether to ordain gay men and women as clergy and whether to require celibacy. Questions surround churches' right to perform or prohibit same-sex wedding ceremonies in their facilities. Still being resolved are federal and interstate governance issues pertaining to tax status, employee benefits, and provision of children and spousal benefits that may have implications for religious organizations. The federal system, separation of church and state, and equal protection provisions make same-sex marriage a particularly complex challenge to governance.

Same-Sex Differences in a Federal System

The U.S. government does not recognize same-sex marriages and is prohibited from doing so by the Defense of Marriage Act (DOMA) passed by Congress and signed into law by the President on September 21, 1996. Same-sex marriages are currently performed in five states: Massachusetts, Connecticut, Iowa, New Hampshire, and Vermont. Legislation authorizing same-sex marriage for the District of Columbia is also being implemented there. The different legal status same-sex marriage is afforded within the U.S. federal system has the potential to generate interstate governance challenges.

Even though DOMA proclaims, no "state needs to treat as a marriage a same-sex relationship considered a marriage in another state" (Section 2) differences do arise (Sanders 2007). One area highlighted in this regard is parental rights. As Joanna Grossman (2009, 1) observes, "two recent cases—one from New York and one from Florida—are a potent reminder of the potential conflicts created by states' taking different approaches to the legal recognition of same-sex parenting." Questions that have arisen include:

- Can an individual adopt the biological children of his or her same-sex partner?
- Is a same-sex spouse entitled to a presumption of parentage for children born to the other partner during the marriage?
- Can a same-sex couple jointly adopt a child that is not biologically related to either?

The collage of emerging rules varies from state to state and can be extremely problematic when same-sex couples with children relocate or separate, and the children are taken to a state that does not recognize their parents' marriage (Grossman 2009).

This problem was evidence in the recent custody case involving former same-sex partners who live in different states. The former partners were joined in a Vermont civil union and are the parents of a young child. After the couple broke up, the birth mother moved to Virginia, denounced homosexuality, and denied her former partner visitation rights prescribed by a Vermont family court when it dissolved their civil union. After the Vermont court switched custody to the other parent, the birth mother disappeared with the child. However, local authorities in Fairfax County, Virginia, refused to investigate the case, citing jurisdictional concerns (CBS/AP, 2010).

Custody and other legal issues between same-sex couples have been actively litigated, and the patchwork of rulings has been very mixed. If forecasts for interstate taxation and employment benefits challenges materialize, governance issues surrounding same-sex marriages will become even more complex in the United States (Black 2008). The global political nature of same-sex relationships also adds to its complexity and challenge for governance.

Global Complexities of Same-Sex Relationships

At least seven countries with which the United States has strong diplomatic, political, and economic relationships allow same-sex marriages: the Netherlands, Belgium, Spain, Canada, South Africa, Norway, and Sweden. Others provide for civil unions or domestic partnerships (Pew Research Center, 2009; Masci et al. 2009). How will citizens who are same-sex couples from these countries be treated in the United States? In contrast, how will same-sex couples from the United States be treated in countries that do not recognize their marriage? Four countries ban same-sex marriage and at least seventy explicitly outlaw homosexuality (Pew Research Center, 2009).

The two countries that border the United States have conflicting policies. Same-sex marriages have been legal nationwide in Canada since 2005. Neither same-sex marriages nor civil unions are recognized at the federal level in Mexico. The Mexican state of Coahuila and the Federal District (Mexico City), however, allow civil unions. The Mexico City government recently passed legislation authorizing same-sex marriage, which is being challenged by the federal government. How will these contrasting laws affect relations among the three countries, which are connected together in an economic federation by the North American Free Trade Agreement? Will they be forced to accept one another's laws, and how will governance issues be reconciled? At least one legal scholar argues that recent legal, economic, social, and technological developments make it nearly impossible for the United States not to recognize same-sex marriage so long as it is lawful in Canada (Spitz 2004).

Multiracial as a Governance Issue

Another complex issue is the United States government's allowance for the classification of individuals as "multiracial." The growing number of minority groups gives individuals a multiplicity of ways to define themselves. Respondents in the 2000 census were given the option to mark one or more races on the questionnaire to indicate their racial identity. While multiracial ancestry is an unquestioned cultural phenomenon for many Americans, some groups question whether or not there are political motives behind establishing it as a new classification. For instance, if this classification is widely embraced, it can significantly reduce the official size of African American and other population groups with diverse ancestry.

Historian Henry Louis Gates (2009), with the help of geneticists, has discerned that most African Americans may be multiracial. As his work reveals:

- 58 percent of African Americans have at least 12.5 percent European ancestry (equivalent to one great-grandparent);
- 19.6 percent of African Americans have at least 25 percent European ancestry (equivalent to one grandparent);
- 1 percent of African Americans have at least 50 percent European ancestry (equivalent to one parent); and
- 5 percent of African Americans have at least 12.5 percent Native American ancestry (equivalent to one great-grandparent)

The option to declare oneself multiracial became an extremely sensitive political issue just prior to the 2000 census. As Kim Williams (2006) asserts in her book on multiracial America, adding a multiracial category to the 2000 U.S. Census provoked unparalleled debates about race. House Speaker Newt Gingrich, affirmative action opponent Ward Connerly, and Project RACE were proponents of "multiracial" as a new racial category, while most civil rights leaders opposed it.

Supporters of the multiracial classification argue that it is vital for both genetic and self-knowledge components. The genetic factor is said to be important for personalized medicine, which will be a basis for much of public health and medicine in the future. The knowledge about oneself, one's family, and one's ancestors is thought vital to individuals because it allows them to "claim and embrace ALL of who they are" (Rand Reed 2009, 1). Opponents insist that it has the potential to diminish the political strength of traditional minority groups. The number of multiracial individuals is increasing, and the compromise option to mark more than one category on the 2000 census does not appear to satisfy either supporters or opponents of the new classification.

According to the U.S. Census Bureau, there were fewer than 500,000 children who could be classified as multiracial in 1960. This number increased to almost 2 million in 1990 and to more than 6 million by 2000 (DeBose and Winters 2002). The complexity of this diversity issue extends far beyond black and white concerns. The 2000 census allowed for sixty-three possible combinations of six basic racial categories, including six categories for those who report exactly one race, and fifty-seven categories for those who report two or more races (Table 23.1).

The census multiracial classification does give recognition to an expanding and diverse group of citizens; however, it still falls short of Rawls's premise that a fully human existence entails the freedom to live according to one's cultural traditions. It also does not facilitate an understanding of cultural behaviors of individuals and communities that constitute this group. Without question,

Table 23.1

Multiracial America

Number of Races Selected on 2000 Census	Number	Percent of Total	Percentage of Multiracial
2	6,368,075	2.26	93.29
3	410,285	0.15	6.01
4	38,408	0.01	0.56
5	8,637	0.00	0.13
6	823	0.00	0.01

Source: Census 2000 analyzed by the Social Science Data Analysis Network (SSDAN).

individuals within these sixty-three categories have cultural rights, but are there limits to the value society places on differences? Or, to paraphrase Herbert Simon, is the embrace of unlimited demographic differences possible, or is it necessary to "satisfice" and accept "bounded diversity"?

Generational Differences and Public Service

Issues surrounding generational differences also represent demographic governance challenges that are receiving significant attention. Generational cohorts have been identified that possess unique cultural, political, and economic orientations that transcend race, ethnicity, and gender. These cohorts are aggregations of individuals with similar experiences into groups, which often have unique values, have competing demands and needs, and make different contributions to society.

The concept of generational cohorts was introduced by Karl Mannheim in the early 1920s and gradually expanded and applied to subsequent population groups. Six main cohort groups are identified in the literature. Each group is said to have experienced a common set of "memorable events," and group members exhibit similar "key characteristics" (Meredith and Schewe 2007). The memorable events experienced by each cohort are believed to produce unique group perspectives and accompanying behavioral characteristics (Strauss and Howe 1992). These generations' memorable events and key characteristics are delineated in Table 23.2 along with each cohort's age range in 2010.

The memorable events, experiences, and accompanying behavioral characteristics unique to each generational cohort have also produced diverse sets of social and political preferences and public service requirements. There are also differences in cohort groups' value for, contribution to, and demand for public services. View of authority and political orientation also vary across generations. While there are transgenerational similarities, there are also significant differences. A brief summary of generational relationships to public service is depicted in Table 23.3.

The diverse perspectives, values, demands, and orientations of generations represent multiple governance challenges that are often contrary to expectations and not easily reconciled. For instance, the baby boomer and millennial generations have similar political orientations and voting patterns. Both generations express strong support for environmental initiatives, diversity, and health care. Nearly three-quarters (74 percent) of millennials and two-thirds of baby boomers (69 percent) who voted in 2008 supported the assertion that there is more that government should be doing (Madland and Teixeira 2009). Collectively, these two generations will make up nearly 55 percent of the voting-age population in the near future. This suggests the possibility for clear policy choices in several areas and a rare governance opportunity to enhance the status

Table 23.2

Generational Cohorts

Cohort Generations	Great Depression	Pre–World War II	World War II	Baby Boomer I	Baby Boomer II	Generation X	Generation Y Millennial
Dates of Birth	1912–1921	1922–1927	1928–1945	1946–1954	1955–1964	1965–1980	1981–2001
Age in 2010	88–98	83–88	65–82	56–64	46–55	30–45	9–29
Memorable events	Great Depression; unemployment; lack of creature comforts; financial uncertainty	War; women working in factories; focus on defeating a common enemy	Economic growth; social tranquility; the cold war; drug culture; McCarthyism	Political unrest, walk on the moon; civil rights; the environmental movement; sexual freedom; social experimentation	Watergate; oil embargo; hypo-inflation; disco; gas shortages; Nixon resigns; the cold war	*Challenger* tragedy; Iran-Contra; AIDS; Reaganomics; MTV; safe sex; home computer; cold war ends; Desert Storm	Rise of the Internet; cultural diversity; two wars in Iraq; 9/11 attack on United States; global financial crisis of 2008–10
Key characteristics	Striving for financial security; risk adverse; waste-not, want-not attitude	Nobility of sacrifice; patriotism; team player	Conservatism and family values	Experimental; individualism; social cause orientation	Less optimism; pragmatism; general cynicism	Quest for emotional security; independent; informality; entrepreneurial	Quest for physical security and safety; heightened fears; acceptance of change; technically savvy

Source: Aging Is an Asset Forum (2009).

Table 23.3

Generational Relationships to Public Service

Cohort Generations	Great Depression	Pre–World War II	World War II	Baby Boomer I	Baby Boomer II	Generation X	Generation Y Millennial
Value for public service	Least government is better	Public service as duty	Government useful for cold war	Public service as an opportunity	Public service as option	Government is the problem	Service as a privilege
Contribution to public service	Employment	Military service	Military and employment	Employment; Peace Corps	Employment Volunteers in Service to America	Work in not-for-profits	Employment volunteerism
Demand for public service	Housing; income; health care	Education; income; health care	Security from communism	Social and economic justice; women's rights	Protection for people with disabilities	Tax relief; rights for people with disabilities	Environmental and economic recovery
View of authority	Respect authority	Respect authority	Respect authority	Question authority	Cynical and disrespectful	Power relationships	Rebellious and own person
Political orientation	Social conservative	Social conservative	Economic conservative	Radical and progressive	Moderately progressive	Economic conservative	Progressive

Source: Aging Is an Asset Forum (2009).

and performance of public service. However, these two generations have significantly different policy preferences in other areas that could be extremely detrimental to collaborations between the two cohort groups.

Same-sex marriages, privatization of Social Security, and the war in Afghanistan are three of these areas (Madland and Teixeira 2009). Baby boomers oppose same-sex marriages, and millennials are more inclined to allow them. There are wide generational differences on Social Security. This division is evident in poll responses to whether Social Security funds should be aggressively invested in the stock market. The millennials (78.3 percent) appear to want their Social Security funds invested aggressively, while baby boomers (54 percent) prefer conservative investment practices (Zogby International 1999).

Afghanistan is another area of significant intergenerational difference. An August 2009, Harris Poll (Voters For Peace, 2009) on support for troop levels exemplifies this difference. Older generations are more likely to support committing more troops and younger generations are more likely to oppose increasing troop levels. Just less than one-quarter of those between the ages of eighteen and thirty-four (23 percent) say they want to commit more troops compared to 44 percent of those fifty-five and older. The reverse is true for sending fewer troops, as almost two in five of those between the ages of eighteen and thirty-four (38 percent) say they believe the United States should commit fewer troops, while only 14 percent of those aged fifty-five and older support sending fewer troops (Zogby International 1999).

As the data in Table 23.3 indicate, the baby boomers are closely aligned with generations that precede them in some issue areas and with millennials in others. Millennials' and generation Xers' views are closely related in some areas and contrast in others. Both the similarities and the differences have policy and governance implications. The size of millennials' and boomers' cohort groups suggest that they have the capacity to build or stifle collaboration and consensus needed for successful policy making and effective governance. The smaller generational cohorts are also positioned to build alliances to advance their interests.

The view of authority is another area of generational difference that has governance implications. In addition to enforcement areas, such as police and fire protection, zoning, and code enforcement, that require citizens' compliance, the uniquely rebellious view toward authority prevalent in the millennial generation has significant management and leadership implications as well. The record number of millennials expected to enter the workforce in the near future will require different types of leadership, management, structures, technology, and work options. It will also require leadership and management practices attuned to the values and needs of this generation. Personnel management, human resources management, and human capital management are embedded with precepts that reflect baby boomers' work behavior, which are often antithetical to the needs of millennials (White 2009). A multigenerational approach is needed.

HUMAN TALENT MANAGEMENT

One approach that is gaining acceptance is human talent management and development, which involves a shift away from valuing employees as resources and capital assets and toward what is described as the more salient tenets of human talents. At the core, human talent management is a fundamental change in how organizations value people and their differences, which includes changing how they recruit, develop, align, assess, and retain employees. As Heidi Spirgi, president of Knowledge Infusion, points out, the new focus on talent management represents "a paradigm shift in the way HR defines its mission and measures its success" (Reuters 2008, 1). This emerging paradigm is enabling organizations with a framework for redesigning and rethinking talent processes, and using new technologies to transform and enhance the way human talent performs (Spirgi and Corsello 2009). The paradigm shift that Spirgi argues for and the corollary embrace of new technologies seem opportune given the generational divide described previously. It also bodes well as a mechanism to help address the diversity of technology that is a challenge for governance.

DIVERSITY OF TECHNOLOGY AND GOVERNANCE

Providing public employees the diverse technologies they need to be productive is a difficult and costly challenge. Compounding this challenge are the range and expanding nature of public services that must be provided; variant skill and experience levels of employees; and skill, competence, and experience of individuals and organizations public administrators must serve. These factors make diversity of technology an important governance consideration.

An indication of the need to consider diverse technologies is the array of tools generational cohorts use in their daily routines. For example, the Depression, pre–World War II, and World War II generations continue to use telephones, letters, and various forms of print materials for most of their communications. These generations were the first primary users of the personal telephone and maintain it as their technology of choice. They also occasionally use the telegraph and fax machine and other wire-related technologies. Baby boomers prefer face-to-face conversations, telephones, and e-mail, with some reliance on print materials. Although members of this generation were the first regular computer users, interpersonal communication continues to be extremely important to them (Aging Is an Asset Forum 2009).

The generation Xers were the first to make extensive use of cell phones but continued to rely on e-mail. The Xers began the move away from the reliance on face-to-face communication, which continues to accelerate with the millennials. The millennials used information technologies to institutionalize text messaging, and popularized MySpace, Facebook, and Twitter (Aging Is an Asset Forum 2009). These diverse communication styles suggest both limits and enhanced possibilities for the provision and production of public services. They are also helpful in discerning the appropriate leadership and management styles for a multi-generational workforce.

From a workforce perspective, the generation Xers' and millennials' affinity for technology suggests the possibility of greater efficiencies in the delivery of public goods and services. These generations have grown up with computers and advanced technologies and expect to use them in their work. Remote collaborations, alternative work options, decision making based on real-time data, and other innovations made possible with information technologies offer promising opportunities for enhancing public services. Hard science technologies and applications from bioengineering, geology, and genetics are facilitating similar advances, particularly in the areas of security, criminology, and environmental remediation.

Reduction in paperwork and paper cost are real possibilities, as is the ability to respond instantaneously to citizens' needs and receive immediate feedback from them. While the promises of technologies are real, so are the challenges. Perhaps the biggest challenge is the diverse technology capacity and willingness of citizens to utilize public services generated with this technology. Citizens will bring their generational preferences with them when they utilize public services, which may clash with the preferences of those providing the services. For example, baby boomers' preference for face-to-face communication contrasts with generation Xers' and millennials' propensity for communicating electronically. The computer literacy of many in the pre–World War II and World War II generations is another challenge. The preferences of these generation groups for print media and telephone services will require a variety of technologies for the provision of public services in the immediate future.

The capacity to manage and deliver services via the Internet is one of the exciting opportunities being realized. For example, the U.S. National Institutes of Health and other federal agencies currently encourage, and in some instances require, online applications and reporting for funded research. Although the savings from technology innovations are significant, the opportunity to transform work processes is perhaps more profound. Accompanying this opportunity is the responsibility of managing information technologies and the expanding array of goods and services they facilitate in a manner that is inclusive and equitable.

DIVERSITY OF SERVICES

The expanding diversity of public services that must be provided is also an area that is a challenge to governance. The 9/11 attacks, Katrina, the Haiti and Chile disasters, cyberattacks, H1N1 influenza (swine flu), global warming, the financial crisis of 2008–10, the Gulf Coast oil disaster, and an array of other events are expanding the demand on public services at an exponential rate. The costs and diverse needs for health care have solicited demands for government to not only place performance criteria on industry but to become a competitor in this market as well. Food and product safety concerns are compelling inspection and enforcement activities to focus on global production of consumer goods. Another area that will require the attention of public service is civilian activity in outer space.

Space tourism is already experienced through the Russian Federal Space Agency with major plans under way in several countries to expand this industry. Serious consideration has been given to the production advantages of a zero-gravity environment, which outer space offers. Also, use of private commercial space cargo enterprises to resupply the International Space Station is expected when the U.S. Space Shuttle program ends its activities in this area. With these space activities will come additional regulatory and management responsibilities for public servants (Date 1992; Pasztor 2008).

The expanding range of responsibilities placed on public servants is a response to the array of social, biological, and technological issues influencing contemporary governance. Whether the collapse of financial markets or natural disasters, differing generational needs, adequate health care, pandemics, energy needs, oil spills, or the emergence of new and exotic concerns related to space tourism, there is an expectation that government will respond. Juxtaposed to this expectation is the libertarian principle of limited government that public administrators must traverse. These countervailing forces represent important differences and management challenges that public administrators are often not prepared to address.

DIFFERENCES AS MANAGEMENT CHALLENGES

Recognizing and appreciating differences have become central aspects of public managers' duties and responsibilities. Critical in this regard is employing management practices that embrace differences and foster an inclusive workforce. The challenge is to understand the ways people differ and utilize these differences to enhance the delivery of public goods and services. This requires developing a consensus on the differences that should be recognized in the public sector workforce and recognizing the sociological phenomenon they represent.

The enhanced participation by women, people of color, persons with disabilities, new and recent immigrants, gays and lesbians, and intergenerational mixes in the workforce represents sociological phenomena that are transforming not only the workplace but the lexicon used to define it. Similarly, technological manifestations are universalizing the workplace and providing access to copious collaborative resources for the provision of public service. Managers must, therefore, expand both their understanding of diversity and its capacity to enhance individual and organizational performance. They must also prepare and manage differently. This includes developing the ability to manage across and within an expanding array of issues and networks that are beyond the traditional domain of public administration. Moreover, effective public managers must be able to skillfully collaborate with and participate in a complexity of diverse technological and sociological networks, peculiar to the twenty-first century.

Management in the context of prevailing technological and sociological phenomena requires multidisciplinary approaches beyond those within traditional management sciences. For instance, public managers must design and implement policies to prevent exclusionary and predatory practices made possible through genetic analyses, bioengineering, and information sciences. In the process they are expanding regulatory activities into new spheres of human endeavor. Similar expansion is emanating from forays into regulation of financial markets, energy, the environment, and health care. The accelerated levels of global warming and environmental degradation are forcing governments worldwide to design and implement new energy and building alternatives.

Public administrators must represent the public's interest in complex issues relating to nanotechnology, molecular engineering, new commons, open-source software, cyberspace governance, intellectual property rights, high-tech-product recycling, and life-extension technologies. They are also tasked with resolving an array of ethical issues, ranging from the distribution of human organs to property rights for new forms of life. Representing the public interest and finding solutions in these areas require knowledge and expertise often unavailable in public organizations.

THE ROAD AHEAD

Governance in the midst of diversity is both a challenge and an opportunity. The diversity challenge for governance is long-standing and has been the source of many societal tensions. These tensions continue to manifest themselves in debates over a variety of policy and administrative issues. They are also present in political and social issues that pervade public service. One of these issues is whether rights afforded some members of a society will not be available to other members because of their differences. A corollary to this issue is the question of whether there are appropriate limits to diversity and if so who has the right to establish these limits.

Variant skill, competence, and experience levels of employees as well as those of individuals and organizations using public services evidence the need for a diversity of technology. Technology competence levels vary across generation groups as do preference and need for public services. Meeting the complex needs and demands for public service also requires drawing upon technological applications from the sciences and humanities, and the expertise available through networks and collaborative management.

Research on the expanding nature of diversity as a governance issue is wanting. Discerning and documenting the specific contributions of diversity for enhancing delivery of public service also needs to be explored. Finally, theoretical and empirical research is sorely needed on questions concerning the limits of differences or bounded diversity and who has the rights to set these limits.

Diversity is both old and new; it transcends time. The issues surrounding diversity represent significant challenges for governance. The dynamics they generate, however, continue to be an important source of energy for sustaining, invigorating, and expanding effective governance, which the social contract requires and public administration helps to achieve. The opportunity to shape these dynamics is what makes public administration such a fascinating and rewarding profession.

REFERENCES

Aging Is an Asset Forum. 2009. Civic engagement for all generations. www.iii.siuc.edu/Aging/index.html.
Antonova, Victoria. 2007. Diversity management and concepts of multiculturalism in Russia. Policy paper, Open Society Institute, International Policy Fellowship Program. www.policy.hu/document/200808/ victoria.antonova.pdf&letoltes=1.
Aristotle. 1932. *Politics.* Trans. by H. Rackham. Cambridge, MA: Harvard University Press. Reprinted 1972.
Black, Stephen T. 2008. Same-sex marriage and taxes. *BYU Journal of Public Law* 22 (2): 327–357. http:// www.law2.byu.edu/jpl/V0122.2/Black.pdf.
Broadnax, Walter D. 2000. *Diversity and Affirmative Action in Public Service.* Boulder, CO: Westview Press.
CBS/AP. 2010. Formerly Gay Birth Mom Defies Court Orders to Turn Over Daughter to Ex-Lover. January 8. http://www.cbsnews.com/8301–504083_162–6067417-504083.html.
Date, Shirish. 1992. NASA seeks outer-space moneymaker. *Spokesman Review* (Spokane, Washington), October 21. http://news.google.com/newspapers?nid=1314&dat=19921021&id=UwUSAAAAIBAJ&sjid =MvADAAAAIBAJ&pg=6858,24029.
DeBose, Herman L. and Loretta I. Winters. 2002. *New Faces in a Changing America: Multiracial Identity in the 21st Century.* Thousand Oaks, CA: Sage Publications.
DOMA. 1996.The Defense of Marriage Act. 28 U. S. Code 1738C. One Hundred Fourth Congress of the United States of America. Section 2.
Frederickson, H. George. 1997. *The Spirit of Public Administration.* San Francisco: Jossey-Bass.
Gabbidon, Shaun L., and George E. Higgins. 2009. The role of race/ethnicity and race relations on public opinion related to the treatment of blacks by the police. *Police Quarterly* 12 (1): 102–115.
Gates. Henry L. 2009. *In Search of Roots.* New York: Random House.
Grissom, Jason A., Jill Nicholson-Crotty, and Scan Nicholson-Crotty. 2009. "Region, Race, and Bureaucratic Representation." *Public Administration Review* 69 (5): 911–919.
Grossman, Joanna L. 2009. When same-sex couples adopt: Problems of interstate recognition. FindLaw, legal commentary, June 9. http://writ.news.findlaw.com/grossman/20090609.html.
Guinier, Lani. 1994. *The Tyranny of the Majority: Fundamental Fairness in Representative Democracy.* New York: Free Press.
Guy, Mary E. 2002. The difference that gender makes. In *Public Personnel Administration: Problems and Prospects.* 4th ed., ed. Steven W. Hays and Richard C. Kearney, 256–270. Englewood Cliffs, NJ: Prentice-Hall.
Hartmann, Douglas, and Joseph Gerteis. 2005. Dealing with diversity: Mapping multiculturalism in sociological terms. *Sociological Theory* 23 (2): 218–240.
Hoffman, John, and Paul Graham. 2009. *Introduction to Political Theory.* 2d ed. Harlow, UK: Pearson Education.
Jun, Jong S. 2006. *Social Construction of Public Administration: The Interpretive and Critical Perspectives.* Albany: State University of New York Press.
Kinder, Donald R., and Lynn M. Sanders. 1996. *Divided by Color: Racial Politics and Democratic Ideals.* Chicago: University of Chicago Press.
Kingsley, J. Donald. 1944. *Representative Bureaucracy.* Yellow Springs, OH: Antioch University Press.
Kranz, H. 1976. *Participatory Bureaucracy: Women and Minorities in a More Representative Public Service.* Lexington, MA: Lexington Books.
Linstone, Harold A. 1984. *Multiple Perspectives for Decision Making: Bridging the Gap between Analysis and Action.* North-Holland: Elsevier Science Pub. Co.
———. 1999. *Decision Making for Technology Executives: Using Multiple Perspectives to Improve Performance.* Norwood, MA: Artech House.
Lipset, Seymour M., and William Schneider. 1983. *Confidence Gap.* New York: Free Press.
Long, Norton E. 1952. Bureaucracy and constitutionalism. *American Political Science Review,* 46: 801–818.

Madland, David, and Ruy Teixeira. 2009. *New Progressive America: The Millennial Generation.* Washington, DC: Center for American Progress.

Makanza, Maggie. 2008. The Majority Are Not Always Right. *Zimbabwe Independent,* June 5. www.theindependent.co.zw/opinion/20461-the-majority-are-not-always-right.html.

Masci, David, Hope Lozano-Bielat, Michelle Ralston, and Elizabeth Podrebarac. 2009. Gay Marriage Around the World. Report, Pew Forum on Religion and Public Life, July 9. http://pewforum.org/Gay-Marriage-and-Homosexuality/Gay-Marriage-Around-the-World.aspx.

Meagher, Sharon M. 2008. *Philosophy and the City: Classic to Contemporary Writings.* Albany: State University of New York Press.

Meredith, Geoffrey E., and Charles D. Schewe. 2007. *Defining Markets, Defining Moments: America's 7 Generational Cohorts, Their Share Experiences, and Why Businesses Should Care.* New York: Hungry Minds. http://www.booklocker.com/pdf/2780s.pdf.

Mosher, F. 1982. *Democracy and Public Service.* New York: Oxford University Press.

Naff, Katherine. 1994. Through the glass ceiling: Prospects for the advancement of women in the federal civil service. *Public Administration Review* 54 (6): 507–514. Reprinted in *Classics of Public Personnel Policy.* 3d ed., ed. F.J. Thompson, 328–345. Belmont, CA: Wadsworth, 2003.

Page, Scott E. 2007. *The Difference: How the Power of Diversity Creates Better Groups, Firms, School, and Societies.* Princeton, NJ: Princeton University Press.

Passel, Jeffrey S., and D'Vera Cohn. 2008. U.S. Population Projections: 2005–2050. Report, Pew Research Center, Social and Demographic Trends, February 11. http://pewsocialtrends.org/pubs/703/population-projections-united-states.

Pasztor, Andy. 2008. NASA takes a leap in outsourcing. *Wall Street Journal,* December 24. http://online.wsj.com/article/SB123006422453630883.html.

Pew Research Center. 2009. The Pew Forum on Religion & Public Life: Gay Marriage & Homosexuality. http://pewforum.org/Topics/Issues/Gay-Marriage-and-Homosexuality/.

Pitts, David W. 2009. Diversity management, job satisfaction, and organizational performance: Evidence from U.S. federal agencies. *Public Administration Review* 69 (2): 328–338.

Rand Reed, Kathleen. 2009. How the multiracial category can be a lifesaver. Letter, April 20. Project Race. www.projectrace.com/urgentmedicalconcern/archive/multiracial_support_medical_concern.php.

Rawls, John, 1993. *Political Liberalism.* New York: Columbia University Press.

Reader, John. 2005. *Cities: A Magisterial Exploration of the Nature and Impact of the City from Its Beginnings to the Mega-Conurbations of Today.* London: Random House.

Reuters. 2008. Cornerstone OnDemand's Client and Partner Conference—Convergence 2008—Highlights. Press release, May 27. www.reuters.com/article/pressRelease/idUS103430+27-May-2008+BW20080527.

Riccucci, Norma M. 1986. Female and minority employment in city government: The role of unions. *Policy Studies Journal* 15 (1): 3–15.

———. 1987. Black employment in municipal work forces. *Public Administration Quarterly* 11 (1): 76–89.

———. 1990. *Women, Minorities and Unions in the Public Sector.* Westport, CT: Greenwood Press.

Riccucci, Norma M. and Judith R. Saidel. 1997. The representativeness of state-level bureaucratic leaders: A missing piece of the representative bureaucracy puzzle. *Public Administration Review,* 57 (5): 423–430.

Rushefsky, Mark E. 2002. *Public Policy in the United States: At the Dawn of the Twenty-first Century.* Armonk, NY: M.E. Sharpe.

Sanders, Steve. 2007. Federalism and same-sex marriage. Paper presented at the annual meeting of the American Political Science Association, Hyatt Regency Chicago and the Sheraton Chicago Hotel and Towers, Chicago, August 30.

Saxonhouse, Arlene W. 1992. *Fear of Diversity: The Birth of Political Science in Ancient Greek Thought.* Chicago: University of Chicago Press.

Schiesinger, Stephen. 2009. Why a league of democracies will not work. *Ethics and International Affairs* 23 (1): 13–18.

Sheeran, Michael J. 1983. *Beyond Majority Rule: Voteless Decisions in the Religious Society of Friends.* Philadelphia: Quaker Books.

Simon, Herbert A. 1976. *Administrative Behavior: A Study of Decision-Making Processes in Administrative Organization.* New York: Macmillan.

Spirgi, Heidi, and Jason Corsello. 2009. An opportunity for change: 10 recommendations for advancing your HR technology strategy. Research Study, Knowledge Infusion Center of Excellence, April.

Spitz, Laura. 2004. At the intersection of North American free trade and same-sex marriage. *UCLA Journal of International Law and Foreign Affairs* 9:163.

Strauss, William, and Neil Howe. 1992. *Generations: The History of America's Future, 1584 to 2069.* New York: William Morrow.

Strivers, Camilla. 2002. *Gender Images in Public Administration Legitimacy and the Administrative State.* Washington, DC: Sage.

Taylor, Charles. 1983. *Sources of the Self: The Making of the Modern Identity.* Cambridge, MA: Harvard University Press.

Van Riper, Paul P. 1958. *History of the United States Civil Service, 1789–1957.* Evanston, IL: Row, Peterson.

Voters For Peace. 2009. AF-PAK War View Depends on Age, Gender. http://votersforpeace.us/press/index.php?itemid=2657.

Walzer, Michael. 1995. *Toward a Global Civil Society.* Providence: Berghahn Books.

White, Harvey L. 2010. Talent Development and Management: Optimizing Human Performance in the Public Sector. In Proceeding of the International Conference on Administrative Development: Towards Excellence In Public Sector Performance. King Faisal Hall for Conferences, Riyadh Kingdom of Saudi Arabia November 1–4, 2009 http://www.fifty.ipa.edu.sa/conf/customcontrols/paperworkflash/Content/pdf/m2/en/11.pdf.

White, Harvey L. and Mitchell F. Rice. 2010. In *Diversity and Public Administration: Theory, Issues and Perspectives,* ed. M. Rice. Armonk, NY: M.E. Sharpe.

Williams, Kim. 2006. *Mark One or More: Civil Rights in Multiracial America.* Ann Arbor: University of Michigan Press.

Zogby International. 1999. New poll: Voters support social security privatization. August 2. www.socialsecurity.org/zogby/fullreport.pdf.

PART V

INTERNATIONAL AND
GLOBAL CHALLENGES

International and global challenges have immersed public administrators in complex patterns of interdependent collaborations, networks, and intersecting relationships that are radically shifting study, research, and practice priorities within the profession. As Fred Riggs (2000) points out in his work on Globalization and Public Administration, the locus and focus of public administration are expanding "both above and beyond states and also below them" into the international arena.[1] While state institutions remain the foundation for public services, their purpose, design, and functions are being reshaped by the influence of accelerating globalization. The contributors in this final section address international and global challenges confronting the profession. They also highlight the exciting possibilities these challenges represent for reinvigorating public administration as a field of study, research, and practice.

The discussion of these challenges begins with Alan Lawton and Frédérique Six's work "New Public Management: Lessons from Abroad." Acknowledging the phenomenal influence of the public management movement on provision of public services, Lawton and Six examine its development as an academic concept, an ideology, and a reform action. Attention is then given to the degree to which the movement has taken hold across the world. At the center of this discussion is whether new public management is an appropriate alternative to public administration. It is concluded that while "efficiency in the delivery of public services has improved, targets have been met, [and] some services are more user friendly," other issues are not addressed. As they explain, the traditional, "first-order questions that public administration addressed were concerned with the relationships between public and private interests, between the citizen and the state, between democracy and bureaucracy, between the rule of law and pragmatic decision making; areas not address by management." New public management is "clearly not a universal panacea for all social ills, not least because the solution to such ills lies in the realm of politics and not management."

Jamil Jreisat's chapter, "Governance: Issues in Concept and Practice," analyzes governance through three sets of issues and questions: (1) What is governance, why is good governance vital for the overall development of a society, and how has globalization effected governance; (2) what are the key attributes of a good governance system and how do we assess them, or measure them; and (3) are there widely recognized imperatives or core values that signify good governance? Two conclusions around these questions are that good governance is ethical and accountable governance. It creates trust and promotes broadly shared values. However, as Jreisat explains, a critical attribute of a "good" governance system includes the capacity to act in the public interest. A major step in this regard would be the international diffusion of common public administration professional standards leading to efficiency, effectiveness, and responsiveness. Jreisat notes, however, "In the final analysis, the most appropriate and reliable indicator of the efficacy of a governance system is its performance and outcome."

The third chapter in this section, "Development Management: Renewal and Discovery in the

Twenty-first Century," by Louis A. Picard, examines the evolution of development management from its roots in post–World War II foreign aid. The role played by the Comparative Administration Group in that process is reviewed to provide a context for an understanding of development management debates in the post–September 11 period. The impact of international donors on development administration is also considered, as is the decline of the state-centric focus of development administration as a framework for development policy. Picard offers several conclusions about development management: Governance and political development are important and remain both controversial and still somewhat neglected; since September 11, 2001, many donors have opted for a whole-of-government approach, which links up the "three Ds of defense, diplomacy and development"; and the post–September 11 focus on links between security, diplomacy, and foreign aid and the trauma of the 2008 economic meltdown have (at least temporarily) reinvigorated assumptions of Keynesian economics and the planning process that accompanies it.

In the final chapter, "The Crisis of Public Administration in a Postglobal World," David Schultz argues that the 2008–9 Western banking crisis and global recession produced a historic event on two counts. First, the state intervention to save banks and the free market from themselves undermines whatever remaining legitimacy there is in the intellectual foundations of neoliberal ideology. Second, the crisis and collapse of the financial sector challenge public administration to better perform its role of regulating the economy and delivering goods and services.

These events, it is argued, suggest the need for a new theory that challenges the current paradigm of globalism and conceptualizes an alternative vision that promotes national public interests that are not adverse to one another. This would require a public administration that addresses global problems such as pollution, depletion of natural resources, poverty, and aggression.

According to Schultz, the stage is set for a new vision of the world in ways that have not been seen since the 1930s. Public administration is a major part of the show. How well it performs will determine the future of the profession.

NOTE

1. W. Fred Riggs, "Globalization and Public Administration," October 23, 2000.

CHAPTER 24

NEW PUBLIC MANAGEMENT

Lessons from Abroad

ALAN LAWTON AND FRÉDÉRIQUE SIX

Writing a chapter on new public management (NPM) has an old-fashioned ring to it. In a special edition of the journal *Public Management Review* published in 2001, the guest editors titled their editorial "Towards a Post–New Public Management Agenda" (Polidano and Hulme 2001). This special edition addressed, specifically, governance reform in developing countries. In 2006, the title of an editorial in the same journal reads, "The New Public Governance?" (Osborne 2006). Clearly things are afoot. Yet in 2009 an article by two eminent scholars in the field begins with the title "The Proverbs of New Public Management" (Meier and O'Toole 2009). There does appear to be life left in the term. Moreover, it continues to engage both academics and practitioners as a "theory in use." The term *theory* is used with caution, recognizing that there is disagreement as to what NPM means, and, indeed, for Polidano and Hulme (2001), "To generalise about the new public management may be about as productive an activity as tilting at windmills" (298).

It is easy to see how scholars might arrive at such a conclusion. In an early, influential discussion of NPM it is described by Hood (1991) as an administrative label, a movement, a "marriage of two different streams of ideas" (5), a joint philosophy, a revolution and a "manifesto," and a "whim of fashion," all within the first four pages of the article! The reader might wonder at the kind of evidence that would confirm, or refute, its success! It is also discussed by Barzelay (2002) in this way: "The New Public management (NPM) began life as a conceptual device invented for purposes of structuring scholarly discussion of contemporary changes in the organization and management of executive government" (16).

In attempting to provide an overview of NPM, a first question is, What exactly is the nature of the thing under investigation? A second question emerging from the literature concerns the extent of its existence around the world. Indeed, one scholar has claimed that "from Korea to Brazil, from Portugal to Sweden, government sector reform has transformed public management" (Kettl 1997, 446).

A third question, and this relates to the article by Meier and O'Toole (2009), is the extent, and type, of evidence that supports the claims made on behalf of NPM. That is, is there any basis for believing that the reforms that fall under the NPM umbrella work in transforming government?

This chapter is interested in the answers to these questions and, just as important, in determining what type of evidence is used to answer such questions. Is the evidence all of the same character? It is suggested that NPM can be understood from three different but interlocking perspectives, each with its own logic and each focusing upon different aspects of NPM. First, NPM can be viewed as an ideology that relies upon a particular rhetoric within a tradition of discourse. The logic of this discourse is continuity, conviction, and conversion. Second, NPM can be examined in action. How does a particular reform, for example, delivering services through arm's-length agencies, work in this country or that? How do issues of design and implementation make it more likely that the reform, indeed any reform, will succeed? Thus, the chapter explores the classic ideas represented in implementation and organizational change studies. Third, NPM is examined from an academic scholarly perspective. In this perspective attention is focused on systematically evaluating what reform initiatives have achieved in terms of results; what works under which circumstances and why? The final section of the chapter examines the degree to which the movement has taken hold across the world. The degree of convergence that may or may not be discerned is, therefore, discussed. The first task is to review what is considered to be included in NPM.

WHAT IS NPM?

Many authors give their definition of what NPM entails. For example, Hughes (2003, 3) summarizes the distinction between public administration and (new) public management this way: "In short, the traditional model of administration is based on bureaucracy; management is based on markets." The Organization for Economic Cooperation and Development (OECD 1998, 5) sees NPM as the new approach to public management that uses "management by objectives and performance measurement, the use of markets and market-type mechanisms in place of centralized command-and-control-style regulation, competition and choice, and devolution with better matching of authority, responsibility and accountability."

In theoretical terms the OECD (1998, 5) formulates NPM as a "new paradigm which attempts to combine modern management practices with the logic of economics, while still retaining core public service values." In Hughes's terms (2003, 6), "public management reforms have been driven by totally different underlying theories: that economic motivations can be assumed for all players in government; that private management flexibility provides lessons for government; and that there can be no separation of politics from administration."

In greater detail, Osborne and Gaebler (1992), who are often considered the first to put forward NPM as a package of reform principles, offer the following:

- Catalytic government: steering rather than rowing;
- Community-owned government: empower communities to solve their own problems rather than simply deliver services;
- Competitive government: injecting competition into service delivery;
- Mission-driven government: be driven by missions, rather than rules;
- Results-oriented government: funding outcomes, not inputs;
- Customer-driven government: meeting the needs of the customer, not the bureaucracy;
- Enterprising government: earning rather than spending;
- Preventive government: invest in preventing problems rather than curing crises;
- Decentralized government: decentralize authority;
- Market-oriented government: solve problems by influencing market forces rather than creating public programs.

Such principles act as a call to action rather than offering a description of the way public services are delivered universally. A feature of early discussions of NPM was this search for principles that might underpin a new way of conducting the government's business. Hood (1991) depicts NPM as consisting of seven doctrines, which are largely similar to the Osborne and Gaebler principles:

1. Hands-on professional management
2. Explicit standards and measures of performance
3. Greater emphasis on output controls
4. Shift to disaggregation of units in the public sector
5. Shift to greater competition in the public sector
6. Stress on private sector styles of management practice
7. Stress on greater discipline and parsimony in resource use

More recent discussions moved away from a search for principles in an attempt to identify what has been really happening. For example, Pollitt and Bouckaert (2004) perform a comparative analysis of public sector reform in twelve countries and distinguish two main groups. The first group, labeled the core NPM group, consists of Australia, New Zealand, the United Kingdom, and, "in words if not always in deeds," the United States: "They all see a large role for private sector forms and techniques in the process of restructuring the public sector. . . . The prophets of the core NPM states envisaged an entrepreneurial, market-oriented society, with a light icing of government on top" (98, 100).

The second group, labeled the neo–Weberian state group, consists of continental European modernizers such as Belgium, Finland, France, the Netherlands, Italy, Sweden, and Germany below the federal level: "They continue to place greater emphasis on the state as the irreplace-able integrative force in society, with a legal personality and operative value system that can-not be reduced to the private sector discourse of efficiency, competitiveness, and consumer satisfaction" (98).

Within this second group a further distinction can be made between the form practiced in the northern countries that "foresaw a citizens' state, with extensive participation facilitated by a modernized system of public law that would guarantee rights and duties" (100).

The form practiced in the central European countries consists of a "professional state—modern, efficient and flexible, yet still uniquely identified with the 'higher purposes' of the general inter-est" (100).

What is striking in the descriptions of these reforms is that none refer to "joined-up government" or the use of the network or collaborative approach. These developments are clearly considered separate from the NPM reforms (see also Pollitt 2009). The extent to which NPM reforms constitute a specific model of public sector reform, limited in time and space, is, therefore, worth examining (see Mathiasen 2007), and this is discussed in the final section.

PERSPECTIVE 1: NPM AS IDEOLOGY

In making sense of NPM as an ideology, issues of tradition, discourse, and rhetoric are of inter-est. Ideology is not seen purely in terms of a political ideology. As critics have pointed out, one of the features of NPM is that it is neutral in terms of its choice of political home, at least along the traditional left-right divide (e.g., Hughes 2003). It is just as likely to be adopted by left- as by right-wing political parties, and governments of different political persuasions. It is claimed to mirror the "end of ideology" as depicted in numerous fin de siècle writings at the end of the twentieth century. Yet there are clear political divisions regarding more or less marketization and privatization. Rather, NPM is presented, in this chapter, as a tradition of thought where different elements make up a reasonably consistent and coherent whole that has some practical use and appeals to the values and emotions of those who already subscribe to it and those who may be attracted, but not yet committed, to it. Regardless of the claims made, it is not the rational implementation of a neutral set of tools. At the same time, it is based on a particular view of human nature, economic individualism, and is framed by a particular view of the world that encompasses neo-institutional theory and transaction-cost economics (see Bozeman 2007). There are different aspects to NPM as ideology.

Continuity over Time

The notion of NPM as part of a tradition of discourse is at the heart of historical approaches to the subject. For example, Hood (2007) provides a history of the term *public management,* drawing upon various themes that have fallen under its umbrella. Similarly, Lynn (2007) visits ancient China, the Middle Ages, eighteenth-century Germany, and the modern-day United States. Ideology can be seen as a tradition of thought and discourse, rather than sets of doctrines to be considered true or false. From this perspective it is not clear what kind of activity would confirm or refute NPM. However, scholars look for continuity over time such that "progress" is charted from traditional bureaucracy to progressive public administration, to NPM, and beyond to new public governance. Thus, Thynne (2003), for example, contrasts what he calls progressive public administration with its heyday in the pre-1980s; NPM with its heyday in the 1980s and 1990s; and enlightened public governance from 2000 onwards. It does not matter whether countries have started from the same point; the question is to what extent do they participate in the same conversation.

The assumption is of a trajectory across time and space and, as with all ideology, there is a sense of movement toward some better future that envisages a more efficient and effective public service that is responsive to the customer. The contrast for all ideologies is with some past that needs to be escaped from, in this case red tape and bureaucracy. It is not the concern of the ideologist whether there is any evidence to support such claims.

One variation of the discussion has been to focus on public service values and the extent to which they have been affected by NPM. Thus, it is claimed that a public service ethos is undermined (Doig and Wilson 1998; Hebson, Grimshaw, and Marchington 2003); professional values have been negatively affected (Powell, Brock, and Hinings 1999); and morale, motivation, and job satisfaction have been lowered (Foster and Wilding 2000). There is, however, a distinct lack of evidence to validate such claims. In fact, Kolthoff (2007) finds a positive relationship between the application of some businesslike management tools and the reduction of integrity violations.

Kernaghan (1994) argues that traditional values will survive, but they will have to contend with new values, particularly those of service, innovation, teamwork, and quality. Both old and new values could be complementary. For example, integrity becomes even more important in the context of the "freedom to manage," empowerment, and service to the public. Similarly, accountability is particularly crucial in partnerships and delivering public services through networks of public, private, and third sector organizations.

Conviction Involving Faith and Believers

More than one scholar has referred to NPM in religious terms, suggesting that faith plays a role in the adoption of NPM (see Meier and O'Toole 2009). As Gray and Jenkins (1995) put it, "Faith is not too strong a word to describe public management and its growth. Many of its advocates are clearly true believers in the power and the sanctity of markets" (82).

Supporters of NPM are prone to see it everywhere (Polidano 1999) while opponents of NPM have a different vision of the world. This is not to say that there is no possibility of a dialogue between supporters and opponents, not least in terms of agreed-upon problems. Inefficiency, corruption, and unemployment can be recognized by all—it is the solutions offered to such problems that are more likely to be the subject of intense debate.

Hood (1991) depicted NPM as consisting of seven doctrines (see the first section of this chapter). According to the OECD, a doctrine is "a principle of religious or political belief," "a dogma." As doctrines they are appeals to the faithful, rather than hypotheses to be tested empirically.

Conversion in Terms of Rhetoric

The debate is often presented in black-and-white terms (either for good or for evil), and opponents of NPM need to have an alternative to convince us of the rightness of their views. There is a gap between proving the truth of a claim and persuading others to accept it. As Graham (1986) suggests, this gap represents the difference between logic and rhetoric; the latter is to be found in the realm of politics. Graham invokes the law of noncontradiction—a single individual cannot accept both the presuppositions of an ideology and the doctrines of another that deny those presuppositions.

According to Graham there are four conditions of a political ideology:

1. Different elements must form a reasonably consistent and coherent whole.
2. Any factual claim made, or implied, or presupposed must be true. "This sounds a rather demanding condition but all it is meant to capture is the idea that falsehood, logical invalidity, and conceptual confusion, are faults of reasoning whatever the subject in hand" (76).
3. It must have some practical use.
4. It must make an appeal to political values shared by those who do not yet subscribe to it.

Why, then, is NPM compelling? Is it because of evidence that it works in solving society's problems or because it appeals to individuals at some level, intellectually or emotionally? Is it convincing as an explanation of reform? Is it believed that NPM will change the lives of citizens for the better? If so, then perhaps it has something in common with ideology. Not only that, but both NPM and ideology address both issues of tradition and issues of reform, with both continuity and change. Ideology is not concerned with a complete break with the past, but rather with explaining current events as a particular reading of the past, and this points the way forward. NPM similarly tries to account for past events, such as the perceived ineffectiveness of traditional public administration, and offers solutions to take us forward.

PERSPECTIVE 2: NPM AS DESIGN AND IMPLEMENTATION

In the previous perspective of NPM as ideology, the rhetoric of launching new reform initiatives is key. The OECD (2002, in Pollitt and Bouckaert 2004) observes that there are clear political advantages to launching such initiatives and political disadvantages in carrying these reforms through. The perspective of design and implementation focuses on actually making the reforms work. In many countries there is a notorious lack of sufficient attention to the actual design and implementation of reforms, probably for the reasons pointed out by the OECD, among others.

Design

The translation of generic organizational principles to the design of specific tasks is not an easy or a straightforward exercise. Market principles are more easily applied to tasks where the desired output can be defined unambiguously, and process requirements—how the output is achieved—are not important. An example of where this is the case is household waste collection; an example of where this is very difficult is health or education, in which the process, that is, the relationship between the doctor and her patient and between the teacher and his student, is a key part of determining the outcome, that is, better health or education. Another example of the design challenge is the performance measurement and management system. In general, a system to systematically measure, and possibly also manage, performance makes sense. The devil, however, is in the details. How can one design such a system for a specific task in a specific context so that it delivers the desired intended effect without (too many) unintended perverse effects? Too often performance systems fail because there are too many unintended consequences. This effect had been described time and time again, in private corporations and public institutions, and long before the start of NPM-type reforms (e.g., Kerr 1975).

Ferlie and Geraghty (2007) argue that more research needs to be done to demonstrate the responses by professionals to public sector reforms. They point to the fact that reforms are welcomed by some but not others. They distinguish between hard and soft NPM; hard NPM focuses on audit and performance and follows an accounting logic. Soft NPM focuses on a user orientation, quality issues, organizational development, and learning. According to Batley (1999), "Reform has tended to focus on organizational structures: more attention needs to be given to supporting more efficient financial and human resource management and the management of services to suit specific customers" (763).

O'Toole and Meier (2009) find evidence that the quality of a public sector organization's human resource management positively affects its performance, as measured by a variety of measures and for a variety of stakeholders.

In rapidly changing societies, organizations need to improve their capacity for continuous learning. This learning occurs at all levels. Most reform initiatives that are part of NPM pay no (explicit) attention to continuous organizational learning. As Pollitt (2009) shows, restructuring of public sector organizations takes place more frequently but, if anything, leads to more memory loss rather than organizational learning. He concludes his analysis of organizational memory loss as follows: "For all their hypothesized benefits in terms of flexibility, [NPM organizations] may well make more avoidable mistakes, unintentionally damage existing strengths, pursue false and glib historical analogies, and muddy the trail of public accountability" (15).

A key theme of NPM in developing countries is the capacity of government organizations to deliver reform. Often skills are not available to properly draft, negotiate, monitor, evaluate, and enforce service contracts (Wenzel 2007). Change management requires bonds of trust and capacity building as well as effective control and political oversight.

Implementation

Baier, March and Sætren (1986) propose two interpretations of implementation problems. The first interpretation concerns bureaucratic incompetence, which could be due to a lack of training, poor organization and management, or inadequate resources. The second interpretation suggests a conflict of interest between policy makers and bureaucratic agents, leading to differences in organizational control. The two interpretations are not mutually exclusive. They argue that some parts of any organization may have incentives for pursuing objectives that deviate from any policy that might be adopted. Thus, policy ambiguities, and organizational dysfunctions, are often ignored by rational policy makers: "Any simple concept of implementation, with its implicit assumption of clear and stable policy intent, is likely to lead to a fundamental misunderstanding of the policy process and to disappointment with efforts to reform it" (211).

In a sweeping critique of the contributions to Ferlie, Lynn, and Pollitt (2007), Hughes (2006) argues that most of the authors do not recognize the difference between public administration and public management and have little understanding of managerial reform. There is a distinction to be made between managers, management, and managing. Managers may be considered as part of a profession, distinct from other professionals, and have skills and knowledge developed through formal training, often with advanced qualifications such as an MBA. They will expect a certain amount of autonomy and, in the language of NPM, will have the "freedom to manage." The extent to which they act in their own interests in a similar fashion to other professions is a moot point. Managers in the public services have been castigated by both politicians and academics. Indeed, scholars have characterized "managerialism" as an ideology (Pollitt 1993; Newman 2002). The authors' experience in working with managers in the public services over a twenty-year period is that in dealing with a multitude of stakeholders, with ambiguity in policy making and competing goals, all with limited resources, the majority of managers should be applauded rather than criticized!

In distinguishing management from managers, the focus is on issues of control, structure, and decision making. That is, management as an organizational layer needs to be understood in terms of power, particularly in relation to politicians. Similarly, it is appropriate to distinguish the practice, the actual act of managing, from management and managers. The act will reflect relations with others, both inside and outside the particular organization that the individual works in. Responsiveness, integrity, duty, loyalty, empathy, sympathy, and so on will characterize the act of managing.

There will be tensions among all of these, and they will operate at different levels. The tensions are not between public and private, nor between traditional public administration and NPM. We need to know more about how reforms affect these different aspects. Pollitt and Bouckaert (2004) examine ten "alleged" contradictions in NPM reform on the degree to which they are truly contradictions and could thus be said to weaken claims of NPM as a successful coherent theory and ideology. They conclude that, aside from some true contradictions, several are "implementation challenges rather than fundamental logical contradictions," for example, "give priority to making savings [versus] improving the performance of the public sector" and "responsibilize government [versus] reduce the range of tasks government is involved with." With some others "there may be a deep-lying tension but the edge can be taken off it by skilled leadership and implementation," for example, "reduce the burden of internal scrutiny and associated paperwork [versus] sharpen managerial accountability" (179–180).

Another gap in reform initiatives is that insufficient attention is paid to the readiness for change of the officials whose behavior needs to change. Cinite, Duxbury and Higgins (2009) identified three indicators of readiness for change—commitment of senior management to the change, competence of change agents, and support of immediate manager—and two indicators of unreadiness for change—poor communication of change and adverse impact of change on work. Their measure contains seventeen items, such as "senior management defines the course of change and stays the course for several years," "change agents have done research to select the right type of change that address the underlying causes of organizational problems rather than just symptoms," "managers acknowledge the impact the change may have on their staff," and "the change process does not involve the phasing out of old duties, and the employee is expected to do both the old and the new duties (reverse coding)" (271). Today's knowledge about effective implementation processes is rarely applied to public sector organizations. Traditionally in the public sector reforms are implemented by way "of a pre-designed top-down implementation process after the content of the new strategy has been formulated," while research shows that "successful implementation

in the public sector also requires a bottom-up approach with some degree of employee participation" (Sminia and Van Nistelrooij 2006, 100–101). Sometimes at the beginning of a change
process, the intention is there, but when the going gets tough, as is almost inevitable in major
change programs, top management often resorts to the old "safe" top-down approach (Sminia
and Van Nistelrooij 2006).

All of this lends credibility to Hood and Peters's (2004) arguments concerning the paradoxes
and surprises, the unintended consequences, the discontinuities and the nonlinearities, of public
service reform. Students of organizations have long known of unintended consequences and the
difficulties in demonstrating causal relationships. This is the result of entering the "middle age" of
NPM, youthful certainties cast aside. They point to the casual adoption of poorly grounded models,
the disregard of historical evidence, and active resistance to learning in any meaningful sense.

PERSPECTIVE 3: NPM AS AN ACADEMIC RESEARCH FIELD

NPM reforms are said to follow evidence-based practice, but often such evidence is lacking. Given
the lack of evidence, then, an ideological understanding has some currency. What is interesting
about Meier and O'Toole's (2009) evidence-based approach to NPM is to critique a proverb with
empirical evidence. For them a proverb is a contention made about best practice or correct management. In the *Oxford English Dictionary* a proverb is a "short pithy saying in general use, held
to embody a general truth." It comes as no surprise that they found mixed evidence.

When looking at NPM from the perspective of academic research, the key challenge is to evaluate
"what works in what situation and why?" (Hodgson, Farrell and Connolly 2007, 378). What are the
underlying mechanisms that make for a particular reform to be considered successful in a particular
context? This simple, straightforward sentence hides many complications. First of all, what are the
criteria to judge a reform's success by? Especially in the public sector, the specific aims and goals
to be achieved by a particular reform may be ambiguous and contested. Second, what exactly is the
reform to be evaluated? Traditionally policy evaluations focus not only on goal achievement, but
also on establishing a causal link between the particular policy and the goal achievement (Dunn
2007). In an increasingly complex society, these direct and simple causal links from intended policy
to achieved result are extremely difficult to prove scientifically. Furthermore, most societal problems,
and hence governments' tasks, are multifaceted and complex, requiring multiple policies. In this
light it makes most sense to evaluate the effectiveness of governance on goal achievement, analyzing
the whole range of government actions and other influences that have contributed to the results that
have been achieved. This approach provides more fruitful avenues for understanding what works and
what does not work in modern governance. In this approach it is important that goals be seen more
broadly than pure content (e.g., number of children lifted out of poverty); they may and probably
will also contain elements of the process and the principles (e.g., equity and integrity) by which the
results in terms of content have been achieved (Bovaird and Löffler 2003).

Another complication is that it is important for academic scholars to distinguish three dimensions in realizing (public sector) reforms: (1) the validity and appropriateness of the theories and
underlying assumptions applied in the reform; (2) the appropriateness of the design, given the
specific task in the specific context; and (3) the appropriateness of the implementation process,
given the specific task and the specific context. The reader may notice that these dimensions have
already been discussed to a degree as different perspectives of NPM. In academic research terms,
a reform can be considered successful only if all three dimensions are found to be appropriate,
because only then will the reform work. The theory and underlying assumptions may be correct,
but if the design principles that follow from the theory are not applied appropriately to the specific

situation, then the reform will fail. Even if the detailed design, based on sound theoretical design principles, is appropriate, it is still possible for the reform to fail, if the implementation process is not attended to. Reform initiatives, in practice, can fail on each of these hurdles. Because academic research so far has not been able to systematically evaluate NPM reforms in the detail needed, taking the different task characteristics and context characteristics into account, or distinguishing between the three dimensions mentioned above, it is currently impossible to make any claims as to the degree that NPM theory holds or not. It is very possible that some critics of NPM have pointed at failed reforms to make their point that NPM should not be applied to that policy field or that public organization, where the failure was due to bad implementation. Similarly it is entirely likely that some critics make sweeping statements about the failure of NPM reform principles, using examples of botched-up designs to make their point, which does not necessarily mean that the underlying theoretical principles are at fault.

Pollitt and Bouckaert (2004, 196) conclude that the main principles of public management "should not be applied sweepingly, as though they were universals, but need rather be tailored to specific organizational contexts." But as Peters (1998) put it, we have not yet done the right type of academic research to build theories at the level that may lead to useful practical advice to practitioners: "Our classification of government organisations tends to be on the basis of what they do—health, defence and so on—rather than on structural or managerial grounds that would provide more of a basis for reform recommendations. While we can think of a number of potentially relevant criteria, such as size, professionalization, client involvement, there is not yet sufficient evidence to make good predictive statements to aid reformers" (96).

Why has this type of research not been commissioned by governments? Practitioners must surely want such evidence-based advice. Or at least that would be the scholar's perspective. Hodgson, Farrell, and Connolly (2007) observe, "Despite the UK's large expenditure programme supporting the delivery of better public services as well as a large political drive promoting this agenda, there is insufficient academic knowledge available on what factors can influence and promote upward shifts in performance" (377).

Pollitt and Bouckaert (2004) observe that economists appear to have been much more ready to offer prescriptions than public administration or management scholars. A possible explanation of this may be that economists tend to theorize more deductively, arguing from abstract theoretical propositions, while the public administration or management scholars tend to work more inductively, arguing from empirical evidence. And this empirical evidence is as yet lacking for solid evidence-based prescriptions.

Jones, Guthrie, and Steane (2001, in Hughes 2003) provide an interesting explanation for why academics tend to be among the most critical of NPM:

> Critics of NPM appear to outnumber advocates in academe, if not in the practitioner environment. Some of this may be related to the fact that academics face professional and career incentives to find fault rather than extol success. . . . Some criticism may derive from the fact that it is perceived to draw conceptually too strongly from a "business school/private management" perspective. This conceptual framework threatens the foundations of much of what is believed to be gospel and is taught in government and public-private sector relationships to students in public administration programmes, in political science and related disciplines. (23–24)

The late management scholar Sumantra Ghoshal (2005) argued that "bad management theories are destroying good management practices." He focused on business schools and their impact on

MBA students who then go into corporate businesses, but the argument applies equally to public management students who are taught these rational-choice theories and then apply them in the public sector. The key theories driving NPM reforms are rational-choice-based theories, and these theories make unnecessarily negative assumptions about people and institutions. These theories are also presented as "amoral." "By propagating ideologically inspired amoral theories, business schools have actively freed their students from any sense of moral responsibility" (76).

Coupled with the pretense of knowledge, these ideology-based theories lead to excessive truth claims based on partial analysis and unbalanced assumptions. These claims influence practitioners, many of whom will adopt the theorists' worldview, and the negative assumptions inherent in the ideologically driven theories become real as the practitioners apply them (Ghoshal 2005). Hence the importance of carefully distinguishing claims based on ideology from those based on sound empirical evidence.

NPM AND CONVERGENCE?

Much of the debate has also centered on the extent to which different countries around the world have adopted NPM, in terms of either its rhetoric or the tools that are said to form part of NPM (see Common 1998; Polidano 1999; McCourt 2008; Steane 2008). One commentator has suggested a "global revolution" despite the fact that the focus of the research appears to be Australia, New Zealand, the United Kingdom, and the United States (Kettl 1997). The claims to universality are said to depend upon a number of conditions: first, the adoption of the same set of doctrines (e.g., Hood's seven doctrines introduced before) as the means to solve the problems of traditional public administration; second, that reforms are apolitical and are supported by politicians of all hues; third, that problems in one country are similar, and linked to, problems in other countries; and fourth, that there is a new global paradigm replacing commonly held assumptions and bringing in a new agenda, values, and policies. All of these are contested.

For many scholars, the main line of inquiry appears to be to identify key aspects of NPM as discussed in the literature and then look for their existence in particular countries. These aspects are said to include the use of markets and deregulation (Steane 2008); contracting and citizen charters (McCourt 2008); and the use of agencies to enhance managerial freedoms (Verschuere and Barbieri 2009). There appears to be general agreement that reforms have been more readily accepted in some countries and have taken hold as a way of doing government business. These countries include Australia, New Zealand, the United States, Canada and the United Kingdom (e.g., Pollitt and Bouckaert 2004). However, even among this group, it is argued, there are differences (Osborne 2006). Lynn (2006), for example, argues that NPM in the United States focused on managerial discretion, quality, and entrepreneurship and far less on market-mimicking reforms that had long been popular anyway.

In other countries individual elements have taken hold. Scholars offer different reasons as to why this might be the case, and these reasons take a number of forms. First, it is the political, social and legal context of the state that determines the kind of reforms that are adopted. Thus, Wenzel (2007) for example, argues that in many countries it is the centralization and personalization of political power that determines whether reform will take place and shapes that reform. Schedler and Proeller (2002) distinguish among unitary, centralist, and federalist states, and Verschuere and Barbieri (2009), in their research on agencies, argue that it is country-specific factors that determine reform processes. Some authors make use of Hofstede's typology of cultural differences to explore country differences (Flynn 2002; Pollitt and Bouckaert 2004; Verschuere and Barbieri 2009). Indeed, Kickert (2005) argues that the study of public administration (not just the practice) differs from country to country depending upon the intellectual context for discussing public sector reform. Thus, continental Europe draws upon a political science background; in southern Europe it is the law; in the Nordic countries it is business administration. In the United Kingdom traditional public administration was taught in social science schools, NPM in business schools.

A second set of reasons for the adoption or otherwise of NPM reforms refers to the capacity of governments, and the competences of public officials, to implement reform. Batley (1999), for example, argues that the capacity of governments to perform market-sensitive regulatory and enabling roles is weak. He argues that senior managerial power has increased but there has not been an equivalent strengthening of accountability mechanisms.

A third set of reasons refers to the imposition of reforms by international agencies on reluctant recipients that causes problems, and scholars working in the development field have long lamented the impact of organizations such as the World Bank, OECD, and the International Monetary Fund. They have pushed an international vocabulary with terms such as "agentification," "contractualization," "performance measurement," and "privatization" (Pollitt and Bouckaert 2004). Polidano (2001) examines the scope of reform, the role of aid donors, and the leadership of change. He argues that "grand design" can often drive out local reforms. In his view the World Bank comes up with a solution in search of a problem—foisting the solution on to a client government is problematic. In a similar fashion, Batley (1999) argues that the reform agenda is too easily captured by those with a stake in doing reform (donors, consultants, etc.).

Common (1998) is equally critical: "What appears to exist is a global policy community that disperses NPM in a piece-meal fashion to receptive political and administrative elites in individual countries. Academics and consultants who are part of this community may tell us that we are witnessing a paradigm shift but the reality for the majority of the countries of the world is the strengthening and maintenance of bureaucratic government" (448). McCourt (2008), for example, argues for a recognition of diversity: "We suggest that it is the enduring power of sovereign states within their own borders which explains the failure of the attempts to induce reform from outside, and which ultimately explains the return of divergence in public management" (474).

The notion of a paradigm shift, drawing upon the groundbreaking work of Thomas Kuhn (1962), is one that has engaged scholars, with some recognizing reform as constituting a paradigm shift as consensus breaks down and we have new agendas, new values, and new personnel (Gray and Jenkins 1995). NPM is seen as a coming together of political ideology, economic theory, and private sector management practices to constitute a new belief system. Others argue that it lacks coherence and continuity and cannot therefore be said to constitute a global paradigm (see Stoker 1999). It is a moot point how it might constitute a paradigm shift when scholars and practitioners still cling to the "old ways" in terms of a concern with enduring themes of accountability, integrity, rules and processes, and some notion of a public interest. There is still some persuading to do to see such concepts in a new light.

Thus, Polidano (1999) argues that, in the context of the developing world, NPM is only one of a number of currents of reform and suggests that its universal character has long been contested. He suggests that a number of questions need to be addressed, and these will include the following:

1. Are developing countries committing themselves to NPM?
2. Are reforms part of the worldwide quest for efficiency and savings or are they being undertaken for different reasons?
3. Are they being implemented or are we being misled by the rhetoric? Lynn (2006) argues that NPM uses similarities in rhetoric to exaggerate similarities in practice.
4. Are there other reforms that are being undertaken that ignore NPM and might, in fact,

run counter to it? For example, is it budgetary reforms rather than management reforms that make a difference?

5. Are the problems that NPM is said to address the same in all countries? For example, in some countries personnel problems are the issue when recruitment and promotion reflect nepotism or seniority rather than competence. In others, low pay of public officials will be a problem.

All of these constitute a research agenda in their own right. Notwithstanding such remarks, Common (1998) argues that policy responses to similar problems in countries that are at a similar stage of economic development do appear to be convergent. Pollitt (2002) focuses on the notion of convergence and identifies four stages of convergence. These are, first, *discursive convergence,* such that more and more people are using the same concepts. Second is *decisional convergence,* where different authorities adopt similar organizational forms or techniques. Third is *practice convergence,* insofar as organizations begin to work in similar ways. Fourth is *results convergence,* where the outputs and outcomes of public service organizations begin to look similar. He argues that while there may be convergence in rhetoric and organizational forms or techniques, there is less evidence of convergence in terms of practice or results. Hughes (2003) argues that even though there may not be much evidence of Pollitt's convergence, theoretical convergence is present and is arguably the more important. The underlying theoretical basis of NPM is economics and private management. But if we go back to Pollitt and Bouckaert's grouping of three—core NPM countries following the marketization strategy, the northern European countries following a modernizing strategy where the supremacy of the state is upheld with a focus on citizen participation, and the central European countries following a modernizing strategy focusing on the professional state—then even a theoretical convergence may be too much to claim. Yes, most countries now do apply more economic theories and more private management "theories" than at the beginning of the twentieth century, but in degrees and scope that vary greatly. Moreover, all of these still also apply rule of law and principles of hierarchy.

It is clear that the convergence debate is closely linked to the ideology perspective. The design and implementation perspective and the academic research perspective have no need to make claims about convergence, as both perspectives are very sensitive to context. The design and implementation perspective is not concerned at all about which theory or ideology wins the day, as long as the practitioners are provided with actionable advice about how to proceed. Also, as long as there is no strong convincing voice that provides scientifically sound evidence-based advice, politicians and top officials will be more likely to listen to other stronger, more ideology-based voices, in particular if these voices claim worldwide convergence of their ideology.

CONCLUSIONS

Almost ten years after Hood (1991) drew upon the Hans Christian Andersen fable to see whether the NPM emperor had any clothes, Pollitt (2000) concluded that he was not completely naked. Efficiency in the delivery of public services has improved, targets have been met, some services are more user-friendly. Its critique of traditional bureaucracy can be justified. And while the heartlands of NPM have never extended beyond Australia, New Zealand, North America, and the United Kingdom, tools have been adopted by other countries, for instance, the Netherlands and the Nordic countries. So critics who argue that NPM is all hype and no substance can find support for their claims. They can find solace in that it is clearly not a universal panacea for all social ills, not least because the solution to such ills lies in the realm of politics and not management.

The traditional, first-order questions that public administration addressed were concerned with the relationships between public and private interests, between the citizen and the state, between democracy and bureaucracy, between the rule of law and pragmatic decision making. Management deals with second-order questions relating to organizational structures, to strategic fit between the organization and its environment, to financial control, to competences and capacity. Clearly, the two sets of issues are interlinked. The problem, we contend, is using a form of evaluation for one set of questions that is appropriate only for another set of questions.

So the first lesson for scholars researching NPM is to be clear about what exactly is being researched. If the concern is with values, then politics cannot be ignored. If the focus is on management, then design and implementation issues need to be addressed.

This chapter examines NPM from three different perspectives. The first perspective, NPM as ideology, may be summarized as "believe that it works." The second perspective, NPM as design and implementation, may be summarized as a pragmatic "make it work," while the third perspective, NPM as an academic research field, may be summarized as "evaluate what works in what situations and why."

Most debate on NPM has revolved around the appropriateness of applying market principles to the domain of the state. Critics have tended to reject any such application, while supporters have tended to want to apply market principles as much as possible. The latter accept bureaucracy or hierarchy as the organizational form only where transaction-cost economics theory indicates that hierarchy is better than the market. This may suggest that transaction-cost economics theory is neutral as to hierarchy versus the market, but it is a rational-choice theory with assumptions that clearly favor markets. So lesson two is to challenge the assumptions that individuals are rational decision makers and that we need to provide a theory of human nature that recognizes the richness of individual decision making in organizations.

Interestingly, most literature on public sector reform and NPM is only recently coming to terms with the move toward more collaboration between public organizations and public-private partnerships that are found increasingly in practice. (See chapter 17, "Collaborative Public Agencies in the Network Era," in this volume.) In the United Kingdom this movement goes under the name "joined-up government." It is a recognition that most societal challenges cut across organizational boundaries. Thus there are not two but (at least) three possible regimes for organizing public tasks, hierarchy, markets, and networks (e.g., Bradach and Eccles 1989; Thompson et al. 1991). A central thesis of that body of literature is the need to find the appropriate balance between the three related coordinating principles, authority (hierarchy), price or contract (market), and trust (network or social relationships). There are no tested theories yet that can explain when the appropriate balance has been achieved, and therefore no evidence-based advice for practice can be formulated.

Lesson three, therefore, is to move beyond the largely unproductive ideological battle between market versus hierarchy and bureaucracy to recognize that the most appropriate way to organize particular tasks is dependent on the task characteristics and the task environment. There will therefore never be a "one best way" or a "one size fits all." For every task and context, there will be a different mix of the three coordinating principles. The more strongly this recognition becomes part of the debate and the rhetoric of politicians, administrators, consultants, and scholars, the better. It may help avoid repetition of some of the mistakes of the past, for example, regulation gone too far because it was applied across the board, or inappropriate contracting out, where market relations were not warranted, but also bureaucracy gone overboard with red tape and goal displacement. However, given the natural tendency for politicians to make ideology-driven rhetorical statements, this may be too much to hope for.

REFERENCES

Baier, V.E., J.G. March, and H. Sætren. 1986. Implementation and ambiguity. *Scandinavian Journal of Management* (May): 179–212.

Barzelay, M. 2002. Origins of the new public management: An international view from public administration/ political science. In *New Public Management: Current Trends and Future Prospects,* ed. K. McLaughlin, S.P. Osborne, and E. Ferlie. London: Routledge, 15–33.

Batley, R. 1999. The new public management in developing countries: Implications for policy and organizational reform. *Journal of International Development* 11:761–765.

Bovaird, T., and E. Löffler. 2003. Evaluating the quality of public governance: Indicators, models and methodologies. *International Review of Administrative Sciences* 69:313–328.

Bozeman, B. 2007. *Public Values and Public Interest: Counterbalancing Economic Individualism.* Washington, DC: Georgetown University Press.

Bradach, J.L., and R.G. Eccles. 1989. Price, authority and trust: From ideal types to plural forms. *Annual Review of Sociology* 15:97–118.

Cinite, I., L.E. Duxbury, and C. Higgins. 2009. Measurement of perceived organizational readiness for change in the public sector. *British Journal of Management* 20:265–277.

Common, R.K. 1998. Convergence and transfer: A review of the globalisation of new public management. *International Journal of Public Sector Management* 11 (6): 440–450.

Doig, R.A., and J. Wilson. 1998. What price new public management? *Political Quarterly* 69 (3): 267–280.

Dunn, W.N. 2007. *Public Policy Analysis: An Introduction.* 4th ed. Upper Saddle River, NJ: Prentice Hall.

Ferlie, E., and K.J. Geraghty. 2007. Professionals in public service organizations: Implications for public sector "reforming." In *The Oxford Handbook of Public Management,* ed. E. Ferlie, L.E. Lynn Jr., and C. Pollitt. Oxford: Oxford University Press, 422–445.

Ferlie, E., Lynn, L.E. Jr., and C. Pollitt, eds. 2007. *The Oxford Handbook of Public Management,* Oxford: Oxford University Press.

Foster, P., and P. Wilding. 2000. Whither welfare professionalism? *Social Policy and Administration* 34 (2): 143–159.

Flynn, N. 2002. Explaining the new public management: The importance of context. In *New Public Management: Current Trends and Future Prospects,* ed. K. McLaughlin, S.P. Osborne, and E. Ferlie. London: Routledge.

Ghoshal, S. 2005. Bad management theories are destroying good management practices. *Academy of Management Learning and Education* 4 (1): 75–91.

Graham, G. 1986. *Politics in Its Place: A Study of Six Ideologies.* Oxford: Clarendon Press.

Gray, A., and Jenkins, B. 1995. From public administration to public management: Reassessing a revolution? *Public Administration* 73 (Spring): 75–99.

Hebson, G., D. Grimshaw, and M. Marchington. 2003. PPPs and the changing public sector ethos: Case study evidence from the health and local authority sectors' work. *Employment and Society* 17 (3): 481–501.

Hodgson, L., C.M. Farrell, and M. Connolly. 2007. Improving UK public services: A review of the evidence. *Public Administration* 85 (2): 355–382.

Hood, C. 1991. A public management for all seasons? *Public Administration* 69:3–19.

———. 2007. Public management: The word, the movement, the science. In *The Oxford Handbook of Public Management,* ed. E. Ferlie, L.E. Lynn Jr., and C. Pollitt. 7–26 Oxford: Oxford University Press.

Hood, C., and G. Peters. 2004. The middle aging of new public management: Into the age of paradox? *Journal of Public Administration Research and Theory* 14 (3): 267–282.

Hughes, O.E. 2003. *Public Management and Administration: An Introduction.* New York: Palgrave.

———. 2006. The state of public management. *Public Management Review* 8 (3): 483–489.

Kernaghan, K. 1994. The emerging public service culture: Values, ethics and reforms. *Canadian Public Administration* 37 (4): 614–630.

Kerr, S. 1975. On the folly of rewarding A, while hoping for B. *Academy of Management Journal* 18 (4): 769–783.

Kettl, D.F. 1997. The global revolution in public management: Driving themes, missing links. *Journal of Policy Analysis and Management* 16 (3): 446–462.

Kickert, W.J.M. 2005. Distinctiveness in the study of public management in Europe: A historical-institutional analysis of France, Germany and Italy. *Public Management Review* 7 (4): 537–563.

Kolthoff, E. 2007. *Ethics and New Public Management: Empirical Research into the Effects of Businesslike Government on Ethics and Integrity.* The Hague: Boom Juridische Uitgevers.

Kuhn, T.S. 1962. *The Structure of Scientific Revolutions.* Chicago: University of Chicago Press.

Lynn, L.E., Jr. 2006. *Public Management: Old and New.* New York: Routledge.

———. 2007. Public management: A concise history of the field. In *The Oxford Handbook of Public Management,* ed. E. Ferlie, L.E. Lynn Jr., and C. Pollitt.Oxford: Oxford University Press, 27–50.

Mathiasen, D. 2007. International public management. In *The Oxford Handbook of Public Management,* ed. E. Ferlie, L.E. Lynn Jr., and C. Pollitt.643–670 Oxford: Oxford University Press.

McCourt, W. 2008. Public Management in Developing Countries: From downsizing to governance. *Public Management Review* 10 (4): 467–479.

Meier, K.J., and L.J. O'Toole Jr. 2009. The proverbs of new public management: Lessons from an evidence-based research agenda. *American Review of Public Administration* 39 (1): 4–22.

Newman, J. 2002. The new public management, modernization and institutional change: Disruptions, disjunctures and dilemmas. In *New Public Management: Current Trends and Future Prospects,* ed. K. McLaughlin, S.P. Osborne, and E. Ferlie. London: Routledge, 77–91.

Organization for Economic Cooperation and Development (OECD). 1998. Public sector management reform and economic and social development, PUMA. Paris: OECD.

Osborne, D., and T. Gaebler. 1992. *Reinventing Government: How the Entrepreneurial Spirit Is Transforming the Public Sector.* Reading, MA: Addison-Wesley.

Osborne, S.P. 2006. Editorial: The New Public Governance? *Public Management Review* 8 (3): 377–387.

O'Toole, L.J., Jr., and K.J. Meier. 2009. The human side of public organizations: Contributions to organizational performance. *American Review of Public Administration* 39 (5): 499–518.

Peters, B. Guy. 1998. *The New Institutionalism.* London: Cassell.

Polidano, C. 1999. The new public management in developing countries. Public Policy and Management Working Paper no. 13, Institute for Development Policy and Management, University of Manchester.

———. 2001. Why Civil Service Reforms Fail. *Public Management Review* 3 (3): 345–361.

Polidano, C., and D. Hulme. 2001. Editorial: Towards a post–new public management agenda. *Public Management Review* 3 (3): 297–303.

Pollitt, C. 1993. *Managerialism and the Public Services,* 2d ed. Oxford: Blackwell Publishers.

———. 2000. Is the emperor in his underwear? An analysis of the impacts of public management reform. *Public Management* 2 (2): 181–199.

———. 2002. Clarifying convergence: Striking similarities and durable differences in public management reform. *Public Management Review* 3 (4): 471–492.

———. 2009. Bureaucracies remember, post-bureaucratic organizations forget? *Public Administration* 87 (2): 198–218.

Pollitt, C., and G. Bouckaert. 2004. *Public Management Reform: A Comparative Analysis.* 2d ed. Oxford: Oxford University Press.

Powell, M.J., D.M. Brock, and C.R. Hinings. 1999. The changing professional organization. In *Restructuring the Professional: Accounting, Health Care and Law,* ed. D.M. Brock, C.R. Hinings, and M. Powell. London: Routledge, 1–19.

Schedler, K., and I. Proeller. 2002. The new public management: A perspective from mainland Europe. In *New Public Management: Current Trends and Future Prospects,* ed. K. McLaughlin, S.P. Osborne, and E. Ferlie. London: Routledge, 163–180.

Sminia, H., and A.T.M. Van Nistelrooij. 2006. Strategic management and organization development: Planned change in a public sector organization. *Journal of Change Management* 6 (1): 99–113.

Steane, P. 2008. Public management reforms in Australia and New Zealand: A potpourri overview of the past decade. *Public Management Review* 10 (4): 453–465.

Stoker, G. 1999. Introduction: The unintended costs and benefits of new management reform for British local government. In *The New Management of British Local Governance,* ed. G. Stoker. Basingstoke: Macmillan Press, 1–21.

Thompson, G., J. Frances, R. Levacic, and J. Mitchell, eds. 1991. *Markets, Hierarchies and Networks, The Coordination of Social Life.* London: Sage Publications.

Thynne, I. 2003. Making sense of public management reform: "Drivers" and "supporters" in comparative perspective. *Public Management Review* 5 (3): 449–459.

Verschuere, B., and D. Barbieri. 2009. Investigating the "NPM-ness" of agencies in Italy and Flanders: The effect of place, age and task. *Public Management Review* 11 (3): 345–373.

Wenzel, P. 2007. Public-sector transformation in South Africa: Getting the basics right. *Progress in Development Studies* 7 (1): 47–64.

CHAPTER 25

GOVERNANCE

Issues in Concept and Practice

JAMIL JREISAT

The profound and far-reaching effects of governance on contemporary societies have stimulated a worldwide interest in the subject (Ahrens 2002; Hyden 2002; Jain 2002; Jreisat 2001, 2004; Donahue and Nye 2002; Rosell 1999). Ineffective and corrupt governance has been blamed for conditions of poverty, economic stagnation, lack of political stability, confused priorities, corruption, and being an obstacle to sustainable development. As Werlin (2003, 329) argues, "Governance rather than natural resources is the primary reason for the wealth and poverty of nations." Similarly, the ability of a society to prosper in a world of rapid change will largely depend on its ability to develop a more participatory and a more effective governance system (Rosell 1999, ix).

This chapter analyzes governance through three sets of issues and questions: (1) what is governance, why is good governance vital for the overall development of a society, and how has globalization effected governance; (2) what are the key attributes of a good governance system and how do we assess them, or measure them; and, (3) are there widely recognized imperatives or core values that signify good governance?

FUNDAMENTALS OF A GOVERNANCE SYSTEM

Despite the apparent amorphousness of the concept of governance, it is possible to sharpen the focus a little by identifying some constant fundamentals of a governance system, and conditions that enhance its effectiveness. A governance system typically consists of structure, process, and outcomes.

1. Structure

The structure is the form and the standard features of the authority system. The structure is comprised of various elements such as centralized and decentralized authority, organizational and institutional settings, agencies performing special tasks, and the pattern of authority and action that connects all such structural requisites of governance. The capacity of institutions and other structures to perform the functions of governance, effectively and efficiently, is a crucial measure of successful governance. The structure also signifies other characteristics of governance such as level of representation of the people and legitimacy of the authority system.

2. Process

The process defines the rules and the authenticity of methods of decision making. In theory, the process is expected to be oriented to deliver equitable outcomes of public policy and to promote common interests. In reality, the contrast is more recurring than generally known, the process becomes captured by powerful special interests, and serves, largely, to accommodate the narrow objectives of such interest groups. The main aspects of the process of governance are often designated by law or legitimated by a constitution. Other aspects of the process may rely on tradition and precedent, be informal, or even obscured. An open and transparent process, however, indicates genuine responsiveness to citizens' preferences in public policy formulation and implementation. Also, an open and well-reasoned process of decision making increases confidence in the integrity of the system of governance and its actions.

3. Outcomes

Outcomes are the measured quality and quantity of the overall results of the performance of governance, particularly in areas of public service delivery, attaining sustainable development, and improving the attributes of a civil society. Outcomes exemplify accountability of public decision making and illustrate the level of commitment to equity in the distribution of benefits as well as uniformity in the application of law and justice in the society.

Thus, governance is a complex web of structures, processes, and outcomes with society-wide impact. Structures and processes of governing are to ensure that outcomes are consistently and equitably responsive to a society's needs and demands. The practice of governance, however, points out that fidelity to rules and processes is not an assurance of the quality and effectiveness of outcomes. Procedural accountability is not equivalent to performance accountability. Over-conformance and excessive compliance to rules and procedures are known to create rigidities, undermine creativity, and weaken performance. A similar situation is widely revealed in critical reviews of literature on dysfunctions of bureaucratic systems.

GOVERNANCE: DEFINITION, SIGNIFICANCE, AND CHANGING CONTEXT

Interest in the theory and the practice of governance is universal, with enduring search for defining concepts and practices within various cultures. Governance is defined by the United Nations Development Program "as the exercise of economic, political, and administrative authority to manage a country's affairs at all levels, comprising the mechanisms, processes, and institutions through which that authority is directed."[1] Similarly, governance is viewed as the general exercise of public authority (Michalski, Miller, and Stevens 2001, 7; Jreisat 2004, 1004). Derived from the Greek—*to steer*—governance is the process by which a society or an organization steers itself (Rosell 1999, 1). Essentially, governance is a system of many dimensions and has been described in different ways, depending on which aspect is the focus of analysis.

Governance is also an appropriate focus of analysis that permits illustration of the dynamic attributes of substantive public decision-making activities while providing a comprehensive view of the interconnections of the political and administrative spheres. In recent years, as Hyden (2002, 14) points out, the public administration literature and scholars have recognized that conventional jurisdictional boundaries of administration no longer have the same relevance as in the past in explaining what happens with formulation and implementation of policy. In many states, administration is bent in the image of governance.

Broadly conceived, governance is an inclusive function that includes, in addition to central government, other players who share in the responsibilities: local authorities, business, interest groups, voluntary organizations, mass media, religious establishments, and a variety of nongovernmental organizations. Governments increasingly rely on the private sector and partner with business for delivery of public policies. Technological innovations have blurred organizational and state boundaries, inducing a continual search for new and more realistic forms of governance to suit the global age. The central government in any society, however, holds the greater powers and responsibilities, facilitated by civil and military services. To succeed in an interconnected and rapidly changing world, societies need "to develop learning-based governance and decision making systems" (Rosell 1999, ix) where more people can participate in systems capable of operating effectively across shifting boundaries.

Focus on governance encourages people to think beyond the routine and incremental steps that do not call for change in existing rules. Like strategic management, Hyden (2002, 18) notes, governance becomes a way of looking at a problem in the context of the "big picture" of adapting systems of rules to changes in the environment, and encouraging leaders to find consensual and creative solutions to problems their constituents encounter.

Although nation-states still formulate policies, they do so in the context of an increasingly dense web of transnational networks, operating at different scales, with different, often overlapping mandates (Mahon and McBride 2009, 83). This context of state governance continually sets in motion demands for change and adaptation. A system of governance rarely stays in a static or fixed condition for a long time. Invariably, the system, the process, and the outcome of governance change, often distinctly rather than uniformly. Many important refinements and realignments of governance structures and functions have taken place in recent years, but disagreements and misconceptions of the most appropriate form and role of effective governance continue.

Historically, change of governance has mostly been progressive and gradual adjustments to citizens' demands for better representation and participation in policy making, and adjustments for more freedom and greater concern for human rights. In contrast, change may be regressive, such as when the military takes over governance, curbs citizens' freedoms, and concentrates political powers in few hands. A different type of change in governance, however, has been stimulated by globalization trends that required reexamination and adaptation of some traditional norms of governance. Similarly, change is prompted by transformation of societal attitudes and values, increasing pressures from within and from without a governance structure to abide by certain sanctioned values such as civil rights, ethics, and accountability. Not surprisingly chances of dissemination and implementation of these values and changes have been enhanced by information technologies, particularly the Internet, that have meaningfully altered tools of communication and effective governance (Jreisat 2004).

As in any social system, including governance, the most reliable source of change is through knowledge and education. Not only because knowledge is power, but also because the production and application of social and scientific knowledge harness social organization to economic growth as they assist policy makers and managers in their managerial activities (Mahon and McBride 2009, 83). An organization that can create, synthesize, legitimate, and disseminate useful knowledge can play a significant role in state and global governance. The interconnections of the technological, economic, and social aspects of modern society have come to be called the "information revolution," a critical factor in the development of a new environment for governance. The image of an information society, however, is far more involved than processing information or offering telecommunication products. The information society is the end result of the interplay and the dynamics of many qualitative and quantitative factors that converge to produce a changed society.

These factors include knowledge and skills, effective public management, improved governance, and better-educated and more informed population (Rosell 1999, 2).

Information and knowledge are also essential for enhanced efficiency and effectiveness of both public and private organizations. But the negative side effects of the use of information technology have to be restrained as well from violations of citizens' privacy. Public outcry in the United States, for example, pressured lawmakers "to protect consumers from shady operators and commercialization run amok" (Dunham 2003, 40). Consumers are demanding that legislators rein in "spammers-jamming," e-mail systems, telemarketers interrupting family time, and credit companies trading in consumer financial data, and routinely intruding in people's privacy (Dunham 2003, 40).

The widening and deepening global integration reinforced mutual relationships among countries to unprecedented levels of "worldwide interconnectedness in all aspects of contemporary social life, from the cultural to the criminal, the financial to the spiritual" (Crocker 2002, 15). In their futuristic study for OECD countries on governance in the twenty-first century, Michalski, Miller, and Stevens (2001, 8) claim that technological breakthroughs and market-driven economic transformation have been potent forces in extending and deepening relationships of market forces. They regard the global economy as influenced by three sets of powerful changes that will sustain growth and wealth creation in the future: "the shift to a knowledge economy, much deeper global integration, and a transformation in humanity's relationship to the environment." From this perspective and within such a context, the rules and behaviors that shape the making and implementation of public decisions are also expected to change.

Convergence of relationships is illustrated by initiatives of the public administration profession in the United States, Europe, and other regions. For example, the American Society for Public Administration and the European Group of Public Administration have held various joint conferences such as the "Transatlantic Dialogue" to address the theme "The Future of Governance in Europe and the U.S." Among the incentives for such cooperation is the general search for new forms of governance that more appropriately serve common interests and improve response to global developments (Fifth Transatlantic Dialogue 2008). Moreover, collaboration with private sector organizations for delivery of public services and for technological innovations has encouraged citizens to become more active as consumers and co-producers of services. The consequence has been elevation of the levels of public concern about basic issues of governance such as ethics, legitimacy, accountability, and control.

A clear impact of globalization and regional integration in Europe, Asia, the Americas, and the Arab world is that national governance as well as international organizations have come to "rely more than ever before on reaching decisions through multilateral negotiations" (Metcalfe and Metcalfe 2002, 267). In part, the reason for increasing reliance on negotiations is the growing importance of certain public policies and issues in areas such as economics, finance, environment, defense, and health. Negotiation is also a managerial process requiring capacity and skills to produce agreement and joint action. Improvement, however, necessitates "overcoming old attitudes and oversimplified assumptions and models of the negotiating process" (Metcalfe and Metcalfe 2002, 269). Within public administration, collaborative public management is gaining thrust from growing collaborative management research, emerging collaborative organizational structures, and search for appropriate managerial skills. The collaborative emphasis in the literature supplements established public management theory (McGuire 2006, 33).

Nevertheless, it would be an oversimplification or a gross misunderstanding to regard globalization trends as moving in a linear path, ever intensifying and speeding up. The position of globalization enthusiasts, or "hyperglobalists," as David Crocker refers to them, is that the phenomenon of globalization is a historically unprecedented and powerful set of processes that certainly result in a more interconnected and organizationally multifaceted world (Crocker 2002, 16). Skeptics, on the other side, argue that regional trading blocs may become alternatives to globalization. The global economic and financial crisis of 2009 is described as "the worst global economic downturn of the post–World War II era; it is the first serious global downturn of the modern era of globalization" (Stiglitz 2009, 11). It has become a real challenge to global economic integration, cross-boundary financial investment, and multinational corporate power. The crisis underlined the fact that with "globalization not only do good things travel more easily across borders; bad things do too" (Stiglitz 2009, 11). One of those negative consequences is that prosperity has not been shared and the gap in wealth and economic growth between developed and developing countries has not been reduced; in many cases it has increased. "The global financial meltdown has pushed the ranks of the world's hungry to a record 1 billion, a grim milestone that poses a threat to peace and security," according to recent estimates by the UN Food and Agricultural Organization (Rizzo 2009).

By the end of 2008, the private sector had won back at the global level the degree of freedom it had lost at the national level with the advent of the welfare state. At the global level, it did not encounter the equivalent of the state, an entity that can tax them, regulate them, and manage a redistributive process. This resulted in what Richard Falk (1999) refers to as "predatory globalization." Skeptics of globalism also encouraged the United States to walk away from international agreements at the turn of this century, such as setting up an international criminal court, the Kyoto Treaty on climate change, and the Anti-Ballistic Missile Treaty with Russia. But the most serious action by Washington was the undermining of the concept and the practice of multilateralism, which has been "an underpinning of the global system since the end of World War II" (Prestowitz 2003, 22). In September 2002, the U.S. Administration, published "The National Security of the United States" as Prestowitz points out, "enshrining the doctrines of preventive war and overwhelming U.S. military superiority" (22). Even free trade among countries has often been used to reward those who yield to certain hegemonic policies and to punish those who do not.

In brief, although globalization is an indisputable reality, equitable globalization remains an illusion. Some important beginnings have been made by developing institutions such as the World Trade Organization to head off trade wars; UN agencies and international offices also set up frameworks to protect against abuse and to legitimate lawful economic, political, and social interactions within established methods (Rosell 1999, 21, 22). Nevertheless, the world was not spared the outcomes of the financial disaster of the 2009. Now, we see reaffirmation of the role of governance for repairing the damage, protecting the public interest, and reviving the regulatory function.

Whether one is an enthusiast or a skeptic, current U.S. policies (after 2008) have been readjusting to a more cooperative global posture, emphasizing dialogue, diplomacy, and multilateralism in resolving global issues and problems. A transformation of the global system into a more active, orderly, and cooperative system is now an official policy as President Obama recently declared, "All of us share this world for but a brief moment in time. The question is whether we spend that time focused on what pushes us apart, or whether we commit ourselves to an effort—a sustained effort—to find common grounds, to focus on the future . . . to respect the dignity of all human beings" (Obama 2009).

The above review defines governance and underlines its far-reaching effects. Also, it points out that in addition to many positive consequences, globalization caused some serious negative side effects ranging from fostering monopolies and domination to advancing ideologically inclined mass media and extremely large corporations. Still, globalization has generated new opportunities and new challenges for human development and the need to refocus the public administration profession. In a sense, globalization is a triumph of capital investment and multinational corporate production, as it is an illustration of the magnificent achievements of technology and the ensuing information revolution. Global cooperation has become a necessity for resisting dangerous global threats to the environment, health, and security of communities everywhere. If countries are to realize the benefits of globalization and a spectacularly connected universe, they have to be enabled by competent management within good governance systems (Jreisat 2009, 42–43). Certainly, adaptation of governance in general and public administration in particular will be a challenging task for the foreseeable future.

MEASUREMENT AND INDICATORS OF GOVERNANCE

What is "good" governance and how do we recognize it? There is no uniform use of the term. Good governance evokes many concepts and practices such as equitable distribution of power and resources in the society instead of excessive centralization of power and concentration of wealth in few hands. Good governance is also effective institutions, equitable policy outcomes, the capacity to aggregate and coordinate various interests to bring about agreements on policy action, and managing political and administrative institutions with accountability and transparency (Jreisat 2004, 1004). Many programs and initiatives have been undertaken to measure governance, develop indicators, and establish benchmarks. The crucial role and the transcendent quality of governance not only intensified the search for better explanations and deeper understanding of the subject, but also precipitated perpetual drives for reform and modernization. Among the widely known activities to define and to measure governance are five initiatives:

1. The World Bank

Worldwide Governance Indicators have been developed by the World Bank as an attempt to build regular governance indicators that can be a crucial tool for policy analysts and decision makers. The indicators seek to facilitate benchmarking and measurement of performance. The World Bank Institute relies on a set of standards for effective governance that consists of six measures: (1) voice and accountability, (2) political stability and absence of violence, (3) government effectiveness, (4) regulatory quality, (5) rule of law, and (6) control of corruption (World Bank 2009).

2. United Nations Development Program

In January 1997 UNDP published a policy document entitled "Governance for Sustainable Human Development," articulating UNDP's commitment to supporting national efforts for good governance for sustainable human development. The policy document followed UNDP's first attempts to define the parameters of good governance in a 1994 document, "Initiatives for Change," which stated that "the goal of governance initiatives should be to develop capacities that are needed to realize development that gives priority to the poor, advances women, sustains the environment and creates needed opportunities for employment and other livelihoods."[2] The UNDP also launched various activities to develop governance indicators that provide applied guidance to users while providing technical assistance in governing to specific regions of the world. Two particular programs have been the focus of field research and have significant practical thrusts: (a) The UNDP Governance Indicators Program (2007) is jointly produced with the Oslo Governance Center to provide a "user's guide" that measures the performance of governments, the quality of public institutions, and people's perceptions of various aspects of governance. The management of this project emphasizes that "an indicator does not have to come in numeric form" (UNDP 2007, 1) such as classification of countries as free or not free. (b) The Program on Governance in the Arab Region was initiated in early 2000, to promote capacity building of governance institutions including legislatures, judiciaries, and civil society organizations. Advice and assistance have primarily focused on three main aspects of governance: participation, rule of law, transparency and accountability.[3]

3. Transparency International

Transparency International has been occupied with developing ethical, transparent, and accountable systems of governance. Progress in fighting corruption at the international level relies considerably on measurement or benchmarking. The most widely recognized tool in this regard is the Corruption Perception Index, which covered 180 countries in 2009. Primarily, Transparency International "seeks to provide reliable quantitative diagnostic tools regarding levels of transparency and corruption at the global and local levels" (Transparency International 2009).

4. Freedom House Survey

Freedom House Survey measures progress in developing political freedoms. The index is widely used by news agencies and researchers, and exclusively reports expert opinions on 192 countries since 1955. Experts, generally not based in the country, allocate a country rating based on responses to a series of questions. The scores for political rights, civil liberties, and combined freedom index run from 1 to 7, with 1 being most free and 7 being least free. Using the average of political rights and civil liberties indices, countries are considered free if they score 1–2.5, partly free with a score of 3–5.5, and not free with a score of 5.5–7.

5. Democratic and Nondemocratic Governance

This classification in the literature often tends to lump together under one descriptive term significantly different systems with diverse forms and practices of governance such as *"democratic," Western*, or *"nondemocratic," authoritarian*. But the democratic constitutional monarchies of Spain, the United Kingdom, or the Netherlands, for example, are not the same as the democratic presidential systems of the United States or France. On the other hand, the French presidential system is not entirely similar to that of the United States. The variation is far greater among non-Western, large systems, such as Japan, Brazil, Mexico, Egypt, China, India, South Africa, and Indonesia.

Over the years, democracy has been loaded with meanings and conceptions, even myths and ideologies that obscure its real values and attributes. The term *democracy* is one of the most widely used and abused characterizations of governance in politics. "The smug assertion that liberal democratic regimes alone are morally acceptable cannot be sustained," as Rohr (2000, 215) points out. Not only would this be unrealistic, Rohr argues, "but, more importantly, it would be a form of historical imperialism that stands aloof in self-righteous judgment on how the vast majority of human beings have organized their civic lives over the centuries." This does not mean that one may not favor a liberal democracy over authoritarian rule. It means, however, that the moral excellence of a liberal democracy cannot deprive a centralized or authoritarian system of moral legitimacy (215).

Inherent in this determination is a healthy regard for and understanding of societal history, culture, and common characteristics. One common characterization of democratic governance is the following: "In the modern world there are no democracies without constitutions" (Chapman 2000, 221). This includes written and unwritten aspects of a constitution to encompass customs and conventions. But, while Chapman recognizes constitutions and elections as determinants of the legitimacy of governance, many examples exist of systems of governance that conduct regular elections and have constitutions, but lack fidelity to democratic values. Questions raised include the following:

- Are conducting a national election and having a constitution sufficient indicators, or do they constitute the main prerequisites, for classifying a state as democratic?
- Does a country remain democratic if its government fails to recognize the particularities of its minorities, oppresses them, openly practices racism, or habitually disregards international laws and conventions?
- Would a system of governance remain democratic when declaring itself a Muslim, Jewish, or Christian state, providing policy preferences to those who are members of the faith (and in such actions disadvantaging those who are not of the same faith)?
- Is democratic governance (constitutional and representative) still a good governance when not effective (lacking in capacity) and not successful in achieving sustainable development or improving conditions for the poor?

These and similar questions should modify an absolutist perspective. A constitution is a basic document that specifies the main structures and functions of a governance system. Nevertheless, history is replete with examples of totalitarian systems that have constitutions and conduct elections. Many examples indicate that governance systems that seek to melt away or exclude certain citizens on the basis of gender, religion, ethnicity, culture, or race, if not reformed, tend to drift to greater chauvinistic, nationalistic, and extremist practices. True, a constitution is a basic prerequisite, but it is an insufficient stipulation for democratic governance. That is why a reformist approach that seeks to align state-society relations by restructuring the rules that guide public action would ultimately resort to establishing and managing constitutional principles. Regardless, a constitution does enhance the democratic characteristics of a governance system when such a constitution explicitly affirms unfettered equality under the law for all citizens, safeguarding principles of equality in word and in deed, while ensuring genuine representation of citizens and free elections (Jreisat 2004).

Concluding that "more countries than ever before are working to build democratic governance," the UNDP is committed to "promoting democracy through reform." The UNDP experience in this regard illustrates that the challenge for the democratizing countries is to develop institutions and processes that are more responsive to the needs of ordinary citizens, including the poor, by building partnerships and "sharing ways to promote participation, accountability and effectiveness at all levels." Also, the UNDP claims: "We help countries strengthen their electoral and legislative systems, improve access to justice and public administration, and develop a greater capacity to deliver basic services to those most in need" (UNDP 2009).

The various studies and political declarations on governance and reform, however, have not produced a universally accepted analytical framework or model. With a more precise meaning of governance, Hyden (2002, 17) points out, it is possible to distinguish between the distributive side of politics (how public resources are allocated), addressing the perennial question of "who gets what, when, and how?" and the constitutive side, which deals with the question of "who sets what rules, when, and how?" This distinction is particularly important to countries emphasizing policies for a sustainable development. The conventional needs approach that has dominated international development assistance, for example, relies more on the distributive side and does not ask for changes in the rules of the game to achieve its objectives (Hyden 2002, 17). But sustainable development that focuses on empowerment and enhanced access to resources, also requires a change in the rules, and, by implication, a shift in power relations.

A practical illustration of governance, by a ruler with a clear purpose, is the following exchange about governance performance in a *Newsweek* interview (2009) with the president of Brazil (Luiz Inácio Lula da Silva known as Lula):

> Question: "You are probably the most popular leader in the world, with 80 percent approval rating. Why?"
>
> Answer: "Brazil is a country that has rich people, as you have in New York City. But we also have poor people, like Bangladesh. So we tried to prove it was possible to develop economic growth while simultaneously improving income distribution. In six years we have lifted 20 million people out of poverty and into middle class, brought electricity into 10 million households and increased the minimum wage every year. All without hurting anyone, without insulting anyone, without picking fights. The poor person in Brazil is now less poor. And this is everything we want." (Zakaria 2009)

Finally, the literature on governance is replete with initiatives and methods to gauge what constitutes good governance or some aspects of it. No one approach is sufficiently valid, comprehensive, and free of preconceived views. Even characterizations such as democratic, or the opposite, are neither value neutral nor free of cultural burdens. A reliable characterization of good governance has to reflect diverse fundamental cultural and political values of the society. Moreover, any dependable measurement of governance has to be a composite of many variables and principles. Nevertheless, apart from conceptual fluidity and lack of uniform application, an examination of governance theory and practice often leads to discernable, integrative, and pivotal dimensions of governance. These dimensions, particularly those related to performance, become the justification for recognizing and differentiating good governance from the opposite.

CORE VALUES OF GOVERNANCE

A basic challenge facing effective governance is the development and implementation of agreed upon core values and policies to guide decision making. It is widely believed that there can be no useful measurement of effective governance without identifying these core values and the degree of fidelity to them in action.

1. *Good governance is ethical and accountable governance.* Ethics permeates all aspects of governance. The "connection between ethics and governance is immediate," Rohr (2000, 203) concludes. A report, *Trust in Government,* for the twenty-nine OECD countries, provides a comprehensive overview of ethics measures, trends, promising practices, and innovative solutions taken by member countries. The report clearly states: "Public ethics are a prerequisite to, and underpin, public trust and are a keystone of good governance" (OECD 2000, 9). Thus, integrity, in addition to capacity, has become a fundamental attribute, indeed, a condition for good governance.

2. *Good governance creates trust and promotes broadly shared values, particularly accountability and sustained openness and transparency.* This means relevant information is openly discussed, mass media are free to report, and professional exploration and learning processes are unbound in conducting their functions. A study by the OECD (2000, 11) offers these specific, additional measures:

- Public servants' behavior is in line with the public purposes.
- Daily public service operations for businesses are reliable.
- Citizens receive impartial treatment on the basis of legality and justice.
- Public resources are effectively, efficiently, and properly used.
- Decision-making procedures are transparent to the public.
- Measures are in place to permit public scrutiny and redress.

3. *Effective leadership is indispensable for establishing an overall framework of collective and strategic goals, interpretations, and shared values, both within government and across society.* It is often said that "leadership defies simple formulations and easy solutions" (Beinecke 2009, 1). But Donna Shalala (2004, 349) offers an insightful perspective, rooted in rich practical experience that sums up the main functions of professional competent organizational leaders and managers as follows: They "set standards, communicate a vision, choose staff based on competence and character, encourage team work, cultivate transparency, care about employees, and respond constructively to feedback." In brief, competent and ethical leadership is a key to a wide range of necessary activities for achieving critical program and policy objectives as well as serving common values, the foundation of good governance.

It is important here to point out that core values that shape governance in all societies and stimulate meaningful shifts in authority relationships clearly stress distribution of power and mechanisms to safeguard against its concentration at the top. The character of governance and the methods of exercising power have changed over time. Authoritarian regimes have been undermined by forces of democratic values, economic competition, new means of communication, education, and far-reaching global interactions (Michalski, Miller, and Stevens 2001, 9–11). In all countries, developed and developing, people expect their leaders to improve quality of life in general but also are concerned with specific issues that matter greatly to most people such as work satisfaction, adequate healthcare, a clean environment, and educational opportunities. Consequently, representation and decentralization have been elevated to the top of the list of values sought by reformers of governance.

4. *Governance is where rules and legal standards for orderly conduct and progressive social transformation are constructed.* During the first decade of this century, conservative political leaders and their associates of ideologically inclined pressure groups, allied with those captivated by the "magic of the market," sought, with some success, to restrict the regulatory role of governance. Such efforts contributed, significantly, to the economic disaster of 2009. The huge size of business corporations compromised healthy competition, became impediments to innovation, and exerted corrupting influence in politics (Greider 2009, 11–12). Weakening antitrust laws allowed concentration of economic power under a few corporate entities, which were deemed "too big to fail" and thus had to be bailed out by taxpayer money.

The incredible size of some firms in the finance and banking field, for example, is illustrated by the following statement from the chief executive officer of Citigroup: "We are in 109 countries around the world. We move $3 trillion to $9 trillion in cash every day around the world, and 99 percent of the Fortune 500 are our clients." This CEO made a remarkable statement when asked whether he was concerned about the potential of government "overregulation." He said: "It is really about governance. You need to ensure that good governance keeps the market going, keeps growth going, and at the same time makes sure that we have systemic stability."[4] Thus, in the end, governance has to contend with economic disasters, avoid mistakes of the past, and free the productive capacities of the society from concentrations of power and mismanagement of capital.

5. *New and modified political and administrative forms and perspectives are displacing early*

models of organization and management, employing hierarchical, command-and- control paradigms. Attempts to reinvent government and to emphasize total quality management, team building, performance measurement, and empowerment of employees have contributed significantly to a meaningful transformation of contemporary governance, even if application of these new organizational and managerial changes has hardly been uniform. The diffusion of techniques of organizational learning played an important role in the evolving transition that is ushering in a culture of governance that fosters delegation, representation, transparency, and accountability. To be sure, the trend has not been linear or painless, but recent history clearly shows that the power to govern has diffused away from the centralized autocratic rule to a broader base of elected representatives, professional public management, and active involvement of the governed (Michalski, Miller, and Stevens 2001, 7).

Finally, a critical attribute of a "good" governance system includes the capacity to act in the public interest. A wide range of governance structures and practices have been presented as good governance attributes. But these attributes by themselves remain insufficient unless they yield effective delivery of public services, improve citizens' trust, and confirm the legitimacy and the capacity of institutions to make decisions with competence and integrity. The list of failures and deficiencies of governance in many settings that did not adhere to core values can be quite lengthy. Too many political leaders fail to advance sustainable and equitable political and economic policies that are institutionally rather than personally based. From countries of the West to Latin America, Asia, and Africa, the similarities of issues and problems of governance are truly remarkable. Ineffective governance repeatedly failed in facing the modern challenges and the growing demands to protect citizens' rights and liberties (Jreisat 2004, 1014).

Many countries seem unable to master the rules of the game in the era of globalization. To be an equal player, not a mere subject of the new global order, effective governance is a condition for cultivating the benefits of the unfolding globalization. Current scholarship on governance is struggling to free its coverage from traditional literature in comparative politics and comparative political theory that only infrequently ventured outside the cultural boundaries of Europe and the United States. Traditional scholarship has also been less interested in institutional reforms and conditions of political thought outside Western democratic models (Macridis and Brown 1990, 2–3). Accordingly, if and when elicited, information about governance in developing societies, for example, has largely been shaped by their failures rather than their achievements or potentials.

Moreover, governance has been measured by the degree of realization of the democratic ideals of the West and of self-sustained growth, relying on the private sector. Reliance on the private sector for steering economic growth and development, however, assumes the presence of a lean state, thriving private nonprofit associations of civil society, and non-monopolistic free domestic and world markets. Achieving this synergy requires other preconditions, particularly checks and balances in the market and a representative government. But actual experiences in many countries undermine assumptions about key instruments of effective governance such as the presence of perfect market competition and adherence to cherished societal values of liberty and the rule of law.

Although public administration institutions and processes are central to effective governance, they are often pejoratively referred to as the bureaucracy, which has been blamed for many failures of today's governance. The literature on bureaucratic failures and shortcomings is too lengthy to document in this analysis.[6] A different question, however, is Baaklini's thesis in which he examines the role of public administration in developing countries, and whether its theories, approaches, and institutions were prepared to face the formidable challenges of the twenty-first century. One particular challenge is the democratic transformation that took place in many of these countries during the last decade of the twentieth century and the institutional and technological change that accompanied this democratic transition (Baaklini 2001, 57–70). Theories suggesting international diffusion of common public administration professional standards leading to efficiency, effectiveness, and responsiveness imply hope for change in nations that are afflicted with dictatorship and personal and predatory rule. The global diffusion of "modern organizational culture" will presumably irreversibly enhance the management capacities of these systems and promote good governance.

Global developments and growing international interconnectedness have been forcing reconsideration of the traditional assumptions, propositions, and principles of public administration. In fact, comparative public administration, the new public management, and the recent international public administration are attempts to discover and to apply best practices. The discourse on global public management capacity enhancement has not resolved issues of how to institutionalize appropriate organizational structures and processes within diverse cultural, economic, and political influences. To what extent organizational structures and processes are culturally determined is not established yet, nor do we know how the norms and conventions of the culture within which an organization is embedded influence the organization's rules of conduct. Success or failure of reform may ultimately depend on the extent to which these rules of conduct promote organizational forms and behaviors that are not too discordant with local institutional contexts. Thus, it is important to adopt an approach to public policy and to governance reform that considers the whole system as an integrated set of structures and functions more than past endeavors have.

An appropriate summary of some critical core values from a consummate practitioner of governance is this statement by U.S. president Obama:

> No system of government can or should be imposed upon one nation by any other. That does not lessen my commitment, however, to governments that reflect the will of the people. Each nation gives life to this principle in its own way, grounded in the traditions of its own people. . . . But I do have unyielding belief that all people yearn for certain things: the ability to speak your mind and have a say in how you are governed; confidence in the rule of law and the equal administration of justice; government that is transparent and doesn't steal from the people; the freedom to live as you choose. (Obama 2009)

CONCLUSION

The various perspectives presented in this chapter are an attempt to formulate a composite picture of good governance, illustrating the complexity of such a task. Certainly, there is no universally accepted model for defining and measuring a proper, effective, and equitable system of governance. Historical and contextual factors brought about what seem to be countless changes of vision and endless variation and contrast of practices of governance in many countries. Such a conclusion, however, should not cloud the many common features, nor deny the trends that have been converging above and beyond the usual exhortations about the virtues of democratization or the panacea of market capitalism that regularly show up in the literature.

Governance is much more difficult to put into one mold, particularly in times of rapid change. The wide range of theories and practices of governance illustrate the need for a continuous adaptation of whatever structures and processes are in place in order to be able to deliver policies and services that respond to society's needs and demands. Thus, institutional dynamics and reform initiatives and strategies are integral parts, if not the ultimate objectives, of most tinkering with theory and practice of governance. Specifically, good governance is not an endowed or a static construct; it continually evolves, adapts, and improves in order to be more responsive to society's needs and reflective of gained knowledge and experience.

In the final analysis, the most appropriate and reliable indicator of the efficacy of a governance system is its performance and outcome. Failures of the state to implement effective reform programs, particularly those that aim at achieving acceptable rates of economic growth, improve accountability and openness, build political and administrative institutional capacities, and develop social and civil society foundations, have profoundly undermined confidence and trust in the contemporary state and its leadership. Such failures provided a rationale for the growing role of the marketplace as an alternative to the berated performance of the institutions of the state. Despite the common realization that the market is not and cannot be a substitute for public policy, one still hears constant calls for "the free market to work its magic."

It is a fact that many countries have a long way to go before building effective institutional frameworks of governance, notwithstanding the abundant prescriptions offered for improvement. A primary objective of most suggested frameworks is to vitalize and integrate the critical functions of the executive, legislature, courts, press, and civil society. While there is only scant evidence on what reforms and policies have succeeded and what have not, governance continues to be more than government and more than the elements of investment and market behavior. A foundation of good governance is outcomes that extend to less discernible aspects of society such as application of equal political, economic, and legal rights as well as harmonizing effects of globalization and modern technical change on communities and cultures.

Thus, governance is a multifaceted, multidisciplinary area of study that encompasses, among other things, elements such as leadership, institutions, public administration, culture, history, politics, and economics. It is an integrated system of many dimensions that delivers basic functions to society. In addition to structures of decision making, governance empowers institutions to serve people and to provide necessary outcomes for their security and welfare. Rules and processes of governance are not neutral in practice and can distort outcomes of a governance system. Thus, independent evaluation, audit, investigation, legislative oversight and similar instruments are regular features of responsible governance. The distinction between governance as an analytical concept and governance as operational processes separates the form from the practice of public authority in managing the resources of the society. It is in this exercise that the capacities of governments to design, formulate, and implement policies are tested. While the processes have been subjected to continual evaluation and appraisal from inside and from outside of countries, such judgments have often been rendered mainly on the form or structure of authority and its shortcomings rather than on the overall performance of the system of governance.

NOTES

1. http://www.undp-pogar.org/resources/publications.aspx?t=0&y=3&p=0 (July 11, 2009). Also see United Nations Development Program (UNDP), *Governance Indicators: A User's Guide,* 2d ed. (Oslo: UNDP Oslo Governance Center, 2007): 1.

2. http://www.undp-pogar.org/resources/publications.aspx?t=0&y=3&p=0 (July 11, 2009).

3. The activities of the Program on Governance in the Arab Region, which include providing policy advice, engaging in institutional capacity building, and testing policy options through pilot projects, revolve around the main concepts of participation, rule of law, transparency and accountability. Website: http:/www.pogar.org/.

4. "Man on a Tightrope," an interview by Maria Bartiromo with Vikram Pandit, CEO of Citigroup, *Business Week* (June 22, 2009):13. Also online (June 10, 2009): http://www.businessweek.com/magazine/content/09_25/b4136000706313.htm.

5. The reinvention of government movement and the new public management are two commonly known illustrations of the attacks on traditional bureaucracy.

REFERENCES

Ahrens, J. 2002. *Governance and Economic Development.* Northampton, MA: Edward Elgar.

Baaklini, A.I. 2001. Administration in developing countries and the democratic challenge. *Journal of Developing Societies* 17 (2): 57–70.

Beinecke, R.H. 2009. Introduction: Leadership for wicked problems. *Innovation Journal: The Public Sector Innovation Journal* 14 (1): 1–17.

Chapman, Richard A., ed. 2000. *Ethics in Public Service for the Millennium.* Burlington, VT: Ashgate Publishing Co.

Crocker, D.A. 2002. Development ethics and globalization. *Philosophy and Public Policy Quarterly* 22 (4): 15.

Donahue, J.D., and J.S. Nye Jr., eds. 2002. *Market-Based Governance: Supply Side, Demand Side, Upside, and Downside.* Washington, DC: Brookings Institution Press.

Dunham, R.S. 2003. A grass-roots revolt against information age intruders. *Business Week,* August 4.

Falk, Richard. 1999. *Predatory Globalization: A Critique.* Cambridge, UK: Polity Press.

Fifth Transatlantic Dialogue. 2008. *Ethics Today: Newsletter of the ASPA Section on Ethics,* 10 (3): 16.

Greider, William. 2009. The future of the American dream. *The Nation* (May 25): 11–16.

Hyden, G. 2002. Operationalizing governance for sustainable development. In *Governance and Developing Countries,* ed. J.E. Jreisat, 13–31. Boston: Brill.

Jain, R.B. 2002. Globalization, Liberalization, and Human Security in India: Challenges for Governance. In *Governance and Developing Countries,* ed. J.E. Jreisat. 111–128. Boston: Brill.

Jreisat, J.E. 2001. Governance and developing countries. *Journal of Developing Societies* 17 (2): 1–12.

———. 2004. Governance in a globalizing world. *International Journal of Public Administration* 27 (13–14): 1003–1030.

———. 2009. Administration, globalization, and the Arab states. *Public Organization Review* 9 (1): 37–50.

Macridis, R.C., and B.E. Brown, eds. 1990. Comparative analysis: Method and concept. In *Comparative Politics: Notes and Readings,* 7th ed. Belmont, CA: Wadsworth.

Mahon, R., and S. McBride. 2009. Standardizing and disseminating knowledge: The role of the OECD in global governance. *European Political Science Review* 1 (1): 83–101.

Metcalfe, L., and D. Metcalfe. 2002. Tools for good governance: An assessment of multiparty negotiation analysis. *International Review of Administrative Sciences* 68 (2): 267–286.

McGuire, M. 2006. Collaborative public management: Assessing what we know and how we know it. *Public Administration Review* 66 (special issue): 33–43.

Michalski, W., R. Miller, and B. Stevens. 2001. Power in the global knowledge economy and society. In *Governance in the 21st Century,* ed. OECD, 7–27. Paris: OECD.

Obama, Barack. 2009. Text: Obama's speech in Cairo. *New York Times,* June 4, 2009. www.nytimes.com/2009/06/04/us/politics/040bama.text.html. Also, http://www.whitehouse.gov/the-press-office/remarks-president-cairo-university-6–04–09.

Organization for Economic Cooperation and Development (OECD). 2000. *Trust in Government: Ethics Measures in OECD Countries.* Paris: OECD.

Prestowitz, C. 2003. *Rogue Nation: American Unilateralism and the Failure of Good Intentions.* New York: Basic Books.

Rizzo, Alessandro. 2009. UN: World hunger reaches 1 billion mark. Associated Press at abcNews.com, June 19. http://abcnews.go.com/International/wireStory?id=7879289.

Rohr, J.A. 2000. Ethics, governance, and constitutions. In *Ethics in Public Service for the New Millennium,* ed. R.A. Chapman, 203–216. Burlington, VT: Ashgate Publishing.

Rosell, S.A. 1999. *Renewing Governance.* New York: Oxford University Press.

Shalala, D.E. 2004. The buck starts here: Managing large organizations with honesty and integrity. *Public Integrity* 6 (4): 349–356.

Stiglitz, J.E. 2009. A real cure for the global economic crackup. *The Nation* (July 13): 11–14.

Transparency International. 2009. Corruptions perception index 2009. www.transparency.org/policy_research/surveys_indices/cpi/2009.

United Nations Development Program (UNDP). 2009.Governance for Sustainable Human Development, www.undp.org/governance/about.htm.

———. 2007. *Governance Indicators: A User's Guide,* 2d ed. (Oslo: UNDP Oslo Governance Center, 2007): 1–92.

Werlin, H.H. 2003. Poor nations, rich nations: A theory of governance. *Public Administration Review* 63 (May): 329–342.

World Bank. 2009. Governance matters, 2009: Release of worldwide governance indicators1996–2008. News release no. 2007/58/DEC, June 29. http://siteresources.worldbank.org/EXTWBIGOVANTCOR/Resources/Pressrelease_7–2009.pdf.

Zakaria, Fareed. 2009. Lula wants to fight: Interview with Brazilian president Luiz Inácio Lula da Silva. *Newsweek* (March 30): 43.

CHAPTER 26

DEVELOPMENT MANAGEMENT

Renewal and Discovery in the Twenty-first Century

LOUIS A. PICARD

This chapter reviews the evolution of development management from its roots in post–World War II foreign aid and the role played by the Comparative Administration Group in that process in order to provide a context for an understanding of development management debates in the post–September 11 period. It examines the impact of international donors on development administration and the decline of the state-centric focus of development administration as a framework for development policy. The chapter then examines the impact and weakness of structural adjustment processes, privatization, and nongovernmental organization–focused development models later labeled "development management." The chapter goes on to discuss the rediscovery of the state in the 1990s and the renewed interest in governance from a public sector reform perspective. The chapter concludes with a brief discussion of the impact of September 11, 2001, on nation building and state building and the development of the government approach to development management and public sector reforms in fragile and collapsed states.

ORIGINS

Any discussion of development management must start with its origins in comparative public administration and comparative politics, since development management assumes that there are principals in operation that are transferable across countries, in terms of methodology, theories, and practice or, at the least, can help us to approach an understanding of countries as case study events (Truman 1951; Heady 2001). The comparative method suggests that there are methodologies of comparison based on structural functionalism that allow the observer to better understand political and administrative processes through comparison of whole systems or system parts (political or administrative) in order to better understand commonalities and differences (Easton 1953; Almond and Powell 1966).

Development administration as a concept grew out of the assumption in the 1950s and 1960s that, with the independence of countries in Asia, the Middle East, Africa, and the Caribbean, and with a resurgence of nationalism in Latin America, the state would take a major role in the management and promotion of economic and social development. The concept was developed by a group of scholar-practitioners who came together as the Comparative Administration Group, supported by the Ford Foundation. The Comparative Administration Group was, since its establishment in 1960, the central focus for the development administration movement, which was led for more than a decade by Fred Riggs[1] (Heady 2001, 6–18). With the end of Ford Foundation support, and controversies over the Comparative Administration Group within the context of the debates about the Vietnam War, discussions about development shifted first to the Section on International and Comparative Development of the American Society of Public Administration and the informal Development Management Network based in Washington, D.C.

By the late 1970s, development administration (the older label, which preceded *development management*) suggested a role for the national governments of less developed countries (LDCs) in the process of promoting social and economic change. Followers of both concepts have long assumed that certain developmental lessons could be learned by comparative analysis of policy and management in order to improve the lives of impoverished people. One of the earliest attempts to systematically promote the concepts was an edited collection by Irving Swerdlow (1963).

The simple assumption that there was a developmental process became a source of controversy over development administration. As a corollary to a broader comparative analysis, development administration popularized many modernization assumptions, including the dichotomy between traditional and modern, agriculture and industry, subsistence and commercial farming, and urban and rural. Growth advocates promoted a trickle-down effect to economic development based on modernization assumptions and state-managed and promoted capital investment (Rostow 1960; Lewis 1955).

Critics of development administration theories suggested that early advocates of development administration ignored two other components of development, the capacity (human skills) of those implementing development programs and the political environment or governance framework that defined policy. Others, with a more fundamental concern with the approach, have argued that development management ignored the structural and power problems of the international regime identified by those later labeled dependency theorists.[2]

The Marshall Plan and President Truman's Point Four Program were both thoroughly Keynesian in the approach to development, designing foreign aid as a part of a development planning and management process. The Marshall Plan assistance was enormous; over a four-year period the U.S. government spent $13.5 billion, or $87.5 billion in 1997 dollars (Sogge 2002). The Point Four Program, with a $25 million budget for fiscal year 1950–51, was equally ambitious. As Walter Sharp (1952, 7) points out, "No survey of the extent of American economic assistance to other countries would be complete without taking account of the vast sums provided for postwar foreign relief, rehabilitation, and recovery" under the Marshall Plan.

The Marshall Plan was successful because it primarily provided capital funds to reconstruct the infrastructure of Europe. It was recognized that Europe already had the needed skills, attitudes, and institutions available to promote economic growth in spite of the destruction of World War II. Except in a limited way, in Taiwan and South Korea during the early years of the Point Four Program, and for political reasons, this existential involvement was never again experienced.

THE EARLY YEARS

Growth strategies predominated in the early postwar period, and "development specialists . . . tended to give the greatest priority to industry, as the sector that was most capital intensive" (Lancaster 1999, 16). A key figure in popularizing the theory of economic growth was Walt Rostow, later a foreign policy adviser to Presidents Kennedy and Johnson (Rostow 1960). All nations are poor, he suggested, but some are able to escape their poverty through their own domestic initiative (with correct policies, development-oriented administrators, and significant amounts of foreign aid).

Rostow argued that economic growth occurs when there is a takeoff point in a country's economy that will lead to self-sustaining capital generation. LDCs are caught in what he called a low-equilibrium trap. There was not enough capital for growth until some means became available to allow developing countries to reach the infamous takeoff point (Martinussen 1997, 28–46).

As early as the 1950s, international donors had assumed that foreign aid–induced development administration would provide a short-term boost to LDCs by filling the financial gap that prevented a country from taking off toward sustained economic growth (Easterly 2001). The search for a formula for government-managed economic growth has been a constant in the debate about development assistance ever since. "Many times over the past fifteen years," according to William Easterly, "we economists thought we had found the right answer to economic growth" (Easterly 2001, 23). The Millennium Challenge Account was the latest iteration of the search for the growth magic bullet that promotes an induced development management approach.

Initially, the magic formula was based on the Harrod-Domar model that aid finance, managed by public sector administrators or contracted out, should be invested in large-scale infrastructure, dams, harbors, roads, and machinery. At various times, capital investment, population control, human resources development, policy reform and structural adjustment, and debt forgiveness have all been identified as the elixir of internationally financed development management. Despite massive amounts of foreign aid and technical assistance in the twentieth century, many heavily aided regions and countries remained among the world's poorest in terms of social indicators, and controversy has continued over the importance of social sector development in health and education. (See discussions in Reilly 1979 and Staudt 1996.)

THE PLANNING FRAMEWORK

Development management is said to be the application of rational ordered choice to social and economic affairs. The model was well described by Albert Waterston et al. (1965). Development planners and development administrators are action-oriented and goal-oriented civil servants, technical assistance specialists and contractors, striving to promote economic and social development. Development planning and management involve the setting of priorities for the use of scarce resources and the careful implementation of a strategic approach to development. The definition is clean, but the practice is often muddy.

The original goal of development administration was to change societal behavior in a way that would impact economic productivity. Thus, development management might include behavioral change through secondary (primary and secondary education) and tertiary (adult—including higher education and on-the-job experiences) socialization but not primary (parent-centered preschool) socialization. As part of the tertiary socialization process, development planning focused on local government authorities, extension services, and district administrations for planning, implementation, and social mobilization of development and human services activities. Human development increasingly became part of the development planning and management portfolio at all levels of government and among nongovernmental groups (Langdon and Karns 1974). This emphasis on human development was reflected in the annual human development reports of the United Nations Development Program and the 2001 United Nations Millennium Development Goals (Picard, Buss, and Belasco 2010).

Many development planning advocates, as noted, have assumed that there can be state-managed social mobilization. The basic premise was that planning was setting priorities for the use of scarce resources through the use of rational rather than political processes, thus setting the stage for the nefarious argument that, from a development management perspective, authoritarian regimes could be good development models, e.g., the Asian model (see Nagel 1994).

Planning is usually seen operationally at three levels of activity. These are:

- Development policy: overall decisions to take action, general outline of choice (decision or nondecision);
- Development programs: ongoing areas of activity within a policy area, a nucleus to carry out program (health, education, microfinance);
- Development projects: discrete time-bound, often sector- or spatially based activity; project managers are responsible for generating specific results within a specific time, space, and budget in a specifically defined set of activities;[3] it is at the project level that international donors tend to intervene.

The major responsibility for development management would lie with the planning and program officials at the national and local levels. The overall assumption was that development change occurred because of planned action. This assumed that political and administrative leaders have made the decision to effect improvement in the social system. Expanded government meant an expanded role for specialized planning organizations and the rise of development economics as a discipline. The issue of grassroots participation, democracy, or entrepreneurialism was often not raised in the planning discussions process, which tended to be top-down prior to 1975. There was often rhetoric, and sometimes the reality of a command economy as opposed to a market economy with the soft (weak) state located somewhere in between (see John Friedmann's critique [1987]).

Planning debates in the 1970s began to focus on the issue of growth versus redistribution (equity). Traditional goals emphasized induced industrialization and state efforts at promoting a high and growing gross national product per capita income as opposed (to its critics) to quality indicators (social development) of life. Other debates included concerns about the nature and consequences of multiyear planning in contrast to the ways in which realistic budget priorities are set (Caiden and Wildavsky 1980). The recurrent budget problem, incrementalism, and debates about the coordination of planning caused academics and practitioners to ignore more fundamental debates about voluntary versus hierarchical authority, the ethics of development assumptions, and who "wins and loses" (Berger 1974).

At the center, in country after country, the overall goals were to be set through the national plan (the "wish list") and through monitoring and "managing" the economy. Prior to 1983, *planning* had become almost a magic term. Five-year plans of more than fifteen hundred pages were observed for a country of fewer than a million people. Planners set targets and measured goals. At the regional and local levels, the goals were to introduce regional planning, coordination, and mobilization, and in some societies, resocialization (Friedmann 1987). This meant that a regional planning official often would have a coordination responsibility that included in some cases forced social mobilization (McHenry 1976). Overall, the key emphasis was on government agents or their contractors to act as change agents, with the state to manage mechanisms that could provide a "stimulus" to society.

Originally, Keynesian planners and managers saw the state taking a major role in providing leadership to improve standards of living in LDCs and accepted the premises of development administration that the state bureaucracy should take a major role in social mobilization, economic transformation, and increases in productivity as well as define policy goals for society. Advocates assumed that political and administrative leadership had made the decision to effect changes in the system, an assumption later critiqued by those who advocated support for rule of law, policy reform, and democratic governance programs. As a result of what is called here the "planning" conundrum (see later in this chapter), development management goals became more modest after 1983.

There has been an overall assumption to those who promote development planning as a framework that the state would continue to serve as the engine of development despite the advent of policy reform demands. The goal remained to change social behavior, the economy, and political structures in order to improve society. It was assumed that development occurs because of planned change. To some extent that has continued to reflect the views of the donor community in the aftermath of the Asian debt crisis of 1997, which brought several Southeast Asian countries, including Indonesia and Japan, to the brink of financial collapse.

CRITICISM

While some have argued that good government and access to education have been important variables in terms of international development, historically, variations in growth across countries have had very little to do with variations in human capital growth alone. As Easterly puts it, "The growth response to the dramatic educational expansion [in LDCs] of the last four decades has been distinctly disappointing" (2001, 73). Economic development occurs only when education grows within the context of political stability and government-managed incentives for economic growth. Within the context of a pro-growth set of policies that will create incentives, and governance principles that ensure the rule of law, the expansion of education and skills can be a powerful developmental tool.

By the 1960s, some development administration specialists had become suspicious of the growth model, and many began to call for more fundamental changes in the international political economy. Both dependency theory and basic needs approaches were seen as alternative interpretations. By 1980, the pendulum had shifted again, and structural adjustment had replaced redistribution theories. Despite policy changes, however, donors continued to look for various techniques labeled development administration and development management to implement their policies.[4]

By 1975, and the end of U.S. involvement in Vietnam, Iran, and several African and Latin American countries, many donors had lost faith in development administration as part of a broader loss of faith in Keynesianism. *Development management* as a term came to replace *development administration*. As Jreisat (2002, 23) points out, however, there is not much difference between the two other than vague images and a broad suggestion, popularized in the 1990s, that public-private partnerships would lead to economic development.

The term *development management* suggested a less state-centric and more collaborative view of development that incorporated privatization, public-private partnerships, and the role of non-governmental organizations in the formulation and implementation of development policy (see Nagel 1994). By 1980, the term *development management* had completely replaced the phrase *development administration* in academic and practitioner circles. Management skills as both art and science were seen as particularly important to the implementation of development policies promoted by international donors.

The next decade brought a decline of faith and confidence in all theories of development management and continued controversy over the role of LDC governments in the development process. This controversy has left a legacy of ambiguity over development management as a tool that remains unresolved at the end of the first decade of the twenty-first century. The end of the cold war also saw newly classified developing nations, sometimes labeled *transitional* by the donors, in Central and Eastern Europe and in the former Soviet Union. While parts of East and South Asia progressed rapidly toward "newly industrializing" status, and a few African and Latin American countries had positive economic growth, most LDCs were worse off in 1990 than they were in 1960. Many political leaders and academics still questioned the assumptions of structural adjustment and policy reform on which capitalized growth is based (see Stiglitz 2002).

THE PLANNING CONUNDRUM

By the late 1980s, the mantra against development management and planning had become intense. The argument was that you cannot make planning better. To neo-orthodox economists, development management was an oxymoron. Planning was no more than writing a shopping list. There were three basic dimensions to the attack against the "antiplanning" machine. First, there was the issue of the soft state and the inability of the state to impose its will on society. Second, the neo-orthodoxy and privatization public/social choice logic became literally orthodoxy. Third, there was no such thing as development management, only good and bad management. Bureaucratic, administrative, and political constraints constituted a major limitation on development planning. It was seen as a two-stage problem. The first part of the problem was that development strategies often paralleled but ignored political realities, and second, authoritarian regimes could and did use planning mechanisms to harvest "rent" and smuggle it out of the country. Bad management was particularly encrusted in the project management system imposed by international foreign aid (Bates 1981).

Development management advocates were caught on the horns of a dilemma at the end of the cold war. For donor-induced development management to occur, there was a need to strengthen administrative capacity in the development economics and planning area. This meant the donor community faced an ongoing human capacity dimension to the development management process in fragile states most threatened by insurgency forces that threatened international terrorism or drug-trade–dependent regimes. If that administrative capacity (including economists, planners, and project management specialists) did not exist, it would have to be created as a cadre. These development management specialists would need to be available to implement the policies of the International Monetary Fund, the World Bank, and the bilateral donors in an opening domestic governance environment. Yet the policy message from international institutions coming out of structural adjustment was privatization, economic reform, and public sector reduction (see Streeten 1987).

Institutional arrangements for planning, planning agencies, management systems, and processes that are innovative continued to be seen by the donor community as part of the requirement for economic and political development even as privatization and policy reform became defined as the process. The donors needed in-country planning capacity in order to meet their own internal project development processes. In the answer to the age-old problem of which comes first, the chicken (economic and social development) or the egg (management development/human resource development), the answer was both at once in an environment of very scarce resources. Often it was to be technical assistance that would fill in the gap.

The criticism of national planning (as distinguished from urban, regional, or program planning) has been multifarious (see Boettke 1994). Critics see the danger of a state-centric authoritarian system with state-level planning degenerating into rent seeking and patronage (Joseph 1987). The basic question was, to what extent was a state-coordinated planning approach possible, especially in terms of equitable social and economic class opportunities, rational economic policies, and balanced regional development? Critics argued that development planning had failed.

There are several explanations why it is claimed that planning failed. One problem is that planning puts limits on political compromise and local-level autonomy. Planning is an allocation process. The definition of politics is the authoritative allocation of values. The debate pits plural-ist politics against central direction. One critic called this conundrum the "anti-politics machine" (Ferguson 1990).

The perceived failure of national development planning was also linked to the limits of applying econometric models to real-life social behavior. Advocates suggested, however, that it is not the models that are the problem; the failures of national planning must be blamed on weak planning and administrative capacity. The separation of planning and management and the lack of implementation were often ignored by planners and policy makers. Criticism of statistical modeling has not led development planning away from quantitative methods but from efforts to fine-tune them (see the essays in Strom, Chesher, and Jackson 2007).

Yet development planning remains a part of the unfulfilled rhetoric of development and remains mandated by technical assistance. The mechanics of donor-mandated planning have become the mechanism for donor involvement via projects with limited money and time commitment but often with a mechanism to control decisions. The whole-of-government approach (integrating management between and among departments), which broadens development management into foreign policy and security from international development, has provided a new mandate for development managers whether in government, in the nonprofit sector, or among contractors (Stewart and Brown 2007).

A TECHNICAL ASSISTANCE FIX

Much of international technical assistance has taken the form of providing technical specialists who are operational experts and advisers who are temporarily on direct contract with government agencies or with private and nongovernmental organizations that provide services to foreign governments and organizations.

By the late 1970s, assumptions of development management had come to focus on temporary strengthening activities, often referred to as technical assistance, in support of capacity building. This meant a shift in technical assistance from the provision of operational experts to the provision of advisers.

Technical assistance can be defined as the provision of professional support on a temporary basis to agencies of government, the nonstate, or the community sector that face specific technical problems. As used here, this would also include technical assistance provided by donors to the private (microcredit) and nongovernmental sectors. Technical assistance has come to assume foreign involvement in the internal affairs of a country, though the same principles apply to technical support provided within a country between one organization and another (Heady 2001, 37–38). It was difficult, as Heady early recognized, to separate development from politics, a problem often faced by those in technical assistance positions (see Brinkerhoff and Brinkerhoff 2005).

The purpose of such technical assistance is often directed at institution building. Consulting, both long and short term, is at the heart of the technical assistance and training processes, and applied research skills are often at the heart of consulting. The technical assistance expert as a development manager is responsible to his or her client. However, under technical assistance, it is not always clear who the client is: the host country, its leadership and its program managers, or the donor agency and its contracting and program officers.

Official foreign aid, to its critics, has been particularly weak when it comes to technical assistance, technological discoveries, and the support of economic growth. Much of the innovation, in terms of international assistance, historically has come from the great private foundations and their programs (Esman and Montgomery 1969). According to Dennis Rondinelli, who addressed the problem in the mid-1980s, "AID's technical assistance for development administration during the 1950s and early 1960s was heavily influenced by the prevailing concepts and theories of economic development, [which originated in the private foundations but were] reflected in the Marshall Plan and Point Four Program, which were primarily aimed at rehabilitating physical infrastructure and industrial plants, temporarily feeding large numbers of people whose sources of income had been destroyed during the war, and re-establishing the economies of industrial societies" (1985, 213).

Beyond technical assistance has been the assumption that there must be a transfer of management skills so that those in charge of implementing development policy are able to do their jobs not just competently but creatively. Technical transfer occurs in strategic interventions in support of increasing development management capacity, including tools, techniques, and technologies, skills in the analysis of the environment, principles of organization and management, and unstructured skills. It is the latter that Gabino Mendoza calls "the synthetic mode of thought" (Mendoza 1977, 66).

The basic tools and techniques of routine administration transfer most rapidly through bridging training and are often not worth high levels of investment, as they can be best provided through the private sector. Unstructured skills, however, are the most difficult to transfer because they require that we have, following Mendoza (66), the "synthetic mode of thought . . . [where] something . . . is viewed as part of a larger system and is explained in terms of its role in that larger system." At the upper levels of management, and for development management, it is the unstructured skills of judgment and analysis (including abstract thinking) that make organizational management skills an art rather than a science and that are most often lost to foreign aid administrators and contractors. Technical assistance and capacity building have often not been able to address this problem (Picard and Buss 2009, 233–248).

Assumptions about the importance of intellectual development were infrequent in many parts of the former colonial world. The assumption at a country's independence was that ten years of basic education often constituted adequate preparation for even the most senior positions in the public and parastatal sectors (see Lee 1967). Three- to six-month bridging courses could be used to bring clerical officers up to speed. Bridging training strategies, however, simply do not foster the intellectual capacity that is critical for development management. Part of the failure of management systems, particularly in Africa, relates to invalid assumptions that such a stopgap management strategy is possible. Much of technical assistance and training efforts were little more than a stopgap.

Along the way, donors had become impatient and at times baffled with the long-term implications of skills development. The myriad of problems that resulted from ineffective donor training intervention in the development process of LDCs remains a neglected area in terms of LDC management skills. Program managers need specific training to deal with donor-supported projects and the problems that come with them. By the early 1990s, donor officials became increasingly aware of the skills needed by LDC program officers to deal with a myriad of donors as part of the development management process. Capacity building came to be taken much more seriously with the development of the UN Human Development Index and the recognition that development management professionals needed high levels of training. Since 1990, skills development has become a much more significant component of development management.

THE CURRENT FRAMEWORK AND DEVELOPMENT REALITIES

The development realities sixty years after the beginning of the Marshall Plan are clear. There were two emerging powerhouses in Asia: China and India. There are a dozen or so success stories: These include the so-called Four Tigers, South Korea, Taiwan, Singapore, and Hong Kong (before it became part of China), and perhaps several of the countries of the Organization of Petroleum Exporting Countries. There were also several emerging markets in Latin America—Brazil, Chile, and Argentina—and perhaps one in South Africa (Sotero 2009).

There is a second tier of countries that have developed economic strength over the last decade but still face significant economic problems. These cases of intermediate success include Malaysia, Thailand, Indonesia, and Costa Rica. There are areas of significant patterns of economic decline in much of Africa, parts of Asia, the Middle East, and the Caribbean. Most important, there are or have been disaster areas with fragile and collapsed states, mostly in Africa but also scattered in other parts of the world (Ethiopia, Somalia, Rwanda, Haiti, Angola, Liberia, Sierra Leone, Burma, Iraq, Afghanistan, East Timor, Guinea [vs. Guinea Bissau]). The latter are seen as a potential threat to international security (Kaplan 2008). Fixing fragile states became the new assignment for development managers, especially after 2001.

Critics have suggested that little of the success but much of the failure for LDCs to grow economically is linked to donor-led development management efforts and that donor-led development management in the 1980s and 1990s included several fallacious assumptions (Martinussen 1997). These included the following:

- Critics, especially in the donor community, spoke of the negative state. Government had become a bad thing, and yet there was little recognition by donors that fixing the state was part of the raison d'être of technical assistance.
- There has been little concern about administrative incapacity among donors. Questions were raised about the efficacy of the state approach, but many donors have paid little heed to the need for public sector competence in their policies.
- Debates focused on privatization, public sector reform, and NGOism (the assumption that NGOs were the focal point of international development work and how that translated into public-private partnerships with little recognition of the nuances of institutional relationships that this required.
- There was a need to address issues of external versus internal solutions to development problems in terms of structural trade, natural resources, and banking elements of the world political economy (domestic capacity versus international redistribution debates). These were development management issues.
- There needed to be greater focus on issues of sustainability and institutional development rather than on the short-term and incomplete fix of the project activity.
- There was a need to search for a creative, flexible, and innovative management system based on the sophisticated mode of thought that would dominate global interchanges in the twenty-first century.
- Implementation and sustainability had become the neglected components of development policy (Pressman and Wildavsky 1973). This remains a weakness for many foreign aid–supported activities.

All of this was grist for the mill of those who argued that ultimately, implementing foreign aid policy remained a development management problem. Implementation issues related to debates about coordination and specialization. Delegating responsibility to other departments or contractors in some situations could threaten political control over the distribution of funds among sectoral fields (see Esman 1991).

There was a concern that the donor community had lost its development management perspective. In the context of the cold war, proposals of special interest to individual governments, groups, or even individuals could monopolize available program resources. Overall, the foreign aid dilemma often appeared to center on the question of whether to co-opt or coerce rather than facilitate or coordinate (Picard and Buss 2009).

By the year 2000, there were a number of major themes that ran through the development management debate. These included the following:

- The relationship between development management and planning and the political process;
- Human resources development as a strategy for development;
- The nature of rural and urban development strategies and policies and the nature of the debate between rural and urban development;
- The impact of international actors (including multilateral and bilateral donors, multinational corporations, and nongovernmental private voluntary organizations); and
- The relevance of demands for structural adjustment and public sector reform in a postdevelopment administration age where democratic governance, civil society, and human security have become dominant themes in international development (Crisis Group 2010).

DEVELOPMENT MANAGEMENT TOWARD THE TWENTY-FIRST CENTURY

In practice, the framework established by development management practitioners and academics continued to define donor views. By the end of the millennium the term *development management* came to refer to two interrelated administrative arrangements. The first was the complex of agencies, management systems, and processes that a government establishes to achieve developmental goals. Second, the term refers to government planning and policies and implementation patterns that foster economic growth, strengthen human and organizational capabilities, and promote greater equality in the distribution of opportunities, income, and power (see Rapley 2007).

There are four components to the donor-supported development management practice in the twenty-first century as supported by international assistance: physical infrastructure development, support for social (health and education) and economic development, humanitarian and security assistance, and support for democratic governance and political development.

Governance and political development are important and remain both controversial and still somewhat neglected. As early as 1950, advocates of foreign aid had made it clear that democratic governance was essential for development aid to succeed. That view atrophied during the cold war period but returned to the fore after 1991. This meant that strategic planning and politics had the potential to clash in the marketplace of ideas (see Olowu and Sako 2003).

Since September 11, 2001, many donors have opted for a whole-of-government approach, which links up the "three Ds of defense, diplomacy and development" (Patrick and Brown 2007). Increasingly, this has included an increased concern for the establishment of an international legitimacy for democracy, in part in order to thwart terror, which has predominated at least conceptually in foreign aid debates. However, there is evidence that foreign aid, if it is inappropriately provided, can make institutional and governance problems much worse. By the early twenty-first century, there was less focus on promoting economic growth directly through foreign aid and more focus on enabling conditions in terms of social relationships and the political environment to promote development (Picard and Buss 2009). Debates about this shift, particularly within the context of conflict mitigation, remain unresolved.

The post–September 11 focus on links connecting security, diplomacy, and foreign aid and the trauma of the 2008 economic meltdown have (at least temporarily) reinvigorated assumptions of Keynesian economics and the planning process that accompanies it. Much has changed and continues to change, however, as images of development management evolve into the twenty-first century (Picard and Buss 2009). The specific role of development management targeted at economic growth and productivity remains problematic.

CONCLUSION

Development management systems are messy and complicated and involve problems of implementation, design, monitoring, and evaluation methodologies; the development of suitable donor, donor mission, and LDC participating agency procedures; and teaching these concepts and procedures to host-country cooperants. Program managers require skills in needs assessment, negotiation, coordination, monitoring, and impact assessment (Rugumamu 1997).

Capacity-building interventions, to be successful, need to include assistance to strengthen local and national-level public management systems, and private sector management capacity, including contracts management, program and project analysis, project identification, design, evaluation and assessment, implementation, and monitoring activities. Public policy concerns include policy analysis and choice, personnel systems development, organizational development, accountancy, human resources development and planning, and project management.

This broad set of needs should be counterposed with the reality of most donors operating within a very restricted project framework. Foreign aid since the development of the project methodology had been trapped in rigid procedures, which often limit effectiveness and creativity. Opting for technical solutions ignored the need to address governance issues, including the management, the monitoring, and if necessary the whistle-blowing process, since good governance broadly defined is the prerequisite to avoiding bad, and poorly implemented, economic and social policies.

In addition to governance, there are four other prerequisites to a successful development management strategy for sustainability and institutional development. First, development management activities must effectively capture the most productive blend of national (government, nongovernmental organizations, and the private sector), local, and grassroots inputs into the program and project planning process. This includes a commitment by host-country and donor stakeholders to a strategy of organizational and geographical decentralization, which takes into account both local conditions and national priorities. Planning for such activities should include the development of management systems and skills development at both the national and subnational levels. Planning activities should be strategic rather than command based, need to ensure the participation of beneficiaries and target groups specified in the program or project, and should provide mechanisms to advise both donor and host-country project managers on the utility of their design and implementation strategies.

Second, management training and human resources development more generally need to be part of a broad strategy for public sector reform and public-private partnerships. Rather than blindly advocating privatization, such a strategy would define the proper role of government in economic and social development, and specifically in the health, education, and training areas. Also included would be policies for placing greater reliance on the private sector in such areas as food production, the delivery of social services, and the marketing of goods and services. Overall, such a strategy should ensure that the social costs to privatization are limited. Management training and education should also include an understanding of the policy reform arguments as well as their limitations.

Third, beyond privatization strategies, there should be a clear strategy for reforming and democratizing central, intermediate, and local government institutions and organizations. The state will not wither away. Strong, efficient, but limited and accountable government is essential to the creation of a viable private sector. Such a strategy would include measures to make public sector organizations economically accountable for their actions and ensure that creativity, a sensitivity to market principles, and individual entrepreneurialism characterize all sectors of the host-country management system. With a renewed focus on human development, experiences with educational and training institutions suggest that there must be financial and institutional autonomy from the civil service structures in order to ensure a modicum of efficiency in performance at all levels of education and training (for both pre-service and in-service professional development). Ideally, focus should be on autonomous (though with adequate public financial support), nongovernmental educational and training institutions (rather than on commercial programs or training units within the public service), which would provide professional management education and training for all sectors—public, parastatal, nonprofit, and private.

Finally, the key to the long-term sustainability of donor-funded programs and projects, particularly in their support for management training, is the development of appropriate systems of cost recovery or indigenous financial support during the project or program period in order to ensure sustainability. Sustainability ultimately must include this viability, which ensures that the activity can be financially sustained after the conclusion of donor support for the project. Effective recovery of recurrent costs (outside the donor system) is critical to ongoing programmatic activity, and special attention needs to be focused on developing innovative approaches to ensure that this occurs before donor funding terminates. The success or failure of foreign aid depends on how effectively and efficiently donor activity is managed by LDC program managers.

Criticism of inappropriate foreign aid and technical assistance has been a meeting point of counterdependency strategy, rational choice and modernization theories of international development, and the practices of development management. A new century has brought few changes in these perceptions. A new practical, and sustainable, foreign aid policy within the context of foreign and security policy realities will be hard to construct; it remains essential to the successful implementation of development management activities.

At the same time, twenty-first-century crises and globalism have brought about an increasing role for international organizations, including the United Nations, the world and regional financial institutions, and security organizations, including NATO and regional security and trade groups. This has meant an expanding role for development management in terms of both theories and operational practices. That said, there is a research gap on the conceptual needs for and practical applications of development management in part driven by the remaining ambiguities about the role of the state and state institutions in government.

NOTES

1. Biography and experience are neglected areas in the social sciences. The origins and experience of those writing about development management are important. Professor Fred Riggs, one of the fathers of development administration, was born in Kuling, China, on July 3, 1917, the son of agricultural missionary parents Charles H. and Grace Riggs. He attended Nanking University in 1934–35. He and several other members of the Comparative Administration Group, most of whom had also had compelling international experiences, coined the term *development administration.* The assumption was simple. As Keynesians, and internationalists, they believed that the institutions of government could be used to promote social and economic development.

2. The literature on dependency theory is voluminous and is not reproduced here. See John Martinussen's (1997) masterful volume on development theory and management.

3. Donor-funded projects are often criticized as central to the failures of development management because of their time-bound limited resources (Picard and Buss 2009, 197–199).

4. The late John Martinussen's encyclopedic book (1997) is an excellent source on the development debate.

REFERENCES

Almond, Gabriel, and G. Bingham Powell. 1966. *Comparative Politics: A Developmental Approach.* Boston: Little, Brown.

Bates, Robert. 1981. *Markets and States in Tropical Africa: The Political Basis of Agricultural Policies.* Berkeley: University of California Press.

Berger, Peter L. 1974. *Pyramids of Sacrifice: Political Ethics and Social Change.* New York: Basic Books.

Boettke, Peter J., ed. 1994. *The Collapse of Development Planning.* New York: New York University.

Brinkerhoff, Derick W., and Jennifer M. Brinkerhoff. 2005. *Working for Change: Making a Career in International Public Service.* Sterling, VA: Kumarian Press.

Caiden, Naomi, and Aaron Wildavsky. 1980. *Planning and Budgeting in Poor Countries.* New Brunswick, NJ: Transaction Books.

Crisis Group. 2010. Reforming Pakistan's civil service. Asia Report 185. Brussels, International Crisis Group, February 16.

Easterly, William P. 2001. *The Elusive Quest for Growth: Economists' Adventures and Misadventures in the Tropics.* Cambridge, MA: MIT Press.

Easton, David. 1953. *The Political System: An Inquiry into the State of Political Science.* New York: Knopf.

Esman, Milton J. 1991. *Management Dimensions of Development: Perspectives and Strategies.* East Hartford, CT: Kumarian Press.

Esman, Milton J., and John D. Montgomery. 1969. Systems approaches to technical cooperation: The role of development administration. *Public Administration Review* 29 (5): 507–539.

Ferguson, James. 1990. *The Anti-Politics Machine: "Development," Depoliticization and Bureaucratic State Power in Lesotho.* Cambridge: Cambridge University Press.

Friedmann, John. 1987. *Planning in the Public Domain: From Knowledge to Action.* Princeton, NJ: Princeton University Press.

Heady, Ferrel. 2001. *Public Administration: A Comparative Perspective.* New York: Marcel Dekker.

Joseph, Richard A. 1987. *Democracy and Prebendal Politics in Nigeria: The Rise and Fall of the Second Republic.* New York: Cambridge University Press.

Jreisat, Jamil E. 2002. *Comparative Public Administration and Policy.* Boulder, CO: Westview Press.

Kaplan, Seth. 2008. *Fixing Fragile States: A New Paradigm for Development.* Westport, CT: Praeger.

Lancaster, Carol. 1999. *Aid to Africa: So Much to Do: So Little Done.* Chicago: University of Chicago Press.

Langton, Kenneth P., and David A. Karns. 1974. Political socialization and national development: Some hypotheses and data. *Western Political Quarterly* 27 (2): 217–238.

Lee, J.M. 1967. *Colonial Development and Good Government.* Oxford: Clarendon Press.

Lewis, William Arthur. 1955. *The Theory of Economic Growth.* London: Taylor and Francis.

Martinussen, John. 1997. *Society, State and Market: A Guide to Competing Theories of Development.* London: Zed Books.

McHenry, Dean. 1976. The Ujamaa village in Tanzania: A comparison with Chinese, Soviet and Mexican experiences in collectivization. *Comparative Studies in Society and History* 18 (3): 347–370.

Mendoza, Gabino. 1977. Education and training for public sector management: An Asian perspective. In *Education and Training for Public Sector Management in Developing Countries,* ed. Lawrence D. Stifel, Joseph Black, and James S. Coleman, 61–71. New York: Rockefeller Foundation.

Nagel, Stuart. 1994. *Asian Development and Public Policy.* London: Macmillan Press.

Olowu, Dele, and Soumana Sako. 2003. *Better Governance and Public Policy Capacity Building for Democratic Renewal in Africa.* Sterling, VA: Kumarian Press.

Patrick, Stewart, and Kaysie Brown. 2007. *Greater than the Sum of Its Parts: Assessing "Whole of Government" Approaches Toward Fragile States.* Washington DC: International Peace Academy.

Picard, Louis A., and Terry F. Buss. 2009. *A Fragile Balance: Re-examining the History of Foreign Aid, Security and Diplomacy.* Sterling, VA: Kumarian Press.

Picard, Louis A., Terry F. Buss, and Chris Belasco. 2010. The effectiveness of aid and the millennium development goals in advancing human development, 1990 to 2010 (draft). Paper prepared for submission to the United Nations Development Program, Human Development Report, Washington, DC, January 16.

Pressman, Jeffery L., and Aaron Wildavsky. 1973. *Implementation.* Berkeley: University of California Press.

Rapley, John. 2007. *Understanding Development: Theory and Practice in the Third World.* 3d ed. Boulder, CO: Lynne Rienner.

Reilly, Wyn. 1979. *Training Administrators for Development.* London: Heinneman.

Rondinelli, Dennis A. 1985. Development administration and American foreign assistance policy: An assessment of theory and practice in aid. *Canadian Journal of Development Studies* 6 (2): 211–240.

Rostow, Walt. 1960. *The Stages of Economic Growth: A Non-Communist Manifesto.* Cambridge: Cambridge University Press.

Rugumamu, Severine M. 1997. *Lethal Aid: The Illusion of Socialism and Self-Reliance in Tanzania.* Trenton, NJ: Africa World Press.

Sharp, Walter R. 1952. *International Technical Assistance.* Chicago: Public Administration Service.

Sogge, David. 2002. *Give and Take: What's the Matter with Foreign Aid?* London: Zed Books.

Sotero, Paulo. 2009. Emerging powers: India, Brazil and South Africa (IBSA) and the future of south-south cooperation. Special report, Woodrow Wilson International Center for Scholars, August.

Staudt, Kathleen. 1996. *Managing Development: State, Society, and International Contexts.* Newbury Park, CA: Sage.

Stiglitz, Joseph. 2002. *Globalization and Its Discontents.* New York: Penguin.

Streeten, Paul. 1987. Structural adjustment: A survey of the issues and opinions. *World Development* 15 (12): 1462–1482.

Strom, Steinar, Andrew Chesher, and Matthew Jackson, eds. 2007. *Econometrics and Economic Theory in the 20th Century: The Ragnar Frisch Centennial Symposium.* Cambridge: Cambridge University Press.

Swerdlow, Irving. 1963. *Development Administration: Concepts and Problems.* Syracuse, NY: Syracuse University Press.

Truman, David B. 1951. *The Governmental Process: Political Interests and Public Opinion.* New York: Knopf.

Waterston, Albert, C.J. Martin, August T. Schumacher, and Fritz A. Stueber.1965. *Development Planning: The Lessons of Experience.* Baltimore, MD: Johns Hopkins University Press.

CHAPTER 27

THE CRISIS OF PUBLIC ADMINISTRATION THEORY IN A POSTGLOBAL WORLD

DAVID SCHULTZ

Nearly a generation ago and soon after the collapse of Soviet Marxism, writers such as Francis Fukuyma (2006) proclaimed in the 1992 *The End of History and the Last Man* that Western capitalism had won. More specifically, Fukuyma and Thomas Friedman in *The World Is Flat* (2005), supported by other neoliberal scholars, heralded that free markets had emerged as the winner in the cold war and that the future was one of less government intervention in market activity and an increasingly globalized capitalist economy. The winners would be those with flat economies fully integrated into the market, the losers those outside.

But the Western banking crisis that began in 2008 and the global recession produced as a result are historic events on two counts. First, state intervention to save the banks and the free market from itself undermine whatever remaining legitimacy there is in the intellectual foundations of neoliberal ideology, setting the stage for a new vision of the world in ways that have not been seen since the 1930s. Second, the crisis and collapse of the financial sector challenge public administration, specifically the role that the government and government officials have in regulating the economy and in delivering goods and services.

Theories of the economy, state, and public administration are interrelated. As conceptualizations of how markets operate change, so do theories about the role of the state or government in relation to economic activity. This then demands a rethinking of the role of public administrators and government officials. The global recession of 2008 has challenged more than a generation of beliefs about free markets and global trade, thereby necessitating a rethinking of the role of governments in promoting policies such as deregulation and privatization. This chapter examines the role of public administration in a postglobal world. Specifically it explores how prevailing public administration theory is challenged and changed by a potentially new global economic order.

WHAT IS THEORY?

A threshold question to ask is, What is meant by theory? The answer is not so clear, and theory can be approached or examined on many different levels. Lynn's "Public Administration Theory: 'Which Side Are You On?'" (chapter 1 in this volume) cogently explores this question across several dimensions. He argues that theory, or at least theorizing, is important to the articulation of a sense of professionalism and necessary to the guidance of practice. Lynn also describes types of theorizing, and he indicates that it may be critical for interpreting, explaining, and criticizing social and political phenomena. Finally, he notes that theorizing, at least in public administration, addresses questions about the uniqueness of the public sector, better achieving client outcomes, ensuring bureaucratic accountability, improving organizational performance, linking policy to implementation, and improving government performance overall. A theory of public administration certainly can do that, and one level of theorizing can be instrumental in securing all these goals.

But there is a deeper sense of theorizing that needs attention. It addresses what philosopher Leon J. Goldstein called the object of inquiry of what we are studying (Goldstein and Schultz n.d.). Specifically, he asks, What are social scientists studying when they are engaged in their disciplinary work? What, for example, is the object of inquiry in economics, sociology, or political science? The same question can be asked about public administration. What is the object of inquiry in the field of public administration? On one level it is policy implementation, organizational performance, or client performance, but all of these queries are guided by an even deeper set of questions about the practice and theory of public administration. The deeper or first-level object of inquiry or theory, which this chapter is directed at, is the state. It contends that the crisis of public administration is ultimately a theoretical question about the nature of the state.

Public administration is really a study about the state. It examines, for example, some basic questions about political power, government, and the officials who operate within it. Daniel Bell in *The Cultural Contradictions of Capitalism* (1996) once delineated the parts of a nation or culture into three entities—society, state, and economy. He argued that each part operated according to a different logic. Society was based on a concept of actualization or growth, the economy on efficiency, and the state on legitimacy. His tripart distinction is reminiscent of arguments by G.W.F. Hegel in *The Philosophy of Right* (1967) that one needs to look at interconnections with the state, civil society, and the economy when seeking to comprehend freedom. The point Bell and Hegel are making is that a theory of the state explicates the relationship among government, society, and the economy. Even more important, their arguments suggest that a study of the state is ultimately a matter of political philosophy and theory, asking fundamental questions about the nature of government. Public administration theory, then, is about theories of the state and how it relates or connects to society and the economy.

One way to think about the question of public administration theory or the object of inquiry within this discipline is to approach the topic from an ontological perspective: "Democratic theories have ontologies. Each defines its object of inquiry, the critical components of what makes a political system work, and what forces, structures, and assumptions are core to its conception of governance. The ontology will not only include a discussion of human nature but also an examination of concepts such as representation, consent, political parties, liberty, equality, and a host of other ideas and institutions that define what a democracy is and how it is to operate" (Schultz 2002, 74).

An ontological discussion of democracy, as with public administration, implicates the most fundamental of all questions regarding government. The most basic questions are, Why government? or Why is government necessary? Addressing these questions goes back to Socrates and the ancient Greeks, including Plato and Aristotle, and addressing them is a salient topic to the present discussion. The Greeks approached these questions by theorizing about human nature. Socrates, Plato, or Aristotle all described humans as social creatures with a desire for knowledge and self-perfection. Plato believed that the task of government was to achieve justice and to find the best role for everyone's talents or skills. His assumptions about human nature led him in his *Republic* to argue for rule by "philosopher kings," who were guided by reason. The ideal republic—one where one's harmony or balance in the soul matched one's soul position or duties—was one where reason as embodied in the philosopher kings ruled the republic.

Other philosophers reached different conclusions about the proper role of government, also based on the differing views they had about human nature. St. Augustine and many of the early Christian thinkers saw humans as basically base and sinful creatures. Accordingly, their view of government was less noble and optimistic than the Greeks'. Government was often viewed as a "punishment and remedy" for human sin. This meant that the primary job of government was to keep peace, maintain order, and, as necessary, enforce moral and religious laws to prevent individuals from sinning, if possible. In the sixteenth century, the famous British philosopher Thomas Hobbes's *Leviathan* deployed a social contract theory to explain the origins of government; like Locke and Rousseau, he envisioned that there was once a state of nature before there was government and civil society. However, this state of nature was a state of war, where life, as Hobbes described it, was "solitary, poor, nasty, brutish, and short." It was a war of all against all. Individuals thus formed a social contract in order to protect themselves. What resulted, though, was a social contract to create a near-absolute monarchy. For Hobbes, only a strong king with unlimited powers could keep order, given how contentious human nature was. John Locke, writing in his *Two Treatises of Government,* described humans as basically good but subject to misjudgments in how they enforce and protect their natural rights to property. Government was instituted to help clarify and protect these and other natural rights of individuals. In contrast to Hobbes, though, the social contract that individuals in the state of nature execute does not produce a monarchy. Instead, it is more of a limited government subject to what now might be called constitutional limits.

Turning to the United States, the best statements regarding the political views and assumptions about human nature and politics that went into the Constitution can be found in *The Federalist Papers.* Government is necessary, as Madison stated in *Federalist* 51.

> But what is government itself but the greatest of all reflections on human nature? If men were angels, no government would be necessary. If angels were to govern men, neither external nor internal controls on government would be necessary. In framing a government which is to be administered by men over men, the great difficulty lies in this: you must first enable the government to control the governed; and in the next place oblige it to control itself. A dependence on the people is, no doubt, the primary control on the government; but experience has taught mankind the necessity of auxiliary precautions (Madison et al. 1937, 337).

Government is necessary to protect property and check against factions and quarrels that are rooted in human nature. The only way to do that is by construction of an elaborate constitutional system of checks and balances, separation of powers, federalism, and other mechanisms meant to break up and limit political power.

Madison's claims about human nature drive a political theory about government, explaining why it is necessary and what some of its critical functions need to be. Within the field of public administration these basic questions have importance too. If political theory or philosophy is about asking, Why government?, a first-order question, there are then a variety of other ordered levels of theory. A second-order level of theory investigates the specific functions of government, asking not, Why government?, but, What should governments do? This question looks to specific functions or tasks to be performed by the government. A third-level of theorizing is about ideology, querying, What values or interests should a government promote? This level of theorizing looks to how majority preferences are translated into public policy or how the public interest is defined. Finally, there are fourth and fifth levels of theorizing, the former investigating what public administrators should do and the latter asking questions such as, How can public organizations or policies perform more efficiently?

All of these five levels of questions are forms of theorizing and involve questions of public administration. One cannot probe fourth- or fifth-level questions without presupposing answers to the previous levels. At one time public administration did explicitly discuss the higher-order questions. *The Federalist Papers* examined first- and second-order levels of theory, and Alexander Hamilton's famous reports, such as the *Report of Manufactures,* are second- and perhaps third-order levels. Both are definitely tracts in public administration because they examine questions about the state and government and have implications for what the public interest is and what public servants should do. Public administration theory now seems to address lower-order questions. It assumes government is necessary and it takes functions and perhaps even ideology as givens.

When in the late nineteenth century Woodrow Wilson and American public administration scholar Frank Goodnow articulated the politics-administration dichotomy, or described neutral competence, they were addressing perhaps fourth-level questions. The new public administration movement of the 1960s did the same. Much of the contemporary public administration scholarship now seems relegated to fifth-level theorizing that examines how specific program or organizational performance can be enhanced. This is the thinnest level of theorizing, directly concerned with translating theory into practice and performance. These questions are important, but recent public administration scholarship focusing on these types of questions ignores deeper levels of theorizing, which are the object of this chapter. Public administration theory, then, cannot be understood without reference to how government is connected to society and, more important for the purposes of this chapter, to the economy. Thus, as will become clear, the crisis of public administration theory is ultimately one rooted in theories of the state and the economy.

MARKETS AND GOVERNMENT

Governments and the economy or markets are intertwined and connected in at least four ways. First, they represent the two dominant ways to distribute goods and services (Lindblom 1980). Except in the case of face-to-face barter economies, the free market and government distribution of goods and services provide rival ways to coordinate their production and distribution. They do that either by decentralizing and privatizing these decisions (in the case of market mechanisms) or by centralizing them (as with planned economies). Often these decisions are not dichotomized, and instead in most societies there is a continuum or hybrid of market-government and decentralized-centralized mechanisms at work.

Second, public power is necessary to create free markets. Polanyi (2001) argued that free markets are not architectonic. They did not just arise and develop on their own. Their establishment, especially during the nineteenth century in Europe, was the product of significant uses of governmental authority and power in order to enforce the rules of free markets. Even Milton Friedman (2002), a conservative free market economist from the United States who was best noted for his arguments in favor of privatization and minimal governmental intervention into the economy, conceded that public authority is necessary to enforce the basic rules of the marketplace. Max Weber's (1979) writings on bureaucratic behavior are often read as lessons for organizational theory. But it should be remembered that he discussed bureaucracy and authority within the context of capitalism and the role of the former in helping to sustain it.

Third, governmental authority is required to address and regulate market failures, such as free-rider problems, (negative) externalities, information asymmetries, and monopolies (Cassidy 2009). For many economists, unregulated free markets produce problems that only government regulation can correct. These may be problems surrounding maintenance of demand (Keynes 1964), distributional issues (Okun 1975), or other pathologies that impede efficiency or the ability of markets to react to disequilibrium.

Fourth, government intervention may be necessary to provide public infrastructure investment

(Smith 1937) or ensure profitability of private businesses (O'Connor 1973). While Adam Smith's *The Wealth of Nations* is best remembered as the first statement defending free markets and capitalism, the book also offers an important defense for government investment in basic infrastructure (roads and canals in Smith's day and perhaps schools and telecommunications today) in order to sustain and support private investment. Moreover, James O'Connor has argued that modern capitalist states serve two basic functions—promoting legitimization or support for the regime and undertaking activities that make it possible for private businesses to maintain profitability or maintain capital accumulation.

Describing these four theories of market-state connection is important for two reasons. First, it establishes an interdependence or connection between markets and governments (or public and private power) that is often overlooked. Second, if markets and government are interconnected, it suggests then that as the relationship between the two changes, so must theories of state, public administration, and the specific role of public administrators.

THE RISE OF NEOLIBERALISM

The twentieth and twenty-first centuries witnessed significant evolution and change in theories regarding the relationship of markets to the state. The most notable point of contrast between the two was highlighted in the ideological struggle between Soviet communism and American capitalism in the post–World War II and cold war eras. The USSR and the United States represented rival theories about economies and politics, creating a bipolar world that divided along a host of principles that extended beyond markets and the state. Fukuyama (2005) described the two models offered by the USSR and the United States as competing metanarratives to structure the world. With the fall of the Berlin Wall in 1989 and soon thereafter the collapse of the Soviet Union, Fukuyama declared the West (capitalism) as having won, leaving it as the lone metanarrative to order and structure the world.

But Fukuyama was not the first to describe the end of history or the triumph of capitalism. During the 1950s, American sociologist Daniel Bell (2000) wrote of the end of ideology. Capitalism won, and those in the West had figured out how to live the good life. The question was not about ideology, only technique; not the ends, but only the means to secure the good life.

The conclusions reached by Fukuyama and Bell were rooted in the belief that the post–World War II rising prosperity of the United States was proof of its superiority. This prosperity, based on liberal-democratic political values and Keynesian economic theory, placed Western governments at the "commanding heights" of the economy (Yergin and Stanislaw 2002). This model of the state and public administration included regulation of many aspects of the economy, a social welfare safety net, limited economic redistributions though transfer payments, and use of government investments and purchasing power to stimulate demand.

But the 1970s shook the foundations of the post–World War II political economic order of the capitalist West. A combination of high unemployment and inflation produced what James O'Connor argued was a fiscal crisis of the state. For O'Connor, the "tendency for government expenditures to outrace revenues" is what he calls the fiscal crisis of the state (O'Connor 1973, 2). The reason for this crisis is rooted in contending class interests that make demands upon the state, necessitating that the government perform two mutually contradictory functions. The first, the accumulation function, demands that the state create the conditions that help to maximize the accumulation of private profits. Accumulation is articulated on behalf of one class, and it involves the socializing of certain investment costs or making other expenditures or purchases that increase profitability. While the government may be pressured into increasing spending or cutting expenditures to maintain profit accumulation, this profit is not socially consumed but is retained by businesses.

While the state is pressured to support business profitability, there is a contradictory demand to make some expenses, such as for welfare, in order to maintain social harmony and peace among unemployed workers. O'Connor sees expenditures for this purpose as fulfilling a legitimation function (O'Connor 1973, 6–7). From capital's perspective, legitimation expenditures are not productive; they are simply expenditures to purchase peace.

O'Connor contended that the capitalist state faced a short- and long-term fiscal crisis that perhaps could not be remedied. Yet the rise of Thatcherism and Reaganism, as a response to the legitimacy and solvency of the post–World War II order, provided one avenue to addressing the fiscal crisis. Their solution was to shed many core state functions, which would reduce expenditures. This was a privatization strategy. Additionally they advocated deregulation, a cutting back of the social welfare system, an anti-union strategy, and tax cuts. The combination of all these was meant to cut expenses businesses had to bear, thereby increasing their profitability and mitigating the fiscal crisis.

The apparent and temporary resurgence of the U.S. and UK economies led many to believe that the strategy had worked. Their economic resurgence, along with the fall of the Berlin Wall, the collapse of European communism, and the apparent triumph of capitalism led some to conclude that the West had won, liberalism had vanquished all its foes, and the end of history had arrived. It is out of these twin events that the core of neoliberalism emerged, along with a theory of public administration.

NEOLIBERALISM PUBLIC ADMINISTRATION

Neoliberalism is a political economic theory committed to the laissez-faire market fundamentalism ideology that traces back to Adam Smith and David Ricardo (Plant 2009). It includes a belief in comparative advantage, a minimalist state, and market freedom, and is, as articulated in the 1990s and 2000s, driven by finance capital. At the state level, neoliberalism defines a theory of public administration. If neoliberalism includes a commitment to market fundamentalism, then that also means that it is dedicated to a politics of limited government. This includes privatization, deregulation, and a scaling back of many traditional functions that capitalist and communist states had performed since at least World War II.

As a theory of public administration, neoliberalism dictated specific roles for government officials. It meant, in the case of privatization, that managers would become contract administrators who oversaw previously performed state functions now being delivered by private actors, or they would be in charge of the sale of state-run businesses to private entities. A neoliberal public administration theory commits managers to cutting regulations or making them more business friendly, crafting them in ways to encourage private capital accumulation. In the United States, one example of this meant adoption in 1999 of the Gramm-Leach-Bliley Act, which deregulated banking. Finally, a neoliberal theory of public administration would also facilitate anti-union rules and those that would make it more difficult for individuals to secure welfare benefits from the state.

A neoliberal theory of public administration in the traditional capitalist West also elicits theories of management such as new public management and reinventing government (Schultz and Maranto 1998). Both of these theories seek to import traditional private sector management theories stressing efficiency into the public sector. In the former communist countries, neoliberal ideology, especially during the transition period, emphasized cold shock therapy and a rapid conversion from central planning to market economies that included privatization, dismantling of price supports, and rapid sell-off of state-owned industries (Åslund 2007, 2009).

But neoliberalism as a theory transcends the state, providing also an international economic theory committed to free trade and globalism. Steger (2002) distinguishes between two phenomena. He describes globalization as a social process or material process referring to a form of a means of production and attendant social relations to organize the forces of production (13). He contrasts it with globalism, which is the dominant political ideology of the day that serves neoliberal interests. Globalism and neoliberalism are best understood through the lens of *New York Times* columnist Thomas Friedman's work, *The World Is Flat: A Brief History of the Twenty-first Century* (2005).

Friedman is not the first writer to describe the emergence of a world global economy. Historians such as Braudel (1979) and Spufford (2002) describe its development during the Middle Ages. Political sociologists such as Wallerstein (1979) discuss it in terms of the emergence of a world capitalist system, and Marxists including Rosa Luxembourg, Rudolf Hilferding, and Vladimir Lenin charted its rise in terms of emphasizing finance and banking. But Friedman is unique in celebrating globalization's emergence in terms of a neoliberal globalism (in Steger's use of the term).

Friedman sees globalization as having gone through three stages that have metaphorically reduced the world from large to small. Version 1.0 (1492–1800) shrank the world from large to medium. The agent of change was brawn, and it was about countries and muscles. Globalization 1.0 was pushed by "how much horsepower, windpower, or steampower your country had and how creatively you could deploy it" (9). Version 2.0 (1800–2000) shrank the world from medium to small. It was directed by multinational corporations going global for markets and labor. It was first driven by falling transportation costs, and then by the telecommunications revolution and then by the Web. Version 3.0 (2000–present) shrinks the world from small to tiny and flattens the playing field. It is directed by individuals seeking to collaborate and compete globally, and it is made possible by software and fiber-optic networks.

Globalization version 3.0 is driven by what Friedman calls ten flatteners, such as the fall of the Berlin Wall, the creation of Microsoft Windows, and Google. These ten flatteners are subject to three convergences (Friedman 2005, 176–177). Convergence I is the "complementary convergence of the ten flatteners, creating this new global playing field for multiple forms of collaboration" (178). Convergence II is the rise of business schools, information technology specialists, CEOs, and workers comfortable with and able to develop horizontal collaborations who developed "business practices and skills that would get the most out of the flat world" (178). Convergence III is the introduction of new players—3 billion—into a new playing field with new processes and horizons for collaboration. Overall, the ten flatteners and three convergences are yielding a frictionless flat world.

A frictionless flat world is the world of the General Agreement on Tariffs and Trade, the European Union, and open borders. For Friedman it is one that makes it possible and easy for business and commerce to cross borders. The question Friedman says countries need to ask is, How flat do you want to be? How much friction should government remove via deregulation to make for a flat world (Friedman 2005, 216). The line between those who are in a flat world and those who are in a nonflat world is the line of hope (376). Overall, the task for governments and public administrators in globalization version 3.0 is to create a world that is immune to political-geographic borders. It will create a free flow of capital, have minimal government regulation and restrictions, and include the development of tax policies to enhance wealth accumulation and profit taking.

Global neoliberalism takes the theories of state and public administration found at the state level and expands them to the world. It encourages creation of borderless states integrated into a larger national economy. Thus, as a theory of public administration, it almost demands surrender of nationality and the national interest to the service of a world economy. The duty of a public servant then is no longer to serve the public good but instead to sacrifice it to a world economic good.

THE CRISIS OF NEOLIBERAL AND PUBLIC ADMINISTRATION

The crisis of contemporary public administration theory is intertwined with the failure of neoliberalism. The collapse of market fundamentalism that defined the Reagan-Thatcher worldview has precipitated a crisis in public administration theory in the sense of implicating core questions about the role of the state in the economy and the attitude and functions that public administrators should assume.

For a time from the 1990s until approximately 2006–7, neoliberalism appeared to reign supreme, but now the world economic crash and the rush for state intervention suggest that Fukuyma and Friedman may not be so right and the rumors of the end of history might be premature. Neoliberalism's deregulation and surrender to the market created the forces that led to its own destruction.

One example of that is the Gramm-Leach-Bliley Act, which repealed the 1933 Glass-Steagall Act. Glass-Steagall had created two classes of banks—commercial and investment. The former would be barred from engaging in stock speculation and instead would be limited to making money generally through home and other types of loans. Investment banks would be permitted to speculate on Wall Street. Glass-Steagall was considered a major banking reform; it erected a firewall to prevent the type of speculation that occurred in the 1920s from repeating itself, thereby protecting financial institutions and the public from the problems that destroyed them with the crash of 1929. Some argue that the repeal of this act laid the groundwork for the world economic crash of 2008 as the credit crisis that began in the United States swiftly moved to banks across the world, affecting financial institutions and credit across Europe, including the Russian Federation. The frictionless flat world that Thomas Friedman and other neoliberals desired literally made it impossible to contain the financial problems from jumping across borders. Globalization means not just the good crosses the borders, but also the bad.

The global crash challenged not just neoliberal thought but public administration in several ways. First, the prevailing paradigm of government and its officials taking a minimalist approach to government regulation was questioned. Not only were first-order questions such as Why government? challenged, but the second-order questions about its functions were also implicated. Massive market failure across the globe was made possible not simply because of the reckless behavior of bankers and speculators. The deregulatory and minimalist government posture toward the economy exacerbated the crisis once it began (if not perhaps even making it possible or enabling the behavior to start). Deregulation was not neutral toward the market but perhaps a major cause of the world financial meltdown.

Second, the government responses to the meltdown also raise a challenge to public administration. Specifically, the significant public bailouts of banks and businesses question whether market fundamentalism makes sense, and they also implicate significant questions about the sustainability of such a strategy without bankrupting the state. Third, the world financial crisis beginning in 2007–8 raises questions about the desirability of a frictionless flat world of open borders. Had there been in place circuit breakers or regulations to prevent the spread of the American financial crisis to the rest of the world, the crash might not have occurred. Contrary to Friedman, then, who argued that the winners of the new economy would be those inside the flat world, the real winners are those outside of it.

Finally, one of the other characteristics of neoliberal public administration was the dramatic increase in the gap between the rich and poor, especially in the United States. Kevin Phillips (1991, 2003), for one, has documented this increase, brought on by supply-side economics and the Reagan (1991, 2003), 1981 tax cuts and then again by the 2001 Bush tax cuts. These policies as well as others in the neoliberal state have hurt the poor and damaged American society. Unlike the role defined for them under the 1960s new public administration movement, which emphasized social equity as a criterion to influence governmental decisions, the new public management theories returned singularly to efficiency as the barometer to judge public choices. Market criteria, as Bell (1996) worried about in his *Cultural Contradictions of Capitalism,* had infected and taken over how government decisions were viewed. Neoliberal public administration had become inured to the ethical and social consequences of its decisions, abandoning legitimacy for efficiency.

Taking these points together, the crisis of contemporary public administration goes back to raising some fundamental questions about the role of the state in relationship to markets. Is government merely an inferior partner in the delivery of goods and services? Should government regulate economic behavior only to prevent market failure? Or is government a critical agent to construct and enforce markets and perhaps even serve as a viable and necessary economic participant in services and goods delivery? To ask these questions is to challenge neoliberal orthodoxy for the last twenty to thirty years, including the desirability of deregulation, privatization, and the sell-off of state-owned enterprises. Does public administration thus need a new theory of the state and therefore a new theory of what role government officials have? This is one major challenge that the global crisis portends for public administration.

Another challenge to contemporary public administration theory questions the desirability of a unipolar world lauded by globalism. Might there still be value to regional political-economic structures, even informal ones such as BRIC (Brazil, Russia, India, and China) as distinct entities? Should the European Union be developing its own public administration values? Even within the European Union, the sacrifice of national economies such as Portugal, Hungary, or others in order to sustain cross-national policies to protect the euro might need to be rethought, because public administrators are being asked to second-guess the natural tendency to protect their people in the interest of serving broader global policies. In effect, the global crisis questions the efficacy and desirability of a flat frictionless world. Had circuit breakers existed to prevent problems in one national set of banks from moving to other institutions around the world, the global financial crisis that began in the United States might have been more easily confined. Neoliberal public administration theory as a normative vision of the role of the state in a global economy collapsed in 2008. Efforts in 2010 to redefine a new international banking system thus are part of an effort to rethink the role of government in the economy and also to reconceptualize the wisdom of a truly economically borderless world.

Although China receives criticism for many of its economic policies and efforts to define its own role in the world economy with a unique measure of state-market relations, such a practice might be given a second thought as an effort to readjust public administration in a new era. This remark is not meant to endorse the repression or denial of civil liberties rights brought about by the Chinese government. But contrary to Thomas Friedman's assertion that the winners in the new global economy would be those whose economies were frictionless, the winners, if any in the past few years, were those who protected themselves from the worst features of full integration into the global economy. Creating a world not dominated by one currency, one set of economic values, or one leader might be a more equitable and intelligent way to manage the world. The economic crisis of 2008 prompts the questions, Is globalization or globalism as we presently know it dead, and is it now necessary to envision a postglobal world? If the answer to these questions is yes, then it is time also to think about what a postglobal theory of public administration might be.

TOWARD A POSTGLOBAL THEORY OF PUBLIC ADMINISTRATION

Theories of public administration are inextricably connected to political and economic arguments regarding the relationship of the state and the market. The crisis of public administration is primarily a first- and second-order theoretical problem. It is a crisis that demands a rethinking and questioning regarding the role of the state within a nation and in an international community that had been defined by neoliberalism for nearly forty years.

From the middle of the 1970s until the emergence of the economic crisis of 2008, neoliberalism defined a public administration theory that prescribed minimalist roles for the state and its officials in the economy, and subordination of the national interest or the public good to global imperatives. The financial crisis of 2008 challenges that theory of public administration. For both the traditional Western capitalist states and the former communist ones, the economic crisis demands a rethinking of roles and strategies that have dominated public administration of late, asking whether they remain viable approaches in a postglobal world. This rethinking includes asking first-order questions about why government should exist, second-order questions about the specific functions states should assume vis-à-vis the economy and society, and addressing other lesser-ordered concerns that look to the role of public administrators and implementers in the delivery of goods and services.

What would a postglobal theory of public administration look like? First, it would need to be a theory that returns to first- and second-order questions about the state. Public administration for too long has conceded these questions to political science and the other social sciences, shying away from the bigger theoretical questions and instead contenting itself to look at mostly fifth-order issues about organizational or policy performance. It has ignored questions about the state and its relationship to the economy and society and the rest of the world. Especially at a time when globalization makes it clearer that everything is interconnected, public administration should return to core questions about the state.

Ali Farazmand (2009) offers good preliminary suggestions regarding how public administration should respond to the changes occurring in a postglobal world. He argues that public administration must respond to the problems caused by predatory globalism and corporate capitalism. It (public administration's task) is about challenging the current paradigm of globalism (Steger's term) and conceptualizing an alternative vision that promotes national public interests that are not adverse to one another. It addresses global problems such as pollution, depletion of natural resources, poverty, and aggression. It is a theory of public administration that recognizes that the frictionless world of Thomas Friedman confuses market autonomy with the public good. Thus, it is a theory that rejects neoliberalism as a failed paradigm and articulates a new one by seeking to provide new answers to the higher-order theoretical questions that public administration seems to have abandoned.

REFERENCES

Åslund, Anders. 2007. *How Capitalism Was Built: The Transformation of Central and Eastern Europe, Russia, and Central Asia.* New York: Cambridge University Press.
———. 2009. *How Ukraine Became a Market Economy and Democracy.* Washington, DC: Peterson Institute for International Economics.
Bell, Daniel. 1996. *The Cultural Contradictions of Capitalism.* New York: Basic Books.
———. 2000. *The End of Ideology: On the Exhaustion of Political Ideas in the Fifties, with "The Resumption of History in the New Century."* Cambridge, MA: Harvard University Press.
Braudel, Fernand. 1979. *Civilization and Capitalism.* 3 vols. New York: Harper and Row.
Cassidy, John. 2009. *How Markets Fail: The Logic of Economic Calamities.* New York: Farrar, Straus and Giroux.
Farazmand, Ali. 2009. Building administrative capacity for the age of rapid globalization: A modest prescription for the twenty-first century. *Public Administration Review* 69 (6): 1007–1020.
Friedman, Milton. 2002. *Capitalism and Freedom.* Chicago: University of Chicago Press.

Friedman, Thomas. 2005. *The World Is Flat: A Brief History of the Twenty-first Century.* New York: Farrar, Straus, and Giroux.

Fukuyma, Francis. 2006. *The End of History and the Last Man.* New York: Free Press.

Goldstein, Leon J., and David Schultz. n.d. Conceptual Tension: Essays on Kinship, Politics, and Individualism. Unpublished.

Hegel, G.W.F. 1967. *Hegel's Philosophy of Right.* Trans. T.M. Knox. New York: Oxford University Press.

Keynes, John Maynard. 1964. *The General Theory of Employment, Interest and Money.* New York: Harcourt, Brace and World.

Lindblom, Charles. 1980. *Politics and Markets: The World's Political Economic Systems.* New York: Basic Books.

Madison, James, Alexander Hamilton, and John Jay. 1937. *The Federalist Papers.* New York: Modern Library.

O'Connor, James. 1973. *The Fiscal Crisis of the State.* New York: St. Martin's Press.

Okun, Arthur M. 1975. *Equality and Efficiency: The Big Tradeoff.* Washington, DC: Brookings Institution Press.

Phillips, Kevin. 1991. *Politics of Rich and Poor: Wealth and the American Electorate in the Reagan Aftermath.* New York: HarperCollins.

———. 2003. *Wealth and Democracy: A Political History of the American Rich.* New York: Broadway.

Plant, Raymond. 2009. *The Neo-Liberal State.* New York: Oxford University Press.

Polanyi, Karl. 2001. *The Great Transformation.* Boston: Beacon Press.

Schultz, David. 2002. The phenomenology of democracy. In *Social Capital: Critical Perspectives on Community and Bowling Alone,* ed. Scott McClean, David A. Schultz, and Manfred B. Steger, 74–98. New York: New York University Press.

Schultz, David, and Robert Maranto. 1998. *The Politics of Civil Service Reform.* New York: Peter Lang Publishing.

Smith, Adam. 1937. *An Inquiry into the Nature and Causes of the Wealth of Nations.* New York: P.F. Collier and Son.

Spufford, Peter. 2002. *Power and Profit: The Merchant in Medieval Europe.* Hong Kong: Thames and Hudson.

Steger, Manfred. 2002. *Globalism: The New Market Ideology.* Lanham, MD: Rowman and Littlefield.

Wallerstein, Immanuel. 1979. *The Capitalist World-Economy.* New York: Cambridge University Press.

Weber, Max. 1979. Bureaucracy. In *From Max Weber: Essays in Sociology,* ed. H.H. Gerth and C. Wright Mills, 196–264. New York Oxford University Press.

Yergin, Daniel, and Daniel Stanislaw. 2002. *The Commanding Heights: The Battle for the World Economy.* New York: Free Press.

NAME INDEX

Italic page references indicate boxed text and charts.

SUBJECT INDEX

Italic page references indicate boxed text and charts.

ABOUT THE EDITORS AND CONTRIBUTORS

Robert Agranoff is professor emeritus, School of Public and Environmental Affairs, Indiana University Bloomington. Since 1990 he has also been a senior professor in the Government and Public Administration Program, Instituto Universitario Ortega y Gasset, Madrid, Spain. He continues to do research in public management, networks, and intergovernmental relations. His latest book is *Local Governments and Their Intergovernmental Networks in Federalizing Spain* (McGill-Queen's University Press, 2010).

James S. Bowman is professor of public administration at the Askew School of Public Administration and Policy, Florida State University. Noted for his work in human resource management and professional ethics, he is author of more than one hundred journal articles and book chapters, as well as editor of six anthologies. He is editor in chief of *Public Integrity,* a journal of the American Society for Public Administration. A past National Association of Schools of Public Affairs and Administration fellow, as well as a Kellogg Foundation fellow, he has experience in the military, civil service, and business.

Stuart I. Bretschneider is the associate dean and chair of the public administration department of the Maxwell School of Citizenship and Public Affairs, Syracuse University. He also holds one of the university's Laura J. and L. Douglas Meredith Professorships for Teaching Excellence. Dr. Bretschneider was the director of the Center for Technology and Information Policy at the Maxwell School from 1994 to 2006. He was the managing editor for the *Journal of Public Administration Research and Theory* from 1992 to 2000. Dr. Bretschneider received his PhD in public administration from Ohio State University in 1980.

Crystal Calarusse is the academic director of NASPAA and has responsibility for academic quality and development. She directs accreditation efforts with the Commission on Peer Review and Accreditation, a specialized accrediting body dedicated to quality assurance in professional graduate education in public affairs and public policy. Calarusse received her MPP degree from the University of Maryland–College Park.

Chung-Lae Cho is assistant professor and chairman of the Department of Public Administration, Ewha Woman's University, Seoul, Korea. His research and teaching interests include intergovernmental relations, local governance, applied statistics, and research methods. He has published articles in *Public Administration Review, Journal of Public Administration Research and Theory, Publius,* and other journals. He received his BA and MA degrees from Korea University and his PhD degree from the University of North Carolina at Chapel Hill.

Beverly A. Cigler, is a professor of public policy and administration at Penn State Harrisburg, and has published 165 articles and chapters and coauthored several books. She has presented two hundred speeches to national and state organizations of government officials and serves on several of their boards of directors and advisory committees. Cigler has received national, state, and university awards for research and public service. She is a fellow of the National Academy of Public Administration.

Louise K. Comfort is a professor of public and international affairs and director of the Center for Disaster Management, University of Pittsburgh. She is a fellow of the National Academy of Public Administration, and author or coauthor of five books, including *Designing Resilience: Preparedness for Extreme Events* (University of Pittsburgh Press, 2010). She has published articles on information policy, organizational learning, and sociotechnical systems, and is book review editor at *Journal of Comparative Policy Analysis.*

Stephen E. Condrey, PhD, is senior associate and program director for human resource management with the University of Georgia's Carl Vinson Institute of Government. He is also adjunct professor of public administration and policy in the School of Public and International Affairs, University of Georgia. He has more than a quarter of a century of professional experience in human resource management and has consulted nationally and internationally with more than seven hundred organizations concerning personnel-related issues. He presently serves as editor in chief of the *Review of Public Personnel Administration* and is the editor of the *Handbook of Human Resource Management in Government,* 3rd ed. (Jossey-Bass, 2010).

Terry L. Cooper, PhD, is the Maria B. Crutcher Professor in Citizenship and Democratic Values. Cooper's research centers on citizen participation and public ethics. He is the director of the USC Civic Engagement Initiative and the author of *The Responsible Administrator: An Approach to Ethics for the Administrative Role,* 5th ed. (Jossey-Boss, 2006) and *An Ethic of Citizenship for Public Administration* (Prentice Hall, 1991). His current research is on the home-owner association movement in China.

Melvin J. Dubnick has been studying accountability for nearly three decades, and his publications on that topic cover a wide range of conceptual and empirical issues related to that elusive topic. His most recent work focuses on performance measurement as an accountability mechanism, the role of accountability in the failure and reform of global financial markets, and a theory of accountable governance rooted in the work of Adam Smith. He is professor of political science at the University of New Hampshire and professor emeritus at Rutgers University–Newark.

Robert F. Durant is professor of public administration and policy in the School of Public Affairs, American University, and chair of the Department of Public Administration and Policy. His latest books are *The Oxford Handbook of American Bureaucracy* (Oxford Press, 2010) and *The Greening of the U.S. Military: Environmental Policy, National Security, and Organizational Change* (Georgetown University Press, 2007). He is an elected fellow in the National Academy of Public Administration.

Beth Gazley is assistant professor of public and environmental affairs at Indiana University–Bloomington. Her research examines volunteerism, management capacity, governance, and collaboration in public and nonprofit contexts. She recently completed a multiyear research project with the American Society of Association Executives on volunteering and giving in trade associations and professional societies.

Wendy Haynes is a full-time faculty and MPA coordinator at Bridgewater State College in Massachusetts. In the classroom, in her research on megaproject management and accountability, and in various management consulting assignments, she draws on her extensive practitioner experience—including thirteen years in the Massachusetts Inspector General's Office—and leadership roles in various professional associations. Dr. Hayes served for more than twenty-five years in public sector leadership and evaluation roles at all levels of government. She is passionately engaged in the pursuit of excellence in teaching, research, service, and leadership development.

Nicholas Henry is a fellow of the National Academy of Public Administration and has served on the National Council of ASPA, on the Executive Council of NASPAA, and as president of Pi Alpha Alpha. He is the founding director of the School of Public Affairs, and founding dean of the College of Public Programs, both at Arizona State University, and served as president of Georgia Southern University. He received a resolution of recognition and commendation from the Georgia State Senate and a special commendation from the governor of Arizona for his administrative work. His academic contributions to public administration include *Public Administration and Public Affairs* (Longman), now in its fourth decade of publication, and he is the recipient of the Laverne Burchfield Award from *Public Administration Review* and the Edwin O. Stene Award.

Leonard J. Huggins is a geospatial postdoctoral (social science) researcher at the Center for Disaster Management, University of Pittsburgh. His research interest is to advance the application of sociotechnical systems for efficient disaster management. His recent work includes the integration of geospatial technology with analysis of organizational networks in projects in the Pittsburgh region as well as island systems in the Caribbean and Indonesia.

Jamil Jreisat is professor of public administration and political science, Department of Government and International Affairs, University of South Florida. He is the author of several books and articles on issues in public administration, comparative government, and administrative reform in the Arab world, including *Comparative Public Administration and Policy* (Westview, 2002). He is the associate editor of *Journal of Asian and African Studies* and a recipient of the USF Award for Professional Excellence.

Alan Lawton is professor of public sector management at Hull University, and he also holds a position as Professor of Integrity of Governance at the VU University in Amsterdam. He has written numerous books and articles on various aspects of public sector management and specializes in public service ethics, on which he has published in *Journal of Public Administration Research and Theory, Public Administration Review,* and *Public Integrity.*

Laurence E. Lynn Jr. is Sid Richardson Research Professor at the LBJ School of Public Affairs, University of Texas; professor of public management at the Manchester Business School; and the Sydney Stein Jr. Professor of Public Management Emeritus at the University of Chicago. His research is concerned with public management theory and research methods. His most recent books are *Public Management: Old and New* (Routledge, 2006); *Madison's Managers: Public Administration and the Constitution,* with Anthony M. Bertelli (Johns Hopkins University Press, 2006), and a textbook with Carolyn J. Hill, *Public Management: A Three-Dimensional Approach* (CQ Press, 2009). For lifetime contributions to public administration research and practice, he has received the John Gaus, Dwight Waldo, Paul Van Riper, and H. George Frederickson awards.

John Marvel is a doctoral student in the School of Public Affairs, American University. His research focuses on public sector employee turnover, representative bureaucracy, and managerial decision making. He has presented the results of his research at the annual conferences of the Association for Public Policy Analysis and Management, the Midwest Political Science Association, and the American Political Science Association.

Steven M. Maser is a professor of public management and public policy at Willamette University's Atkinson Graduate School of Management in Salem, Oregon. He chaired the Standards Committee for the National Association of Schools of Public Affairs and Administration and served on the steering committee supervising the revision of NASPAA's accreditation standards from 2007 to 2009. Previously, he had spent four years on NASPAA's Commission on Peer Review and Accreditation and participated in multiple accreditation site visits.

Donald C. Menzel is president of Ethics Management International and emeritus professor of public administration, Northern Illinois University. He served as the 2005–6 president of the American Society for Public Administration. He holds a PhD from Pennsylvania State University, a master's degree from Miami University (Ohio), and a bachelor's degree in mathematics from Southern Illinois University. He served in the U.S. Air Force from 1962 to 1967 as a navigator/bombardier on B-52s. His most recent books are *Ethics Moments in Government: Cases and Controversies* (Taylor and Francis 2010) and *Ethics Management for Public Administrators: Building Organizations of Integrity* (M.E. Sharpe, 2007).

Ines Mergel is an assistant professor of public administration in the public administration department of the Maxwell School of Citizenship and Public Affairs, Syracuse University. She holds a DBA (2005) from the University of St. Gallen, Switzerland, and a master's degree in business economics (1999) from the University of Kassel, Germany. Dr. Mergel's research focuses on the use of social media applications in the public sector, and she is investigating how public managers are using their informal social networking ties to fulfill the mission of their agencies.

Louis A. Picard is professor and director of the International Development Division, Graduate School of Public and International Affairs, University of Pittsburgh. His research and consulting specializations include governance, development management, decentralization, civil society, and human resource development. He has had extensive fieldwork in the Middle East and in North, Western, Eastern, and Southern Africa, including three years in South Africa and Uganda, two years in Botswana and Tanzania, and intermittently in the Horn of Africa. He has served as a UNDP, USAID, and World Bank adviser on regional, local government, and public sector capacity building in Guinea-Conakry, Ethiopia, and Eritrea. He has worked in forty-two countries and is the author or editor of nine books and forty-six articles.

Jeffrey A. Raffel is the Charles P. Messick Professor of Public Administration and immediate past director of the School of Urban Affairs and Public Policy at the University of Delaware. He is the lead editor of *Public Sector Leadership: International Challenges and Perspectives* (Edward Elgar, 2009). Dr. Raffel is the president of the National Association of Schools of Public Affairs and Administration (NASPAA) and previously served as the chair of the accreditation commission and the standards revision committee.

Nandhini Rangarajan is an assistant professor of political science at Texas State University. She earned a PhD in public administration from the Rockefeller College of Public Affairs and Policy, State University of New York at Albany. Her research interests are in creativity and innovation, public management, human resources, and organizational behavior.

Norma M. Riccucci is a professor of public administration at Rutgers University in Newark. Her research and teaching interests lie in the areas of human resources and public management. She is a fellow of the National Academy of Public Administration.

David H. Rosenbloom is distinguished professor of public administration at American University (Washington, DC) and chair professor of public management at City University of Hong Kong. A member of the National Academy of Public Administration, he is recipient of the Waldo, Gaus, Brownlow, and Mosher awards, among others, for his scholarly contributions to the field of public administration. Rosenbloom is internationally known for his competing-lenses model of public administration as management, politics, and law.

Irene S. Rubin is a professor emerita from the Public Administration Division of Northern Illinois University. She has published widely on the politics of public budgeting, with a particular focus on fiscal stress and crisis. Recent books include *The Politics of Public Budgeting: Getting and Spending, Borrowing and Balancing,* 6th ed. (CQ Press, 2010); *Balancing the Federal Budget: Eating the Seed Corn or Trimming the Herds?* (Chatham House/Seven Bridges, 2003); and an edited collection, *Public Budgeting: Policy, Process, and Politics* (M.E. Sharpe, 2008).

Judith R. Saidel is associate professor of public administration and policy and senior research associate, Center for Women in Government and Civil Society, University at Albany, State University of New York. She has published numerous articles, chapters, and reports on government-nonprofit relationships, nonprofit governance, and the representativeness of the gubernatorial appointee leadership cohort. Dr. Saidel won the 2006 Rita Mae Kelly Award for Distinguished Research conferred by the Section for Women in Public Administration, American Society for Public Administration.

Steve Scheinert completed his PhD at the University of Pittsburgh. He earned a master's degree in public policy from the Thomas Jefferson Program in Public Policy in 2006 at the College of William and Mary. Scheinert joined the IISIS Team in 2007, where he focused on data management and research methods. He focuses on the impact of conflict intervention systems and is now looking to apply the research methods associated with complex adaptive systems to postconflict nation building.

David Schultz is a professor in the Hamline University School of Business. He is the author of more than twenty-five books and seventy articles on various aspects of law, public administration, and ethics. Among his current projects, he is coauthor with Sheila Kennedy of *American Public Service: Constitutional and Ethical Foundations* (Jones and Bartlett Publishers, 2010).

Patricia M. Shields is a professor and MPA director at Texas State University. She has authored book chapters and articles on privatization, pragmatism and public administration, user fees, research methodology, military recruitment, military organizations, and women in the military. Her work in this volume is an extension of her study of women in the military and early pragmatists like Jane Addams. She has also edited the journal *Armed Forces and Society* since 2001.

Frédérique Six is assistant professor at VU University Amsterdam, Department of Governance Studies. Her research interests lie in the role of integrity and trust in achieving good governance. Next to several books—one of which includes *Local Integrity Systems,* coedited with Leo Huberts and Frank Anechiarico (Boom Juridische Uitgevers, 2008)—and book chapters on these subjects, she has published in, among others, *Journal of Management Studies, European Management Journal,* and *International Journal of Human Resource Management.*

Carl W. Stenberg is professor of public administration and government at the School of Government, University of North Carolina at Chapel Hill, and director of the Master of Public Administration Program. Formerly, he served as executive director of the Council of State Governments and assistant director of the U.S. Advisory Commission on Intergovernmental Relations. Dr. Stenberg is past national president of ASPA and a fellow and former chair of the board of directors of NAPA. He is the recipient of the Dimock, Brownlow, and Stone awards from ASPA.

Montgomery Van Wart is professor and chair at California State University, San Bernardino. As a scholar, Dr. Van Wart has more than sixty publications including seven books and a substantial number of articles in leading journals. One of his books on leadership, *The Dynamics of Leadership: Theory and Practice* (M.E. Sharpe, 2005), was highly recommended in *Choice* as a "very impressive and successful effort" and was later designated as a *Choice* Outstanding Academic Title for 2005. He is the associate editor of *Public Performance and Management Review* and serves on numerous other editorial boards, including *Public Administration Review.*

William L. Waugh is professor of public management and policy in the Andrew Young School at Georgia State University. He has written extensively on emergency management and homeland security and has been a consultant to federal, state, and local agencies and nongovernmental organizations. He is a member of the Emergency Management Accreditation Program Commission, which sets standards for and accredits state and local emergency management agencies, and editor in chief of the *Journal of Emergency Management.*

Jonathan P. West is a professor of political science and director of the graduate public administration program at the University of Miami. He has published eight books and more than one hundred articles and book chapters. For twelve years he has been the managing editor of *Public Integrity,* an American Society for Public Administration journal cosponsored by the International City/County Management Association, the Council of State Governments, the Ethics Resource Center, and the Council on Governmental Ethics Laws.

Harvey L. White is an associate professor and director of the Roscoe Robinson Initiative for Diversity and Public Service in the Graduate School of Public and International Affairs at the University of Pittsburgh. He also is professor of health and preventive medicine at the University of South Alabama. He served as dean of the School of Public and Urban Affairs at Southern University, Baton Rouge, and city manager for the town of Princeville, North Carolina. Dr. White has directed public administration programs at Southern University and the University of Pittsburgh. He is the founder and past director of the Center for Healthy Communities at the University of South Alabama. Other professional roles have included editor of the *Journal of Public Management and Social Policy;* general chair of the International Consortium for Public Management, Policy and Development; president of the National Conference of Minority Public Administrators; and president of the American Society for Public Administration. Dr. White is also a fellow in the National Academy of Public Administration.

Deil S. Wright was alumni distinguished professor emeritus of political science and public administration, University of North Carolina at Chapel Hill. He authored or coauthored more than one hundred articles, and his text *Understanding Intergovernmental Relations* helped define the field in the 1970s and 1980s. Dr. Wright's recognitions include the Mosher, Waldo, and Rita Mae Kelly awards from the American Society for Public Administration, and he was elected fellow of the National Academy of Public Administration in 1975. Dr. Wright passed away on June 30, 2009.

Clayton Wukich is completing his PhD at the Graduate School of Public and International Affairs, University of Pittsburgh. His research and teaching interests include public administration, public policy, intergovernmental relations, federalism, and state and local governance. His dissertation focuses on the factors that promote or inhibit interorganizational cooperation. Wukich also serves as an intelligence officer in the U.S. Navy Reserve.

Kaifeng Yang is an associate professor and MPA program director of the Askew School of Public Administration and Policy, Florida State University. He is the managing editor of *Public Performance and Management Review,* and his current research interests include public and performance management, citizen participation, and organizational theory.